LESBOS

THREE THOUSAND YEARS ON AN AEOLIAN ISLAND

by
Konst. Inos Fallieros

ISOS INTERNATIONAL, P.C.
1995

ISOS INTERNATIONAL, P.C.
Denver and Vail, Colorado; Athens, Greece

COVER: Center: Sappho, Hellenistic Roman fresco; Top left and clockwise: Greek fifth century B.C. vase, singer with lyre; Aristotle's successor, Theophrastos of Lesbos; Epicuros, fourth century philosopher; Constantine IX, eleventh century Byzantine emperor; Manuel II, fourteenth century emperor; Ignatios of Lesbos, nineteenth century bishop of Hungary and Wallachia; Theophilos, twentieth century folk artist; O. Elytis, twentieth century Nobel laureate poet of Lesbos.

Library of Congress Cataloguing-in-Publication Data
Fallieros (aka Falliers, Phallieros), Konst. Inos (aka Constantine), 1924–
  Lesbos three thousand years on an Aeolian island.
   Lesbos, Aegean Greek island: history, literature, arts, life.
Ancient Greek, Byzantine, and modern Greek themes, philosophy, poetry, erotic modes.
   Reference data: Gods, muses, musical instruments, sages, women writers in antiquity, barbarian invasions, multiple language translations and critique.
   Includes index.
ISBN 0-9627950-1-1

© Copyright 1995, Isos International.
All rights reserved. No part of this book may be reproduced in any form or by any electronic or mechanical means, including information storage and retrieval systems, without permission in writing from the publisher, except by a reviewer who may quote brief passages in a review.

Isos International, P.C.
360 S. Garfield Street
Denver, Colorado 80209-3136
Tel (303) 321-3434   Fax (303) 321-3435

Printed in the United States of America

CONTENTS

Preface - Olvia E. MacCarr, M.A.		vi
Foreword - Constantine J. Falliers, M.D.		ix
Introduction - K.I. Fallieros		xi

I. *The Head of Orpheus*   1
    A. How Aeolians and Others Became Lesbians   3
        Hellenic genesis and Deukalion's flood   3
        Aeolus [*Aiolos*], Macar, and the Amazons   5
        The daughters of Macar and the songs of Homer   6
        Lesbos in the Odyssey   9
        The flying chariot of Pelops   12
        Penthilos and a rescue by dolphins   13

    B. Orpheus, the Muses and the Mad Women of Thrace   15
        The head of Orpheus   15
        The rhythm of the Argonauts, the lure of the Sirens   17
        Orpheus and Euridice   18
        Orphic poetry, religion and philosophy   19

II. *Lesbian Lyrics*   25
    A. Communications' Explosion Around 600 B.C.   27
        New words, new music, new letters   27
        The "Little Iliad"   27
        Terpandros of Lesbos   28
        Arion, the lyre [*kithara*] singer   30
        Compilation and recording   33
        Continuity and controversy   38

    B. Lesbian Love Lyrics   40
        The discovery of the Self [*ego*]   40
        Lyres and other tools for music   41
        Sappho and the women on Lesbos   42
        Alkaios, politics and drinking songs   65
        Lasting lyrics   73

III. *Sages, Soldiers, Slaves and Scholars*   77
    A. The Rule of the "Sages"   79
        Pittakos, the wise ruler on Lesbos   79

		Pherekydes and Pythagoras—Gods vs. mathematics	83
		Merchants, mercenaries and a girl's erotic art	84
	B.	**Hellenic Holocaust: Slaughter, Slavery and Survival**	85
		Civil strife and the Persian wars	85
		Lesbos between Athens and Sparta	87
		Greeks against Greeks: the Battle of Arginousai	96
	C.	**Lesbos and the Hellenic Schools of Thought**	105
		The Academy of Plato	106
		The Lyceum of Aristotle and Theophrastos	109
		The Epicurean Hermarkhos of Lesbos	123
		Stoics of the Painted Arcade [*Stoa*]	126
IV.	*Hellenistic Twilight and Roman Romantic Loves*		131
	A.	**Waves of Wars**	133
		Alexander to the conquest of Asia	133
		Memnon in the enemy's service	133
		The Romans on Lesbos	138
		Pompey and Cornelia	150
	B.	**Erotic Romances**	158
		Hellenistic historians, librarians and "stylists"	158
		Erotic Passions by Parthenios	160
		The Lesbian pastoral about *Daphnis and Chloe*	162
		The adventures of *Apollonios*	179
	C.	**Early Christian Contacts and Comments**	191
		Saint Paul on Assos and Lesbos	191
		Clement's *Exhortation to the Greeks*	193
Maps		Greece and Asia Minor	198
		The Mediterranean World	200
		Lesbos	202
COLOR PLATES			203
V.	*Medieval Masters, Mystics and Monsters*		219
	A.	**Apostasy and Apotheosis**	221
		Julian "the Apostate", a young philosopher-king	221
		Barbarians through the gates	224
		The horrid reign of "Saint" Irene	232
	B.	**Ruthless and Romantic Rulers**	245
		The end of iconoclasm	245

	A medieval hellenic renaissance	247
	Intrigues of a scholarly king	250
	An imperial erotic triangle	255
	Death in Constantinople	268
VI.	*Collapsing Fences and Defenses*	271
	A. Agony and Progeny	273
	The "first woman historian": Anna Komnena	273
	A Turkish rebel on Lesbos	275
	The crossing of the Crusades	283
	B. Fatal family feuds	289
	Byzantine civil wars	289
	Latins in the Levant	291
	Lesbos Genoese	296
	C. The Ottoman conquest	302
	The Turks in Europe	302
	The fall of Lesbos, 1462 A.D.	304
VII.	*On the Verge of Freedom*	319
	A. On the verge of extinction	321
	Under the "Franks" and the Turks	321
	A painful coexistence	327
	Aeolian "enlightenment"	332
	Free at last!	337
	B. Liberation and literary ferment	340
	Ethnic re-awakening	340
	Some ordinary people	343
	The novels of S. Myrivilis: *Daskala*; *Mermaid Madonna*	345
	C. Now—and then …	368
	Lesbos now	368
	A Lesbian-French art connection	375
	The Nobel-laureate poet from Lesbos	380
	Recycling the past	390
Appendix: The Greek Alphabet		393
Notes		394
References		409
Reference Tables A to M		419
Index		457

PREFACE

The names of *Lesbos* and of almost all the Greek islands are feminine. This is because the generic word for island in Greek, *nesos* (from which we derive Peloponnesos, Polynesia, Indonesia, etc., but not . . . amnesia), as in many other languages, is feminine also. But my connection with Lesbos, both the island and the book, is not due to my own womanhood, nor to the origins of my name, Olvia (blissfully happy) MacCarr (blessed) which can be traced to ancient Greek texts about this Aeolian island. I am writing these lines actually to stress the opposite of the sharp male-female distinction prevalent in Greek antiquity (1). What impresses me is the lack of difference, the virtual identity between women and men in the course of these 3,000-year stories associated with Lesbos.

Lyricism, romanticism, liberalism, as well as lesbianism, dilettantism and hedonism are some of the *isms*, (besides cataclysms!) which commonly open up paths of escape from the rules and rigors of reality. But the return to Lesbos is not a retreat or withdrawal. It is a celebration, a feast. Not everything or everyone at a party is of course good or even tolerable. In *Lesbos* too we have situations and people with a mixture, as Homer rhapsodized (Chapter I-A), of blessings and evil. Orpheus, the son of a muse, created the lyrical tradition for Lesbos but his purity and mysticism brought on his destruction and death in the hands of maniacal women. The love of young girls inspired Sappho of Lesbos to compose lines "unsurpassed in 2500 years" (Chapter II-B) but she also suffered the political hatred and even the theatrical ridicule not only of her contemporaries but of many generations after her lifetime. The "sages" of antiquity including the Lesbian Pittakos (Chapter III-A) have remained famous for their wise sayings but also for their imperfections and for the hostility they aroused among their compatriots. Some of the most profound philosophers the world has ever seen came from, or spent some time on Lesbos. They also had their lives stained by the civil wars and slaughters among their cities and by their own sensuous and sexual overindulgence (Chapter III-C), or, on the contrary, by their negativism and their denial of the "real" world.

The light of the "dark" ages saw on Lesbos a combination of the most devout Christian spirituality with types of human behavior and with personal lives full of banality and brutality. An outstanding medieval female ruler, the Byzantine empress Irene "the Athenian," died in exile on Lesbos after having ordered the blinding of her own son in the purple chamber of the palace in Constantinople, where he was born of her. Soon after the year 1000 A.D., Constantine IX and his mistress spent years on the island, also in exile, before they returned to the capital. There he became king by marrying the aged empress, but still kept his mistress to form a ruling trio. Things got worse for women—and, it seems, also for men—in late medieval times when a pretender to the Byzantine throne forced his daughter to marry a Turk, in order to obtain Moslem military assistance against another Greek emperor. This opponent then gave his sister in marriage to a Genoese adventurer, offering the island of Lesbos as part of her dowry after he received from him the help he needed to regain the throne.

The "holo-grafts" of people and traditions continued on Lesbos up to the twentieth century. The Olympic Airlines jets now land on the airport by Mytilene five times daily. The streets of the city and the improving highways of the island are congested with private Audis and Hondas as well as with big busses and trucks. A new road was even constructed in 1988 leading to the village of Pelopi (near where, we assume, the winged chariot of Pelops landed about 3,000 years ago), mainly because the father of the U.S.A. presidential candidate, Michael Dukakis, came from that mountainous community. Yet things have not changed and I will go back to Lesbos anytime, to have the special *mezedes* (hors d'oeuvres) of sardines, octopus, eggplant or souvlaki, and to imbibe the uniquely delicious *Ouzo* flavored with the herbs which still grow as in ancient times (Sappho's girls decorated their hair with these) in the Lesbian valleys.

Among the many changes of modernization and side-by-side with the continuity of the tradition of hospitality and pleasurable living, some deep-seated explosive patterns also seem to characterize the island. According to Plato's *Symposium* a man who loved a woman was only half a man and the most masculine of men could only love other males. If that were to be true we might consider a woman's love of other women also the epitome of femininity. Some virulent tongues even from ancient times have accused the Lesbian poetess Sappho of being a "man-like sex maniac pornic [sic] lover of girls" (2). This vice of calling names (it is not a vice to love girls) has persisted until our own days. Lesbianism has been considered by some a disease, by others a perversion or sin. An overreaction has raised the word as a banner for a movement of "liberation" (3), as if private preferences, whether for chocolates, for fancy dresses, or for young women, were of any public concern! Hopefully books such as *Lesbos*, so well reflecting reality and true values, may place life's impulses and pulses in proper perspective and prevent both arbitrary praise and punishment. Poetry can be an extraordinary guiding light to achieve this. Lesbos is the home of Odysseas Elytis, a poet of modern Greece and of the modern world, who has been awarded the Nobel Prize for literature. Among Elytis's works is a book of translations to modern Greek of the poetry of Sappho (4). Even those with a limited knowledge of modern Greek can transcend ethnic ethics and appreciate the musicality, the meaning and the mystique of these lyrical lines and through them the "adoration of tender delicate feelings" (Chapter II-B) that has overcome holocausts and "homocausts" (Chapter III-B) for at least three thousand years.

Olvia E. MacCarr, M.A.,
Venice, Italy, and Vail, Colorado

REFERENCES

1. Cantarella, E.: *Pandora's Daughter: The Role and Status of Women in Greek and Roman Antiquity* (translated by M. B. Fant), Baltimore, Johns Hopkins Univ. Press, 1987.
2. Barnstone, W.: *Sappho and the Greek Lyric Poets*, New York, Stocken Books, 1988, p. 274 (quoting Ovid).
3. Abbott, S., Love, B.: *Sappho was a Right-On Woman: A liberated view of lesbianism*, New York, Stein and Day, 1972.
4. Elytis, O.: *Sappho—Recomposition and Rendition [Anasynthesi kai Apodosi]* (in modern Greek verses), 2nd Edition, Ikaros, Athens, 1985.

FOREWORD

The switch from biology and medicine to . . . Lesbiology, poetic love and historical dissection (or dys-sexion!) in the writing of *Lesbos*, has not been a case of self-indulgent pleasurable preoccupation, or *post*occupation of a physician, who having done his duty as a clinical consultant (caring for thousands of patients, writing about 200 professional articles and books, teaching and lecturing) decided that personal feeling, affection and emotional involvement are more important than medical services and rigid (frigid?) scientific knowledge. This is not just another case like that of the medieval Faust, who dedicated his younger years to the pursuit of factual or fictitious learning and later had to contract with the Devil (Mephistopheles), in order to gain the ability to love and to satisfy his passionate desire for a young maiden's erotic embrace. The writing of *Lesbos* has not been a change of directions, an abandonment of Kos, the Hippocratic island of medicine, for the sake of Lesbos, the Aeolian island of lyrics and love. Instead, it is a combined culmination of both. Lesbos, the island and the book, represent the natural goal, the evolution and expansion backward and forward, of a person's search for meaning in life, for love and poetic expression and also of the capacity to comprehend the "artificial stupidity" of many historic events.

Many people, including some outstanding individuals, have had different and often contrasting existential experiences in a single lifetime. These do not reflect abnormal, schizoid traits and they involve much more than a simple succession of phases, common in artistic creativity. Such "double lives" go as far as changing religious faiths, political views, moral principles and even sex. Arkhilohos, a pioneer poet before 600 B.C. died in battle as a paid mercenary soldier. An earlier Greek, the mythical seer Teiresias, was turned into a woman for several years and then again became a man. This is how he was able to settle the argument between the gods, Zeus and his wife Hera, comparing male and female erotic experiences and deciding, incidentally, in favor of femininity. In the author of *Lesbos* we have someone who has been both a rational scientist and a sensitive poet, a passionate and compassionate lover of individual human beings and an objectively detached aesthetic connoisseur. For that he could be considered an expert "aesthesiologist," as he aims at the enhancement rather than the suppression (as in anesthesiology) of feeling and awareness.

The need for a certain humility must not obscure a sense of growing pride at the realization of an exceptional achievement. This is the ability to combine an unfailing rationality, unlimited encyclopedic knowledge and a critical sorting of facts with a highly developed intuitive sensitivity for artistic values and an emotional appreciation for all human efforts to express beauty in a diversity of media. The study of original, first experiences of pleasurable sensations and of new vistas of human sensitivity involves an analytical study of "the pleasures and pains of virginal experiences," which is the topic of a forthcoming publication by the same author. Paralleled by the delight of new developments however, is a critical and skillful appraisal of the increasingly prevalent failure of most "mature" artists and writers to express human feelings, moods, aspirations and inspirations adequately and well. A possible explanation for the resulting "poemetics" is to be found in the "poetiology" of human creativity. In the past two or three hundred years, and particularly in our twentieth century, young people with "brains" have directed themselves to the predictable, solid, comforting and yet not often inspiring fields of the sciences and administrative or business activities. Poets, painters, musicians and other artists commonly emerged only among the rebels, reacting against either the social "system", or against their own inability to conform to the demanding disciplines. It is now wonderful that we are able to prove that the sharp nails and intersecting beams of the scientific "cross" do not necessarily destroy artistic inspiration. Conversely, a reluctance to master practical reason, knowledge and skills is not a determining dynamic basis for escapist artistic activity.

The publication of "Lesbos" is the result of a synthetic process, an interweaving of many approaches, rational, intuitive and sentimental. Virginal experiences in poetry and music (the discovery of the first lyrical lines, as well as of the first case of plagiarism), in politics (first democracy and first dictators), in social structures and in national destinies are here combined with a careful selection, by twentieth century criteria, from the Greek words and sounds that are not only ingenious but enjoyable and modern. The unearthing or "unsalting" of Lesbian legends and of the island's history, offer us the uninterrupted, though knotty thread of life that continues to pulsate in all of us who are now here and able to read this book. This thread, the same as that of the ancient Fates, can and should be transmitted to others who will follow, if life as we know it continues on this earth. It is here that biology and lesbiology merge, to meet the urge of making life not only livable but also delightful, lucid and luxurious.

Constantine J. Falliers, M.D., Denver, Colorado, U.S.A.

INTRODUCTION

The rediscovery of Lesbos, a real island full of feelings, felicity, humiliations and horrors, began about the time when, not discontent with medical science but still wondering about the mysteries of the "self", I was exploring (a) the basic units of pleasure, which I had decided to call "hedons" in reference to other elementary particles, such as electrons and protons, and (b) the many "firsts" and "never agains" of life, virginal experiences both pleasurable and painful, involving the body, the emotions and the intellect. At the same time I found myself deploring (a) the misconceptions and miscarriages of word-values, particularly the degradation and distortion of expressions such as "classical" and "romantic", "lyrical", "epicurean", "stoic" and on to "apocalypse" and "holocaust", (see Chapters III & IV re. Greek "homocaust"), "lesbian", "gay" and many others, and (b) the inconsistent and confused views of Greek antiquity, ranging from an unrestrained admiration of the "birthplace of democracy" and of the classical world of marble-white purity, to the bewilderment and shock with the endless civil and fratricidal wars, with a civilization based on slavery and with the striking prevalence of unconventional sexual practices. Despite a more detached and kind contemporary comprehension of opposites, the continuity of contrasts through the medieval Byzantine mysticism and malice, down to the current twentieth century materialistic myths, scintillating science and self-induced "artificial stupidity", remained puzzling. The resolution and the result was the writing of *Lesbos*.

The first encounters with the actual island of Lesbos were accidental, having to do with the polarity of philosophy and food. Rechecking Pythagoras' theory of music I realized that the first—"virginal"—experience of cosmologic rational thinking by the man who first used the word "philosophy" was on Lesbos (Chapter II-A). I also then recalled that Theophrastos, the great philosopher and student of nature, who also has been credited for the preservation of much of Aristotle's work, was a Lesbian and that his "peripatetic" (wandering, as much as promenading) teacher, Aristotle himself, spent some years on Lesbos (Chapter III-C). Closer to "home" and to modern life, on a return visit to Athens over ten years ago, I found the most intriguing and intensely satisfying taverna (where the tentacles of fresh octopus hanging over the entrance almost brushed our hair as we walked in) located where my own grandmother's ground floor apartment used to be in the 1940s on a side alley off a narrow downtown street. That delightful place was called "Mytilene" and was run by a man from that city on Lesbos. His enormous black moustache was like that of Nietzsche, the German philosopher who in my student days made me first aware of the conceptual contrast between Apollo and Dionysos, purity and passion, a duality which I would reencounter on Lesbos (Chapter I-B). The tavern-man served us the best Lesbian ouzo, the well-known aperitif, which is still flavored with the seeds of the same anise [the Aeolic *aneton*] herbs that Lesbian girls 2500 years ago used to decorate their hair. Singing to her attractive young ladyfriends, the Lesbian poetess Sappho around 600 B.C. commanded:

> AND NOW . . . DECK YOUR LOVELY CURLS
> WITH CROWNS OF TENDER STALKS OF ANISE
> WOVEN TOGETHER WITH YOUR DELICATE HANDS . . .
> Elytis, 1973, p.70; Lobel/Page 1963, 82; Edmonds 1928, 117.

The brand name "Mini" of a Lesbian ouzo seems to refer not only to the mini-skirt (the prefix *mini-* is Latin, not Greek) on the label, but also to the first and last syllables in the name of the Lesbian city Mytilene, in which all vowels sound like the "i" in mini, Mi-ti-li-ni (Appendix I).

Between the Lesbos of the classical Greek philosophers and the ouzo of the late twentieth century (Ref. Table A) is the year 1044 A.D., when a Byzantine princess who had lived on Lesbos (Chapter V-B) died of asthma, the first known historical person to succumb to the illness that has concerned much of my medical work (Falliers, C.J., *J. Asthma* 23:97 & 239, 1986) and still perplexes clinical scientists with its worldwide increase in morbidity and mortality. Moving from medicine to myth, I was impressed to note that the recipient of the first human transplant, the mythical Pelops, also landed on Lesbos. There, his charioteer was dead upon arrival, due to the rapidity of their flight on the winged chariot and that event established another first, a death due to "jetlag" (Chapter II-B). The head of Orpheus 3,000 years ago, carried by the waves to the island's shore, marked the beginning of Lesbian lyrical tradition, which still exists (Chapter I-B). Of the two modern Greek poets awarded the Nobel prize for literature in the twentieth century, one, Odysseas Elytis, is of Lesbian origin and has a home on the island. The family of the other poet-laureate, George Seferis, came from the Ionian shores of Asia Minor a few miles east of Lesbos. As for Orpheus, his *persona*—if not his religion (Chapter I-B)—has conquered the world. The countless musical compositions, the works of art and literature of the past five hundred years for or about Orpheus include the early 20th century poems and collections of sonnets by Paul Valéry in French and R.M. Rilke in German. Among the leading composers in this century who took Orpheus as their theme (Porter, A., *The New Yorker*, June 23, 1986; June 6, 1988; July 1, 1991) were K. Weill (*The New Orpheus*, double concerto, 1925-27), D. Milhaud (*Les Malheurs d' Orphée*, opera 1926-27), I. Stravinsky (*Orpheus*, ballet, 1947), A. Hovhaness (*Meditation on Orpheus*, 1958), Wm. Schuman (*The Song of Orpheus*, cello sonata, 1958), L. Foss (*Orpheus and Euridice* two-violin concerto, 1972/83), E. Bond (*Canzoni to Orpheus*, 1980), and H-W. Henze (*Orpheus behind the wire*, ballet, 1981-83). After the 1948 French film *Orphée* by J. Cocteau and the Brazilian musical motion picture *Black Orpheus* [*Orfeo du Carnival*], in the 1980s there was the award-winning opera *The Mask of Orpheus* by H. Birtwistle and currently the one-act opera *Orphée* by Ph. Glass, premiered in Cambridge, Ma. in May 1993. The 1940/58 play by Tennessee Williams, *Orpheus Descending*, and the 1988 novel of Robertson Davies, *The Lyre of Orpheus*, used the name of the legendary musician-mystic not entirely in vain.

Evidently one may "come"—a climax of consummating love, or a second coming of salvation from existential tormenting trivia—to Lesbos through many paths, including love of lyrics, or love of any kind, or empathy for another human person, or intrigue with history's persistent perversity, or simply through the pleasures, glories and disasters of human society and individual lives. Lesbos, the island and the concept may still, without much doubt, remain unknown or faintly recognized by millions of people. The reader can decide whether this ignorance is a failure or a virtue (back to the concept of virginal experiences!), possibly preferable to overdiscovery. Lesbos, in fact, has been examined and overdiscovered with such distorting magnifying glasses that both the virtues and the vices connected with this island can be viewed as the invention of some "miscreants." Excessive and idealized adoration is one of these trespasses. Over one hundred years ago, the English author of "Studies of the Greek Poets" (first edition 1873), John Addington Symonds, declared:

> For a certain space of time, the Aeolians occupied the very foreground of Greek literature, and blazed out with a brilliance of lyrical splendor that has never been surpassed. There seems to have been something passionate and intense in their temperament. Lesbos, the centre of Aeolian culture, was the island of overmastering passions: the personality of the Greek race burned there with a fierce and steady flame of concentrated feeling. The energies which the Ionians divided between pleasure, politics, trade, legislation, science, and the arts, and which the Dorians turned to war and statecraft and social economy, were restrained by the Aeolians within the sphere of individual emotions, ready to burst

forth volcanically. Nowhere in any age of Greek history, or in any part of Hellas, did the love of physical beauty, the sensibility to radiant scenes of nature, the consuming fervour of personal feeling, assume such grand proportions and receive so illustrious an expression as they did in Lesbos. At first this passion blossomed into the most exquisite lyrical poetry that the world has known: this was the flower-time of the Aeolians, their brief and brilliant spring. But the fruit it bore was bitter and rotten. Lesbos became a byword for corruption. The passions which for a moment had flamed into the gorgeousness of Art, burning their envelope of words and images, remained a mere furnace of sensuality, from which no expression of the divine in human life could be expected.

Several circumstances contributed to the development of lyric poetry in Lesbos. The customs of the Aeolians permitted more social and domestic freedom than was common in Greece. Aeolian women were not confined to the harem like Ionians, or subjected to the rigorous discipline of the Spartans. While mixing freely with male society, they were highly educated , and accustomed to express their sentiments to an extent unknown elsewhere in history—until, indeed, the present time. The Lesbian ladies applied themselves successfully to literature. They formed clubs for the cultivation of poetry and music. They studied the arts of beauty, and sought to refine metrical forms and diction. Nor did they confine themselves to the scientific side of art. Unrestrained by public opinion, and passionate for the beautiful, they cultivated their senses and emotions, and indulged their wildest passions. All the luxuries and elegances of life which that climate and the rich valleys of Lesbos could afford, were at their disposal; exquisite gardens, where the rose and hyacinth spread perfume; river-beds ablaze with the oleander and wild pomegranate; olive-groves and fountains, where the cyclamen and violet flowered with feathery maidenhair; pine tree-shadowed coves, where they might bathe in the calm of a tideless sea; fruits such as only the southern sun and sea-wind can mature; marble cliffs, starred with jonquil and anemone in spring, aromatic with myrtle and lentisk and samphire and wild rosemary through all the months; nightingales that sang in May; temples dim with dusky gold and bright with ivory; statues and frescoes of heroic forms. In such scenes as these the Lesbian poets lived, and thought of love. When we read their poems, we seem to have the perfumes, colours, sounds, and lights of that luxurious land distilled in verse. Nor was a brief but biting winter wanting to give tone to their nerves, and,by contrast with the summer, to prevent the palling of so much luxury on sated senses. The voluptuousness of Aeolian poetry is not like that of Persian or Arabian art. It is Greek in its self-restraint, proportion, tact. We find nothing burdensome in its sweetness. All is so rhythmically and sublimely ordered in the poems of Sappho that supreme art lends solemnity and grandeur to the expression of unmitigated passion."

Symonds, JA, in Page, D. 1955, pp. 140-142.

INTRODUCTION

The glory of Aeolic literature, Lesbian lyrics and particularly of Sapphic verses has been subject to unrestricted admiration throughout the Greek-speaking world from early classical times, by Plato, the Hellenistic and Roman literary critics, as well as the relatively closer to us 12th century A.D. Byzantine scholar Tzetzes. Other excesses went in the opposite direction. The passionate eroticism, liberal or "loose" morality on the island and the sexual preferences or practices of its most famous woman poet have been the subject of ethical disapproval and also of theatrical ridicule. Only one generation after Sappho, the Ionian poet Anacreon, who wrote boy-loving poems to please his patron, the dictator of Samos Polycrates, lamented in verse about his rejection by a young woman and blamed it on her "lesbian" preference for other girls:

SHE, BEING FROM THE STYLISH WELL-BUILT LESBOS, REJECTS ME ON ACCOUNT OF MY HAIR TURNING WHITE AND RUNS OPEN-MOUTHED TO SOME OTHER (NAUGHTY) GIRL.
(Quoted in Greek by Page, 1955, page 143)

If these lines simply try to comfort an aging man rejected by a charming girl who prefers female company, much worse "anti-lesbian" expressions were to appear for centuries. No fewer than five comedies were presented in ancient Greece (Chapter II-B) making fun of Sappho and of her "lesbian", as well as presumed multiple heterosexual love affairs. The well known Roman poet, Ovid, commented that Lesbian girls had become infamous for their love relationships and in Byzantine times the reference compendium called *Suidas* or *Suda* (Oxf. Class. Dict. p.1019) stated that Sappho "had a bad reputation for her shameful love affairs" (Chapter II-B).

The ancients went well beyond the modern practice of applying the adjective "lesbian" to female homosexual love. They, and particularly the writers of Attic comedy, used a verb "to lesbize" [lesbizein or *lesbiazein*] for a sexual practice other than homoeroticism and specifically for the oral sex activity called fellatio. These Athenian playwrights evidently attributed the invention of fellatio to the luxury-loving Lesbians.

THAT OLD AND FAMOUS TRICK OF APPLYING OUR MOUTHS WAS, AS THEY SAY, INVENTED BY THE SONS OF LESBIANS
(Quoted in Greek by Henderson, 1975, pg. 183)

The verb "to lesbize" is encountered at least three times in the plays of Aristophanes, the leading Athenian comedy writer. His characters talk about a flute girl "who is about to lesbize" the drinking partners—not an uncommon practice, it seems (Henderson, 1975). The muse inspiring Euripides "did not lesbize", which indicated (double-meaning) that she did not follow the Lesbian singing modes and also that she did not perform fellatio. Then there was a girl insulting a hag with the lines "It seems to me you place the lambda [λ = L] as the Lesbians do", the word for the letter "L" also being an obscene reference to the male organ (Henderson, 1975 pp. 129, 183, etc).

In assembling the collage of text-styles about Lesbos, however, there was no particular need to condemn or to defend "lesbian" practices of any kind. When a modern commentator and translator in the USA stated that "sexual frenzy was as respectable [*sic*] a passion to Sappho as rapacious selfishness to an American" (Davenport, 1984, p. 10), he did not make it clear whether both attitudes were to be accepted or rejected. Most of us, trying to be impartial—though not indifferent—consider "frenzy", or ecstasy, perhaps a little more commendable or enviable than selfish greed. In the writing of "Lesbos" there was no preconceived plan either to glorify or to criticize the literary products, the arts, the politics or any individual or social lifestyles on this Aeolian island. Nothing about Lesbos, from our eclectic, timidly tolerant and tentatively respectful twentieth century perspective invites absolute admiration or total abhorrence. What has been and remains wonderfully fascinating is human life itself in its fullest expression, its realized or shattered expectations and its self-exploring awareness. In answer to the question whether this book is about history, literature, eroticism or philosophy, ethnic pride or modernistic moralizing, the answer should be that *Lesbos* is basically a candelabrum of life.

The building blocks, the "bricks" of this work are established texts, generally in Greek, from the early antique and classical to the medieval and modern times, referring to Lesbos, or written by people on or from the island. The classical texts are all printed in CAPITAL letters to distinguish them from the interspersed narrative and also to evoke the writings on ancient monuments, plaques and papyri. Validation of the authenticity of each fragment is discussed in each section, whenever this seems pertinent. There is a story in Isak Dinesen's *Out of Africa* (Davenport, 1984, p. 13) of a parrot trained to recite rhymes of Lesbian lyrics in Greek. Whether the accent was Aeolic, English, the author's Danish, or the owner's Chinese, people evidently took the parrot's "word" that his lines were authentic. Unfortunately the acceptance of some contemporary translations of ancient poetry (Chapter II-B and Ref. Table H) as noteworthy, relies on the same degree of poorly justified trust.

The "cement" of this 3,000-year history, the information about places and people and the comments about events are in regular type, with references to other more specialized publications and also to Tables, Maps and Illustrations. Names and works with alternative spelling, translated or transliterated, are given in parentheses. When, following a current dominant trend (Levi, 1986), it appears necessary to return to a spelling closer to the original Greek and different from the more or less established Latin (in particular to avoid the prevalent Latin spelling ending in -us instead of the Greek -os, or the Latin "ae" for the Greek "ai"—e.g. *Aiolos* vs. *Aeolus*) the preferred transliteration is included in brackets. The main difficulty in transliterating from the Greek is not with the relatively unknown names but with those that are now quite common. For the sake of consistency next to the name of Homer the Greek [*Homeros*] is added, with no intention or expectation that this, or *Platon* for Plato, *Aristoteles* for Aristotle and *Alexandros* for Alexander will prevail. A certain inconsistency will persist but rather than perpetuate the distortion with new names, we have, like most current writers, adopted generally the Hellenized spelling, even dropping both "ch" and "kh" in favor of "h" (Greek = chi), when that sounded right, especially between vowels (e.g. Sappho's brother *Larihos*, not Larichos or Larikhos). The traditional Latinizing style has been given preference mostly for the "famous" established names or words now part of everyday English, such as Homer, Phillip, Alexander, etc.

A major problem in the phonetic transliteration from Greek to English is the existence of only one acceptable letter, for two or more corresponding sounds in Greek. The letter "e," for instance, in English denotes what in Greek and most other western languages is the sound "ay" as in the name of Sappho's daughter—and mother—Cleis [*Kleis*] which ought to be pronounced Klay-ees. Also, however, "e" in English and other languages is used instead of the Greek "eta," which in the spoken Greek of at least the past 2,000 years sounds like a long "ee." In the case of the cities on Lesbos specifically, Mytilene is in Greek pronounced with all vowels sounding between the "i" in *mini* and the long "ee" in *me*, essentially like a French, Italian or Spanish "i." In the name of the other Lesbian city, Methymna, the first syllable should sound "ee" as in me, and not like the "me-" in metric. Another very common transliteration problem (others are listed in the Appendix) involves the distinction between the sound "th" in *the*, and in *the*ater. In Greek this is written with two different letters, delta or theta. Even though the delta is often rendered with a "d" in English, the sound is closer to the "th" of *the* or *the*n. The pronunciation of "b" is also softer in Greek, so in modern printing even Lesbos [ΛΕΣΒΟΣ] is often transliterated as Lesvos (Eleftheriadis, 1987). Anglicized phonetics, of course, would be unnecessary if the exact pronunciation of the Greek letters and their combinations could be learned by everyone. This seems a relatively simple task, especially if attention is paid mainly to the living language of the past 1,000–2,000 years and if speculations about ancient pitch-oriented sounds are left for the scholars. The option concerning the possible acquisition of this additional verbal tool, the 24 letters of the Greek alphabet (Appendix)—most of which are identical to those in other western or Latin-derived languages—is left up to the individual reader, with the promise that the difficulties will be minor compared to the many rewards of being able to read Greek, at least phonetically. The full meaning of certain medieval and modern Greek words might only be appreciated literally, so they have been cited, usually in brackets.

After the basic orientation with respect to chronological times (Reference Table A), places (Maps I, II and III) and names (Reference Tables B, C, etc.) certain precise historical markers may be important guides for the 3,000-year journey to and through Lesbos. Major dates are given in terms of B.C. and A.D., which for those who prefer it, could be taken to signify Before the Current and then the Actual Dating systems. The ancients dated events in relation to the Olympic games, the 4-year periods between the "Olympiads" and a few significant correlations of the two dating systems are given on Reference Table A. Dates, which critically determined the course of human history and must be remembered include the victory of the Greeks against the Persians at Marathon, the beginning and the end of the war of Athens and Sparta, the establishment of major philosophical schools, the campaigns of Alexander the Great, the Roman conquest of Greece, the recognition of Christianity as the official religion of the Roman empire, Latin, Arab, Slavic, Turkish and other in-roads into the Greek world; the disappearance and re-emergence of Hellas as a nation and finally the events of our twentieth century, the major world wars and social or ethnic upheavals, with the declarations and the decline of national independence movements. Individual lives, the development and interpretation of historical personalities, changes in social and national structures and, in fact, the evolution of the language in which the history and the literature related to Lesbos have been recorded will then be naturally understood and appreciated. In our "brick and mortar" structure consisting of authentic literal translations and narrative commentaries binding them, we will then also find doors and windows to penetrate life's situations inside Lesbos and, looking out to the world, to gain new perspectives and vistas of the three millennia of our history.

Each chapter of *Lesbos* can be read in sections according to the reader's time and primary interests. For specific information it may be best to start from the Index and to find important notations about, say, Aristotle or Zeno, Orpheus or Epicuros, forms of love and types of death, music and the Muses, metaphysics and ethics, metamorphoses or metaphors. While the cross-indexing has not been allowed to become overwhelmingly detailed, interested readers should be able to create their own multidimensional concept correlations, making a note, for instance, of ambisexuality among the philosophers, cruelty in relation to the fine arts, poetry in politics and so on without stop. Next to being a 3,000 year history of life on Lesbos, this book actually presents an embroidery of concepts and conditions which can easily prepare the ground for further mental structures or . . . deconstructions. Self-service from the 3,000-year displays of *Lesbos* should be as easy and pleasurable as going through or choosing from a sumptuous buffet table. Some items on this selection array may seem strange but can prove delectable. Other pieces that appear attractive may be hard to digest, at least by some unprepared information-consumers. Although overindulgence can cause mental indigestion, proper selectivity and perhaps a second or third visit to the Lesbian "buffet table" should ensure an unlimited enjoyment without trespassing the boundaries of individual comprehension or tolerance.

For an overview or a "wide angle" approach it may be good to look at *Lesbos* from the beginning to the end from a proper distance. The Table of Contents may serve as the guideline, although, as already pointed out, some readers may prefer to start with the Index and then go on to the chapter sequence. There, as in the case of our "mixed" philosopher Pherekydes, who explained the world partly in rational and partly in mythical terms, the stories of the Amazons, Macar and Orpheus blend folk fantasies with the better-documented events of the Iliad and the Odyssey. What follows these is not only solid and crystal clear historical information but sometimes a spectrum of multifaceted views, which include pervasive gossip, still intriguing, informative and occasionally irritating more than 10 or 25 centuries later. Chapters III and IV place next to each other historical war reports and popularized sentimental romances with varying degrees of explicit details. The otherworldly mysticism and savage selfishness of medieval times may be particularly strange for modern readers, yet they form an essential and factual link between antiquity and modern times. The survival of Greek tradition in coexistence with many invaders and conquerors offers important lessons both about the significance and the futility of national and religious beliefs. As we arrive to the time of independence for Lesbos in 1912, we begin to see how, as in the case of Orpheus and Euridice 3,000 years ago, what is about to be gained can be irretrievably lost. The Greek spirit, and even the Greek language in the second part of the twentieth century seemed to be losing much of what they had been able to retain during the previous millennia.

In essence, as it has already been pointed out, "Lesbos" presents a collage of continuity, if seen from a certain distance, or a mosaic of dissimilar data, if close-up sections are viewed separately. Throughout this disconcerting "concert" (Gk. *synaulia*, see Chapter IV-B) of events, superb and unequalled beauty in words, feelings and works can be detected and should be not only appreciated but assimilated. Despite the self-destruction of the Greeks—called "homocaust" in Chapter III—there is nothing repulsive in the personal lives of the Lesbian lore. It can be claimed in fact that in the Hellenic expression of human existence the absence of offensive features is comparable to the virtual lack of ugliness in nature, whether in a weed or a flower, a cloud or a rock, an insect or a volcano. The "Lesbian Lessons" (that was intended initially to be the title of this book) provide us with penetrating sketches of human personal and political behavior, of the expanding awareness of existence, of love, surrender and survival, which can faithfully follow us on our path to the worldly light of our self-discovery, provided that we do not, like Orpheus, look back in doubt. If this foundation of trust and faith is lost, Lesbos also, like Euridice, will disappear in the dark mists of the irrevocable past and the elements of our mental reconstruction will be dimmer than the lifeless stars, because the lyre of Orpheus—or of Arion—will not be shining in our firmament.

K. Inos Fallieros
Englewood, Colorado, and Athens, Greece

ACKNOWLEDGMENTS

From the beginning, the understanding, encouragement and support of my dear wife Electra kept *Lesbos* going. The trips with her to the island of Lesbos, to the antiquarians in Athens (Greece) and to the venerable American libraries in New York City, in Cambridge, Ma. (Houghton) and in Georgetown, D.C. (Dumbarton Oaks) were milestones for this three-thousand-year journey. Most valuable information and material were provided by Pan. Christopoulos, director of the Library of Congress in Athens, Greece. Our mutual friend, J. Paranikas kindly gave me a copy of his great-uncle's book on Greek education for the past few hundred years. Through these Athenian friends we were fortunate to receive the warm hospitality of Takis and Stella Tsorvadellis of Mytilene on Lesbos. First and foremost have been the services of the Denver Public Library system and those of the University of Denver. Their comprehensive and comprehending information retrieval often enabled me to obtain volumes from ordinarily inaccessible sources and thus made my work much more complete.

Skillfully switching from modern medicine to Greek literature, Jean Vrchota-Holland typed and processed the entire text on our clinical word processing system. The close and conscientious cooperation of the experienced staff at Johnson Printing Co. in Boulder, Colorado, and the meticulous attention to every detail has contributed significantly to the success of this publishing effort.

Due credits for any texts quoted are rendered to the original authors and publishers. Translations in English are my own with incidental reference to earlier translation efforts, in several languages. Illustrations and photographs, other than my own, are reproduced with proper indication of the source and, whenever possible, after written permission. In some instances, both pertaining to texts and to illustrations, neither the original nor the current address of the (mostly foreign) publisher was obtainable. Acknowledgment of all these valuable contributions (cited specifically in the bibliography) is made with deep appreciation.

– *KIF / CJF*

Lip cup, chariot race, mid sixth century B.C., Pl. 49 in Arias, 1961.

CHAPTER I

THE HEAD OF ORPHEUS

A. How Aeolians and others became Lesbians
　　Hellenic genesis and Deukalion's flood
　　Aeolus [*Aiolos*], Macar, and the Amazons
　　The daughters of Macar and the songs of Homer
　　Lesbos in the Odyssey
　　The flying chariot of Pelops
　　Penthilos and rescue by dolphins

B. Orpheus, the Muses and the Mad Women of Thrace
　　The head of Orpheus
　　The rhythm of the Argonauts, the lure of the Sirens
　　Orpheus and Euridice
　　Orphic poetry, religion and philosophy

Orpheus, from a bronze statue of *Orpheus and Euridice*, by the Colorado sculptor Edgar Britton, 1960. Courtesy of The Denver Art Museum.

Overleaf: Woman prompting Herakles (Hercules) to battle, late sixth century B.C. krater (mixing bowl); Louvre, Paris (in Arias/Shefton, 1961, Fig. 111.)

A. HOW AEOLIANS AND OTHERS BECAME LESBIANS

Hellenic Genesis and Deukalion's Flood

The prehistoric petrified woods on the island show that the triangular spot of land we call *Lesbos* has existed for millions of years (Elef. 1986). At one time it may have been connected, like a bulging peninsula, with the Asiatic mainland, now only 5 to 8 miles to the east across the sea. For thousands of years, the human presence has also left its marks in the stone and bronze tools and the intriguing artifacts still dug up here and there, intentionally or accidentally (1). It was only a little over thirty centuries ago, however, that the super-human, semi-mythical heroes, Macar, Lesbos, Achilles, Orestes and before them the Amazons, arrived on these shores (Ref. Table A). According to Hellenic tradition, these pioneers, or their offspring, settled on the island and lent their names to the places or to the events of our 3,000-year-long excursion.

Before 3000 B.C. "civilized," i.e., city-centered human communities grew on the island along the lines of those in Troy across the water on the Asiatic coast. The Pelasgians were probably there before 1500 B.C. (Ref. Table A). Then came a cataclysmic flood—perhaps the same one that the Biblical Noah survived with the help of God—which presumably wiped out all human life on Lesbos. The Achaean Greeks [*Akhaioi*] began to arrive in the late fourteenth century B.C. and already by "around 1300 B.C." (Wood, M., 1985, p. 180) Hittite inscriptions referred to "Lazpas"—the Hittite name for Lesbos—as the source of cult idols, possibly representing "the great pre-Greek god of Lesbos, Smintheus" (Wood, M., 1985, p. 180), which were brought to their Asiatic kingdom to save their plague-stricken king. Following the Achaeans came from Thessaly in Central Greece the Aeolians, (Table I-A) who spoke their own soft and lyrical dialect of the Greek language (Roche, 1966). These early Greek settlers traced their ancestry to Aeolus [*Aiolos*], a third generation descendant of the only man and woman that survived the Hellenic flood. These sons and daughters of Aeolus were enriched by scattered minorities from elsewhere. Sappho, the most famous Lesbian poetess, may have been in part of Asiatic Phrygian (the kingdom of Midas) background. Her senior contemporary, the political leader and sage Pittakos, was the son of a man from Thrace, who came to Mytilene on Lesbos and married a native woman. Orpheus too, who is credited for the lyrical tradition and poetic excellence of the people of Lesbos, was a native of the northern mainland, Thrace. Eastern non-Hellenic influences were reflected in the name of the island itself, which scholars have attributed to the Carian, or Lydian *Lazba*, or to the Phoenician-

Semitic *esbu* (Paulys, 1925, p. 2107). In earlier times Lesbos was also known as *Aiolis*, *Pelasgia*, *Lasia* (for the luscious vegetation), *Himerte* (enviable, desirable), *Macaria* (blessed), *Issa* and *Mytonis*, perhaps the root for the name of the city *Mytilene* (Paulys, 1925, p. 2108).

Aeolus, who often has been identified with the Lord of the Winds (a namesake?) was the son of a Nymph (Table 1) and his father was one of the earliest Greek heroes, Hellen. Hellen's parents—the grandparents of Aeolus—were Deukalion and Pyrrha (her name, meaning flame-haired, redhead, was possibly related to the town of Pyrrha on Lesbos), whom the gods according to Greek mythology had kept alive when the rest of the population of Greece perished in the flood. The four Hellenic tribes, the Achaeans, the Aeolians, the Ionians and the Dorians, took their names after Hellen's two sons and two grandsons (Table I-1). Macar (meaning blessed or blissful), a king of Lesbos mentioned in Homer's

Hercules [*Herakles*] battling with an Amazon. Metope from Selinus.
National Museum, Palermo.

Iliad, was supposedly a son of Helios (the sun) and he came to Lesbos from the island of Rhodes. This king is often identified with Macareus (3), the son of Aeolus, who became notorious for an incestuous relation with his sister. Later, another Macareus was a priest of the god Dionysos in Mytilene, where, as in other parts of Greece, this Dionysiac worship and passionate philosophy of life conflicted and at times intermingled with that of the Orphics (section I-B), which was pure, serene and intellectually Apollonian (Guthrie, 1935/52, Chapt. II–VI; Hogart, 1993).

Aeolus [Aiolos], Macar and the Amazons

Maybe the first to establish permanent human communities on Lesbos and on Aeolis were the Amazons. This was a mythical race of women warriors who, in order to fight and to ride better (they were thought to be always on horseback), had one breast removed. This is why they were named Amazons [*a-mazon*, without a breast] (Graves, 1958; Oxf. Class. Dict. 1978). Before they were all destroyed by Hercules [*Heracles*], the Amazons invaded the lands of the eastern Aegean coast and, under their leader, Myrina, won many battles against the local natives. The prolific historian of the first century A.D., Diodoros of Sicily [the "Sikeliot"] included both the Amazon and the Macar stories in his writings about the early settlements on Lesbos (Oldfather, 1968).

> **A LIBRARY OF HISTORY**
> BY DIODOROS OF SICILY, 1ST CENTURY A.D.
>
> **BOOK III**
> **55.5-7.** THEN SHE (MYRINA, THE AMAZON LEADER) OCCUPIED THE COASTAL REGION . . . AND BUILT MANY CITIES, ONE CALLED AFTER HERSELF AND OTHERS AFTER HER LEADING COMPANIONS, KYME, PITANE (2), PRIENE. . . . SHE ALSO CONQUERED SOME OF THE ISLANDS AND SPECIFICALLY LESBOS, WHERE SHE BUILT THE CITY OF MYTILENE, NAMED AFTER HER SISTER, WHO ALSO HAD TAKEN PART IN THE CAMPAIGN.
>
> From the Greek in Oldfather, C. H., Vol. II, p. 258.

Continuing his review of the mythologic origins of the Greek world, Diodoros wrote about other islands and particularly Crete. Then he returned to Lesbos with more factual details and even contradicted himself regarding the origins of some names, such as Mytilene.

> **BOOK V**
> **81.1-6.** NOW WE SHALL UNDERTAKE TO TALK ABOUT LESBOS. THIS ISLAND IN ANCIENT TIMES WAS INHABITED BY MANY PEOPLES AND MANY MIGRATIONS TOOK PLACE ON IT. WHILE

IT WAS STILL UNINHABITED THE PELASGIANS CAME AND WERE THE FIRST TO OCCUPY IT. IT HAPPENED THIS WAY. XANTHOS, SON OF TRIOPAS, REIGNING OVER THE PELASGIANS OF ARGOS, TOOK OVER PART OF LYCIA AND THERE HE BECAME THE KING OF THOSE WHO HAD COME WITH HIM. THEN CROSSING OVER TO LESBOS, WHICH WAS EMPTY, HE DIVIDED THE LAND AMONG HIS PEOPLE AND NAMED THE ISLAND, FORMERLY CALLED ISSA, AFTER THE SETTLERS, PELASGIA. SEVEN GENERATIONS LATER, AFTER THE FLOOD OF DEUKALION AND THE DESTRUCTION OF MOST OF MANKIND, LESBOS TOO WAS LEFT DESOLATE BY THE DELUGE. THEN CAME MACAREUS (3) . . . WITH PEOPLE GATHERED FROM MANY ETHNIC GROUPS. HE FIRST SETTLED ON LESBOS BUT LATER HE WAS ABLE TO EXPAND, BOTH DUE TO THE PRODUCTIVITY OF THE ISLAND AND TO HIS OWN FAIR AND JUST RULE. SO HE TOOK POSSESSION OF THE NEARBY ISLANDS, WHICH WERE NOT OCCUPIED AND HE DISTRIBUTED THE LAND THERE. ABOUT THAT TIME, (A MAN NAMED) LESBOS, SON OF LAPITHES, THE SON OF AIOLOS, . . . SAILED TO THE ISLAND WITH OTHER SETTLERS, AS ORDAINED BY AN ORACLE. LESBOS MARRIED METHYMNA, A DAUGHTER OF MACAREUS AND TOGETHER WITH HER, HE MADE HIS HOME ON THE ISLAND. LATER, AFTER HE BECAME VERY PROMINENT, HE NAMED THE ISLAND LESBOS AFTER HIMSELF AND ADDRESSED HIS PEOPLE AS LESBIANS. AMONG THE DAUGHTERS OF MACAREUS WERE MYTILENE AND METHYMNA AND FROM THEM TWO CITIES ON THE ISLAND GOT THEIR NAMES.

82 . . . THE ISLANDS, CROSSED BY FAIR WINDS AND ENJOYING A HEALTHFUL AIR FOR THE RESIDENTS, AS WELL AS BEING FERTILE AND PRODUCTIVE OF GOOD CROPS, WERE CONSISTENTLY FILLED WITH PROSPERITY. SO IT WAS THAT SOON THE INHABITANTS SEEMED ENVIABLY BLISSFUL AND THE ISLANDS WERE CALLED ISLANDS OF THE BLESSED. SOME SAY HOWEVER, THAT THE WORD "OF THE BLESSED" [GK. MAKARON] WAS FROM THE NAME OF MACAREUS. IN GENERAL THESE ISLANDS HAVE IN FACT LIVED IN SUCH HAPPINESS. . . . NOT ONLY IN OLD TIMES BUT IN OUR AGE TOO . . . THAT FOR GOOD REASON THEY HAVE BEEN CALLED WHAT THEY TRULY ARE, BLISSFUL.

Oldfather, C.H., Vol. III, pp. 318–20.

The daughters of Macar and the songs of Homer

The original King Macar had five daughters, Antissa, Issa, Arisbe, Methymna and Mytilene. Three of the five ancient cities—"Pentapolis"—on Lesbos were named after them (Table I-1) with the long "e" changed in Aeolic to a long "a" sound, as in Mathymna and Mytilana. Macar also had four sons, one of whom, Eresos, gave his name to another Lesbian town. Methymna (4) married a man named Lesbos, son of the mythical hero Lapithes. Lesbos migrated from Thessaly (5) on the advice of an

Homer [*Homeros*]; in Munich, from Richter 1965/84.

oracle and his name in feminine (islands in Greek are feminine), became that of the whole island. Sadly, the two sons of Lesbos and Methymna were later killed by Achilles (Chapter IV-C) when he invaded the island on his way to join the other Achaean Greeks in the war against the Trojans. The long and everlasting epic about that war, the Iliad, the campaign at Ilium (the district of Troy), refers several times to Lesbos, to the Lesbians and to Macar. The almost legendary author, the poet–bard Homer [*Homeros*, originally named *Melisigenes*] may have been a native of the Ionian island of Chios [*Hios*], just south of Lesbos. But the "father of history," Herodotos, believed that Homer was, like the Lesbians, an Aeolian (Lefkowitz, 1981, pp. 12–24). A long ancient Greek biography of Homer by an author using the name of the fifth century historian, Herodotos, related the birth of the poet to the chronology of the Trojan war and of the settlement of Lesbos.

THE LIFE OF HOMER
BY "HERODOTOS" (LATE ANTIQUITY WRITER USING THE NAME OF HERODOTOS OF HALICARNASSOS)
[35] AFTER THE EXPEDITION AGAINST TROY, LED BY AGAMEMNON AND MENELAOS, ONE HUNDRED AND THIRTY YEARS PASSED BEFORE CITIES WERE BUILT ON LESBOS. THE ISLAND HAD NO CITIES BEFORE THEN. TWENTY YEARS AFTER LESBOS WAS SETTLED, AEOLIAN KYME ... WAS SETTLED AND EIGHTEEN YEARS LATER SMYRNA WAS COLONIZED ... AND AT THAT TIME HOMER WAS BORN ... SO HOMER WAS BORN 168 YEARS AFTER THE TROJAN WAR.
(Text also cited in English by Lefkowitz, 1981, Appendix 1, p. 155).

But the "real" Herodotos wrote (History II.53): I BELIEVE THAT HOMER'S TIME WAS FOUR HUNDRED YEARS BEFORE MINE AND NOT MORE. Currently it is estimated that Homer lived between 800 and 700 B.C., more than 400 years after the Trojan war he rhapsodized (Oxf.

Class. Dict. p. 524). The starting and basic theme of the Iliad is the dispute between the leader of the Greeks Agamemnon and the young hero Achilles. In an effort to settle it the wise senior counsellor, Nestor, intervened. To his advice, King Agamemnon responded:

THE ILIAD BY HOMER [HOMEROS], 8TH CENTURY B.C.
BOOK IX, 115-130
"MY LORD, YOU HAVE NOT DESCRIBED MY OWN FOLLY FALSELY. I WAS OUT OF MY MIND, I CANNOT DENY IT MYSELF . . . NOW, HOWEVER, THAT I KNOW HOW WRONG I WAS IN MY PITIFUL PASSION, I AM WILLING TO MAKE UP FOR MY WRONGDOING AND TO REPAY WITH OVERABUNDANT GIFTS. IN THE PRESENCE OF ALL OF YOU I WILL DECLARE MY OUTSTANDING PRESENTS: SEVEN BRAND-NEW TRIPODS, TEN GOLDEN TALENTS (COINS) . . . TWELVE POWERFUL HORSES . . . ALSO I WILL OFFER SEVEN LESBIAN WOMEN ESPECIALLY SKILLED IN ARTISTIC HANDIWORK, WHO SURPASS ALL OTHERS IN BEAUTY AND WHOM I CHOSE FOR MYSELF AFTER HE (ACHILLES) HAD CONQUERED THE WELL-BUILT ISLAND OF LESBOS.

Later on (about Achilles):

ILIAD IX 663-665
. . . ACHILLES WENT TO SLEEP IN THE DEEP CORNER OF THE STURDY CABIN AND BY HIM LAY A WOMAN WHOM HE HAD BROUGHT FROM LESBOS, THE GOOD-LOOKING DIOMEDE, DAUGHTER OF PHORBAS.

From the original Greek, in Murray, AT, Vol. I, pp. 390–2 and 430.

After Achilles had killed in battle Hector, the hero of the Trojans and son of King Priam [*Priamos*] he felt sorry for the bereaved old father and said to him:

ILIAD, XXIV (FINAL BOOK OF THE EPIC) 522-548
"COME NOW AND REST ON THIS CHAIR, SO THAT FOR ALL OUR PAIN, WE MAY AIR THE SUFFERING IN OUR HEARTS AND PUT IT ASIDE . . . THERE ARE TWO URNS STANDING BY ZEUS . . . ONE FULL OF ILLS, THE OTHER OF BLESSINGS. WHEN THE MASTER OF THE THUNDERBOLTS MIXES THESE, SOMETIMES HE GRANTS ONE PERSON MORE BAD THINGS AND SOMETIMES MORE GOOD . . . (MY FATHER) PELEUS SURPASSED ALL MEN IN HAPPINESS AND WEALTH . . . YET EVEN UPON HIM THE GODS BROUGHT MISFORTUNE . . . HE ONLY HAD ONE SON (ME) DESTINED TO HAVE A SHORT LIFE. I AM NOT THERE TO CARE FOR HIM IN HIS OLD AGE, BUT (INSTEAD) HERE IN TROY, VERY FAR FROM MY COUNTRY, MAKING WAR AGAINST YOU AND YOURS. WE HEAR THAT YOU TOO, MY LORD, WERE HAPPY IN DAYS PAST. ALL THE LANDS, FROM

LESBOS, THE KINGDOM OF MACAR, TO INLAND PHRYGIA AND UP THE BOUNDLESS HELLESPONT WERE YOURS, PROOF OF THE SUPERIORITY OF YOUR WEALTH AND OF YOUR SONS . . . NOW, HOWEVER, EVEN AROUND YOUR CITY THERE IS FIGHTING AND MANSLAUGHTER".

Murray, AT, Vol. II, pp. 600–2.

Table I-1
GENEALOGY OF THE EARLY GREEK SETTLERS ON LESBOS

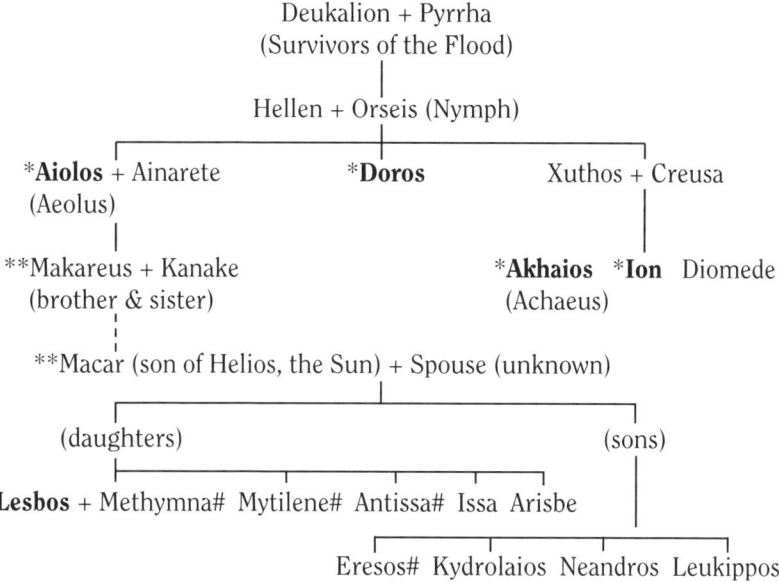

---

* Originators of the names of the four Hellenic tribes, the Aeolians, Dorians, Achaeans, and Ionians.

** Makareus, the son of Aiolos, and Macar, son of Helios, have often been viewed as one and the same person.

The names of three daughters and one son (in feminine) were given to cities on Lesbos. The island, formerly called *Issa*, was renamed (in feminine) after the hero *Lesbos*, son of Lapithes.

Lesbos in the Odyssey

According to Homer, it was on Lesbos that the Trojan war heroes Achilles and Ajax [*Aias*] buried the cleverest among the Greeks, Palamedes, who had invented weights and measures and also had adapted the Phoenician alphabet with vowels for the Greek tongue. He was maliciously killed in revenge for having tricked Odysseus of Ithaca into joining the war. After the sack of Troy, the victorious Greeks, Menelaos (whose wife Helen, had

Achilles killing the Amazon Penthesilea, 6th century amphora, London, British Museum (in Arias/Shefton, 1961, Pl. XVIII).

triggered the expedition by eloping with the Trojan prince Paris) and Nestor, held a meeting on Lesbos to determine the best way for returning home. King Nestor of Pylos recounted the departure from Troy to the son of Odysseus, Telemakhos, who had come from Ithaca, (where his mother was desperately trying to avoid remarriage, still hoping to see her husband return) in search for information about his father's fate. The predominance of women and of feminine details in the Odyssey has, in fact, raised the possibility that it was composed by a woman—Nausicaa?—and only later attributed to the eighth century bard (Graves, R. *Homer's Daughter*, 1955).

> **ODYSSEY** BY HOMER [HOMEROS], 8TH CENTURY B.C.
>
> **III. 159-160** ... ARRIVING IN TENEDOS, WE OFFERED SACRIFICES TO THE GODS, PRAYING FOR A SMOOTH RETURN TRIP HOME. AFTERWARDS SOME TOOK OFF ON THEIR CURVE-LINED SHIPS, INCLUDING THE CLEVER AND CRAFTY ODYSSEUS (YOUR FATHER) ... BUT WE, WITH ALL THE SHIPS THAT FOLLOWED MINE, LEFT AND WITH FAIR-HAIRED MENELAOS BEHIND US WENT TO LESBOS. THERE WE STOPPED TO STUDY THE BEST WAY TO SAIL PAST ROCKY HIOS ...

Still without news about his father, who had been gone for twenty years, Telemakhos went to Sparta, where king Menelaos told him:

> **ODYSSEY** BY HOMER, 8TH CENTURY B.C.
>
> **IV. 335-344** ... LIKE A MIGHTY LION ... WHO BRINGS A CRUEL DEATH TO SOME BABY-DEER, ODYSSEUS WILL COME TO INFLICT A TERRIBLE FATAL BLOW ON THESE MEN (PENELOPE'S SUITORS) ... I PRAY THAT THIS MAY HAPPEN THE WAY HE WRESTLED AND ROSE VICTORIOUS ON WELL-DEVELOPED LESBOS, IN HIS FIGHT AGAINST PHILOMELEIDES, AND CAUSED THE ACHAEANS GREAT JOY.
>
> Murray, AT, Vol. I, pp. 78, 130.

It is a reflection of the island's historical importance and also its strategic location that, among the Homeric heroes, not only Achilles and Ajax, but also Odysseus, Nestor and Menelaos stopped on Lesbos and that the brilliant intellectual, Palamedes, was buried there. Sappho suggested

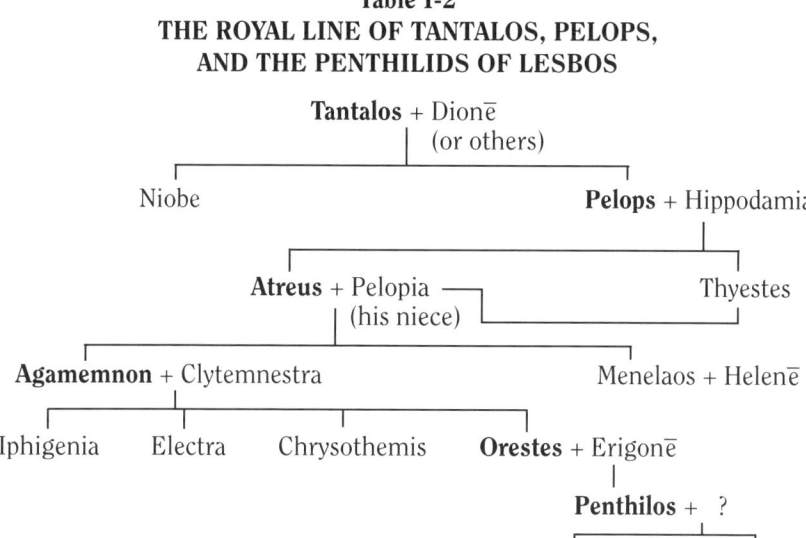

Table I-2
THE ROYAL LINE OF TANTALOS, PELOPS, AND THE PENTHILIDS OF LESBOS

NOTES

TANTALOS:
king of Phrygia and Lydia, condemned by the gods to endless unsatisfied hunger and thirst in Hades, for stealing divine secrets, etc.

PELOPS:
cut to pieces in childhood by his father, Tantalos, and served to the Gods for dinner. Later put together by Poseidon, who gave him a flying golden chariot to migrate (stopping first on Lesbos) to Peloponnesos.

ATREUS:
killed his nephews and served their flesh to their father, his brother Thyestes. Married Thyestes' daughter, who was already pregnant with a son conceived incestuously when her father unknowingly raped her.

AGAMEMNON:
killed his cousin, Clytemnestra's first husband, and took her as his wife. Returning home after leading the victorious Greeks against the Trojans, he was murdered by his wife and her lover, who ruled Mycenae until they were killed by Orestes, prompted by Electra.

ORESTES:
 tormented by guilt for the murder of his mother, he was pursued by "evil spirits" for years but later returned to reign. He, or Penthilos, or their descendants, established Greek settlements on Lesbos.

ENALOS AND **PHINEIS:** lovers, rescued and taken to Lesbos by friendly dolphins.

Odysseus, sketch from T.E. Lawrence, *The Odyssey of Homer*, Oxford, 1991.

that the Lesbian version of the story differed in certain important details (Page, 1959, p. 60). Agamemnon was present beside Menelaos on Lesbos, whereas according to the Odyssey the two brothers had parted company long before. Sappho's version either told nothing of the quarrel, or supposed a reconciliation before the arrival at Lesbos. Further, the Atridae brothers in Sappho's poem pray not to Zeus only, as in the Odyssey, but to the peculiar Lesbian trinity of Zeus, Hera, and Dionysos. The foundation of their precinct and altars is described in a poem of Alcaeus (Chapter II-B).

The flying chariot of Pelops

It is not clear who, if anybody, lived on Lesbos when years before the Trojan war, a flying golden chariot landed on the island. Pelops, king of Paphlagonia and of Lydia had been forced by the invading king of Troy, Ilos (after whom the whole country was named Ilion and the epic of the Trojan war became the "Iliad") to withdraw on the hills to the South. Eventually he decided to move across the Aegean Sea to the lands of southern Greece and to sue for the hand of Hippodamia, daughter of the king of Arcadia and Elis. To accomplish this he had to meet an almost impossible challenge and to compete against Hippodamia's father—who may have been in love with his daughter and not willing to let her go—in a fierce chariot race. Many suitors before Pelops had lost the race and then according to the contract, also their lives. Their skulls were beginning to pile up, frightening all prospective candidates. Poseidon, the god of the seas, disgusted with the slaughter, gave Pelops—with whom evidently he was in love—a marvelous flying chariot, drawn by tireless winged horses. Pelops and his charioteer were on their way to the mainland but so fast was the trip over the waters off the coast of Asia Minor that on their first landing on Lesbos (6), the charioteer expired (Graves, 1957, Vol. II, p. 33). Pelops built a temple to Apollo over the grave of this first-known victim of "jet lag" and continued the voyage alone. Eventually he was able to win the heart and the kingdom of the beautiful and wild Hippodamia. Ever since, that part of southern Greece has been known as Pelops' Island, or Peloponnesos.

Penthilos and (one more) rescue by dolphins

According to one story (there are several) the great-grandson of Pelops, (Table I-2) Orestes, was the first Achaean to bring Greek settlers to Lesbos. Or it may have been one of the sons of Orestes, Penthilos, or the grandson, Kras [or Gras] and their offspring—the "Penthilids"— that came east to colonize the island (Graves, 1957, Vol. II, p. 82; Elef. 1986). Among these descendants of Orestes on the ship sailing to Lesbos was a young woman, Phineis. She had to be thrown overboard, as a sacrifice to placate the sea nymph Amphitrite, who was angry and was causing a heavy storm. The young man in love with Phineis, Enalos, also a Penthilid, could not let her drown and jumped in the Aegean waters after her. Luckily they were both rescued by two friendly dolphins—like the Lesbian Arion was to be saved from drowning later on (Chapter II-A)—and, arriving safely on Lesbos, established the noble-blooded Penthilid royal dynasty there. That was between 1100 B.C. and 1000 B.C., about sixty years after the end of the Trojan war. The dynasty of Penthilos then ruled until 659 B.C. when the last king was murdered and the government of most Lesbian city-states was taken over by a succession of dictators ["*tyrants*"].

In his extensive historical "Tour Book" of Greece, the Lydian-Greek Pausanias also mentioned the settlement of Lesbos by people from Laconia, in south-central Peloponnesos.

TOUR (DESCRIPTION) OF GREECE
BY PAUSANIAS, DIED CA. 180 A.D.
BOOK III. LACONIA.
I.1. AFTERWARDS . . . WE REACH LACONIA TO THE WEST . . . (FROM THERE . . .)
II.1. GRAS, WHO WAS THE SON OF EKHELAS, SON OF PENTHILOS, (HIMSELF) SON OF ORESTES, WAS THE LEADER OF THOSE

SENT ON SHIPS TO ESTABLISH A COLONY. HE WAS TO SETTLE THE LAND BETWEEN IONIA AND MYSIA, WHICH IS STILL CALLED AEOLIS. EVEN BEFORE HIM, HIS ANCESTOR PENTHILOS HAD CONQUERED THE ISLAND OF LESBOS, WHICH IS OVER AGAINST THAT PART OF THE MAINLAND.

Jones, W.H.S., Vol. II, 1926, pp. 1–8.

In a later volume, the traveling author again referred to Lesbos and described an archaic idol of the god Dionysos, which had been found in the bottom of the sea by fishermen from Methymna and then deposited in a sanctuary in the Lesbian city of Antissa (Pausanias, *Book X*, 19.3—Ref. in *Munzen u. Medaillen* Vente Publ. No. 76, 1991, p. 52). That head was depicted on a coin of Antissa from 220–160 B.C.

About one thousand years afterwards, the historian-priest Plutarch had his dining sages recount the story of Enalos and his love.

DINNER OF THE SEVEN SAGES
BY PLUTARCH 50–AFTER 120 A.D.

163. A–C . . . I REMEMBER HEARING FROM PEOPLE OF LESBOS THAT A YOUNG MAID WAS RESCUED FROM THE SEA BY DOLPHINS. AS I CANNOT BE VERY PRECISE ABOUT THIS, PITTAKOS RIGHTFULLY OUGHT TO TELL US THE STORY.

PITTAKOS THEN SAID THAT IT WAS A FAMOUS STORY, MENTIONED BY MANY. AN ORACLE GIVEN TO THOSE GOING TO SETTLE ON LESBOS HAD COMMANDED THAT WHEN THEY REACHED A REEF CALLED "MEDITERRANEAN" (MIDLAND) THEY OUGHT TO THROW INTO THE SEA A BULL FOR POSEIDON AND A LIVING VIRGIN FOR AMPHITRITE AND THE NEREIDS (NYMPHS) . . . THOSE WHO HAD UNMARRIED DAUGHTERS CAST LOTS AND THE DAUGHTER OF SMINTHEUS WAS THE ONE CHOSEN. DECORATING HER WITH A FINE DRESS AND WITH GOLD, AS THEY CAME TO THE SPOT, AND AFTER DUE PRAYERS, THEY WERE READY TO THROW HER INTO THE SEA. BUT ONE OF THE FELLOW PASSENGERS, A YOUNG MAN OF NO MEAN BIRTH, HAPPENED TO BE IN LOVE WITH HER. HIS NAME IS REMEMBERED TO HAVE BEEN ENALOS. NOT KNOWING WHAT TO DO IN HIS DESIRE TO HELP HER IN HER TROUBLE, AT THE LAST MOMENT HE RUSHED AND HOLDING HER LET HIMSELF SINK WITH HER INTO THE SEA. AN UNCONFIRMED RUMOR SPREAD QUICKLY AND CONVINCED MANY IN THE SETTLEMENT ABOUT HOW THEY WERE SAVED AND RESCUED. THEY SAID THAT LATER ENALOS APPEARED ON LESBOS AND REPORTED THAT THEY WERE CARRIED BY DOLPHINS ACROSS THE SEA AND WERE DEPOSITED UNHARMED ON DRY LAND. HE TOLD EVEN MORE DIVINE SUPERHUMAN STORIES WHICH ASTONISHED AND ENTERTAINED MOST EVERYONE'S CONFIDENCE WITH WHAT HE DID. WHEN A TOWERING WAVE LIFTED ITSELF BY THE ISLAND AND EVERYONE WAS IN A STATE OF TERROR, HE WENT BY HIMSELF TO CONFRONT THE SEA AND TOWARDS

THE TEMPLE OF POSEIDON ESCORTED BY POLYPI (OCTOPUS). THE BIGGEST OF THEM BROUGHT A ROCK, WHICH ENALOS TOOK AND DEDICATED THERE, SO WE STILL CALL THAT (MONUMENT) ENALOS. SO, IN GENERAL, . . . A PERSON WHO KNOWS THE DIFFERENCE BETWEEN THE IMPOSSIBLE AND THE EXTRAORDINARY, OR BETWEEN THE ILLOGICAL AND THE PARADOX, WOULD NEITHER BELIEVE NOR DISBELIEVE ARBITRARILY AND WOULD OBSERVE THE COMMAND "NOTHING IN EXTREMES" THAT YOU HAVE PRONOUNCED YOURSELF.

Babbitt, F.C., 1928-56, Vol. II, p. 440–42.

The Egyptian Greek Athenaeus [*Athenaios*], about two generations after Plutarch, had a slightly different version of the myth associated with the settlement of Lesbos.

DINING SCHOLARS [DEIPNOSOPHISTS]
BY ATHENAEUS [ATHENAIOS] OF NAUCRATIS, C. 200 A.D.
XI.466, C–D. ANTICLEIDES OF ATHENS, IN HIS SIXTH BOOK ABOUT "HOMECOMING" DESCRIBES . . . THE SETTLEMENT OF LESBOS. HE STATES THAT AN ORACLE WAS GIVEN TO THEM (THE COLONISTS) ON THEIR SAILING ACROSS, TO THROW A VIRGIN INTO THE OPEN SEA AS AN OFFERING TO POSEIDON. THIS IS WHAT HE WRITES: "SOME PEOPLE IN METHYMNA TALK ABOUT THE LEGEND [MYTH] OF A VIRGIN WHO WAS DROPPED INTO THE SEA AND SAY THAT ONE OF THE LEADERS, NAMED ENALOS, BEING IN LOVE WITH HER, JUMPED AND SWAM, TRYING TO SAVE THE GIRL. THEY WERE BOTH THEN COVERED BY THE WAVES AND DISAPPEARED, BUT SOME TIME LATER, WHEN METHYMNA HAD ALREADY BEEN SETTLED, ENALOS APPEARED AND DESCRIBED HOW THEY HAD REMAINED ALIVE. HE SAID THAT THE GIRL WAS STAYING WITH THE SEA NYMPHS [NEREIDS] AND THAT HE HAD BECOME THE SHEPHERD FOR POSEIDON'S HORSES. THEN IT HAPPENED THAT A HUGE WAVE CAME UPON THE COAST AND HE (ENALOS) SWAM ON TOP OF IT AND CAME OUT HOLDING A CUP OF GOLD SO WONDERFUL THAT BY COMPARISON THE GOLD THEY (IN METHYMNA) HAD WAS NO DIFFERENT FROM COPPER."

Gulick, CB, Vol. V, pp. 32-34.

B. ORPHEUS, THE MUSES, AND THE MAD WOMEN OF THRACE

The head of Orpheus

The head of Orpheus, after his body was savagely torn apart by the maniacal women, the Maenads—or Bassarids (West, 1983, p. 4)—floated on the north Aegean waves, along with this mystical musician's magical lyre, all the way from his Thracian homeland or nearby Macedonia, to a secluded cove on the island of Lesbos. The severed head kept singing and the lyre

The death of Orpheus and his dismemberment by the Maenads, fifth century B.C. Attic vase, Boston Museum of Fine Arts, from Guthrie, 1952.

continued to accompany the melodies until they both touched land, possibly near Antissa, on the north coast facing towards Troy. Afterwards the lyre was turned by the gods into a constellation, ever since shining on the northern skies, but for awhile in ancient times a lyre, said to be that of Orpheus, was displayed in one of the holy temples on Lesbos. The head was given a ceremonial burial by the few early Hellenic inhabitants of that blessed spot. According to Lucian [*Loukianos*] a temple of Bakkhos (Bacchus)—Dionysos was built on the spot where the head was buried and Philostratos, as late as the third century A.D. described its fame as a giver of oracles (Guthrie 1935/52, 35). Ever since antiquity, the Orphic spirit was considered responsible for the lyricism, poetry and music on Lesbos. The creative talent of a Lesbian "melody maker" [*melopoios*], could not be surpassed, as the Lesbian poetess, Sappho declared:

STANDING HIGH ABOVE THE OTHERS,
LIKE THE SINGER FROM LESBOS
OVER THOSE FROM FOREIGN LANDS
(Cam. 106, see also Chap. II-B)

The magical power of the songs and of the lyre music of Orpheus enchanted not only people but animals, plants and inanimate nature as well (West, 1983, pp. 3–5). His musical instrument, which he invented, or received as a gift from Apollo, was the seven-string lyre. The number seven seemed to match the harmony of the seven planets known then. The lute, the kithara (7) and the phorminx (Ref. Table C) were also mentioned in relation to Orpheus by the ancients, who viewed him as the first and earliest musician and poet, an "inventor" perhaps of both music and poetry. A belief that Orpheus introduced writing too seemed unfounded, but his healing and medicinal knowledge and skills were widely recognized (Graves, 1957, Vol. I, pp. 111–115; Oxf. 1978; Class. Myth. 1986).

The rhythm of the Argonauts, the lure of the Sirens

These events took place about 3,000 years ago, soon after the voyage of the Argonauts and shortly before the Trojan war. Orpheus, the son of Oeagrus [*Oiagros*] and Kalliope, head of the Muses (Ref. Table D) also was one of the Argonauts, the Greek sailors who, led by Jason, travelled on the ship "Argo" to the East end of the Black Sea to retrieve the Golden Fleece. Because of his musical talent and also his relative lack of sailing ability, Orpheus was not asked to row but was put in charge of sounding the rhythm, the command—a *"keleustes"* (Ref. Table E)—for the oarmen's strokes. Also with his music he was able to save the men from total destruction by the seductive Sirens [*Sirenae*], when the "Argo" sailed by their rocky island. Orpheus sang and played the lyre much more beautifully than these inviting melodious man-eating creatures (8), half-women and half-birds. So the crew kept rowing past this almost fatal attraction.

For centuries, the poems attributed to Orpheus or to his disciples were memorized and transmitted orally or with notes on wooden tablets. Eventually, in the sixth century B.C. under the direction of the dictator Hipparkhos the "Orphic" texts were collected and put down in writing by a committee in Athens headed by a man named Onomakritos. Previous to that, during the rule of Hipparkhos' father, scribes had assembled and recorded the Homeric epics, the Iliad and the Odyssey. Those however were kept faithfully in their original archaic style, while in the Orphics there were many Attic-Athenian changes of the earlier Achaean-Aeolic language. Onomakritos was accused of altering the text and introducing his own lines and, as a result, he was exiled from Athens. This action is thought by some to have ensured the authenticity of the text (Orphika, 1987). Even in ancient times, however, "fake" Orphic texts began to circulate and the great philosopher Pythagoras himself was accused of publishing some of his works using the name of Orpheus (West, 1983, p. 7). Modern research, including the study of recently unearthed papyri, has led some scholars to conclude that the existing "Orphic Hymns" were composed—or at least rewritten—in Roman Imperial times (West, 1983, p. 1). The early Christian writer Origenes, compared Orpheus to the religious leaders Moses and Zoroaster, as well as to the Greeks Museus, Linos, Pherekydes and Pythagoras (West, pp. 63-64). Whether original or later inventions of classical antiquity, the Orphic lines do relate to the spirit that landed on Lesbos with the evidently mythical head of Orpheus. One of the "Orphic" works narrated the expedition and adventures of the Argonauts (Orphika, 1987—Ref. to Leipzig ed. 1829—p. 136). In it Orpheus described his encounter with Jason, the head of the Argonauts.

> **ARGONAUTICS,** LINES 75–120 (EXCERPTS)
>
> ... (JASON) ENTERED MY OWN BELOVED GROTTO, AND WITH A MELLOW VOICE FROM HIS HAIRY CHEST HE SAID: "ORPHEUS, DEAR SON OF KALLIOPE AND OIAGROS ... GREETINGS. ... AS A FRIEND AND YOUR GUEST [XENOS] I INVITE YOU TO JOIN THE ARGONAUTS ..." AND I REPLIED ...
>
> "YOU ARE TRYING TO CONVINCE ME TO SAIL OVER THE DARK UNKNOWN SEAS TO KOLCHIS ... BUT I HAVE HAD MY SHARE OF THE TOIL AND STRUGGLE OF CROSSING THE SEAS WHEN I TRAVELLED TO DISTANT LANDS AND CITIES, REVEALING TO PEOPLE MY DIVINE MESSAGE ALL THE WAY TO EGYPT AND LIBYA ...
>
> IT IS TRUE THAT MY MOTHER, TO SAVE ME FROM THE RESTLESSNESS AND FROM THE URGE TO WANDER, HAS LED ME TO MY OWN HOME, SO THAT HERE I MIGHT COME TO THE END OF MY LIFE BEYOND THE SORROWS OF OLD AGE. BUT IT IS NOT POSSIBLE TO AVOID WHAT IS MEANT TO BE ... I SHALL COME ..."
>
> AND TAKING MY PHORMINX I LEFT MY CAVE AND FOLLOWED HIM ...

Orpheus and Euridice

The greatest triumph of Orpheus' song was on his trip to the Underworld, in search for his wife Euridice, who had died from a snake bite (Graves, 1957; Class. Myth. 1986). His music charmed the Lords of Hades so much that they allowed Euridice to follow her husband back to Earth, provided that he did not look at her on the way. As everybody has known for centuries ever since, Orpheus did turn as they approached daylight, to make sure that Euridice had followed his steps guided by his melodies. So (doubt destroys love) he lost his beloved forever.

Afterwards Orpheus showed no interest in women and either remained chaste, or turned to the love of other men. This was said to have so enraged the women of Thrace worshiping Dionysos, that in a maniacal frenzy, these "Maenads" attacked him and tore him apart. Another version related the death of Orpheus to his opposition to the passionate, orgiastic and irrational worship of Dionysos, god of wine, with the introduction of his new religion based on Apollo's light (Ref. Table B), reason, purity and serenity. This infuriated the Maenads. Certain similarities however between the Orphic and Dionysiac traditions had been noted since antiquity (9). The Orphic "Hymns," it must be noted, included a prayer to Dionysos.

Orphic poetry, religion and philosophy

Orpheus and Euridice, Greek marble relief, ca. 400 B.C. (Naples Museum), from Guthrie, 1952.

Orpheus, regardless of the myths surrounding his life, was apparently a real historical (Guthrie, 1952; Hogart, 1993) person. Of greater importance than the romance with Euridice and the musical enchantment of wild beasts, was in antiquity the role of Orpheus as the originator, or importer and interpreter, of a religious attitude and ritualistic cult. After the irretrievable loss of Euridice, he advocated sexual and spiritual purity—and travelling extensively, he preached a religion of ecstasy and mystical trance-formation. The famous Eleusinian Mysteries (10) owe much to Orphism. The head of Orpheus, as has been reported, landed on Lesbos, but the Orphic religion "landed" almost everywhere. Despite the ridicule of Christian church leaders (chapter IV-C), Orphism can be found to contain much of the moral and liturgical basis of Christianity and of other faiths founded on selfless virtues and ecstatic "beyond one's self" (Ref. Table E) devotion. A selection of "Hymns," again from the sixth-century compilation ordered by Hipparkhos, which are addressed to the divinities (11) often mentioned in this volume may demonstrate the spirit of Orphism and will show a major aspect of ancient Greek religious practice (Orphika, 1987, pp. 195–250). A recent collection of ninety-eight "mutations" (liberal rendering in English) of the Hymns of Orpheus (Hogart, 1993) provides a broader, even though historically less faithful display of the Orphic tradition. A strictly literal translation of the Orphic Hymns has also been published (Athanassakis, 1977).

XI. TO PAN
I CALL UPON PAN, THE POWERFUL SHEPHERD, ESSENCE OF THE WORLD.
ALL HEAVEN AND THE OCEANS AND OUR QUEEN EARTH
AND THE IMMORTAL FIRE, THEY ARE ALL MEMBERS OF PAN.
COME, BLESSED THOU, WHO LEAP ALL OVER
AND SHARE A THRONE WITH THE SEASONS [HORAI]
GOAT-FOOTED CAVE-DWELLING GOD, ENTHUSIASTIC SEDUCER
YOU WHO WEAVE THE HARMONY OF THE UNIVERSE WITH PLAYFUL TUNES,
FEED US WILD FANTASIES AND STUN MORTALS WITH TERROR . . .
YOU CHANGE THE NATURE OF THINGS AS YOU SEE FIT
AND TEND TO THE RACE OF MAN IN THIS INFINITE WORLD, . . . COME,
YOU BLESSED BACCHIC SEDUCER, FOND OF ECSTASIES
JOIN IN OUR HOLY LIBATIONS AND ENABLE US
TO COMPLETE OUR LIVES IN NOBLE GOODNESS
CHASING AWAY THE MANIACAL DRIVES BEYOND THE END OF THE EARTH.

XXX. TO DIONYSOS
I INVITE DIONYSOS, THE BOISTEROUS JOYFUL CALLER,
THE PRIMARY BACCHIC LORD WITH THE TWO NATURES,
WHO WAS BORN THREE TIMES . . .
. . . IMMORTAL SPIRIT [GK. DAIMON], LISTEN . . . TO OUR VOICE
AND COME GENTLY AND SWEETLY TO INSPIRE US
[LIT. BLOW UPON US]
WITH YOUR DIVINE GOOD-WILL, JOINED BY YOUR COMPANIONS (12)
WEARING THEIR BEAUTIFUL BUCKLES.

XXXIV. TO APOLLO
COME, BLESSED PAEAN . . . YOU PHOEBOS, ALWAYS
SPLENDIDLY HONORED, RESPONDING TO OUR CALLS AND BESTOWING HAPPINESS WITH YOUR GOLDEN LYRE, WATCHING OVER OUR GRAIN
AND PLOUGHS . . .
LEADER OF THE MUSES, CARRIER OF JOY, PURE KING OF DELOS,
YOUR SIGHT ENLIGHTENS THE MORTALS
YOU SET THE ROOTS AND CONTROL THE ENDS OF THE UNIVERSE,

AND YOURS IS EVERY NEW BEGINNING AND ALL FUTURE
   END,
YOU LIVE FOREVER . . .
AND HARMONIZE THE SONOROUS HIGHS AND LOWS ON
   YOUR KITHARA OFTEN ALSO COMBINING YOUR TUNES
   IN THE DORIAN MODE,
YOU ALSO WEAVE THE DESTINY OF MANY WITH HAR-
   MONY
AS YOU BALANCE THE SEASONS OF THE YEAR
AND SO YOU HOLD THE SEAL OF THE ENTIRE WORLD . . .
ALLOW US TO CALL UPON YOU, OH BLESSED ONE
AND SAVE (13) THOSE INITIATED IN THE MYSTERIES,
   [GK. MYSTES] WHOSE VOICE NOW IMPLORES YOU.

LXXVI. TO THE MUSES
DAUGHTERS OF REMEMBRANCE [MNEMOSYNE] AND OF THE
THUNDERING ZEUS, RENOWNED PIERIAN MUSES
WITH THE BRILLIANT FAME,
MULTIFORM, MOST DESIRABLE TO ANY MORTALS YOU
   APPROACH,
YOU GENERATE THE PERFECT VIRTUES OF ALL EXPERIENCE,
YOU NOURISH THE SOUL, DIRECT TO STRAIGHT THINKING
AND ARE THE RULING GUIDES TO A POWERFUL MIND . . .
. . .
KLEIO, EUTERPE, THALEIA, MELPOMENE,
TERPSICHORE, ERATO, POLYMNIA, OURANIA (14)
AND MY OWN MOTHER, KALLIOPE, YOU PURE AND KINDLY
POWERFUL [EUDYNATE] GODDESSES,
COME VISIT THE MYSTIC WORSHIPPERS
AND BRING TO THEM WELL-BEING [EUKLEIA]
AND THE DESIRED LAUDABLE AMBITIOUS ZEAL [ZELOS]

LXVIII. TO HYGEIA (HEALTH)
ESSENCE OF OUR WISHES, BELOVED MANY-NURTURING
QUEEN OF EVERYTHING,
BLESSED HYGEIA, LET YOURSELF BE INVOKED,
YOU, CARRIER OF HAPPINESS, MOTHER OF ALL
THROUGH YOU THE AILMENTS OF MANKIND SUBSIDE
EVERY HOME JOYFULLY PROSPERS
AND THE ARTS AND SKILLS MULTIPLY . . .
YOU ARE OUR COMFORT AND SUPPORT,
WITHOUT YOU ALL IS USELESS,
WEALTH AND POSSESSIONS CANNOT BE ENJOYED IN
   CELEBRATIONS,
NOR CAN A MAN ATTAIN THE REWARDS OF HIS WORK IN
   OLD AGE;
YOU RULE EVERYTHING.
COME, THEREFORE, OH GODDESS
ALWAYS HELP YOUR WORSHIPPERS
AND PROTECT US ALL FROM THE MISFORTUNES AND
   CONCERNS
OF DISASTROUS DISEASES.

With the weakening of religious faith and the strengthening of the belief in rationality—another religion?—it was suggested that Orpheus was in fact the first philosopher, from the "wild" (according to the ancient Greeks) north in Thrace. In his "Lives and Opinions of Philosophers" Diogenes Laertios (Prologue, Book I, sect. 4–5) commented:

> ... PHILOSOPHY STARTED WITH THE GREEKS AND EVEN ITS NAME CANNOT BE TRANSLATED INTO OTHER LANGUAGES ... THOSE WHO ATTRIBUTE THE INVENTION OF PHILOSOPHY TO FOREIGNERS OFFER AS AN EXAMPLE ORPHEUS FROM THRACE, CALLING HIM A PHILOSOPHER AND A VERY ANCIENT ONE, INDEED. BUT FROM HIS DECLARATIONS ABOUT THE GODS, I REALLY DON'T KNOW HOW HE COULD BE CONSIDERED A PHILOSOPHER.

Perhaps the Muses, Pan, Dionysos, or Apollo, or the Love of Wisdom—"philosophy"—may now still be called upon to provide the inspiration [*en-thusiasm*], the zeal [*zelos*] and the basic urge [*estros*] to go on with this volume so that we may encounter the real women and men in the living "Museum" (the Muses' habitat) of Lesbos.

The legend of Orpheus 2,500 years later: Surviving the Dark Ages, Orpheus plays the guitar-like *vihuela* in an illustration from Luis Milan's *El Maestro*, 1536. From *The Hymns of Orpheus*, trans. by R. C. Hogart, 1993. Grand Rapids, MI: Phanes Press.

Orpheus in the twentieth century: a three-thousand-year survival. Above, the poster for the world première of *Orphée*, a modern opera by the American composer Philip Glass, based on the scenario by the French writer Jean Cocteau. Presented by the American Repertory Theatre, Cambridge, MA, May–June 1993.

CHAPTER II

LESBIAN LYRICS

A. Communications' Explosion Around 600 B.C.
New words, new music, new letters
The "Little Iliad"
Terpandros of Lesbos
Arion, the lyre [*kithara*]-singer
Compilation and recording
Continuity and controversy

B. **Lesbian Love Lyrics**
The discovery of the Self [*ego*]
Lyres and other tools for music
Sappho and the women on Lesbos
Alkaios, politics and drinking songs
Lasting lyrics

Musician and dancer (holding a drinking cup over his head), from a late sixth century B.C. kylix (drinking cup), in *Kunstwerke der Antike*, D3, Schwabe, Basel, Switzerland; not dated.

Overleaf: Muse playing a seven-string lyre (*kithara*), from a fifth century B.C. Attic vase (lekythos). Private collection, Lugano, Switzerland (in Arias/Shefton, Pl. XXXIX).

A. COMMUNICATIONS' EXPLOSION AROUND 600 B.C.

New words, new music, new letters

Suddenly, within relatively few years in the seventh century B.C. new manners of communication and exchange erupted in the Greek world. Money began to replace bartering when coinage was introduced for business and commerce, starting in Lydia, on the mainland east of Lesbos (1). A new script with an alphabet adapted to the sounds of the Greek language (2), made it possible to record in writing actions and transactions, contracts, traditions, epics, myths and history as well as moods, feelings and desires. Some words were also new, including some evocative verbs and beautiful adjectives (Ref. Table E), sparkling like jewels, which met the need for expressing new ideas, sensations and values. Painted and sculptured images of gods, heroes and nature, illustrations of mythical and historical events plus the new structures and designs of everything, from soldiers' helmets to religious temples, presented novel visual messages in public places, homes, ships and portable objects. The range of communication at all levels was completed with new sounds and musical instruments (Ref. Table C) often developed by the composers-poets themselves (Oxf. Class. Dict. "Music"; Mountford et al., 1984). The Lesbian poetess Sappho, herself the inventor of a small handheld harp-like instrument, the *pectis,* could then sing, perhaps in the new mixolydian mode also introduced by her (Roche, 1966, Introduction, p. xii, Campbell, 1982, pp. 34–35):

> COME MY LYRE ["TURTLE-SHELL"] SING TO ME
> AND FIND YOURSELF A VOICE.

The "Little Iliad"

Before the singing lyrical voice of Sappho, other poetic sounds and songs came from her island. It is well known that Homer's Iliad was not the complete story of the Trojan war. Lesches [*Leskhes*] of Mytilene, or possibly Pyrrha, in the seventh century B.C. composed an epic poem in four books, which was called "Little Iliad," to distinguish it from the Homeric work (Oxf. Class. Dict. 1978). In this, Leskhes recited in detail the stories of Ajax, Philoctetes and others and also of the gigantic wooden horse, in which the Greeks hid to enter and capture Troy. This Lesbian poet may have been also the author of a sequel in two books, describing the sack of Troy and the departure of the victorious Greeks.

Terpandros of Lesbos

Terpander [*Terpandros*] was another man from Lesbos to achieve fame as a musician and poet mainly far from his home, in the city of Sparta, in Laconia. According to the *Suda*—a tenth century A.D. medieval Greek literary encyclopedia (Oxf. Class. Dict., p. 1019)—the art of Terpandros brought internal peace to Sparta.

> **SUDA LEXICON** 10TH CENTURY A.D.
> "NEXT TO THE SINGER FROM LESBOS"; THAT WAS THE PROVERBIAL SAYING FOR THOSE WHO CAME SECOND. FOR THE LACEDAEMONIANS ALWAYS CALLED IN FIRST THE LESBIAN LYRE-SINGERS. WHEN THERE WAS DISORDER IN THEIR CITY (SPARTA), AN ORACLE BID THEM TO SEND FOR A LESBIAN SINGER. SO THEY BROUGHT TERPANDER, WHO HAD TO LEAVE ANTISSA DUE TO A BLOOD-FEUD AND AFTER THEY HEARD HIM AT THEIR PUBLIC DINNERS, THEY QUIETED DOWN. ANOTHER ACCOUNT (CONFIRMS) THAT THE PEOPLE OF SPARTA WERE FIGHTING EACH OTHER AND THEN INVITED THE MUSICIAN TERPANDROS FROM LESBOS. HIS COMING MADE THEIR MINDS CALMER AND SO THE QUARRELS ENDED. WHEN, LATER, THE SPARTANS HEARD A (LESSER) MUSICIAN, THEY WOULD SAY THAT "HE WAS NOT COMPARABLE TO THE POET FROM LESBOS."
>
> (Edmonds, 1928, Vol. I, p. 26–28; Barnstone, 1988, p. 44)

Terpandros (possibly an adopted name meaning "entertainer of men") was born in Antissa, on the north side of Lesbos, not far from the coast where the head of Orpheus (Chapter I) was said to have landed hundreds of years earlier. According to the *Parian Marble* (3) he was in his prime around 645 B.C. Terpander set his own and also Homeric verses to lyre music and it has been stated that ancient Greek music begins with him (Oxford Class. Dict., p. 710), transcending a background of religious and folk songs. One type of composition introduced by Terpander was the "nomos," characterized by a distinct style rather than defined melodies. It consisted of vocal solos accompanied by the kithara. These songs and also some composed for solo *aulos* (type of flute) were often performed during public musical competitions. Much of Terpander's work in Sparta was for choral uses. He also composed "preludes" somewhat resembling the Homeric Hymns, which were sung with kithara (Ref. Table C) accompaniment. Also, Terpander introduced and continued to compose "*skolia*," a type of individual party, or drinking songs, which can be viewed as the precursors of lyrical poetry and music. Very few fragments remain which may be attributed (still very questionably) to Terpander. To show how tradition continued, it should be mentioned that another man from Lesbos, Phrynis of Mytilene "revolutionized" the *nomos* with kithara, when by his time, around the middle of the 5th century B.C., "individualism was in the air" (Oxf. Class. Dict. p. 711). From a rigid religious form, Phrynis changed the nomos and added much variety [*poikilia*], aiming to please the audiences.

> ORPHEUS, SON OF THE PIERIAN KALLIOPE WAS FIRST TO CREATE THE TORTOISE-SHELL FOR MUSICAL DIVERSITY.
> THEN CAME THE FAMOUS TERPANDER BORN AT ANTISSA ON AEOLIAN LESBOS AND CAPTURED THE MUSE IN TEN ODES.
> (In Persae by Timotheus, cited by Edmonds, Vol. I, 1928, p. 18).

ON MUSIC BY PLUTARCH [Plutarkhos], CA. 46—CA. 120 A.D.

18.3 . . . TERPANDER . . . WAS A POET OF NOMES SUNG WITH THE LYRE [kithara], WHO NAMED THEM ALL, HIS OWN AND ALSO SONGS OF HOMER, TO BE SUNG AT ATHLETIC CONTESTS . . .

THE LYRE-SUNG NOMES, ESTABLISHED . . . DURING TERPANDER'S TIME, WERE FIRST NAMED BY HIM, ONE BOETIAN, OTHERS AEOLIAN. TROCHAIC . . . A BEAUTIFUL TERPANDREAN . . . AND ONE QUARTET. TERPANDER ALSO COMPOSED PRELUDES FOR SONG-AND-LYRE IN EPIC LINES.

(Quoted by Edmonds, Vol. I, 1928, p. 22)

In more technical terms the philosopher Aristotle wrote:

PROBLEMS BY ARISTOTLE, 384-322 B.C.

19.32. WHY THE OCTAVE IS CALLED DIA-PASON (ACROSS ALL) AND NOT BY THE NUMBER OF THE INTERVAL OF EIGHT AS IS DONE FOR (INTERVALS OF) FOUR AND FOR FIVE? IT IS BECAUSE IN ANCIENT TIMES THE STRINGS WERE SEVEN AND TERPANDER TOOK OUT THE THIRD AND ADDED A nete, THE HIGHEST, SO THE SCALE HAS BEEN CALLED "ACROSS-THEM-ALL" AND NOT "ACROSS EIGHT," BECAUSE THE STRINGS REMAINED SEVEN.

(Quoted by Edmonds, Vol. I, 1928, p. 18).

Some lines attributed to Terpander have been preserved by later writers.

GEOGRAPHY BY STRABO [Strabon], 63? B.C.—21? A.D.

13.618 TERPANDER . . . WAS THE FIRST TO USE A SEVEN-STRING INSTEAD OF THE FOUR-STRING LYRE, AS THE EPIC LINES ATTRIBUTED TO HIM INDICATE:

> WE SHALL REJECT THE FOUR-TONE SONGS
> AND SOUND NEW HYMNS ON THE SEVEN-STRINGED PHORMINX.

Quoted by Edmonds, Vol. I, 1928, p. 32.

The Christian author of Alexandria in Egypt commented:

MISCELLANEA
BY CLEMENT OF ALEXANDRIA, ABOUT 200 A.D.
STR.6.784 THE HARMONIES OF THE FOREIGN PSALTERY (OF DAVID) THAT DISPLAY SUCH SOLEMNITY OF MELODY AND ARE MOST ANCIENT, REPRESENTED AN EXCELLENT PROTOTYPE FOR TERPANDER, WHO PRAISED ZEUS IN THE DORIAN MODE AND SUNG THIS WAY:
  ZEUS, THE BEGINNING OF EVERYTHING,
  THE COMMANDER OF ALL
  ZEUS, TO YOU I BEGIN
  TO SEND THIS SONG OF PRAISE [HYMN].
In Edmonds, Vol. I, 1928, p. 30.

In his long account of "Dining Scholars" the Alexandrian Greek Athenaios reported:

DINING SCHOLARS [DEIPNOSOPHISTS]
BY ATHENAIOS, ABOUT 200 A.D.
XIV. 635D. . . . PINDAR CLEARLY STATED THAT TERPANDER INVENTED THE BARBITOS TO PLAY ALONG (HARMONIZE) WITH THE LYDIAN PECTIS . . .
635E. MENAIKHMOS . . . REPORTED THAT TERPANDER WAS OLDER THAN SAPPHO AND ANACREON . . . AND THAT HE WAS THE FIRST TO WIN A VICTORY AT THE KARNEAN FESTIVAL (HONORING APOLLO), . . . WHICH WAS INAUGURATED DURING THE 26TH OLYMPIAD. IN HIS WORK "ABOUT LYRE-SINGERS" [PERI KITHARODON] HIERONYMOS SAYS THAT TERPANDER WAS A CONTEMPORARY OF LYCURGOS THE LAW-GIVER, WHO, AS EVERYONE AGREES, WAS RESPONSIBLE FOR SETTING THE OLYMPIC GAMES IN NUMERICAL ORDER.
Gulick, C.B., Vol. VI, pp. 428–430

Arion the lyre [kithara]-singer

Arion, the "*kitharodos*" the singer with the kithara (Ref. Table C), later had his life enveloped by myths (a common communications medium in antiquity). He was, however, a real historical person from Methymna on Lesbos, who went to become the court musician of Periander [*Periandros*], ruler of Corinth (Ref. Table F, "Seven Sages").

Arion composed dithyrambs (4), wild and irregular chants celebrating Dionysos, god of wine and gave new popularity to these. With his patron's permission, Arion went on a singing tour of the Greek communities in Sicily and southern Italy, where he earned enviable fees and became rich. On the voyage back to Corinth, the sailors decided to get

Herodotos (Dresden)
in Bowder 1984

rid of him and to take his money. Before they threw him overboard in order to keep his treasure, Arion asked them, as his last wish, to allow him to sing a hymn to Apollo. A dolphin, probably sent by the gods, heard Arion's music and was so enthralled that when the poor poet-singer was about to drown, took him on his back and gave him a rapid ride to safety. So Arion arrived in Corinth unhurt, before the sailors. When the ship reached port, the crew was made to confess, the money was retrieved and the sailors punished. The "father of history," Herodotos, wrote about the event.

HISTORY
BY HERODOTOS, 484-420 B.C.
BOOK A

1. THE HISTORY BY HERODOTOS OF HALICARNASSOS IS PRESENTED HERE SO THAT EVENTS MAY NOT VANISH FROM HUMAN MEMORY BY THE PASSAGE OF TIME AND THAT THE RENOWN OF THE GREAT AND WONDROUS ACTS OF BOTH GREEKS AND BARBARIANS MAY NOT BE LOST . . .

. . .

23. PERIANDER [PERIANDROS] . . . WAS THE RULER [TYRANT] OF CORINTH. IN HIS LIFETIME, THE CORINTHIANS SAY (AND THE LESBIANS AGREE WITH THEM), THAT A MAJOR MIRACLE TOOK PLACE, WHEN ARION OF METHYMNA WAS CARRIED BY A DOLPHIN AND LANDED ON (CAPE) TAINARON. THAT MAN WAS A LYRE-PLAYER SECOND TO NONE OF HIS CONTEMPORARIES AND WAS THE FIRST HUMAN BEING WE KNOW WHO COMPOSED A DITHYRAMB (4), GAVE A NAME TO IT AND TAUGHT IT IN CORINTH.

24. THEY SAY THAT THIS ARION, AFTER SPENDING MUCH TIME NEAR PERIANDER, FELT A DESIRE TO SAIL TO ITALY AND SICILY. AFTER HIS PERFORMANCES EARNED HIM MUCH MONEY THERE, HE WANTED TO RETURN TO CORINTH. BECAUSE HE TRUSTED NO OTHERS MORE THAN THE MEN FROM CORINTH, HE HIRED A SHIP WITH A CORINTHIAN CREW TO TAKE HIM BACK FROM TARAS (TARENTO). THESE MEN, HOWEVER, WHEN OUT AT SEA, PLOTTED TO GET RID OF ARION AND TO KEEP HIS FORTUNE. WHEN ARION BECAME

AWARE OF THIS, HE BEGGED THEM TO BE SATISFIED WITH HIS MONEY FOR THEMSELVES BUT TO SPARE HIS SOUL. BUT THE SAILORS COULD NOT BE PERSUADED AND THEY ORDERED HIM EITHER TO KILL HIMSELF AND SO GET TO BE BURIED ON LAND, OR TO JUMP INTO THE SEA RIGHT AWAY. DRIVEN INTO SUCH AN IMPASSE, BECAUSE OF THE SAILORS' DETERMINATION, ARION BEGGED THEM TO ALLOW HIM TO WEAR HIS FULL STAGE REGALIA AND, STANDING ON A BENCH, TO SING. HE PROMISED THAT AFTER HE HAD FINISHED HIS SINGING HE WOULD DO AWAY WITH HIMSELF. THE MEN WERE EXTREMELY PLEASED AT THE PROSPECT OF HEARING THE BEST SINGER OF MANKIND AND THEY MOVED AWAY FROM THE STERN, TOWARDS THE MIDDLE OF THE SHIP. ARION PUT ON ALL HIS ELEGANT CLOTHES, TOOK HIS LYRE AND, STANDING ON A BENCH, DELIVERED THE FAMOUS "HIGH-STANDING" ODE (4). THEN, WHEN HE FINISHED THE TUNE, HE THREW HIMSELF IN THE WATERS, FULLY DRESSED. THE CREW THEN SAILED ON TO CORINTH, WHILE, AS THE STORY GOES, A DOLPHIN TOOK ARION ON HIS BACK AND CARRIED HIM TO TAINARON. AFTER LANDING THERE, ARION PROCEEDED TO CORINTH, STILL WEARING HIS FESTIVE ATTIRE AND, UPON HIS ARRIVAL, HE TOLD HIS FULL STORY. PERIANDER, NOT TRUSTING ARION'S UNBELIEVABLE TALE, PLACED HIM UNDER GUARD AND KEPT WATCHING CAREFULLY FOR THE SAILORS' ARRIVAL. AS SOON AS THEY GOT THERE, THEY WERE SUMMONED AND ASKED TO REPORT WHAT THEY KNEW ABOUT ARION. THEY WERE SAYING THAT HE WAS SAFE IN ITALY AND THAT THEY LEFT HIM DOING WELL IN TARAS, WHEN SUDDENLY ARION SHOWED UP, EXACTLY AS HE WAS WHEN HE JUMPED FROM THE SHIP. THE MEN WERE TOTALLY SURPRISED AND HAD NOTHING TO SAY TO DENY WHAT THE INQUIRY HAD ALREADY PROVEN. THIS IS WHAT BOTH CORINTHIANS AND LESBIANS SAY. THERE IS ALSO A BRONZE MONUMENT ON CAPE TAINARON, NOT VERY LARGE, DEDICATED TO ARION, WITH A MAN RIDING ON A DOLPHIN.

Godley, A.D., Vol. I, pp. 2, 24–28

On several other occasions friendly dolphins came to the rescue of Greek sea voyagers. They saved the lives of two of the first Greek settlers on their way to Lesbos (Chapter I-A) and took to safety Phalanthos, who then founded the city of Taras (Tarento) in southern Italy. Even the poet Hesiod was said to have been carried by dolphins (Lefkowitz, 1981, p.4). Arion is not known to have ever returned to Lesbos. After his death, his image and that of his lyre (others say it was Orpheus' lyre) were set by Apollo among the stars (Graves, Vol. I, Ch. 87, pp. 290–292).

Only a few lines from Arion's "Hymn to Poseidon" have been preserved, composed in gratitude for his rescue by a dolphin. These may have been rewritten and amplified by a much later author. Aelian [*Ailianos*] in his book on "The Properties of Animals" written shortly after 200 A.D. (almost

900 years after Arion's lifetime), quoted the poem when he discussed dolphins and their love of music and of human beings.

THE PROPERTIES OF ANIMALS
BY AELIAN [Ailianos], AFTER 200 A.D.

DOLPHINS . . . LOVE SINGING AND FLUTE MUSIC. A GOOD PROOF OF THIS CAN BE FOUND IN THE STATUE OF ARION THE METHYMNEAN AT CAPE TAINARON, AND THE WRITING ON IT. THAT INSCRIPTION READS: "THIS RIDE (THE DOLPHIN'S), SENT BY THE IMMORTALS, SAVED ARION, SON OF KYKEUS, FROM THE SICILIAN SEA." ARION HIMSELF WROTE A THANKSGIVING HYMN TO POSEIDON, WHICH IS A TESTIMONY OF THE DOLPHINS' LOVE FOR MUSIC AND WHICH ALSO EXTENDS HIS EXPRESSION OF GRATITUDE TO THESE CREATURES. THIS HYMN IS AS FOLLOWS:

"HIGHEST OF GODS,
SEA-LORD POSEIDON WITH THE GOLDEN TRIDENT,
EARTH-SHAKING RULER OF THE PREGNANT BRINE
AROUND WHOM THE SWIMMING BEASTS DANCE IN
 CIRCLES
AND LIGHTLY JUMP WITH SLIGHT FLIPS OF THEIR TAILS,
SNUB-NOSED BRISTLE-NECKED FAST-RUNNING SHARKS,
AND THE MUSE-LOVING DOLPHINS, SEA-CREATURES
OF NEREUS' DIVINE DAUGHTERS
BORN OF HIM BY AMPHITRITE.
THESE CARRIED A CASTAWAY FROM THE SICILIAN SEAS
TO THE SHORES OF TAINARON IN PELOPS' LAND
LETTING HIM RIDE ON THEIR CURVED BACK
AS THEY PLOUGHED THROUGH THE WET SURFACE
CUTTING A PASSAGE ACROSS NEREUS' UNTRODDEN
 DOMAIN
(THEY SAVED ME)
WHEN CROOKED MEN CAST ME OVER
THE HOLLOW SEA-FARING SHIP
INTO THE SWOLLEN SALT-WATER OF THE PURPLE-BLUE SEA.
(In Edm., Vol. III, p. 478)

Another reference to Arion, by the Roman philosopher-king Julian "the Apostate," is quoted in Chapter V-A.

Compilation and recording

Before the end of the seventh century B.C. the Athenian ruler Peisistratos, set up a committee to compile and record in writing for the first time the Homeric epics, the Iliad and the Odyssey, which until then were mostly transmitted orally and memorized from one generation to the other. The son of Peisistratos, Hipparkhos, also ruling Athens as a dictator, had the Orphic works assembled and transcribed by the same group, under Onomakritos (Levi, 1985, p. 99, Orphika, 1987). This man subsequently was accused of changing some of the Orphic lines and adding some of his own. Therefore he was banished from the city of Athens. The work was later finished and most people accepted it (Hogart, R.C. 1993, Notes and Bibliography, pp. 161–184) as authentic (cf. Ch I-B).

The scintillating dawn of rational thinking and of the ability to express personal feelings and desires, which took place about 2500 years ago, has been associated with the intense interaction between the traveling Greeks and the relatively more stable and culturally advanced populations of Asia Minor and the Eastern Mediterranean (Durant, 1939). The first known rational philosopher of nature, the "physicist" Thales of Miletos, may have been in part of Semitic—Carian? -origin and some of his knowledge of geometry and nature had been acquired in Egypt. The father of Pittakos, the "sage" ruler of Mytilene, came from the northern mainland of Thrace and Pittakos himself later was fighting the Athenians in Asia Minor for control of the vital trade passages to the Black Sea. This migration within and outside the Hellenic world never ceased and was well-documented by historical writers, often travellers themselves.

A better appreciation and proper perspective of the intellectual developments of the sixth and seventh centuries B.C. in the Hellenic world can be derived from texts written centuries later. In late Hellenistic and early Roman times and as late as the third century A.D. historians, grammarians and particularly writers about correct language style—and some actually "in style" themselves such as the prolific Athenaios (Gulick, 1980)—praised, criticized and generally commented on the works of their predecessors. They also often quoted exact passages as examples. These are included as valuable "testimonia" in modern publications of ancient writings. In fact, by the time Alexander's conquests spread Greek culture very widely, the pattern and quantity of recorded communication was so encyclopedic and over-abundant that it came close to the modern diversity and complexity. Strabo [*Strabon*], an Asiatic Greek from Pontos who lived between 64 B.C. and about 21 A.D., wrote a detailed historical geography of selected parts of the world known to him. This work, which has been available in an eight-volume set (Jones, HL, 1929) described both the physical setting and the history of the people in each location. Strabon's passage about Mytilene may serve as the reader's "passage" to the land and legends of the Lesbian Lyrics.

GEOGRAPHY
BY STRABO [Strabon], 64/63 b.c.- 21(?) a.d.
BOOK XIII, SECTION II.

1. SINCE LESBOS, WHICH IS MUCH WORTH DISCUSSION, AND THE ISLANDS AROUND IT LIE ALONGSIDE AND OPPOSITE THE COAST... IT IS NOW TIME TO DESCRIBE THESE. THEY ARE ALL AEOLIAN AND LESBOS IS LIKE A MOTHER-CITY [metropolis] OF THE AEOLIAN SETTLEMENTS.

2. FOR SOMEONE SAILING FROM LECTON TO ASSOS THE BEGINNING OF THE LESBIAN LANDS IS NEAR SIGRION, THE POINT FACING NORTH. THE LESBIAN CITY OF METHYMNA IS IN THIS GENERAL AREA, ABOUT SIXTY STADIA (5) FROM THE COAST... MITYLENE (6), THE LARGEST CITY, LIES BETWEEN METHYMNA AND MALIA AT A DISTANCE OF SEVENTY STADIA FROM MALIA AND... ONE HUNDRED AND TWENTY... FROM ARGINOUSSAI, THREE NOT VERY LARGE ISLANDS NEXT TO THE MAINLAND... BETWEEN MITYLENE AND METHYMNA, NEAR A METHYMNEAN VILLAGE CALLED AIGEIRON, THE ISLAND IS THE NARROWEST WITH A CROSSING... OF ONLY TWENTY STADIA. THE CITY OF PYRRHA IS SET ON THE WESTERN SIDE OF LESBOS, ONE HUNDRED STADIA AWAY FROM MALIA. MITYLENE HAS TWO HARBORS; OF WHICH THE SOUTHERN IS ENCLOSED AND HOLDS FIFTY TRIREMES, WHILE THE ONE ON THE NORTH IS LARGE, DEEP AND IS SHELTERED BY A MOLE. IN FRONT OF BOTH HARBORS IS A SMALL ISLE WITH PART OF THE CITY SETTLED ON IT. EVERYTHING IN THIS CITY HAS BEEN CONSTRUCTED AND EQUIPPED WELL.

THE CITY (MYTILENE) HAS PRODUCED FAMOUS PEOPLE. IN OLDER TIMES IT WAS PITTAKOS, ONE OF THE SEVEN SAGES. THERE WAS ALSO THE POET ALKAIOS AND HIS BROTHER ANTIMENIDES, WHO, AS ALKAIOS HAS SAID... PERFORMED A GREAT FEAT FIGHTING ON THE SIDE OF THE BABYLONIANS AND SO HE SAVED THEM FROM MUCH STRESS, WHEN

> "HE DESTROYED A MAN, A WARRIOR, THE ENORMOUS ROYAL WRESTLER, WHO (AS HE SAYS) WAS ONLY ONE SHORT OF FIVE CUBITS TALL."

ABOUT THE SAME TIME WITH THEM FLOURISHED SAPPHO... A WONDERFUL HUMAN BEING. DURING THE ENTIRE PERIOD OF THIS SURVEY I HAVE KNOWN OF NO OTHER WOMAN WHO COULD COMPARE TO HER EVEN REMOTELY IN THE GRACE OF HER POETRY.

IN THOSE YEARS THE CITY (OF MYTILENE) CAME UNDER THE RULE OF SEVERAL TYRANTS (DICTATORS) DUE TO CIVIL DISCORD. THE SO-CALLED REBELLION-SONGS OF ALKAIOS ARE ABOUT THESE. PITTAKOS WAS ONE OF THE TYRANTS AND ALKAIOS MADE FUN OF HIM AS HE DID OF MYRSILOS AND MELANKHROS, THE CLEANAX CLAN AND A FEW OTHERS, ALTHOUGH HE WAS NOT INNOCENT HIMSELF OF SIMILAR ATTEMPTS TO CHANGE THE GOVERNMENT. PITTAKOS, IN

FACT, USED HIS ONE-MAN RULE [MONARCHY] TO ABOLISH THE ESTABLISHED POWERFUL CLANS [DYNASTIES] AND WHEN HE DID THAT HE RESTORED SELF-DETERMINATION [AUTONOMY] FOR THE CITY.

(Quoted in Greek by Campbell, p. 206,
also in Jones, Vol. VI,
pp. 138-146)

We may continue to rely on the chroniclers of the turn of the millennium, from the first century B.C. to the second or third centuries A.D., not only because they are closer to us than the early Lesbians by five or six hundred years but also because their reliability and reporting style are much more "modern." We can take Strabon's word that Sappho, Alkaios and Pittakos were approximately contemporaries. According to him, Alkaios was born about 625–620 B.C. and Sappho was said to have been "made," or accomplished (meaning at the prime of life, not her time of birth) in the 42nd Olympiad, which was in the four years between 612 and 608 B.C. From 604/3 to 595/4 B.C. she and her family had left Mytilene and lived in exile in faraway Sicily, where she felt welcome by the conservative landowners' party still in power. In Mytilene the common people, hostile to the aristocrats like her, had placed their own man in control of the state. Moving to the west side of Lesbos, to the city of Eresos, Strabon referred to it in his "Geography" as the birthplace of the philosophers (Chapter III-C) Theophrastos and Phainias (Strabon spelled it Phanias) but he did not mention Sappho. There must have been a "communications gap" there, because Eresos did pride itself of being the poetess's birthplace and had in fact minted coins with her portrait inscribed "Sappho of Eresos." A much larger number of coins, however, came from Mytilene, many of them dating from the first to the third centuries A.D. Six to eight hundred years after Sappho's death these monetary exchange media placed the message of lyrical poetry in the Lesbian merchants' hands.

The inspired originality of the archaic Greek world of the sixth and seventh centuries B.C. was succeeded centuries later by a respect for authority, a repetition and rumination of the old stories and expressions. Philostratos, in the first century A.D. wrote a semi-realistic and semi-fictitious biography of Apollonios of Tyana, a spiritual leader, prophet, holy man and miracle worker, whose life was presented as something comparable to that of Jesus Christ. There is a passage in that book referring to women poets.

THE LIFE OF APOLLONIOS OF TYANA
BY PHILOSTRATOS, 170-247 A.D.

I, PAR. 30. YOU ASKED ME AWHILE AGO, HE SAID, WHAT WAS THE NAME OF THE WOMAN FROM PAMPHYLIA, WHO WAS REPORTED TO HAVE ASSOCIATED WITH SAPPHO AND TO HAVE COMPOSED THE HYMNS IN THE AEOLIAN AND PAMPHYLIAN MODES, THAT PEOPLE SING TO ARTEMIS ... WELL, THIS SKILLED WOMAN WAS CALLED DAMOPHYLE AND THEY SAY THAT SHE FORMED A GROUP OF GIRLS AND COMPOSED LOVE-POEMS AND HYMNS. SOME OF HER SONGS TO ARTEMIS ARE HER OWN VARIATIONS [PARODIES] AND SOME ARE SAPPHO'S.

(Quoted in Greek by Cam. No. 21, p. 20)

Even a famous Greek physician and researcher, Galen, communicated to his Greek and Roman pupils and readers the messages of Sappho.

EXHORTATION TO LEARNING
BY GALEN [GALENOS] OF PERGAMUM, 129-199 A.D.

SINCE WE KNOW THAT THE PLEASURES OF YOUTH, LIKE THE ENJOYMENT OF SPRING FLOWERS, DO NOT LAST LONG, WE MUST COMMEND THE LESBIAN WOMAN (SAPPHO) WHO SAID: "A PERSON'S BEAUTY EXISTS ONLY WHEN IT CAN BE SEEN, BUT WHOEVER IS GOOD SHALL REMAIN BEAUTIFUL FOREVER."

(Quoted in Greek by LP 50, Cam. 50,—cf. Balmer 119, Rayor 41)

The appreciation of beauty which makes life complete and death not frightening is mentioned by an anthologist of these years of late antiquity, referring back to the sixth and seventh centuries B.C. The Athenian law-giver and sage (Ref. Table F), Solon (7) was reported to be ready to die only after he could memorize a song of Sappho—or, interpreted slightly differently, *not* to be willing to die unless he first learned the beautiful composition by Sappho.

ANTHOLOGY, BY STOBAEUS,
QUOTING AELIAN [AILIANOS], 170-235 A.D.

SOLON OF ATHENS ONE TIME HEARD HIS NEPHEW SING FOR HIM A SONG OF SAPPHO AND HE WAS SO DELIGHTED THAT HE ASKED THE YOUNG BOY TO TEACH IT TO HIM. WHEN SOMEONE THEN ASKED SOLON WHY HE WANTED TO DWELL ON IT AND STUDY IT, HE REPLIED: "SO THAT AFTER I HAVE LEARNED IT I MAY (BE READY TO) DIE."

(Quoted in Greek by Cam, No. 10, p. 12)

The great Athenian philosopher, Plato, respectfully had Socrates refer to Sappho:

PHAIDROS
BY PLATO [Platon], 425-347 B.C.
235B ... MEN AND WOMEN IN EARLIER TIMES HAVE SPOKEN OR WRITTEN ON THE SUBJECT ... AND WILL CHALLENGE ME IF I GIVE IN AND AGREE WITH YOU ... THE BEAUTIFUL SAPPHO AND THE WISE ANACREON (WERE) AMONG THEM.
(Quoted in Greek by Edmonds, pp. 158-160)

This did not stop Pausanias, more than seven hundred years later, to comment coldly and objectively:

DESCRIPTION OF GREECE
BY PAUSANIAS, 2ND CENTURY A.D.
9.27.3 ... SAPPHO OF LESBOS MADE MANY REFERENCES TO LOVE [eros] BUT THEY DID NOT CONSISTENTLY AGREE WITH EACH OTHER
(Greek passage in Cam. 198, p.184)

References to Sappho as an extraordinary woman poetess, to works of art inspired by her and to a general ability or inability to communicate in Greek during the Roman times, are found also in the Latin literature, as shown by an excerpt from Cicero (8), in which this Roman orator accused the Roman proconsul of Sicily (73-71 B.C.) of looting, or "abducting" a statue of Sappho.

AGAINST VERRES
BY CICERO, 106-43 B.C.
II, PAR. 4. 125-127. THE STATUE OF SAPPHO WHICH WAS TAKEN FROM THE CITY HALL (IN SYRACUSE, SICILY) ... THE WORK OF SILANION, SO PERFECT, SO ELEGANT AND EXQUISITELY FINISHED ... WHO SHOULD OWN IT RATHER THAN THE MOST DISTINGUISHED AND ERUDITE VERRES? IT IS HARD TO EXPRESS IN WORDS HOW MUCH THIS STOLEN SAPPHO WILL BE MISSED.... THE FAMOUS GREEK INSCRIPTION ON ITS BASE WOULD ALSO HAVE BEEN REMOVED WITH THE STATUE, IF THE THIEF HAD UNDERSTOOD ONE SINGLE LETTER OF GREEK. NOW THESE LINES ARE STANDING THERE A SIGN OF WHAT USED TO BE ABOVE IT AND THEY DECLARE THAT IT HAS BEEN TAKEN AWAY.
(Quoted in Latin by Campbell, 1982, p. 24)

Continuity and controversy

Works of poets, dramatists, philosophers and historians referring to the beginnings of our 3,000-year-old Lesbian history will be cited mostly in a timely fashion. The perspective from the first century A.D.

however, remains interesting and may appropriately serve to close this section on how it all began. The views of Plutarch about the virtues of women (Ref. Tables E and G) must first be pointed out.

VIRTUES OF WOMEN
BY PLUTARCH [Plutarkhos], 50–C. 120 A.D.
... ALSO IN THE ARTS OF POETRY, OR OF DIVINATION, COULD ANYONE ARGUE FAIRLY AGAINST OUR CONCLUSION THAT THE SKILLS OF MEN AND WOMEN ARE NOT DIFFERENT BUT TRULY THE SAME, WHEN WE COMPARE THE SONGS OF SAPPHO TO THOSE OF ANACREON, OR THE SAYINGS OF SIBYLLA TO THOSE OF BAKIS?
(Quoted in Greek by Cam. 54, p.46)

Conflicts, contradictions and conspiracies are part of any expanding communications system. So Plutarch [*Plutarkhos*] in the first century A.D., (his work on Pompey is quoted extensively in Chapter IV-A), was not only well aware of the history of Herodotos, written over four hundred years before, but felt the need to argue with the older historian.

THE UNPRINCIPLED MALICE OF HERODOTOS
BY PLUTARCH, 50–C. 120 A.D.
WHEN ATHENS AND MYTILENE WERE AT WAR OVER SIGEON AND THE ATHENIAN GENERAL, PHRYNON (AN OLYMPIC CHAMPION), CHALLENGED ANYONE . . . TO SINGLE COMBAT, PITTAKOS CAME FORWARD AND THEN WAS ABLE TO TRAP THE MAN IN A NET AND TO KILL HIM, EVEN THOUGH HE WAS SO BIG AND STRONG . . .
NOW WHAT DOES HERODOTOS REPORT ABOUT THE EVENT? INSTEAD OF DESCRIBING THE OUTSTANDING BRAVERY OF PITTAKOS, HE MENTIONS THE FLIGHT OF THE POET ALKAIOS FROM THE BATTLEFIELD AND HOW HE DROPPED HIS ARMS BEHIND HIM. BY NEGLECTING TO WRITE ABOUT GOOD DEEDS AND BY NOT REFRAINING FROM COMMENTING ON A DISGRACEFUL ACTION, HERODOTOS PROVES AGAIN THAT BOTH ENVY AND VICARIOUS ENJOYMENT FROM OTHER PEOPLES' MISFORTUNES COME FROM THE SAME BASIC VICIOUSNESS (9).
(Quoted in Greek by Campbell, D.A., 1982, p. 208)

Clearly, Plutarch, a thoughtful and objective writer who was also a priest in the temple at Delphi (see Chapter IV-A) felt the same justifiable irritation for the biased reporting (10) of "bad news" as any modern cultivated individual exposed to the distorted and unbalanced communications of the pervasive contemporary news media.

B. LESBIAN LOVE LYRICS

The Discovery of the Self [Ego]

The greatest discovery—or invention—in this excited and exciting pre-classical age of the Greek world, perhaps more important than the introduction of new political systems and the development of original musical modes and instruments, was the recognition of the immense potential of individual self-awareness and self-expression. The Iliad, the Odyssey and other epics described the deeds, the labors and the fate of outstanding heroes who were glorified at an idealized super-human level. Terpander still worked as part of a community group. Arion may have been a pioneer, going on his own (though with his master's permission) to display his musical talents, to sing and to entertain for personal profit. The poet-soldier from the Aegean island of Paros, Arkhilokhos (Davenport, 1984; Rayor, 1991, pp. 4–5), who sang forcefully and emotionally about his loves, his tastes (for figs and wine), his nostalgia for his home and his hatreds, fears and torments, in the middle of the seventh century B.C., was a new ground-breaking voice. He was also the one to recognize the already existing leadership of Lesbos, at least with respect to the martial tunes of the paean, when he said:

> I WILL LEAD THE WAY WITH A LESBIAN PAEAN ON MY FLUTE.
> (Bowra, 1961, p. 131;
> Davenport, 1981, Fragm. Nov. 6, 199).

As the seventh century ended, Alkaios of Lesbos raised his personal poetic sounds in celebration of convivial feasts, uninhibited revelry and also in rebellion against the new rulers from the upstart social class, who had forced him into exile from his hometown of Mytilene. That city, with the exception of the sufferings of the exiled aristocrats, enjoyed considerable prosperity, though not quite at the level of the luxurious styles of Lydia, the riches of Egypt and the commercial wealth of Corinth. The singing poets of Lesbos were among the first to perceive and to declare that there was something more precious than military victories and worldly goods. Human feeling, affection, adoration of beauty, love for another human being and the mysterious melancholy of introspective existence had to be expressed in song. The poetess Sappho was singing for the whole Greek-speaking world to hear:

> FOR SOME PEOPLE A PARADE OF HORSEMEN, OR INFANTRY,
> OR NAVY SHIPS ARE THE BEST SIGHTS ON THIS BLACK EARTH,

BUT I [EGO] AM TELLING YOU THAT TRUE BEAUTY
IS ONLY FOUND IN WHAT ONE LOVES.
(LP 16, Cam. 16, Edm. 38, WB 5,
cf. also Balmer 21, Rayor, 4, etc.)

With "the subtle and complex use of 'I' in poetry" (Balmer, 1988, p. 11), Sappho not only sang about "the ephemeral pleasures and pains of an idle but graceful society" (D. Page, 1955/79, quoted by Balmer, 1988, p. 19), but did demonstrate her "awareness of the poet's function in society" (Rayor, 1991, p. 160). At the highest level of esthetic sensitivity, unsurpassed in 2,500 years and probably unsurpassable, the woman poet from the Aeolian island could say about herself:

EGO . . . PHILEM' ABROSYNAN . . .

That can be translated (note again the "I"—"ego") by amplifying *abrosynan*—what Rayor (1991) calls "luxuriance"— with the three words "tender, delicate sensations" (Ref. Table E) as:

I ADORE TENDER, DELICATE SENSATIONS . . .
FOR ME LOVE [EROS] HAS CAPTURED
THE BRILLIANCE AND BEAUTY OF THE SUN.
(LP 58, Cam. 58, Edm. 118, WB 117, Roc. 158, SG 38,
WB 117, Rayor 29)

Lyres and other tools for music

These rising and arousing feelings of love, tenderness, beauty and the rainbow of inner moods, were sung in verses and music accompanied by string instruments, generally called *lyres*. Hence such poetry and the moods themselves have ever since been considered as lyric or lyrical. With small changes, new instruments were also created, such as the barbitos, the magadis, the pectis and the sambyka or iambyka (Ref. Table C). Athenaios, in extended sessions of his "Dining Scholars," went into much detail.

DINING SCHOLARS [DEIPNOSOPHISTS]
BY ATHENAIOS, ABOUT 200 A.D.
IV.182F THE BAROMOS AND THE BARBITOS, WHICH ARE MENTIONED BY SAPPHO AND ANACREON, AND ALSO THE MAGADIS, THE TRIANGLES AND THE SAMBYCA ARE ALL ANCIENT (MUSICAL INSTRUMENTS).
(Quoted in Greek, Cam. 176, p. 176)

XIV. 634E,F ... MAGADIS IS THE FLUTE ATTUNED TO THE LYRE [KITHARA] ... OR ... AN INSTRUMENT PLAYED TO ACCOMPANY SONGS, LIKE THE LYRE, AS ANACREON SAID ...

635A,B ... MAGADIS WAS AN OLD INSTRUMENT WHICH SOMETIME AGO WAS MODIFIED AND THEN RENAMED SAMBYCA. THIS INSTRUMENT WAS SO COMMON IN MITYLENE (11) THAT THERE WAS EVEN A STATUE BY THE ANCIENT SCULPTOR LESBOTHEMIS OF ONE OF THE MUSES HOLDING IT. IN HIS WORK "ABOUT ARTISTS" MENAIKHMOS STATED THAT THE PECTIS, WHICH HE SAID WAS THE SAME AS MAGADIS, WAS INVENTED BY SAPPHO. ARISTOXENOS INDICATED THAT THE MAGADIS OR PECTIS CAN BE PLAYED WITHOUT A PLECTRUM, TO ACCOMPANY SONGS.

636.B PHILLIS OF DELOS, IN HIS SECOND VOLUME "ON MUSIC," STATED THAT THE PECTIS [PACTIS IN AEOLIC] IS DIFFERENT FROM THE MAGADIS ... (AND THAT) ANY NINE-STRINGED INSTRUMENT ACCOMPANYING IAMBIC SINGING WAS CALLED IAMBYCA, (BUT) ... THE MAGADIS WAS TO SOUND AN OCTAVE APART FROM THE SINGING VOICE.

637.A SOPHOCLES IN HIS PLAY "THAMYRAS" DECLARED:
"THE WELL-BUILT LYRES AND MAGADIDS ARE WHAT THE GREEKS USE FOR DELIGHTFUL MELODIES."

Gulick, C.B., Vol. VI, pp. 422–26, 432, 436.

Sappho and the women on Lesbos

Lesbos would be lost to us if we could not penetrate the mood and the meaning of at least a few words, such as love, beauty, tenderness in the original Greek (Ref. Table *E*). We also might wish that we had access to the original musical tunes as well. Next of course we would want to appreciate the full message of the poetry, the rhythm and the emotional intonations of it and if possible, to admire the existing manuscript lines the way we revere the white marbles of the ancient temples and sculptures, similarly deprived of their colorful embellishments. Few fragments and only one complete poem remain of the lyrical output of Sappho, the wonderful woman of Lesbos, the "tenth muse" (Ref. Table D) according to Plato (Campbell, 60, p. 48). Time alone cannot account for the loss, considering that of many other poets, dramatists, historians, philosophers, etc. we have volumes of intact manuscripts. Willful destruction of much of Sappho's work took place under the prompting of medieval morality, because of the erotic content and also of the "bad" reputation of the poetess herself, as an unnatural "lover of women" (Campbell, 1982, *Introduction*; Barnstone, 1965, *Introduction*). Fortunately, the admiration of literary critics, grammarians and other ancient Greek language scholars for many centuries after her death, has pre-

Women, music and wine, exterior of a sixth century B.C. Greek kylix (drinking cup, like the one pictured); Archeological Museum, Madrid, Spain.

served selected instructive and respectful quotations, as well as some facts about the poetess' life.

Her fame already during her lifetime was so widespread that it gave rise not only to scholarly citations but also to malicious rumors and indecent jokes (Balmer, 1988, pp. 7–8). Yet some later Greeks—down to the twentieth century—and also the Romans named a girl *Lesbia*, to indicate pure love. The Roman poet Catullus (c. 84–c. 54 B.C.) used the word "Lesbia" as a substitute for Claudia, the name of a prominent married woman with whom he was in love, when he wrote: "My Lesbia, you ask how many kisses would be enough to satisfy me . . ." (Knox, 1993,

---

Table II-1
SAPPHO OF LESBOS, HER FAMILY AND GIRL-COMPANIONS

```
            Skamandros* + Kleis (pronounced Klay-ees)
              (father)    |    (mother)
      ┌─────────────────┬──┴──────────────────────────────┐
┌---- Sappho + Kerkylas (?)      Larihos  Haraxos  Erigyios
|              |                       (Sappho's brothers)
|            Kleis
|          (daughter)
|
Anactoria, Atthis, Gongyla, Mnasidika, Praxinoa
(some of Sappho's beloved pupils and companions)
```

---

*Or Scamander, or Simon (Skamon), or Euregios (Erigyios)

p. 605). On the other hand ancient comedians tried to entertain semi-informed audiences with distorted caricatures. At least five comedies had been staged in antiquity dealing with Sappho (Campbell, 1982, p. 27). Many comedians took incredible liberties with their plots.

DINING SCHOLARS [DEIPNOSOPHISTS]
BY ATHENAIOS, ABOUT 200 A.D.
XIII.598B, C. DIPHILOS, THE WRITER OF COMEDIES, IN HIS PLAY "SAPPHO" MADE BOTH ARKHILOHOS AND HIPPONAX (12) LOVERS OF SAPPHO.
(Quoted in Greek by Cam. 8, p. 8)

Sappho, or Psappha (Barnstone, 1965 *Introduction* p. xviii) as she called herself in the Aeolic dialect (the name has been thought to suggest a Phrygian origin), was born on Lesbos, possibly in the town of Eresos, shortly before 620 B.C. A recent reconstruction of her life gives the dates of her birth and death as approximately 612 to 558 B.C. (Roche, 1966, *Introduction*, p. xiii). Most likely however, she was already a mature woman and famous for her poetry by the time of her first exile to Sicily about 604–600 B.C. Except for such forced temporary absences, Sappho lived most of her life in the city of Mytilene, where her family (Table II-1) belonged to the prominent aristocracy. Her father was Euregios—or Simon, or Skamon, or Skamander or a variant of this (*Suidas*, quoted by Edmonds, 1928, Vol. I, p. 114)—and her mother's name was Kleis (pronounced *Klay-ees*), the same as Sappho's beloved daughter, her only child. Her parents probably died young, if we can rely on Ovid.

I WAS SIX YEARS OLD WHEN MY PARENTS' BONES WERE PREMATURELY DRENCHED WITH THE DRINK OF MY TEARS.
(Ed. quoting Ovid, in Latin, "Life of Sappho," p. 144).

A younger brother, Larihos, apparently a good-looking lad, was assigned the task of pouring the wine at city festivals, a privilege accorded only to attractive youths from the nobility.

DINING SCHOLARS [DEIPNOSOPHISTS]
BY ATHENAIOS, ABOUT 200 A.D.
X.425A. THE LOVELY SAPPHO ON MANY OCCASIONS PRAISED HER BROTHER LARICHOS [LARIHOS] FOR POURING WINE IN THE TOWNHALL FOR THE CITIZENS OF MYTILENE (11).
Gulick, C.B., Vol. IV, p. 424 (also quoted in Greek, by Cam. 203, p. 188)

CLOCKWISE FROM TOP LEFT: Sappho—Hellenistic marble (Copenhagen); Sappho—mosaic from Sparta; Sappho—romanticized Roman fresco (Naples); Sappho on a Greek vase (Athens); bust of Sappho on a coin. From Richter 1965/84.

Another brother, Charaxos [*Haraxos*], caused the poetess much distress, with his love affairs and money-spending in Egypt, as her poems (to be quoted) testify. About her own loves and death, persistent stories in antiquity referred to Sappho's suicide off the cliffs of the island of Lefkas, due to her desperate desire for the young boatman, Phaon. But Herodotos assigns this episode to another Sappho, a courtesan (Campbell, 1982; Barnstone, 1965, *Introductions*).

HISTORY
BY HERODOTOS, 484-425(?) B.C.
XIII. 596E. THE COURTESAN, ALSO FROM ERESOS, WHO HAD THE SAME NAME AS THE POETESS SAPPHO, WAS FAMOUS FOR HER LOVE OF THE HANDSOME PHAON.

The medieval Greek encyclopedia, called "Suda," or "Suidas," reported that Sappho had a reputation for "shameful liaisons with women" (Balmer, 1988, p. 8). Another entry referred to another (?) Lesbian Sappho "from Mitylene" (Campbell, 1982, p. 6).

SAPPHO
Entry in the *Suda* (also *Suidas*) Encyclopedia, 12th century A.D.

107.iv322s. Sappho . . . a Lesbian from Eressos, a lyric poetess, flourished around the 42nd Olympiad (612–08 B.C.), at the same time as Alkaios, Stesikhoros and Pittakos. She had three brothers, Larihos, Haraxos and Eurygios. She was married to a very wealthy man, Kerkylas, who came originally from Andros and she had a daughter by him, who was named Kleis. She (Sappho) had three very close companions and friends, Atthis, Telesippa and Megara and was accused of having a shameful relationship with them. Among her students were Anagora from Miletos, Gongyla from Kolophon and Eunica from Salamis. She wrote nine books of lyric poems and was the first to invent the plectrum. She also wrote epigrams and elegies and iambics and monodies.
Quoted in Greek by Campbell, 1982 pp. 4–6.

Second entry—*Suda*

108.iv 323. Sappho, a Lesbian from Mitylene, a singer. She threw herself into the sea from the Leukadian rock due to her love for Phaon of Mitylene. Some have also attributed to her certain lyrical poems.
Quoted in Greek by Campbell, 1982, p. 6.

According to most reliable sources, Sappho the poetess did not kill herself for love but died a natural death in old age and was buried on Lesbos. An appropriate epigram was inscribed on her tombstone.

EPIGRAM BY PINYTOS, DATE UNKNOWN
THE BONES AND THE EMPTY NAME OF SAPPHO ARE IN
  THIS GRAVE
BUT HER WISE WORDS REMAIN IMMORTAL
                    (Quoted in Greek by Edmonds, p. 166)

Sappho has been described as beautiful, possibly in reference to her person and her work. Physically we know she was petite and of rather dark complexion. Her contemporary Alkaios sang about the "pure, sweet-smiling Sappho with the violet-braided hair" (Barnstone, 1965). No known portrait, statue or other realistic picture of her has been preserved from her lifetime. Later images were idealized or simply imagined. Her own comment about her character was "I have a child's heart." She married a wealthy merchant from the island of Andros with the rather "funny" name—at least in ancient Greek—of Kerkylas (Barnstone, 1965, *Introduction*, p. xix). He died early of unknown causes, or possibly he left the family, or disappeared. As a young widow and single parent, Sappho was very much attached to her only daughter, Kleis, but also was busy in politics and social functions. Later, probably after her return from her first exile in Sicily, she started a special "finishing school" for girls (Campbell 1982; Barnstone 1965, 1988; Jenkyns 1982). Some modern scholars thought that this was also a nucleus of a religious cult but this seems unlikely. Young female students came to her not only from all over the island of Lesbos but also from prosperous Greek cities on the Asiatic mainland.

THEN IN LEISURELY CALM [HESYKHIA] SHE INSTRUCTS THE BEST (YOUNG WOMEN) NOT ONLY OF THE LOCALS BUT ALSO OF IONIA AND SHE RECEIVES AN APPROPRIATE REWARD (PRAISE?) FROM THE CITIZENS, ACCORDING TO KALLIAS OF MYTILENE (13).
                    (Frag. Nov. 1981, G. Davenport p. xxi)

Sappho loved them all, but for a few she felt an extraordinary warm passion. She was exited by their mere presence, longed for them when they were away, was intensely jealous of others coming near them, resented their occasional indifference and reminisced with painful nostalgia about her own passing feelings of love. Not only her fame but her life itself can be found in her poems. Even the fragments, now read in the original or in the many translations without music and with uncertain pronunciation and rhythm, are alive, naturally more so in Greek. Reference Table H, with a few selected lines in several English translations and samples of the same in French, German, Italian, Spanish, Catalan and Modern Greek, shows how Aeolic lyrics have been rendered—with questionable success—by twentieth-century poets, including two modern Nobel laureates, the Italian Quasimodo and the Greek Elytis.

In the introduction to her own translation of Sappho's poems, a British contributor to this ever-expanding literature cited a famous Latin work by Ovid (43 B.C.–17 A.D.)—translated in English by Alexander Pope (1688–1744)—and concluded that "The concept of vicious forbidden love, of shame and guilt and the rejection of a deviant life for a man who does not love her all became standard features of the mythology of Sappho" (Balmer, 1988, p. 8). Balmer also felt that in the nineteenth century, in France, Charles Baudelaire, "obsessed by decadent sexuality" (!), in his poem *Lesbos* allows Sappho to "indulge in lurid frenzied relationships with women until she is overcome with passion for Phaon" (*ibid*. p. 8). Not much later, another symbolist French poet, Paul Verlaine (1844–96) in his poem *Sappho* "follows a similar pattern" (*ibid*. p. 8). Evidently the current English commentator had not read, or did not understand, the superb French originals, which radiate a tender identification—regardless of sex or sexuality—and lyrical admiration for the admittedly hypothetical Lesbian life. Baudelaire started by declaring Lesbos "the mother of . . . Greek voluptuousness [*volupté*]," where famous courtesans—the likes of the "Phryne" prototype—"lured each other." The *poète maudit* alluded to the stories about Sappho's lewd loves and in exquisite verses glorified her rebellion against ritualistic convention.

LES FLEURS DU MAL—PIÈCES CONDAMNÉES
by Chas. Baudelaire, 1821–67

***Lesbos* (1857)** *Stanzas 12 and 14*

. . .

Of the lover and poet, the man-like Sappho
With her doleful pallor more beautiful than Venus
The blue eye is defeated by the black that is spotted
With the dismal dark circles traced by the travails
Of the lover and poet, male-like Sappho.

Of Sappho who was dead the day of her blasphemy
When she offended the invented rites and cults
Making her lovely body the ultimate pasture
Of a brute whose conceit is to punish the impiety
Of Sappho who was dead the day of her blasphemy.

> Translated from the French for the present work; for other—even less faithful—translations, cf. Flores, 1958, Mathews, 1989, etc.

Near the end of that century, a popular "semi-pornographic work" (Balmer, 1988, p. 8) by Pierre Louÿs (1870-1925) *Les Chansons de Bilitis* (The Songs of Bilitis), published in 1895, "contained the familiar description of life on Lesbos; Bilitis, a newcomer to the island, is seduced on arrival by Sappho" (*ibid.* p. 8). That, according to Balmer, showed how "Sappho had become a sexual rather than a literary celebrity" (*ibid.* p. 8). On the contrary, however, a more sympathetic reading of the French original—which, amusingly, was first presented as a "translation" from a nonexistent Greek work—and an additional appreciative audition of the exquisite music composed for selected *Chansons* in 1897–98 by Louÿs' friend, Claude Debussy—including incidental music for *The Memory of Mnasidika*, that most beautiful girl in Sappho's entourage, with whom, according to the *Chansons*, Bilitis "lived a sweet and passionate" (Preface, by Goujon, 1990, p. 12) homoerotic love and to whom Louÿs dedicated at least four poems plus some "secret" ones (Goujon, 1990, p. 215)—should leave no doubt that in aesthetic sensitivity and erotic expression ancient Lesbos and nineteenth century France were much closer and at a higher level than some late twentieth century critics seem to think. One of the subtly homoerotic *Chansons*, in "rhythmical prose" (Goujon, Preface, p. 7) was about *Psappha*, the pre-classical way of calling Sappho. Bilitis, the girl from the Asiatic side in Pamphylia, wakes up and realizes that she had spent the night in bed with the Lesbian celebrity.

LES CHANSONS DE BILITIS
by Pierre Louÿs, 1870-1925.

XLVIII. *Psappha*

I rub my eyes . . . It's already daytime,
I think. Ah! who is next to me?
A woman? By the Paphian (goddess
Aphrodite), I had forgotten . . . Oh Graces!
how I am ashamed.

. . . Is it possible that she is Psappha!

She is asleep . . . she is certainly beautiful
even though her hair is cut short like an
athlete's. But this strange face . . .
    Translated from the French (Gallimard, 1990, p. 88)
      for the present work.

Sappho's works were arranged in nine books according to their meter (Edmonds 1928, Campbell 1982, *Introductions*) by the grammarians and literary scholars in the Library of Alexandria, Egypt, during the reign of the Macedonian-Greek royal house of the Ptolemies. Book I alone contained 60 to 70 poems, with 1320 lines. A separate volume—Book IX—contained choral works called "Epithalamia," which were sung by groups of young people in the course of a wedding ceremony and also during the wedding night (*Epi-thalamia*, meaning by the bed-chamber). Most modern translators follow an arrangement by topic, often with invented (silly) titles, which may correspond to the tune or structure of the original. A modern Greek political scientist (Kordatos, 1942) attempted to arrange Sappho's work in chronological order. After an intriguing dialectic materialistic (Marxist) analysis but poorly founded suppositions, Kordatos wrote that the Lesbian poetess' feelings, inclinations and lyrics were determined by the social and political situation on Lesbos at the time. Sappho, like other women of the Lesbian aristocracy, felt lonely and bored when the men were gone, killed, exiled, or traveling, after the people's party took over. According to that writer, the presumed Lesbian female homosexuality was a result of the revolution, a "habit" imposed on the ladies of the upper class.

The first printing of the then available texts of Sappho, in 1554, started with the "Ode to Aphrodite," a singularly beautiful poem in Aeolic, or irregularly Ionic meter, the "soft meter of languor" (Roche, p. 223). This was probably the first poem in her Book I. It started with the line, in transliterated Greek:

POIKILOTHRON' ATHANAT' APHRODITA

Sappho's *Invocation to Aphrodite*, or, in the Aeolian dialect *Aphrodita*, is the only poem—out of "some five hundred" (Rayor, 1991, p. 2) in the nine volumes compiled by Alexandrian scholars three or four centuries later—by the Lesbian "melody-maker" [*melopoios*] preserved in its entirety.

APHRODITE IMMORTAL ON YOUR MULTISPLENDORED THRONE
INTRIGUE-WEAVING DAUGHTER OF ZEUS
I BEG YOU NOBLE MISTRESS
DO NOT TORTURE ME AND DON'T TAKE PLEASURE
IN SUBDUING MY HEART
BUT DO COME AS YOU ONCE DID
WHEN FROM A DISTANCE YOU HEARD MY VOICE
AND WILLINGLY LEFT YOUR FATHER'S DOMAIN
ON YOUR CHARIOT OF GOLD DRAWN BY BEAUTIFUL BIRDS (14)
THEIR FEATHERED WINGS BEATING SWIFTLY
AND, CROSSING THE SKIES PROMPTLY, ARRIVED
ON THIS BLACK EARTH.
YOU, BLESSED LADY, WITH A SMILE ON YOUR IMMORTAL FACE
INQUIRED WHAT WAS THE MATTER WITH ME,

WHAT WAS THE REASON I CALLED YOU
AND WHAT IN MY MAD WILD MOOD
I MOST WANTED TO HAPPEN.
"WHOM DO I HAVE TO CONVINCE
TO COME BACK TO YOU NOW BELOVED?
WHO IS IT SAPPHO THAT IS DOING YOU WRONG?
IF SHE NOW AVOIDS YOU SHE SHALL SOON BE PURSUING
SHE REFUSES YOUR PRESENTS BUT SHE'LL BE THE ONE TO
  GIVE GIFTS

SHE MAY NOT LOVE YOU NOW BUT SHE WILL SOON FALL
  IN LOVE
EVEN IF SHE (15) MAY NOT WANT IT."
SO COME NOW AGAIN AND FREE ME FROM PAIN
AND UNBEARABLE TORMENT
PLEASE LET ALL THE DESIRES IN MY HEART
COME TRUE AND BE FULFILLED
WITH YOU ALL THE TIME MY COMPANION IN BATTLE.
(LP 1, Cam. 1, Edm. 1, Lat. 1, MB 38, Roc. 17, SG p. 3, Dav. 1,
Balmer 78, Snyder 1, Rayor 1)

Even without music, this single poem gives an indication of what Dionysios of Halicarnassos meant, when more than five hundred years after Sappho's lifetime (about 20 B.C.) he wrote:

I SHALL GIVE YOU EXAMPLES OF HARMONY, BY WHICH I MEAN REFINED AND VIBRANT COMPOSITION, CHOOSING AMONG THE POETS THE MELODIST SAPPHO... THE MELODY AND CHARM OF HER WORKS ARE DUE TO THE SMOOTH COMBINATION OF WORDS AND SOUNDS, WHICH ARE INTERWOVEN IN SEQUENCES FOLLOWING THE NATURAL RELATIONSHIPS AND BALANCE OF THE LETTERS...
(Campbell, pp. 52-55).

Modern metaphors connecting Sappho's pursuit and conquest of her beloved (whose sex is only indicated by one word) to the martial deeds of the Homeric heroes might appear far-fetched but actually contain elements of historical reality. In "Sappho and the heroic ideal" Marry (1979) compared the *Ode to Aphrodite* with the *Iliad* and pointed out that words such as "subdue" (the Greek word also means taming an animal), "flee," "chase," "ally" [*symmakhos*, comrade in battle] reveal "resemblances between early Greek psychology of the erotic and the heroic" (p. 77) and "the treatment of a love affair as a duel" (p. 79). But in most other songs, Sappho did transcend this "agonistic way of loving" (p. 78), "raising the erotic... higher... than the military" (p. 79) and exploring "what kinds of activity are worthwhile for a human being" (p. 81). It was "the emergence of the individual voice" and "Sappho's different version of how a woman could live" (p. 83) that are universally admired today, even though "later generations of Greek males . . ." felt that "to be subversive" and made Sappho "a low character . . . in Attic comedy" (p. 83).

Somewhat later, in the first century A.D. a Greek-speaking Sicilian literary critic, with a Roman name and possibly Jewish background, *Longinus*, in his popular and often quoted book "On the Sublime"—literally "On the Highest" (form of language)—described Sappho's expression as "eloquent and efflorescent" (Greek terms in Ref. Table E). He elegantly analyzed this way the poem that followed his comments:

> . . . SAPPHO TAKES THE EVENTS AND EXPERIENCES OF EROTIC FRENZY FROM EACH REAL SITUATION AND DEMONSTRATES HER TALENT IN SELECTING AND CONNECTING TO EACH OTHER EXTREME OPPOSITE TENSIONS . . . YOU WILL ADMIRE HOW AT THE SAME TIME SHE EXPLORES HER SOUL AND HER BODY, HER HEARING, HER TONGUE, WHAT SHE SEES, WHAT COLOR IS HER SKIN, ALL AS IF THIS WAS SOMEONE ELSE'S VARYING SENSATIONS. IN CONTRASTING WAYS SHE FREEZES AND BURNS, IS IRRATIONAL AND SANE, TENSE WITH ANXIETY, YET LIMP AS IF ABOUT TO DIE, SO THAT IN HER WE SEE NOT ONE SINGLE EMOTION BUT A COMPLEX OF PASSIONATE FEELINGS. THIS OF COURSE IS WHAT HAPPENS TO PEOPLE IN LOVE, BUT HERE, AS I SAID, EXCELLENCE CONSISTS IN TAKING THE EXTREMES AND COMBINING THEM IN ONE (WORK):
>
> TO ME HE SEEMS EQUAL TO THE GODS
> THAT MAN WHO SITS FACING YOU AND NEAR YOU
> CAN LISTEN TO YOUR SWEET VOICE AND LOVELY
>   LAUGHTER.
> THAT MAKES MY HEART INSIDE MY CHEST PALPITATE;
> THE MOMENT I SEE YOU I LOSE MY VOICE,
> MY TONGUE IS TIED AND THAT VERY MOMENT
> A SUBTLE FIRE CROSSES MY FLESH,
> MY EYES SEE NOTHING, I HEAR A HUM,
> I AM SWEATING AND SHAKING
> ALL OVER, I LOOK GREENER THAN GRASS
> AND I FEEL THAT I AM ABOUT TO DIE.
>
> (LP 31, Cam. 31, Edm. 2, Lat. 2, MB 39, Roc. 27, SG p.10, WB 9, Dav. 20, Balmer 20, Snyder 31, Rayor 8; cf. Ref. Table H)

A psychoanalytic interpretation of Sappho's feelings about the man seated by the (unnamed) beloved girl (Devereux, 1970, pp. 17–31) represented this as a typical "anxiety attack" caused by a "male rival" for her "masculine" lesbian "perversion." According to this paper, Sappho viewed the man as "god-like" not because—cf. also Ref. Table H—he was in a position to recognize and to be charmed by exquisite beauty but because of her own lesbian "phallic awe." Sappho envied the sexuality of her male rival who "had something she did not have" (cited by Marcovich, 1972, p. 20). The subsequent critique (*ibid.*, pp. 19–32) of that distorted "text-book case" analysis, however, aptly reviewed the linguistic history of the key words in the poem, including the Greek terms for the supposed "symptoms of anxiety," or the "seizure" of the Lesbian lyricist and it concluded that the superb Sapphic verses were nothing more or less than a vivid, passionate but not pathological "declaration of love" (Marcovich, 1972, pp. 25–28). But there is more than that. Sappho did not simply express her envy of the man and her desire for the girl; she also *defined divinity* ("equal to the gods") as the unlimited appreciation of charm, beauty and love (Ref. Table H).

Sappho's choice of common everyday words expressed these and actually helped release the mind from the constraints of consciousness. Emphatic repetitions, seeming redundancies, such as "my harsh trouble," "my desires want . . . " (Roche, 1966, Introduction pp. x-xi and *Appendix*, pp. 143-148) become not only acceptable but precious and natural if, closer to the Greek, the lines are translated as "my heavy worries," "my mood longs for . . . ." Other expressions, like "whiter than snow," "greener than grass," "shinier than gold" (Edm. 59-62) have become poetic clichés, but were much admired as literary innovations of the 7th and early 6th centuries B.C. The poetic meters, the rhythms, the tempo, the music, all seemed to be new approaches to the art of self-expression. Sappho may have written down her own poems—in capitals "because lower case had not yet been invented" (Barnard, 1958, p. 104)—but copies certainly were "passed on to professional singers wherever Greek was spoken" (Barnard, 1958, p. 104). "The flexibility of the Greek allowed Sappho a complicated tense structure and swift movement," "fresh colloquial divertissement" with mixtures of overtones, ambiguity and occasional puns, which always "seemed right" (Barnard, 1958, p. 102). With . . . "a great range of different meters" she "moved with perfect ease" (Bowra, 1961, p. 246) and her words . . . "seemed as if invented in that moment" (Barnard, 1958, p. 103). From a twentieth century perspective, Sappho's verses can still be viewed as "not surpassed in any language" (Roche, 1966, p. 180) and her Aeolic idiom "remains beautiful in any variation of pronunciation and stress" (Roche, 1966, Introduction, p. xxiv). What matters most now is the range of subjects celebrated and sung by her. The totality of her imagery, the completeness of her verbal tableaux may not be shattered if specific selections are cited, inspired by nature, love, personal moods, loneliness and, with equal intensity by family festivities and by other social events. Writing about "Styles", Hermogenes (second century A.D.) showed that

One can express the pleasure of seeing the beauty of a landscape, the different plants, the variety of running waters, with simple words that are also a pleasure to hear, as did Sappho:

> HERE COOL DEW-DROPS MURMUR THROUGH THE APPLE
>   TREE TWIGS,
> ROSE BUSHES SHADE THE GROUND
> AND FROM THE QUIVERING LEAVES DESCENDS
> A DREAMER'S UNDISTURBED SLEEP . . .
>   (LP 2, Cam. 2, Edm. 4, Lat. 4, MB. 37, Roc. 45, SG p. 4, Dav. 2,
>   Balmer 79, Snyder 2, Rayor 2)

The above poem of Sappho started by inviting Aphrodite, the goddess of love (Ref. Table B):

> COME TO US NOW FROM CRETE TO THIS HOLY TEMPLE
> IN THE MIDDLE OF THIS MARVELOUS APPLE TREE GROVE
> ITS ALTARS, AS ALWAYS, SMOKING WITH INCENSE . . .
>   (LP 2, Cam. 2, Edm. 4 & 6, Roc. 45, WB 29, etc.)

The Lesbian poetess knew how the wind could become song and expressed it in a way very reminiscent of Homer (16).

> I START WITH WINDY WORDS BUT SO DELIGHTFUL TO HEAR
>   (Edm. 1a, Roc. 1, WB 2, Balmer 100)

She plucked the chords of her "turtle-shell" lyre, or "kithara," saying:

> COME DIVINE TURTLE-SHELL (LYRE) SPEAK TO ME
> AND GET YOURSELF A VOICE.
>   (LP 118, Cam. 118, Balmer 99, Rayor 67)

Julian, (331-363 A.D.) a classical scholar and youthful Roman emperor, referred to the following passage by Sappho in his *Letters*, concerning a young woman outshining in beauty all others:

> THE STARS AROUND THE BEAUTIFUL MOON
> GET DIMMER AND HIDE THEIR SPARKLE
> WHEN IN HER FULLNESS SHE SHINES ON EARTH
>   (LP 34, Cam. 34, Edm. 3, Dav. 73,
>   MB 24, Roc. 32, WB 14, Balmer 111,
>   Snyder 34, Rayor 7)

Spring and dawn, nighttime and winter winds, all became topics for Sappho's poetry:

IN GOLDEN SANDALS DAWN
JUST WOKE ME UP
(Edm. 19, Roc. 3, MB 3, Balmer 28)

HERALD OF SPRING, THE SWEET-VOICED NIGHTINGALE
(Cam. 136, Edm. 138, MB 62, Roc. 8, Dav. 79)

SPLENDIDLY DECORATED EARTH, WITH MANY GARLANDS
(Cam. 168C, Roc. 10)

THE MOON WENT DOWN AND SO DID THE PLEIADES;
IT'S THE MIDDLE OF THE NIGHT, THE HOURS PASS
AND I LIE ALONE
(Cam. 168B, Edm. 111, MB 64, WB 6,
Dav. 213, Balmer 38, Rayor 27; Ref. Table H)

PEACE, I HAVE NEVER FOUND YOU MORE FRUSTRATING . . .
(Edm. 116, Roc. 130, WB 121)

LOVE [Eros] HAS SHAKEN MY MIND LIKE A MOUNTAIN WIND
FALLING UPON THE OAK TREES
(LP 47, Cam. 47, Edm. 54, MB 44, Roc. 21, SG p. 26, WB 8, Dav. 15,
Snyder 47, and Ref. Table H)

Nature introduces Love, the most lyrically inspiring natural feeling and Sappho's favorite topic. Her emotional and physical response to the simple sight of her beloved, sitting next to someone else, was poetically and pathetically clear in the passage quoted by Longinus and cited earlier, which starts with the famous (for any admirer of the Lesbian lyricist):

TO ME HE SEEMS EQUAL TO THE GODS . . .
(Ref. Table H-1)

The hard-to-reach apple was used as a metaphor for the unapproachable maturing woman.

LIKE THE SWEET APPLE TURNING RED UP AT THE VERY END
OF THE HIGHEST BRANCH, MISSED BY THE FRUIT-PICKERS;
BUT NO, THEY DID NOT MISS IT, THEY WERE NOT ABLE TO
REACH.
(LP 105a, Cam. 105, Dav. 40, Balmer 68, Snyder 105a, Rayor 48)

For her beloved girl, Gongyla, she was telling herself:

> ... TAKE YOUR LYRE [PACTIS] ABANTHIS AND SING
> OF GONGYLA, AS THE DESIRE (17)
> ENCIRCLES AND SURROUNDS YOU
> FOR HER BEAUTY; TRULY HER POISE AND ATTIRE
> OVERWHELMED YOU WHEN YOU SAW HER ...
> THAT GIVES ME GREAT JOY.
> (Cam. 22, Edm. 45, MB 46, Dav. 112, Balmer 22)

Gongyla is mentioned again in other poems, once as the "spouse" [*syndygos*, or *synzyx*] of another woman, Gorgo (Campbell 1982, p. 195). Another beloved disciple of Sappho—the time separating or linking these loves is not known—was Mnasidika, or, in the Ionic-Attic dialect, Mnesidike (cf. *Chanson de Bilitis*, cited earlier). According to Sappho

> MNASIDIKA IS PRETTIER THAN TENDER (17) GYRINNO
> (LP 82a, Cam. 83, MB 18, Roc. 64, Balmer 17).

Calling her "Dika," Sappho urged her young companion to decorate her hair with garlands of anise, the delicate herb (the Aeolian *aneton*, or *anethon* in Ionic, known in botanical terms as *Pimpinella Anisum* and by some translated as dill, i.e. the closely related *Anethum graveolus*).

> AND YOU MY DIKA DECK YOUR LOVELY LOCKS WITH WREATHS
> OF ANISE TWIGS WOVEN TOGETHER WITH YOUR GENTLE
> HANDS
> (DP p. 135, Cam. 81, Edm. 117, AW p. 110, MB 19, Roc. 65, WB 95,
> Balmer 16, Snyder 81b, Rayor 5)

The poem about cavalry, soldiers, ships and "what one loves," (not "whatever" as rendered by Balmer, 1988, *21* and by Rayor, 1991, *4*) mentioned earlier, continued about Sappho's love (17) for Anactoria:

> ... ON THIS BLACK EARTH, I AM TELLING YOU,
> THAT TRUE BEAUTY IS ONLY FOUND IN WHAT ONE LOVES.
> HELEN, IN BEAUTY UNSURPASSED, LEFT
> HER NOBLE HUSBAND BEHIND AND SAILED TO TROY
> HER MIND FLYING HIGH IN LOVE ...
> AND NOW I AM MYSELF REMINDED OF ANACTORIA
> WHO IS NO LONGER HERE ...
> I SO WISH I COULD SEE HER LOVELY STRIDE
> AND HER BRIGHT SHINY FACE
> RATHER THAN ALL THE LYDIAN CHARIOTS AND ARMED MEN.
> (LP 16, Cam. 16, Edm. 38, Lat. 3, MB 41, Roc. 55, SG 7, WB 5,
> Dav.25, Balmer 21, Snyder 16, Rayor 4)

In a penetrating essay on "Sappho and Helen," Page DuBois (*Arethusa*, Vol. 11, 1978, pp. 89–97) saw in this poem "one of the few texts which break the silence of women in antiquity, an instant in which women become more than objects of man's desire." A striking difference is noted between the passive Helen of Homer and the passionately independent Helen of Sappho, a woman much like Sappho and her students themselves. "Sappho's poem . . . reverses the pattern . . . of the Homeric poems, men trading women . . . ." Helen is "one who acted pursuing the thing she loved. . . ." In loving Anactoria "Sappho acts as did Helen" by placing her individual feelings, or herself, or her *ego*, "against the background of choices" (p. 89). Her lines then become more than a love poem for Anactoria, as she "universalizes her insight" and is thus "defining desire" (p. 91). As the revolutionary changes in her aristocratic society "freed her from the rigidity of traditional marriage," Sappho was able "to see Helen as an autonomous subject, the hero of her own life" (DuBois, 1978, p. 97).

"Anactoria" was the title of a poem by A.C. Swinburne (1837-1909) supposedly narrated by Sappho. When that was published in England in 1866 it was "branded by the critics as libidinous" (Snyder, 1991, p. 35), even though it was much more subdued than the *Chansons de Bilitis* cited above. Closer to the Lesbian lyrics, the English poet included in his work a paraphrase of Sappho's *Hymn to Aphrodite* (*ibid.*, p. 35).

For a beloved friend who returned, Sappho sang:

> YOU CAME, AS I WAS LONGING FOR YOU
> AND YOU COOLED MY HEART (17) THAT WAS BURNING WITH
> PASSION
> (LP 48, Cam. 48, Edm. 89, MB 46, Roc. 49, SG 27, Dav. 113,
> Balmer 26, Snyder 48, Rayor 24)

And in another "sample" of erotic passion (17):

> . . . AND YOU MUST KNOW, I PRAYED
> THAT THE NIGHT MIGHT HAVE BEEN DOUBLED FOR US
> (Edm. 84a, Roc. 148, MB 47)

She also sang about a young girl overwhelmed by love for a boy.

> SWEET MOTHER I CANNOT WEAVE ON MY LOOM
> SUBTLE APHRODITE OVERWHELMED ME
> WITH DESIRE FOR A BOY.
> (LP 102, Cam. 102, Dav. 9, Balmer 40, Snyder 102, Rayor 18)

But some of her beloved girls left, never to return, like the one who got married in distant, wealthy Sardis, and made Sappho declare:

> FRANKLY I WANT TO DIE;
> SHE WAS GOING AWAY AND FULL OF TEARS SHE SAID:
> "PSAPPHO, I SWEAR I DON'T WANT TO LEAVE YOU . . ."
> AND I REPLIED: " . . . I WANT YOU TO REMEMBER
> WHAT BEAUTIFUL MOMENTS WE HAD TOGETHER
> . . . WHEN YOU USED TO DECORATE YOUR DELICATE NECK
>   WITH
> GARLANDS OF FLOWERS, ANOINT YOURSELF WITH REGAL
>   PERFUMES,
> AND ON THE SOFT MATTRESSES YOU LET LOOSE A YOUNG
>   WOMAN'S TENDER PASSION.
> (LP 94, Cam. 94, Edm. 83, MB 42, Roc. 54, WB 130, Dav. 78,
> Balmer 32, Snyder 94, Rayor 14)

This poem may have opened with a line not confirmed to be authentic.

> SO I SHALL NEVER SEE ATTHIS AGAIN
> (Edm. 83, WB 24)

Some erotic torment was left without a specified object:

> EROS MAKES ME TREMBLE AND LOOSENS MY LIMBS,
> THIS BITTER-SWEET, UNMANAGEABLE CREATURE
> (LP 130, Cam. 130, Edm. 81, MB 53, Roc. 109, WB 25, Dav. 65,
> Balmer 2, Snyder 130, Rayor 16)

Some collections have combined these two stanzas with two more:

> ATTHIS YOU NOW HATE MY CARING FOR YOU
> AND YOU RUN AFTER ANDROMEDA.
> (Edm. 81, WB 25, LP 131, and poss. Cam. 130 & 131, Snyder 131)

> I DON'T KNOW WHICH WAY TO GO;
> MY MIND IS SPLIT IN TWO
> (LP 51, Cam. 51, MB 69, Roc. 28, Dav. 114, Balmer 48, Snyder 51)

And some loves became a thing of the past, without any loss of lyrical intensity:

> I LOVED YOU ATTHIS, LONG TIME AGO,
> WHEN TO ME YOU SEEMED SUCH A CLUMSY LITTLE GIRL . . .
> (LP 49, Cam. 49, Edm. 48, MB 50, Roc. 116, WB 26,
> Dav. 4 & 16, Balmer 35, Snyder 49, Rayor 35)

Another poem was possibly addressed to Atthis—the first three lines are questionable (Edmonds, 1928; Barnstone, 1965)—and referred to her beloved Anactoria who was away in Lydia.

> NOW SHE STANDS OUT AMONG THE WOMEN OF LYDIA
> LIKE THE ROSE-FINGERED MOON AFTER THE SUN IS GONE
> OUTSHINING THE STARS SPREADS HER LIGHT
> OVER THE SALTY SEA AND THE FLOWERY FIELDS.
> . . . .
> OFTEN AS SHE ATTENDS (17) TO THIS OR THAT
> SHE RECALLS HER TENDER LOVE FOR ATTHIS
> AND HER GENTLE HEART IS CONSUMED (17) BY SADNESS.
>   (LP 96, Cam. 96, Edm. 86, Lat. 7, Page 96, MB 40, Roc. 53, WB 28,
>   Dav. 43, SG p. 47, Balmer 33, Rayor 15)

The name of lovely Atthis—the "clumsy little girl"—can be found at least six times (two or three additional references are doubtful) in the existing fragments of Sappho's verses (Campbell 1982, pp. 62, 94, 114, 120, 148, 204). Mnasidika—resurrected in the nineteenth century by P. Louÿs—or "Dika" appears only twice. Love poems addressed to other pupils (Table II-1) or "companions" (Balmer 1988, p. 110) indicate that the passionate affection of the Lesbian poet-singer-teacher either concerned several girls at the same time, or was aimed at different ones in succession.

But Sappho also knew how to hate and to ridicule, especially her rivals. Andromeda was one of them.

> **DINING SCHOLARS**
> BY ATHENAIOS CA. 200 A.D.
> **I.21C.** SAPPHO MADE FUN OF ANDROMEDA, SAYING:
> THAT KIND OF PEASANT WOMAN CHARMS YOUR MIND, WHO DOES NOT EVEN KNOW HOW TO PULL HER DRESS OVER HER ANKLES?   Gulick, 1969, Vol. I, p. 92.

As with everyone, so it was with Sappho, that some loves were only erotic fantasies. It is not known how many women would love to go to bed with their Endymion, and this is not because few recognize the name. The Greek myth is about a passive male loved by an aggressive, active female. Endymion was a handsome young shepherd and the moon goddess, Selene, fell in love with him. So she caused him to fall asleep forever in a secret cave on Mount Latmos and every night, or whenever she wished, she would visit and actively make love to this sleeping, yet alive and excitable male body. Sappho admits her own desire for a passively responsive male by saying:

> I AM NOT THE ONLY WOMAN, IT SEEMS, WHO WANTS TO VISIT
> THE LATMIAN CAVE   (Roc. 72)

Sappho's tender love for her own daughter, Kleis (pronounced Klay-ees) was also sensitively expressed in her lyrics (Re. "love," "beloved," "desire," see Ref. Table E):

> MINE IS A BEAUTIFUL CHILD THAT LOOKS
> LIKE A GOLDEN FLOWER, MY BELOVED KLEIS;
> I WOULD NOT DESIRE ALL OF LYDIA IN HER STEAD . . .
> (LP 132, Cam. 132, Edm. 130,
> MB 17, Roc. 62, WB 112, Dav. 57,
> Balmer 75, Snyder 132, Rayor 45)

And during their exile, she was saying plaintively:

> I HAVE NO WAY, KLEIS, NOW
> TO GET YOU A FANCY DECORATED HEAD GARLAND . . .
> . . . WE HAVE TO REALIZE THAT THE CLEANAX FAMILY
> MADE US TURN FUGITIVES
> (LP 98, Cam. 98, MB 83, Roc. 133, WB 113, Dav. 30,
> Balmer 74, Snyder 98b, Rayor 46)

At one time, when Sappho was sick and thought she might die, she advised Kleis not to cry:

> IT'S NOT RIGHT, IN A HOME THAT SERVES THE MUSES
> TO ALLOW LONG LAMENTS;
> THIS FOR US IS NOT BECOMING.
> (LP 150, Cam. 150, Edm. 108, Roc. 170,
> MB 99, WB 135, Balmer 76, Rayor 64)

At times, frustrated with her own milieu, she projected that posterity would acknowledge her talent.

> I AM TELLING YOU THAT SOMEONE IN DIFFERENT TIMES
> WILL REMEMBER US
>   (LP 147, Cam. 147, Lat. 6, Dav. 90, MB 60, Snyder p. 37, Rayor 68)

To this others append more lines:

> OBLIVION MAY HAVE LIED TO OTHERS
> BUT THE JUDGMENT OF GOOD MEN HAS NEVER MISSED ONE.
>   (Edm. 76, 77)

Her group collectively attracted much of Sappho's attention:

> HERE NOW, FOR MY DEAREST COMPANIONS
> BEAUTIFULLY I SHALL SING ABOUT PLEASURE
>
> (LP 160, Cam. 160, Edm. 12, MB 1, Roc. 2,
> Dav. 97, Balmer 98, Rayor 66)

One of the most explicit passages of Sappho, about two women living together concerned her friends Gorgo and Arkheanassa, possibly also known as Pleistodike.

> ARKHEANASSA THE SPOUSE (17) OF GORGO;
> AND PLEISTODIKE WILL BE CALLED A MATE OF GORGO
> ALONG WITH GONGYLA, BECAUSE SHE WAS GIVEN THE SAME NAME.
>
> (LP 213, Cam. 213, Dav. 54)

A series of "Epithalamia" (literally "By the bed-chamber") were sung by a group of girls, friends of the bride—bride's maids—during a wedding ceremony and often all night, by the door of the new couple's bedroom.

> UP AND HIGH THE ROOF MUST GO—BLESSED WEDDING!
> RAISE IT HIGH MASTER CRAFTSMEN—BLESSED HOURS!
> THERE IS THE BRIDEGROOM, LOOKING LIKE ARES
> SO MUCH TALLER THAN THE TALLEST OF MEN,
> STANDING HIGH ABOVE THE OTHERS
> LIKE THE SINGER FROM LESBOS
> OVER THOSE FROM FOREIGN LANDS.
>
> (Edm. 148, LP 111 & 106, Cam. 111,
> MB 29, Roc. 86, Dav. 102 & 50, Balmer 65 & 101,
> Snyder 111, Rayor 57 & 32)

> JOY TO THE BRIDE, JOY TO THE VALIANT BRIDEGROOM
> MUCH JOY FOREVER!
>
> (Edm. 162, Cam. 116, Roc. 101)

It seems that Sappho felt the need to discuss in intimate verses with her companions the questions of virginity and of the wedding night.

> I WOULD TELL YOU THIS:
> "I SWEAR BY THE GODDESS THAT EVEN THOUGH,
> LIKE YOU, I HAD NOT MANY BUT ONE ONLY VIRGINITY
> I DID NOT FEAR THE STEP TO GIVE IT AWAY
> WHICH HERA INTENDED FOR ME."
> SENSING THAT I COMFORTED YOU A LITTLE
> I WOULD MORE LOUDLY ADD: "THAT NIGHT
> WAS NONE OF A BURDEN FOR ME,

> DARLING GIRL, SO YOU TOO
> SHALL HAVE NOTHING TO FEAR."
>
> (Edm. 84, Roc. 94)

And with somewhat lighter verses, in a "dialogue."

> VIRGINITY, VIRGINITY, WHERE HAVE YOU GONE AND LEFT ME?

There echoes a response:

> I WILL NEVER RETURN TO YOU AGAIN, NEVER AGAIN . . .
> (Edm. 164, LP 114, Cam. 114, MB 32, Dav. 121, Balmer 71, Snyder 114, Rayor 59)

Some songs may sound relatively commonplace.

> FOR YOU, LUCKY BRIDEGROOM THE WEDDING TOOK PLACE,
> THE WAY YOU WANTED, NOW YOU HAVE HER, THE GIRL OF YOUR PRAYERS.
> YOU LOOK VERY GRACEFUL, YOUR EYES ARE MELLOW
> LIKE HONEY AND LOVE COVERS YOUR HANDSOME FACE
> . . . APHRODITE HAS IN FACT ENDOWED YOU SUPERBLY.
> (Edm. 155, LP 112, Cam. 112, MB 30, Roc. 99, Balmer 62, Rayor 54)

> YOUNG BRIDE, WITH YOUR GRACEFUL LOOKS
> SOFT-COLORED EYES AND LOVE
> SHINING THROUGH
> YOUR BEAUTIFUL FACE . . .
> (Edm. 158, Roc. 89)

> WILL BE SLEEPING ON THE BOSOM OF MY TENDER COMPANION
> (Edm. 128, Cam. 126, Snyder 126, Rayor 25)

> WE, THE GIRLS, THEN SHALL STAY BY THE DOORS
> OF THE HAPPIEST BRIDEGROOM AND WILL PARTY ALL NIGHT
> SINGING AS ALWAYS ABOUT YOUR LOVE
> AND ABOUT THE BRIDE'S SOFT BOSOM.
> WHEN THE DAWN LATER COMES
> AND YOU GET UP AND GO
> MAY THE GOD [HERMES] GUIDE YOUR STEPS
> TO AS LITTLE MISFORTUNE
> AS THIS NIGHT'S RARE SLEEP.
> (Edm. 47, Roc. 96, Balmer 59, Rayor 61)

The adventures of Sappho's older brother, Kharaxos (Haraxos) in Egypt and his love affair with—and possible marriage to—a famous slave and erotically "skillful" courtesan are described in Chapter III-A. There, Herodotos is quoted as rather admiring the woman, her lovemaking and her devotional gifts to the Delphic temple. Sappho had different feelings. In fact she was quite mad for the waste of Haraxos' time and money and for the embarrassment to their family. She addressed him in her poetry like this:

> . . . IF YOU MINGLE WITH HIGH-CLASS PEOPLE
> BUT WITH NO ONE NOBLE AND GOOD,
> IF YOU SAY GOOD-BYE TO THOSE WHO DO LOVE YOU
> AND CAUSE SERIOUS GRIEF TO ME TOO,
> WHEN WITH YOUR ARROGANT PRIDE
> CLAIM THAT IT WAS I, WHO EMBARRASSED AND SHAMED YOU
> YOU MAY DO AS YOUR HEART STILL DESIRES
> AND PLEASE YOURSELF FULLY.
> AS FOR ME, MY TEMPER MAY PASS LIKE A CHILD'S BAD MOOD.
>
> BUT DO NOT BE MISTAKEN
> (THE SNARE WILL NOT CATCH THE WISE OLD BIRD!)
> I AM AWARE OF THE MESS YOU WERE IN UNTIL NOW
> AND THE VICIOUS OPPONENT I WILL HAVE TO CONFRONT.
> YOU'D BETTER RETHINK IT AND HAVE YOUR MIND CHANGED.
> I HAVE NO DOUBT THAT MY MANNERS, SO GENTLE,
> WILL MAKE THE GODS STAND FIRM BY MY SIDE.
>
> (LP 3, Cam. 3, Edm. 35, MB 103, Roc. 135, Dav. 104)

But always, as a forgiving sister, she hoped to see him back, a good citizen and married well.

> CYPRIAN (GODDESS) AND GOLDEN SEA-MAIDS [NEREIDS]
> MAKE MY BROTHER
> COME SOON SAFELY HOME.
> IT'S ALRIGHT IF ALL THAT HIS HEART EVER WANTED
> HAS BEEN FULLY ACCOMPLISHED.
>
> IMMORTALS, I DO SWEAR THAT WHATEVER HAS HAPPENED
> WILL BE FULLY DISMISSED AND TO THOSE WHO STILL LOVE HIM
> HE WILL BRING ONLY JOY, SAVING PAINFUL ANGUISH
> FOR ONLY HIS FOES. AS FOR US OF HIS FAMILY
> THERE SHOULD NOT BE ANY EMBARRASSMENT
>
> I STILL HOPE HE IS WILLING TO HONOR HIS SISTER.
> THE DISMAL DISTRESS HE HAS CAUSED ME BEFORE,
> AND HIS WORDS AS HE LEFT ME I MAY BE GLAD TO FORGET . . .
> . . . IF HE IS BACK IN DUE TIME
> GETS RID OF HIS BAD FRIENDS AND BECOMES A GOOD CITIZEN.
> ALSO FINDS A BED-MATE, IF HE TRULY WANTS ONE,
> A WORTHY AND GOOD WIFE.
> AS FOR YOU, DIRTY BITCH,
> STICK YOUR FOUL SNOUT TO THE GROUND

TO SNIFF FOR ANOTHER MALE-VICTIM
WHOM YOU'LL CATCH AND THEN HARNESS.
(LP 5, Cam. 5, Edm. 36, MB 71,
Roc. 134, Dav. 103, Snyder 5)

The "dirty bitch" Sappho wrote about was the famous "love professional," courtesan, or prostitute, in Naucratis, Egypt. Yet Herodotos—who called her "Rhodopis," perhaps a nickname for "Rosy Cheeks"—admired her and in the second century A.D., the chronicler Athenaios commented, with a touch of melancholy:

THE DINING SCHOLARS
BY ATHENAIOS, ABOUT 200 A.D.
XIII. 596B-D. FAMOUS COURTESANS (17), DISTINGUISHED FOR THEIR BEAUTY, WERE PRODUCED BY (THE CITY OF) NAUCRATIS TOO. THERE WAS DORIKHA, WHO BECAME THE MISTRESS OF SAPPHO'S BROTHER HARAXOS WHEN HE WENT TO NAUCRATIS ON BUSINESS. THE FAIR SAPPHO DENOUNCED HER IN HER POETRY BECAUSE SHE TOOK MUCH MONEY FROM HER BROTHER . . . HERODOTOS CALLS HER RHODOPIS NOT KNOWING THAT THIS WAS A DIFFERENT WOMAN FROM DORIKHA [Doriha], WHO HAD DEDICATED THE FAMOUS OBELISKS (OXEN SPITS) IN DELPHI. POSEIDIPPOS (18) MENTIONS THIS DORIKHA OFTEN AND ALSO WROTE THIS EPIGRAM (MEMORIAL INSCRIPTION) FOR HER:

YOUR BONES HAVE BEEN SLEEPING A LONG TIME DORIKHA
BOUND SOFTLY BY THE CURLS OF YOUR HAIR
AND BY YOUR SCARF FULL OF PERFUMES,
WITH WHICH ONCE YOU HAD WRAPPED CHARMING
   HARAXOS
JOINING HIM TO YOURSELF TILL 'TWAS TIME
FOR THE DAWN'S WINE CUP.

FROM SAPPHO'S BRIGHT PAGES HER SONGS' LOVELY
   SOUNDS
ARE ALL STILL WITH US AND ALWAYS WILL BE
(BUT) YOUR NAME (TOO) WILL BE BLESSED
AND PRESERVED HERE IN NAUCRATIS
FOR AS LONG AS THE SHIPS FROM THE NILE
PASS BY AND THROUGH TO THE SALTY OPEN SEAS.

   . . . IN SOME WAY, AS HERODOTOS SAYS, NAUCRATIS WAS LIKELY TO HAVE VERY SEXY (17) COURTESANS.

XIII. 596E. THE COURTESAN FROM ERESOS TOO, WHO HAD THE SAME NAME AS THE POETESS SAPPHO, WAS RENOWNED FOR HER LOVE OF THE HANDSOME PHAON.
(Parts quoted in Greek by Campbell, Testm. No. 15,
p. 15 and No. 202, p. 188)

The traveling geographer, Strabo [*Strabon*] visited Egypt and confirmed the fact that Doriha, her lovers, Sappho and the others, were all real people, with existing tombstones at the turn of the millennium.

> **GEOGRAPHY**
> BY STRABON, ABOUT 63 B.C.–21 A.D.
> **XVII.1.33** IT (A PYRAMID NEAR MEMPHIS, IN EGYPT) IS CALLED THE TOMB OF THE COURTESAN, ERECTED BY THE LOVERS OF A WOMAN, WHOM THE LYRIC POETESS SAPPHO CALLS DORIHA. SHE BECAME THE MISTRESS OF HER (SAPPHO'S) BROTHER HARAXOS, WHO IMPORTED AND MARKETED LESBIAN WINE TO NAUCRATIS. OTHERS CALLED THE SAME WOMAN RHODOPIS.
> (Quoted in Greek by Cam. 202, p. 186)

Clearly the two women, Sappho and Dorikha, represented two worlds far apart, one the lyrical love of Lesbos and the other the skilled sexuality of Hellenized Egypt. Yet they both, side-by-side, remained very much in the center of Greek feeling and thought, for many centuries.

Alkaios [Alcaeus], politics and drinking songs

Alkaios (commonly transliterated Alcaeus) was a man from Mytilene, a Lesbian poet approximately contemporary of Sappho and almost as famous (Bowra, 1961, Campbell, 1982). Ancient biographers placed his birth about 652–48 B.C. (32nd Olympiad)—or later—and his death, in his seventies, about 570–69 B.C. Alkaios, too, composed and sang lyric poetry, that is songs accompanied by lyre music, although their content was not as "lyrical" in the modern sense, as that of Sappho. If a citation by the philosopher Aristotle, almost 250 years later, is correct, Alkaios may have been at the time amorously attached to his female contemporary lyricist.

> **RHETORIC**
> BY ARISTOTLE, 384–322 B.C.
> **1367A.** SOME MEN ARE EMBARRASSED TO SAY, TO DO OR TO CONTEMPLATE (WHAT THEY CONSIDER) SHAMEFUL THINGS. NOTE SAPPHO'S REPLY WHEN ALKAIOS SAID:
> "I WOULD LIKE TO SAY SOMETHING TO YOU BUT SHAME WILL NOT LET ME"
> ". . . IF YOUR DESIRE WAS HONORABLE AND GOOD, AND YOUR TONGUE HAD NOTHING EVIL TO SAY, SHAME WOULD NOT COVER YOUR EYES BUT YOU WOULD CLEARLY EXPRESS WHAT YOU WANT"
> (Quoted in Greek by Campbell 137, p. 152; also LP 137)

Alkaios and Sappho, each holding a lyre and plektron, on a kalathos-psykter from Agrigentum; in Munich, Staatliche Antikensammlungen und Glyptothek. From Richter 1965/84.

The two Lesbian poets are shown together on vase paintings. Alkaios, like Sappho, also sang about the beautiful girls on Lesbos and he described the established "kallisteia," which were young maidens' beauty contests (19).

> THERE, LESBIAN MAIDENS IN TRAILING ROBES
> WALK UP AND DOWN, TO BE JUDGED FOR THEIR BEAUTY
> AND ENCHANTING WOMEN'S SONGS AROUND THEM
> SOUND THE DIVINE ANNUAL FEAST...
> (Ath. XIII.16a; LP 130, Cam. 130b, Rayor 1:12-20)

Alkaios may have been too young to help his brothers in the rebellion of the aristocracy aimed at the overthrow of the dictator Melanchros even though his prime—"acme"—was placed about the 42nd Olympiad, i.e. 612–608 B.C. and that was the time the tyrant was overthrown (Campbell, *Introduction* xiii–xiv) by Myrsilos and Pittakos.

Later, Alkaios did follow Pittakos in the expedition against the Athenians at Sigeon (Campbell, *Introduction*). That is where he fled, dropping his arms and shield (cf. Plutarch, II-A, p. 21).

HISTORY
BY HERODOTOS, 484-420 (?) B.C.

A WAR WAS GOING ON . . . BETWEEN MYTILENE AND ATHENS . . . OVER SIGEON (ON ASIA MINOR) . . . AND AMONG ALL KINDS OF BATTLE INCIDENTS THERE WAS ONE INVOLVING ALKAIOS, THE POET. AS THE ATHENIANS WERE WINNING HE RAN AND ESCAPED, BUT THE ATHENIANS GOT HOLD OF HIS ARMOR, WHICH THEY HUNG UP ON THE TEMPLE OF ATHENA AT SIGEON. ALKAIOS MADE A POEM ABOUT THIS AND SENT IT TO MYTILENE, TO TELL HIS CLOSE FRIEND MELANIPPOS WHAT HAPPENED TO HIM.

(Quoted in Greek by Cam. 428 (b), p. 420)

Alkaios took part in another unsuccessful attempt to depose the next "tyrant" of Mytilene, Myrsilos. As a result, to escape punishment, he had to leave the city and then spent some time in exile in Pyrrha, a city in the center of Lesbos (Bowra, 1961, pp. 130–175; Campbell, 1982, *Introduction*, xv), where he wrote some of his political and sea-faring songs. The poet's lines, written later during the rule of Pittakos, described the spot, in which there was a sanctuary for the three gods, Zeus, Hera and Dionysos.

. . . THE LESBIANS SET UP
THIS HIGH-STANDING LARGE COMMON SANCTUARY
AND PLACED IN IT ALTARS TO THE BLESSED IMMORTALS
CALLING ZEUS THE PROTECTOR
YOU, THE GLORIOUS AEOLIAN GODDESS (HERA?), CREATRIX
    OF ALL
AND THIRD, NAMING ZONNYSSOS [DIONYSOS] KEMELIOS,
RAW-MEAT-EATER.
IN KIND SPIRIT NOW LISTEN TO OUR PLEAS
AND DELIVER US FROM OUR HARDSHIPS AND PAINFUL
    EXILE.
SEND THE SPIRITS OF VENGEANCE AFTER THE SON OF
    HYRRHAS (PITTAKOS)
. . . THAT BLOATED RASCAL
WHO NEVER SPOKE TO THE MEN'S HEARTS
YET HE SLOWLY DEVOURS THE CITY
TRAMPLING ON THE OATHS . . .

(LP 129, Cam. 129)

That may have been the same "prominent and clearly visible location," where, according to Homer, (chapter I-A) Nestor and Menelaos landed and made further plans for sailing back to their respective kingdoms. The notable [*eudeilon*] sanctuary may have been on the peninsula east of the entrance to the large bay of Kalloni facing south (Quinn 1961), where the only modern markers are a few broken marbles and a tiny chapel dedicated to Saint Phokas. Possibly the poet arrived there from Mytilene, sailing around the east coast of Lesbos (Quinn 1961). Perhaps it was this or maybe another rough trip, that made him say:

> HERE COMES ANOTHER WAVE, RIGHT AFTER THE ONE BEFORE
> IT WILL BE HARD TO PUMP THE WATERS OUT
> WHEN OUR BOAT IS FLOODED.
> LET'S BOARD IT UP QUICKLY
> AND RUSH TO A SAFE HARBOR.
> LET NO ONE RELAX OR BE TIMID
> AN ENORMOUS ORDEAL IS CLEARLY AHEAD OF US
> BUT REMEMBER OUR EARLIER TROUBLES
> AND LET EVERYONE NOW PROVE THEMSELVES
> NOT TO DISGRACE OUR NOBLE ANCESTORS...
>
> (LP 6, Cam. 6, Rayor 1)

In another song Alkaios' allegorical reference to the shifting, unpredictable winds and waves has been interpreted to reflect his views of the political changes on Lesbos.

> I AM CONFUSED BY THE THRUST OF THE WINDS; WHILE ONE WAVE ROLLS FROM THIS SIDE ANOTHER ONE COMES FROM THAT, AND WE, WITH OUR BLACK SHIP ARE RIGHT IN THE MIDDLE STRUGGLING HARD IN THE BIG STORM...
>
> (Cam. 208, Rayor 1)

A commentary by Heraclitos points out the clear allusions.

> WE FIND THE MYTILENEAN LYRICIST USING ALLEGORY IN MANY PASSAGES; HE COMPARES SIDE-BY-SIDE THE STORMY SEAS TO THE DICTATORIAL UPHEAVALS.
>
> Quoted by Campbell, p. 322.

About 590 B.C. Myrsilos died and Alkaios celebrated it in a drinking song, of which he composed many. But when the nobility attempted a return to power they failed again. Pittakos, a popular hero and populist leader was freely elected as absolute ruler, dictator, or, in Greek, "tyrant" of Mytilene and governed the city for ten years (Chap. III-A). Although formerly his friend, the young aristocrat-poet now left out, expressed his anger, contempt and frustration against *Ph*ittakos (as he spelled it, with a Greek *phi*) with numerous verses.

Alcaeus [*Alkaios*]; (Vienna), in Richter 1965/84.

... THEN LET THIS MAN, WHO MARRIED AN ATREID (20)
GOBBLE UP THE CITY AS HE DID JOINING MYRSILOS
UNTIL, WITH THE WILL OF ARES
WE TAKE UP ARMS AGAIN.

LET'S FOR NOW FORGET OUR ANGER
RELAX FROM THE HEART-DEVOURING STRIFE
AND THE CIVIL WARS, WHICH SOME OLYMPIAN STIRRED UP,
LEADING THE PEOPLE TO CALAMITY
AND PHITTAKOS TO PLEASURABLE PRESTIGE.

(LP 70, Cam. 70)

Before Pittakos eventually pardoned him, Alkaios traveled to Egypt and also probably to Thrace and Lydia. His brother too left Lesbos for political reasons and became a mercenary of the king of Babylon (Oxf. Clas. Dict., p. 35).

The complete poems of Alkaios were edited by Alexandrian scholars in the last two centuries B.C. and were probably divided in ten books, of which at least one was known to contain more than 1,000 verses (Campbell, 1982, *Introduction*, p. xvii). They included lyrical, festive and plain drinking songs, "sometimes with a meditative tinge" (Oxf. Clas. Dict. p. 35). Many pertained to the poet's contemporary politics and others were hymns to the Gods. The language was vernacular

Aeolic, "with occasional Homerisms" (*ibid.*, p. 35). Aristotle relied on the poetry of Alkaios for details about the political history of Mytilene.

POLITICS
BY ARISTOTLE, 384–332 B.C.
BOOK III, 1285A, 35SS
ALKAIOS VERIFIES, IN HIS OWN SKOLIA (DRINKING SONGS), THAT THE CITIZENS OF MYTILENE ELECTED PITTAKOS TYRANT AND HE BLAMES THEM FOR PUTTING UP WITH HIM:

"THEY ELECTED PITTAKOS THE LOW-BORN, AS THE
ABSOLUTE RULER OF THIS APATHETIC ILL-FATED CITY"
(Quoted in Greek by Campbell, 1982, No. 348, p. 382)

After Pittakos felt sufficiently secure in his government, he allowed Alkaios to return to the city and apparently forgave him for his political action and his poisonous poetry.

THE LIBRARY OF HISTORY
BY DIODOROS OF SICILY, 1ST CENTURY B.C.
THEN ALSO WHEN HE (PITTAKOS) GOT HOLD OF THE POET ALKAIOS, WHO HAD BEEN HIS WORST ENEMY AND HAD RIDICULED HIM BITTERLY IN HIS POEMS, HE LET HIM GO, DECLARING THAT PARDON IS BETTER THAN PUNISHMENT.
(Quoted in Greek by Campbell, 1982, p. 212)

In a survey of the total poetic output of Sappho and of Alkaios, it may be worth pondering why a woman like her wished to surrender to love and a man, her contemporary and compatriot, preferred to submit to wine. The surviving examples of Alkaios' drinking songs are numerous.

DRINK AND GET DRUNK WITH ME, MELANIPPOS,
UNLESS YOU EXPECT THAT AFTER YOU CROSS
THE RIVER OF DEATH, ROUGH TWISTING ACHERON,
YOU WILL STILL BE ENJOYING THE SUN'S BRIGHT LIGHT.
COME ON, DO NOT SET YOUR AIMS TOO HIGH,
FOR EVEN WHEN SISYPHOS (21), THE AEOLID KING
MOST CLEVER OF MEN AND HIGHLY KNOWLEDGEABLE,
THOUGHT THAT HE HAD MASTERED DEATH
TWICE HE WAS FORCED TO CROSS THE ACHERON,
AND WAS DOOMED BY KRONOS' SON (ZEUS)
TO TOIL FOREVER IN THE DARK UNDERWORLD.
COME ON, DO NOT HOPE FOR SOMETHING UNREAL
NOW, IF EVER, WE MUST MAKE THE BEST
OF OUR OWN EXISTENCE ...
AND ENDURE AS WE CAN, WHAT THE GODS MAKE US
  SUFFER ...
(LP 38, Cam. 38A, Rayor 1)

Athenaios was a late second century A.D. Greek from Naucratis, Egypt, who wrote a very long work, with a total of 40 volumes (Gulick, 1968), about "Dining Scholars" (variously translated as Sages at Dinner, The Dinner of Wise Men, etc.). In it he went into much detail about banquets, about what people ate on various occasions and also of their conversation. This ranged from popular wisdom to debates about ancient musical instruments and famous prostitutes. It included innumerable valuable quotations from the works of prominent poets, dramatists, philosophers. In a long section about wines and drinking (not neglecting a description of various cups and utensils) there were many quotations from the poetry of Alkaios.

DINING SCHOLARS [DEIPNOSOPHISTS]
BY ATHENAIOS, ABOUT 200 A.D.

THIS POET (ALKAIOS) IS FOUND DRINKING IN EVERY SEASON AND ALL CIRCUMSTANCES . . . ON HAPPY OCCASIONS HE CELEBRATES THIS WAY (ATH. X 430.A-C):

"NOW WE MUST GET INEBRIATED
AND DRINK WITH ALL OUR STRENGTH,
SINCE MYRSILOS (THE TYRANT) IS DEAD."

(LP 332, Cam. 335)

AND WHEN THINGS WERE BAD (ATH. 430 B-C)

"WE MUST NOT SURRENDER OUR HEART TO BAD LUCK
WE CANNOT GO AHEAD IN GRIEF
. . . THE BEST REMEDY IS
TO BRING IN THE WINE AND TO GET DRUNK."

. . . FOR WINTERTIME TOO, THESE WERE HIS LINES (X 430 A-B)

" . . . A WINTRY STORM COMES DOWN FROM THE SKY
RUNNING WATERS ARE FROZEN
BUT WHAT DOES IT MATTER?
LET'S CONQUER THE WINTER, START NOW A GOOD FIRE
FILL WITHOUT STOP THE BLENDERS WITH SWEET WINE
AND SHADE YOUR TEMPLES BOTH RIGHT AND LEFT
WITH SOFT OBSCURE VEILS.

(Cam. 332, 335, 338, also LP 335, 338)

AND HE SAID (ATH. X 430 C-D)

"LET'S DRINK! WHY WAIT FOR THE LAMP-LIGHTS?
ONE FINGER IS ONLY LEFT OF THE DAY.
BRING HERE, MY FAVORITE FRIEND, THE LARGE FANCY
  CUPS.
THE DIVINE SON OF ZEUS AND SEMELE (DIONYSOS)
HAS GIVEN FOR MEN THE WORRY-CHASING WINE.

> POUR IN THE MIXERS ONE HEAD (PART, OF WATER) TO MORE THAN TWO (OF WINE)
> AND LET EACH ONE GOBLET CHASE DOWN THE OTHER."
>
> (LP 346, Cam. 346)
>
> AND AS A MATTER OF GENERAL ADVICE HE (ALKAIOS) SAID (ATH. X 430C)
>
> "YOU SHOULD PLANT NOTHING ELSE BEFORE THE VINE"
>
> (LP 342, Cam. 342)

That was what Alkaios had been quoted as saying about wine and drinking. To balance this, a quote suggesting sober behavior was:

> "IF YOU SAY WHAT YOU LIKE, YOU MAY HEAR WHAT YOU DO NOT LIKE"
>
> (LP 341, Cam. 341, citing a quote by Proclos)

Centuries later, the Byzantine writer John [*Ioannes*] Tzetzes also referred to Alkaios' views about wine.

> **LYKOPHRON**
> by John Tzetzes, 12th century A.D.
>
> Under the influence of wine people reveal their most secret thoughts. This is what Alkaios said:
>
> FOR WINE IS A SEE-THROUGH INTO A MAN
>
> Quoted by Campbell 1982, p. 372.

At the end of a drinking party, there was often a game, when the last drops in a cup were aimed at a target (Ath. xi 480f-481a) and Alkaios said, referring also to the fancy cups from Teos:

> "DROPS FLY OUT OF THE TEIAN GOBLETS"
>
> (LP 322, Cam. 322)

In an earlier section discussing wines in general, the "Dining Scholars" talked much about the Lesbian varieties.

> **DINING SCHOLARS**
> BY ATHENAIOS, CA 200 A.D.
>
> **I.22E.** MNESITHEUS OF ATHENS SAYS THAT THE PYTHIAN PRIESTESS DIRECTED THE ATHENIANS TO HONOR DIONYSOS AS PHYSICIAN-HEALER. ALKAIOS TOO, THE POET FROM MITYLENE, DECLARED:
>
> SOFTEN YOUR LUNGS WITH WINE,
>   BECAUSE THE STAR IS RISING;

> THE HOUR IS HEAVY AND EVERYTHING IS THIRSTY
> FROM THE HEAT.
>
> Gulick 1969, Vol. I, p. 98.

The Lesbian wine still invited the praise of Athenaios' *Dining Scholars* almost eight hundred years after Alkaios' songs.

> **DINING SCHOLARS**
> BY ATHENAIOS, CA 200 A.D.
>
> **I.28E-F.** THERE IS NOT ANOTHER WINE TO DRINK MORE POTENT THAN THE LESBIAN DRAUGHT
>
> SAYS ALEXIS. AND THE SAME ONE:
>
> HE SLOWLY DRINKS THE LITTLE . . . LESBIAN WINES
>   FOR THE REST OF THE DAY
>   WHILE HE NIBBLES.
>
> THE BROMIAN GOD (BACCHUS) WAS SWEET TO MAKE LESBIAN WINE DUTY-FREE FOR IMPORT HERE. BUT WHOEVER IS CAUGHT SENDING EVEN A CUP TO ANOTHER TOWN WILL HAVE HIS HOLDINGS SEIZED.
>
> Gulick 1969, Vol. I, p. 124.
>
> (AND) EPHIPPOS (SAYS):
>
> I LOVE THE PRAMNIAN WINE OF LESBOS
>   MANY ARE THE LESBIAN DROPS
>   TO DRAIN AND DRINK WITH DELIGHT.
>
> EUBOULOS (SAYS):
>
> TAKE SOME . . . OLD LESBIAN WINE
>   ITS DROPS ARE LIKE NECTAR
>
> AND ARKHESTRATOS THE CULINARY EXPERT:
>
> **I.29B.** I PRAISE ALSO THE WINE OF BYBLOS FROM THE SACRED PHOENICIAN LAND. . . . ONE MAY THINK AT FIRST THAT IT IS EVEN MORE FRAGRANT THAN LESBIAN WINE. BUT AFTER YOU TASTE IT YOU WILL FIND IT MUCH INFERIOR. THAT LESBIAN WINE GIVES YOU THE REWARDS OF AMBROSIA, MORE SO THAN JUST WINE.
>
> Gulick 1969, Vol. I, pp. 126-28.

Lasting lyrics

Lesbian locations, lyrics and traditions have been cited endlessly during the centuries of Greek antiquity up to our modern age. Discussing current findings concerning the renowned temple of the 6th–7th century B.C. dedicated to the "Triple Deities" of Zeus, Hera and Dionysos [*Zonnysos*] a Greek newspaper (*Kathemerini*, "The

Daily," Dec. 23, 1962) quoted the lines from the "Palatine Anthology" about the ancient Lesbian beauty contests.

> **THE PALATINE ANTHOLOGY**
> **IX-189**
> COME TO THE SERENE TEMPLE OF THE BULL-EYED HERA
> YOU, LESBIAN MAIDS, SWINGING BY THE STEPS
>   OF YOUR DELICATE LEGS
> THERE START FOR THE GODDESS A BEAUTIFUL DANCE
> FOR YOU IT WAS THAT SAPPHO HAS SUNG
> HOLDING IN HER HANDS HER GOLDEN LYRE

For hundreds of years the songs of the early Greek lyricists, the words of Alkaios, the poetry of Sappho, also remained immensely popular. They were often part of an evening's entertainment and topics of lively conversation and comments. At a party in Plutarch's time (around 100 A.D.) men talked about Sappho and how Love [*Eros*] made a poet out of a boor (Edmonds, 1928, Vol. I, p. 168, quoting Plutarch's *Symposium*, 1.5.1).

> AFTER THE SINGING OF SOME OF SAPPHO'S SONGS, THERE WAS A DISCUSSION AT SOSSIOS' ABOUT HOW LOVE TEACHES EVEN SOMEONE CRUDE AND UNINSPIRED [AMOUSOS—REF. TABLE E] TO BECOME A POET.

Not much later, another commentator wrote:

> **ATTIC NIGHTS**
> BY AULUS GELLIUS, 2ND CENTURY A.D.
> AFTER WE FINISHED OUR DINNER AND IT WAS TIME FOR WINE AND CONVERSATION ... THE EXCELLENT SINGERS AND LYRE PLAYERS OF OUR HOST, YOUNG MEN AND WOMEN, GAVE A WONDERFUL PERFORMANCE OF MANY SONGS OF ANACREON AND OF SAPPHO AND ALSO OF SOME SWEET AND CHARMING EROTIC ELEGIES BY MODERN COMPOSERS.
>   (Quoted in Greek by Campbell No. 53, p. 44)

After another six hundred years we still can find the names of our Lesbian poets in the writings of prominent men of letters. Photios was a Byzantine scholar, who assembled and then published his own "library," before he became ecumenical patriarch (22), head of the millions of Eastern Orthodox Christians (Chapter V-B).

LIBRARY
BY PHOTIOS, 820-891 A.D.

161. VARIOUS EXCERPTS WERE READ FROM THE TWELVE BOOKS OF SOPATER THE SOPHIST . . . THE SECOND VOLUME INCLUDES PASSAGES FROM THE FIRST BOOK OF THE "COMPENDIA" BY PAMPHILE, DAUGHTER OF SOTIRIDAS AND FROM THE "STORIES OF WORTHY ACCOMPLISHMENTS AMONG WOMEN," BY ARTEMON, AS WELL AS . . . SPECIAL SECTIONS FROM THE EIGHTH BOOK OF SAPPHO.
(Quoted in Greek by Cam. No. 32, p. 30)

Three more centuries passed and another Byzantine man of letters, Tzetzes, writing about "all the meters of Pindar" (Sect. 20-22) lamented that:

. . . SAPPHO AND SAPPHO'S WORK, HER LYRE AND HER SONGS HAVE BEEN DESTROYED BY THE PASSAGE OF TIME.
(Quoted in Greek by Cam. No. 61, p. 50)

Enough lines and historical material remain, however, to fill dozens of books on Sappho alone, in modern English and other western European languages (23). No fewer than twenty fairly comprehensive English translations of Lesbian poetry have been published within the past seven decades. Many lines from Sappho were included in a recording of E. Carter's composition "Syringa" (Composers' Recordings, New York, 1982). Examples of selected Sapphic verses in English—some translated word-by-word and others interpreted rather fancifully—plus other translations in widely spoken modern tongues are included in Ref. Table H for appreciation, comparisons and critique.

Musicians accompanying a ram to the altar for sacrifice.
Corinthian painting (ca. 540 B.C.), with archaic lettering.
M. Andronikos et al., *The Greek Museums*, 1975, p. 69.

Chapter III

SAGES, SOLDIERS, SLAVES AND SCHOLARS

A. **The Rule of the "Sages"**
   Pittakos, the wise ruler of Lesbos
   Pherekydes and Pythagoras—Gods vs. mathematics
   Merchants, mercenaries and a girl's erotic art

B. **Hellenic Holocaust—Slaughter, Slavery and Survival**
   Civil strife and the Persian wars
   Lesbos between Athens and Sparta
   Greeks against Greeks: The Battle of Arginousai

C. **Lesbos and the Hellenic Schools of Thought**
   The Academy of Plato
   The Lyceum of Aristotle and Theophrastos
   The Epicurean Hermarkhos of Lesbos
   Stoics of the Multicolored Arcade [*Stoa*]

Hoplites (soldiers) going into battle, seventh century B.C. Corinthian olpe (in Arias/Shefton, 1961, Pl. IV).

Overleaf: Theophrastos, Lesbian philosopher, successor of Aristotle as head of the Lyceum in Athens.

SAGES, SOLDIERS, SLAVES AND SCHOLARS

A. THE RULE OF THE "SAGES"

Pittakos, the wise ruler on Lesbos

Pittakos (Louvre) from Richter 1965/84.

One of the Seven Sages of ancient Greece (Ref. Table F), Pittakos (Pittacus) ruled Mytilene on Lesbos for ten years. He was freely elected "tyrant" (absolute dictator) by the people and then voluntarily resigned when his work was done. This popular leader and law maker was also a poet and a teacher (1). Some later famous philosophers came to the island when young to learn from him. Even though he aroused the hatred and the ridicule of members of the aristocracy, which included the poets Sappho and Alkaios—both of whom had to leave Mytilene and to spend some time in exile—Pittakos was already renowned in his lifetime and has been known as one of the Greek "sages" ever since. Personal biographical notes and comments on the work and sayings of Pittakos are found in the first of the ten books (2) by Diogenes Laertios (Hicks, 1965).

LIVES AND OPINIONS OF EMINENT PHILOSOPHERS
BY DIOGENES LAERTIOS, FIRST HALF OF THIRD CENTURY A.D.
BOOK I, CHAPTER 4
PITTAKOS
74-81. PITTAKOS WAS A NATIVE OF MYTILENE; HIS FATHER . . . WAS FROM THRACE. WITH THE HELP OF ALKAIOS' BROTHER HE OVERTHREW MELANKHROS, THE TYRANT (DICTATOR) OF LESBOS. AS THE GENERAL IN CHARGE OF THE MYTILENEAN TROOPS DURING A TERRITORIAL WAR WITH ATHENS, HE MANAGED BY A TRICK TO CATCH THE ATHENIAN GENERAL IN A NET AND TO KILL HIM. AFTER THIS THE CONFLICT WAS SETTLED BY ARBITRATION . . . BY PERIANDER (OF CORINTH, ANOTHER "SAGE").

THE CITY OF MYTILENE HONORED PITTAKOS GREATLY AND TRUSTED HIM WITH ABSOLUTE RULING POWER. BUT AFTER HE GOVERNED FOR TEN YEARS AND BROUGHT THE CONSTITUTION TO ORDER, HE LAID DOWN HIS OFFICE AND LIVED (PRIVATELY) FOR ANOTHER TEN YEARS . . . HE WAS CONTENT WITH LITTLE AND . . . WHEN (THE LYDIAN KING) KROISOS OFFERED HIM A GIFT OF MONEY HE REFUSED IT, SAYING THAT HE HAD TWICE AS MUCH AS HE WANTED. WHEN ALKAIOS

(THE POET WHO OPPOSED HIS RULE) WAS TAKEN TO HIM CAPTIVE, PITTAKOS LET HIM GO SAYING "PARDON IS BETTER THAN PUNISHMENT"...

PITTAKOS IMPOSED LAWS, ONE PROVIDING THAT ANY OFFENDER FOUND TO BE INTOXICATED, WOULD HAVE HIS PENALTY DOUBLED. THAT WAS TO DISCOURAGE DRUNKENNESS, ESPECIALLY IN VIEW OF THE FACT THAT THERE WAS PLENTY OF WINE ON THE ISLAND. HE WAS KNOWN FOR SAYING "IT IS DIFFICULT TO BE CONSISTENTLY GOOD" AND "THE OFFICE SHOWS THE MAN." TO SOMEONE WHO CLAIMED TO BE LOOKING FOR A PERFECT PERSON, PITTAKOS COMMENTED "IF YOU SEARCH TOO CAREFULLY YOU WILL NEVER FIND ONE." HE ADVISED "PRUDENT PEOPLE MUST TRY TO PREVENT DIFFICULTIES BEFORE THEY ARISE" . . . "DO NOT ANNOUNCE YOUR PLANS BECAUSE IF YOU FAIL YOU WILL BE RIDICULED" . . . "SAY NOTHING BAD ABOUT A FRIEND AND NOT EVEN ABOUT AN ENEMY." HE ALSO WROTE ABOUT SIX HUNDRED POETIC ELEGIES AND A COMPILATION OF LAWS IN PROSE FOR THE CITIZENS. THE PEAK OF HIS ACTIVITY (GREEK ACME) WAS ABOUT THE 42ND OLYMPIAD (612-608 B.C.) AND HE DIED IN THE THIRD YEAR OF THE 52ND OLYMPIAD (569 B.C.), HAVING LIVED OVER SEVENTY YEARS . . . HIS WIFE WAS OF A NOBLER BIRTH . . . AND SHE TREATED HIM WITH EXTREME CONTEMPT. ALKAIOS CALLED HIM NAMES BECAUSE OF HIS (PRESUMED) FLAT FEET, COARSE HANDS, POT BELLY, FUNNY GAIT AND FOR BEING UNKEMPT AND DIRTY.

THIS IS A SHORT LETTER OF PITTAKOS TO KROISOS (CROESUS, KING OF LYDIA):

"YOU INVITE ME TO COME TO LYDIA SO THAT I MAY ADMIRE YOUR PROSPERITY (3). BUT EVEN WITHOUT SEEING IT I AM CONVINCED THAT YOU . . . HAVE MORE GOLD AND RICHES THAN ANY ROYALTY. THIS WILL NOT BE A REASON FOR ME TO COME TO SARDIS (THE CAPITAL OF LYDIA). I HAVE NO NEED FOR GOLD AND I HAVE ENOUGH PROPERTY FOR MYSELF AND EVEN FOR MY COMPANIONS. HOWEVER I MAY COME JUST TO BE YOUR HOST AND TO HAVE A NICE CONVERSATION WITH YOU."

Hicks, R.D., Vol. I, pp. 74-84.

Aristotle (4), in his book on Politics [*Politika*], described the rule of Pittakos more precisely.

BOOK III, IX 5-6.

1285A. THERE WAS ANOTHER KIND OF MONARCHY AMONG THE ANCIENT HELLENES . . . THIS WAS, TO STATE IT SIMPLY, AN ELECTIVE DICTATORSHIP [TYRANNY] WHICH WAS NOT HEREDITARY. SOME PEOPLE HAVE RULED THIS WAY FOR LIFE AND OTHERS UNTIL A DEFINED TIME AND EVENT, AS WAS THE CASE WITH PITTAKOS, WHOM THE CITIZENS OF MYTILENE ELECTED TO STAND UP TO THE EXILES LED BY (THE

BROTHERS) ANTIMENIDES AND ALKAIOS. IN FACT, ALKAIOS MENTIONS IN ONE OF HIS DRINKING SONGS THAT PITTAKOS WAS ELECTED TYRANT AND BLAMES THE MYTILENEANS BECAUSE "THEY SET UP THE LOW-BORN PITTAKOS AS THE GOVERNOR OF THE APATHETIC AND MINDLESS CITY AND ALL OF THEM APPLAUDED HIM STRONGLY."

Rackham, H., 1977, p. 250

And about the laws, which have been compared to those of the Athenian Solon (also one of the Seven Sages), Aristotle reported:

POLITICS, BOOK II, IX-9

1274B. PITTAKOS ALSO CREATED LAWS, THOUGH NOT A CONSTITUTION FOR THE CITY. CHARACTERISTIC WAS AN UNUSUAL LAW OF HIS, WHICH REQUIRED A GREATER PENALTY FOR AN OFFENSE WHEN THE CULPRIT WAS DRUNK THAN WHEN SOBER; WITH THAT LAW PITTAKOS WAS DISREGARDING THE EXCUSE THAT AN INTOXICATED PERSON IS MORE PRONE TO OFFEND AND WAS INSTEAD AIMING AT PROTECTING THE INTERESTS OF THE CITY.

Rackham, H., 1977, p. 170.

Both before and after the stable ten-year rule of Pittakos, there were revolutions and coups in the city-states of Lesbos, as also elsewhere in Greece (the "cradle" of dictatorship as well as of democracy). Book V of Aristotle's *Politics* (Rackham, 1932-1977, pp. 370–483) is about "Revolution: its causes and prevention" and it includes examples from Lesbos.

POLITICS
BY ARISTOTLE [Aristoteles], 384–322 b.c.

BOOK V, I-VIII

1301A. WE MUST NOW CONSIDER HOW MANY AND WHICH ARE THE CAUSES THAT UPSET (ALTER) THE CONSTITUTIONS, WHAT BRINGS ABOUT THE DESTRUCTION OF EACH CONSTITUTION [polity] AND SPECIFICALLY FROM WHAT FORMS TO WHAT OTHER FORMS THEY DO CHANGE. ALSO FROM THE ABOVE (WE MUST INQUIRE) WHETHER THERE ARE WAYS TO SAFEGUARD ANY CONSTITUTION IN GENERAL AND EACH ONE IN PARTICULAR . . . **26.** TO BEGIN WITH, WE MUST ASSUME THAT MANY CONSTITUTIONS HAVE BEEN ESTABLISHED WHEN EVERYONE AGREED ON WHAT IS RIGHT [dikaion = just] AND FAIR [analog = proportionally equal], BUT THEN FAILED TO ACHIEVE THIS. DEMOCRACY DEVELOPED ON THE PREMISE THAT IF PEOPLE ARE EQUAL IN SOME RESPECTS, THEY ARE EQUAL IN EVERYTHING . . .

1311A, 23 . . . WHAT STARTS A REVOLUTIONARY MOVE APPEARS TO BE THE SAME IN THE CASE OF CONSTITUTIONAL AND

MONARCHICAL RULES. PEOPLE RISE AND ATTACK THEM BECAUSE OF INJUSTICES, FEAR AND HUMILIATIONS, THE WORST AMONG UNJUST TREATMENTS BEING PERSONAL INSULTS [HYBRIS] AND SOMETIMES SEIZURE OF PRIVATE PROPERTY.

1311B, 23-32. MANY PEOPLE, INFURIATED BY THE INDIGNITY OF CORPORAL PUNISHMENT, HAVE AVENGED THEMSELVES FOR THE INSULT BY DESTROYING OR TRYING TO DESTROY THE RULERS. FOR EXAMPLE, WHEN IN MYTILENE, THE (RULING NOBLES) PENTHILIDS (CHAPTER I-A) WENT AROUND BEATING PEOPLE WITH CLUBS, MEGACLES WITH HIS FRIENDS ATTACKED THEM AND GOT RID OF THEM. LATER ON, SMERDIS KILLED PENTHILOS, AFTER HE HAD BEEN WOUNDED AND DRAGGED OUT FROM HIS WIFE'S PRESENCE.

Rackham, H., 1977, pp. 370 and 440-446.

Reference to the above is also made by Page (pp. 150–152) concerning the life of Alkaios (see Chapter II-B)

In his thirty-seven volume *History* (5), Diodoros (Oldfather, 1968) added his comments.

THE LIBRARY OF HISTORY
BY DIODOROS THE SICILIAN, FIRST CENTURY B.C.

BOOK IX

11.1-2 PITTAKOS OF MYTILENE WAS NOT ONLY ADMIRABLE FOR HIS WISDOM BUT ALSO A CITIZEN SUCH AS THE ISLAND NEVER HAD AND, I THINK, MAY NEVER PRODUCE AGAIN—(AT LEAST) NOT UNTIL IT ALSO PRODUCES MORE ABUNDANT AND EVEN MORE DELICIOUS WINE. HE WAS AN EXCELLENT LAW-GIVER, DEALT PERSONALLY AND KINDLY WITH EACH CITIZEN AND, FURTHERMORE, HE FREED HIS HOMELAND FROM THE THREE GREATEST EVILS, TYRANNY, REBELLION AND WAR.

PITTAKOS WAS PROFOUNDLY STABLE, CALM AND GENTLE, OFTEN BEING PRONE TO BELITTLE HIMSELF. HE WAS REGARDED BY ALL, UNANIMOUSLY, AS A PERFECT MAN WITH RESPECT TO EVERY VIRTUE.

Oldfather, C.H., Vol. IV, pp. 16-18.

Still later, at the beginning of the second century A.D. the historian and Delphic priest Plutarch referred to Pittakos of Lesbos in his writings.

DINNER OF THE SEVEN SAGES
BY PLUTARCH [PLUTARKHOS], 50 TO AFTER 120 A.D.

147.B. . . . THEN, . . . SAID NEILOXENOS . . . YOU HAVE BEEN ACCUSED OF BEING A KING-HATER AND SOME INSULTING COMMENTS OF YOURS HAVE BEEN MENTIONED . . . WHEN YOU WERE ASKED WHAT IS THE MOST UNUSUAL THING YOU EVER SAW, YOU REPLIED "A DICTATOR WHO LIVED TO BE OLD."

> BUT, REPLIED THALES, THIS WAS A JOKING STATEMENT BY PITTAKOS, REFERRING TO MYRSILOS. PERSONALLY, I WOULD BE SURPRISED IF I SAW EVEN A GOVERNOR, NOT A TYRANT, BEING OLD . . . THIS IS WHY I CONSIDER SOLON MOST WISE FOR NOT CONSENTING TO BECOME A DICTATOR. ALSO IF PITTAKOS, RIGHT HERE, DID NOT HAVE AN OPPORTUNITY TO GOVERN ALONE, HE WOULD NOT HAVE SAID "IT IS HARD TO BE CONTINUOUSLY GOOD AND PERFECT [ESTHLOS]."
> Babbitt, F.C., Vol. II, 1928/56, pp. 352-354.

Pherekydes and Pythagoras—Gods vs. Mathematics

Among the students of Pittakos on Lesbos was Pherekydes, a young man from the island of Syros (Kirk and Raven, 1966, pp. 48–72) whom Diogenes Laertios included in his book.

> **LIVES AND OPINIONS OF EMINENT PHILOSOPHERS**
> **BOOK I, CHAPTER 11: PHEREKYDES**
> **118-119.** PHEREKYDES . . . A NATIVE OF SYROS, ATTENDED THE LECTURES OF PITTAKOS . . . HE WAS THE FIRST TO WRITE ABOUT NATURE AND ABOUT THE GODS . . . THE BOOK THAT PHEREKYDES WROTE IS PRESERVED AND BEGINS THIS WAY, "ZEUS AND CHRONOS [KHRONOS, TIME] AND KHTHONIE (EARTH) HAVE ALWAYS EXISTED . . ."
> Hicks, R.D., Vol. I, pp. 120-124.

The Roman Cicero remarked that Pherekydes was the first to call the human soul eternal. The neo-platonist philosopher, Proclos, provided a very poetic image on the creation of the world according to Pherekydes (Kirk & Raven, 1966, p. 61):

> PHEREKYDES STATED THAT WHEN ZEUS WAS ABOUT TO CREATE THE WORLD ["DEMIURGEIN"] HE TRANSFORMED HIMSELF INTO EROS (LOVE).

Pherekydes traveled much through the Greek islands but it was his pupil, the famous Pythagoras, who covered most of the then-known world, including Egypt and Assyria (Kirk & Raven, 1966, pp. 217–231). The main relationship of Pythagoras to Lesbos is that, according to Diogenes Laertios (Hicks, 1965), he studied there.

> **LIVES AND OPINIONS OF EMINENT PHILOSOPHERS**
> **BOOK VIII, CHAPTER 1: PYTHAGORAS**
> **1-2.** HE CAME TO LESBOS WITH AN INTRODUCTION TO PHEREKYDES BY HIS UNCLE . . . HE WAS A STUDENT OF PHEREKYDES

> AND AFTER HIS TEACHER DIED PYTHAGORAS WENT BACK TO SAMOS (6) . . .
>
> Hicks, R.D., Vol. II, pp. 320-322.

As is well known, Pythagoras later moved to southern Italy where he established himself as a leader of a school (almost a cult), ruled the city of Croton and also became famous for his mathematical works, harmonic analysis of music and metaphysical philosophy in general (Kirk & Raven, 1966). According to Diogenes Laertios, Pythagoras was the first "philosopher" (lover of wisdom).

> **LIVES AND OPINIONS OF EMINENT PHILOSOPHERS**
> BY DIOGENES LAERTIOS, THIRD CENTURY A.D.
>
> **PREFACE**
>
> **12.** PYTHAGORAS WAS THE FIRST TO FIND A NAME FOR PHILOSOPHY AND TO CALL HIMSELF A PHILOSOPHER . . . BECAUSE (HE SAID) NO HUMAN BEING, ONLY A GOD, CAN BE ABSOLUTELY WISE [SOPHOS] . . . A PHILOSOPHER IS SIMPLY ONE WHO LOVES AND EMBRACES WISDOM (REF. TABLE E).
>
> **14.** THE TEACHER OF PYTHAGORAS WAS PHEREKYDES . . . AND BECAUSE HE PRACTICED PHILOSOPHY MOSTLY IN ITALY PYTHAGORAS IS CONSIDERED AS THE FOUNDER OF THE ITALIAN SCHOOL..
>
> Hicks, R.D., Vol. I, pp. 12–14.

Merchants, mercenaries and a girl's erotic art

The seed [Greek *sperma*] and spark of rational thinking, natural science and philosophy, from the Eastern Aegean coast, Ionia and Lesbos, moved on west to Athens and beyond, to Sicily and southern Italy (Kirk & Raven, 1966). At the same time, people from Lesbos, especially members of the old aristocracy, displaced or dispossessed by the upstart dictators including Pittakos, went sailing toward the eastern Mediterranean shores, to Egypt, Phoenicia and Babylonia (Durant, 1939). Some of them were merchants or traders and others became hired mercenaries in foreign armies. A brother of the Lesbian poet Alkaios fought as a paid soldier in the Babylonian army (Campbell 1982, Introduction, p. xiv). Another traveler was the brother of the poetess Sappho, Charaxos [*Haraxos*], who found himself in Egypt, where the Greeks were developing an active trading post in the city of Naucratis. There, profits, pleasures and prostitution proliferated under the benevolent rule of the Egyptian pharaoh, Amasis (Campbell 1982, Introduction, p. xi).

SAGES, SOLDIERS, SLAVES AND SCHOLARS

HISTORY
BY HERODOTOS, 484-420 (?) B.C.
BOOK II
177. UNDER KING AMASIS, EGYPT PROSPERED GREATLY . . . ACCORDING TO A NEW LAW PASSED BY AMASIS, EVERYONE WAS REQUIRED TO DECLARE HIS INCOME ANNUALLY . . . SOLON (THE ATHENIAN LAW-MAKER) INTRODUCED THE SAME LAW INTO ATHENS AND I HOPE IT WILL REMAIN IN FORCE FOR A LONG TIME (7).

178. AMASIS WAS VERY FOND OF THE GREEKS AND HE PROVED IT IN MANY WAYS, INCLUDING HIS GRANT OF A CITY, NAUCRATIS, FOR THOSE WHO CAME TO EGYPT FROM GREECE . . . HE GAVE LAND . . . FOR SANCTUARIES, THE BIGGEST OF WHICH WAS HELLENION. MANY CITIES WORKED TOGETHER TO BUILD IT, INCLUDING IONIANS, DORIANS AND AMONG THE AEOLIANS ONLY THE CITY OF MYTILENE.

Godley, A.D., Vol. I, pp. 490–492.

II.134. A GREEK COURTESAN, RHODOPIS, WAS EXTREMELY POPULAR DURING THE REIGN OF KING AMASIS . . . SHE CAME FROM THRACE AND WAS A SLAVE OF IADMON OF SAMOS. A FELLOW SLAVE OF HERS ALSO BELONGING TO IADMON WAS AESOP [AISOPOS], THE STORYTELLER, WELL-KNOWN FOR HIS FABLES.

II.135. AFTER RHODOPIS CAME TO EGYPT . . . SHE GOT HER FREEDOM TO PURSUE HER OWN BUSINESS, WHEN A MAN FROM MYTILENE, HARAXOS, BROTHER OF THE POETESS SAPPHO, PAID THE VERY LARGE PRICE REQUIRED TO FREE HER. RHODOPIS AS A FREE WOMAN STAYED IN EGYPT. HER EROTIC TALENTS WERE SO SUPERIOR THAT SHE BECAME VERY RICH . . . ANXIOUS TO HAVE A PERMANENT MEMORIAL OF HERSELF IN GREECE . . . SHE SPENT ONE-TENTH OF HER FORTUNE TO SET UP IRON SPITS IN DELPHI, NEAR THE ALTAR FROM HIOS, MANY OF WHICH WERE BIG ENOUGH TO ROAST A WHOLE OX . . . IN SOME WAY THE COURTESANS IN NAUCRATIS WERE PARTICULARLY SKILLFUL IN SEXUALITY. THIS WOMAN, RHODOPIS, FOR INSTANCE, BECAME SO FAMOUS THAT EVERYONE IN GREECE KNEW HER NAME. AS FAR AS HARAXOS IS CONCERNED, AFTER HE HAD PAID TO FREE RHODOPIS, HE WENT BACK HOME TO MYTILENE, WHERE HE WAS BITTERLY ATTACKED FOR HIS ACTION BY SAPPHO (HIS SISTER) IN ONE OF HER POEMS (CHAPTER II-B).

Godley, A.D. Vol. I, pp. 436–8.

B. HELLENIC HOLOCAUST—SLAUGHTER, SLAVERY AND SURVIVAL

Civil strife and the Persian Wars

The ten-year rule of Pittakos turned out to be only a short peaceful interlude for Lesbos. A time of troubles again followed, both due to the rivalry among the Greek cities and islands and to the expansion of the Persian kingdom which gradually reached the coast of nearby Ionia (Durant, 1939). Mytilene renewed the war against Athens and was defeated. As a result, the territories on the mainland which Pittakos had effectively defended, were lost. Afterwards, when the tyrant of Samos, Polykrates—the one who forced the philosopher Pythagoras to leave that island and to move to Italy—in his piratical wars against the mainland attacked the Ionian city of Miletos, Mytilene became involved. Herodotos in his "History" (Grene, 1987) wrote about the events.

HISTORY
BY HERODOTOS, 484-420 (?) B.C.

III-39 ... POLYCRATES ... KILLED ONE OF HIS BROTHERS, BANISHED THE YOUNGER ONE AND TOOK CONTROL OF ALL SAMOS ... AFTERWARDS ... HE ATTACKED AND PLUNDERED EVERY STATE ... SAYING THAT HE COULD MAKE MORE PEOPLE GRATEFUL BY RETURNING ... WHAT HE HAD SEIZED, THAN BY NOT TAKING ANYTHING IN THE FIRST PLACE ... ALSO IN A SEA BATTLE HE OVERPOWERED AND CAPTURED THE LESBIANS WHO HAD COME TO HELP THE MILESIANS. THESE PRISONERS, IN CHAINS, WERE FORCED TO DIG THE LONG TRENCH AROUND THE FORTIFICATIONS OF SAMOS.

Godley, A.D. Vol. II, p. 52.

Greeks commonly hired themselves out as mercenaries to the eastern barbarians (8). Someone from Mytilene, named Coes, helped the Persian king Darius (about 513–512 B.C.) in his expedition against the Northern Scythians.

HISTORY
BY HERODOTOS, 484-420 (?) B.C.

IV. 97-98 COES, WHO WAS THE LEADER OF THE MEN FROM MYTILENE, SAID TO DARIUS (AFTER FIRST CHECKING WHETHER THE KING WOULD ALLOW SOMEONE TO PRESENT HIS VIEWS) "MY LORD, YOU OUGHT TO LET THIS BRIDGE STAND HERE ... IF WE DEFEAT THE SCYTHIANS THIS WILL BE OUR WAY BACK HOME ... IF WE CANNOT FIND THE ENEMY AND WANDER ABOUT, WE MAY STILL BE ABLE TO RETURN TO SAFETY ...." DARIUS WAS VERY GLAD TO HAVE THIS ADVICE AND ANSWERED: "MY FRIEND FROM LESBOS, WHEN I RETURN SAFELY TO MY HOME YOU MUST COME AND PRESENT YOURSELF TO ME SO THAT I CAN REWARD YOU WELL" ... WHEN DARIUS RETURNED TO SARDIS, HE REMEMBERED COES OF MYTILENE ... WHO, THOUGH ONLY AN ORDINARY CITIZEN, ASKED TO BE APPOINTED RULER OF MYTILENE.

Godley, A.D., Vol. II, p. 298.

V. 36-38 ARISTAGORAS (TYRANT OF MILETOS) CONTRIVED TO HAVE . . . COES, TO WHOM DARIUS HAD GIVEN MYTILENE, AND . . . MANY MORE LEADERS ARRESTED . . . HE INTRODUCED A CONSTITUTION OF EQUALITY . . . SO PEOPLE MIGHT JOIN IN THE REVOLT . . .
WHEN THE PEOPLE OF MYTILENE GOT HOLD OF COES, THEY TOOK HIM OUT AND STONED HIM TO DEATH.

Godley, A.D. Vol. II, P. 40–42.

That happened about 500-499 B.C. at the outset of the widespread and ultimately unsuccessful uprising of the Ionian cities against the Persians, who had earlier managed to divide and to conquer them (9).

Lesbos between Athens and Sparta

About ten years later, the Persians organized two major campaigns to complete their domination of the Greeks. The failure of these determined the future course of history and of civilization. The first time the Greeks were successful in stopping the invasion was in the battle of Marathon, famous ever since for the long distance runner, who covered the 41+ kilometers (26 miles) non-stop to announce the victory to the people in Athens.

Ten years after that defeat, the Persians made a second and greater effort to conquer Greece crossing with their armies over to Europe and sending their fleet across the Aegean to the Greek mainland. Many islands and the Eastern Greek provinces already were under Persian rule and so they were obliged to send ships and men to support the Persian expedition against their own countrymen.

THE LIBRARY OF HISTORY
BY DIODOROS THE SICILIAN, FIRST CENTURY B.C.
BOOK XI
3.7 . . . THE NUMBER OF HIS (THE PERSIAN KING'S) LAND FORCES WAS OVER 800,000 AND THE TOTAL OF HIS SHIPS MORE THAN 1,200, OF WHICH 320 HAD GREEKS MAKING UP THE CREWS WHILE THE KING SUPPLIED THE VESSELS. . . . AMONG THE GREEKS . . . THE AEOLIANS, INCLUDING THE LESBIANS SENT FORTY SHIPS . . .

Greer, R.M., Vol. IX, pp. 128–30.

The Persian fleet, with its Greek island contingent then sailed on to Artemision, on the north of the island of Euboea, where the critical sea battle with the Greeks defending their country was to take place in 480 B.C. The Persians managed to capture and destroy Athens but then were overwhelmingly defeated by the allied Greeks, under Athenian leadership, in a crucial sea battle fought in the straits of Salamis. That was the island where the Athenian law-giver, poet and sage (one of the "seven sages") Solon, was born almost one-hundred years earlier. Afterwards the independent Greek city-states formed a sort of loose alliance, the Delian League, headquartered on the island of Delos (10). Lesbos had taken the initiative in establishing the league but later the city of Mytilene twice made attempts to secede (Oxf. Class. Dict. p. 319). Bitter antagonism soon developed primarily between the leading Hellenic city-states, Athens and Sparta. After intermittent hostilities and attempts to conclude workable peace treaties, the twenty-seven-year-long "Peloponnesian" war (so named by the Athenians because the town of Sparta and the district of Lacedaemon are in Peloponnesos) broke out. The Athenians eventually lost, due to repeated mistakes and misfortunes. One major problem was created by the determination of Athens, a democracy, to treat her allies in very authoritarian and often oppressive ways. This caused deep resentment and several revolts. In the fourth year of the war between Athens and Sparta, the city of Mytilene on Lesbos changed sides, rejected Athenian leadership and welcomed a Spartan military commander. The revolt had been contemplated for a long time because the Lesbians were afraid that if they waited, they would eventually suffer the same fate as other allies, who were totally subjugated by Athens. In conjunction with the break of the alliance, plans were made for a confederation of the city-states of Lesbos with the exception of Methymna, always an antagonist of Mytilene (Chapter IV-B), which remained loyal to Athens.

At the last moment, when the Athenians discovered the plans and attacked, Mytilene was found unprepared. Its ports were blockaded and the city besieged by an Athenian army under general Pakhes. This unexpected war effort against a former ally—while the real enemy, Sparta, was devastating the lands of Attica, closer to home—strained the finances of Athens to the limit and a new property tax had to be imposed on the citizens. This naturally increased very much their resentment and their hatred of Mytilene.

To give hope to the encircled city, Sparta sent to Mytilene a representative, Salaithos, who managed to pass unnoticed through the Athenian lines. However no real military assistance was provided. It was then decided to make a sortie and arms were given to the people for this purpose. But the armed population rebelled against their rulers—who had instigated the uprising against Athens—and this forced a capitulation, in the expectation of leniency on the part of the victorious Athenian general. The impartial, critically analytical historian of the events, the

SAGES, SOLDIERS, SLAVES AND SCHOLARS

Thycydides (Holkhm Hall), Richter 1965/84.

Athenian Thucydides, wrote in detail about the incident, which concluded with a race of ships as exciting as any modern suspense story. For the benefit of anyone wishing to "train in democracy", "the debate that provides a vivid image of Athenian, or any other advanced democracy at work and which resulted in saving thousands of lives on Lesbos" is quoted here, in translation from the original Attic Greek (C.F. Smith, 1920/75).

HISTORY OF THE PELOPONNESIAN WAR
BY THUCYDIDES, ABOUT 460-400 B.C.

BOOK III

XXVIII. THOSE IN CHARGE REALIZED THAT THEY COULD NOT PREVENT THE PEOPLE FROM COMING TO TERMS WITH THE ATHENIANS AND FROM SURRENDERING THE CITY. TO AVOID BEING BYPASSED, THEY JOINED IN THE AGREEMENT . . . WHICH PROVIDED THAT ATHENS WOULD HAVE THE POWER TO DECIDE THE FATE OF MYTILENE, THAT ITS ARMY WOULD BE ADMITTED INTO THE CITY BUT ALSO THAT THE MYTILENEANS WOULD SEND A DELEGATION TO ATHENS TO NEGOTIATE THEIR FUTURE. IN THE MEANTIME THE ATHENIAN GENERAL, PAKHES, WAS NOT TO SEIZE, IMPRISON OR EXECUTE ANYONE FROM MYTILENE.

XXXV-L. COMING BACK TO MYTILENE PAKHES SUBDUED THE CITIES OF PYRRHA AND ERESOS. HE ALSO FOUND AND CAPTURED THE AGENT OF LACEDAEMON, SALAITHOS HIMSELF, HIDING IN MYTILENE AND SENT HIM TO ATHENS ALONG WITH THOSE CITIZENS OF THE CITY AND OTHERS WHO HAD BEEN HELD UNDER GUARD BECAUSE OF THEIR SUSPECTED ROLE IN THE REVOLT.

WHEN THESE MEN ARRIVED IN ATHENS, SALAITHOS WAS PUT TO DEATH RIGHT AWAY . . . THE FATE OF THE OTHERS WAS DEBATED IN THE ASSEMBLY AND IN THE EXCITEMENT OF THE MOMENT IT WAS DECIDED TO EXECUTE NOT ONLY THOSE DEPORTED TO ATHENS BUT ALL MYTILENEAN MALES OF MILITARY AGE AND TO SELL THE WOMEN AND CHILDREN TO SLAVERY. THE ATHENIANS WERE PARTICULARLY ANGRY WITH THE PEOPLE OF MYTILENE BECAUSE THEY HAD

REVOLTED DESPITE THE FACT THEY HAD NEVER BEEN DEPRIVED OF THEIR LIBERTY AS WAS THE CASE WITH OTHER ALLIES OF ATHENS; AND THE VINDICTIVENESS OF THE ATHENIANS WAS MADE WORSE WHEN THEY WERE LED TO BELIEVE THAT THE REVOLT DID NOT OCCUR ON THE SPUR OF THE MOMENT BUT HAD BEEN CONTEMPLATED FOR SOME TIME. ACCORDINGLY THEY SENT A WARSHIP TO PAKHES TO INFORM HIM OF THE VOTE AND TO ORDER HIM TO PUT IT PROMPTLY INTO EFFECT. THE NEXT DAY HOWEVER, THERE WAS A REVERSE REACTION, AS THE VOTERS REALIZED THE ENORMOUS ATROCITY OF THIS DECISION TO EXTERMINATE AN ENTIRE COMMUNITY . . . IT WAS EVIDENT THAT THE MAJORITY OF THE PEOPLE WANTED TO HAVE AN OPPORTUNITY FOR MORE DISCUSSION. THE ASSEMBLY MET AGAIN AND A DEBATE ENSUED WHICH STARTED WITH A SPEECH BY CLEON, WHO THE DAY BEFORE HAD CARRIED THE VOTE FOR THE DEATH PENALTY AND WHO WAS ONE OF THE MOST VIOLENT AND ALSO MOST INFLUENTIAL CITIZENS. HE CAME FORWARD AND SPOKE AS FOLLOWS:

XXXVII (1-5) "ALREADY MANY TIMES BEFORE I HAVE REALIZED THAT A DEMOCRATIC STATE CANNOT POSSIBLY RULE OTHERS (OUTSIDE OF IT), BUT MORE THAN EVER I DO SO NOW, SEEING YOUR CHANGE OF MIND ABOUT MYTILENE. THE LACK OF FEAR AND MUTUAL INTRIGUE IN YOUR DAILY LIVES, MAKES YOU BEHAVE THE SAME WAY TOWARD YOUR ALLIES. WHETHER YOU BELIEVE IN THEIR WORDS OR YOU GIVE IN TO PITY, YOU MAKE A MISTAKE AND YOU FORGET THAT YOUR LEADERSHIP IS LIKE A DICTATORSHIP, AGAINST THE WILL OF INTRIGUING SUBJECTS, WHO DO NOT OBEY YOU BECAUSE OF ANY FAVOR YOU DID THEM, OR OUT OF GOOD WILL, BUT BECAUSE OF YOUR STRENGTH. IT WILL BE TERRIBLE TO TAKE NO ACTION ABOUT WHAT WE BELIEVE IS RIGHT AND WHAT CERTAINLY YOU VOTED UPON . . . REMEMBER THAT MOST ORDINARY PEOPLE ARE BETTER THAN THE SMARTEST ONES FOR THEIR STATES. THE LATTER WANT TO APPEAR WISER THAN THE LAWS AND TO DOMINATE PUBLIC DEBATE . . . WHILE THOSE WHO DO NOT TRUST THEIR OWN ABILITY TO UNDERSTAND EVERYTHING, ACCEPT THE FACT THAT THEY KNOW LESS THAN THE LAW SYSTEM AND . . . BEING IMPARTIAL JUDGES RATHER THAN CONTESTANTS, THEY DO MOST THINGS RIGHT . . . SO IN THIS CASE ALSO, WE MUST NOT BE CARRIED AWAY BY RHETORIC OR BY A CONTEST OF WITS AND TRY TO ADVISE YOU AGAINST YOUR OWN POPULAR CONVICTIONS.

XXXVIII (1) MY PERSONAL OPINIONS HAVE NOT CHANGED AND I AM AMAZED THAT SOME PEOPLE HAVE PROPOSED TO DEBATE AGAIN THE CASE AGAINST THE MYTILENEANS. THIS WILL CAUSE A DELAY WHICH FAVORS THE CULPRITS (BECAUSE THE ANGER OF THE VICTIMS SUBSIDES WITH TIME, WHEREAS AN IMMEDIATE PUNISHMENT FOR THE INSULT DOES MATCH IT MORE CLOSELY) . . .

XXXIX (1-5). I WILL TRY TO TURN YOU AWAY FROM THE PLEASURABLE DISTRACTIONS OF ORATORY AND TO PROVE TO YOU

THAT MYTILENE HAS DONE YOU MORE HARM THAN ANY OTHER CITY. WE MAY FORGIVE THOSE WHO REBEL BECAUSE OF AN UNBEARABLE RULE, OR BECAUSE OUR ENEMIES FORCE THEM TO DO IT, BUT WHEN PEOPLE IN A WELL-FORTIFIED ISLAND . . . WHO HAVE LIVED IN FULL AUTONOMY AND HAVE BEEN HIGHLY RESPECTED BY US ACT THAT WAY, WHAT IS THIS BUT PREMEDITATED REVOLUTION RATHER THAN A MERE WITHDRAWAL FROM OUR ALLIANCE? THEY PLACED THEMSELVES ON THE SIDE OF OUR WORST ENEMIES IN ORDER TO DESTROY US. NEITHER THE DISASTERS OF OTHERS WHO REBELLED AGAINST US NOR THEIR PRESENT PROSPERITY COULD STOP THEM FROM GETTING INTO THIS AWFUL SITUATION. IT IS A FACT THAT STATES WHICH HAVE PROSPERED UNEXPECTEDLY AND WITH LITTLE EFFORT ARE COMMONLY MORE PRONE TO TURN TO OFFENSE. WE SHOULD HAVE TREATED THE MYTILENEANS FROM THE BEGINNING NOT DIFFERENTLY THAN OTHERS AND THEN THEY WOULD HAVE RESPECTED US RATHER THAN INSULT US. PEOPLE NATURALLY DISRESPECT THOSE WHO CATER TO THEM AND ADMIRE THOSE WHO ARE FIRM AND UNYIELDING.

NOW THEREFORE WE MUST PUNISH THEM AS BEFITS THEIR CRIME, WITHOUT PLACING THE BLAME ON THE FEW AND ABSOLVING THE REST. THEY ALL ATTACKED YOU . . . THINK ABOUT OUR ALLIES . . . WHO MIGHT REVOLT WITH THE SLIGHTEST PRETEXT IF THEY SEE A CHANCE TO SECURE THEIR INDEPENDENCE AND THEY KNOW THAT IF THEY FAIL THEY WILL SUFFER NOTHING IRREPARABLE.

XL (1-2) SO WE MUST OFFER THEM NO HOPE, RESPONDING TO THEIR WORDS OR TO PAYMENT OF MONEY, THAT THEY WILL BE FORGIVEN WITH THE EXCUSE THAT WHAT THEY DID WAS ONLY A HUMAN ERROR. THEY DID NOT INJURE US UNINTENTIONALLY BUT THEY PLOTTED DELIBERATELY AGAINST US. SO LET THE SPEAKERS WHO WANT TO DELIGHT YOU WITH THEIR RHETORIC EXERCISE THEIR SKILL ON SOME OTHER LESS SERIOUS OCCASION OR CONFLICT . . .

XL (4) . . . IF YOU FOLLOW MY ADVICE YOU WILL DO WHAT IS JUST TO THE MYTILENEANS AND IS ALSO TO YOUR OWN ADVANTAGE. IF YOU DECIDE OTHERWISE, YOU WILL NOT WIN THEIR GRATITUDE BUT YOU WILL BRING JUDGMENT UPON YOURSELVES.

XL (7-8) SO DO NOT BECOME TRAITORS TO YOUR OWN CAUSE BUT COME CLOSE TO HOW YOU FELT WHEN YOU SUFFERED THE ATTACK AND HOW YOU WANTED ABOVE ALL TO DESTROY THEM. PAY THEM BACK WITHOUT SOFTNESS . . . AND WITHOUT FORGETTING THE SERIOUS DANGER RECENTLY HANGING OVER YOU. PUNISH THEM AS THEY DESERVE AND MAKE IT CLEAR TO YOUR OTHER ALLIES THAT FOR ANY UPRISING THE PENALTY IS DEATH. IF THEY ALL RECOGNIZE THIS YOU WILL BE LESS PRONE TO DISREGARD YOUR ENEMIES BY FIGHTING AGAINST YOUR OWN ALLIES."

XLI. THIS IS HOW CLEON SPOKE. AFTER HIM DIODOTOS, THE MAN WHO HAD SPOKEN TO THE PREVIOUS ASSEMBLY

AGAINST PUTTING THE MYTILENEANS TO DEATH, STEPPED FORWARD AND SPOKE THIS WAY.

XLII. (1,2) "I CANNOT ARGUE AGAINST THOSE WHO HAVE PROPOSED ANOTHER DISCUSSION ABOUT MYTILENE AND I CANNOT PRAISE THOSE WHO OBJECT TO REPEATED CONSIDERATION OF THE MOST IMPORTANT ITEMS. HASTE AND ANGER, IN MY OPINION, ARE MOST CONTRARY TO GOOD JUDGMENT, THE FIRST BEING ASSOCIATED WITH THOUGHTLESSNESS AND THE SECOND WITH AN UNCONTROLLABLE AND QUICK RESOLVE [GNOME] . . .

XLIII. (2-5) . . . IT IS NOW ESTABLISHED THAT GOOD COUNSEL EXPRESSED DIRECTLY IS NO LESS SUSPECT THAN A BAD ONE. SO A SPEAKER WHO WANTS TO PERSUADE THE PEOPLE DECEITFULLY ABOUT THE MOST TERRIBLE MEASURES, AND ONE WHO OFFERS THE BETTER ADVICE MUST BOTH LIE IN ORDER TO BE BELIEVED. OUR CITY IS THE ONLY ONE WHERE IT IS IMPOSSIBLE TO BE OF GOOD SERVICE OPENLY AND WITHOUT DECEIT. IF SOMEONE OFFERS YOU SOMETHING GOOD IN THE OPEN HE IS STILL SUSPECTED OF TRYING SECRETLY TO GET SOMETHING FOR HIMSELF. NEVERTHELESS, WHEN IT COMES TO SUCH IMPORTANT MATTERS AS THIS, WE WHO ADVISE YOU MUST LOOK FURTHER AHEAD THAN YOU WHO ONLY BRIEFLY CONSIDER THE QUESTION. WE ARE THE ONES WHO ARE RESPONSIBLE FOR OUR PROPOSALS WHILE YOU ARE THE LISTENERS, WITHOUT DIRECT RESPONSIBILITY. IF INDEED, BOTH THE PERSON SOLICITING YOUR FAVORABLE VOTE AND YOU WHO FOLLOW THIS RECOMMENDATION AND VOTE FOR IT, WERE SUBJECT TO THE SAME PENALTY FOR ANY WRONG ACTION, YOU WOULD CERTAINLY BE EXERCISING YOUR JUDGEMENT WITH MORE CARE. AS IT IS, WHEN YOU DETECT AN ERRONEOUS DECISION, YOU GIVE IN TO YOUR ANGER AND PUNISH THE PERSON WHOSE ADVICE YOU FOLLOWED BUT DO NOT PENALIZE YOURSELVES EVEN THOUGH YOU ARE EQUALLY AT FAULT.

XLIV. I APPEAR BEFORE YOU NOW NEITHER AS A DEFENDER NOR AS AN ACCUSER OF MYTILENE. OUR DEBATE, IF WE ARE WISE, SHOULD NOT BE ABOUT THEIR WRONGDOING BUT ABOUT OUR CORRECT PLANNING. NO MATTER HOW GUILTY I PROVE THEM TO BE, I WILL NOT PROPOSE THAT WE PUT THEM TO DEATH UNLESS THIS WILL BE TO YOUR BENEFIT. NEITHER WOULD I SUGGEST, IF THERE WAS SOME EXCUSE ON THEIR PART, THAT WE FORGIVE THEM, IF THAT WOULD NOT BE GOOD FOR OUR STATE. I BELIEVE THAT WE ARE DELIBERATING ABOUT THE FUTURE, NOT JUST THE PRESENT. IF THE STRONGEST POINT OF CLEON WAS THAT THE DEATH PENALTY WOULD BE IN OUR FUTURE INTEREST, BECAUSE IT WOULD LESSEN THE RISK OF FURTHER UPRISINGS, I WILL COUNTER WITH EXACTLY THE OPPOSITE. HIS ARGUMENT MAY SEEM FAIRER TO YOU IN VIEW OF YOUR PRESENT ANGER AGAINST MYTILENE. HOWEVER WE ARE NOT HERE IN A LAWSUIT TO EXPRESS JUDGEMENT AGAINST THEM AND

TO DECIDE WHAT IS WRONG AND WHAT IS RIGHT, BUT WE ARE IN A DEBATE ABOUT HOW WE CAN HANDLE THE MATTER IN A WAY USEFUL TO US.

XLV. (1-7) THE DEATH PENALTY IS IN THE LAWS OF EVERY STATE FOR VARIOUS CRIMES, SOME OF WHICH ARE NOT AS GRAVE AS THE PRESENT ONE. YET, HOPING TO SUCCEED, PEOPLE TAKE RISKS . . . IT IS IN HUMAN NATURE TO MAKE ERRORS, BOTH INDIVIDUALLY AND COLLECTIVELY AND THERE IS NO LAW TO PREVENT THESE. MANKIND HAS IMPOSED A SERIES OF PUNISHMENTS, MORE AND MORE SEVERE, IN EFFORTS TO LESSEN THE CRIME RATE, BUT EVEN SO THERE ARE INFRACTIONS. WE MUST THEN FIND A PUNISHMENT MORE SEVERE THAN DEATH OR SIMPLY ADMIT THAT THERE IS NO RELIABLE DETERRENT. POVERTY AND WANT CAUSE PEOPLE TO DARE; POSITION, PRIDE AND INSOLENCE GENERATE GREED AND OTHER CIRCUMSTANCES, ANGER AND HUMAN PASSION, ALL MAY LEAD PEOPLE TO TAKE CHANCES WITH CRIME.

XLVI. (1-6) SO WE MUST NOT CONSIDER THE DEATH PENALTY AS A GUARANTEE AND PASS THE WRONG DECISION, NOR MAKE THE REBELS BELIEVE THAT THEY HAVE NO HOPE . . . ACCORDING TO THE EXISTING LAWS, IF A CITY REBELS AND THEN REALIZES THAT IT WILL BE SUBDUED, IT MAY COME TO TERMS WHILE STILL ABLE TO PAY AN INDEMNITY AND LATER A REGULAR TRIBUTE. BUT OTHERWISE, WHAT CITY WOULD NOT TRY TO BEST PREPARE ITSELF AND TO ENDURE SIEGE UNTIL THE END IF IT MAY EXPECT THE SAME FATE WHETHER IT CAPITULATES QUICKLY OR AFTER A LONG TIME? AS FOR OURSELVES, HOW CAN WE AVOID DAMAGING OUR OWN INTERESTS WHEN WE BESIEGE A CITY THAT WILL NOT SURRENDER, WHICH WE FIND IN RUINS WHEN WE CAPTURE IT, AND SO WE ARE DEPRIVED OF FUTURE INCOME FROM IT? . . . WE CANNOT BE SUCH SEVERE JUDGES OF THE CULPRITS THAT WE END UP HURTING OURSELVES. LOOKING TOWARD THE FUTURE WE MUST PUNISH IN MODERATION SO THAT WE MAY CONTINUE TO HOLD CITIES STRONG IN RESOURCES. WE CAN GUARD OURSELVES AGAINST UPRISINGS NOT WITH FRIGHTENING LAWS BUT WITH THE VIGILANCE OF OUR ADMINISTRATION . . . INSTEAD OF PUNISHING SEVERELY INDEPENDENT PEOPLE UNDER OUR RULE WHEN THEY REVOLT AGAINST US, WE MUST WATCH THEM CLOSELY AND TRY TO PREVENT THEM FROM EVEN THINKING ABOUT AN UPRISING. THEN, IF THEY REVOLT AND WE PREVAIL, WE MUST PLACE THE BLAME ON AS FEW AS POSSIBLE.

XLVII. (1-5) THINK ALSO ABOUT ANOTHER MISTAKE YOU WILL BE MAKING IF YOU FOLLOW CLEON. THE GENERAL POPULATION IN ALL THE CITIES IS AT PRESENT FAVORABLY INCLINED TOWARD US AND EITHER IT WILL NOT GO ALONG WITH THE FEW LEADERS OPPOSING US, OR, IF FORCED TO DO SO, IT WILL BE FROM THE BEGINNING HOSTILE TO THEM . . . IF NOW YOU DESTROY THE ENTIRE POPULATION OF MYTILENE, including those who did not take part in the rebellion and who, as soon as they got hold of arms, willingly came over to us, in the first place you will commit an injustice by killing those who helped you and then you will establish a precedent, which all men in power will want to present to their cities. When they rebel, the population will be immediately on their side, because you will have shown to them that the same punishment is inflicted upon the guilty and upon the innocent. Actually, even if some of the people are guilty, you should pretend not to know it so that this class of people that are still friendly to us will not become our enemies. It will be more conducive to the maintenance of our leadership, believe me, if we are willing to have some injustice done to us, instead of punishing, no matter how justly, those whom we should not destroy. Cleon claimed that the proposed punishment is both just and to our benefit but I find that in such a policy the two cannot be combined.

XLVIII. (1-2) You must know now that my proposal is the better course and, without being influenced by feelings of either pity of clemency, which even I will not propose, be persuaded by my presentation that we must calmly pass judgement on the Mytileneans whom Pakhes sent to us, as the guilty ones and allow the rest to continue living at home. Doing that will be beneficial for our future and will cause alarm among our enemies, because he who exercises good judgement is stronger against his adversaries than anyone who rushes on with a show of strength, without thinking."

XLIX. (1-4) That is how Diodotos spoke. Following these two contrasting [Greek antithetical] presentations, the Athenians in their show of hands found themselves almost equally divided, but eventually the view of Diodotos prevailed. Immediately and in a hurry they dispatched another boat [trireme] hoping that the first one, which had a head start of one day and one night, might not have already arrived and then have the city destroyed. The delegates from Mytilene provided wine and barley for the crew and promised them a big reward if they arrived on time. The crewmen sailed in such a hurry that they ate their special cakes of barley, wine and olive oil while rowing and even when some slept others kept going. Fortunately there was no contrary wind and because also the first boat, carrying such an unwelcome message, was sailing in no hurry, while the second was going with such an urgency, the first one had just arrived on time for Pakhes to read the decree and prepare to take action

AS INSTRUCTED, WHEN THE SECOND ONE ARRIVED AND PREVENTED THE DESTRUCTION. IT WAS SO NARROWLY THAT MYTILENE ESCAPED THIS DISASTER.

L. (1-3) IN ACCORDANCE WITH CLEON'S PROPOSAL THE ATHENIANS EXECUTED THE MEN FROM MYTILENE WHOM PAKHES HAD ALREADY SENT AND WHO WERE CONSIDERED CHIEFLY RESPONSIBLE FOR THE UPRISING. THESE WERE A LITTLE MORE THAN ONE-THOUSAND (11). THEY ALSO DEMOLISHED THE WALLS OF MYTILENE AND CONFISCATED ITS NAVY. AFTERWARDS INSTEAD OF IMPOSING A TAX ON THE LESBIANS THEY DIVIDED THE LAND—EXCEPT THAT OF METHYMNA—INTO 3,000 LOTS. OF THESE THEY DEDICATED 300 TO THE GODS AND THE OTHERS THEY DISTRIBUTED BY LOT TO ATHENIAN COLONISTS WHOM THEY SENT TO THE ISLAND. THE LESBIANS IN TURN MADE AN ARRANGEMENT TO CULTIVATE THE LAND, EACH PAYING TWO MNAS (13) ANNUALLY PER LOT. IN ADDITION, THE ATHENIANS TOOK POSSESSION OF ALL THE AREAS THAT MYTILENE CONTROLLED ON THE MAINLAND AND THESE BECAME SUBJECT TO ATHENS. THIS WAS THE COURSE OF EVENTS RELATED TO LESBOS.

Smith, C.F. 1975, pp.44-88.

The war continued and the Athenians launched a disastrous expedition against Syracuse in Sicily. That was 413 B.C. and the defeated Athenians begged for mercy. The historian Diodoros from Sicily described the speech of a Spartan leader arguing against any clemency (12).

THE LIBRARY OF HISTORY
BY DIODOROS THE SICILIAN, FIRST CENTURY B.C.

BOOK XIII

XIII. 28.3-6 . . . FORGIVE MY FRANK TALK, I AM FROM SPARTA AND SPEAK LIKE A SPARTAN . . . HOW CAN ONE SAY TO SHOW MERCY TO THE ATHENIANS? . . . LOOK AT THE LARGE NUMBER OF THEIR UNFORTUNATE VICTIMS. THE PEOPLE WHO HAVE BEEN DEPRIVED OF THEIR OWN KINSMEN AND MUST HATE THE ATHENIANS AS MUCH AS THEY LOVED THEIR OWN.

29.1 WILL IT NOT BE STRANGE AND IMPROPER, MEN OF SYRACUSE, IF, THOSE WHO HAVE PERISHED, WILLINGLY CHOSE DEATH ON YOUR BEHALF, YET YOU WILL NOT INFLICT PUNISHMENT EVEN ON YOUR WORST ENEMIES? . . . LET THEM NOT BLAME THEIR BAD FORTUNE FOR THEIR WICKEDNESS AND GREED . . . MERCY IS RESERVED FOR PEOPLE WHO HAVE A PURE HEART AND WHO HAVE MET WITH BAD LUCK. BUT THESE MEN (THE ATHENIANS), WITH THEIR LIVES FULL OF UNJUST ACTS, HAVE NO GROUNDS FOR MERCY AND PROTECTION LEFT TO THEM.

30.1-6 . . . THEY HAD BEEN THE MOST FORTUNATE OF ALL THE GREEKS, YET THEY WERE UNABLE TO TOLERATE THEIR HAPPI-

NESS AS IF IT WERE A HEAVY BURDEN. DESPITE THE WIDE SEA THAT SEPARATES US, THEY WANTED TO SUBDUE SICILY, DIVIDE IT INTO LOTS (FOR THEMSELVES) AND REDUCE OUR PEOPLE TO SLAVERY. IT IS AWFUL TO START A WAR WITHOUT HAVING SUFFERED ANY PREVIOUS INJUSTICE, BUT THAT IS EXACTLY WHAT THEY DID . . . WHEN IN THE SAME MEN WE FIND GREED, TREACHERY AND ARROGANCE, WHO IN HIS RIGHT MIND WOULD SHOW THEM MERCY? HOW THEN, PLEASE NOTE, DID THE ATHENIANS TREAT THE MYTILENEANS? EVEN THOUGH THESE PEOPLE HAD NO INTENTION OF DOING THEM ANY WRONG AND THEY ONLY DESIRED TO BE INDEPENDENT, AFTER THE ATHENIANS GOT CONTROL OF THEIR CITY, THEY VOTED TO BUTCHER EVERYONE IN IT. A CRUEL AND BARBAROUS ACTION FOR SURE, PARTICULARLY WHEN COMMITTED AGAINST GREEKS, ALLIES WHO HAVE FREQUENTLY DONE THEM MANY FAVORS . . . IT IS NOW ONLY FAIR THAT WHATEVER LAW THEY HAD IMPOSED UPON OTHERS, THE ATHENIANS SHOULD ACCEPT WITHOUT INDIGNATION WHEN IT IS APPLIED TO THEMSELVES.

Oldfather, C.H., Vol. V, pp. 198-204.

After describing the events in Sicily and citing the previous example mentioned by the speaker, Diodoros returned his narrative to the eastern Aegean scene, including Lesbos.

BOOK XIII

73.3-6 ALCIBIADES (ATHENIAN LEADER) WITH ALL HIS SHIPS SAILED FROM SAMOS TO KYME AND, WANTING TO FIND AN EXCUSE TO PLUNDER THAT TERRITORY, HE HURLED FALSE CHARGES AGAINST THE KYMEANS. IN THE BEGINNING HE WAS ABLE TO TAKE MANY CAPTIVES AND HAUL THEM TO THE SHIPS. BUT WHEN THE WHOLE POPULATION CAME OUT OF THE CITY TO RESCUE THE PRISONERS AND THEY FELL UNEXPECTEDLY ON ALCIBIADES' TROOPS, AFTER A WHILE . . . THE ATHENIANS WERE FORCED TO ABANDON THE PRISONERS AND RUN FOR SAFETY TO THEIR SHIPS. ALCIBIADES WAS VERY DISTRESSED FOR THE REVERSES AND SUMMONING HIS ARMY FROM MYTILENE HE PLACED IT BEFORE THE CITY AND CHALLENGED THE KYMEANS TO BATTLE. HOWEVER NOBODY CAME OUT AND SO HE RAVAGED THE COUNTRYSIDE AND SAILED OFF BACK TO MYTILENE.

Oldfather, C.H., Vol. V, p.326.

Greeks against Greeks: the Battle of Arginousai

Athens and Sparta continued their mutually destructive hostilities until, after a twenty-seven-year war, the Athenians lost all their fleet and were obliged to capitulate in 403 B.C.

Four years before the end, the biggest sea battle of Greeks against Greeks took place near Lesbos. Not a naval power originally, the Spartans and their allies by 407–406 B.C. had built a strong fleet of 140 ships and managed to gain control of the eastern Aegean coastal region. Methymna on Lesbos was captured and the Athenian admiral Conon, with only seventy ships, was forced into battle outside Mytilene. He lost thirty triremes in action and those left were blockaded by the Spartans in the harbor of Mytilene. Athens, understandably alarmed, had to melt the gold and silver dedications on the Acropolis to pay for more ships and armaments. Later that year, with a new fleet of 150 triremes, the Athenians engaged the Peloponnesians near the small islands next to Lesbos called Arginousai (14) and won decisively. A storm stopped them from sailing to Mytilene to destroy the rest of the enemy's ships and also from rescuing the men from the twenty-five ships they had lost in the battle and burying the dead. For this failure, the Athenian assembly, angry and misguided, voted to condemn eight of the victorious leaders to death and had six of them executed (two escaped), regretting this action bitterly later on. Socrates was one of the few who voted against this unjust death penalty.

THE LIBRARY OF HISTORY
BY DIODOROS THE SICILIAN, FIRST CENTURY B.C.

BOOK XIII.

76.4-6 THEN HE (THE SPARTAN COMMANDER CALLICRATIDAS) SAILED TO LESBOS AND WITH HIS FORCES ATTACKED METHYMNA, WHICH HAD A GARRISON OF ATHENIANS. CONTINUOUS ASSAULTS AT FIRST WERE UNSUCCESSFUL BUT SOON AFTERWARDS SOME MEN BETRAYED THE CITY TO THE SPARTANS SO THEY WERE ABLE TO BREAK INSIDE THE WALLS, WHERE THEY SEIZED ALL WEALTH AND POSSESSIONS. BUT THEY SPARED THE POPULATION AND RETURNED THE CITY TO THE METHYMNIANS. AFTER THESE EVENTS CALLICRATIDAS RUSHED TO MYTILENE LEAVING HIS ARMY IN CARE OF THE LACEDAEMONIAN (NAMED) THORAX WITH AN ORDER TO ADVANCE AS FAST AS HE COULD ON FOOT, WHILE HE SAILED ALONG THE COAST WITH HIS NAVY.

77. CONON, THE ATHENIAN GENERAL, HAD SEVENTY SHIPS WHICH HE HAD EQUIPPED FOR BATTLE BETTER THAN ANY OTHER GENERAL HAD DONE IN THE PAST. IT JUST HAPPENED THAT HE HAD GONE OUT TO SEA TO HELP METHYMNA AND WHEN HE LEARNED THAT IT HAD BEEN CAPTURED HE ANCHORED BY AN ISLAND CALLED "OF THE ONE HUNDRED." EARLY THE NEXT DAY, REALIZING THAT THE ENEMIES' SHIPS WERE COMING AGAINST HIM HE DECIDED THAT IT WOULD HAVE BEEN DANGEROUS TO ENGAGE IN BATTLE IN THAT SPOT AGAINST A FLEET TWICE AS LARGE. HE MADE A PLAN TO AVOID ENGAGEMENT BY SAILING ON THE OTHER SIDE OF THE ISLAND AND BY DRAWING SOME OF THE ENEMY TOWARD HIM TO GIVE BATTLE OFF MYTILENE.

77.1-5 THIS WAY HE FIGURED THAT IF HE WON HE COULD TURN ABOUT TO CHASE AND IF HE WAS DEFEATED, HE COULD FIND SHELTER IN THE HARBOR. THEREFORE, AFTER HE HAD HIS MEN BOARD THE SHIPS, HE BEGAN TO NAVIGATE LEISURELY USING ONLY THE OARS, IN ORDER TO MAKE THE PELOPONNESIANS GET NEARER. THEY, ON THE OTHER HAND, AS THEY APPROACHED HAD THEIR SHIPS GOING FASTER AND FASTER, HOPING TO CATCH THE END LINE OF THE ENEMY. AS CONON THEN BEGAN TO PULL BACK, THE PELOPONNESIAN COMMANDERS WITH THE BEST SHIPS, RUSHED TO THE CHASE, WHICH NOT ONLY EXHAUSTED THE OARSMEN DUE TO THE CONTINUOUS ROWING, BUT ALSO SEPARATED THEM FROM THE REST OF THE FLEET. RECOGNIZING THIS, CONON, WHO WAS ABOUT TO REACH MYTILENE, RAISED FROM HIS FLAGSHIP A RED BANNER AS THE SIGNAL TO THE TRIREME CAPTAINS. THUS, JUST AS THE ENEMY WAS ABOUT TO CONTACT THEM, THE ATHENIANS TURNED SUDDENLY AROUND ALL AT THE SAME TIME WHILE THE CREW ROARED THEIR BATTLE SONG [PAEAN] AND THE TRUMPETERS SOUNDED THE WAR SIGNAL. VERY SURPRISED WITH THIS, THE PELOPONNESIANS TRIED IN A HURRY TO PLACE THEIR SHIPS IN A DEFENSIVE POSITION, BUT AS THERE WAS NO TIME TO TURN ABOUT, THEY FOUND THEMSELVES IN A GREAT CONFUSION, MADE WORSE BY THE FACT THAT THEIR OWN SHIPS, COMING UP BEHIND THEM HAD ABANDONED THEIR CUSTOMARY ARRANGEMENT.

78.1-7 TAKING ADVANTAGE OF THIS OPPORTUNITY, CONON RUSHED UPON THEM TO PREVENT ANY ORDERLY FORMATION, DIRECTLY INJURED SOME OF THE SHIPS AND OF OTHERS HE SHEARED OFF THE OARS. YET NONE OF THE SHIPS OPPOSING CONON TURNED TO FLIGHT BUT WAITED HOLDING THEIR BOWS STEADY, EXPECTING THE ARRIVAL OF THE REST (OF THE SPARTAN FLEET). ONLY THE ATHENIANS ON THE LEFT WING OF THE FORMATION FORCED THEIR OPPONENTS TO RETREAT AND THEN EAGERLY PURSUED THEM FOR A LONG TIME. BUT ALREADY, THE ENTIRE PELOPONNESIAN FLEET WAS GATHERING TOGETHER AND CONON, IN AWE OF THE LARGE NUMBER OF THE ENEMY'S VESSELS, STOPPED HIS PURSUIT AND SAILED BACK TO MYTILENE WITH FORTY SHIPS. HOWEVER THOSE ATHENIAN SHIPS WHICH HAD GONE ON A CHASE, FOUND THE PELOPONNESIANS SWARMING AROUND THEM AND BLOCKING THEIR RETURN TO THE CITY. CAUGHT BY SURPRISE, THEY WERE FORCED TO RUN TOWARDS THE NEAREST LAND. WITH THE PELOPONNESIANS CLOSE AFTER THEM, THE ATHENIANS SAW NO OTHER WAY TO SAVE THEMSELVES BUT TO RUN ASHORE FOR SHELTER. SO DESERTING THEIR VESSELS THEY FOUND REFUGE IN MYTILENE.

Oldfather, C.H., Vol. V, pp.334–338.

With the capture of thirty Athenian ships, the Spartan general Callicratidas realized that the naval power of his enemy had been destroyed.

The Spartans then organized by land and sea a siege of Mytilene, which was defended by its citizens and by the Athenian expeditionary force.

...

79.2 THE ATHENIANS AND MYTILENEANS, SEEING THAT THE ONLY WAY THEY COULD BE SAVED WAS WITH A VICTORY, WERE DETERMINED TO DIE NOBLY RATHER THAN TO GIVE UP THEIR POSITION. SINCE A SUPREME DETERMINATION POSSESSED BOTH SIDES, THERE WAS MASSIVE KILLING, AS EVERYONE WITHOUT HESITATION EXPOSED THEIR BODIES TO THE DANGERS OF THE BATTLE. THE MEN ON THE SHIPS' DECKS WERE WOUNDED BADLY BY THE SHOWERS OF ARROWS THROWN AGAINST THEM. SOME, MORTALLY STRUCK, FELL IN THE WATER, WHILE OTHERS NOT FEELING YET THEIR FRESH AND STILL HOT WOUNDS, CONTINUED TO FIGHT. MANY WERE FELLED BY THE HUGE ROCKS WHICH THE ATHENIANS LAUNCHED FROM THEIR COMMANDING POSTS. DESPITE THIS, THE FIGHTING WENT ON FOR A LONG TIME, WITH MANY DEATHS ON BOTH SIDES, UNTIL CALLICRATIDAS HAD THE TRUMPET [SALPINX] SOUND THE RECALL, IN ORDER TO GIVE HIS SOLDIERS SOME REST. THEN AFTER A WHILE HE MANNED AGAIN HIS FLEET AND, MAINLY DUE TO THE LARGE NUMBER OF HIS SHIPS AND TO THE STRENGTH OF HIS MARINES, AFTER FURTHER PROLONGED STRUGGLE HE MANAGED TO EXPEL THE ATHENIANS FROM THE (OLD PART OF THE) CITY. WHEN THEY HAD SOUGHT SHELTER IN THE LITTLE PORT WITHIN THE CITY, HE (THE SPARTAN CHIEF) SAILED THROUGH THE BARRIERS AND ANCHORED NEAR THE TOWN OF MYTILENE. IT SHOULD BE MADE CLEAR THAT THE INLET, OVER WHICH THEY FOUGHT, LED TO A HARBOR WHICH WAS VERY GOOD BUT WAS LOCATED OUTSIDE THE CITY. THE ANCIENT CITY OF MYTILENE WAS ON A SMALL ISLAND AND ONLY LATER IT EXPANDED ACROSS ONTO THE MAINLAND OF LESBOS. BETWEEN THE TWO CITIES (THE OLD AND THE NEW) THERE WAS A NARROW STRAIT, WHICH RENDERED THE CITY MORE IMPREGNABLE. ONCE INSIDE THE HARBOR, CALLICRATIDAS LANDED HIS FORCES, HAD THEM CAMP ALL AROUND THE CITY AND THEN LAUNCHED ATTACKS FROM ALL SIDES.

Oldfather, C.H., Vol. V, pp. 342–344.

Diodoros devoted the next sixteen chapters to the military affairs in Sicily between 407 and 406 B.C. Then he returned to the continuing war between the Athenians and the Spartans on and near Lesbos.

97.1-7 WHILE ALL THIS WAS GOING ON (IN SICILY) THE ATHENIANS, AFTER THEIR CONTINUING SERIES OF REVERSES, GRANTED CITIZENSHIP TO IMMIGRANTS AND OTHER FOREIGNERS WHO WERE WILLING TO JOIN THEM IN THEIR WAR EFFORT. SOON MANY PEOPLE ACQUIRED CITIZENSHIP AND THE GENERALS BEGAN TO ENLIST THOSE FIT FOR MILITARY

SERVICE. THE ATHENIAN LEADERS ALSO GOT SIXTY SHIPS READY, WHICH WERE EQUIPPED AT GREAT COST AND THEN SAILED TO SAMOS. THERE, THEY JOINED THE OTHER GENERALS WHO HAD ASSEMBLED EIGHTY TRIREMES FROM THE OTHER ISLANDS. THEY ALSO ASKED THE SAMIANS TO MAN AND OUTFIT TEN TRIREMES AND WITH THE TOTAL OF 150 SHIPS THEY SAILED TOWARD THE ARGINOUSAE (14) ISLANDS, EAGER TO GO ON TO RAISE THE SIEGE OF MYTILENE. WHEN THE LACEDAEMONIAN ADMIRAL CALLICRATIDAS LEARNED OF THE (ATHENIAN) SHIPS' APPROACH, HE LEFT ETEONIKOS IN CHARGE OF THE LAND FORCES AND HE EMBARKED HIS CREW ON 140 SHIPS, WITH WHICH IN A HURRY HE SAILED OUT TO SEA TOWARDS THE OPPOSITE SIDE OF ARGINOUSAE. THOSE ISLANDS AT THAT TIME WERE INHABITED AND THERE WAS A SMALL AEOLIAN COLONY ON THEM. THE ISLANDS LIE BETWEEN MYTILENE AND KYME (15), A VERY SHORT DISTANCE FROM THE MAINLAND OFF THE CANIS POINT.

THE ATHENIANS KNEW IMMEDIATELY THAT THE ENEMY HAD ARRIVED, SINCE THEY WERE AT ANCHOR NOT FAR FROM THEM, BUT DUE TO THE HIGH WINDS THEY DECIDED TO AVOID AN ENCOUNTER. THEY MADE PREPARATIONS FOR A SEA BATTLE ON THE FOLLOWING DAY AND THE LACEDAEMONIANS DID THE SAME, EVEN THOUGH THE ORACLES ON BOTH SIDES WERE FORBIDDING IT. ON THE LACEDAEMONIAN SIDE THE HEAD OF THE SACRIFICIAL ANIMAL, WHICH LAY ON THE BEACH, DISAPPEARED WHEN THE WAVES REACHED IT AND THIS SIGNAL MADE THE SEER PREDICT THAT THEIR ADMIRAL WOULD DIE IN BATTLE. HEARING THIS, CALLICRATIDAS WAS REPORTED TO HAVE SAID THAT HIS DEATH IN THE UPCOMING FIGHT WOULD CERTAINLY NOT LESSEN THE GLORY OF SPARTA. AMONG THE ATHENIANS, THE GENERAL THRASYLLOS, WHO WAS IN CHARGE THAT DAY, SAW DURING THE NIGHT THE FOLLOWING DREAM. IT SEEMED THAT THEY WERE IN A CROWDED THEATER IN ATHENS AND HE WITH SIX OF THE OTHER GENERALS WERE THE ACTORS IN THE TRAGEDY OF EURIPIDES (16) "PHOENICIAN WOMEN." THEIR OPPONENTS (ALSO ON STAGE IN HIS DREAM) WERE PLAYING THE "SUPPLIANTS" (ALSO A PLAY BY EURIPIDES) AND THE RESULT WAS A "CADMEAN VICTORY" IN WHICH EVERYBODY DIED, AS IT HAPPENED IN THE OLD STORY ABOUT THE WARRIORS AGAINST THEBES. WHEN THE SEER HEARD THIS, HE MADE IT CLEAR THAT SEVEN OF THE GENERALS WERE GOING TO PERISH. HOWEVER, SINCE THE OMENS HERALDED VICTORY, THE COMMANDERS PREVENTED ANY ANNOUNCEMENT OF THEIR OWN PREDICTED END TO ANYONE ELSE AND ONLY DECLARED TO THE ENTIRE ARMY THE NEWS ABOUT THE VICTORY OMENS.

98.1-5 CALLICRATIDAS, THE SPARTAN ADMIRAL, GATHERED ALL HIS FORCES AND ENCOURAGED THEM WITH THE RIGHT WORDS, SAYING AT THE END: "I AM PERSONALLY SO EAGER TO FACE THIS DANGER OF OUR FATHERLAND, THAT ALTHOUGH

THE ORACLES PREDICT VICTORY FOR YOU BUT DEATH FOR ME, I AM NONETHELESS READY TO PERISH. KNOWING THAT AFTER THE COMMANDER'S DEATH THE FORCES ARE PRONE TO CONFUSION, I AM NOW APPOINTING CLEARKHOS ADMIRAL AND MY SUCCESSOR, IN CASE SOMETHING HAPPENS TO ME. HE IS A MAN WHO HAS GIVEN PROOF OF HIS ABILITY IN WARFARE." BY SAYING THIS, CALLICRATIDAS MADE NOT FEW OF HIS MEN WANT TO PROVE THEMSELVES AS VALIANT AND TO BECOME MORE EAGER FOR THE BATTLE. SO THE LACEDAEMONIANS, PROMPTING EACH OTHER, WENT UP ON THEIR SHIPS. THE ATHENIANS TOO, AFTER LISTENING TO THE CALLS OF THEIR GENERALS, RAPIDLY BOARDED THEIR TRIREMES AND THEY ALL TOOK THEIR POSITIONS. THRASYLLOS WAS IN CHARGE OF THE RIGHT WING, ALONG WITH PERICLES, SON OF THE PERICLES WHO WAS CALLED "OLYMPIAN" FOR HIS MAJESTIC POWER (17) . . . THE OTHER GENERALS WERE STATIONED ALONG THE ENTIRE LINE AND THE ARGINOUSAE ISLANDS WERE MADE PART OF THE ARRANGEMENT, BECAUSE THRASYLLOS WANTED TO EXTEND HIS FLEET AS MUCH AS POSSIBLE. CALLICRATIDAS ON HIS PART, SAILED OUT KEEPING TO THE RIGHT AND DELEGATED HIS LEFT WING TO THE BOEOTIANS, UNDER THE COMMAND OF THRASONDAS FROM THEBES. SINCE HE COULD NOT STRETCH THE LENGTH OF HIS FORMATION AS MUCH AS THE ENEMY HAD WITH THE LARGE SPACE OCCUPIED BY THE ISLANDS, THE SPARTAN ADMIRAL DIVIDED HIS FORCE TO FORM TWO SQUADRONS, WHICH FOUGHT TWO BATTLES, ONE ON EACH SIDE. THIS GREATLY AMAZED THOSE WHO SAW IT ON MANY SIDES, BECAUSE IT WAS AS IF FOUR FLEETS WERE ENGAGED IN BATTLE, WITH A TOTAL NUMBER OF ASSEMBLED SHIPS NOT MUCH BELOW THREE HUNDRED. IN FACT, THAT WAS THE GREATEST SEA BATTLE ON RECORD OF GREEKS AGAINST GREEKS.

99.1-6 THE MOMENT THE ADMIRALS GAVE ORDERS TO SOUND THE TRUMPETS, ALL THE MEN ON EACH SIDE IN TURN RAISED THE WAR CRY FILLING THE AIR WITH THUNDEROUS SOUND. SPEEDING THROUGH THE WAVES THEY ALL RUSHED ON, EACH STRIVING TO BE THE FIRST TO START THE FIGHT. BECAUSE THE WAR HAD LASTED SO LONG, MOST OF THE MEN HAD MUCH BATTLEFIELD EXPERIENCE AND THEY DISPLAYED AN UNSURPASSED DRIVE, ESPECIALLY SINCE THESE WERE THE BEST TROOPS THAT HAD BEEN GATHERED FOR THIS CRITICAL CONTEST. IT WAS GENERALLY ASSUMED THAT WHOEVER WON THAT BATTLE WOULD PUT AN END TO THE WAR. ABOVE ALL CALLICRATIDAS, HAVING HEARD THE SEER FORETELL HIS OWN END, WAS RUSHING TO OBTAIN FOR HIMSELF A MOST OUTSTANDING DEATH. CONSEQUENTLY, HE WAS THE FIRST TO DRIVE AT THE SHIP OF GENERAL LYSIAS AND RUSHING UPON IT HE PIERCED IT AND SANK IT. HE DISABLED SOME OF THE OTHER TRIREMES SAILING NEXT TO THEM, BATTERING THEM WITH THE SHIP'S NOZZLE AND OTHERS HE MADE USELESS FOR THE FIGHT BY BREAKING OFF OR PULLING AWAY THE OARS. LASTLY HE RAN INTO THE TRIREME OF PERICLES SO VIOLENTLY that he cut a big hole into it. Then since the nozzle of his ship was stuck in the gap and his crew could not pull back, he gave a chance to Pericles to throw an "iron hand" (ancient grappling war machine) and to fasten it. So the Athenians were able to surround the Spartan admiral's ship and jumping on it they cut all the Spartans to pieces. They say that Callicratidas continued to fight brilliantly and resisted for a long time but finally being hit from all sides by the enemy crowd he succumbed (18). When the admiral's loss became clear it caused the Peloponnesians to lose their courage and begin to turn back. While the right wing of the Peloponnesians was withdrawing, the Boeotians on the left held on for sometime and fought vigorously. In fact, both they and all others fighting on their side, who had seceded from Athens, were fearing that if the Athenians regained their leadership, they would be penalized for their rebellion. But when they saw that most ships had been hit and the entire navy of the victors was moving against them, they were forced to take flight. Some of the Peloponnesians ran for safety to Hios and others to Kyme.

100.1-6 The Athenians continued the chase of the defeated fleet for a great distance and the sea of the whole area was filled with the dead and the wreckage of ships. Subsequently, some of the (Athenian) generals thought that they ought to pick up the dead, since the Athenian people hated those who left their dead unburied. Others however declared that they should sail to Mytilene, to raise the siege as soon as possible. In the meantime, a great storm arose tossing about the triremes and the soldiers objected to the effort of gathering the dead, both because of the hardships of the battle and of the size of the waves. Finally, as the storm was getting worse, the Athenians did not sail to Mytilene nor did they collect their dead but instead they were forced by the winds to put in at Arginousae. In the sea battle the Athenians lost twenty-five ships with most of their crew and the Peloponnesians seventy-seven of theirs. Due to the loss of so many ships and of the men aboard, the coastline along Kyme and Phokaia was full of dead bodies and wreckage.

When the (Spartan) general besieging Mytilene, Eteonikos, learned of the defeat of the Peloponnesians, he sent his ships to Hios and with his land forces he withdrew to the city of Pyrrha, which was his ally. He was concerned that if the Athenian fleet should sail and attack them and if the besieged from the city would also make a sortie, he

WOULD LOSE HIS ENTIRE ARMY. AFTERWARDS THE ATHENIANS DID SAIL TO MYTILENE AND PICKING UP CONON WITH HIS FORTY SHIPS, THEY PUT IN AT SAMOS. FROM THAT BASE THEY LAUNCHED ATTACKS AND LAID WASTE THE ENEMY TERRITORIES.

. . .

101.1 WHEN THE NEWS OF THE GOOD TURN OF EVENTS BY ARGINOUSAE REACHED ATHENS, THE CITIZENS COMMENDED THE GENERALS FOR THE VICTORY BUT WERE VERY DISTRESSED BECAUSE THEY HAD ALLOWED THE MEN WHO LOST THEIR LIVES FOR THE SAKE OF ATHENIAN SUPREMACY TO REMAIN UNBURIED . . .

101 . . . 5. CONSEQUENTLY THE PEOPLE NOTIFIED THE GENERALS OF PLANS TO PUT THEM ON TRIAL AND ORDERED THEM TO TRANSFER THE COMMAND TO CONON AND TO RETURN IMMEDIATELY TO ATHENS.

Two of the generals, fearing the anger of the crowd, fled, but the others returned with much of the fleet to Athens, hoping that the large number of crewmen would also help defend them in their trial.

101.6 WHEN THE PEOPLE GATHERED IN THE ASSEMBLY, THEY LISTENED TO THE ACCUSATION AND TO THOSE WHO SPOKE IN ITS FAVOR BUT WHEN THE DEFENDANTS APPEARED THEY MADE MUCH NOISE AND WOULD NOT LET THEM TALK . . . AT THE END THE FRIENDS AND RELATIVES OF THE DEAD WITH THEIR POLITICAL LEADERS . . . PREVAILED AND THE VERDICT WAS TO CONDEMN THE GENERALS TO DEATH AND TO CONFISCATE THEIR PROPERTY.

102.1-3 WHEN THIS DECISION WAS CONFIRMED AND THEY WERE ABOUT TO BE LED AWAY BY THE OFFICIALS TO THEIR EXECUTION, ONE OF THE GENERALS, DIOMEDON, A MAN WITH MUCH WAR EXPERIENCE AND RECOGNIZED FOR HIS JUSTICE AND OTHER VIRTUES, TOOK THE FLOOR IN THE MIDDLE OF THE CROWD. WHEN EVERYONE QUIETED DOWN HE SAID: "MEN OF ATHENS, MAY THE VERDICT AGAINST US PROVE TO BE TO THE CITY'S ADVANTAGE. SINCE OUR FATE, HOWEVER, IS PREVENTING US FROM SATISFYING OUR SACRED VOWS FOR OUR VICTORY, IT WILL BE GOOD IF YOU WOULD TAKE CARE AND RENDER THEIR DUE TO ZEUS THE SAVIOR, AND TO APOLLO AND THE HOLY GODDESSES, BECAUSE IT WAS WITH OUR PRAYERS AND VOWS TO THEM THAT WE WERE ABLE TO DEFEAT THE ENEMY AT SEA." WHILE DIOMEDON, HAVING SPOKEN THIS WAY, WAS TAKEN AWAY ALONG WITH THE OTHER GENERALS TO THE APPOINTED PLACE OF EXECUTION, HE LEFT MANY DECENT CITIZENS FULL OF PITY AND TEARS. . . . TO SUCH A DEGREE WERE THE (ATHENIAN) PEOPLE OUT OF THEIR MINDS THAT UPON UNJUST PROVOCATION BY DEMAGOGUES, THEY VENTED THEIR ANGER AGAINST MEN WHO DESERVED NOT PUNISHMENT BUT MANY PRAISES AND LAURELS INSTEAD.

103.1-2 SOON AFTERWARDS BOTH THOSE WHO PROPOSED THIS ACTION AND THOSE WHO WERE PERSUADED TO VOTE FOR IT REPENTED, AS IF A DIVINE SPIRIT PERSECUTED THEM. . . . THE MAN WHO MISLED THE PEOPLE WAS BROUGHT TO TRIAL FOR DECEIVING THE CITIZENS AND WITHOUT PERMISSION TO SPEAK IN HIS DEFENSE HE WAS THROWN IN JAIL. ALTHOUGH HE . . . MANAGED TO ESCAPE HE LIVED ONLY TO HAVE HIS WICKEDNESS CONTINUE TO BE POINTED OUT, NOT ONLY IN ATHENS BUT BY ALL THE GREEKS . . .

Oldfather, C.H., Vol. V, pp. 396-416.

The Hellenic holocaust—it is tempting to call it "homocaust," considering that the Greeks were destroying their own kind [*homo*-]—continued as the new century began. The Athenians were joined now by their archenemy, the Persians, in an effort to weaken or subdue Sparta. In 392 B.C. a new general, Thrasybulos, was elected in Athens and sailed with the Athenian forces to Lesbos.

THE LIBRARY OF HISTORY
BY DIODOROS THE SICILIAN, FIRST CENTURY B.C.

BOOK XIV
94.3-4. FROM THE HELLESPONT HE (THRASYBULOS) SAILED TO LESBOS AND ANCHORED BY THE COAST NEAR ERESOS. BUT HEAVY WINDS THEN AROSE AND TWENTY-THREE OF HIS TRIREMES WERE DESTROYED. HAVING SURVIVED THE STORM, THRASYBULOS ADVANCED WITH THE REST OF HIS SHIPS AGAINST THE CITIES OF LESBOS IN ORDER TO BRING THEM OVER TO HIS SIDE. ALL THESE CITIES, WITH THE EXCEPTION OF MYTILENE, HAD REVOLTED (AGAINST ATHENIAN DOMINANCE).
FIRST HE SHOWED UP BY METHYMNA AND ENGAGED IN BATTLE AGAINST THOSE IN THAT CITY, WHO WERE UNDER THE COMMAND OF THE SPARTAN THERIMAKHOS. IN A BRILLIANT COMBAT HE SLEW THERIMAKHOS HIMSELF AND NOT A SMALL NUMBER OF METHYMNIANS. FORCING THE REST OF THEM INSIDE THE WALLS, HE THEN RAVAGED THE LAND AROUND METHYMNA AND OBTAINED THE SUBMISSION OF (THE OTHER CITIES) ERESOS AND ANTISSA. AFTERWARDS WITH THE ADDITION OF MORE SHIPS FROM HIS ALLIES IN MYTILENE AND HIOS, HE SAILED FOR RHODOS.

After the endless slaughter he had to include in his history, Diodoros understandably introduced one of his last chapters (Oldfather, 1968) with some philosophical remarks.

THE LIBRARY OF HISTORY
BY DIODOROS THE SICILIAN, FIRST CENTURY B.C.

BOOK XXV 1.
WHEN THE PHILOSOPHER EPICUROS, IN HIS WORK ENTITLED "PRINCIPAL DOCTRINES," DECLARED THAT

THE JUST LIFE REMAINS UNPERTURBED WHILE THE UNJUST EXISTENCE IS FILLED WITH COMMOTION, HE PUT IN A SHORT SENTENCE MUCH TRUE WISDOM WHICH MIGHT ULTIMATELY BE ABLE TO CORRECT HUMAN EVIL.

Walton, F.R., Vol. XI, p. 144.

C. LESBOS AND THE HELLENIC SCHOOLS OF THOUGHT

Four main schools of philosophy (Table III-1), not simply educational establishments but groups with distinct views and principles, emerged in Greece and specifically in Athens during the fourth century B.C. In all four, men from Lesbos and Aeolis played prominent roles. Theophrastos from Eresos had succeeded Aristotle in the "Lyceum" and Polemon (from 314–276 B.C.) was holding the chair of Plato in the "Academy" when two more and quite different philosophical teams were established in Athens, the Epicureans in 306 and the Stoics in 301 B.C. Following the death of Epicuros, Hermarkhos from Mytilene became the second director of the Epicureans' "Garden." The Stoics continued to hold their sessions in their "Stoa" (colonnaded arcade) after the passing of the founder, Zeno, who had named as his successor Kleanthes from Assos in Aeolis, across the straits from the east coast of Lesbos.

Table III-1
THE PRINCIPAL PHILOSOPHICAL SCHOOLS OF ATHENS AND THEIR LESBIAN-AEOLIAN LEADERS

School and Site / Founder and Year	Lesbian-Aeolian Leader
Platonists - The Academy* Plato [*Platon*], 385 B.C.*	Arkesilaos of Pitane** b. 318, d. 242 B.C.
Peripatetics - The Lyceum [*Lykeion*] Aristotle [*Aristoteles*], 335 B.C.	Theophrastos of Eresos b. 370, d. 287/5 B.C.
Epicureans# - The Garden [*Kepos*] Epicuros, 306 B.C.	Hermarkhos of Mytilene ca. 340, after 270 B.C.
Stoics - The Stoa (Arcade) Zeno of Citium (Cyprus), 300/1 B.C.	Kleanthes of Assos b. 331, d. 232 B.C.

*By the time the schools of Athens were closed in 529 A.D. by the order of the Byzantine emperor Justinian I, the Academy had existed and operated for 916 years.
** In the still prevalent Latinized spelling of Greek names, "c" stands for "k," "ch" for "kh" (Greek chi, with a—hard or soft—*h* sound), and the -os ending becomes -us, e.g., Arcesilaus, Theophrastus, etc.
# The epicurean school freely admitted women and also included the first African-Hellenic black philosopher, Ptolemy the Black from Egypt (Diog. Laertios, II.x.25–26; Sarton, G. I., p. 595).

The Academy of Plato

The name of Plato [*Platon*] is widely known but not everyone realizes that "Plato" was a nickname referring to the wide forehead, or the broad mind [Greek *platy-*] of the young Athenian originally named Aristocles (Diog. Laert. III, 4) after his grandfather, according to a prevalent Greek tradition. The only native Athenian among the founders of the four major schools of philosophy there, Plato, following his teacher and fellow Athenian, the intellectual "gadfly" Socrates (who started no school and wrote nothing), turned philosophical inquiry "inward" from the study of nature and the universe to the understanding of the human mind,

Plato [*Platon*] (Cambridge, Fitzwilliam) from Richter 1965/84.

the limitations of knowledge, the relativity of ethics ("no one is intentionally bad" said Socrates), and the possibility of an ideal society (Jaspers, 1957/ 1962). The Platonic system—which made reference to non-carnal (later called "platonic") love in only one work, the "Symposium," that described a banquet devoted to the subject of love—was taught in the Academy [*Academeia*], a park outside Athens dedicated to the hero Academos. Plato officially established the school in 385 B.C., fourteen years after Socrates had been condemned by the Athenians for impiety and died drinking poison. With the exception of his trips to Sicily, Plato rarely left his city. The Academy, as an organization for philosophical study including mathematics, natural science, ethics and metaphysics, continued to function for over 900 years. It was dissolved in 529 A.D. by edict of the Christian East Roman emperor, Justinian I (Oxf. Class. Dict. p. 1).

The sixth head of the Academy after Plato was Arkesilaos of Pitane in Aeolis (15). He could be associated with Lesbos both because of his Aeolian origin and also because he studied with the successor of Aristotle, Theophrastos of Eresos. As a young man, Arkesilaos studied at home, then went on to Sardis, the capital of Lydia. After his father's death, he moved to Athens and became a student of Theophrastos. Later, an intimate friendship with a prominent platonist, Krantor, made him move to the Academy. According to Diogenes Laertios (Book IV, chapter 4, par. 22)

> ARKESILAOS LIVED WITH KRANTOR AND POLEMON WITH KRATES. . . . AS HAS BEEN SAID ALREADY, KRATES WAS THE LOVER OF POLEMON AND ARKESILAOS OF KRANTOR.
> Hicks, R.D., Vol. I, p. 398.

And (Book IV, Chapter 3, par. 17)

> ANTIGONOS . . . SAYS THAT . . . POLEMON WAS SUED BY HIS WIFE FOR ABUSE BECAUSE HE HAD LOVE AFFAIRS WITH YOUNG BOYS. HOWEVER HIS CHARACTER WAS SO MUCH STRENGTHENED WHEN HE ENGAGED IN PHILOSOPHY, THAT HIS EXPRESSION AND DEMEANOR WERE ALWAYS THE SAME. HIS VOICE TOO NEVER CHANGED AND THAT IS WHAT CAPTIVATED KRANTOR.
> Hicks, R.D., Vol. I, p. 394.

Polemon and Krates, in succession, headed the Academy. Krantor died early and so Arkesilaos became the next director, before the middle of the third century B.C. and he held that position until his death in 242 B.C. He gave to the school's philosophy a more skeptical or argumentative (dialectical) turn (Oxf. Class. Dict. p. 1, 95). Arkesilaos was a man of wide interests, rejected dogmatic approaches and was known both for his sense of humor and for being an interesting but also a demanding teacher. Due to his skepticism he wrote no books. His morals were based on the concept of the *eulogon*, which he defined as the clearly logical principle of thought and behavior.

THE LIVES AND OPINIONS OF EMINENT PHILOSOPHERS
BY DIOGENES LAERTIOS, FIRST HALF OF THIRD CENTURY A.D.
BOOK IV, CHAPTER 6
ARKESILAOS (ARCECILAUS), 318–242 B.C.
28-30. ARKESILAOS . . . CAME FROM PITANE IN AEOLIS. HE MARKS THE BEGINNING OF THE "MIDDLE ACADEMY" AND WAS THE FIRST TO SUSPEND JUDGEMENT WHEN CONFRONTED WITH CONTRADICTORY PRESENTATIONS. HE WAS ALSO THE FIRST TO TAKE POSITIONS ON BOTH SIDES OF AN ARGUMENT AND THE FIRST TO MODIFY THE SYSTEM ESTABLISHED BY PLATO AND MAKE IT MORE LIKE A DEBATE WITH QUESTIONS AND ANSWERS. INITIALLY, BEFORE HE LEFT FOR ATHENS, HE ATTENDED THE CLASSES OF A MATHEMATICIAN, WHO WAS ALSO A CITIZEN OF PITANE AND WITH HIM HE WENT TO SARDIS. LATER (IN ATHENS) HE WAS A STUDENT OF XANTHOS, AN ATHENIAN MUSIC TEACHER AND AFTER-

WARDS HE BECAME A STUDENT OF THEOPHRASTOS. THEN HE TRANSFERRED TO THE ACADEMY AND JOINED KRANTOR. ALTHOUGH HIS BROTHER . . . WANTED HIM TO CONCENTRATE ON RHETORIC, HE PREFERRED PHILOSOPHY. KRANTOR, WHO WAS IN LOVE WITH HIM, QUOTED (ONE DAY) THE LINE FROM EURIPIDES' (PLAY) ANDROMEDA:

> "OH MAIDEN, IF I SAVE YOU, WILL YOU BE GRATEFUL?"

TO WHICH ARKESILAOS ANSWERED WITH THE (PLAY"S) NEXT LINE:

> "TAKE ME STRANGER, WHETHER YOU WANT ME AS A SERVANT OR AS A WIFE"

FROM THEN ON THE TWO MEN LIVED TOGETHER. THEY SAY THAT THEOPHRASTOS, STUNG BY THE LOSS OF HIS STUDENT, REMARKED "WHAT A BRIGHT AND RESPONSIVE YOUTH LEFT MY SCHOOL." IN FACT, BESIDES BEING EXTREMELY LEARNED AND VERY FOND OF LITERATURE, ARKESILAOS ALSO GOT INVOLVED IN POETRY . . .

32 . . . ARKESILAOS TOOK OVER THE ACADEMY WHEN KRATES DIED . . . HE WROTE NO BOOKS BECAUSE, AS SOME SAY, HE REFRAINED FROM ANY CONCLUSIONS . . . IT SEEMS THAT HE ADMIRED PLATO AND OWNED ALL OF HIS BOOKS . . . BUT ALSO HE WAS CAPTIVATED BY DIALECTIC AND . . . BY ARGUMENTATION. FOR INSTANCE WHEN AN UGLY MAN FROM HIOS, WHO CONSIDERED HIMSELF GOOD-LOOKING AND WORE FANCY CLOTHES, DECLARED THAT NO WISE MAN SHOULD EVER FALL IN LOVE, ARKESILAOS REPLIED "YOU MEAN NOT EVEN WITH SOMEONE AS HANDSOME AND WELL-DRESSED AS YOU ARE?."

34. . . . . AND WHEN SOMEONE NOTORIOUSLY "GAY" (19) IMPLIED THAT ARKESILAOS WAS TOO PONDEROUS [BARYS] AND ARROGANT AND SAID TO HIM: "MY NOBLE LADY, WILL YOU ALLOW ME A QUESTION OR MUST I KEEP QUIET?" THE PHILOSOPHER REPLIED (WITH ANOTHER QUOTE):

> "WHY THIS ROUGH TALK, WOMAN, SO IMPROPER FOR YOU?"

37. MOST TALENTED IN FINDING THE RIGHT WORDS AND IN RESPONDING ON THE MARK, ARKESILAOS WAS ABLE TO BRING ANY DISCUSSION TO THE POINT AS THE OCCASION DEMANDED. HE WAS MORE PERSUASIVE THAN ANYBODY AND THIS ATTRACTED MORE STUDENTS YET TO HIS SCHOOL, EVEN THOUGH HIS SHARP WIT OFTEN HURT THEM. THEY PUT UP GLADLY WITH THIS, BECAUSE BASICALLY ARKESILAOS WAS EXTREMELY KIND AND HE FILLED HIS AUDIENCE WITH POSITIVE EXPECTATIONS. IN HIS WAY OF LIFE HE WAS VERY SOCIABLE AND READY TO BE A BENEFACTOR, ALTHOUGH HE MADE AN EFFORT TO HIDE ANY FAVORS HE GRANTED.

40. . . . HE LOVED LUXURY AND ENJOYED SPECIAL DINNERS WITH THOSE WHO SHARED HIS TASTES. HE LIVED OPENLY

WITH THEODOTE AND PHILA, TWO FEMALE COURTESANS FROM ELIS . . . BUT HE WAS ALSO VERY FOND OF BOYS AND MOST SUSCEPTIBLE TO THEIR CHARMS. MORE THAN MOST, HE LOVED DEMETRIOS . . . AND CLEOHARES. DEMOHARES, SON OF LAHES, WAS ALSO IN LOVE WITH CLEOHARES AND ONCE, WHEN ARKESILAOS CAUGHT THEM (IN THE ACT) HE LET THEM GO WITHOUT RESENTMENT. ON ANOTHER OCCASION DURING A DRINKING PARTY, WHEN HE WAS ASKED TO DISCUSS A CERTAIN THEORY HE REFUSED BY SAYING "THIS IS EXACTLY THE FEATURE OF PHILOSOPHY, TO KNOW WHEN IT IS TIME FOR SOMETHING."

43. ANOTHER CHARMING STORY IS THIS. WHEN SOMEONE ASKED ARKESILAOS WHY SO MANY STUDENTS SWITCHED OVER TO THE EPICUREAN SCHOOL BUT NEVER OUT OF IT TO ANOTHER SCHOOL, ARKESILAOS COMMENTED "A MAN CAN BECOME A EUNUCH (BE CASTRATED), BUT FROM A EUNUCH ONE CANNOT MAKE A MAN."

44. ACCORDING TO HERMIPPOS, ARKESILAOS DIED FROM DRINKING TOO LIBERALLY MUCH UNMIXED WINE WHICH AFFECTED HIS MIND. HE WAS OVER SEVENTY-FIVE YEARS OLD AT THAT TIME.

Hicks, R.D., Vol. I, pp. 404-422.

The Lyceum of Aristotle and Theophrastos

Originally the family came from Chalkis [*Halkis*], not far from Athens and went north, settling in the city of Stageira in Macedonia. Aristotle, the son of a medical practitioner and physician in the court of the Macedonian kings, was born there in 384 B.C. (Edel. 1967, p. 27). At the age of about eighteen he went to Athens to study with Plato who, comparing his quick mind and rapid learning to those of other students, said admiringly that this one required a harness while others needed a whip. Aristotle later said the same thing about his student Theophrastos in comparison to slower pupils. Perhaps due to a rising anti-Macedonian trend in Athens after the death of king Philip, or to disappointment for not being elected a successor of

Aristotle [*Aristoteles*] (Vienna) from Richter 1965/84.

Plato (Plato's nephew got the job), or according to another view (Edel, 1967, pp. 35–36) even before the death of Plato in 347 B.C. Aristotle left Athens and went to Assos, perhaps to establish a branch of the Academy there. After three years, about 345–344 B.C., he left Assos and went to Mytilene, probably influenced by Theophrastos, who came from the city of Eresos, on the western part of Lesbos. Many of Aristotle's biological observations date from that time, as indicated by the prevalence of place names from this area in his biological writings (Edel. 1967, p. 38). Theophrastos was with him then and has been considered as "a central figure in Aristotelian philosophy" (Edel. 1967, p. 38; Oxf. Class. Dict. p. 1058). An eminent philosopher in his own right, Theophrastos has also been credited for his editorial labors in putting together Aristotle's work from notes he found at the time of his teacher's death. On the basis of his pioneering studies of the habitats on Lesbos, Theophrastos is considered the first scientific ecologist (Hughes, 1988). After Mytilene, when Aristotle went to Macedonia, Theophrastos went with him and even acquired property in Stageira, Aristotle's hometown (Edel. 1967, p. 39).

It was in 343 or 342 that Aristotle accepted the invitation of King Philip to tutor his young son Alexander, who was then thirteen years old. So he went to Macedonia and for three years he was the teacher of the future conqueror of Asia. Although Aristotle did not follow Alexander in his campaigns, his nephew Callisthenes went along, until years later he was suspected of conspiracy and executed. Aristotle, after a brief stay again in his home at Stageira, returned to Athens in 335–34, at which time Alexander, now king, had established his dominance over the Greek city-states. Students of philosophy gathered around him in a grove sacred to Apollo Lykeios (meaning "of the wolves"), so the school was called the Lyceum [*Lykeion* in Greek]. Discussions were held all morning during long walks around the park or back and forth in the course of what was called a peripatos, meaning promenade. So the school was known as "peripatetic." The institution which developed around Aristotle became a research facility and had the first large reference library. For the actual establishment of a permanent school credit is given by some to Aristotle's successor, Theophrastos (Oxf. Class. Dict. p. 1058–9).

The ailments and weaknesses of old age, which Aristotle described in his "Rhetoric" II, such as distrust of people and indifference in their feelings, attention to what is useful more than to what is noble, living with memories rather than with expectations, the peripatetic philosopher did not experience. He died relatively young (almost all other Greek philosophers lived into their late seventies and some were more than 80–100 years old when they died) at the age of 62, in 322 B.C., the year after the death of Alexander the Great. Convinced that "only the good life," and not any life is of value and that human existence should not be accepted on simply any terms, Aristotle in his discussion of death also referred to Sappho (Rhetoric 1398b27). In his "Ethics" he showed again his familiarity with Lesbos by citing the example of a "flexible rule":

NIKOMAKHIAN ETHICS
BY ARISTOTLE [Aristoteles], 384–322 b.c.

V.-X 6 . . . THE PURPOSE OF ADJUSTMENTS IS TO RESTRUCTURE ANY LAW WHICH IS DEFICIENT DUE TO ITS ABSOLUTE GENERALITY. THE REASON THAT NOT EVERYTHING GOES ACCORDING TO A LAW IS THAT IN SOME CASES IT IS IMPOSSIBLE TO IMPOSE A (PREDEFINED) LEGAL SYSTEM. THEN A SPECIAL RULING IS NECESSARY, BECAUSE FOR SOMETHING THAT CANNOT BE DEFINED PRECISELY, THE RULES MUST ALSO BE FLEXIBLE, LIKE THE RULER OF THE LESBIAN BUILDERS, WHICH IS MADE OUT OF LEAD. THIS RULER DOES NOT REMAIN THE SAME BUT CAN BE CHANGED AND BENT TO FIT THE SHAPE OF THE STONES. THE SAME WAY A SPECIAL LEGAL RULING MUST BE ADAPTED TO EACH SITUATION.
Rackham, H., Vol. XIX, p. 316.

On the subject of political harmony or "concord," Aristotle cited the example of Pittakos of Mytilene:

NIKOMAKHIAN ETHICS
BY ARISTOTLE [Aristoteles], 384–322 b.c.

IX, VI
. . . THERE IS CONCORD [homonoia] IN A STATE WHEN EVERYONE AGREES THAT THE GOVERNMENT MUST BE (FREELY) ELECTED, OR THAT AN ALLIANCE MUST BE CONCLUDED OR THAT ONE MAN, LIKE PITTAKOS, OUGHT TO RULE (ALONE), PROVIDED THAT HE ALSO WANTS THAT.
Rackham, H., Vol. XIX, p. 542.

Aristotelian philosophy pervaded Christian theology from the early middle ages and has continued to exert a strong influence on all sciences, from pure and applied logic to aesthetics and ethics, until our own days. Posterity honors a Lesbian, the philosopher Theophrastos (370–286 b.c.), for continuing the tradition of Aristotle, the most rational and "scientific" school of thought in antiquity.

The historical geographer, Strabo [*Strabon*], taking his readers along the southern coast of Lesbos, mentioned Eresos (he spelled it Eressos) and its famous citizens.

GEOGRAPHY
BY STRABO [STRABON], 64/63 B.C.-21(?) A.D.

THEN AFTER PYRRHA IS ERESSOS FOUNDED ON A HILL AND STRETCHING TO THE SEA ... FROM ERESSOS CAME THE PERIPATETIC PHILOSOPHERS THEOPHRASTOS AND PHANIAS (20), WHO KNEW ARISTOTLE WELL. ORIGINALLY THEOPHRASTOS WAS CALLED TYRTAMOS AND IT WAS ARISTOTLE WHO RENAMED HIM THEOPHRASTOS, BOTH TO AVOID THE BAD SOUND [CACOPHONY] OF THE FORMER NAME AND TO INDICATE THE POWER OF HIS SPEECH [PHRASES].

Jones, Vol. VI, p. 144.

THE LIVES AND OPINIONS OF EMINENT PHILOSOPHERS
BY DIOGENES LAERTIOS, FIRST HALF OF THIRD CENTURY A.D.

BOOK V, CHAPTER 2

THEOPHRASTOS

SECTIONS 36-41. THEOPHRASTOS WAS A NATIVE OF ERESOS (ON LESBOS), THE SON OF A FULLER. HE FIRST ATTENDED LECTURES IN HIS NATIVE CITY, THEN AFTER STUDYING WITH PLATO IN ATHENS HE TRANSFERRED TO ARISTOTLE. LATER, WHEN ARISTOTLE WITHDREW TO CHALKIS, THEOPHRASTOS SUCCEEDED HIM AS HEAD OF THE SCHOOL IN THE 114TH OLYMPIAD (323 B.C.). THEOPHRASTOS WAS A VERY LOGICAL, WISE AND INDUSTRIOUS MAN AND, AS PAMPHILE (21) STATES, HE TAUGHT MENANDER, THE WRITER OF COMEDIES. ALSO HE WAS KNOWN FOR HIS CHARITABLE WORKS AND FOR HIS FONDNESS OF LITERATURE. CASSANDER (KING OF MACEDONIA, A SUCCESSOR OF ALEXANDER) GRANTED HIM AN AUDIENCE AND PTOLEMY (KING OF EGYPT AFTER THE DEATH OF ALEXANDER) SENT INVITATIONS TO HIM. THEOPHRASTOS WAS SO WELL ACCEPTED BY THE ATHENIANS THAT WHEN SOMEONE TRIED TO PROSECUTE HIM FOR IMPIETY, THE ACCUSER HIMSELF ALMOST GOT PUNISHED. ABOUT 2,000 STUDENTS IN ATHENS WERE ATTENDING THE LECTURES OF THEOPHRASTOS. BUT AS FAMOUS AS HE WAS, HE, LIKE ALL THE OTHER PHILOSOPHERS IN ATHENS, WAS FORCED TO LEAVE THE CITY TEMPORARILY, WHEN A NEW LAW WAS PASSED FORBIDDING ANYONE TO HEAD A SCHOOL OF PHI-

Theophrastos (Villa Albani, Rome)
Richter, 1965/84

SAGES, SOLDIERS, SLAVES AND SCHOLARS

LOSOPHY WITHOUT THE CONSENT OF THE ASSEMBLY AND OF THE PEOPLE, ON PENALTY OF DEATH. BEFORE LONG HOWEVER, THE PHILOSOPHERS RETURNED, WHEN THAT PROPOSAL WAS DECLARED ILLEGAL AND THE LAW WAS REPEALED. THE MAIN REASON FOR THAT ACTION IN FACT WAS TO ENABLE THEOPHRASTOS TO COME BACK AND BE AMONG HIS FOLLOWERS.

ACTUALLY THE PHILOSOPHER'S REAL NAME WAS TYRTAMOS. HE WAS CALLED THEOPHRASTOS BY ARISTOTLE, ON ACCOUNT OF HIS SUPERB VERBAL EXPRESSIONS OR PHRASINGS (THEO, DIVINE; PHRASE, EXPRESSION). ACCORDING TO THE BOOK BY ARISTIPPOS ON "LEISURES AND PLEASURES OF OLD TIME," EVEN THOUGH ARISTOTLE WAS HIS TEACHER, THEOPHRASTOS WAS SEXUALLY ATTRACTED BY HIS SON NICOMACHOS [NICOMAKHOS]. AMONG THE FAMOUS EXPRESSIONS OF THEOPHRASTOS WORTH REPEATING ARE, "I TRUST MORE AN UNHARNESSED HORSE THAN AN UNSTRUCTURED DISCUSSION" AND "TIME IS THE COSTLIEST OF ALL CONSUMER GOODS."

THEOPHRASTOS DIED OLD AT THE AGE OF EIGHTY-FIVE, SOON AFTER HE HAD RETIRED FROM HIS WORK. THEY SAY THAT WHEN HIS STUDENTS ASKED IF HE HAD ANY FINAL WORDS, HE REPLIED "I HAVE NO FINAL MESSAGES EXCEPT THAT LIFE SEEMS TO PROMISE MANY PLEASURES BUT IN FACT AS SOON AS WE BEGIN TO LIVE WE ARE READY TO DIE . . . THE VOID OF OUR LIFE IS BIGGER THAN ANY REWARDS FROM IT." THE ENTIRE POPULATION OF ATHENS ESCORTED HIS FUNERAL, SO MUCH THEY HONORED THIS MAN.

SECTION 42-50. THEOPHRASTOS LEFT A LARGE NUMBER OF BOOKS AND I BELIEVE THEY ARE WORTH LISTING, BECAUSE THEY ARE SO EXCEPTIONALLY FULL OF EVERY QUALITY AND VIRTUE. THESE ARE THE TITLES OF HIS BOOKS (DIOGENES LISTS 228 BOOK TITLES OF WHICH THE FOLLOWING SEEM TO BE MOST INTERESTING):

ABOUT THE SENSES OR SENSATION
THE VARIETY OF VIRTUES
ABOUT LOVE [EROTIC]
ABOUT OLD AGE
CONCERNING HAPPINESS
ABOUT SPIRITUAL EXCITATION AND FRENZY [ENTHUSIASM]
ABOUT (THE ART OF) ARGUMENT, VOLS. 1-18
ON WILL-POWER AND WHAT IS VOLUNTARY
ABOUT PLEASURE [HEDONE]
ABOUT DIZZINESS AND FAINTING
ABOUT PERSPIRATION
ON MELANCHOLY
ABOUT HONEY
ABOUT INTOXICATION [METHE] - (REF. TABLE E)
COMPENDIUM OF LAWS, VOLS. 1-10
ABOUT WINE AND OIL
LEGISLATURE AND POLITICS
ON CUSTOMS (ETHICS)
ABOUT INSANITY
ABOUT PASSIONS

ABOUT PUNISHMENT
ABOUT FRIENDSHIP
ON NATURAL SCIENCE
ABOUT FALSE PLEASURES
ABOUT HARMONY
ON GOOD JUDGEMENT
ON HUMOR (WHAT IS RIDICULOUS OR FUNNY)
THEORIES OF THE PHYSICISTS VOLS. 1-16

ALL THESE WRITINGS AMOUNT TO 232,802 LINES.

SECTION 51. I HAVE ALSO FOUND THEOPHRASTOS' LAST WILL AND TESTAMENT WHICH READ AS FOLLOWS:

"LET ALL BE WELL, BUT SHOULD ANYTHING HAPPEN THESE ARE MY INSTRUCTIONS FOR THE DISPOSITION OF MY PROPERTY. EVERYTHING IN MY HOME SHALL GO TO THE SONS OF LEON. OF THE TRUST FUNDS MANAGED BY HIPPARKHOS, APPROPRIATIONS SHOULD BE MADE TO COMPLETE AND REDECORATE THE MUSEUM WITH THE STATUES OF THE GODDESSES AND TO DO WHATEVER IS NECESSARY TO EMBELLISH THEM. THE BUST OF ARISTOTLE SHOULD BE PLACED BACK IN THE TEMPLE ALONG WITH THE REST OF THE OBJECTS DEDICATED TO THE TEMPLE WHICH WERE FORMERLY THERE. NEXT, THE SMALL ART CLOISTER ADJACENT TO THE MUSEUM SHOULD BE RESTORED IN SUCH A WAY AS NOT TO LOOK ANY WORSE THAN BEFORE. THAT SHOULD INCLUDE A RESTORATION OF THE TABLES AND ILLUSTRATIONS IN THE LOWER ARCHWAYS WHICH SHOW THE TRAVELS OF THE EXPLORERS. THE ALTAR SHOULD BE REPAIRED SO THAT IT WILL BE SHAPELY AND PERFECT. IT IS ALSO MY WISH THAT A LIFE-SIZE BUST OF NICOMAKHOS SHOULD BE COMPLETED. PRAXITELES (THE SCULPTOR) HAS ALREADY RECEIVED THE CONTRACT PRICE BUT ANY ADDITIONAL COST SHOULD BE TAKEN FROM THE TRUST FUND . . . THE GARDEN AND THE PROMENADE AND ALL OF THE HOUSES ADJOINING THE PARK I BEQUEATH TO MY FRIENDS LISTED BELOW SO THAT ANYTIME THEY WISH THEY CAN HAVE DISCUSSIONS AND PHILOSOPHIZE TOGETHER THERE . . . I SHOULD BE BURIED ANYWHERE IN THE GARDEN THAT SEEMS APPROPRIATE, WITH NOTHING UNUSUAL FOR MY FUNERAL OR FOR THE MONUMENT ON MY GRAVE. AFTER MY DEATH EVERYTHING AROUND THE TEMPLE, THE MONUMENT, THE GARDEN AND THE PROMENADE SHOULD CONTINUE TO BE UNDER THE CARE OF POMPYLOS, WHO LIVES CLOSE BY, AND THE OTHER SLAVES WHOM I HAVE FREED . . . TO THEM ALSO I BEQUEATH THE YOUNG MAID, SOMATALE . . . (LISTED FRIENDS TO RECEIVE MONEY, SLAVES TO BE FREED, PROPERTY TO BE ALLOCATED, ETC.).

THIS IS HOW HIS WILL READ.

SOME PEOPLE SAY THAT ERASISTRATOS THE PHYSICIAN [IATROS] ALSO ATTENDED HIS (THEOPHRASTOS') LECTURES AND THIS IS LIKELY.

Hicks, R.D., 1966, Vol. I, pp. 482–508.

In their dinner talk about the dress and appearance of famous people, the "Dining Scholars" of Athenaeus [*Athenaios*] described Theophrastos in rather flamboyant terms.

> **DINING SCHOLARS [DEIPNOSOPHISTS]**
> BY ATHENAIOS OF NAUCRATIS, CA. 200 A.D.
> **I.21.A-B.** HERMIPPOS SAYS THAT THEOPHRASTOS USED TO COME TO THE SCHOOL [PERIPATOS] AT THE REGULAR TIME, SHINING AND DRESSED BRILLIANTLY. AFTER HE HAD BEEN SEATED, HE WOULD DELIVER HIS LECTURES WITH UNRESTRAINED MOVEMENTS AND GESTURES. AT ONE TIME, IMITATING A GOURMET EATER, HE STUCK HIS TONGUE OUT AND LICKED HIS LIPS.
> Gulick, C.R., 1969, Vol. I, p. 90.

Another comment about permissible or extravagant body movement is characteristic of the times.

> **DINING SCHOLARS [DEIPNOSOPHISTS]**
> BY ATHENAIOS OF NAUCRATIS, CA. 200 A.D.
> **I.22C.** ACCORDING TO THEOPHRASTOS, THE FIRST MAN TO MOVE HIS BODY RHYTHMICALLY WHILE PLAYING WAS THE FLUTE-PLAYER ANDRON OF CATANIA; SO FOR THE ANCIENTS TO "ACT LIKE A SICILIAN" MEANT TO DANCE.
> Gulick 1969, Vol. I, p. 96.

The same group of Athenaios' "dining experts," in an extended discussion of wines and wine-making, referred to Theophrastos and also to Phanias (mostly spelled Phainias, or Latinized as Phaenias), another philosopher from Eresos on Lesbos (20).

> **DINING SCHOLARS [DEIPNOSOPHISTS]**
> BY ATHENAIOS OF NAUCRATIS, CA. 200 A.D.
> **I.31(F)-32(A-B).** CONCERNING THE MAKING OF AROMATIC WINES, THIS IS WHAT PHANIAS OF ERESOS HAD TO SAY: "ONE PITCHER OF SEA-WATER, ADDED TO FIFTY PITCHERS OF GRAPE MUST, PRODUCES A FLOWERY BOUQUET [ANTHOSMIA]." AND AGAIN: "THE BOUQUET IS STRONGER IN THE WINE FROM YOUNGER THAN FROM OLDER VINES." THEN HE CONTINUED: "THEY STEPPED ON THE HARDER GRAPES AND STORED THE JUICE, WHICH BECAME FRAGRANT." THEOPHRASTOS HAS SAID THAT THE WINE SERVED AT THE TOWN HALL ON THASOS IS WONDERFULLY DELICIOUS AND THIS IS DUE TO ITS SEASONING: "IN THE CLAY WINE-JAR [KERAMION] THEY PLACE A WHEAT-FLOUR DOUGH MIXED WITH HONEY. THIS WAY THE WINE MAINTAINS ITS OWN FRAGRANCE WHILE IT RECEIVES ITS SWEETNESS FROM THE DOUGH." FURTHER ON HE SAYS: "IF

> ONE MIXES HARD BUT FRAGRANT WINE WITH A SMOOTH BUT ODORLESS TYPE... THE LATTER SUPPLIES THE SMOOTHNESS AND THE FIRST ONE THE FRAGRANCE."
>
> Gulick, C.R., 1969, Vol. I, pp. 138-140.

According to Athenaios, Theophrastos also bequeathed funds for the continuation of philosophical symposia.

DINING SCHOLARS [Deipnosophists]
BY ATHENAIOS OF NAUCRATIS, CA. 200 A.D.
BOOK V, 185C-186A.
> WINE HAS PROPERTIES CONDUCIVE TO FRIENDSHIP AS IT WARMS THE SOUL AND MAKES IT MORE EFFUSIVE. SO THEY (THE HOSTS) DID NOT FIRST ASK THE UNKNOWN VISITORS WHO THEY WERE BUT ONLY LATER. THIS WAY THEY HONORED THE ACT OF HOSPITALITY ITSELF AND NOT EACH ONE INDIVIDUAL PERSONALLY... MANY OF THE PHILOSOPHERS IN THE CITY (OF ATHENS) HAVE GATHERINGS OF THIS TYPE... AND THEOPHRASTOS LEFT FUNDS FOR SUCH MEETINGS, NOT, BY ZEUS, TO GATHER FOR ORGIES AND DEBAUCHERY BUT TO CARRY OUT WISELY AND AFTER PROPER EDUCATION THE PRACTICES THAT MEET THE REQUIREMENTS FOR A SYMPOSIUM.
>
> Gulick 1967, Vol. II, p. 320.

A prominent authority of our times and translator of many Greek works, including those of Theophrastos (Edmonds, 1966, *Introduction*, p. 10), considers the philosopher's will "... an historical document of the greatest interest. We gain from it among other things a clear notion of the Garden (meaning Aristotle's Lyceum), which was the undoubted ancestor of the modern college." Edmonds, citing Theophrastos' extended botanical works, calls him "a great classifier" and describes the philosopher's ever-popular small book on "Characters" as another example of classification, sorting out the "species" of human personalities in a somewhat lighter, humorous style. The text is admittedly rigid—a philosopher trying to be funny!—with oversimplifications and caricature which by modern standards often seem dull. Yet it is Theophrastos' most famous and imitated work, not so much as a series of "moral essays" but as a reference for handbooks on rhetoric and for comic plays (Oxf. Class. Dict. p. 1058). "Characters" which is a transliteration of the original title (meaning more exactly "Human Personality Traits," from the Greek word "character," a carving, a trait) was written in 319 B.C., four years after Theophrastos had taken over the directorship of the Peripatetic school. The names of the thirty "Personality

Characteristics" (the titles of all sections are abstract nouns, feminine in Greek) are difficult to translate. The rendering by Edmonds at times is more amusing (unintentionally) than the Greek original. It seems almost impossible to make literal comparisons between ancient Greek, modern Greek and modern English personality labels.

CHARACTERS
BY THEOPHRASTOS, 370(?)-287/5 B.C.
INTRODUCTION (22)
EVERY TIME I HAVE STUDIED HUMAN MENTALITY IN THE PAST I HAVE WONDERED AND I MAY NEVER STOP WONDERING WHY, EVEN THOUGH THE CLIMATE IS THE SAME EVERYWHERE IN GREECE AND ALL GREEKS ARE BROUGHT UP ALIKE, WE DO NOT HAVE THE SAME BEHAVIOR PATTERNS. I HAVE OBSERVED HUMAN NATURE FOR A LONG TIME, I HAVE INTERVIEWED MANY DIVERSE PERSONALITIES AND I HAVE MADE PRECISE COMPARISONS BOTH OF GOOD AND OF VICIOUS INDIVIDUALS, SO I HAVE UNDERTAKEN TO WRITE A BOOK ON HOW EACH OF THEM HANDLE THEMSELVES IN LIFE. I WILL OUTLINE THE MAJOR TYPES OF BEHAVIOR AND HOW THESE FIT THE REQUIREMENTS OF LIVING. . . . I WILL DISCUSS FIRST THE WORST TENDENCIES, AVOIDING LENGTHY INTRODUCTIONS AND ANYTHING THAT IS BESIDE THE POINT . . .

Of the thirty "characters" described, excerpts from six are quoted here in English [transliteration of the Greek in brackets].

I. DISSIMULATION ["IRONY"]
IT APPEARS THAT DISSIMULATION, OR DISSEMBLING, AS A FORM OF BEHAVIOR GENERALLY IS THE WORST TYPE OF AFFECTATION IN ACTS AND IN WORDS. A DISSEMBLER IS A PERSON WHO WILL COME UP AND TALK TO HIS ENEMY, NOT SHOWING HIS HATRED. HE WILL COMPLIMENT IN THEIR PRESENCE THOSE WHOM HE WAS SECRETLY ATTACKING. HE WILL FEIGN REGRET TOWARDS SOMEONE WHO HAS JUST LOST A CASE AGAINST HIM, AS IF THE LOSS WAS UNDESERVED. HE WILL GO ALONG WITH THOSE SPEAKING EVIL AGAINST HIM AND WILL SMILE AS IF HE APPROVED WHAT THEY SAID . . . HE WILL NOT ADMIT TAKING ANY ACTION BUT WILL SAY HE IS STILL CONSIDERING THE MATTER, OFTEN CLAIMING THAT HE HAS JUST ARRIVED, OR THAT ONLY LATELY HE JOINED THE GROUP, OR THAT HE HAD NOT BEEN WELL . . . HE PRETENDS NOT TO HAVE HEARD WHAT HE ACTUALLY HEARD AND NOT TO HAVE SEEN WHAT HE SAW. AFTER AGREEING TO SOMETHING HE COUNTERS THAT HE DOES NOT REMEMBER. SOME THINGS HE PROMISES TO THINK ABOUT, OTHERS HE SAYS HE DOES NOT KNOW, OTHERS APPEAR TO PUZZLE HIM. IN GENERAL HE IS NOTORIOUS FOR REPEATING OFTEN "I DON'T BELIEVE IT," "I DO NOT UNDERSTAND," "I AM

AMAZED" . . . "THIS IS NOT WHAT I WAS TOLD," "HOW STRANGE," "TELL THAT TO SOMEONE ELSE" . . .

IV. BOORISHNESS ["AGROIKIA," MEANING PEASANT MANNERS]

BOORISHNESS OR CRUDENESS SHOWS AN IGNORANCE OR DISREGARD OF WHAT IS NOT APPROPRIATE AND A CRUDE PERSON IS SUCH THAT HE WILL DRINK A KYKEON (INTOXICATING BEVERAGE—SEE CHAPTER IV-C, NOTE 25) BEFORE GOING TO THE ASSEMBLY. HE IS PRONE TO SAY THAT A PERFUME SMELLS NO BETTER THAN THYME. HE WEARS SHOES TOO BIG FOR HIS FEET AND HE TALKS WITH A VERY LOUD VOICE. HE DOES NOT TRUST HIS FRIENDS AND RELATIVES, YET CONFIDES IMPORTANT MATTERS TO HIS SERVANTS. HE DISCUSSES THE DEBATES OF THE ASSEMBLY WITH HIRED LABORERS ON HIS FARM AND HE SITS WITH HIS COAT ABOVE THE KNEES SO THAT HIS NAKED PARTS SHOW UNDER IT. HE PAYS NO ATTENTION . . . TO EVENTS OR TO PEOPLE IN THE STREETS BUT STOPS AND ADMIRES A PASSING BULL, OR A DONKEY, OR A GOAT. HE IS LIKELY TO EAT STRAIGHT FROM THE CUPBOARD AND TO DRINK HIS WINE STRONG (UNDILUTED). HE SECRETLY MAKES LOVE TO THE GIRL IN THE BAKERY, THEN HELPS HER GRIND THE GRAIN FOR EVERYONE, INCLUDING HIMSELF. HE FEEDS THE ANIMALS WHILE HE EATS AND PERSONALLY ANSWERS A KNOCK ON HIS DOOR. . . . HE IS THE ONE TO SING IN THE PUBLIC BATHS . . .

VI. SHAMELESSNESS, INSENSITIVITY ["APONOIA"]

SHAMELESSNESS IS THE ACCEPTANCE OF OR INDULGENCE IN DISHONORABLE ACTION AND WORDS. THE SHAMELESS PERSON IS SUCH THAT WILL SWEAR TO ANYTHING, WILL LISTEN TO ABUSIVE TALK AGAINST HIM WITH INDIFFERENCE, RIDICULE THE AUTHORITIES, AND HIS GENERAL ATTITUDE [ETHOS] IS VULGAR, INDECENT AND READY FOR ANYTHING. HE IS SO UNINHIBITED THAT HE WILL DANCE THE KORDAX (AN INDECENT VULGAR DANCE) EVEN WHEN SOBER. . . . HE IS PRONE TO RUN INNS, MANAGE PROSTITUTES [A PORNOHERD] HANDLE TAX COLLECTIONS AND WILL NOT AVOID OR DISAPPROVE OF ANY DEGRADING JOB BUT WILL BE A PUBLIC ANNOUNCER [KYRYX, TOWN-CRIER], A COOK, OR A DICE-THROWER. HE WILL NOT TAKE CARE OF HIS MOTHER, MAY BE ARRESTED FOR THEFT AND IS LIKELY TO SPEND MORE TIME IN JAIL THAN IN HIS OWN HOME. . . . HE MAY APPEAR OFTEN IN COURT SOMETIMES AS A DEFENDANT, OTHER TIMES AS A PLAINTIFF, IN SOME CASES REFUSING TO TESTIFY AND IN OTHERS COMING WITH BOXES AND BUNDLES OF WRITTEN DOCUMENTS IN HIS HANDS. . . . HE DOES NOT DISAPPROVE OF THE MARKET AND WILL BE A BROKER HIMSELF, READY TO LEND MONEY AND THEN CHARGE HUGE INTEREST DAILY. HE IS NOT RELUCTANT TO MAKE THE ROUNDS AND BE A SUPPLIER FOR TAVERNS, FISH-HOUSES AND DELICATESSEN STORES AND THEN PUT HIS SALES' COMMISSION IN HIS MOUTH.

XI. LOATHSOMENESS OR RIDICULOUSNESS ["BDELYRIA"]

IT IS NOT DIFFICULT TO DEFINE LOATHSOMENESS. IT IS SHALLOW AND EMBARRASSING BUFFOONERY AND THE LOATHSOME, DISGUSTING PERSON IS SUCH THAT COMING ACROSS FREE WOMEN HE LIFTS HIS CLOAK TO SHOW HIS PRIVATE PART. IN THE THEATER HE CLAPS WHEN ALL OTHERS STOP, WILL HISS THE ACTORS WHOM THE OTHERS ADMIRE AND WHEN THE WHOLE AUDIENCE IS QUIET HE WILL STICK HIS HEAD UP AND HICCUP, TO MAKE EVERYONE LOOK. . . . HE WILL CALL BY NAME SOMEONE IN THE COMPANY WHOM HE HARDLY KNOWS. IF HE SEES SOMEONE WHO IS IN A HURRY HE WILL TRY TO MAKE HIM WAIT. HE DOES HIS OWN SHOPPING AND HIRES FLUTE-GIRLS HIMSELF. THEN HE SHOWS WHAT HE HAS BOUGHT TO PASSERS-BY AND INVITES THEM TO SHARE THE FEAST. STANDING IN FRONT OF A BARBER-SHOP OR A PERFUMERY HE DECLARES THAT HE IS ABOUT TO GET DRUNK. HE CUSSES IN FRONT OF HIS MOTHER JUST AS SHE IS BACK FROM THE DIVINE-ORACLE. . . . AT A FLUTE RECITAL HE IS THE ONLY ONE CLAPPING WITH HIS HANDS TO BEAT TIME AND LATER REPRIMANDS THE FLUTIST BECAUSE SHE STOPPED TOO SOON. IF THIS MAN EVER WANTS TO SPIT HE WILL DO IT ACROSS THE TABLE AT THE WINE-SERVER.

XVI. SUPERSTITION ["DEISIDAIMONIA"]

NEEDLESS TO SAY THAT SUPERSTITIOUSNESS CAN BE CONSIDERED A FORM OF COWARDICE IN RELATION TO THE DIVINE SPIRIT. THE SUPERSTITIOUS PERSON WILL NOT START HIS DAY WITHOUT WASHING HIS HANDS AND SPRINKLE HIMSELF WITH (HOLY) WATER FROM THE "NINE SPRINGS" AND WITHOUT PUTTING A SACRED LAUREL LEAF IN HIS MOUTH. IF A CAT CROSSES HIS PATH HE WILL NOT GO ANY FARTHER UNTIL SOMEONE ELSE GOES FIRST OVER THAT ROAD, OR UNTIL AFTER HE TOSSES THREE STONES IN THAT DIRECTION. . . . HE IS EVER PURIFYING HIS HOUSE . . . . . . AND IF AN OWL HOOTS AS HE GOES BY, HE BECOMES VERY UPSET AND WILL NOT CONTINUE ON HIS WAY BUT WILL CALL (THE GODDESS) ATHENA FOR PROTECTION. HE WILL NOT STEP CLOSE TO A GRAVE OR NEAR A DEAD PERSON, NOT EVEN NEAR A WOMAN AFTER CHILDBIRTH, TO PREVENT—AS HE WOULD SAY—CONTAMINATION. ON THE FOURTH AND SEVENTH DAYS OF EVERY MONTH HE WILL ORDER WINE RITUALLY POURED AT HOME AND WILL GO TO BUY MYRTLE, INCENSE AND A SACRED FIGURE, THEN WILL RETURN TO HIS HOUSE TO DECORATE AND MAKE OFFERINGS TO THE HERMAPHRODITE STATUES ALL DAY LONG. WHENEVER HE SEES A DREAM HE MARCHES ON TO THE DREAM INTERPRETERS, OR TO THE SOOTH-SAYERS, OR TO THOSE WHO EXPLAIN THE SIGNS OF THE BIRDS AND WILL INQUIRE ABOUT WHICH ONE OF THE GODS HE OUGHT TO ADDRESS IN HIS PRAYERS. . . . HE WOULD BE EXPECTED TO BE AMONG THOSE WHO FAITHFULLY GO TO THE BEACH TO POUR SEA-WATER ON THEMSELVES. . . . AND IF HE ENCOUNTERS A MAD PERSON OR AN EPILEPTIC HE SHUDDERS AND SPITS ON THEIR CHEST.

XXIV. ARROGANCE ["HYPEREPHANIA"]

ARROGANCE IS THE DISDAIN FOR EVERYONE BUT ONE'S SELF AND THE ARROGANT PERSON IS SUCH AS WILL TELL A FRIEND COMING TO TALK TO HIM AFTER HAVING DINNER TOGETHER, THAT HE WILL ONLY SPEAK TO HIM WHILE WALKING (OUT). IF HE HAD HELPED SOMEONE HE REMEMBERS TO TALK ABOUT IT. HE REFUSES TO ACCEPT ASSIGNMENTS SAYING THAT HE DOES NOT HAVE TIME FOR THEM. HE IS UNWILLING TO APPROACH AND TO SPEAK TO OTHERS FIRST.... WHEN HE INVITES PEOPLE FOR DINNER HE DOES NOT SIT WITH THEM BUT HAS SOMEBODY WORKING FOR HIM TAKE CARE OF THE GUESTS. WHEN HE TRAVELS HE SENDS SOMEONE AHEAD TO ANNOUNCE HIS ARRIVAL. NO ONE IS ALLOWED TO COME IN WHEN HE IS ANOINTING HIMSELF, OR BATHING, OR EATING. NEEDLESS TO SAY THAT WHEN HE IS CONDUCTING BUSINESS HE HAS A CLERK DO THE ACCOUNTING.... IN HIS CORRESPONDENCE HE DOES NOT WRITE "PLEASE DO ME A FAVOR," BUT "I WANT THIS DONE"...

Edmonds, J.M., 1946, pp. 36-104.

Four centuries later, Plutarch made respectful reference to Theophrastos, citing the philosopher's theory of music.

ON LISTENING TO LECTURES
BY PLUTARCH [Plutarkhos] C. 46–C. 120 A.D.

I BELIEVE THAT YOU WILL NOT FIND OBJECTIONABLE SOME PRELIMINARY REMARKS ABOUT THE SENSE OF HEARING [acoustics], WHICH THEOPHRASTOS CONSIDERED AS THE MOST SENSITIVELY EMOTIONAL [pathetic] OF ALL. NOTHING WE SEE, OR TASTE, OR TOUCH BRINGS ON SUCH ECSTASY, TURMOIL AND EXCITEMENT AS POSSESS THE SOUL WITH THE BEATS AND BANGS AND SOUNDS THAT REACH OUR HEARING. BUT HEARING CAN BE MORE RATIONAL THAN EMOTIONAL.

Babbitt, F.C., 1927-49, Vol. I, p. 206.

Another Lesbian pupil of Aristotle and friend of Theophrastos was Phanias (22) or *Phainias* (Encyc. Brit., Vol. 17) of Eresos. He flourished around 300 B.C. and wrote books on Logic, Botany, Socratic philosophy and also on historical events in the Greek world from the chronological reference point of the succession of magistrates in his native city on Lesbos. His treatises on the rule of dictators [*tyrants*] were noted for their "moral judgements" (Oxf. Class. Dict. 1970/78, p. 809).

Phainias was quoted in the *Dining Scholars* by Athenaios (I,16e–f) in reference to ancient games of dice, with the claim that Leon of Mitylene—*sic* (ref. to notes 6 and 11, Chap. II and IV no.6)—"was never defeated at draughts" (Gulick, Vol. I., p. 72). The writings of both Theophrastos and Phainias of Eresos *About Plants* were quoted repeatedly by

Athenaios of Naucratis in his *Dining Scholars*. This third century Hellenistic author used the Lesbian philosopher-botanists' data about the growing and classification of mushrooms and truffles (II, 61f-62a, Gulick, Vol. I, p. 268) and again in relation to a "round-table" discussion of fruit, specifically peaches [*persics*] and citrus (III, 82-83, Gulick, Vol. I, p. 356). Altogether, the cosmopolitan Egyptian-Greek writer about pleasure, wisdom, good food and wine, mentioned Theophrastos' work and opinions over eighty times in fifteen "Books" of his *Dining Scholars* [*Deipnosophists*]. One of the longest sections in this extensive work was about figs and it referred in detail to the work of Theophrastos.

DINING SCHOLARS [DEIPNOSOPHISTS]
BY ATHENAIOS OF NAUCRATIS, CA. 200 A.D.
BOOK III, 77.A-C
IN THE SECOND BOOK OF HIS "HISTORY OF PLANTS" THEOPHRASTOS SAID THAT THERE IS A VARIETY OF FIG-TREE WHICH IS LIKE THE SO-CALLED ARATEIAN. IN THE THIRD BOOK HE TOLD ABOUT A BUSH-LIKE FIG-TREE WITH LEAVES LIKE THOSE OF THE LINDEN TREE, WHICH GROWS IN THE REGION OF THE TROJAN MOUNT IDA; IT BEARS RED FIGS ABOUT THE SIZE OF AN OLIVE BUT MORE ROUND, WHICH TASTE LIKE A MEDLAR. THE SAME THEOPHRASTOS, IN THE FOURTH BOOK OF HIS "HISTORY OF PLANTS" WROTE AS FOLLOWS ABOUT THE SO-CALLED CYPRIAN FIG-TREE FOUND ON CRETE: "THE SO-CALLED CYPRIAN FIG-TREE ON CRETE BEARS THE FRUIT ON THE STEM AND ON THE THICKEST END-BRANCHES, BY SENDING OUT SMALL LEAFLESS SHOOTS RESEMBLING A ROOTLET, TO WHICH THE FRUIT IS ATTACHED. THE STEM IS LARGE, SIMILAR TO THAT OF THE WHITE POPLAR AND THE LEAF IS MORE LIKE THAT OF THE ELM. IT PRODUCES FOUR CROPS, THE SAME NUMBER AS ITS SPROUTINGS. ITS SWEETNESS IS CLOSE TO THAT OF THE (COMMON) FIG-TREE AND THE FLESH INSIDE MORE LIKE THAT OF THE WILD FIG; THE SIZE IS ABOUT THE SAME AS THAT OF A PLUM."

Gulick, 1969, Vol. I, p. 332.

The word *cactus* can be traced to the writings of Theophrastos and of Phainias from Eresos, according to Athenaios' *Dining Scholars*.

DINING SCHOLARS [DEIPNOSOPHISTS]
BY ATHENAIOS OF NAUCRATIS, CA. 200 A.D.
BOOK II, 70.D-E.
PHAINIAS, IN HIS FIFTH BOOK "ABOUT PLANTS" CALLED A CERTAIN THORNY PLANT A "SICILIAN CACTUS" AND SO DID THEOPHRASTOS IN THE SIXTH BOOK OF HIS TREATISE ON PLANTS: "THE CACTUS, AS THEY CALL IT, IS FOUND IN SICILY AND IT DOES NOT EXIST IN GREECE. IT SENDS FORTH ABOVE

GROUND STALKS DIRECTLY FROM THE ROOT AND ITS LEAF IS FLAT AND THORNY. THE STALK IS WHAT IS CALLED CACTUS. WHEN PEELED IT IS EDIBLE ALTHOUGH SLIGHTLY BITTER AND CAN BE PRESERVED IN BRINE. ANOTHER SPECIES, CALLED PTERNIX, SENDS UP ERECT STALKS AND IS ALSO EDIBLE. WHEN THE DOWNY PRICKLES ARE REMOVED THE FRUIT-SHELL RESEMBLES THE BRAIN (HEART) OF PALMS AND IS ALSO GOOD TO EAT; THAT THEY CALL ASKALERON." BUT WHO, NOT CONVINCED BY THESE DESCRIPTIONS, WOULD NOT SAY WITH CONFIDENCE THAT THE CACTUS IS WHAT THE ROMANS, WHO ARE NOT FAR FROM SICILY, CALL CARDUS AND, CLEARLY, WHAT THE GREEKS NAME KINARA (ARTICHOKE)?

Gulick, 1969, Vol., I, pp. 306-308.

In connection with seafood, the writings of Theophrastos of Eresos and also of two other Lesbians, Kallias and Kharis of Mytilene, are quoted concerning the classification of species, their places of origin, tasting qualities and, peripherally, the production of pearls.

DINING SCHOLARS [Deipnosophists]
BY ATHENAIOS OF NAUCRATIS, CA. 200 A.D.

BOOK III, 85.F.

KALLIAS OF MITYLENE (SIC, CF. NOTE 6 AND ALSO CHAP. V AND NOTE VI-5) SAID IN CONNECTION WITH THE USE OF THE WORD LIMPET [LEPAS] BY ALKAIOS THAT THERE IS AN ODE AMONG ALKAIOS' WORKS THE BEGINNING OF WHICH IS: "CHILD OF THE ROCKS AND OF THE GREY SEA" AND ITS END IS WRITTEN SO: "OH LIMPET OF THE SEA, YOU OPEN LOOSE THE SPIRITS OF CHILDREN."

Gulick, 1969, Vol. I, p. 368.

Anticipating some of the excesses of the Epicureans (not endorsed by Epicuros himself), Theophrastos had some comments about perfumes, pearls and sexuality, too.

DINING SCHOLARS [Deipnosophists]
BY ATHENAIOS OF NAUCRATIS, CA. 200 A.D.

I.18D. GOURMET-COOKING AND ALSO PERFUME-MAKING HAVE REACHED SUCH EXCESSIVE REFINEMENT THAT EVEN BATHING IN A TUB FULL OF PERFUMES MAY NOT BE ENOUGH TO SATISFY SOME PEOPLE . . . ALSO IN FULL BLOOM ARE THE CREATIVE CRAFTS FOR PASTRIES AND THE SKILLS OF SEXUALITY, TO THE POINT THAT MEN HAVE DEVISED SPONGE SUPPOSITORIES, PRESUMING THAT THESE LEAD TO MORE NUMEROUS ORGASMS. THEOPHRASTOS TALKS ABOUT CERTAIN STIMULANTS SO POTENT THAT THEY ACHIEVE UP TO SEVENTY SEXUAL ACTS, IN THE LAST OF WHICH THE DISCHARGE IS BLOOD.

Gulick, 1969, Vol. I, p. 80.

BOOK III 93.A-C.
CONCERNING SHELLFISH FOUND IN THE AREA AROUND INDIA—IT WILL NOT BE UNTIMELY TO MENTION THESE, IN VIEW OF THE CURRENT VOGUE OF PEARLS—THEOPHRASTOS, IN HIS WORK "ABOUT STONES" WROTE AS FOLLOWS: "AMONG THE STONES THAT ARE MUCH ADMIRED ARE THE SO-CALLED MARGARITES (PEARLS), OF A TRANSLUCENT NATURE, FROM WHICH THEY MAKE LUXURIOUS NECKLACES. THEY ARE FOUND IN SHELLS SIMILAR TO THE PINNA BUT SMALLER AND THEIR SIZE IS THAT OF A LARGE FISH EYE."
. . . IN THE SEVENTH VOLUME OF HIS "TALES OF ALEXANDER" KHARIS OF MITYLENE (SIC, REF. NOTES CHAP. II AND VI) SAID THAT A CREATURE SIMILAR TO THE OYSTER IS CAUGHT IN THE INDIAN SEA AND ALSO IN THE WATERS AROUND ARMENIA, PERSIA, SUSA AND BABYLONIA. IT IS LARGE AND OBLONG WITH A GOOD AMOUNT OF FLESH INSIDE, WHICH IS WHITE AND VERY FRAGRANT. FROM THESE THEY TAKE OUT WHITE BONY PARTICLES CALLED MARGARITES (PEARLS), USED TO MAKE NECKLACES AND BRACELETS FOR THE WRISTS AND FOR THE ANKLES. THE PERSIANS, THE MEDES AND ALL THE PEOPLE OF ASIA VALUE THESE MUCH MORE THAN OTHER OBJECTS MADE OF GOLD.

Gulick, 1969, Vol. I, pp. 398-402.

The Epicurean Hermarkhos of Lesbos

The Epicurean school in Athens, established by Epicuros in 306 B.C., gave expression to the desire for a refined type of happiness. This was considered as the reward of the cultured man, who could take pleasure in the joys of the mind, over which he had greater control than over those of a material or sensuous nature (Oxf. Class. Dict. p. 390). The Epicureans refused to be perturbed by metaphysical or religious doctrines, which, by imposing predetermined duties, interfered with the freedom of pure enjoyment. Epicuros, whose philosophy only much later was associated with hedonism, did not advocate the pursuit of all or any

Epicuros (Metropolitan Museum, New York) Richter, 1965/84.

pleasures but only of those consistent with intelligence and moderation. The basic condition for a perfectly calm state of mind (imperturbability, or in Greek *ataraxia*) is virtue and without it happiness (*eudemonia*) is not possible.

In 310 B.C. Epicuros had "founded the oldest sanatorium, in Mytilene, for persons suffering from psychic or nervous disorders, depressions, or the consequences of failure or disappointment" (Runes, 1959 p. 101). This may be a twentieth-century view of the Epicurean "sanatorium," which in 306 B.C. was transferred to Athens. But, in fact, Epicuros and his disciples considered philosophy as the care and cure of the mind, the only way to endure pain and misfortune and to maintain a pleasurable equanimity.

Although the epicureans often found themselves opposed to the stoics, there were many points of philosophy the two schools had in common. The writings of Epicuros filled over three-hundred cylinders or volumes but little has been preserved. He died in 271 B.C. and was succeeded by Hermarkhos from Lesbos approximately his contemporary (est. 340-after 270 B.C.) with whom he "GREW OLD TOGETHER IN (THE PRACTICE OF) PHILOSOPHY" (Richter, 1965, Vol. II, p. 203).

THE LIVES AND OPINIONS OF EMINENT PHILOSOPHERS
BY DIOGENES LAERTIOS, FIRST HALF OF THIRD CENTURY A.D.
BOOK X
EPICUROS, 341-271 B.C.

1-4. EPICUROS . . . WAS AN ATHENIAN OF THE (NOBLE) FAMILY OF PHILAIDAE. HE GREW UP ON SAMOS AMONG THE ATHENIAN SETTLERS THERE AND AT THE AGE OF EIGHTEEN HE CAME TO ATHENS . . . AT THAT TIME . . . ARISTOTLE WAS IN KHALKIS. WHEN ALEXANDER (THE GREAT, KING OF MACEDON) DIED AND THE ATHENIANS WERE EXPELLED FROM SAMOS, EPICUROS JOINED HIS FATHER IN KOLOPHON, WHERE HE BEGAN TO ATTRACT STUDENTS. HE THEN RETURNED TO ATHENS . . . WHERE HE CONGREGATED WITH OTHER PHILOSOPHERS, UNTIL HE ESTABLISHED HIS OWN SCHOOL, NAMED AFTER HIM. ACCORDING TO HIM, HIS FIRST CONTACT WITH PHILOSOPHY WAS WHEN HE WAS FOURTEEN. THE EPICUREAN APOLLODOROS IN THE FIRST VOLUME OF HIS "LIFE OF EPICUROS" REPORTS THAT EPICUROS TURNED TO PHILOSOPHY BECAUSE HE WAS IRRITATED WITH THE SCHOOL-MASTERS ["GRAMMARIANS"] WHO WERE UNABLE TO EXPLAIN TO HIM THE MEANING OF CHAOS IN HESIOD'S WORK. BUT ACCORDING TO HERMIPPOS, EPICUROS WAS A SCHOOL TEACHER HIMSELF AND THEN SWITCHED TO PHILOSOPHY AFTER HE READ THE BOOKS OF DEMOCRITOS (THE ATOMIST) . . . SOME (OF HIS ENEMIES) ALLEGED THAT EPICUROS PRESENTED THE ATOMIC THEORY OF

DEMOCRITOS AND THE VIEWS OF ARISTIPPOS ABOUT PLEASURE [HEDONE] AS HIS OWN.

6. HE WAS ALSO ACCUSED, ADMITTING THIS HIMSELF IN A LETTER TO THE PHILOSOPHERS IN MYTILENE, THAT HE SPENT A WHOLE MNA (13) DAILY ON HIS MEALS . . . AND THAT AMONG THE MANY OTHER FEMALE COURTESANS WHO CONSORTED WITH HIM WERE MAMMARION, HEDEIA, EROTION AND NIKIDION (23).

9. BUT THESE ACCUSATIONS ARE MADNESS. THERE ARE ENOUGH WITNESSES TO CONFIRM THIS MAN'S UNSURPASSED GOOD WILL . . .

13. . . . EPICUROS HIMSELF DENIES HAVING STUDIED WITH ANYBODY AND CLAIMS TO HAVE BEEN SELF-TAUGHT.

15-16. HE WAS BORN . . . SEVEN YEARS AFTER THE DEATH OF PLATO. WHEN HE WAS THIRTY-TWO HE STARTED A SCHOOL OF PHILOSOPHY, FIRST IN MYTILENE AND IN LAMPSAKOS AND AFTER FIVE YEARS HE TRANSFERRED TO ATHENS . . . HE DIED THERE AFTER A LIFE OF SEVENTY-TWO YEARS AND HERMARKHOS OF MYTILENE SUCCEEDED HIM. THE DEATH OF EPICUROS WAS DUE TO A KIDNEY STONE AND URINARY RETENTION, AS IS STATED IN HERMARKHOS' LETTERS. NEAR THE END, AFTER A FOURTEEN DAY ILLNESS EPICUROS WAS BATHING IN A BRONZE TUB FILLED WITH WARM WATER AND ASKED FOR UNDILUTED WINE, WHICH HE SWALLOWED. THEN ADVISING HIS FRIENDS TO REMEMBER HIS DOCTRINES, HE ENDED HIS LIFE.

17. HIS LAST WILL WAS AS FOLLOWS: "WITH THIS I BEQUEATH ALL MY PROPERTY TO (LISTS NAMES) . . . ON CONDITION THAT THEY MAKE THE GARDEN [KEPOS] AND EVERYTHING IN IT AVAILABLE TO HERMARKHOS OF MYTILENE AND TO THOSE WHO JOIN HIM IN THE PURSUIT OF PHILOSOPHY, AS WELL AS THOSE WHOM HERMARKHOS MAY DESIGNATE AS HIS SUCCESSORS, SO THAT THEY MAY CONGREGATE AND STUDY TOGETHER MATTERS PERTAINING TO PHILOSOPHY . . ."

18. "AND FROM THE REVENUES . . . IN CONSULTATION WITH HERMARKHOS, TO MAKE SEPARATE PROVISIONS FOR MEMORIAL OFFERINGS TO MY FATHER, MOTHER AND BROTHERS AND FOR MYSELF, TO COMMEMORATE MY BIRTHDAY EVERY YEAR . . . ."

19-20. "LET THEM ALSO PROVIDE FOR THE SUPPORT OF THE DAUGHTER OF METRODOROS (A PROMINENT YOUNGER EPICUREAN WHO DIED FIRST) AND WHEN SHE IS OF AGE TO GIVE HER IN MARRIAGE TO A PHILOSOPHER FROM OUR SCHOOL, CHOSEN BY HERMARKHOS, SO LONG AS SHE BEHAVES WELL AND OBEYS HIM. HERMARKHOS SHOULD BE MADE TRUSTEE OF THE FUNDS . . . SO THAT EVERYTHING MAY BE DONE ACCORDING TO THE WISHES OF THIS MAN WHO HAS GROWN OLD IN PHILOSOPHY ALONG WITH ME AND WHO IS TO BECOME THE HEAD OF OUR GROUP OF PHILOSOPHERS."

HERMARKHOS OF MYTILENE WHO SUCCEEDED EPICUROS, WAS THE SON OF A VERY POOR MAN AND INITIALLY STUDIED RHETORIC. THERE ARE THESE EXCELLENT BOOKS WRITTEN BY HIM:

ESSAYS [LETTERS] ABOUT EMBEDOCLES IN 22 VOLUMES
ON MATHEMATICS
VERSUS PLATO
VERSUS ARISTOTLE

HERMARKHOS DIED OF PARALYSIS WELL-ADVANCED IN AGE.
Hicks, R.D., Vol. II, pp. 528-48 and 552.

Hermarkhos
(British Museum) Richter 1965/84.

Zeno [*Zenon*]
(Copenhagen), Richter 1965/84.

Stoics of the Multicolored Arcade [Stoa]

Many "stoics" today do not belong to any school of thought and may not have attended philosophical sessions! In Hellenistic and Roman times however, a stoic was primarily a trained philosopher, with dedication and a certain recognizable lifestyle, often with a self-promoted image or personality cult. Roman political leaders, senators and emperors were confirmed stoics and some of them (Seneca, Marcus Aurelius) wrote long treatises and books about their philosophy of life (Panzani, 1988). Stoicism, as a philosophical school that fitted the times of collapsing values, social instability and political chaos was originated by Zeno [*Zenon*] who came to Athens from a Phoenician settlement on the island of Cyprus. Beginning in 301 B.C. (an earlier date is given by some) sessions were held in a covered archway [stoa], a colonnaded portico decorated with brilliant paintings which for this reason was called *Poikile* (multi-colored, painted) Stoa.

According to the stoics, philosophy is the practice and study [*askesis*] of virtue [*arete*] and a truly moral life must be founded on intellectual exercise and theoretical research (Oxf. Class. Dict. p. 1015). True morality is not possible without this knowledge, so a person is "moral" only if he is also wise and learned [*sophos*]. But while Zeno considered scientific knowledge and logic (a term that he was the first to introduce) as an absolute requirement for ethical action, some of his followers tended to dismiss the importance of factual or theoretical knowledge and so they approached the cynic philosophers. The virtuous person finds satisfaction and happiness in himself and is independent and most indifferent to the outside world. This he accomplishes by mastering himself, his emotions, desires and passions. A fundamental divine "World-Reason" (24) determines the rational order by which a stoic philosopher is trained and able to regulate his life. Because it was so particularly well-adapted to the expectations and needs of the later phase of classical antiquity, stoicism became very popular and branches of the stoa were established by the students of the successor of Zeno, Kleanthes in the second century B.C. in places as far as Babylon (Oxf. Class. Dict. p. 1016).

THE LIVES AND OPINIONS OF EMINENT PHILOSOPHERS
BY DIOGENES LAERTIOS, FIRST HALF OF THIRD CENTURY A.D.

BOOK VII, CHAPTER 4
167.... THESE WERE THE MEN WHO DEVIATED FROM ZENO'S PHILOSOPHY. HIS (FAITHFUL) SUCCESSOR WAS KLEANTHES, ABOUT WHOM WE ARE NOW TO SPEAK.

V. KLEANTHES
KLEANTHES ... WAS A NATIVE OF ASSOS. HE WAS INITIALLY A BOXER ... WHO ARRIVED IN ATHENS WITH ONLY FOUR DRACHMAS AND CAME IN CONTACT WITH ZENO. AFTER THAT HE PURSUED PHILOSOPHY VIGOROUSLY AND REMAINED FAITHFUL TO HIS TEACHER'S DOCTRINES. HE WAS FAMOUS FOR HIS HARD WORK. POVERTY FORCED HIM TO HIRE HIMSELF FOR A LIVING AND AT NIGHT HE PUMPED WATER IN THE GARDENS WHILE DURING THE DAY HE PRACTICED IN DEBATES AND IN LOGIC. THEY SAY HOWEVER THAT ANTIGONOS (KING OF MACEDON) GAVE HIM A GRANT OF 3,000 DRACHMAS. STILL, WHEN ONE DAY HE WAS TAKING A GROUP OF TEENAGERS TO A SHOW AND THE WIND BLEW OPEN HIS COAT, PEOPLE NOTICED THAT HE WORE NO SHIRT,

AND THAT MADE THEM (THE ATHENIANS) TO HONOR AND APPLAUD HIM (FOR HIS SIMPLE WAYS).

170-171. . . . ALTHOUGH A HARD WORKER, KLEANTHES HAD NO SKILLS IN PHYSICS AND WAS GENERALLY SLOW. HE OFTEN MADE FUN OF HIMSELF AND WHEN SOMEONE ASKED HIM "WHOM ARE YOU REPROACHING?" HE REPLIED (MEANING HIMSELF) "AN OLD MAN WITH GRAY HAIR AND NO BRAINS." WHEN SOMEONE SAID THAT ARKESILAOS (HEAD OF PLATO'S ACADEMY) WAS NOT DOING HIS DUTY, KLEANTHES REPORTED "STOP THAT AND DO NOT BLAME (ANYONE); EVEN IF HE NEGLECTS HIS DUTY IN WORDS, AT LEAST HE ACCOMPLISHES IT IN HIS ACTS." WHEN ARKESILAOS (HEARING THIS) COMMENTED, "I AM NOT TO BE FLATTERED," KLEANTHES ADDED "YES, I DO COMPLIMENT YOU BECAUSE YOU SAY ONE THING BUT YOU DO SOMETHING ELSE (WHICH MAY BE BETTER)."

172. WHEN SOMEONE ASKED WHAT COUNSEL HE OUGHT TO LAY DOWN FOR HIS SON, HE QUOTED FROM "ELECTRA":

KEEP QUIET, QUIET, SUBTLE BE THY TRACE.

AND WHEN A MAN FROM LACONIA DECLARED THAT STRESS [PONOS] WAS GOOD HE WAS OVERJOYED AND SAID:

YOU ARE OF NOBLE BLOOD, DEAR CHILD.

173 . . . HE DECLARED THAT PERIPATETIC PHILOSOPHERS WERE LIKE LYRES, MAKING BEAUTIFUL SOUNDS BUT UNABLE TO PERCEIVE THEM. THERE IS A STORY TOO PERTAINING TO HIS CLAIM THAT, ACCORDING TO ZENO, A PERSON'S CHARACTER [ETHOS] COULD BE KNOWN FROM HIS APPEARANCE. IN RESPONSE TO THAT, SOME YOUNG MEN WITH A SENSE OF HUMOR BROUGHT TO HIM A KNOWN "FAG" (19) WITH FEATURES HARDENED BY FARMING AND ASKED HIM WHAT WAS HIS PERSONALITY. KLEANTHES SEEMED CONFUSED AND FINALLY ASKED THE MAN TO LEAVE. AS THAT FELLOW WAS GOING AWAY, HE SNEEZED, WHEREUPON KLEANTHES EXCLAIMED: "I GET IT, HE IS AN EFFEMINATE SOFTIE [MALAKOS]."

174-175. IT HAS BEEN SAID THAT KLEANTHES MADE NOTES OF ZENO'S LECTURES ON SEASHELLS AND OXEN SHOULDER BLADES, BECAUSE HE HAD NO MONEY TO BUY WRITING SCROLLS. SUCH AS HE WAS, KLEANTHES PREVAILED AND EVEN THOUGH THERE WERE MANY WORTHWHILE STUDENTS OF ZENO, HE WAS THE ONE TO SUCCEED HIM.

HE LEFT MANY EXCELLENT BOOKS, WHICH ARE THE FOLLOWING:

(Fifty titles were listed, of which these seem most interesting):

CONCERNING TIME
ZENO'S PHYSIOLOGY (PHILOSOPHY OF NATURE)
ABOUT THE SENSES
ABOUT ART
ABOUT IMPULSES
ABOUT MARRIAGE
ABOUT INTELLIGENCE

ABOUT LOVE [EROS]
ABOUT FREEDOM
THE ART OF LOVE [TECHNIQUES]
ON EDUCATION
ON BEAUTY
ON KNOWLEDGE (SCIENCE)
ON THE IDENTITY OF VIRTUE FOR MAN AND WOMAN
ON PLEASURE [HEDONE]
ON INSOLUBLE PROBLEMS

176. THIS IS HOW HE DIED. HIS GUMS WERE SWOLLEN AND A PHYSICIAN ORDERED HIM NOT TO EAT, SO HE AVOIDED FOOD FOR TWO DAYS. THEN HE RECOVERED AND THE DOCTOR ALLOWED HIM TO TAKE HIS USUAL MEALS. BUT HE DID NOT FOLLOW THIS INSTRUCTION. SAYING THAT HE HAD ALREADY GONE FAR DOWN THIS ROAD, HE CONTINUED TO ABSTAIN FROM FOOD AND ENDED HIS LIFE AT THE SAME AGE AS ZENO, HAVING LIVED EIGHTY YEARS. NINETEEN OF THESE HE SPENT AS A STUDENT OF ZENO.

Philosophy, as a way of life common in ancient Greece and as one of our contemporary options, too, is not simply a search for the meaning of existence, but it is that meaning itself. Life becomes meaningful, full of meaning, through the act—the Greek verb *philosophein* is more reflective of it—of philosophizing. The spirit of fervent mental ferment, dedication, seriousness and concern, combined with a sense of humor and a feeling of casual comfort, which characterized the ancient philosophers, was in fact a form of religious faith, not dependent of a rigid ritual, irrational beliefs or miraculous occurrences. The scintillating brilliance and the floating freedom of this philosophical spirit and also its relative inaccessibility to the masses may have contributed to its inability to survive eventually the political, military and religious developments of late antiquity. Philosophy may also have caused its own demise, burning itself out or stifling through fossilized scholarship. But it was still alive when attempts were made to bury it by authoritarian edicts and social pressures in an era more inclined to worship fixed, transfixed and crucifixed prototypes. The schools continued to exist for centuries along with the spreading religions from the East, which had borrowed much—often undigested—material from them (24). The devoutly Christian empress of the East Roman empire, Athenais-Eudokia, who was in part responsible for the preservation and expansion of Hellenism in the early Byzantine—"dark"—ages of the fifth century A.D. (Tsatsou, 1980), was the daughter of an Athenian philosopher. When her husband, the East Roman emperor Theodosius II (408–450 A.D.) attempted to close the schools of Athens, the philosophers accepted the invitation of the king of

Persia—a bitter enemy of the Byzantine Greeks—and as a group went to this foreign capital. Before long however they returned homesick to Greece, when their own ruler had changed his mind about the expulsion. The final blow and the extinction of all official philosophical teaching in Athens and elsewhere, came in the sixth century, 529 A.D. (136 years after the emperor Theodosius I had ordered the end of the Olympic games in 393 A.D.), when the Byzantine emperor Justinian I abolished all pagan teaching establishments in the Greek and Roman world.

Chapter IV

HELLENISTIC TWILIGHT AND ROMAN ROMANTIC LOVES

A. **Waves of Wars**
   Alexander to the conquest of Asia
   Memnon in the enemy's service
   The Romans and Lesbos
   Pompey and Cornelia

B. **Erotic Romances**
   Hellenistic historians, librarians and "stylists"
   "Erotic Passions" by Parthenios
   The Lesbian pastoral about *"Daphnis and Chloe"*
   The adventures of *"Apollonios"*

C. **Early Christian Contacts and Commentaries**
   Saint Paul on Assos and Lesbos
   Clement's *"Exhortation to the Greeks"*

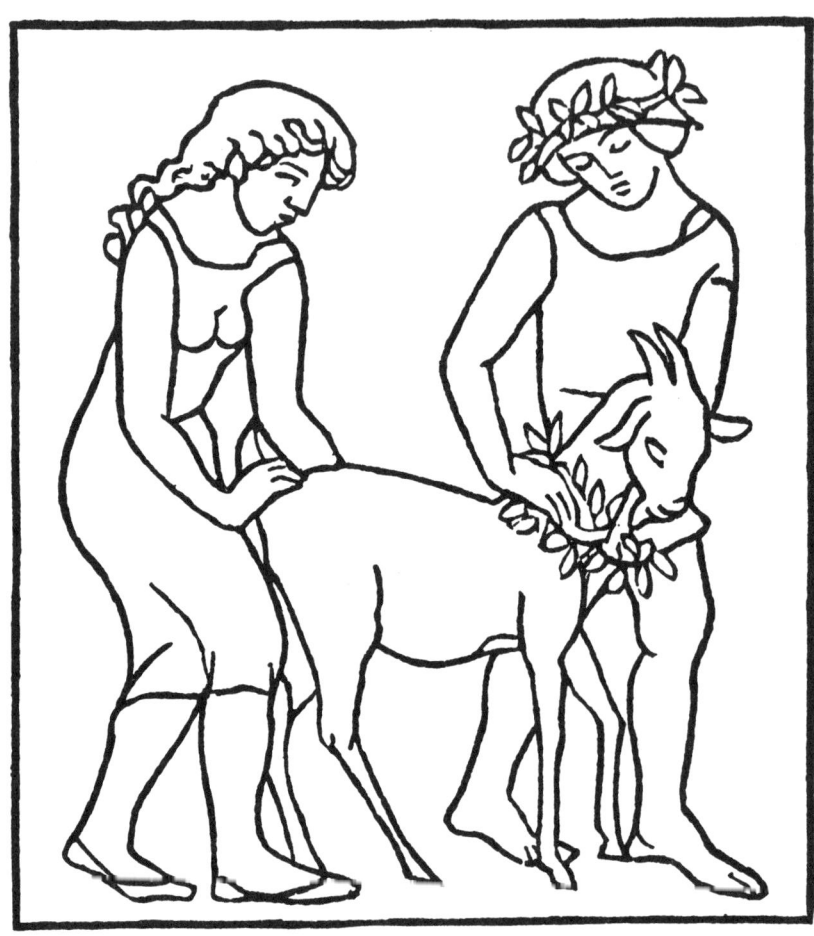

Daphnis and Chloe—in gratitude, the lovers sacrifice a male goat to Pan (Book II). Woodcut, Aristide Maillol, 1938. Dover Publications, 1979 (*see also* pp. 165, 179, this volume).

Overleaf: Pompey the Great (*Pompeius Magnus*), marble, in the Ny Carlsberg Glyptothek, Copenhagen, Denmark (from Durant, 1936, Fig. 6)

A. WAVES OF WARS

The constant wars of city against city came to an end when the Greek city-states one by one were conquered—some destroyed and others only subdued—by the Macedonians under King Philip [*Philippos*] and later under his son Alexander [*Alexandros*] "the Great" who reigned from 336 to 323 B.C. (Ref. Table A). Individual citizens of the Greek cities were divided in their attitudes concerning Macedonian leadership. Some feared and then resented the loss of independence but others welcomed the unification of all Hellenes under the vigorous Greek state from the north. Aristotle, the founder of the peripatetic school of philosophy, the "Lyceum" in Athens, was the son of the physician in the court of the Macedonian king and himself—after leaving Athens and spending a short time on Lesbos (Chapter III-C)—became the tutor of the young Alexander. Mostly, political or social class concerns determined which side people preferred. In mainland Greece the conservatives or oligarchs (rule of the few) sympathized with Macedon, while the democratic parties opposed it. But in Ionia, Aeolis and other eastern Greek centers the whole population welcomed Macedonian expansion against the Persians. Only certain rulers and some mercenaries ignored the ethnic identity and fought with the Persians against Alexander, as some of their Greek ancestors had also helped the Persians invade Greece about 150 years earlier (Bury, 1913; Durant, 1939, and subsequent editions). Most of the historians of the Alexandrian and Hellenistic times focused on major wars and political events but at least one Lesbian writer, Myrsilos of Methymna (about 250 B.C.), in his *Lesbika*, i.e., the History and Affairs of Lesbos (text not available) paid more attention to early traditions and folk movements (Oxf. Class. Dict. p. 716).

Alexander to the conquest of Asia; Memnon in the enemy's service

Lesbos was not in the center of action when the Macedonian armies crossed the sea in their thrust toward the center of Asia Minor and then on to Phoenicia, Egypt and Persia. Alexander only stopped in nearby Troy, to offer sacrifices to the ancestors of his Greek troops fallen there almost 1000 years earlier. But the commander-in-chief of the Persian armies, a Greek from Rhodos named Memnon, greatly admired by king Darius for his military skills, planned to circumvent the Macedonians, to sail north and to attack their home country behind their lines. He occupied several Greek islands trying to make their people revolt against Alexander and, counting on the cooperation of some leading Lesbian conservatives, he chose Lesbos for a series of battles (Bury, 1913/ff., p. 738–742). Memnon

Alexander [*Alexandros*] the Great, Hellenistic marble (Louvre, Paris), in Richter 1965/84.

invaded the island, captured Eresos and Pyrrha, then laid siege to Mytilene. But there suddenly he fell ill and died and his forces, after initially occupying the city, had to abandon the field because Alexander, with extraordinary speed, was conquering the rest of Asia Minor and going on to Syria and Egypt.

The sudden death of Memnon on Lesbos was "a severe loss for Persia" (Oxf. Class. Dict. 1970/78, p. 669) and may have affected the course of history. Memnon's wife, Barsine, later became the mistress of the victorious Alexander and for a while a strong influence on him. An important connection of Alexander with Lesbos was through one of his generals, who was a relative of the poetess Sappho, a descendant of her brother Larihos. His name was Erigyios, and according to Plutarch, he was a friend of the young Alexander in the court of Macedon.

PARALLEL LIVES
BY PLUTARCH [PLUTARKHOS], CA. 46 – CA. 120 A.D.

ALEXANDER [ALEXANDROS]

X.1-3. PIXODAROS, THE SATRAP OF CARIA (1), TRYING TO BECOME AN ALLY OF PHILIP (KING OF MACEDON) THROUGH A FAMILY CONNECTION, WISHED TO GIVE HIS OLDEST DAUGHTER IN MARRIAGE TO ARRHIDAIOS, PHILIP'S SON . . . GREATLY DISTURBED, ALEXANDER SENT THESSALOS, THE DRAMATIC ACTOR, TO CARIA, TO ARGUE THAT HE (ALEXANDER) SHOULD BE THE ONE TO BE CONSIDERED, AND NOT HIS BASTARD BROTHER, WHO, BESIDES, WAS NOT IN HIS RIGHT MIND (2) . . . BUT PHILIP BECAME AWARE OF THIS AND ASKED FOR THESSALOS . . . TO BE BROUGHT BACK IN CHAINS. HE ALSO EXPELLED FROM MACEDONIA, AMONG THE OTHER COMPANIONS OF ALEXANDER, ERIGYIOS AND PTOLEMY [PTOLEMAIOS]. LATER (WHEN HE BECAME KING AFTER THE ASSASSINATION OF PHILIP) ALEXANDER BROUGHT THESE MEN BACK AND GRANTED THEM HIGHEST HONORS.

Perrin, B., 1967, Vol. VII, pp. 248–250.

The historian Diodoros mentioned Erigyios many times, starting with the crossing of the Macedonians to Asia Minor in 334 B.C.

THE LIBRARY OF HISTORY
BY DIODOROS THE SICILIAN, FIRST CENTURY B.C.
BOOK XVII
17.4 THE CAVALRY CONSISTED OF 1800 MACEDONIANS . . . AND A TOTAL OF 600 FROM THE REST OF GREECE UNDER THE COMMAND OF ERIGYIOS.

Erigyios again is listed by Diodoros as one of the generals in the crucial battle against the Persians, in 331 B.C.

BOOK XVII
57.3-4 THE ARRANGEMENT OF THE CAVALRY . . . WAS COMPLETED WITH THOSE FROM PELOPONNESOS . . . AND FROM (SEVERAL) AREAS OF GREECE UNDER THE LEADERSHIP OF ERIGYIOS FROM MYTILENE.
Welles, C.B., Vol. VII, p. 164, 282.

By the year 328 B.C. Alexander's troops had crossed the eastern borders of Persia (also called Aria, i.e., Iran) into Bactria (3) and beyond.

BOOK XVII
83.5-6 . . . THE BARBARIANS WERE HOLDING THEIR OWN WHEN THEIR LEADER, SATIBARZANES, REMOVING HIS HELMET WITH HIS OWN HANDS TO SHOW WHO HE WAS, CHALLENGED TO SINGLE COMBAT ANYONE OF THE (GREEK) GENERALS. ERIGYIOS RESPONDED AND FOLLOWING AN HEROIC STRUGGLE HE MANAGED TO WIN. STUNNED BY THEIR LEADER'S DEATH, THE BARBARIANS, AFTER RECEIVING THE REQUIRED ASSURANCES, SURRENDERED THEMSELVES TO THE (MACEDONIAN) KING.
Welles, C.B., Vol. VIII, pp. 358–360.

According to the editor and commentator of Plutarch's work (Perrin, 1967 Vol. VII, Ch.17) Erigyios of Mytilene was killed in battle in 328 B.C.

One of the easily accessible Greek writings about Alexander's campaigns, called "Alexander's Anabasis," was the work of Arrian [*Arrianos*]. A Greek born in Nicomedia in Asia Minor about 96 A.D., Arrian completed his history more than three centuries after the death of the Macedonian king (Brunt, 1976, *Introduction* pp. ix–xiv). The author had the unusual honor for a Greek in the Roman empire, to be appointed first governor of Cappadocia and then in 147 A.D., archon of Athens. He died probably in 180 A.D. in Athens. As student of the famous stoic philosopher Epictetos, he kept notes of the philosopher's lectures. The current publication of "Alexander's Anabasis" refers back to 15th century codices and manuscripts from Constantinople (4). The text is based on earlier eye-witness histories and is written in somewhat imperfect (from the classical point of view) Greek. It has been considered to represent an "official view" of the Greek conquest of the eastern Mediterranean world, at a time when all that world had become part of the Roman empire. Like other writers of his—and later—times, Arrian reversed the "y" and "i" and spelled the name of the city on Lesbos *Mitylene* (Note 5; cf. II-6 and 11).

ALEXANDER'S ANABASIS (ASCENT)
BY ARRIAN [Arrianos] SECOND CENTURY A.D.

BOOK TWO
1:1–5 AFTERWARDS, MEMNON (A GREEK FROM RHODOS IN THE SERVICE OF PERSIA), HAVING BEEN APPOINTED BY (THE PERSIAN) KING DARIUS COMMANDER-IN-CHIEF OF THE ENTIRE PERSIAN NAVY AND LORD OF THE COASTAL AREA, PLANNED A STRATEGY TO DIVERT THE WAR (FROM ASIA MINOR) TO MACEDONIA AND GREECE AND FOR THIS PURPOSE HE TOOK POSSESSION OF HIOS, WHICH WAS SURRENDERED TO HIM BY TREACHERY. FROM THERE HE SAILED TO LESBOS AND ALTHOUGH MITYLENE DID NOT SUBMIT TO HIM, HE MANAGED TO BRING OVER TO HIS SIDE THE OTHER CITIES ON LESBOS. AFTER HE HAD SECURED THESE HE CONCENTRATED ON MITYLENE, WALLED OFF THE TOWN WITH A DOUBLE STOCKADE FROM SEA TO SEA AND THEN, SETTING UP FIVE ARMY CAMPS, HE CONTROLLED THE COUNTRYSIDE WITHOUT DIFFICULTY. PART OF HIS FLEET GUARDED THE HARBOR AND OTHER VESSELS WERE SENT TO CAPE SIGRION, THE POINT OF LESBOS WHERE MERCHANT SHIPS WOULD COME TO DOCK. THIS WAY NO HELP COULD REACH MITYLENE FROM THE SEA. WHILE THIS WAS GOING ON, HOWEVER, MEMNON FELL ILL AND DIED, WHICH AT THAT TIME HURT THE AFFAIRS OF THE (PERSIAN) KING VERY BADLY. YET THE SIEGE CONTINUED WITH UNDIMINISHED VIGOR BY AUTOPHRADATES AND PHARNABAZUS . . . TO WHOM MEMNON, AS HE WAS DYING, HAD TURNED OVER HIS COMMAND UNTIL DARIUS HAD A CHANCE TO MAKE FINAL DECISIONS. THE CITIZENS OF MITYLENE, BLOCKADED FROM THE LAND AND GUARDED FROM THE SEA-SIDE BY AGGRESSIVELY PATROLLING VESSELS, SENT DELEGATES TO PHARNABAZUS AND MADE AN AGREEMENT TO SEND BACK HOME THE FOREIGN AUXILIARY TROOPS SUPPLIED BY ALEXANDER AS PART OF THEIR ALLIANCE PACT, TO TEAR DOWN THE COLUMNS ON WHICH THE TREATY WITH ALEXANDER WAS INSCRIBED AND, INSTEAD, TO BECOME THE ALLIES OF DARIUS . . . THE EXILES WHO HAD FLED MITYLENE WERE TO BE ALLOWED TO RETURN AND GET BACK HALF OF THE PROPERTY THEY OWNED BEFORE THEY HAD LEFT. THESE WERE THE TERMS OF THE AGREEMENTS BETWEEN MITYLENE AND THE PERSIANS. BUT AUTOPHRADATES AND PHARNABAZUS, ONCE THEY ENTERED THE CITY, SET UP A GARRISON (OF THEIR OWN) . . . AND INSTALLED A DICTATOR, DIOGENES, WHO WAS ONE OF THE (PRO-PERSIAN) EXILES. IN ADDITION THEY COLLECTED MONEY FROM THE MITYLENEANS, TAKING IT

BY FORCE FROM THE WEALTHY AND IMPOSING A GENERAL TAX ON THE REST OF THE COMMUNITY.

II:1–2. ALEXANDER IN THE MEANTIME HAD REACHED GORDION AND THERE HE FELT A STRONG DESIRE TO GO UP TO THE ACROPOLIS ON WHICH WERE THE PALACES OF (KING) GORDIOS AND OF HIS SON MIDAS (6A) AND TO SEE THERE THE CHARIOT OF GORDIOS AND THE KNOT ON ITS YOKE. THERE WAS A WIDESPREAD TRADITION IN THE AREA ABOUT THE CHARIOT . . .

6–8. . . . THAT WHOEVER WOULD UNTIE THE KNOT ON THE CHARIOT'S YOKE WOULD BE DESTINED TO BECOME LORD OF ASIA . . . ALEXANDER DID NOT MANAGE TO FIND A WAY TO UNTIE THE KNOT YET HE DID NOT WANT TO LEAVE IT TIED IN CASE THAT MIGHT MAKE THE CROWDS UNRULY OR DISTRUSTFUL. THEN, SOME SAY, HE STRUCK THE KNOT WITH HIS SWORD AND CLAIMED TO HAVE UNTIED IT. ANOTHER REPORT HAD IT THAT ALEXANDER REMOVED THE POLE PIN . . . HOLDING THE KNOT TOGETHER AND THEN PULLED THE YOKE OUT . . . WHATEVER MIGHT HAVE HAPPENED, WHEN HE AND HIS ENTOURAGE LEFT THE CHARIOT, THE GENERAL IMPRESSION WAS THAT THE SAYING ABOUT THE GORDIAN KNOT HAD BEEN FULFILLED. FURTHER SIGNS CAME THAT SAME NIGHT, WITH THUNDER AND LIGHTNING FROM THE SKY. ALEXANDER MADE SACRIFICES THE NEXT DAY TO MARK THESE WELCOME SIGNALS FROM THE GODS AND TO CELEBRATE THE UNTYING OF THE KNOT (6B).

BOOK THREE

I. 1. ALEXANDER NOW MARCHED ON TO EGYPT, HIS ORIGINAL GOAL, AND ARRIVED THERE SEVEN DAYS AFTER HE LEFT GAZA . . .

II. 2–7. SOON THEREAFTER HEGELOHOS SAILED ONTO EGYPT AND REPORTED TO ALEXANDER THAT . . . THE PEOPLE OF HIOS HAD WELCOMED THE MACEDONIANS, AGAINST THE GOVERNOR WHO HAD BEEN PLACED THERE FORCIBLY BY AUTOPHRADATES AND PHARNABAZUS. HE ALSO ANNOUNCED THAT PHARNABAZUS HAD BEEN CAPTURED THERE AND WITH HIM ALSO ARISTONIKOS, THE TYRANT OF METHYMNA, WHO HAD SAILED INTO THE PORT OF HIOS WITH FIVE PIRATE SHIPS, NOT KNOWING THAT IT WAS NOW UNDER MACEDONIAN CONTROL . . . THE PIRATES HAD ALL BEEN MASSACRED BY THE MACEDONIANS OF HEGELOHOS BUT ARISTONIKOS WAS BROUGHT TO ALEXANDER ALONG WITH APPOLONIDES OF HIOS AND OTHERS WHO HAD TAKEN AN ACTIVE PART IN THE (ANTI-MACEDONIAN) REVOLT OF HIOS AND WHO RULED FOR A WHILE THE ISLAND BY FORCE. HEGELOHOS ALSO STATED THAT HE HAD TAKEN MYTILENE FROM HARES, WHO WAS HOLDING IT AND THAT HE HAD OBTAINED A PLEDGE OF SUPPORT FROM THE OTHER CITIES ON LESBOS . . . ALEXANDER (LATER) SENT THE CAPTIVE TYRANTS BACK . . . TO THEIR CITIES, SO THAT THE PEOPLE MIGHT DO WITH THEM ANYTHING THEY WANTED.

Brunt, P.A., 1976, Vol. I, pp. 122–130 & 222–226.

Kharis (pronounced *Harris*, often written *Charis*) of Mytilene also wrote books of history about Alexander. He was quoted by Athenaios when his "Dining Scholars" discussed the use of snow for drinking and for cooling food and beverages.

DINING SCHOLARS
BY ATHENAIOS OF NAUKRATIS, THIRD CENTURY A.D.
BOOK III, 124.E
... KHARIS OF MITYLENE (SIC, CF. NOTE 5 AND CHAP. V AND VII, NOTE 8) IN HIS "TALES OF ALEXANDER" INDICATED HOW SNOW COULD BE PRESERVED WHEN HE DESCRIBED THE SIEGE OF THE INDIAN CITY OF PETRA. HE SAID THAT ALEXANDER HAD DUG THIRTY COOLING WELLS WHICH HE FILLED WITH SNOW AND COVERED WITH OAK BRANCHES. THIS WAY THE SNOW COULD LAST A LONG TIME.
Gulick, 1967, Vol. II, p. 76.

The Romans and Lesbos

Alexander the Great died in Babylon in 323 B.C. A year later Aristotle, his former teacher, also ended his life not far from Athens (he stayed away from the city where an anti-Macedonean political climate was prevalent) in Halkis, home of his ancestors. While philosophy and the arts continued to flourish and Hellenistic culture spread all over the Mediterranean world, the generals who divided Alexander's empire among themselves fought each other incessantly, claiming and reclaiming their respective territories until, before long, they all lost their kingdoms to the invading Romans. The ancient Lesbian city of Antissa was completely destroyed by the Romans in 167 B.C. because it had sent provisions to the fleet of their enemy, the Macedonian king Perseus (Nesiotis, M. *Eleftheros Kosmos*—"Free World," Athenian newspaper, June 23, 1963).

As the Romans advanced east to the conquest of all the world known to them, one of the toughest enemies they had to face was Mithridates VI "the Great," king of Pontos, in eastern Asia Minor. The conflict came to a climax about 88 B.C. The historian of the first century B.C., Diodoros, described the attempt of Lesbian youths to seize the Roman commander on Lesbos, Aquillius. That officer was probably the son of another Roman by the same name, who had been sent to Asia in 89 B.C. at the head of the Roman delegation, to help the rulers of two smaller kingdoms against Mithridates. The older Aquillius was captured by Mithridates and the king had him killed by pouring hot melted gold down his throat, declaring that this was a form of punishment for Roman greed (Appian, quoted by Oldfather, in Diodoros of Sicily, 1933-68).

THE LIBRARY OF HISTORY
BY DIODOROS THE SICILIAN, FIRST CENTURY B.C.
BOOK XXXVII
27.1-2 AS MITHRIDATES WAS GAINING CONTROL OF ASIA AND THE CITIES IRRESISTIBLY WERE DECLARING THEIR INDEPENDENCE FROM THE ROMANS, THE PEOPLE ON LESBOS DECIDED NOT ONLY TO ALIGN THEMSELVES WITH THE KING (OF PONTOS), BUT ALSO TO ARREST (THE ROMAN) AQUILLIUS, WHO HAD SOUGHT SHELTER IN MYTILENE FOR MEDICAL TREATMENT THERE AND TO HAND HIM OVER TO MITHRIDATES. SO THEY CHOSE SOME OUTSTANDING VIGOROUS YOUNG MEN AND SENT THEM TO THE ROMAN'S RESIDENCE. THE WHOLE GROUP FELL UPON AQUILLIUS INTENDING TO GRAB HIM AND TIE HIM UP. THEY BELIEVED THAT HE WOULD BE A PERFECT AND MUCH APPRECIATED PRESENT, IF HE WERE TO BE SENT TO THE KING.

AQUILLIUS, HOWEVER, ALTHOUGH VERY YOUNG, HAD THE COURAGE TO PERFORM AN HEROIC ACT. FORESTALLING THOSE WHO WERE TO SEIZE HIM, HE CHOSE DEATH INSTEAD OF HUMILIATING AND SHAMEFUL TREATMENT (BY HIS ENEMY). SO HE KILLED HIMSELF AND BY THIS TERRIBLE ACT HE STUNNED HIS ASSAILANTS SO MUCH THAT THEY DID NOT EVEN DARE GO CLOSE TO HIM. WITHOUT HESITATING HE DELIVERED HIMSELF FROM LIVING AND FROM THE FORTHCOMING EVILS. BY DOING THIS HE GAINED WIDESPREAD REPUTATION AND GLORY FOR HIS RIGHT SPIRIT [EUPSYCHIA].

Oldfather, C.H., Vol. XII, pp. 230-232.

Pompey [*Pompeius*] the Great (Copenhagen) from Durant 1936.

The Roman leader of the first century B.C., Pompey "the Great" [*Pompeius Magnus*], fighting for supreme power, stayed near Mytilene, before and after his decisive battles with Julius Caesar on the mainland (7). Caesar himself had spent some time on Lesbos. To avoid political turmoil in Rome and to study Greek, rhetoric and the martial arts, he went to Rhodes and then to the service of the Roman governor of Asia Minor. From there the twenty-year-old Caesar crossed over on a military operation to Lesbos and afterwards, in 80 B.C., he was awarded the oak-wreath Roman Civic Crown, presumably for "an act of gallantry"

(Grant, M.: *Julius Caesar*, 1969/92, p. 7). Pompey's wife too lived for some time on Lesbos and the couple admired the island, its culture and architecture so much that Pompey, while still in power, had an exact copy of the large marble theater in Mytilene replicated in Rome. It was said to be the first theater in stone there.

Lesbos was fortunate that the personal historian of Pompey, Theophanes, who lived from about 80—or about 100 (Elef. p. 32)—to 30 B.C. and escorted, advised and aided the Roman general in his campaigns, was a native of Mytilene on the island.

In his historical discussion of Lesbos the geographer Strabo [*Strabon*] referred to the famous Theophanes.

> **GEOGRAPHY**
> BY STRABO [STRABON], 64/63 B.C.-21(?) A.D.
> LONG AFTERWARDS ... IN OUR TIMES (THERE WERE) POTAMON, LESBOKLES AND KRINAGORAS AND THE WRITER THEOPHANES. HE WAS ALSO A STATESMAN, A MAN OF POLITICS, WHO, DUE MAINLY TO HIS ABILITY, BECAME A FRIEND OF POMPEY THE GREAT AND SHARED IN ALL HIS ACTIONS AND ACCOMPLISHMENTS. FROM THESE HE ADORNED HIS NATIVE LAND, PARTLY THROUGH POMPEY AND PARTLY ON HIS OWN, AND HIMSELF BECAME THE MOST PROMINENT OF ALL GREEKS.
> Jones Vol. VI, p. 148.

As a reward for Theophanes' services to the Roman leader, Lesbos was exempted from taxation and was granted autonomy (Richter, III, 1965, p. 283). In his written history detailing Pompey's expeditions, Theophanes had much to say about Lesbos (Oxf. Class. Dict. p.1058). Details about the life of Theophanes himself are only available from the date when, in 62 B.C., he was officially granted Roman citizenship by Pompey, the most powerful military and political leader of that time. If we can trust the antagonistic comments of Cicero, Theophanes came from the "plebeian" low class of Lesbos. That prominent Roman statesman, orator and thinker (Cicero had an excellent education in Greek philosophy), who strongly opposed any suspected dictatorial ambitions, in his writings, speeches and in the more than 900 existing letters, provided a penetrating view of his expanding world and referred to "The Greek" Theophanes many times.

> **ON BEHALF OF ARKHIAS THE POET** [PRO ARCHIA POETA]
> BY M. T. CICERO, 106–43 B.C.
> **X.24** ... WHAT THEN? DIDN'T OUR SO-CALLED "GREAT" MAN (POMPEY), WHO HAS MANAGED TO MATCH HIS VALOR

HELLENISTIC TWILIGHT AND ROMAN ROMANTIC LOVES 141

> WITH HIS FORTUNE, DIDN'T HE GRANT THE HISTORIAN OF HIS CAMPAIGNS, THEOPHANES OF MITYLENE (5) ROMAN CITIZENSHIP, IN FRONT OF HIS GATHERED TROOPS? AND WEREN'T OUR BRAVE MEN, BEING SIMPLE PEASANTS AND SOLDIERS, SO THRILLED BY THE SPLENDOR OF GLORY, THAT THEY APPLAUDED THE ACT VERY LOUDLY, AS IF THEY TOO HAD THEIR SHARE OF THAT HONOR?
>
> Quoted in Latin by Watts, 1935–65 (in Latin), p. 33

In his voluminous correspondence, Cicero also often referred to Theophanes in a more or less gossipy manner.

> **LETTERS TO ATTICUS**
> BY M. T. CICERO, 106-43 B.C. (WRITTEN IN DECEMBER 50 B.C., PROTESTING CAESAR'S AMBITIONS)
>
> **SECTION VII**
>
> **VII,6** . . . THEN I WILL HAVE TO APPROVE OF MY OWN BANISHMENT . . . (AS WELL AS) THE ADOPTION OF A PATRICIAN BY A PLEBEIAN, . . . BY THE MAN FROM MYTILENE.
>
> Winstedt, 1913-66, Vol. II (in Latin), pp. 40-42

More about that adoption later. Concerning the origins of Theophanes, an inscription in Mytilene indicated that he was the son of Hieroitas (Mirmont, p. 172) and that in his youth he wrote poetry. Two of his epigrams have survived (Greek Anthology, quoted by Mirmont, p. 173).

> I WISH THAT HEAVEN WOULD MAKE ME TURN
> INTO A PRETTY WHITE LILY,
> SO THAT YOU MIGHT COME AND PICK ME UP
> TO PLACE ME UPON YOUR BOSOM (8)

And

> NOT FOR HIS FATHER BUT FOR HIS SON HAS LYSIS,
> IN GRIEVING PAIN, ERECTED HERE THIS EMPTY TOMB
> AND WETS IT WITH HIS TEARS.
> IT IS A GRAVE OF ONLY A NAME, BECAUSE THE PARENTS
> HAVE NEVER FOUND THE BODY OF MANTITHEOS
> WHO DIED IN A SHIPWRECK.

It is possible that like "many needy and mediocre poets" (Mirmont, p. 174), Theophanes traveled from place to place and earned a living by reciting his verses or by composing new poems on commission.

Pompey evidently met his future biographer in Asia before the final victory against Mithridates of Pontos in 64 B.C. From then on, the young Lesbian must have been with the Roman general in all the major campaigns through Asia Minor. Much information about the geography of the area, all the way to the Caucasian Mountains, as well as about the life of Pompey and related events in the works of later authors such as Strabo and Plutarch, was taken second-hand from the original writings of Theophanes. Strabo, a half-Greek native of Asia Minor, in his monumental twelve-volume work on the geography and people of the Greek and Roman world, dwelt much on Lesbos (Chapter II). In writing about that island, he expressed unrestrained admiration for its prominent native and later Roman citizen, Theophanes of Mytilene.

GEOGRAPHY
BY STRABO [Strabon], 64/63 B.C.-21(?) A.D.

BOOK XIII, CHAPTER II

(Note: The beginning of this chapter by Strabo has been included in an earlier section of this book on Lesbos.)

PART 3. THIS CITY (MYTILENE) HAS PRODUCED FAMOUS PEOPLE . . . CLOSER TO OUR TIMES POTAMON, LESBOCLES AND . . . THE WRITER THEOPHANES. HE WAS A MAN OF POLITICS (STATESMAN), WHO BECAME A FRIEND OF POMPEY THE GREAT, MOSTLY DUE TO HIS OWN ABILITY AND WENT ALONG WITH HIM ON ALL HIS EXPEDITIONS AND ACCOMPLISHMENTS. HENCE HE WAS ABLE TO ADORN HIS NATIVE CITY, BOTH THROUGH POMPEY AND ON HIS OWN AND SHOWED HIMSELF TO BE THE MOST OUTSTANDING AMONG ALL THE GREEKS. HE LEFT A SON, MARCUS POMPEY [Pompeios], WHO AT ONE TIME WAS APPOINTED GOVERNOR OF ASIA BY AUGUSTUS CAESAR AND WHO NOW IS COUNTED AMONG THE BEST FRIENDS OF (THE EMPEROR) TIBERIUS.

Jones, Vol. VI, pp. 142-144

But the "father" of geography felt obligated to question some of the Lesbian traveler's accounts about the Amazons. The entire ancient text on this subject is so interesting and characteristic about life on the distant mountains that it deserves a relatively extensive quotation.

GEOGRAPHY
BY STRABO [Strabon], 64/63 B.C.-21(?) A.D.

BOOK XI

SECTION II, 1-2 . . . FURTHER ON COMES KOLKHIS, LOCATED DOWN BELOW THE CAUCASIAN MOUNTAINS AND THOSE CALLED MOSKHIAN. AS THE RIVER TANAIS IS CONSIDERED THE BOUNDARY BETWEEN EUROPE AND ASIA, I WILL BEGIN FROM HERE MY DETAILED DESCRIPTION. THIS RIVER FLOWS FROM THE NORTHERLY SIDE (OF THE MOUNTAINS) AND, LIKE THOSE OF THE NILE, ITS ORIGINS ARE UNKNOWN . . . ALSO, IN THE CASE OF TANAIS . . . VERY LITTLE IS KNOWN BESIDES ITS OUTLETS, BECAUSE OF THE COLD AND THE BARREN-

NESS OF THE COUNTRY, WHERE ONLY THE NATIVES CAN SUPPORT THEMSELVES IN A NOMADIC WAY, LIVING ON FLESH AND MILK. PEOPLE FROM OTHER AREAS CANNOT STAND THIS AND BESIDES, THE NOMADS BEING AVERSE TO MIXING WITH OTHER PEOPLE AND ALSO SUPERIOR IN NUMBER AND STRENGTH, HAVE BLOCKED OFF ANY SECTION OF THAT COUNTRY THAT COULD BE CROSSED AND PARTS OF THE RIVER THAT MIGHT BE NAVIGABLE. FOR THIS REASON SOME HAVE ASSUMED THAT THE SOURCES OF THE RIVER ARE ON MOUNT KAUKASOS (CAUCASUS) . . . AND WITH THEM AGREES THEOPHANES OF MITYLENE (5) . . .

Jones, Vol. V, pp. 190–192

BOOK XI

SECTION V, 1. THE AMAZONS, PEOPLE SAY, ALSO LIVE ON THE MOUNTAINS ABOVE ALBANIA. SO THEOPHANES, WHO CAMPAIGNED WITH POMPEY AND WAS IN THE ALBANIANS' LANDS, SAYS THAT BETWEEN THE AMAZONS AND THE ALBANIANS LIVE THE SCYTHIAN GELAE AND THE LEGAE AND THAT THE RIVER MERMADALIS FLOWS BETWEEN THESE PEOPLE AND THE AMAZONS. HOWEVER OTHERS . . . SAY THAT THE AMAZONS MAKE THEIR HOME ON THE NORTH SIDE OF THE CAUCASIAN MOUNTAINS AND THERE THEY SPEND PART OF THEIR TIME WORKING ON THEIR LANDS, PLOWING, PLANTING AND TENDING THEIR HERDS, ESPECIALLY THEIR HORSES, WHILE THE FITTEST AMONG THEM ALSO GO HUNTING ON HORSEBACK AND PRACTICE WAR. ALL OF THEM HAVE THEIR RIGHT BREASTS CAUTERIZED IN THEIR INFANCY, SO THAT THEY CAN USE THEIR ARMS PROPERLY FOR EVERYTHING AND PARTICULARLY FOR THROWING THE JAVELIN.

2. IN TWO DESIGNATED MONTHS IN THE SPRING, THE AMAZONS GO UP THE NEARBY MOUNTAINS THAT SEPARATE THEM FROM THE GARGARIANS. THESE MEN TOO CLIMB UP, ACCORDING TO AN OLD CUSTOM, THEY ALL OFFER SACRIFICES TOGETHER AND FOR THE SAKE OF CHILDBEARING THEY MATE WITH THE WOMEN, HIDING IN THE DARK, ANY MAN AT RANDOM WITH ANY WOMAN. THEN, AFTER THEY ARE MADE PREGNANT, THE WOMEN ARE SENT BACK. IF THEY GIVE BIRTH TO GIRLS, THE AMAZONS KEEP THEM, BUT THE BOYS THEY SEND TO THE MEN TO BE BROUGHT UP THERE . . .

3. SOMETHING EXTRAORDINARY HAS HAPPENED IN THE TALES ABOUT THE AMAZONS. IN OTHER CASES, THERE IS A CLEAR DISTINCTION BETWEEN MYTH AND HISTORY. BUT CONCERNING THE AMAZONS, THE SAME THINGS ARE BEING TOLD NOW AS IN OLDER TIMES, EVEN THOUGH THEY ARE WEIRD AND BEYOND BELIEF.

4. . . . THE MOST NORTHERLY AREAS ADJACENT TO MOUNT KAUKASOS ARE HIT BY THE GREATEST SNOW STORMS. THERE, IT IS SAID, ON THE MOUNTAIN PASSES, OFTEN ENTIRE CONVOYS ARE SWALLOWED BY THE SNOW AND PEOPLE CARRY HOLLOW CANES TO BREATHE THROUGH THEM BY REACHING THE SURFACE ABOVE AND ALSO TO SIGNAL TO ANY PASSERSBY

FOR HELP, SO THAT THEY MAY BE DUG OUT AND SAVED. PEOPLE ALSO SAY THAT ICE BALLS FORM IN THE SNOW, WHICH CONTAIN GOOD (DRINKABLE) WATER . . . AND THAT SOME LIVING CREATURES, CALLED "SKOLEKES" (WORMS) BY APOLLONIOS AND "THRIPES" BY THEOPHANES, MAY BREED INSIDE THE SNOW . . . LIKE SOME MOSQUITOES CAN COME OUT OF THE FLAMES OF FURNACES.

Jones, Vol. V, pp. 232-236

According to another ancient author, Appian (quoted by Mirmont, p. 179), the name "Amazon" was given to any woman warrior in that "barbarian" region. In their expedition through those distant mountains Theophanes and Pompey showed a strong interest not only in the Amazons but in other mythological characters. It was told that on Mount Kaukasos they kept searching for the rock where Zeus had chained Prometheus.

Mythology was only one of the areas where the credibility of Theophanes was questioned. Since his own days, he had been attacked for his presumed misrepresentation of facts, meant to glorify his chief, Pompey, and to degrade their common enemies (Mirmont, p. 180). One of these enemies was the Roman stoic philosopher P. Rutilius Rufus, whom others considered "one of the best citizens, not only of his century, but of all times" (Mirmont, p. 180). This prominent Roman also spent some time on Lesbos.

After serving as a consul in Rome, Rutilius was sent to help in the administration of the new Roman conquests in Asia. But later, when he returned to Rome, he was accused (unfairly, it seems) of extortion and bribery and then was exiled to Mytilene. Rutilius was still there when many Romans were massacred by the men of Mithridates and by the Lesbians who had taken the side of this enemy of Rome, the king of Pontos. Rutilius was able to escape death only by renouncing his Roman citizenship.

ON BEHALF OF RABIRIUS [Pro Rabirio Postumo]
BY M.T. CICERO, 106–43

X, 27. NECESSITY EXCUSES THE CONDUCT OF RUTILIUS. WHEN THREATENED IN MYTILENE TO BE PUT TO DEATH BY MITHRIDATES, HE WAS ABLE TO AVOID THE SAVAGERY OF THE KING ONLY BY GIVING UP THE TOGA. SO THEN THIS MAN RUTILIUS, WHO FOR US ROMANS WAS A MODEL OF VIRTUE, WISDOM AND OLD-FASHIONED HONESTY, THIS CONSULAR PERSONALITY, HAS NOW ADOPTED THE SHOE-WEAR AND THE MANTLE OF THE GREEKS! YET NOBODY HAS THOUGHT TO ACCUSE HIM OF A CRIME; IT IS JUST THE MISFORTUNES OF OUR TIMES THAT ONE CAN BLAME.

Quoted by Mirmont (in French translation), pp. 181–182.

The rumors about the false accusations against Rutilius by Theophanes, apparently were accepted as fact by the Greek biographer Plutarch, even though the information came to him second-hand, through the writings of others and especially the historian Timagenes (Mirmont, p. 183). That episode, which was blamed on Theophanes, presumably took place after the Romans under Pompey had defeated Mithridates and proceeded to the conquest of the entire kingdom of Pontos.

LIFE OF POMPEY
BY PLUTARCH [PLUTARKHOS], C. 46–C. 120 A.D.

SECTION XXXVII
3. IN THE FORTRESS OF KAINON ("NEW CASTLE") POMPEY ALSO CAME ACROSS SOME SECRET RECORDS OF MITHRIDATES, WHICH HE REVIEWED NOT WITHOUT PLEASURE, BECAUSE THEY HAD MUCH TO DO WITH AN UNDERSTANDING OF THE CHARACTER OF THAT KING. AMONG THESE DOCUMENTS WERE MEMORANDA SHOWING THAT HE (MITHRIDATES) HAD POISONED MANY PEOPLE AND THAT WAS HOW ALSO HE HAD CAUSED THE DEATH OF HIS OWN SON, ARIARATHES, AS WELL AS ALKAIOS OF SARDIS, BECAUSE HE HAD OUTDONE HIM IN A HORSE RACE. THERE WERE ALSO (NOTES ABOUT) INTERPRETATIONS OF DREAMS, SOME THAT THE KING HIMSELF HAD SEEN AND OTHERS THAT WERE DREAMT BY HIS WIVES. ALSO FOUND WERE SOME LETTERS FROM MONIME TO HIM AND AGAIN FROM HIM (THE KING) TO HER. THEOPHANES ALSO CLAIMED TO HAVE DISCOVERED AN INFLAMMATORY MESSAGE FROM RUTILIUS, URGING THE EXTERMINATION OF THE ROMANS IN ASIA. MOST PEOPLE RIGHTFULLY CONSIDER THAT A VICIOUS FABRICATION, COMMITTED BY THEOPHANES PERHAPS BECAUSE HE HATED RUTILIUS FOR BEING SO UNLIKE HIM, OR, PROBABLY, FOR THE BENEFIT OF POMPEY, WHOSE FATHER HAD BEEN PRESENTED AS A VERY WICKED MAN BY RUTILIUS IN HIS HISTORIES.

Perrin, B., Vol. V, p. 212

When, in January 61 B.C., the victorious Pompey returned to Italy, his historian, Theophanes, was with him. By then, the Lesbian Greek not only could claim Roman citizenship but also was able to join the order of the equestrians (knights), having acquired the sizable fortune required for that social status (Mirmont, p. 183). Facing the complex political intrigues and struggles in the Roman capital, Theophanes quickly became the counsellor and negotiating agent of Pompey, who was increasingly being suspected of antirepublican dictatorial ambitions and, consequently, was not even allowed to celebrate a public triumph for his victories until nine months later, in September of that year (Mirmont, p.

185). While the public and the senate were concerned about the preservation of the republic, another victorious army general, Gaius Julius Caesar was emerging as the major personal rival of Pompey. In his own *History of the Civil Wars* (in which he always referred to himself in the third person) Caesar acknowledged the leading role of Theophanes in the efforts first to avert the conflict and later to organize the campaign and to save the defeated and hopeless Pompey from total annihilation.

THE CIVIL WARS [DE BELLUM CIVILE]
BY G. JULIUS CAESAR, C. 100–44 B.C.
BOOK III
18. . . . AFTER THE COMMOTION CAUSED BY THE SUDDEN APPEARANCE OF CAESAR HAD SUBSIDED, VIBULLIUS (ONE OF THE NAVY CHIEFS OF POMPEY), PLANNED A CONFERENCE WITH LIBO AND LUCCEIUS AND THEOPHANES, WHOM POMPEY CUSTOMARILY CONSULTED ABOUT HIS MOST IMPORTANT AFFAIRS. THE PURPOSE OF THE MEETING WAS TO STUDY CAESAR'S PROPOSALS (OF SAFE CONDUCT FOR HIS DELEGATES AND A POSSIBLE TRUCE). HOWEVER, SHORTLY AFTER VIBULLIUS HAD STARTED HIS PRESENTATION, POMPEY INTERRUPTED AND PREVENTED HIM FROM SPEAKING ANYMORE. "WHAT IS THE VALUE OF LIFE AND OF CITIZENSHIP FOR ME," HE DECLARED "IF I OWE THESE TO THE BENEVOLENCE OF CAESAR?." . . . CAESAR LEARNED ABOUT THESE PROCEEDINGS FROM THOSE WHO WERE PART OF THE MEETING. NEVERTHELESS HE KEPT TRYING TO FIND OTHER WAYS TO MAINTAIN THE PEACE.
Quoted in Latin by Peskett, 1921/66, pp. 220-222

While away from Rome, Caesar had delegated the handling of his affairs to Balbus, a man of patrician birth, from Gades in Spain (Mirmont, p. 186). After both victorious leaders, Caesar and Pompey, returned to Rome, the negotiations between them were conducted by two men, whom they trusted completely, Balbus, the Spaniard nobleman, and Theophanes, the Lesbian Greek, with "equal diplomatic skills" (Mirmont, p. 189). Theophanes may have been particularly interested in bringing the two rival leaders together, because the Roman citizenship bestowed upon him by Pompey needed to be confirmed by law and Caesar was the man to help them do it (Mirmont, p. 188). To develop closer ties between the two factions, Caesar not only gave his own daughter, Julia, to Pompey for a wife (Pompey later divorced her to marry the much younger Cornelia) but also had Balbus become the adopted son of Theophanes. At that time (59–58 B.C.), Balbus was approaching forty years of age and Theophanes' age could only be guessed. According to Roman law, to be allowed to adopt a son, he must have been considered old enough not to expect to have children of his own (Mirmont, p. 189), yet a later marriage of Theophanes produced the son mentioned by Strabo. The Roman orator, Cicero, could not hide his displeasure with this temporary alliance of his two enemies and with his apparent exclusion from it. In an anxious letter he expressed the concern shared by the entire senatorial ranks of the republic.

LETTER TO ATTICUS
BY M.T. CICERO, 106–43 B.C. (WRITTEN IN APRIL 59 B.C.)
I AM ANXIOUS AND HAVE BEEN FOR SOME TIME, TO VISIT ALEXANDRIA AND THE REST OF EGYPT, GETTING AWAY FROM HERE WHERE PEOPLE ARE TIRED OF SEEING ME AND RETURNING WHEN THEY MISS ME A LITTLE. BUT CONSIDERING THE CIRCUMSTANCES . . . WHAT WILL PEOPLE ON OUR SIDE (IF THERE ARE ANY LEFT) SAY? . . . HOW WILL HISTORY JUDGE ME 600 YEARS FROM NOW? I WORRY MORE ABOUT THAT THAN ABOUT THE PETTY GOSSIP OF OUR CONTEMPORARIES. HOWEVER I SUPPOSE I MUST SIT LOW AND SEE WHAT DEVELOPS. IF ANY OFFER IS MADE TO ME . . . EVEN REFUSING MIGHT NOT BE WITHOUT SOME GLORY. SO MAKE A NOTE THAT IF THEOPHANES (CICERO USED THE GREEK ALPHABET FOR THIS NAME) HAPPENS TO CONSULT YOU DO NOT DISMISS HIM RIGHT AWAY.
Winstedt, 1962 Vol. I, pp. 120-122.

LETTER TO ATTICUS
BY M.T. CICERO, 106–43 B.C. (WRITTEN IN APRIL 59 B.C.)
ISN'T SO MUCH NONSENSE WHAT WE HEAR IN LIVE CONVERSATION? I LEARNED A DOZEN TIMES MORE ABOUT CURRENT AFFAIRS FROM YOUR LETTER THAN FROM HIS TALK, THE DAILY GOSSIP, THE PLANS OF PUBLIUS, . . . THE CONVERSATIONS OF THEOPHANES AND MEMNIUS; AND YOU EXCITED MY WILD CURIOSITY ABOUT THAT ORGIASTIC DINNER . . . I WOULD LIKE TO HEAR MORE ABOUT IT.
Winstedt, 1962 Vol. I, pp. 142-144

LETTER TO ATTICUS
BY M.T. CICERO, 106–43 B.C. (WRITTEN IN APRIL 59 B.C.)
IF, AS YOU WRITE, YOU WILL COME HERE TO SEE ME, I WISH YOU COULD FIND OUT FROM THEOPHANES WHAT ARE THE FEELINGS OF THE BIG CHIEF TOWARDS ME.
Winstedt, 1962 Vol. I, pp. 158-160

The correspondence between Cicero and Atticus continued and in a letter from Athens, Cicero again discussed Pompey and Theophanes.

LETTER TO ATTICUS
BY M.T. CICERO, 106–43 B.C. (WRITTEN IN APRIL 59 B.C.)
I AGREE . . . THAT POMPEY IS SURELY GOING TO SPAIN. I DO NOT APPROVE OF THIS AT ALL; ON THIS POINT I CONVINCED THEOPHANES EASILY THAT NOTHING WOULD BE BETTER THAN TO REMAIN IN ROME. CONSEQUENTLY THE GREEK WILL PUT PRESSURE ON POMPEY. HE (POMPEY) VALUES HIS AUTHORITATIVE ADVICE MOST OF ALL.
Winstedt, Vol. 1, p. 362.

More than a year-and-a-half later, as time went by and as troubles (which eventually ended in his death) piled up, Cicero again mentions "The Greek" with regrets about not relying on his earlier advice.

LETTER TO ATTICUS
BY M.T. CICERO, 106–43 B.C. (WRITTEN IN APRIL 59 B.C.)
SO THEN I, EVEN THOUGH I TRY TO JUDGE EVERYTHING BY THE STANDARDS OF DUTY, WILL STILL REMEMBER YOUR ADVICE. IF I HAD FOLLOWED IT I WOULD NOT HAVE SUFFERED SUCH SORROWFUL AND SAD TIMES. I RECALL THE COUNSEL YOU SENT ME ON THE PART OF THEOPHANES AND THE MEMORY MAKES ME MOAN.
Winstedt, Vol. II, p. 148

Five years later, as the civil war between the Roman forces of Caesar and Pompey was going to be pursued and to end with the latter's total defeat on the mainland of Greece, the name of Theophanes still appeared in Cicero's continuing correspondence.

LETTER TO ATTICUS
BY M.T. CICERO, 106–43 B.C. (WRITTEN IN APRIL 59 B.C.)
. . . THERE IS NOTHING CLEARER THAT WAR IS IMMINENT. LET ME THEN RUN AWAY, THE WAY YOU SUGGEST. I DO NOT KNOW WHY THEOPHANES WANTS TO SEE ME. BUT HE DID WRITE TO ME. I ANSWERED AS WELL AS I COULD. HE HAS BEEN TELLING ME THAT HE WANTS TO COME TO ME TO DISCUSS HIS OWN AFFAIRS AND SOME THAT CONCERN ME. I WILL BE WAITING FOR YOUR LETTER. PLEASE SEE TO IT THAT NOTHING IS DONE HASTILY.
Winstedt, Vol. III, pp. 344-346.

Details about the civil war and Pompey's assassination are given in the next section.

After Pompey's death, Theophanes was pardoned by the victorious Caesar. Upon his own death, which occurred after 44 B.C., the famous native of Mytilene received divine honors from his countrymen (Perrin,

HELLENISTIC TWILIGHT AND ROMAN ROMANTIC LOVES 149

Left: Theophanes of Lesbos, "Theos," ca. first century B.C.;
Right: Arkhedamis, wife of Theophanes. Lesbian coins, in Richter 1965/84.

1968, Vol. V, p.543). He was called "savior, benefactor and builder of his country" and also "theos" (not an uncommon practice in Roman times), "God liberator" and *"philopatris,"* "lover-of-his-country" (*Inscr. Insul. Mar. Aegaei*, Fasc. No. 150, 163, quoted by Mirmont, p. 203). Coins were struck (Richter, III 1965, Figs. 2023, 2024, 2028) with his portrait on the obverse and that of his wife Arkhedamis on the reverse. A contemporary of Theophanes was the philosopher Lesbonax, also of Mytilene (Richter, 1965, p. 283 and Figs. 2029–2031). None of the many books of this Lesbian philosopher now exist. His son, named Potamos, later was the head of delegations from Lesbos to Julius Caesar, according to inscriptions found on the island (Richter, III, 1965, p. 283). The son of Theophanes, Marcos Pompeios, or, in Latin, Pompeius Macer, was appointed by the first Roman emperor, Augustus, as supervising councilman of Asia and, before that, he had served as chief library administrator in Rome. Later he became a close friend of Augustus' successor, emperor Tiberius. The ancient texts leave some doubt whether this Romanized Greek was in fact the son, or the grandson of the first Lesbian to be granted Roman citizenship (Mirmont, p. 203–204). Through his father or grandfather Theophanes, Pompeius Macer must have been familiar with the geography of Asia Minor, and as a young man of twenty he served as a guide through that area for the eighteen-year-old Ovid, the future renowned Latin poet. Afterwards both young men also traveled together through Sicily and remained good friends (Mirmont, pp. 203–204).

In 33 A.D. when the poet Ovid was seventy-five years old, Pompeios (then approaching eighty) and his family fell victims to Tiberius' wrath, perhaps due to the extraordinary honors they had received in the Greek world. The old Pompeios Makrinos (as the name was spelled on an inscription from Lesbos) was put to death along with his son-in-law and his daughter was exiled. But almost 100 years later, in 127 A.D., a daughter of "Theophanes the Younger"—grandson or great-grandson(?) of the Lesbian historian and Roman counsellor—was celebrated as a "benefactress of the city" of Mytilene (*Inscr. Gr. Insul. Mar. Aegaei*, Fasc. No. 2346, 237, quoted by Mirmont, p. 206), a demonstration of the continuing gratitude and admiration of the Lesbians for Theophanes' family.

Pompey and Cornelia

The biographer of Pompey, of Caesar, of Cicero and of many others, Plutarch [*Plutarkhos*] of Cheronea [*Heronea*] in Central Greece, lived from about 46–50 to some years after 120 A.D. mostly in Greece, but he also travelled to Egypt and to Italy. In Rome he taught and made many prominent friends. For the last thirty years of his life he was a priest at Delphi, not far from his hometown. Not only a biographer and historian but also a philosopher, Plutarch was considered a platonist, although his moral philosophy, published under the title "Ethics" (in Latin "Moralia") included eclectically well-integrated concepts from Aristotle, from the stoics and from the epicureans (Chapter III-C). Plutarch's best known work, the "Parallel Lives" (biographies side-by-side) contain twenty-three pairs of biographies comparing outstanding Greek and Roman individuals. This valuable work—a "mine of information" according to the *Oxford Classical Dictionary*—was introduced into Italy in the fifteenth century A.D. by Greek scholars fleeing the invading Turks (4). The first English translation of the "Lives" appeared in 1579 A.D. and from the sixteenth to the nineteenth centuries Plutarch was "the most popular of the classic authors" (*Encyclopedia Britannica*, Vol. 18). The life of Pompey the Great referred to the Roman general's and his wife's stay on Lesbos and also to his reliance on his Lesbian counsellor and historian, Theophanes.

Plutarch [*Plutarkhos*] (presumed portrait) (Delphi Museum), in Richter 1965/84.

HELLENISTIC TWILIGHT AND ROMAN ROMANTIC LOVES 151

PARALLEL LIVES
BY PLUTARCH [PLUTARKHOS], C. 46 – C. 120 A.D.
POMPEY [POMPEIUS MAGNUS]
I.1. THE ROMAN PEOPLE MUST HAVE FELT FROM EARLY ON TOWARDS POMPEY THE WAY AISKHYLOS (AESCHYLUS) EXPRESSED THE FEELINGS OF PROMETHEUS FOR HERAKLES, WHEN HE HAD HIM SAY:
"MY MOST BELOVED SON OF A FATHER I HATE"
. . .

Plutarch referred here to the Romans' hatred for Pompey's father, comparing it to Prometheus' hatred of father Zeus, (who had chained him on a rock on Mount Caucasus [*Kaukasos*] for life). Herakles, the son, had freed him and his gratitude was likened to the Romans' feelings toward Pompey the Great [*Pompeius Magnus*]. But after many victorious campaigns from Spain and Gaul to Asia Minor, the eastern Mediterranean and the Caucasian mountains, Pompey seemed to have become a threat to the Roman Republic and a popular rival emerged in the person of Julius Caesar.

LV. 1-3. ON HIS RETURN TO ROME POMPEY MARRIED CORNELIA . . . LATELY LEFT A WIDOW. THE YOUNG WOMAN HAD OTHER ATTRACTIONS BESIDES YOUTH AND BEAUTY. SHE WAS HIGHLY EDUCATED, PLAYED THE LUTE WELL, UNDERSTOOD GEOMETRY AND HAD MADE IT A HABIT TO ATTEND AND BENEFIT FROM TALKS ON PHILOSOPHY, WITHOUT BECOMING, AS A RESULT, UNFRIENDLY OR PRETENTIOUS LIKE SOME WOMEN WHO PURSUE SUCH STUDIES. NEITHER WAS THERE ANY FAULT IN HER FATHER'S FAMILY OR REPUTATION. THE AGE DIFFERENCE HOWEVER, WAS NOT LIKED BY EVERYONE, BECAUSE CORNELIA WAS YOUNG ENOUGH TO BE A CLOSER MATCH FOR POMPEY'S SON.

LVI.1. . . . SOME OF CAESAR'S FRIENDS THOUGHT THAT HE TOO, WHO HAD PROVIDED SUCH OUTSTANDING SERVICES . . . DESERVED TO BECOME AT LEAST SECOND CONSUL . . .

LVII.3-4 (THEN) . . . POMPEY (FOLLOWING PUBLIC DEMONSTRATIONS OF ADMIRATION . . .) ABANDONING THE PRUDENT ATTITUDE THAT HAD GUIDED HIM BEFORE, DISPLAYED AN EXCESSIVE CONFIDENCE IN HIS OWN POWER AND A CONTEMPT FOR CAESAR'S. THIS WAS NOT A MINOR FACTOR IN CAUSING THE CIVIL WAR . . .

LX.1-2. THEN . . . NEWS ARRIVED THAT CAESAR . . . WAS MARCHING DIRECTLY TOWARDS ROME WITH ALL HIS ARMIES . . . BUT IN FACT HE HAD NO MORE THAN 300 CAVALRY AND 5,000 FOOT SOLDIERS WHEN HE CAME TO THE BANKS OF THE RUBICON RIVER. LIKE MEN HEADED FROM A ROCK TOWARDS A DEEP CANYON, HAVING CLOSED HIS MIND'S EYES TO THE THOUGHTS OF DANGER, CAESAR SIMPLY

DECLARED IN GREEK "ANARRHIPHTHO KYBOS" (LET THE DIE BE CAST) AND LED HIS FORCES THROUGH THE RIVER.

There was confusion in Rome and

LXI.4 POMPEY DETERMINED TO PUT AN END TO ALL THE RUMORS BY LEAVING THE CITY...

LXII.1. SOME DAYS LATER... CAESAR CAME INTO THE CITY... AND (LATER) TAKING WHAT FUNDS WERE AVAILABLE HE STARTED A CAMPAIGN TO PURSUE POMPEY.

Pompey and Caesar after him sailed with their troops across the sea to the Greek mainland where a final confrontation was to take place. When Caesar withdrew due to lack of provisions, Pompey's men were very anxious to attack but for a while Pompey preferred not to engage in battle and to keep his armies at the enemy's heels with caution, marking only a few temporary successes. According to Plutarch, Caesar was contemptuous of his opponent's hesitancy and remarked:

LXV.5... "VICTORY WOULD HAVE BEEN ON THE SIDE OF OUR ENEMIES IF THEY HAD A VICTOR AS THEIR LEADER."

Yet most of Pompey's followers still believed that victory was theirs and

LXVI.3... MANY ALSO SAILED TO LESBOS TO BRING THE GOOD NEWS ABOUT THE END OF THE WAR TO CORNELIA, WHOM POMPEY HAD SENT THERE FOR HER SAFETY.

Caesar, however, returned and the two Roman armies confronted each other in the plain of Pharsala—or *Pharsalus* (*Encycl. Brit.*, Vol. 17)—in central Greece (7).

LXVIII.1. BUT... WHEN THEY REACHED THE PLAIN OF PHARSALA THEY (THE SENIOR OFFICERS) FORCED POMPEY... TO CALL A WAR COUNCIL AND... THEY SWORE NOT TO LEAVE THE BATTLEFIELD UNTIL THEY ROUTED THE ENEMY... CAESAR'S ARMY CONSISTED OF 22,000 AND POMPEY'S OF MORE THAN TWICE THIS MANY... THE TRUMPETS BEGAN TO SOUND FOR THE ATTACK... A FEW OF THE ROMAN HIGH NOBILITY AND SOME GREEKS WHO WERE THERE AS SPECTATORS NOT INVOLVED IN THE CONFLICT, WERE WONDERING HOW THE EMPIRE HAD BEEN BROUGHT TO SUCH A STATE (OF CIVIL WAR) THROUGH UNRESTRAINED PERSONAL AMBITION AND RIVALRY.

The decisive battle followed—August, 48 B.C.—and Pompey, due to poor strategy and his inexperienced and undisciplined troops, was defeated.

LXXII.1. THROUGH THE DUST... POMPEY... DISTRACTED AND BESIDE HIMSELF, RETIRED TOWARDS HIS CAMP, WITH-

HELLENISTIC TWILIGHT AND ROMAN ROMANTIC LOVES

OUT SAYING A WORD TO ANYBODY . . . PUTTING ON SOME OLD CLOTHES APPROPRIATE FOR HIS BAD FORTUNE, HE MADE HIS WAY OUT IN SECRET.

LXXIII.1-3 THE NEXT MORNING AT DAWN, POMPEY WENT TO THE RIVER (PINEIOS, BETWEEN THESSALY AND MACEDONIA) AND AFTER HE DISMISSED MOST OF HIS FOLLOWERS AND ALL HIS SERVANTS, HE RODE A BOAT . . . TO A LARGE MERCHANT SHIP, READY TO SAIL. THE CAPTAIN, A ROMAN CITIZEN, TOOK HIM ABOARD WITH TWO OF HIS COMPANIONS . . . AND HOISTED SAIL.

One of Pompey's companions, later seeing him untie his own shoes felt sorry for him without servants and went to untie them and also to anoint his chief. From the coast of Greece, Pompey and his few followers sailed to Lesbos. A messenger was sent from the harbor of Mytilene to find Cornelia. The scene may have taken place in the house of Theophanes, Pompey's historian and counsellor, where Cornelia was thought to have been staying (Mirmont, p. 198).

LXXIV.1-3. POMPEY, SAILING BY . . . AMPHIPOLIS, CROSSED OVER FROM THERE TO MYTILENE, PLANNING TO TAKE BACK (HIS WIFE) CORNELIA AND HIS SON. AS SOON AS HE ARRIVED IN THE HARBOR OF THE ISLAND, HE SENT A MESSENGER TO TOWN CARRYING THE NEWS, WHICH WAS VERY DIFFERENT FROM WHAT CORNELIA EXPECTED. FROM ALL THE MESSAGES AND LETTERS SENT TO HER PREVIOUSLY FOR THE PURPOSE OF KEEPING HER HAPPY, SHE WAS HOPING THAT THE WAR HAD ENDED AND THAT ALL THAT WAS LEFT FOR POMPEY WAS TO CHASE AND CAPTURE CAESAR. THE MESSENGER, NOTICING HER HOPES AND EXPECTATIONS, WAS UNABLE TO GREET HER OR TO SPEAK AND ONLY MADE HER UNDERSTAND THE MAGNITUDE OF THE DISASTER BY HIS TEARS, RATHER THAN ANY WORDS. THEN, AFTER AWHILE, HE MADE IT CLEAR TO HER THAT SHE HAD TO RUSH TO POMPEY, WHO WAS THERE WITH ONLY ONE SHIP AND EVEN THAT NOT HIS OWN. HEARING THIS, THE YOUNG WOMAN COLLAPSED AND FAINTED, REMAINING SPEECHLESS AND UNCONSCIOUS FOR A LONG TIME. AS SOON AS SHE REGAINED CONSCIOUSNESS SHE REALIZED THAT THERE WAS NO TIME FOR TEARS AND LAMENTATIONS AND SHE RAN THROUGH THE CITY DOWN TO THE SEA. POMPEY MET HER AND WELCOMED HER IN HIS ARMS JUST AS SHE BEGAN TO TOTTER AND WAS ABOUT TO FALL. "I SEE YOU, MY HUSBAND," SHE CRIED, "NOT DUE TO YOUR DESTINY BUT BECAUSE OF MY BAD LUCK, NOW REDUCED DOWN TO ONE SHIP, YOU WHO BEFORE YOUR MARRIAGE TO CORNELIA WERE NAVIGATING THIS SEA WITH FIVE HUNDRED VESSELS. WHY DID YOU COME TO SEE ME AND YOU DID NOT LEAVE TO HER HEAVY DOOM THE WOMAN WHO HAS OVERWHELMED YOU WITH SUCH A MISFORTUNE? HOW GLAD I WOULD HAVE BEEN IF I HAD DIED BEFORE LEARNING THAT

POPLIUS, MY VIRGINAL HUSBAND, LAY DEAD AMONG THE PARTHIANS; AND HOW WISE IF, AFTER HIM, I WOULD HAVE PUT AN END TO MY OWN LIFE, AS I WANTED TO DO. BUT IT SEEMS THAT I WAS SPARED, TO BECOME THE RUIN OF POMPEY THE GREAT."

LXXV.1-4. THAT WAS HOW CORNELIA WAS REPORTED TO HAVE SPOKEN AND POMPEY THEN ANSWERED: "SO IT IS, CORNELIA, THAT YOU HAVE KNOWN ONLY ONE FORTUNE OF MINE AND THAT WAS THE BETTER ONE. THIS PERHAPS HAS DECEIVED YOU TOO, IN THAT IT LASTED WITH ME LONGER THAN IT IS USUAL. AS ORDINARY HUMANS, HOWEVER, WE MUST ALSO BEAR OUR MISFORTUNES AND TEST AGAIN OUR CHANCES. IT IS NOT BEYOND HOPE THAT I MIGHT RECOVER FROM THIS SITUATION, CONSIDERING THAT I GOT HERE FROM WHERE I WAS BEFORE."

SO THE WIFE SENT FOR HER BELONGINGS AND FOR HER SERVANTS FROM THE CITY. BUT EVEN THOUGH THE CITIZENS OF MYTILENE EMBRACED POMPEY AND INVITED HIM TO ENTER THEIR CITY, HE DID NOT WISH TO DO SO AND ADVISED THEM INSTEAD TO SUBMIT TO THE CONQUEROR AND TO BE COURAGEOUS, BECAUSE CAESAR SHOULD PROVE TO BE FAIR AND KIND. THEN, TURNING TO THE PHILOSOPHER KRATIPPOS, WHO HAD COME DOWN FROM THE CITY TO SEE HIM, HE COMPLAINED AND WONDERED WITH HIM BRIEFLY ABOUT PROVIDENCE. KRATIPPOS TRIED TO COME UP WITH SOME BETTER PROSPECTS, YIELDING SOMEWHAT IN ORDER TO AVOID CAUSING ANYMORE GRIEF, OR BEING ARGUMENTATIVE AT THE WRONG TIME. FOR WHEN POMPEY WAS RAISING QUESTIONS ABOUT PROVIDENCE, KRATIPPOS MIGHT HAVE DECLARED THAT BECAUSE THE STATE ADMINISTRATION WAS SO BAD, A SINGLE RULER [MONARCHY] WAS NEEDED; AND HE MIGHT ALSO HAVE ASKED: "HOW, POMPEY, AND BY WHAT PROOF COULD YOU CONVINCE US THAT YOU COULD HAVE MADE A BETTER USE OF YOUR LUCK, HAD YOU WON AGAINST CAESAR?" BUT THESE MATTERS BELONGED TO THE GODS AND IT WAS BETTER TO LEAVE THEM AS THEY WERE, WITHOUT DISCUSSION.

LXXVI.1. TAKING HIS WIFE AND HIS FRIENDS ON BOARD, POMPEY SAILED AWAY, ANCHORING ONLY IN SMALL HARBORS TO GET THE NECESSARY SUPPLIES AND WATER . . .

LXXVI.4-5. . . . HE BEGAN TO CONSIDER WHERE WOULD BE THE SAFEST PLACE TO RETREAT FOR THE TIME. A CONFERENCE WAS HELD AND EVERYONE AGREED THAT NO ROMAN PROVINCE WOULD BE SAFE ENOUGH . . . THEOPHANES THE LESBIAN, INDICATED THAT IT WOULD MAKE NO SENSE TO GO ANYWHERE BUT EGYPT, FROM WHICH THERE WERE AT A DISTANCE OF ONLY THREE DAYS' SAILING AND WHERE THEY COULD RELY ON (KING) PTOLEMY, WHO WAS STILL A YOUNG BOY AND SHOULD HAVE BEEN VERY MUCH INDEBTED TO POMPEY FOR THE FRIENDSHIP HE HAD GRANTED TO HIS FATHER.

LXXVII.1. AS SOON AS IT WAS DECIDED TO LOOK FOR A SHELTER IN EGYPT, POMPEY SET SAIL FROM CYPRUS TOGETHER WITH CORNELIA ... ON LEARNING THAT KING PTOLEMY (THE 12TH, REF. TABLE I) WAS WITH AN ARMY MAKING WAR AGAINST HIS SISTER (CLEOPATRA VII), HE SENT A MESSENGER TO INFORM THE KING OF HIS ARRIVAL. PTOLEMY CALLED A COUNCIL IN WHICH THEODOTOS OF HIOS, A SALARIED TEACHER OF RHETORIC, DEMONSTRATED TO THEM THAT NEITHER HOSPITALITY NOR REJECTION WERE SAFE FOR EGYPT AND THAT THE WISEST COURSE WOULD BE TO TAKE POMPEY'S LIFE, ADDING WITH A SMILE THAT "A DEAD MAN CANNOT BITE."

LXXVIII.1-4. THEY DECIDED ON THIS PLAN AND ASSIGNED ITS EXECUTION TO ACHILLAS. TAKING ALONG SOMEONE NAMED SEPTIMIUS, WHO HAD ONCE BEEN A COMMANDER UNDER POMPEY, ANOTHER CENTURION, SALVIOS AND THREE OR FOUR SERVANTS, HE TOOK OFF TOWARDS POMPEY'S SHIP. THE MOST EXPERIENCED MEN ON BOARD ... NOTICED THAT THERE WAS NO SIGN OF SPECTACULAR AND ROYAL RECEPTION LIKE THEOPHANES HAD EXPECTED, BUT ONLY A FEW MEN WERE COMING, IN A SMALL FISHING BOAT. THEY BECAME VERY SUSPICIOUS AND URGED POMPEY TO SAIL BACK TO THE OPEN SEA, BEYOND THE REACH OF ANY PROJECTILES. BUT IN THE MEANTIME THE APPROACHING FISHING BOAT HAD ALREADY ARRIVED AND SEPTIMIUS STOOD UP AND ADDRESSED POMPEY IN THE ROMAN LANGUAGE AS IMPERATOR. THEN ACHILLAS GREETED HIM IN GREEK AND INVITED HIM TO COME ABOARD THE FISHING BOAT ... AT THE SAME TIME IT WAS NOTED THAT SOME ROYAL SHIPS WERE TAKING THEIR CREWS ABOARD AND THAT THE SHORE WAS OCCUPIED BY ARMED SOLDIERS, SO THAT IT WOULD HAVE BEEN IMPOSSIBLE TO ESCAPE, EVEN IF THEY HAD CHANGED THEIR MINDS. BESIDES ANY SUCH SHOW OF DISTRUST MIGHT HAVE GIVEN THE ASSASSINS AN EXCUSE FOR THEIR CRIME. CONSEQUENTLY, AFTER HE EMBRACED CORNELIA, WHO WAS WEEPING ALREADY FOR HIS ANTICIPATED DEATH, HE ORDERED TWO CENTURIONS TO EMBARK FIRST AND ALSO PHILIP, ONE OF THE FREEMEN AND A SERVANT NAMED SKYTHES. WHILE THOSE AROUND ACHILLAS WERE READY TO RECEIVE HIM ON THE FISHING BOAT. HE TURNED TOWARDS HIS WIFE AND SON AND QUOTED THE VERSES OF SOPHOCLES:

> "WHO GOES TO DEAL WITH A TYRANT BECOMES HIS SLAVE, ALTHOUGH FREE ON HIS WAY THERE."

LXXIX.1-3. AFTER RECITING THESE LAST WORDS TO HIS ENTOURAGE, HE BOARDED THE LITTLE BOAT. THE DISTANCE FROM THE TRIREME TO THE LAND WAS LONG AND SINCE NO ONE ON BOARD HAD ANYTHING KIND TO SAY ... AND THERE WAS DEEP SILENCE, POMPEY STARTED TO READ FROM A BOOKLET A SPEECH HE HAD HIMSELF WRITTEN IN GREEK, TO ADDRESS PTOLEMY. AS THEY WERE APPROACHING THE SHORE, CORNELIA WATCHED WITH THEIR FRIENDS FROM

THE TRIREME, FILLED WITH ANXIETY ABOUT WHAT WAS TO HAPPEN. SHE BEGAN TO FEEL A LITTLE ENCOURAGED WHEN SHE SAW MANY OF THE KING'S MEN GATHERING AS IF TO HONOR AND WELCOME POMPEY. BUT AS HE GRABBED PHILIP'S HAND TO DISEMBARK MORE EASILY, SEPTIMIUS RAN HIS SWORD THROUGH HIM AND THEN OTHERS STABBED HIM WITH THEIR DAGGERS. PULLING HIS TOGA WITH BOTH HANDS OVER HIS FACE, POMPEY SUBMITTED TO THE BLOWS ONLY WITH A MOAN AND WITHOUT SAYING OR DOING ANYTHING UNWORTHY OF HIM. HE HAD LIVED ONE YEAR LESS THAN SIXTY AND ENDED HIS LIFE ONE DAY BEFORE HIS BIRTHDAY.

LXXX.1-6. WATCHING THE ASSASSINATION, THOSE ON THE SHIP LET OUT A WAILING CRY THAT COULD BE HEARD AS FAR AS THE SHORE. THEN QUICKLY WEIGHING ANCHORS THEY FLED. A STRONG WIND HELPED THEM REACH SAFELY THE OPEN SEA AND SO THE EGYPTIANS WHO WANTED TO CHASE THEM HAD TO TURN BACK. BUT THEY CUT OFF POMPEY'S HEAD AND THREW OUT OF THE BOAT THE REST OF THE BODY, NAKED, LEAVING IT FOR THOSE WHO CARED TO SEE SUCH A SIGHT. PHILIP STAYED BY IT UNTIL VIEWERS GOT TIRED WATCHING. THEN HE WASHED IT WITH SEA-WATER AND WRAPPED IT WITH ONE OF HIS OWN TUNICS. HAVING NOTHING ELSE, HE SEARCHED ALONG THE BEACH AND FOUND THE REMNANTS OF A SMALL FISHING BOAT, WHICH, THOUGH OLD, COULD SERVE TO PREPARE A FUNERAL PYRE FOR THE NAKED CORPSE, ALTHOUGH BARELY. AS HE WAS GATHERING THE WOOD AND BUILDING THE PYRE, A NOW OLD ROMAN CAME BY, WHO WHEN YOUNG HAD SERVED IN THE EARLY CAMPAIGNS WITH POMPEY. "WHO ARE YOU, MY FRIEND, TO THINK OF DOING THE BURIAL OF POMPEY THE GREAT?" AND WHEN PHILIP ANSWERED THAT HE WAS AN EMANCIPATED SLAVE (FREEDMAN) THE MAN SAID, "BUT YOU SHALL NOT HAVE THE HONOR ALL ALONE; LET ME TAKE PART IN A PIOUS PRIVILEGE OFFERED TO US. I WILL NOT TOTALLY REGRET MY BEING IN A FOREIGN COUNTRY IF, TO COMPENSATE FOR MANY HARDSHIPS, I HAVE THE OPPORTUNITY TO TOUCH WITH MY OWN HANDS AND ARRANGE FOR THE BURIAL OF THE GREATEST OF ROMAN IMPERATORS." THAT WAS POMPEY'S FUNERAL . . .

. . .

THE REMAINS OF POMPEY WERE TAKEN TO CORNELIA WHO THEN HAD THEM DEPOSITED AT HIS ALBAN VILLA.

Perrin, V. 1968, pp. 116-325.

Pompey's opponent and former father-in-law, Julius Caesar, in his book *De Bellum Civile* (The Civil War, in Latin) described the final battle in extraordinary detail referring to himself in the third person and not with total impartiality. The end of Pompey is also mentioned, but more briefly. The available manuscripts date from the tenth to twelfth centuries A.D.

THE CIVIL WAR
BY JULIUS CAESAR, C. 100–44 B.C.

BOOK III, 93–95 WHEN THE SIGNAL WAS GIVEN, OUR SOLDIERS WITH SPEARS STRAIGHT RUSHED FORWARD BUT THEN, SEEING THAT THE POMPEIANS WERE NOT ADVANCING . . . THEY SLOWED DOWN AND STOPPED ABOUT HALF-WAY SO THAT THEIR ENERGY MIGHT NOT BE ALL EXHAUSTED BY THE TIME THEY MADE CONTACT WITH THE ENEMY. AFTER A SHORT INTERVAL THEY RENEWED THEIR RAPID ADVANCE AND ON CAESAR'S COMMAND THEY DISCHARGED THEIR SPEARS AND QUICKLY DREW THEIR SWORDS.

A detailed description of the battle at Pharsala—or *Pharsalus* (*Encyl. Brit.* Vol. 17)—was next given by Caesar, concluding with Pompey's defeat.

AFTER THE POMPEIANS WERE FORCED TO FLEE . . . CAESAR URGED HIS SOLDIERS TO TAKE ADVANTAGE OF THEIR GOOD FORTUNE AND TO ATTACK THE ENEMY CAMP. THE RAMPARTS WERE WELL-DEFENDED BY THE GUARDS . . . BUT THE SOLDIERS WHO HAD FLED FROM THE BATTLEFIELD WERE PANIC-STRICKEN AND EXHAUSTED, MANY HAD THROWN AWAY THEIR ARMS . . . AND WERE THINKING MORE OF FURTHER FLIGHT THAN OF DEFENDING THE CAMP.

. . . POMPEIUS, GETTING A HORSE AND TEARING OFF HIS INSIGNIA, ESCAPED THROUGH A BACK GATE AND HURRIED DIRECTLY TO LARISA. WITHOUT SLOWING DOWN HE THEN RODE THROUGH THE NIGHT AND CAME TO THE SHORE.

99. IN THIS BATTLE HE (CAESAR) LOST NO MORE THAN TWO HUNDRED FOOT SOLDIERS, BUT ALSO ABOUT THIRTY BRAVE CENTURIONS. . . . OF THE POMPEIAN ARMY ABOUT FIFTEEN THOUSAND LOST THEIR LIVES AND MORE THAN TWENTY-FOUR THOUSAND WERE TAKEN PRISONERS . . . MANY, BESIDES, FLED TO THE SURROUNDING COMMUNITIES . . .

102. CAESAR, PUTTING EVERYTHING ASIDE, PURSUED POMPEIUS. . . . POMPEIUS HIMSELF, AFTER STOPPING OVERNIGHT AT AMPHIPOLIS TO CONFER WITH OLD COMRADES AND TO COLLECT MONEY FOR NECESSARY EXPENSES, HE BOARDED A SHIP AND IN A FEW DAYS CAME TO MYTILENE. HE WAS DETAINED THERE BY A STORM FOR TWO DAYS AND THEN, AFTER ADDING SOME OTHER SMALL CRAFT TO HIS FLEET, HE SAILED TO . . . CYPRUS . . . A REPORT OF CAESAR'S APPROACH WAS ALREADY SPREADING . . .

103. . . . POMPEIUS GAVE UP THE IDEA OF GOING TO SYRIA . . . AND WITH AN ARMY OF TWO THOUSAND MEN . . . ARRIVED AT PELUSIUM IN EGYPT. THERE, KING PTOLEMY, STILL A

> YOUNG BOY, WAS AT WAR AGAINST HIS SISTER CLEOPATRA, WHOM A FEW MONTHS BEFORE HE HAD DEPOSED FROM THE THRONE, WITH THE HELP OF RELATIVES AND FRIENDS. MANY OF PTOLEMY'S MEN WERE FORMER SOLDIERS OF POMPEIUS...
> ... BUT THE KING'S PREFECT... A MAN OF UNIQUE AUDACITY, AND A MILITARY TRIBUNE CONSPIRED TO ASSASSINATE POMPEIUS. LURED BY THEIR COURTEOUS GREETINGS, HE BOARDED A SMALL BOAT WITH FEW FRIENDS AND AS HE LANDED, HE WAS KILLED BY THE KING'S OFFICERS.
> Peskett, A.G., 1921-66, Vol. III, pp. 326-344.

Theophanes was closely involved with the "Egyptian question" (Mirmont, p. 190) concerning the succession of the young Ptolemy XII Auletes ("The Flute Player") to the throne of his natural father, Ptolemy XI Soter ("The Savior"). The young prince, who was eventually responsible for the murder of Pompey, back in the year 59 B.C. had to pay 1,000 talents to induce the Romans to support his right to the Egyptian throne. Previous to that, in about 62 B.C., Theophanes had been the middle man in arranging for gifts to Pompey from Ptolemy Auletes, who was known to be a repulsive individual and was later chased by his own people and forced to seek refuge by the Romans of Pompey. It was rumored that Theophanes instigated the king's flight in order to extract more gifts and payments from the fugitive Egyptian prince. That experience obviously did not deter the young Ptolemy from consenting to Pompey's assassination when the defeated Roman in turn asked for protection in Egypt.

B. EROTIC ROMANCES

Hellenistic historians, librarians and "stylists"

The Roman peace—*Pax Romana*—for most average persons lasted almost 500 years and citizens, freemen, even slaves in the empire from Britain and Spain to Egypt and Mesopotamia had for a while the sensation of a private as well as political and military calm. Hellenism (9) was in the roots as well as the blossoms of the cosmopolitan, comfortable and perhaps complacent and somewhat corrupt mentality of the first century B.C. and the three first centuries of our era. Religious restraints began to fade but scholarship and learning shone with great brilliance. An earlier example of the coming age of scholarship was Hellanikos of Lesbos (fourth century B.C.), who published systematic accounts of the heroic mythology and surveys of foreign nations, along the lines of Herodotos. He also prepared a catalog of all the priestesses of Hera at the temple of Heraion of Argos—one of many examples of the urge to record and to classify—and an early history of Athens (Levi, 1985, p. 291-2). It is not known where Hellanikos lived and where or when he died. His life and work, however, are typical of the trend and personal goals of hundreds of intellectuals and scholars in the 500–600 years around the turn of the millennium. Notably, the recreation of the life on Lesbos and of the Lesbians is only possible thanks to the extensive historical writings of people like Diodoros the Sicilian, Plutarkhos, Arrianos, Praxilla and Diogenes Laertios, dated one or two centuries before or after the beginning of our era. Among the many others who also contributed to the recording and preservation of stories, facts and phrases—almost with a fanatic collector's compulsion—were grammarians, rhetoricians, writers about proper language styles and encyclopedic lexicographers (Brunt, 1929-76; Fyfe 1927-82; Hicks, 1925-66; Oldfather, 1933-68; Robson, 1954). The use of lines from ancient poetry, as examples of style, spelling and grammar, has continued to provide shining examples of creative genius, which otherwise would have been totally lost (Edmonds, 1922-80; Campbell, 1982). Surprisingly too, prolific Hellenistic and Roman writers, aiming primarily to amuse and to entertain,—such as Athenaios—have turned out to be the richest treasure chests of ancient Greek wisdom, knowledge and art (Gulick, R.B. 1969, Vol. I, Introduction, p. ix–x). The fifteen-volume work of the Egyptian-Greek from Naukratis has been quoted many times in previous chapters. More on fish and seafood in "The Dining Scholars" referred to Lesbos.

DINING SCHOLARS
BY ATHENAIOS OF NAUKRATIS, THIRD CENTURY A.D.
BOOK III, 92.D.
IN HIS BOOK ON "GASTRONOMY" ARKHESISTRATOS SAID: "BIG MUSSELS COME FROM AINOS, OYSTERS FROM ABYDOS, PARION HAS CRABS AND MITYLENE SCALLOPS . . . KALKHEDON GIVES US ITS OWN OYSTERS [TETHEA] BUT AS FOR HERALDS (PERIWINKLES) MAY ZEUS DESTROY THEM, BOTH THOSE TAKEN FROM THE SEA AND OTHERS FROM THE MARKET, WITH THE EXCEPTION OF THOSE OF ONE MAN: HE IS MY CLOSE FRIEND, HIS HOME IS ON LESBOS AND HIS NAME IS AGATHON."
. . . PHILYLLIOS TOO—OR WHOEVER WAS THE AUTHOR OF "THE ISLAND-TOWNS"—REFERRED TO "COCKLES, LIMPETS, TUBE-FISH, MUSSELS, PINNAS AND SCALLOPS FROM METHYMNA."

Gulick, 1969, Vol. I, pp. 396-398.

Among the diversions or entertainment that people wanted were stories of exploits, adventures and love, not like the heroic myths of antiquity but more like what Photios, the ninth century Byzantine sage and later patriarch of the orthodox church (note no. 8, Chap. II), called "Bucolic Dramas." Roman authors and poets wanted summaries of Greek stories, true or imagined, so that they might develop them into Latin texts, poems, plays or books for their compatriots. One of the Greeks who met this literary demand was Parthenios.

Erotic Passions *by Parthenios*

Parthenios, a Greek from the city of Nicaea [*Nikaia*] in northwest Asia Minor was taken to Rome as a prisoner of war in 73 B.C. He was later released but stayed in Italy writing poetry and teaching (Gaselee, S., 1978, Introduction). The famous Roman poet Virgil was one of his students. The poems of Parthenios, which have been lost, were thought to be more original than his book *Adventures of Erotic Passion* [*Erotica Pathemata*], which has been preserved. This is a collection of rather simple outlines of love stories, apparently put together as a reference manual for other writers. Two of the short stories in the available Greek text relate to Lesbos.

> **ADVENTURES OF EROTIC PASSION**
> BY PARTHENIOS, FIRST CENTURY B.C.
>
> **STORY XXI: ABOUT PEISIDIKE**
>
> **1.** THEY SAY THAT ACHILLES [Ahilleus], IN THE COURSE OF SAILING ALONG THE MAINLAND (10) AND SUBDUING THE ISLANDS NEAR IT, ARRIVED AT LESBOS. THERE HE ATTACKED THE CITIES ONE BY ONE AND PLUNDERED THEM.
>
> **2.** THE CITIZENS OF METHYMNA RESISTED VERY STRONGLY AND ACHILLES WAS FRUSTRATED FOR NOT BEING ABLE TO STORM THE CITY. THEN THE DAUGHTER OF THE KING OF METHYMNA, PEISIDIKE, SEEING HIM FROM THE TOP OF THE CITY WALLS FELL IN LOVE WITH HIM AND SENT HER ATTENDANT TO PROPOSE TO SURRENDER THE CITY TO HIM, IF HE WOULD TAKE HER AS HIS WIFE. ACHILLES ACCEPTED IMMEDIATELY BUT AFTER HE BECAME MASTER OF THE CITY HE BEGAN TO HATE WHAT SHE HAD DONE AND URGED HIS SOLDIERS TO DESTROY THE WOMAN. THE POET (11) WRITING ABOUT THE FOUNDATION OF LESBOS MENTIONS THIS PASSION WITH THESE WORDS:
>
> THE YOUNG WOMAN'S HEART FLUTTERED AS SHE WATCHED ACHILLES WITH HIS ACHAEAN CHAMPIONS REVELLING IN THEIR LUST FOR THE BATTLE AND MANY TIMES SHE STRETCHED HER ARMS IN THE MOIST AIR LONGING FOR HIS LOVE.

4. A LITTLE FURTHER DOWN HE GOES ON: SOON AFTERWARDS THE MAIDEN ALLOWED THE ACHAEAN PEOPLE TO ENTER HER HOMETOWN, HAVING STEALTHILY UNLOCKED THE CITY GATES. SHE COULD STAND TO SEE WITH HER OWN EYES HER COUNTRY'S ELDERS SLAIN WITH THE ENEMY'S BRONZE SWORDS AND THE WOMEN BOUND TO SLAVERY AND DRAGGED TO THE SHIPS AS ACHILLES WAS COMMITTED TO DO. ALL THIS SO THAT SHE MIGHT BE THE DAUGHTER OF THETIS OF THE DEEP BLUE SEA, TO HAVE THE FAMILY OF AEACUS [Aiakos] AS HER KIN (12), AND TO LIVE IN THE ROYAL CHAMBERS AT PHTHIA AS THE DEVOTED WIFE OF THE MOST OUTSTANDING MAN. BUT THIS WAS NOT MEANT TO HAPPEN, BECAUSE WHILE ACHILLES WAS CELEBRATING THE CONQUEST OF HER CITY, HER MAD WISH TO MARRY HIM BECAME THE CAUSE OF HER DEATH IN HIS SOLDIERS' HANDS. THEY SLEW HER (ON ACHILLES' ORDERS), ALL OF THEM THROWING THE BIGGEST ROCKS AT HER.

STORY XXVI: ABOUT APRIATE

1. ON LESBOS, TRAMBELOS, THE SON OF TELAMON, FELL IN LOVE WITH A GIRL, APRIATE, AND TRIED ALL HE COULD TO MAKE HER HIS OWN. HOWEVER, SHE DID NOT GIVE IN AT ALL AND SO HE THOUGHT OF A DEVIOUS WAY TO WIN HER BY DECEIT.

2. AS SHE WAS WALKING ONE DAY BY THE SEASHORE TO ONE OF HER FATHER'S ESTATES, WITH HER ATTENDING HANDMAIDS, HE HID IN AMBUSH AND ATTACKED HER. THEN, BECAUSE SHE STRUGGLED A LOT DEFENDING HER VIRGINITY, TRAMBELOS GOT MAD AND THREW HER IN THE SEA, WHICH HAPPENED TO BE VERY DEEP AND CAUSED THE POOR GIRL TO PERISH. ACCORDING TO OTHERS IT WAS IN FACT HERSELF THAT JUMPED IN THE WATER WHILE SHE WAS BEING CHASED.

3. SOON AFTERWARDS TRAMBELOS GOT HIS PUNISHMENT FROM THE GODS. IN AN EFFORT TO STOP ACHILLES, WHO WAS CARRYING AWAY FROM LESBOS AN ENORMOUS AMOUNT OF BOOTY, HE GATHERED A TROOP OF NATIVES AND MET HIM IN BATTLE.

4. THEN AND THERE HE WAS STRUCK IN HIS CHEST AND INSTANTLY FELL. WHILE HE WAS STILL BREATHING, ACHILLES, ADMIRING HIS STRENGTH AND VALOR ASKED WHO HE WAS AND FROM WHERE. WHEN HE LEARNED THAT THIS WAS THE SON OF TELAMON (12) HE MOURNED HIM DEEPLY AND HAD A LARGE MOUND BUILT FOR HIM ON THE BEACH, WHICH HAS BEEN CALLED THE MONUMENT OF TRAMBELOS EVER SINCE.

Parthenios also included in his writings several stories for which he credited others. One of them he attributed to Phanias (13) of Eresos, on Lesbos.

VII. ABOUT HIPPARINOS

1. IN THE ITALIAN CITY OF HERACLEA, ANTILEON FELL IN LOVE WITH A BOY OF EXQUISITE BEAUTY AND OF A DISTINGUISHED BACKGROUND, WHOSE NAME WAS HIPPARINOS. THAT MAN TRIED EVERYTHING BUT COULD NOT GET A CLOSE RELATIONSHIP WITH THE BOY. HE SPENT MUCH TIME AROUND HIPPARINOS IN THE GYMNASIUM AND FINALLY TOLD HIM THAT HIS DESIRE FOR HIM WAS SO GREAT THAT HE WOULD NOT FAIL TO DO ANYTHING HE REQUESTED.

2. HIPPARINOS, QUITE JOKINGLY, ORDERED HIM TO CARRY BACK THE BELL FROM A FORTIFIED TOWER WHICH, BESIDES, WAS UNDER GUARD BY THE RULER OF HERACLEA. HE WAS SURE THIS FEAT WAS IMPOSSIBLE. BUT ANTILEON WAS ABLE TO ENTER THE CASTLE SECRETLY AND THEN AMBUSHED AND KILLED THE GUARD OF THE BELL. WHEN HE RETURNED TO THE YOUNGSTER WITH THE MISSION ACCOMPLISHED HE BECAME HIS FAVORITE AND FROM THEN ON THEY LOVED EACH OTHER VERY MUCH.

3. SOMETIME AFTERWARDS THE RULER ("TYRANT") OF THE TOWN ALSO DESIRED AND PURSUED THE BOY AND SEEMED LIKELY TO TAKE HIM BY FORCE. ANTILEON WAS MUCH DISTRESSED AND WHILE HE URGED HIPPARINOS NOT TO RISK A REFUSAL, HE JUMPED UPON THE TYRANT AS HE WAS LEAVING HIS RESIDENCE AND KILLED HIM.

4. AFTER HE DID THIS HE FLED AND MIGHT HAVE ESCAPED IF HE HAD NOT FALLEN IN THE MIDDLE OF A FLOCK OF SHEEP WHICH WERE TIED TOGETHER, WHERE HE WAS CAPTURED. WHEN SUBSEQUENTLY THE ANCIENT CONSTITUTION OF HERACLEA WAS RESTORED, THE CITIZENS ERECTED BRONZE STATUES IN LIKENESS OF THE TWO LOVERS AND A LAW WAS WRITTEN THAT NO ONE SHOULD DRIVE SHEEP TIED TOGETHER.

Gaselee, S., 1978, pp. 318-320, 328-330 and 276-278.

The Lesbian pastoral about Daphnis and Chloe

Love romances, elementary or sophisticated, intertwined with ordinary or fantastic adventures, continued to be produced and remained popular for hundreds of years (Perry, 1967). They were somewhat analogous to the twentieth century cinematic dramas or the "soap operas" of television. Some works possessed outstanding literary qualities and achieved literary fame. Of the two stories to be presented, both dating from the third century, one, *Daphnis and Chloe*, has been called "little short of a masterpiece" (Edmonds, 1916-78) and the famous eighteenth century German poet W. Goethe was recommending that it ought to be read at least once a year (Oxf. Class. Dict. p. 619). The other, *Apollonios of Tyre*, regrettably is not available in the original Greek but the Latin text has been translated into numerous modern languages (including modern Greek and several Slavic tongues) and has been said to be "the story with the longest tradition in the English language" (Encycl. Brit., Vol. II). It was reshaped into a novel by Lawrence Twine in 1576 called "The Patterne of Painefull Adventures" and also transformed by Wm. Shakespeare into the drama "Pericles" (with a change of names but not substance) in 1608 (Oxf. Class. Dict. p. 124).

Daphnis and Chloe, a prose narrative written in Greek, presumably between 200 and 300 A.D. is, according to the original subtitle, a lesbiac pastoral story. The author is known only by this work and his Roman sounding name Longus (Greek Longos) may not have actually been how he was originally called in Greek (Edmonds, 1916-78). Longos was possibly a freeman, teacher in a Roman household and was either born on Lesbos or knew the island well, as is evident from the descriptions in his ever-popular four-book romance. It is possible (Perry, 1967, p. 351) that he was a descendant of a distinguished Lesbian family, which was named after the Roman patron of the island (Chapter IV-A), Pompey the Great [*Pompeius Longus*—or *Magnus*]. According to Edmonds, Longos has "earned his fame by something more than a pretty story." The narrative followed the trend of the Hellenistic and Hellenizing Roman style of overabundant sentimentality, temporary adventures and adversities eventually concluding with good luck and rewards for the "good" and punishments for the "bad" characters in the story. Daphnis and Chloe is the product of imagination and is not based on mythology or history as in the earlier "classical" Greek literature. But this novel is less concerned with surprising events and concentrates more so on the idyllic description of scenery and the portrayal of the main characters (Table IV-1), especially their virginal feelings of erotic impulses and experiences. The young Daphnis, the maturing virgin Chloe (the spelling Khloë would be closer to the sound of the Greek) and their entourage, continue to inspire artists composers, choreographers and others till now (14).

The manuscript available to us was first compiled from three originals in the Vatican library by the Renaissance scholar and collector F. Orsini around the year 1595. The first Greek printing, in 1598, in Florence, had been preceded by a printed translation in French, in 1559. In 1657 an English "gentleman" (this distinction was printed after his name), George Thornley, published a book with the title *"Daphnis and Chloe— a most sweet and pleasant pastoral romance for young ladies,"* but failed to indicate that this was in fact a translation from a bilingual Greek-and-Latin edition of the original story by Longos. An annotated and indexed critical volume with parallel Greek and English texts is currently available in the Loeb Classical Library series. The parts cited in exact translation (CAPITALIZED), or in summary, are from the Greek text of the 1978 reprinting (Edmonds, 1916-78).

Table IV-1
THE GAME OF THE NAMES IN DAPHNIS AND CHLOE

Almost all the names in this Hellenistic romance by Longos relate directly to peasant or social life on Lesbos and to nature and natural urges. Such invented names may sound simple or silly, but they reveal the author's double purpose of (a) presenting crude and clear labels for all, and (b) amusing himself and the sophisticated readers with some subtle ridicule of the naming game in any literature.

The hero and the heroine
Daphnis: from the laurel tree; or a winner of laurels.
Chloe: tender lawn, blade of grass, new foliage.

Shepherds and adoptive parents
Lamon: possibly an abbreviation for colt.
Dryas: of the oak tree.
Nape (wife of Dryas): a wooden glen, narrow valley.
Dorcon: antelope-man.

Sex instructors and sex fiends
Philetas: loving fellow, lover.
Lykainion ("it," neutral, though a woman's name): from the Arcadian mountain Lykaion; or of the early dawn, *lyke*; or a little wolf [*lykos*].
Gnathon: big jaw.
Lampis: bright, shining; or [from *lampe*] scum.

Noble masters, the true family of Daphnis and Chloe
Dionysophanes: manifestation of Dionysos, God of wine and feasts.
Cleariste (his wife): illustrious and best.
Astylos (their son): from the city [*asty*], or independent with no support [*a-stylos*].
Megacles: of great prominence and fame.

THE LESBIAC PASTORALS OF DAPHNIS AND CHLOE
BY LONGOS—ABOUT 300 A.D.

FOREWORD
1. WHEN I WAS HUNTING ON LESBOS, I SAW IN THE PARK OF THE NYMPHS THE BEST SPECTACLE I HAVE EVER SEEN, A PAINTING ILLUSTRATING A LOVE STORY. ALTHOUGH THE PARK WAS VERY BEAUTIFUL, WITH MANY TREES, FULL OF FLOWERS AND RUNNING WATER . . . THE PAINTING WAS

HELLENISTIC TWILIGHT AND ROMAN ROMANTIC LOVES   165

EVEN MORE DELIGHTFUL DISPLAYING NOT ONLY OVER-ABUNDANT ARTISTRY, BUT EROTIC SCENES, SO THAT MANY PEOPLE, INCLUDING FOREIGN VISITORS, PRESUMABLY COMING TO WORSHIP THE NYMPHS, WERE THERE ACTUALLY TO SEE THE PICTURE . . .

2. AFTER I SAW AND ADMIRED ALL THESE VARIOUS AND EROTIC IMAGES, I FELT A STRANGE DESIRE TO PUT THE PICTURE INTO WRITING. I FOUND A WELL-INFORMED INTERPRETER OF THE ILLUSTRATIONS AND THEN I WORKED ON THESE FOUR BOOKS, WHICH ARE DEDICATED TO LOVE [EROS] AND TO THE NYMPHS AND TO PAN, THOUGH THEY CAN BE ANYONE'S ENJOYABLE POSSESSION. MY WORK MAY BE A REMEDY FOR THE SICK, CONSOLE A PERSON IN SORROW, BRING BACK MEMORIES OF AN OLD LOVE TO THOSE WHO HAVE LOVED AND INSTRUCT THOSE WHO HAVE NOT LOVED YET. IN GENERAL NO ONE HAS EVER ESCAPED OR CAN ESCAPE EROS, SO LONG AS BEAUTY EXISTS AND EYES CAN SEE. ON MY PART I PRAY THAT GOD MAY GRANT ME THE GOOD SENSE AND WISDOM TO WRITE ABOUT OTHER PEOPLE'S STORIES.

BOOK I.
ON LESBOS THERE IS A CITY, MYTILENE, QUITE LARGE AND BEAUTIFUL. IT IS TRAVERSED BY CANALS, INLETS FROM THE SEA AND IS ADORNED WITH BRIDGES OF CARVED WHITE STONE . . . NOT FAR FROM THE CITY A BLESSED MAN HAD A VERY BEAUTIFUL ESTATE, WITH MOUNTAINS SHELTERING WILD ANIMALS, FIELDS GROWING ALL KINDS OF GRAIN, GRAPEVINES ON THE HILLSIDE AND PASTURES FOR THE FLOCKS. WITH THE SEA SPLASHING ON ITS FAR-REACHING SHORES, THIS WAS TRULY A SOUL'S MOST GENTLE DELIGHT.

2. ON THIS FIELD LAMON, THE GOAT-HERD, ONE DAY TAKING A LONG WALK DISCOVERED AN INFANT BEING NURSED BY ONE OF HIS GOATS . . .

Summary, Section 2-31: Lamon took the baby boy home. He kept him and named him Daphnis. Two years later another shepherd, Dryas, found in the grotto of the Nymphs on Lesbos an abandoned baby girl fed by a sheep, took her home to raise her and called her Chloe. As the youngsters grew older, Daphnis and Chloe learned to tend the flocks. They also played together and had occasional misadventures without consequences. One day Chloe saw Daphnis bathing and admired his good looks. Daphnis pursued Chloe and she gave him a first kiss.

But another shepherd, Dorcon, had now his eyes on the adolescent Chloe, showered her with gifts and asked her adopted father Dryas to let him marry her. When rejected he tried to kidnap Chloe disguised in a wolfskin but the shepherd dogs fell upon him and wounded him seriously. In the meantime pirates ravaged the fields and carried away Daphnis. Chloe was desperate and went for help to Dorcon who was dying of his wounds. He gave her a magic flute and when she played it, the stolen cattle on the pirates' ship went wild and caused it to capsize. The heavily armed pirates drowned while Daphnis swam safely to shore, where he found Chloe, all shaken up, laughing and crying at the same time. Dorcon died and was given an emotional funeral, at which shepherds broke their pipes over his body, flowers covered the tomb and even the goats and the cattle moaned as a kind of lamentation for their dead master.

32. AFTER DORCON'S BURIAL CHLOE LED DAPHNIS TO THE GROTTO OF THE NYMPHS AND THERE SHE GAVE HIM A BATH. SHE ALSO WASHED HERSELF WHILE DAPHNIS WATCHED FOR THE FIRST TIME HER PURE WHITE BODY. AFTERWARDS THEY BOTH GATHERED FRESH FLOWERS AND CROWNED THE STATUES OF THE NYMPHS. ON ONE OF THE STONES THEY ALSO HUNG DORCON'S GIFT, THE PIPE. MUCH LATER THEY CAME OUT TO FIND THEIR GOATS AND SHEEP WAITING FOR THEM. THE ANIMALS JUMPED HAPPILY WHEN THEY SAW THEM AND BEGAN TO GRAZE . . . BUT DAPHNIS COULD NOT MAKE HIS SOUL FEEL ANY JOY, AFTER HE HAD SEEN CHLOE NAKED AND HER FORMERLY HIDDEN BEAUTY UNCOVERED. HIS HEART ACHED AS IF HE HAD SWALLOWED SOME POISONOUS DRUG. EVEN HIS BREATH AT TIMES BECAME VERY HEAVY AND LABORED AS IF SOMEONE HAD BEEN CHASING HIM AND AT OTHER TIMES IT ALMOST STOPPED AS IF IT HAD BEEN EXHAUSTED FROM HIS EARLIER ADVENTURES. HE FOUND THE BATH IN THE GROTTO MORE INTIMIDATING THAN THE DEEP OPEN SEA. IT SEEMED TO HIM THAT HIS SOUL WAS STILL BEING HELD BY THE ROBBERS, BECAUSE HE WAS TOO YOUNG AND INEXPERIENCED TO KNOW WHAT A ROBBER IS LOVE.

BOOK II

1. NOW THAT THE FRUIT SEASON HAD REACHED ITS PEAK AND IT WAS ABOUT VINTAGE TIME, EVERYONE WAS OUT WORKING IN THE FIELDS . . . DAPHNIS AND CHLOE TOO PAID LESS ATTENTION TO THEIR GOATS AND SHEEP IN ORDER TO OFFER A HELPING HAND. DAPHNIS CARRIED GRAPES IN HIS BASKET, DROPPED THEM IN THE BINS AND AFTER STEPPING ON THEM AND SQUEEZING THEM CARRIED THE JUICE TO THE BARRELS. CHLOE PREPARED MEALS FOR THE VINTAGERS AND POURED FOR THEM SOME OLD WINE. SHE ALSO GATHERED SOME GRAPES FROM THE LOWER VINES, BECAUSE ON

HELLENISTIC TWILIGHT AND ROMAN ROMANTIC LOVES

LESBOS ALL THE VINES GROW SMALL AND DO NOT HANG HIGH OR CLIMB ON TREES BUT SPREAD LOW AND CREEP LIKE IVY...

2. THEN CAME THE FEAST DAY CELEBRATING THE BIRTHS OF DIONYSOS AND OF WINE. THE WOMEN WHO HAD BEEN CALLED FROM THE NEARBY FIELDS TO HELP WITH THE WINE SERVICE KEPT THEIR EYES ON DAPHNIS, COMPLIMENTING HIM FOR HIS GOOD LOOKS AND SAYING THAT HE WAS AS BEAUTIFUL AS THE DIVINE DIONYSOS. ONE OF THE BOLDEST EVEN KISSED HIM, WHICH EXCITED DAPHNIS VERY MUCH BUT HURT THE FEELINGS OF POOR CHLOE. ON THE OTHER HAND THE MEN WHO WORKED ON THE WINE PRESSES WERE AFTER CHLOE, CALLING ALL KINDS OF THINGS TO HER AND JUMPING, LIKE SATYRS IN A FRENZY AROUND A BACCHANTE, WISHING, THEY SAID, TO BE SHEEP SO THAT SHE WOULD TEND TO THEM. THIS ATTENTION SHE LIKED BUT DAPHNIS RESENTED IT. BOTH OF THEM FINALLY WISHED THE VINTAGE AND THE FESTIVITIES TO BE OVER . . . SO THAT INSTEAD OF THE UGLY NOISES OF THE CROWD THEY COULD HEAR, BACK IN THEIR FAMILIAR LAND, THE WINDPIPES OF THE SHEPHERDS AND THE BLEATING OF THE FLOCK.

Interim Summary Section 2 (continued)–3 (beginning): When vintage was over Daphnis and Chloe returned to the flocks and with great joy paid tribute to the Nymphs, bringing to them the best bunches of grapes, as they always had taken to them flowers and fruit, wreaths of green leaves or milk offerings. In their rejoicing came to see them an old man dressed like a poor peasant, who talked to them about his youth and love affairs.

3 . . . "I AM PHILETAS," HE SAID, "AND LIKE YOU I HAVE GIVEN MUCH TO THESE NYMPHS AND ALSO PLAYED MY TUNES FOR THE GOD PAN AND LED MY HERDS OF CATTLE WITH MY MUSIC ALONE . . . EVEN NOW IN MY OLD AGE I TOIL IN MY GARDEN TO GROW ROSES AND LILIES AND HYACINTHS AND VIOLETS . . . AS WELL AS PEARS AND ALL KINDS OF APPLES, GRAPES, FIGS, POMEGRANATES AND GREEN MYRTLE . . . "

4. "ONE DAY AT NOON (PHILETAS CONTINUED) A BOY, AS WHITE AS MILK AND BLOND LIKE FIRE . . . APPEARED TO ME, SHINING NAKED . . . I RUSHED TO CATCH HIM AS I HAD OFTEN RUN AFTER SUCKLING KIDS OR NEWBORN CALVES BUT HE WAS CHANGEABLE, ELUSIVE AND IMPOSSIBLE TO CHASE. WATCHING HIM SO THAT HE MIGHT NOT GET AWAY I ASKED WHO HE WAS."

5. "WITH A DRY LAUGHTER HE SPOKE AND HIS VOICE WAS NOT LIKE ANYTHING I KNOW, NOT THAT OF A NIGHTINGALE, A SWALLOW OR AN OLD SWAN. 'PHILETAS,' HE SAID, 'I WOULD NOT MIND GIVING YOU A LOVING KISS, BUT SEE WHETHER THIS SUITS YOUR AGE, BECAUSE YOUR YEARS WILL NOT ALLOW YOU TO PURSUE ME AFTER THAT ONE KISS . . . I

AM NOT A BOY, THOUGH I LOOK LIKE ONE AND IN FACT I AM OLDER THAN KRONOS (15) AND THE UNIVERSE ITSELF . . . I STOOD BY YOU WHEN YOU PLAYED YOUR PIPE AND WERE IN LOVE WITH AMARYLLIS . . . NOW I AM SHEPHERDING DAPHNIS AND CHLOE . . .'

6. "HAVING SAID THAT . . . HE FLEW FROM BRANCH TO BRANCH AND I NOTICED THE WINGS ON HIS SHOULDERS AND HIS BOW WITH DARTS . . . THEN I SAW HIM NO MORE. IF IT IS TRUE THAT I HAVE NOT GROWN THIS WHITE HAIR IN VAIN AND THAT WITH OLD AGE THERE IS NO VANITY IN MY THOUGHTS, I AM TELLING YOU KIDS YOU ARE MARKED BY EROS, LOVE, AND EROS IS WATCHING AFTER YOU."

7. . . . AND THEY ASKED HIM "WHAT IS EROS AND WHAT CAN HE DO?" "HE IS A GOD," PHILETAS REPLIED, "YOUNG AND BEAUTIFUL AND ABLE TO FLY. THAT IS WHY HE DELIGHTS IN YOUTH, PURSUES BEAUTY AND MAKES ONE'S SOUL FLY HIGH . . . MYSELF WHEN YOUNG WAS IN LOVE WITH AMARYLLIS AND COULD NOT REMEMBER TO EAT, NOR TO TAKE A DRINK NOR COULD I HAVE A RESTFUL SLEEP. MY SOUL WAS ACHING, MY HEART WAS BEATING FAST AND MY BODY HAD CHILLS . . . I BROKE MY PIPES BECAUSE THEY SEEMED TO PLEASE MY CATTLE BUT DID NOT ATTRACT AMARYLLIS. FOR LOVE, I AM TELLING YOU, THERE IS NO MEDICINE YOU CAN DRINK OR EAT, NOTHING YOU CAN SAY IN SONGS FOR CONSOLATION, BUT THERE IS ONLY KISSING AND EMBRACING AND LYING DOWN NAKED TOGETHER."

8. AFTER PHILETAS GAVE THEM THIS LESSON ABOUT LOVE HE WENT AWAY, TAKING AS GIFTS SEVERAL CHEESES AND A WHOLE BABY GOAT. WHEN THEY WERE LEFT ALONE, HAVING HEARD FOR THE FIRST TIME ABOUT LOVE, THEY FELT THEIR MINDS VERY STRAINED AND AT LOOSE ENDS. BACK HOME AT NIGHT THEY BEGAN TO COMPARE WHAT THEY HAD HEARD WITH THEIR OWN SENSATIONS: "THOSE IN LOVE ARE IN PAIN AND SO ARE WE; THEY ARE ABSENT-MINDED AND WE TOO ARE DISTRACTED; THEY CANNOT RELAX AND THIS IS OUR PROBLEM; THEY FEEL THAT THEY ARE BURNING AND WE TOO FEEL IN FLAMES; THEY WANT TO CONTEMPLATE EACH OTHER AND THIS IS WHY WE TOO CAN HARDLY WAIT FOR THE DAWN OF EACH DAY . . . WE ARE IN LOVE WITH EACH OTHER WITHOUT QUITE KNOWING WHAT LOVE IS AND IF WE ARE TRULY LOVERS. THEREFORE WE MUST EXPLORE THE REMEDIES THAT PHILETAS MENTIONED, WHICH ARE KISSING, EMBRACING AND LYING DOWN NAKED . . .

9. . . . NEXT DAY AS SOON AS THEY HAD LED THEIR HERDS TO PASTURE, THEY STARTED KISSING AS THEY HAD NEVER BEFORE AND HELD THEMSELVES TIGHTLY TOGETHER WITH THEIR ARMS AROUND EACH OTHER; BUT THEY WERE TOO SHY TO TRY THE THIRD REMEDY, TO UNDRESS AND LIE DOWN, WHICH SEEMED TOO DARING NOT ONLY TO THE VIRGIN GIRL BUT ALSO TO THE YOUNG SHEPHERD-BOY. AS A

RESULT THEIR NIGHT WAS AGAIN WITHOUT SLEEP AND THEY PONDERED THE MEANING OF WHAT THEY HAD DONE AND BLAMED THEMSELVES FOR WHAT THEY LEFT UNDONE. "WE HAVE KISSED WITH NO BENEFIT; EMBRACED AND NOTHING MORE. THAT MEANS THAT LYING DOWN TOGETHER IS THE ONLY RELIEF FROM THE PAINS OF LOVE. WE WILL HAVE TO TRY IT FOR THAT MUST BE SOMETHING BETTER THAN A KISS."

10. WHILE ALL THIS WAS IN THEIR MINDS THEY SAW MANY EROTIC DREAMS, WITH KISSES AND EMBRACES, AND ALSO ACTING IN THEIR DREAMS WHAT THEY HAD NOT ATTEMPTED IN THE DAYTIME . . . [BUT] THE THIRD REMEDY WAS STILL BEING DELAYED BECAUSE DAPHNIS DID NOT DARE TO MENTION IT AND CHLOE WAS UNWILLING TO MAKE A START, UNTIL BY CHANCE THEY TRIED TO ACT IN THE FOLLOWING WAY:

11. AS THEY SAT CLOSE TO EACH OTHER SAVORING THE PLEASURES OF KISSING, THEY WERE OVERWHELMED BY VOLUPTUOUSNESS WITHOUT RESTRAINT. WITH HIS ARMS AROUND HER, DAPHNIS HELD CHLOE CLOSE TO HIM MORE TIGHTLY THAN EVER AND AS SHE RECLINED ON HER SIDE HE LAY BY HER CONTINUING TO KISS HER. REMEMBERING THE VISIONS OF THEIR DREAMS THEY LAY DOWN BOUND TO EACH OTHER. BUT NOT KNOWING WHAT OUGHT TO HAPPEN NEXT AND BELIEVING THIS TO BE THE END OF EROTIC PLEASURE THEY PARTED HAVING SPENT MOST OF THE DAY USELESSLY AND HATING TO GO BACK SEPARATELY TO THE TORTURE OF THE NIGHT. THEY MIGHT NEXT HAVE DONE SOMETHING MORE REAL BUT A GREAT DISTURBANCE OVERCAME THE ENTIRE LAND.

Concluding Summary, Book II, Sections 12-39: Some rich young men from the city of Methymna (northwest coast of Lesbos) arrived with their boat to fish and to enjoy themselves in the good harbors and beautiful coastline near Mytilene, with its well-built mansions and prosperous farmland. While they were having much fun the boat got loose and was blown off to sea because a goat chewed on the lines holding it to shore and cut them. The visitors blamed Daphnis for this and tried to capture him but his local friends rushed to his help. The skirmish between the visiting party and those defending Daphnis threatened to escalate into a war between Methymna and Mytilene. The Methymneans sent a fleet ready for battle and after their men landed they managed to capture Chloe. A nightmarish scene followed, when sheep and goats howled like wolves, flocks were trapped in nets of ivy, the ships' anchors stuck to the rocks, oars broke like straws and the joints of the barges got loose, struck by the tails of leaping dolphins. Among all these strange happenings, high from the rocks over the promontory of the harbor came the sound of pipes, not pleasant as usual but more like a frightening blast from a trumpet. These were the doings of the god Pan who, to protect his shepherds, spread an awful terror, a true panic (16) among the men from Methymna. He also visited their captain in a dream and ordered him to return Chloe to her people.

Chloe and Daphnis were then happily reunited. There were thanksgiving ceremonies to the god Pan and much rejoicing, gift giving and storytelling. Lamon narrated the old myth of how a beautiful maid, Syrinx (16), was turned into a reed to avoid surrendering to Pan, the goat-footed god. Philetas praised Lamon and said that his storytelling was sweeter than the singing of a melody and then himself started playing a variety of pastoral tunes on an old pipe with the largest possible reeds, which made people believe that they were hearing the harmonies of a concert [Greek: *synaulia*—Ref. Table E], not of a single musical instrument. Whereupon Dryas, increasingly inebriated, asked Philetas to play a Dionysiac rhythm and then he danced wildly the series of the wine-maker's steps, from the harvesting and squeezing of the grapes to the tasting of the sweet molasses. Afterwards there was a musical pantomime, in which Daphnis played the role of Pan, pursuing Chloe in the role of Syrinx. Later Daphnis grabbed the big pipe of Philetas and played himself a series of love songs ranging from plaintive or searching moods to those overtly erotic. Philetas admired them so much that he jumped up, kissed Daphnis and offered him his big pipe as a gift, with the wish that someday he would pass it on to someone else who could play equally well. That night everyone, including Daphnis and Chloe, walked slowly back to their homes with the flocks. The next day, after taking the goats and sheep out to pasture very early and again kissing and hugging passionately, Daphnis and Chloe took solemn oaths of eternal devotion. Daphnis swore by the god Pan that he would never live alone, without Chloe . . . and Chloe, after she had entered the grotto of the Nymphs, swore by them that she would share with Daphnis both life and death.

Book III

Summary, Sections 1-13: War maneuvers still continued in the meantime and the Mytileneans, having learned about the incursion of the ships from Methymna and the plundering and ravaging of their fields, prepared an army of revenge to march by land, as they distrusted the sea in winter. Their leader did not allow any destruction and looting or taking the enemies' livestock, believing these to be the acts of a robber, rather than of an army general. Then he camped in front of the city of Methymna and sent delegates to present his grievances and to ask for reparations. Methymna's citizens decided that peace was preferable to war and they returned all the captives and the plundered goods. So this war that was both strange and unexpected to start with, came also to a quick and sudden resolution.

That winter, however, seemed to Daphnis and Chloe much more bitter than war. A heavy snowfall blocked the roads and forced all the farmers to stay indoors, keeping warm by huge wood fires and doing domestic chores. Most of them were very relaxed and glad to have a brief chance to rest, to sleep long hours at night and to enjoy big breakfasts at leisure. But Chloe and Daphnis spent their days sadly only with memories of kissing and embracing, they would not eat and their nights were without sleep. They could hardly wait for spring so that they might be reborn from such living death. Only once a brief reunion gave them new hopes, when Daphnis with the excuse of going out to get firewood and to hunt birds, came by the home of Chloe and was invited in to a big dinner with a chance to see his beloved girl. But that night he had to share a bed with Dryas, Chloe's stepfather, while she slept with her stepmother in another room.

Finally there were signs of an early spring, the snow began to melt, the earth to reveal herself and grass to turn green. The shepherds took their flocks back to pasture and first among them were Chloe and Daphnis, under the command of a greater shepherd. When they met, they kissed madly and in their joy cut flowers for the Nymphs while listening to the nightingales that were recalling their songs after the long winter silence. One could see the newborn lambs and kids nursing under the mother's belly and when rams could find females that had not yet mated they chased them and mounted them. Billy goats were even sexier, jumping wildly and fighting for the she-goats and, after they mated, watching carefully so that no other goat could molest their own. After seeing such erotic frenzy among animals even old people felt the urges of Aphrodite but it was especially the young, longing for love, that were on fire and desired much more than a kiss and a hug. Daphnis in particular, as he had now reached full adolescence during his winter homebound days, was greatly aroused by the kisses and excited by the embraces, acting now with greater impetuosity and curiosity.

14. THEREFORE HE BEGGED CHLOE TO GRANT HIM WHAT HE WANTED AND TO LIE DOWN WITH HIM NAKED MUCH LONGER THAN THEY HAD DONE BEFORE BECAUSE THAT, HE THOUGHT, WOULD TURN OUT TO BE THE ONLY REMEDY FOR THE EROTIC DRIVE. WHEN SHE ASKED WHAT MORE THERE WAS TO KISSING, EMBRACING AND EVEN LYING DOWN AND WHAT HE THOUGHT HE WOULD DO WHEN HE LAY DOWN

IN THE NUDE WITH HER ALSO NAKED, "HERE," HE SAID, "WHAT RAMS DO TO THE EWES AND BILLY GOATS TO SHE-GOATS. YOU SEE HOW THE CHASE IS OVER WHEN THEY DO THAT AND SHARE A COMMON VOLUPTUOUS PLEASURE. THIS ACT SEEMS TO BE DELIGHTFUL AND CAN OVERCOME THE BITTER SIDE OF LOVE."

"BUT CAN'T YOU SEE DAPHNIS THE SHEEP AND GOATS, THAT THE MALES DO JUMP ON THE FEMALES STANDING UP AND THE FEMALES TOO RECEIVE THEIR MATES UPRIGHT. YET YOU DEMAND THAT I LIE DOWN WITH YOU AND FOR THAT MATTER NAKED EVEN THOUGH THESE ANIMALS HAVE MORE COAT ON THAN I DO EVEN WHEN I AM DRESSED?" BUT DAPHNIS CONVINCED HER AND HE LAY DOWN WITH HER FOR A LONG TIME, AFTER WHICH, STILL NOT KNOWING WHAT TO DO, HE MADE HER GET UP AND CAME BEHIND HER IMITATING THE BILLY GOATS. EVEN AFTER THAT HOWEVER HE STILL FELT GREATLY PERPLEXED AND STARTED TO CRY, BEING MORE IGNORANT THAN RAMS IN THE ACT OF LOVE.

15. IN THE NEIGHBORHOOD THERE WAS AN OLDER FARMER . . . WITH A YOUNG AND BEAUTIFUL WIFE WHO CAME FROM THE CITY AND WAS MUCH MORE REFINED THAN THE COUNTRY FOLK AROUND. HER NAME WAS LYKAINION AND SHE, SEEING DAPHNIS DAY IN AND DAY OUT, FELT A DESIRE TO MAKE HIM HER LOVER. FINDING HIM ALONE SHE TRIED TO SEDUCE HIM FIRST WITH GIFTS SUCH AS A FLUTE-PIPE, HONEY IN BEE'S WAX AND A BEAUTIFUL DEER HIDE. HOWEVER SHE HESITATED TO SPEAK TO HIM ABOUT LOVE, GUESSING HOW MUCH HE WAS IN LOVE WITH CHLOE WHEN SHE SAW HIM ALWAYS ATTACHED TO THE YOUNG MAIDEN. THEN ONE DAY, TELLING HER HUSBAND THAT SHE WAS TO VISIT A NEIGHBOR . . . SHE FOLLOWED THE YOUNG COUPLE AND HIDING IN SOME BUSHES, SHE HEARD EVERYTHING THEY SAID AND SAW EVERYTHING THEY DID. SHE DIDN'T EVEN MISS DAPHNIS CRYING WHEN HE FELT SO FRUSTRATED WITH HIS SEXUAL CLUMSINESS. SHE FELT SORRY FOR THE MISERABLE COUPLE AND DECIDED THAT THIS WAS A PERFECT OPPORTUNITY TO ACCOMPLISH TWO THINGS, BOTH TO SOLVE THE PROBLEM OF THE YOUNG LOVERS AND ALSO TO SATISFY HER OWN DESIRES, SO SHE THOUGHT UP A DECEITFUL PLAN TO DO THIS.

16. THE NEXT DAY, AGAIN PRESUMABLY GOING TO VISIT THE WOMAN IN THE NEIGHBORHOOD, SHE CAME OPENLY TO THE OAK TREE WHERE DAPHNIS AND CHLOE WERE SITTING AND ACTED EXACTLY AS IF SHE WERE IN GREAT TROUBLE SAYING "HELP ME DAPHNIS I AM IN TROUBLE. AN EAGLE TOOK MY BEST GOOSE . . . THEN NOT ABLE TO CARRY THIS HEAVY LOAD HE CAME DOWN WITH HIS PREY IN THE WOODS BACK THERE . . . COME AND SAVE MY GOOSE AND MAYBE YOU CAN KILL THE EAGLE TOO, SO THAT HE WILL NOT STEAL OUR LAMBS AND KIDS ANYMORE."

17. NOT SUSPECTING WHAT WAS GOING TO HAPPEN, DAPHNIS FOLLOWED LYKAINION, WHO TOOK HIM AS FAR FROM CHLOE AS POSSIBLE, WHERE THE WOODS WERE THE THICKEST, AND THERE SITTING BY A FOUNTAIN SHE CALLED HIM AND SAID "DAPHNIS, YOU ARE IN LOVE WITH CHLOE AS I HAVE LEARNED FROM THE NYMPHS IN A DREAM LAST NIGHT. THEY ALSO TOLD ME ABOUT YOUR TEARS AND ASKED ME TO SAVE YOU BY TEACHING YOU THE ACTS OF LOVE. THIS INVOLVES NOT ONLY KISSING AND EMBRACING AND WHAT RAMS AND BILLY GOATS DO, BUT ALSO DIFFERENT STEPS MUCH SWEETER AND WITH A LONGER-LASTING PLEASURE. SO IF YOU WISH TO GET RID OF YOUR EVIL TENSIONS AND BECOME EXPERIENCED IN THE PLEASURES YOU SEEK, COME GIVE YOURSELF UP TO ME AS MY PUPIL AND I WILL TEACH YOU ALL THERE IS TO KNOW ABOUT LOVE FOR THE SAKE OF THE NYMPHS."

18. DAPHNIS COULD HARDLY WAIT . . . AND HE BEGGED LYKAINION TO TEACH HIM THE ART WHICH HE COULD APPLY ON CHLOE AS SOON AS POSSIBLE. HE ASSUMED THAT HE WAS GOING TO BE TAUGHT SOMETHING GREAT AND GODSENT AND HE PROMISED TO GIVE HER MANY EXQUISITE CHEESES MADE FROM THE VERY BEST MILK AND, IN FACT, THE GOAT HERSELF. LYKAINION FOUND DAPHNIS' NAIVETE QUITE UNEXPECTED AND SHE BEGAN HER LESSON RIGHT AWAY. SHE ASKED HIM TO SIT BY HER AND TO KISS HER AS HE HAD BEEN DOING TO CHLOE, THEN TO TAKE HER IN HIS ARMS AND TO LIE DOWN. WHEN SHE NOTICED THAT HE WAS WELL AROUSED AND HIS BODY STIFF AND STRONG SHE HAD HIM MOVE FROM HER SIDE TO A POSITION OVER HER AND THEN SKILLFULLY POSITIONING HERSELF BELOW SHE GUIDED HIM INTO THE PATH THAT HE HAD BEEN TRYING TO FIND ALL ALONG. AFTER THAT THERE WAS NO NEED FOR ANY TRIALS OF UNFAMILIAR MANEUVERS. NATURE HERSELF WELL-INSTRUCTED DAPHNIS HOW TO ACT.

19. WHEN THIS SEXUAL EDUCATION WAS COMPLETED, DAPHNIS, STILL THINKING LIKE A SIMPLE GOAT-HERD, HAD AN URGE TO RUN TO CHLOE AND DO WITH HER WHAT HE HAD JUST LEARNED, BEING CONCERNED THAT IF HE DELAYED HE MIGHT FORGET IT. BUT LYKAINION HELD HIM BACK AND SAID "THERE IS MORE FOR YOU TO LEARN DAPHNIS. I HAPPEN TO BE A MATURE WOMAN AND THERE WAS NO DISTRESS FOR ME NOW. A LONG TIME AGO ANOTHER MAN TAUGHT ME THIS LESSON AND TOOK MY VIRGINITY AS HIS REWARD. IF CHLOE WERE TO ENTANGLE HERSELF WITH YOU LIKE THIS SHE MAY MOAN AND CRY AND BLEED AS IF SHE HAD BEEN WOUNDED. YOU SHOULD NOT BE SCARED . . . BUT YOU BETTER TAKE HER WITH YOU TO THIS QUIET SPOT SO NOBODY CAN HEAR OR SEE HER IF SHE WERE TO CRY OR WEEP AND ALSO, IF SHE BLED, SHE COULD WASH HERSELF BY THIS FOREST FOUNTAIN. REMEMBER TOO THAT I WAS THE ONE TO MAKE YOU A MAN, BEFORE CHLOE."

20. AFTER SHE GAVE ALL THIS ADVICE LYKAINION LEFT FOR ANOTHER PART OF THE WOODS AS IF SHE WERE STILL LOOKING FOR HER GOOSE. DAPHNIS THINKING AGAIN ABOUT ALL SHE HAD SAID FOUND THAT HIS EARLIER URGE WAS GONE BECAUSE HE DID NOT WANT TO HURT CHLOE BY DOING MORE THAN KISSING AND EMBRACING, TO MAKE HER SCREAM AS IF HE WERE HER ENEMY, OR TO WEEP IN PAIN OR TO BLEED . . . SO DECIDING ONLY TO HAVE THE USUAL PLEASURES WITH HER HE CAME OUT OF THE WOODS AND WENT TO HER AS SHE WAS WEAVING A CROWN OF VIOLETS. HE TOLD HER A LIE THAT HE HAD SAVED THE GOOSE FROM THE CLAWS OF THE EAGLE AND THEN PUT HIS ARMS AROUND HER KISSING HER AS HE HAD DONE WITH LYKAINION, KNOWING THAT THIS PART WAS NOT RISKY. SHE THEN PUT THE CROWN OF VIOLETS ON HIS HEAD AND KISSED HIS HAIR WHICH SHE LIKED BETTER THAN VIOLETS. TAKING OUT OF HER BAG HER MEAL AND BREADS SHE GAVE DAPHNIS TO EAT AND AS HE WAS EATING SHE GRABBED SOME FOOD FROM HIS MOUTH, NIBBLING LIKE A NEWLY HATCHED BIRD IN THE NEST.

Summary, Section 21-34: As they were eating and kissing all along, a fisherman's boat was seen passing by the coast and because there was no wind and the sea was calm Daphnis and Chloe could hear the sailors' songs, which Daphnis tried to memorize so that he could later play them on his flute. They also heard the echo from the hills behind, whereupon Daphnis started telling Chloe the ancient myth of Echo, who was the daughter of one of the Nymphs. Days passed and the weather was getting warmer, so Daphnis often swam in the rivers and Chloe bathed in the springs. He played his flute while she sang. They both picked flowers, shook the trees and ate the ripe fruit. At times they slept together naked under a goatskin and Chloe could easily have become a full woman but Daphnis was still upset with the thought of blood. In fact he was so worried that his desire might overcome his resolution not to hurt Chloe, that most of the time he did not let her undress, which puzzled her though she was too shy to ask for the reasons.

That summer many suitors with many gifts and promises came for Chloe and asked her adopted father Dryas for permission to marry her. Dryas was often quite pleased because the presents were extraordinary but then, realizing that his girl was superior to any of these young farmers he kept putting off his decision. Daphnis despaired of his chances of ever being allowed to marry Chloe because he was so poor. He seemed so close to giving up hope that his own mother feared that he might try to kill himself. Luckily he got the help he needed from the Nymphs, who in a dream guided him how to find a big purse of 3,000 drachmas hidden under a shipwreck among the seaweeds on the beach. That ship in fact was the one that had gotten loose when the goat chewed the mooring lines and afterwards was blown to the shore by heavy storms. Without delay Daphnis ran and asked Dryas and his wife Nape for Chloe's hand, outlining all the things he could offer and all he could do for them and for her. Then the two fathers, Dryas and Lamon got together and came to a full agreement, which they celebrated by hugging and kissing each other and drinking together some superior wine. The wedding however had to be postponed until Lamon, who was a servant, had informed his master and got his permission. Perhaps secretly he was also hoping that in the meantime the true parents of Daphnis and Chloe could be found.

While the parents were celebrating, Daphnis, without eating or drinking, ran to Chloe who was milking the sheep and getting ready to make cheese. He brought her the good tidings of the marriage contract and kissed her now as his wife-to-be and not hiding as before. In the season's abundance of fruit ripening on the trees there was one apple tree with all the fruit harvested but one huge and very aromatic golden apple on the very top branch. Daphnis climbed to the top, cut it and offered it to Chloe, comparing her to Aphrodite and himself to Paris of Troy. Then he placed the apple inside her bosom while she, pulling him close to her, covered him with kisses, which were for him much more precious than the golden apple he had given her.

Book IV

Summary, Sections 1-11: Expecting the estate lord from Mytilene to visit before vintage time, Lamon worked very hard to make the whole land look like a paradise. He even weaved a crown for the statue of the god Dionysos in the temple located in the middle of the magnificent orchards, flower beds and sparkling creeks. Daphnis was instructed to make the goats as fat as possible and he took such good care of them that he even combed their hair and polished their horns. Yet both he and Chloe were very worried about the visit and the kind of impression they might make, poor shepherds that they were. Then came a terrible shock, when one morning before the visit, Lamon found his gardens ruined by a madman, Lampis, a young farmer who in the past had been rejected in favor of Daphnis, when he had asked to marry Chloe. Lamon and Daphnis feared the lord's worst punishment but a messenger from the city advised them to speak first to Astylos, his son, who was to arrive the next day. Astylos in fact felt sorry for them when he heard the story and promised to tell his father that some wild horses had caused all the damage.

Later on, Astylos, a dashing young man and a sports fan, went to hunt while his older companion and sidekick [in Greek "*parasite*"], Gnathon, who was only interested in the pleasures of his mouth and of his belly and of the parts below it, stayed behind. This Gnathon liked young boys and was much impressed with Daphnis, as he had never seen anyone so handsome in the city. So he decided to make advances on Daphnis thinking it would be easy to seduce a simple-minded shepherd. He followed him, praised his goats, said how much he admired his playing on the pipe and then promised to speak to the estate lord about his skills.

12. HAVING GAINED THE YOUNG MAN'S TRUST, GNATHON ONE NIGHT CAME OUT OF HIDING AS DAPHNIS WAS GUIDING HIS GOATS BACK FROM PASTURE, RAN UP TO HIM AND AFTER FIRST KISSING HIM HE TOLD HIM THAT HE WANTED TO MOUNT HIM FROM BEHIND, AS BILLIES MOUNT SHE-GOATS. DAPHNIS WAS SLOW TO UNDERSTAND AND REPLIED THAT IT IS RIGHT THAT SHE-GOATS ARE MOUNTED BY BILLIES BUT HE HAD NEVER SEEN A BILLY GOAT MOUNTING ANOTHER MALE, NOR A RAM DO IT TO ANOTHER RAM, NOR A ROOSTER ON A ROOSTER, INSTEAD OF A HEN. BUT SUCH WAS GNATHON THAT HE TRIED TO FORCE DAPHNIS AND LAY HANDS ON HIM. AT THIS POINT DAPHNIS PUSHED TO THE GROUND THIS DRUNKEN FELLOW, WHO COULD HARDLY STAND STRAIGHT AND LEAVING HIM WONDERING WHETHER HE HAD APPROACHED A BOY OR A VERY STRONG MAN, HE RAN QUICKLY TO TAKE CARE OF HIS FLOCK. SINCE THEN HE AVOIDED GNATHON AND ALSO WATCHED CHLOE AGAINST HIM . . .

13. . . . NOW CAME DIONYSOPHANES, THE LORD OF THE ESTATE, A TALL AND HANDSOME MAN, WHO, ALTHOUGH TURNING GRAY, COULD BE A MATCH FOR ANY YOUNGER MAN AND WHILE EXCEPTIONALLY RICH, WAS ABOVE ALL HONEST AND JUST. HE INITIALLY OFFERED SACRIFICES TO THE GODS OF AGRICULTURE, DEMETER, DIONYSOS, PAN AND THE NYMPHS AND THEN SET UP A LARGE WINE MIXING BOWL [Greek: Krater] FOR EVERYONE THERE. THE FOLLOWING DAYS DIONYSOPHANES INSPECTED ALL OF LAMON'S WORKS, THE WELL-PLOUGHED FIELDS, THE VINES LOADED WITH GRAPES, THE BEAUTY OF THE ENTIRE PARADISE (HIS SON ASTYLOS HAD TAKEN THE BLAME FOR THE DESTRUCTION OF THE FLOWER BEDS). THE MASTER WAS EXCEEDINGLY PLEASED, PRAISED LAMON AND PROMISED TO GRANT HIM HIS FREEDOM . . .

Summary, Sections 14-15: Dionysophanes and his wife Cleariste then went to see and to admire the herds and particularly appreciated Daphnis' music on the pipe. Cleariste promised special rewards for his labors and his talent and gave him all kinds of food and sweets from the city.

16. DAPHNIS THEN WENT TO HAVE LUNCH WITH CHLOE AND SHARED WITH HER THE DELICACIES HE HAD RECEIVED. NOW HE FELT MUCH MORE HOPEFUL ABOUT OBTAINING THE LORD'S CONSENT FOR MARRYING CHLOE. BUT GNA-

THON WAS NOW BURNING WITH AN EVEN STRONGER DESIRE FOR THE GOATHERD AND FELT THAT HIS LIFE WOULD NOT BE WORTH LIVING IF HE COULD NOT WIN DAPHNIS . . .

17. TO GET WHAT HE WANTED GNATHON BEGGED ASTYLOS TO HAVE HIS FATHER TRANSFER DAPHNIS TO THE CITY, WHERE HE COULD BE A SERVANT IN THE FAMILY MANSION AND ALSO EASILY BECOME THE LOVER OF GNATHON . . .

Summary, Sections 17- (continued) 39: Dionysophanes was about to approve Daphnis' removal to the city but Lamon was forewarned and went ahead to reveal the secret that Daphnis was not his natural son. By the luxurious way he was clothed and adorned when found, he could be considered to belong to a noble family and, Lamon thought, would be shameful for him to become a servant in the city and also to play the role of a woman for Gnathon. To convince his master, Lamon displayed the baby's purple dress, golden buckle and an ivory little dagger he had carefully kept all those years. The landlords recognized them as those of their own baby boy, whom they had abandoned in the woods when they thought that their first three children were enough for them. Astylos, the only one surviving, now ran to get his newly found brother Daphnis, who then was dressed in luxurious clothes and seated next to his real father. After thanksgiving sacrifices to Zeus the Savior, there was a big banquet and the only one missing from it was Gnathon who, quite scared, went hiding in the temple of Dionysos. Everyone else was present partaking of the abundant wine, breads, waterfowl, suckling pigs and a variety of sweets. Among the guests was Dryas, who was the one first to find and nurture Chloe. That poor girl was now worried that Daphnis had forgotten her, or perhaps had found a prettier girl among his real mother's housemaids.

Just as she was wondering and worrying, there came Lampis, the cowboy, who attacked and kidnapped her, believing that Daphnis would not now want to marry her and Dryas should be glad to accept him as a son-in-law. Someone saw him however and ran and told Dryas and Daphnis. The young man went out of his mind (Greek: *exo-phrenon*— Ref. Table E) ran to the front yard and cried: "Oh how much happier I was as a shepherd tending my flock and seeing Chloe, whom now Lampis will rape and will sleep with her at night, while I am here leisurely eating and drinking." His cry was heard right then by Gnathon, who was now hiding behind the greenery. He decided that this might be an opportunity to be reconciled with Daphnis and taking along some friends, he arrived in the house of Lampis and stopped him as he came in, dragging the still-screaming Chloe. They set her free and before dark Gnathon took her back to the weeping Daphnis, begging forgiveness and also predictably for some food so that he would not "starve."

After Daphnis apologized to Chloe for his temporary neglect, they decided to tell only his mother Cleariste about the proposed wedding. But Dryas intervened and announced to all that, like Lamon with Daphnis, he also was not the real father of Chloe but had found her in the grotto of the Nymphs. Her rich clothes and her delicate beauty suggested that she was not of peasant stock and so she would be worth marrying Daphnis. Cleariste then decided to take over and to dress and decorate Chloe as would be appropriate for her son's future wife. Dionysophanes, in the meantime, took Daphnis aside and asked to be reassured that Chloe was still a virgin and that nothing more than kissing had taken place between them. When Chloe returned everyone was amazed to see how beauty is enhanced when properly adorned. She was so well dressed-up, her face washed and her hair stylishly combed that even Daphnis could barely recognize her.

After many days of feasting and religious ceremonies with dedications to the gods—they even poured wine into the fountain from where they drank water and where they bathed—Daphnis and Chloe and the entire entourage departed for the city of Mytilene, to look for Chloe's parents and to make plans for the wedding. Another big banquet was organized and as it was about to end, the servants brought on a silver platter the items, clothes and jewelry, that were found with the baby and which might help identify Chloe's background. No one recognized them until Megacles, who due to his old age sat in the place of honor and was reached last, saw them and cried out: "What do I see? My little daughter might still be alive! . . ." He then said how as a young man, having spent all his money funding ships for the navy and sponsoring theatrical performances, he could not afford to raise and to educate his baby daughter properly so he had abandoned her to the care of the Nymphs. Later he became rich but he and his wife were not blessed to have another child who might inherit them . . . while, in a dream, the gods seemed to make fun of him, declaring that a sheep would make him a father.

Dionysophanes then brought in Chloe dressed magnificently and with a loud voice he said "This is your daughter, a sheep nursed her by divine providence, the same way a goat fed my own son Daphnis and helped him survive. We exposed them but now we found them both because Pan, the Nymphs and Eros looked after them." All parents then joyfully approved the forthcoming wedding. The next day Daphnis and Chloe, finding it hard to endure the city turmoil, left for the country to plan a truly pastoral wedding. That took place on a beautiful day, before the actual grotto, on carpets of flowers and greenery. Everyone was there, including Philetas and Lykainion, some playing music, others dancing and everybody feasting and reveling. Even the goats came by and Daphnis, calling them each by name, fed them and warmly kissed them. In fact, not only for the wedding ceremony but for the rest of their lives, Daphnis and Chloe remained on the countryside. They lived the life of pastoral peace, multiplied their flock, had their own children and also built an altar to Eros, "Love the Shepherd."

40. BUT THAT CAME LATER. ON THE NIGHT OF THE WEDDING EVERYONE ESCORTED THEM TO THE BRIDAL CHAMBER, SOME PLAYING THE PIPE, OTHERS THE FLUTE AND OTHERS HOLDING HIGH BIG TORCHES. THEN DAPHNIS AND CHLOE WENT TO BED NAKED, EMBRACED AND KISSED EACH OTHER AND STAYED AWAKE ALL NIGHT, LONGER THAN EVEN OWLS DO. DAPHNIS ACTED EXACTLY THE WAY LYKAINION HAD TAUGHT HIM AND CHLOE REALIZED THAT WHAT THEY HAD BEEN DOING HIDING IN THE WOODS WAS ONLY A CHILD'S PLAY.

Edmonds, JM, 1916/78, pp. 6–246.

The adventures of Apollonios

"*Apollonios of Tyre*" is another prose romance from about the third century A.D., but it has been preserved only in Latin. From that it has been translated and adapted in many modern languages. The story is identified as Greek (17) from the social and topographical context, certain features in the vocabulary and style and also from the characteristic motifs of late Hellenistic romances, such as the separated families and lovers, their trials and tribulations, the kind and the evil people they encounter and the final reunion and mutual recognition of the protagonists. A fairly detailed narrative in English has been presented in a modern review (Perry, 1967, pp. 294–320) exclusively considering the Latin authorship of the original and mentioning an ancient claim that Apollonios himself wrote his story and deposited one manuscript in the temple of Diana at Ephesus. The hero, Apollonios, was forced to escape in a hurry from the city of Antioch when he aroused the fury of the king by solving a riddle and disclosing that his royal majesty was living incestuously with his own daughter. While in North Africa, Apollonios married the daughter of the king of Cyrene. This young woman, for some unknown reason, remains unnamed in the Latin texts (Perry, 1967, p. 303). She, on the journey back to Tyre, gave birth to a daughter and then supposedly died on the ship. The body was placed in a chest and thrown overboard but when it was washed up at Ephesos on the coast of Asia Minor, south of Lesbos, a local physician revived the woman. She then became a priestess in the Temple of Artemis, or, in Latin, Diana. The daughter, whom Apollonios left in the care of foster parents while he went to Egypt, was kidnapped by pirates who sold her to a brothel in Mytilene on Lesbos. Apollonios, thinking that both his wife and daughter were dead, happened to visit Mytilene and there he joyfully found his daughter, surprisingly still a virgin. Their happiness was complete when after receiving a message in a dream, Apollonios and his daughter went to Ephesos where they were reunited with his wife, her mother.

As the original Greek text does not exist, a small example of the opening lines is cited in Latin, and for curiosity's sake, in old English. Both texts employ the Latin ending *-us* for the Greek names ending in *-os* (*Antiokhos*, *Apollonios*, etc.).

THE STORY OF APOLLONIOS KING OF TYRE
Greek author unknown, written late third century A.D.

LATIN TEXT (sample)
I. In civitate Antiochia rex fuit Antiochus nomine a quo et ipsa civitas nomen Antiochia accepit. Hic habuit ex amissa coniuge filiam . . . speciosissimam incredibili pulchritudine.

OLD ENGLISH TRANSLATION (sample)
I. An Antiochia þare ceastre wæs sum cyningc Antiochus gehaten: æfter þæs cyninges naman wæs seo ceaster Antiochia geciged. Þises cyninges cwen wearð of life gewiten, be ðare he hæfde ane swiðe wlitige dohter ungelifedlicre fægernesse.

Goolden, P. 1958, pp. 2-3.

The existing Latin text is probably from the fifth century A.D. A copy of the "Story of Apollonios" was on the list of books in the library of Wando, who became an abbott in 742 A.D. English versions, some from the Latin and others translated from the French, date from the 1100 to 1600s A.D.

(Goolden, 1958). An Old English translation with several adaptations (grammatical changes and religious Christian additions, references to angels and the One God) has been published recently (Goolden, 1958), with annotations and a parallel Latin text. Regrettably, more than half of the story, with the parts describing the events in Mytilene, is not included in this publication and is presented by the editor only in the form of a summary (Goolden, pp. 59-60). According to the editor, the Old English version of *Apollonius of Tyre* "is not only a landmark in the history of English literature" but also "one of the better specimens of Old English prose" (Goolden, *Preface*). With its many touches of human tender feelings and humor, it is considered as "the first book of romantic adventure in English literature" (Goolden, *Introduction*, pg. xxv). Yet Chaucer (1340?–1400 A.D.) called Apollonius a "cursed" story, a tale "horrible . . . for to rede" (Goolden, p. 44).

The same story was told by Lawrence Twine in his novel "*The Patterne of Painefull Adventures*" (1576) and with a few name changes, by George Wilkins in 1608, in his novel "*The Painefull Adventures of Pericles Prince of Tyre*" (Encycl. Brit., Vol. 2; Goolden, *Introduction* p. xiii). Shakespeare's drama, *Pericles, Prince of Tyre* also includes the same sequence of events, essentially in the same locations (18). Pericles (same as Apollonius) suing for the hand of King Antiochus' daughter, was compelled to solve a riddle, which all previous suitors had failed to do and were put to death by Antiochus, who this way was able to continue his incestuous relationship with his daughter. Pericles had the answer, which revealed the King's sin and was then forced to escape to save his life. He travelled to Pentapolis and there he married the king's daughter, Thaisa. When later they learned that Antiochus and his daughter were struck dead by a god-sent thunderbolt, they sailed back to Tyre to claim their realm. In the middle of a terrible storm at sea, Thaisa gave birth to a daughter and then seemed to have died. The superstitious sailors placed the regally-clad body in a heavy chest and threw it overboard. It floated to Ephesus, where a skilled physician revived Thaisa and she remained there to become high priestess in the famous Temple of Diana. Pericles left his daughter, named Marina, in the care of friends but by the age of fourteen, she had become so much more beautiful than their own girls, that they hired an assassin to kill her. Before he did that, pirates arrived, kidnapped Marina and sailed away to Mytilene on Lesbos, where they sold her to the keeper of a brothel. Miraculously she was able to remain a virgin and bravely tried to make the customers change their sexual habits. Finally, the Governor of Mytilene, Lysimachus, coming as a client, fell in love with Marina and gave her enough gold to buy her freedom. Pericles, having been told that his daughter had died, was forced by strong winds to sail to Mytilene. There, his deep depression and despair turned to exaltation and joy when he and Marina recognized each other as father and daughter. Together they went to the Temple of Diana in Ephesus (see also Chapter IV-D, Saint Paul's visit to Ephesus) where Thaisa was revealed to them as the presumably dead wife and mother. Shortly afterwards Pericles announced the betrothal of Marina and Lysimachus and the couple then became the rulers of Tyre.

A few passages from *Pericles* may provide a Shakespearean view of Lesbos.

PERICLES, PRINCE OF TYRE
by William Shakespeare, 1564–1616 A.D.
Act IV Scene II. *Mytilene. A room in a brothel.*
. . . .
PANDAR. Search the market narrowly; Mytilene is full of gallants. We lost too much money this mart by being too wenchless.
BAWD. We were never so much out of creatures. We have but poor three, and they can do no more than they can do; and they with continual action are even as good as rotten.
. . . .
        Re-enter BOULT, with the PIRATES and MARINA
BOULT (to Marina). Come your ways. My masters, you say she's a virgin?
FIRST PIRATE. O, sir, we doubt it not.
. . . .
PANDAR. . . . my masters, you shall have your money presently. Wife, take her in; instruct her what she has to do, that she may not be raw in her entertainment.
. . . .
Scene VI. The same. A room in the brothel.
        . . . *Enter LYSIMACHUS*
LYSIMACHUS. How now! How a dozen of virginities?
BOULT. I am glad to see your honour in good health.
. . . .
BAWD. We have here one, sir, if she would—but there never came her like in Mytilene.
LYSIMACHUS. If she'ld do the deed of darkness, thou wouldst say.
. . . .
BAWD . . . Come, we will leave his honour and her together. Go thy ways.
LYSIMACHUS. Now, pretty one, how long have you been at this trade? . . . Why, the house you dwell in proclaims you to be a creature of sale.
. . . .
MARINA . . . That I am a maid, though most ungentle fortune Have placed me in this sty, where, since I came, Diseases have been

sold dearer than physic, O, that the gods Would set me free from this unhallow'd place . . .
LYSIMACHUS. I did not think Thou couldst have spoke so well; ne'er dream'd thou couldst. Had I brought hither a corrupted mind, Thy speech had alter'd it. Hold, here's gold for thee.
BOULT. I beseech your honour, one piece for me.
LYSIMACHUS. Avaunt, though damned door-keeper! Your house, but for this virgin that doth prop it, would sink, and overwhelm you. Away!
BOULT. I must have your maidenhead taken off, or the common hangman shall execute it. Come your ways. We'll have no more gentlemen driven away. Come your ways, I say.
BAWD. How now! what's the matter?
BOULT. The nobleman would have dealt with her like a nobleman, and she sent him away as cold as a snowball, saying his prayers too.
BAWD. Boult, take her away; use her at thy pleasure: crack the glass of her virginity, and make the rest malleable.
BOULT. An if she were a thornier piece of ground than she is, she shall be ploughed.

Act V Scene I. On board PERICLES' ship, off Mytilene . . .

LYSIMACHUS (being taken on board to see PERICLES). I am the governor of this place you lie before.
HELICANUS (Lord of Tyre). Sir, Our vessel is of Tyre, in it the king; A man who for this three months hath not spoken to any one, nor taken sustenance but to prorogue his grief.
LYSIMACHUS. Upon what ground is his distemperature?
HELICANUS. 'Twould be too tedious to repeat; but the main grief springs from the loss of a beloved daughter and a wife.
. . . .
LYSIMACHUS. Sir king, all hail! the gods preserve you! Hail, royal sir!
HELICANUS. It is in vain; he will not speak to you.
FIRST LORD. Sir, We have a maid in Mytilene, I durst wager, would win some words of him.
. . . .
MARINA. Sir, I will use My utmost skill in his recovery, provided That none but I and my companion maid be suffer'd to come near him.
. . . .
LYSIMACHUS. See, she will speak to him.
. . . .
MARINA. If I should tell my history, it would seem like lies disdain'd in the reporting.
PERICLES. Prithee, speak: Falseness cannot come from thee; for thou look'st Modest as Justice, and thou seems'st a palace for the crown'd Truth to dwell in: I will believe thee, and make my senses credit thy relation to points that seem impossible; for thou look'st like one I loved indeed. . . .
. . . .

MARINA. My name is Marina.
. . . .

PERICLES. But are you flesh and blood? Have you a working pulse? and are no fairy? Motion! Well; speak on. Where were you born? And wherefore call'd Marina?

MARINA. Call'd Marina. For I was born at sea.

PERICLES. At sea! what mother?

MARINA. My mother was the daughter of a king; who died the minute I was born. . . .
. . . .

PERICLES (to Helicanus) Thou art a grave and noble counsellor, most wise in general: tell me, if thou canst, what this maid is, or what is like to be, that thus hath made me weep.

HELICANUS. I know not; but here is the regent, sir, of Mytilene speaks nobly of her.

LYSIMACHUS. She never would tell her parentage; being demanded that, she would sit still and weep.

PERICLES. O Helicanus, strike me, honour'd sir; give me a gash, put me to present pain; lest this great sea of joys rushing upon me o'erbear the shores of my mortality, and drown me with their sweetness. O, come hither, thou that beget'st him that did thee beget; though that wast born at sea, buried at Tarsus, and found at sea again! O Helicanus, down on thy knees; thank the holy gods as loud as thunder threatens us: this is Marina. What was thy mother's name? tell me but that, for truth can never be confirm'd enough, though doubts did ever sleep.

MARINA. First, sir, I pray, what is your title?

PERICLES. I am Pericles of Tyre: but tell me now my drown'd queen's name, as in the rest you said thou hast been godlike perfect, the heir of kingdoms, and another like to Pericles thy father.

MARINA. Is it no more to be your daughter than to say my mother's name was Thaisa? Thaisa was my mother, who did end the minute I began.

PERICLES. Now, blessing on thee! rise; thou art my child. Give me fresh garments. Mine own, Helicanus; she is not dead at Tarsus, as she should have been, by savage Cleon: she shall tell thee all; when thou shalt kneel, and justify in knowledge she is thy very princess. Who is this?

HELICANUS. Sir, 'tis the governor of Mytilene, who, hearing of your melancholy state, did come to see you.

PERICLES. I embrace you. Give me my robes. I am wild in my beholding. O heavens bless my girl! But, hark, what music? Tell Helicanus, my Marina, tell him o'er, point by point, for yet he seems to doubt, how sure you are my daughter. But, what music?

HELICANUS. My lord, I hear none.

PERICLES. None! The music of the spheres! List, my Marina.

LYSIMACHUS. It is not good to cross him; give him way.

PERICLES. Rarest sounds! Do ye not hear?

LYSIMACHUS. My lord, I hear.

Shakespeare, Wm. Complete Works,
W.A. Wright, ed. 1936, pp. 1202–1211.

HELLENISTIC TWILIGHT AND ROMAN ROMANTIC LOVES 185

Book cover for *Apollonios*, a sixteenth century Greek version, published in Venice in 1745

Almost contemporary with the Shakespearean work and (though lacking the Elizabethan English style and polish) notably warmer, endearing and, perhaps, closer to the lost original Greek, was "A most beautiful tale"—as labeled on the title page—composed about 1500 A.D., in rhyming verses, on the Greek island of Crete. At that time Crete was under Venetian rule. When after twenty-two years of fighting, it was captured by the Turks in 1669 (19), many Greeks followed the Venetian colonists and migrated to Venice. There the colloquial Greek (very close to the modern Greek language) "Apollonios" was reprinted a number of times. Two names associated with this work are now believed to identify later eighteenth century copyists (20). My English translation of a selection from the total number of 1894 verses attempts to convey the essence of the original story and to emulate the literary style of the unknown poet.

THE STORY OF APOLLONIOS OF TYRE:
A MOST BEAUTIFUL TALE
by Konstantinos Themenos, or Gabriel Kontianos (20).

Sect. A-2, p. 3 (first page of the text)
The glory of Jesus Christ our Lord, whom all of us revere
May give me strength to say the words for everyone to hear
An ancient story of great charm the world will sure admire,
Of Apollonios, Lord and Prince of faraway Tyre,
On how his fate so many woes on him for long compiled
Far from his own homeland he was driven and exiled,
Until the cycle turn'd again and back his way he found.
So listen now, if you will, to how my tale will sound.

Continuing in idiomatic and often charmingly clumsy rhyming verses, the early sixteenth-century (21) Greek folk-poet narrated the familiar old story. Apollonios was forced to leave his estate in Tyre (*Tyros*, a seaport in ancient Phoenicia, modern Lebanon) when, challenged to solve a riddle imposed by the great king of Antioch as a condition for marrying the princess, his daughter, he understood and revealed that she and her royal father were having an incestuous sexual liaison. Following a moralizing but intriguing description of how the king managed to seduce his own child, the writer introduced Apollonios.

> **A-4,5, p. 8**
> So Apollonios then declared: "It's like a crystal clear,
> The riddle that you gave me, but secretly I fear
> That if I don't say what it means, my neck will feel the knife,
> Yet if I tell the truth I know, do I get the girl for wife?
> It can't be helped, the awful sin I must to all announce:
> This king's bed-mate is his daughter, them strongly I denounce."

To avoid the king's fury and vengeance, Apollonios escaped but was shipwrecked off the coast of North Africa. Recognized by a fisherman as a prince, he was taken to that kingdom's royal palace. The king's only daughter, Arkhistrata, and Apollonios fell in love and after numerous difficulties and tribulations, they obtained her father's, king Arkhistrator's (21) permission to marry. The wedding was magnificent with the bishop officiating and an enormous banquet, lasting for hours.

> **Sect. B-8, p. 30-31**
> Then every day was a feast, their weeks were full of pleasure,
> Being part of all the palace life in luxury and leisure
> In bliss and ardor Apollonios his wife's joys received
> And Arkhistrata very soon a child had conceived.

A few months later and despite the king's objections, the young couple took off to try to reclaim Tyre for Apollonios, after they learned that the king of Antioch and his daughter were killed by a God-sent thunderbolt. On board the ship taking them to Tyre and in the middle of a terrible storm, Arkhistrata gave birth to a baby girl.

> **C-2, p. 35**
> The clouds cover'd everything, a heavy storm broke out
> Much rain fell and snow too, big hailstones all about.
> And in that moment full of risks began the labor pains.
> The princess seemed almost dead, with all the stress and strains
> For all on board the journey's woes, the misery and the trouble
> Were getting worse, a doom of hell the horror made double.
> Then after lots of pains and pangs a little babe she bore.
> The princess had a little girl for everyone to adore.

For the poor mother "everything went dark," she lost consciousness and was thought to be dead. Apollonios, weeping inconsolably, dressed her in the most luxurious clothes, put a bejewelled crown on her head and placed her in a thick wooden casket, which with the help of the crew, was thrown into the dark deep sea waters and carried away by the raging waves.

C-3, p. 37
But the All-merciful's concern and His Divine Grace
The casket brought to a sandy beach, a truly quiet place
There it was found by a man, a doctor, a physician,
Extremely learn'd about the world and also a logician,
Who, by that distant shelter'd shore, away from the crowd
Had many students come to learn of wisdom to be proud.

The medical professor and his students took the casket to the school where after much effort they managed to open it.

The very learned medical men to look inside were curious
And all were stunned to behold such clothes and gems luxurious.

They found a note and on it they read that the young woman was a princess, had married Apollonios and that she had died after giving birth to a child on board the ship. A large crowd arrived to see the mysterious and marvelous casket and the dead princess, then preparations were made for a proper burial.

C-3, p. 38
But a young doctor with greater skills than even his own master
Began to think she was not dead, he questioned the disaster.
He bet his life that he could help her instead recover.
He sent for a miraculous salve, her body all to cover.
And soon the unlucky woman moved and opened her eyes,
She took deep breaths and one could hear her very plaintive sighs.

The young doctor wanted to marry her but Arkhistrata could not be consoled for the loss of her husband and of her baby. She decided to become a nun. In the meantime Apollonios continued his trip and landed near the estates of an old friend named Strangylos, with whom he felt he had to leave his infant daughter, if he were to continue his travels.

C-6, p. 42
"I worry that she may be lost, I want now to baptize her
And then to leave her in your hands, to raise and to advise her."

They took the baby to the church and christened her Tarsia. Apollonios tearfully departed and Tarsia was left with Strangylos and his wife. The couple had also a daughter who became Tarsia's companion in school and play. Years later, as Tarsia's *nona* (god-mother, or maybe nurse) was ill and near death, told Tarsia who were her real father and mother. Not long afterwards it became quite clear that:

C-7, p. 44
In all her studies she was the best, at human nature's peak,
No matter what one asked her, she knew well how to speak.

Because Tarsia's talents and beauty were notably much superior to those of their own daughter, her foster parents became more and more jealous and decided to have her killed, feeling sure that "nobody would ever ask for her." The hired assassin took Tarsia to a secluded cove but while she cried and begged to be spared, pirates arrived, captured her and carried her off to their boat. She was reported by Strangylos to have died a natural death and "everyone dressed in black" to mourn her.

D-1, p. 49
Please make a note of this, all you in this dark world of ours
Who raise children and believe that blind fate devours
Whatever knowledge, skills and works have on their lives been paved,
That the Divine Mind decides who is lost and who is saved.
And so too Tarsia, with fair winds, the galleon as her fort,
Was safely taken by the waves to Mytilene's port.
. . . .
She's taken to the big bazaar, slave buyers to entice.
A ruffian ready there for her was quick to pay the price.
He took her home with vicious plans, jumping with wild joy,
To teach her skills and make her good to be for men a toy.
"My girl I want you to be well, eat, drink, as you desire
And then allow any man to come and be your sire.
I'll give you clothes and jewelry that every woman craves,
But let's be sure you take in all of these excited braves
And make them pay, do never give a single friend discount,
Or else your fun will end and you will have to give account.
. . . .

D-1, p. 50
The great lord and town head, who was called Thenagoras (21)
After he heard about her while crossing the agoras,
Went by to visit her and found her very sad and weeping.
"I warmly welcome you and your charms, which truly are in keeping
With what I've heard, but tell me please what makes you now cry?
"And she, in her sobs to answer well she managed to try.

She told him how she got to the island and all she knew about her birth and her background.

D-2, p. 51
"Please, Sir, in the name of God, do not torment me worse,
What can you more get out of me—think of a child of yours."

Thenagoras felt sorry and also a deep respect and maybe love for Tarsia. He gave her a precious gift and, weeping himself, left her. But other men were waiting and her master, the ruffian Makarios, was mad because he still had not made any money.

HELLENISTIC TWILIGHT AND ROMAN ROMANTIC LOVES   189

> Then, more than mad, he went to find a very loathsome man,
> He brought him home, gave him a knife and told him: "If you can
> Go sleep with Tarsia, the young maid, my slave do violate
> And if she doesn't allow you that, kill her before it's too late."

Tarsia wept and prayed, so even the hired killer felt sorry for her and gave up. Her master first planned to kill her himself but then he too listened to her prayers. He agreed to get for her a guitar, so that she may earn some money singing in the marketplace.

> **D-3, p. 53**
> "Oh, let me out, please let me go to the central big bazaar,
> Where I can sing and play the lute and also a guitar."

That is what Tarsia ended up doing and earned much more money than anyone had expected. Her singing, especially her wailing "songs of fate" [*moirologia*] at wakes and her lamenting her misfortunes in her own words, made everyone cry.

> **D-4, p. 54**
> Now let's go back to Tarsia's lord, her long-lost dear father
> Who had been able to get a ship and all new crew to gather
> To look for her across the seas, to find and have her married.
> Back in the land of Stangylos he rushed and never tarried.

Arriving there, Apollonios noted that people were wearing black. He learned that they were still mourning the death of his daughter Tarsia. He was taken to see her grave and was carried back to his ship in utter despair, wanting to die.

> **D-4, p. 55**
> "I care not about the world, if I at all survive,
> This moment all I want is death, in darkness now I dive.
> Let's all go back to our ship, the open seas to sail
> And never touch the steering helm, let any wind prevail."
> . . . .
>
> **D-5, p. 56**
> But folks you must now see our God's Good Will and Great Power,
> How if he wants to save a man, He builds for him a tower.
> And so for Apollonios the woes at last he ended.
> To Mytilene He brought his ship, the goal He had intended.

The governor of Mytilene, followed by many citizens, went to inspect the mysterious galley and they found Apollonios there, listless, silent and ready to die.

> **D-5, pp. 56-57**
> The only way, they decide, to change the prince's mind
> And to assist this gentle lord, some hope and goals to find,

Would be for Tarsia to come aboard and sing for him a song,
With her guitar perhaps to soothe a heart in pain so long.

Tarsia arrived but her song and music had no effect. She was ready to leave but was made to try once more, when promised her freedom if she managed to get Apollonios out of his depression and death wish. Again her words and melodies were in vain and, desperate, she tried to grab him and make him stand up.

D-5, pp.57-58
He then became extremely mad and kicked her in the face
In shock and pain the unlucky girl then wanted to retrace
The chain of all her fortune's blows, with sighs to complain
Still badly hurt, with bleeding nose and moaning with pain:
"Upon your house, Stangylos, a curse should quick fall
You were the one most vicious cause of my misfortunes all.
A curse upon my doomed life and that ill-starred day
When by my father I was left at your foreboding bay
And here I am, most miserable, by everyone suppressed.
On top of all the embarrassments now beaten and oppressed.
. . . .

D-6, pp.58-59
That instant Apollonios knew that she was his own child
The one who was the reason why his life was wasted, wild.
He jumped at once, embraced her with tears overloaded
And as he sobbed he began, with words his girl he goaded.
"Alas, my daughter, my own soul and source of all my courage,
My light and my deepest love, my hope, my life's steerage,
. . . .
Alas, they told me long ago that you had died young,
While you, instead, were stranded here, by vice almost stung."
. . . .
When Tarsia then knew who he was, for sure her own parent,
She felt a joy so immense, first time for her apparent.
She jumped up, embraced him, her arms his neck to bind
And he, poor Apollonios, practically lost his mind.
Like him she started then to weep with joy and to cry.
No more I will now say with words, you to imagine try.

Thenagoras, the Lord of Mytilene, heard about the miraculous reunion and came to learn the details and to wish father and daughter well. Apollonios, with deep emotion, told his story and also extended his tale with analogies to the ancient adventures of the Greeks in that area near Troy.

D-6 ff. pp. 60-61
Then Thenagoras asked them to join him in the palace,
Not only for festivities and for their sorrows' solace,

> But so that he could there request for Tarsia's fair hand
> To marry her and jointly with her to rule the land.

The wedding took place with magnificent pomp. In the meantime, the "ruffian" of the whorehouse was seized, bound behind a black horse and dragged to his miserable death. Soon afterwards, a dream made Apollonios persuade his daughter and son-in-law to equip a ship and sail with him across the straits to the mainland.

D-7, p. 61
> After a couple days' trip with God's Divine Grace,
> They sailed across and found a convent, a very holy place (21).
> There, in the chapel where they went to worship and to pray
> An aging casket they beheld, lit by the sun's rare ray.
> On it they read some lettering, which spelled Arkhistrata.
> There was no doubt about that, no chance for any errata.
> At once then Apollonios stood up from his deep prayer
> To find the mother superior, the casket did betray her.
> He saw and recognized her, his own long-lost wife,
> Who broke down in tears and sobs, to tell him about her life.
>
> N. Glykes of Jannina [*Ioannina*], Greek publisher, Venice, 1745.

Tarsia and Thenagoras joined them, to hear the rest of the story. Later, they all sailed back to Tyre, where Apollonios made the young couple governors, to succeed his rule. Not long afterwards, they all made a trip to find the criminal Strangylos and his wife, who repeated their lies about Tarsia's death, until they were confronted by the young woman alive. The population went mad and stoned the culprits to death. Before returning to Tyre, Apollonios and his family went to visit the old king Arkhistrator (21), who shed tears of joy seeing again his daughter and son-in-law and meeting his grand-daughter and her husband from Mytilene.

C. EARLY CHRISTIAN CONTACTS AND COMMENTARIES

Saint Paul on Assos and Lesbos

Remarkably, the pastoral romances and adventure stories like Daphnis and Chloe and Apollonios, continued to be written and read close to the date when the Roman emperor Constantine—and a dramatic change in public mentality—made christianity the official state religion, in the early part of the fourth century A.D. More than 250 years before that, Saint Paul the apostle was travelling through the gentile Greek and Roman world spreading the new Christian message of love, humility and self-sacrifice. On his third trip, covering major Greek cities around the Aegean Sea, Saint Paul visited Lesbos. Earlier, near the beginning of that tour, the apostle had stopped in Ephesos, the famous city on the mainland and there he was confronted by a rioting crowd of craftsmen, who were incited to protest the possible loss of their trade, of making and selling statues and shrines of their city's patron goddess Artemis (Diana), as a result of the spread of Paul's new religion. A town magistrate had to come out to calm the crowds (Toynbee, 1953, p. 119–120; also in *The Acts of the Apostles*, XIX, 23–41).

The "Acts of the Apostles" is the fifth book of the New Testament. Its author, presumably Saint Luke, provided a day-by-day description of Saint Paul's travels, which is "historically of unique interest" (Encyclopedia Britannica, Vol. I) and, indeed, essential for following the missions and the series of the Epistles of Saint Paul. The "Acts" was written in Greek and was addressed—as was also the Gospel of St. Luke—to Theophilos, a Greek convert to Christianity. A draft probably was prepared before Saint Paul's final journey to Rome and his death there. Some authorities date the final manuscript about 75-80 A.D. The author, Saint Luke, was a travelling companion of Saint Paul, a close friend and his "beloved physician" (Col. iv, 14).

THE ACTS OF THE APOSTLES
BY SAINT LUKE, ABOUT 70–80 A.D.

1-12. AND AFTER THE UPROAR HAD STOPPED (22), PAUL CALLED HIS FOLLOWERS AND EMBRACED THEM AND THEN HE LEFT (EPHESOS) FOR MACEDONIA. . . . AFTER PREACHING THERE, HE WENT TO GREECE . . . AND STAYED THERE THREE MONTHS . . . AND RETURNED TO ASIA THROUGH MACEDONIA . . . (SOME OF) HIS COMPANIONS WENT FIRST AND WAITED FOR US. WE SAILED FROM PHILIPPI . . . AND IN FIVE DAYS CAME TO TROAS (TROY), WHERE WE REMAINED SEVEN DAYS. WHEN WE HAD GATHERED ON A SATURDAY TO BREAK BREAD, PAUL BEGAN A LONG DISCOURSE, AS HE WAS DUE TO LEAVE THE NEXT DAY, AND HE EXTENDED HIS SERMON UNTIL MIDNIGHT. IN THE MEZZANINE WHERE WE HAD CONGREGATED THERE WERE NUMEROUS LIT CANDLES. A YOUNG MAN SITTING THERE AGAINST A SMALL OPENING WAS OVERWHELMED BY SLEEP WHILE PAUL KEPT ON TALKING AND FELL DOWN THREE STORIES, WHEREUPON HE WAS CONSIDERED DEAD. BUT PAUL CAME DOWN TO HIM, HELD HIM IN HIS ARMS AND SAID "DO NOT WORRY, HIS SOUL IS IN HIM." AND THE YOUNG MAN GOT UP AGAIN, BROKE BREAD, ATE IT AND TALKED A LOT UNTIL DAWN, AFTER WHICH HE WENT AWAY. EVERYONE ESCORTING THE YOUNG MAN ALIVE FELT REASSURED AND COMFORTED MORE THAN A LITTLE.

13. WE THEN TOOK THE BOAT AND SAILED TO ASSOS (23) WHERE WE PLANNED TO MEET PAUL, WHO WAS DETERMINED TO GO THERE ON FOOT.

14-16. WHEN HE MET WITH US AT ASSOS WE TOOK HIM ABOARD AND SAILED TO MYTILENE. THE NEXT DAY WE SAILED FROM THERE OVER TO HIOS AND THE FOLLOWING DAY WE ARRIVED AT SAMOS, AFTER WHICH WE CAME TO MILETOS. PAUL HAD DECIDED TO BYPASS EPHESOS, IN ORDER TO AVOID DELAYS IN ASIA. HE WAS IN A HURRY TO ARRIVE IN JERUSALEM, IF POSSIBLE, THE DAY OF THE PENTECOST.

From The New Testament (Greek original), first century A.D.

Clement's "Exhortation to the Greeks"

Certain attitudes, ideas, and situations generate or provoke their opposite. The Roman Peace eventually ended with barbarian invasions (Gibbon, E., 1909/ff.). Hellenistic philosophical skepticism and amorous or amorphous amorality was overcome by the rising Christian fervor. The adoration of bodily beauty and strength was succeeded by a condemnation of the flesh and all its desires and needs. The aesthetic merits of classical, Hellenistic and Roman art and literature already by the time of the writing of Daphnis and Chloe and of Apollonios of Tyre had become the targets of attacks, criticism, ridicule and condemnation not just by ignorant religious fanatics (they could not have the faintest notion about the past) but by learned Christian leaders, trained in the Athenian schools of philosophy and very familiar with Greek tradition, literature and art. Such rejection of the classical past has in turn been considered unacceptable from the time of the Renaissance. Yet in our own twentieth century we cannot take sides, but must respect and try to understand the mentality of the great Christian church fathers, such as Clement [*Clemes*] from Alexandria in Hellenized Egypt. He had much to say about the faults and failures of pagan Greek religion, starting with Orpheus and the Olympian gods.

Clement was born about 150 A.D., possibly in Athens, where he had his education in the classical Greek tradition. Later he became a Christian presbyter and head of a school in Alexandria. His work *The Exhortation to the Greeks* was written in that city, which he was forced to leave in 202 A.D. due to the persecution of the Christians by the Roman rulers.

THE EXHORTATION TO THE GREEKS
BY CLEMENT OF ALEXANDRIA, ABOUT 200 A.D.

CHAPTER I. PARAGRAPH 4. TO ME THAT ORPHEUS FROM THRACE AND ALSO THOSE MEN FROM THEBES AND FROM

METHYMNA (24) ARE NOT WORTHY TO BE CALLED "MEN." THEY WERE SWINDLERS, USING MUSIC TO RUIN LIVES, BRINGING THE DEMONS OF CORRUPTION WITH ARTFUL DECEPTION, INCLUDING VIOLENT INSULTS IN THEIR (RELIGIOUS) ORGIES AND GLORIFYING SADNESS AND SORROW. THEY WERE THE FIRST TO LEAD PEOPLE TO (THE WORSHIP OF) IDOLS, IN STONE AS WELL AS IN WOOD, THAT IS STATUES AND PICTURES MEANT TO SUSTAIN THE CRUDENESS OF CUSTOMARY ETHICS. WITH THEIR CHANTS AND ENCHANTMENTS THESE INDIVIDUALS TOOK THE PRECIOUS FREEDOM OF OUR CITIZENS WHO LIVE UNDER HEAVEN AND SUBJECTED THEM TO THE LOWEST FORM OF SLAVERY . . .

THESE MINDLESS PEOPLE ARE LIKE STONE AND WOOD THEMSELVES. IN FACT A MAN IMMERSED (IN GREEK "BAPTIZED") IN IGNORANCE IS EVEN MORE SENSELESS (IN GREEK "ANESTHETIZED") THAN STONES. OUR WITNESS IS THE PROPHETIC VOICE (OF THE EVANGELIST) SINGING ALONG THE MESSAGE OF TRUTH WHICH COMES FORTH TO EXPRESS PITY FOR THOSE OVERWHELMED BY IGNORANCE AND MINDLESSNESS: "FOR GOD IS ABLE TO RAISE FROM THESE STONES THE CHILDREN UNTO ABRAHAM."

CHAPTER II.

SECTION 17. . . . (THE GODDESS) DEMETER REFUSED TO DRINK THE KYKEON (25) OFFERED TO HER BECAUSE SHE WAS IN MOURNING. HER HOSTESS, BAUBO, SEEMINGLY VERY HURT, THEN DECIDED TO EXPOSE HER PRIVATE PARTS AND TO DISPLAY THEM TO THE GODDESS, WHO ENJOYED THE SIGHT AND TOOK THE DRINK. THIS IS WHAT THE SECRET ATHENIAN RITUALS (26) ARE AND WHAT ORPHEUS DESCRIBED. I WILL QUOTE YOU THE ACTUAL VERSES OF ORPHEUS SO THAT YOU HAVE AS WITNESS THIS CREATURE OF SHAMELESSNESS:

HAVING SAID THIS SHE RAISED HER ROBE TO SHOW EVERYTHING. AN IMPROPER BODY EXPOSURE; THEN THERE WAS CHILD IACCHUS WHO LAUGHINGLY DIPPED HIS HAND UNDER BAUBO'S BOSOM. WHEREUPON THE GODDESS SMILED AND IN A SMILING MOOD ACCEPTED THE DELIGHTFUL CUP WITH THE KYKEON IN IT. AND THIS IS, BELIEVE ME, THE SYMBOLISM OF ELEUSINIAN (26) MYSTERIES . . . BEAUTIFUL SPECTACLES, TRULY PROPER FOR A GODDESS!

CHAPTER II.

SECTION 21. THE EXTREME POINTS OF IGNORANCE ARE THEREFORE ATHEISM AND SUPERSTITION OR DEMON WORSHIP AND WE MUST CONSTANTLY STUDY HOW TO KEEP AWAY FROM THEM . . . THE PERSON WHO SUBSCRIBES TO MANY FALSELY-NAMED GODS INSTEAD OF THE ONE REAL GOD IS LIKE THE SON OF A PROSTITUTE, WHO MAY HAVE TO ACCEPT MANY FATHERS BECAUSE HE DOES NOT KNOW WHO HIS TRUE FATHER IS . . .

THEN THE MUSES, WHOM POETS AND AUTHORS PRAISE AND RESPECT AND TO WHOM ALL CITIES DEDICATE TEMPLES,

WERE IN FACT SERVANT GIRLS BOUGHT BY MEGACLO, THE DAUGHTER OF MACAR, KING OF THE LESBIANS. THIS MACAR WAS CONSTANTLY FIGHTING WITH HIS WIFE AND MEGACLO FELT SORRY FOR THAT. SO SHE BOUGHT THESE MAIDS FROM MYSIA (27), WHOM SHE CALLED "MUSES" AND TAUGHT THEM TO SING, TO PLAY THE GUITAR AND TO ACT THE OLD-FASHIONED WAY WITH MUSIC. BY DOING THAT THEY WERE ABLE TO PLEASE MACAR AND STOP HIS ANGER. THESE ARE THE MUSES TO WHOM MEGACLO HERSELF DEDICATED BRONZE STATUES, SIMPLE SERVANT GIRLS AND ENTERTAINERS.

CHAPTER III.
SECTION 36 . . . HUMAN SACRIFICES (ACCORDING TO MANY AUTHORS) WERE OFFERED BY A RACE OF CRETANS AND DOSIDAS (ANOTHER AUTHOR) SAYS THAT THE LESBIANS OFFERED A SIMILAR SACRIFICE TO DIONYSOS.

CHAPTER VII.
BUT EVEN THE THRACIAN PRIEST AND ALSO POET, ORPHEUS, AFTER ALL THE ORGIASTIC RITUALS AND THE THEOLOGY OF THE IDOLS, HE RETRACTS AND INTRODUCES THE TRUTH, AT LAST CHANTING THE SACRED WORD:

> I WILL SPEAK ONLY TO THE JUST AND PURE; LOCK THE DOORS TO THE PROFANE . . .

> . . .

> I PRONOUNCE THE TRUTH AND YOU MUST NOT LET THE BURDENS ON YOUR CHEST STOP YOU FROM EMBRACING ETERNITY . . . THERE IS ONE CREATOR, WHO HAS CREATED HIMSELF ["AUTOGENOUS"] AND ALL THINGS ARE BORN FROM ONE. . . . NO MORTAL EVER SEES HIM BUT HE SEES EVERYTHING.

THIS IS THEN WHAT ORPHEUS WAS SAYING. AFTER MUCH TIME HAD PASSED, HE REALIZED THAT HE HAD WANDERED IN ERROR.

Butterworth, G.W., 1960, pp. 8, 36, 42, 50, 64, 166.

The pious Clement tried to salvage something of Orpheus—although not much of the muses, or the gods—but it was too late. Society, and with it Lesbos, was already abandoning the feasts of the ancient Pantheon and entering the age of faith and christologic conformity. The entire ancient world, not unlike our contemporary societies, "wandered in error." Yet through the wandering and meandering, the brilliance of antiquity has kept flickering in the minds and the writings of medieval scholars, including emperors and princesses, bishops and monks. This meaningful coexistence of inspiration and erudition, affectation and affection, hatred and love, pleasure and pain, may still be part of the Lesbian heritage for the days to come.

The Hellenistic romantic story of *Apollonios* in a Shakespearean dramatic version—*Pericles*—on the modern stage. Above, Hope Chernov as Marina and Walter Stanford as Lysimachus from the souvenir program of the Colorado Shakespeare Festival, costume design Holly Cole, production director Joel G. Fink, summer 1993 (see excerpts of the play, chapter IV-B).

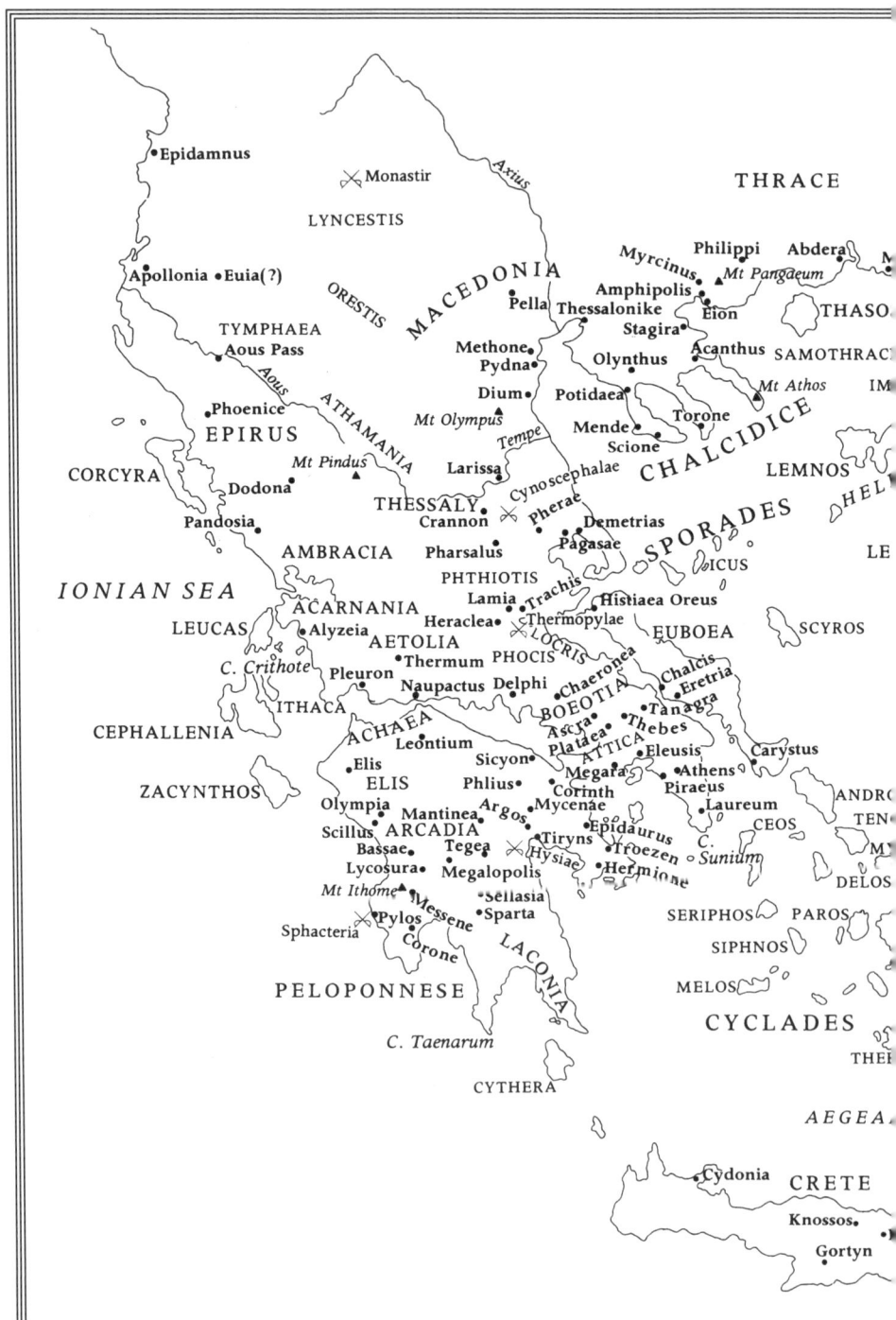

GREECE AND ASIA MINOR

THE MEDITERRANEAN WORLD

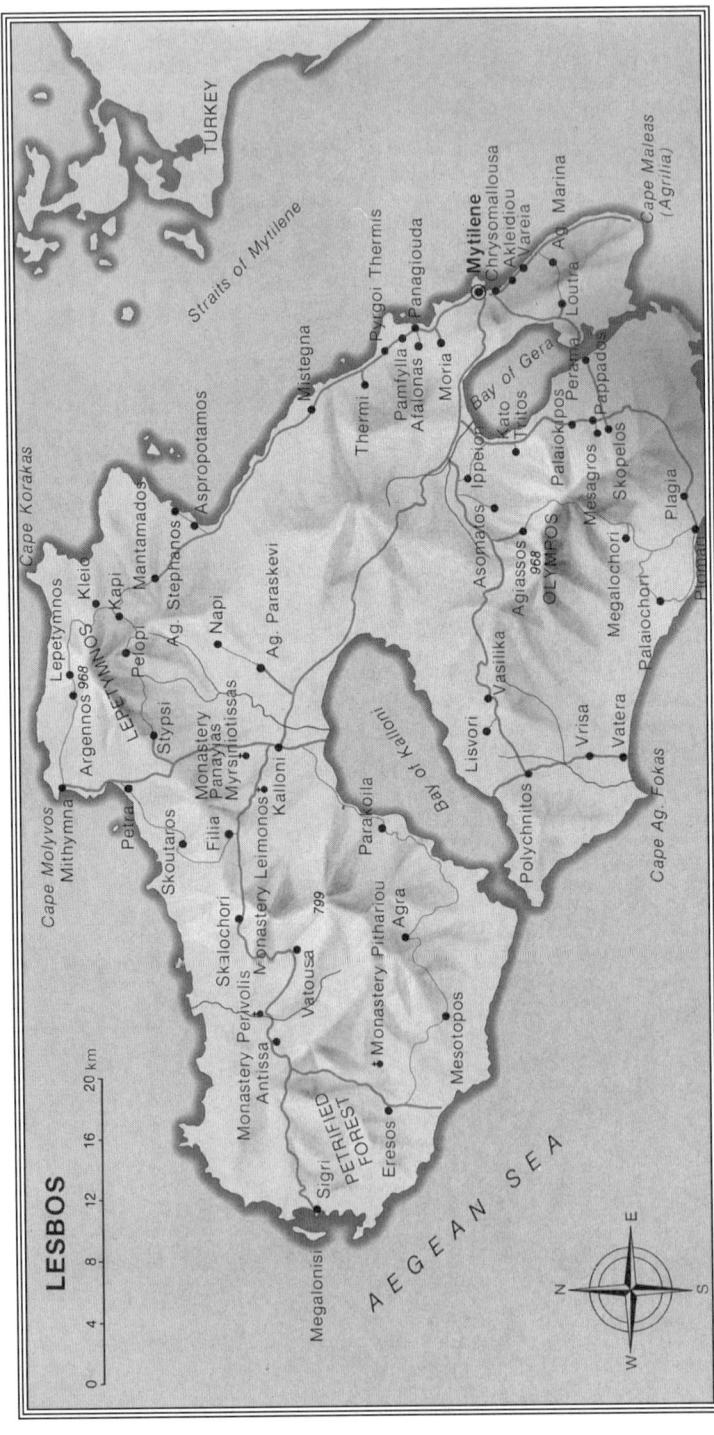

North coast of Lesbos, by Antissa, where the head of Orpheus landed three thousand years ago.

Remains on the site of the "prominent" temple described by Alkaios, around 600 B.C. Lesbos' south coast.

Another possible site of the temple of the triple divinity, Zeus, Hera, and Dionysos, central Lesbos.

Roman aqueduct near the city of Mytilene, Lesbos.

LEFT: The site of the ancient Greek theater, admired and copied by the Roman Pompey the Great. RIGHT: The throne of the arch-priest—or ruler—from the theater at Mytilene, Museum of Mytilene.

The fourth century B.C. Greek comedy writer, Menander [*Menandros*]; Roman mosaic, Museum of Mytilene.

Ancient and medieval coins related to Lesbos. (1) Lyre, silver drachm, Methymna, fifth century B.C. (2) Riding a dolphin to safety, Taras, fourth century B.C. (3) Quadriga, gold stater, Phillip of Macedon, fourth century B.C.

(4) Roman emperor Julian "The Apostate," fourth century A.D. (5) Byzantine empress Irene, eighth–ninth century A.D. (6) Constantine VI, son and co-emperor with Irene.

(7) Emperor Constantine IX Monomakhos, eleventh century A.D. (8) Emperor Alexios I Komnenos, eleventh–twelfth century A.D. All from the author's collection.

Left: The Madonna of Ayiasos. Kleombrotos, 1982. Right: Saint Paul, mosaic in the Moni Horas, Constantinople, thirteenth century A.D.

Saint Theodore of Mytilene, a nineteenth century Orthodox martyr. Soteriou, 1991.

From the twelfth century illustrated manuscript by J. Skylitzes. Top: The five daughters of emperor Theophilos secretly worship a holy icon presented to them by their grandmother. Middle: Emperor Constantine VII tells his brothers-in-law that they will be exiled (one of them to Lesbos). Bottom: The rebellious Leon and Nikephoros attempt to leave Lesbos for Constantinople.

Emperor Constantine IX Monomakhos, eleventh century A.D. Saint Sophia, Constantinople.

Emperor Alexios I Komnenos, eleventh–twelfth century, Constantinople.

Chapel of the Virgin "Trouloti" (with the dome) near where empress Irene died on Lesbos.

The "blessed" town of Ayiasos, in the foothills of the Lesbian Mt. Olympos.

Top: The medieval fort—*Kastro*—of Mytilene on Lesbos.
Bottom: The entrance to the *Kastro* of Methymna on Lesbos.

LEFT: View of Asia Minor (where the crusading French king Louis VII and his wife, Eleanor of Aquitaine, camped) from an arch of the Mytilene *kastro*.
RIGHT: An abandoned "house of pleasure" below the *kastro* of Mytilene.

Combination of Byzantine and Genoese stone carvings on the *kastro* walls.

A panel of the Saints of Lesbos, twentieth century, Mytilene Orthodox cathedral.

The home of the businessman and poet, A. Eftaliotis, in Methymna, now the Community Art Museum. The poet's bust in front.

A turn-of-the-century mansion by the port of Mytilene.

Statue of the liberator of Lesbos, admiral Koundouriotis, by the port of Mytilene.

Commemorative stamp, 50 drachmas, with the Greek cruiser "Averoff" and Admiral P. Koundouriotis, liberator of Lesbos, 1932 (from the author's collection).

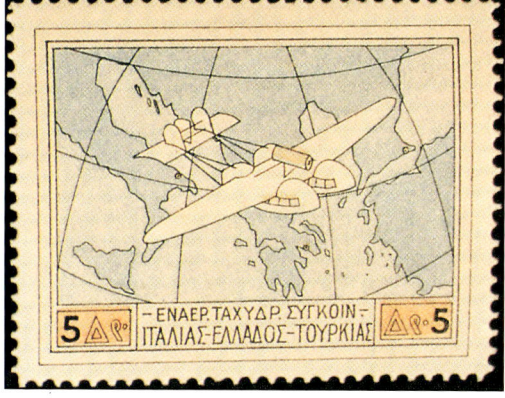

Greek 5 drachma postage stamp inaugurating airmail service, Italy–Greece–Turkey (flight over Lesbos), 1926.

Statue of Liberty, on the coast near Mytilene.

3000 YEARS ON A GREEK ISLAND 217

Ancient olive trees by the Teriadis Museum, Varia, Lesbos.

Goats remain undisturbed by the airport traffic nearby.

The face of the United States 1988 presidential candidate, Michael Dukakis, covers the door of a taverna in his father's native village of Pelopi on Lesbos.

The author and his wife Electra by the deep bay of Yera (Gera) during their 1988 trip to Lesbos.

Chapter V

MEDIEVAL MASTERS, MYSTICS AND MONSTERS

A. **Apostasy and Apotheosis**
Julian "the Apostate," a young philosopher-king
Barbarians through the gates
The horrid reign of "Saint" Irene

B. **Ruthless and Romantic Rulers**
The end of iconoclasm
A Medieval Hellenic Renaissance
Intrigues of a scholarly king
An imperial erotic triangle
Death and tenderness in Constantinople

Arion, seventh century B.C. Lesbian singer, shown standing on a "dolphin," playing a violin-like instrument; from the cover of a sixteenth century edition of the *Annals* by the eleventh century A.D. Greek-Byzantine historian G. Cedrenus [*Kedrenos*].

Overleaf: Michael Psellos, eleventh century Byzantine statesman and historian, in a monk's garb. From *ms. 234* in the monastery of Pantocrator (f. 254), courtesy of Prof. S. Marketos.

A. APOSTASY AND APOTHEOSIS

Julian "the Apostate," a young philosopher-king

After more than three hundred years of clandestine worship and persistent underground conversions, Christianity in the beginning of the fourth century A.D. was declared a legitimate and then the official state religion of the Roman Empire, which at that time covered almost all the civilized world around the Mediterranean Sea. In 334 A.D. the capital of the empire was transferred from Rome to the ancient Greek city of Byzantium (1) on the Straits of Bosphorus separating Europe from Asia. In honor of the emperor Constantine "The Great," who commanded this move and was also the first ruler to recognize and later to adopt Christianity, the city was renamed Constantinople [*Constantinoupolis*, i.e., Constantine's city]. The third Roman emperor to succeed Constantine was Julian (Flavius Claudius Julianus), afterwards labeled "The Apostate"—"The Defector"—because he abandoned Christianity, attempted to revive a rapidly declining religious tolerance and himself favored the restoration of the ancient pagan Greek and Roman religion and rituals.

Julian was born in Constantinople in 331 A.D., the only son of a half-brother of Constantine the Great and of a very educated, devoutly Christian mother, who died when the future king was a baby (Wright, 1962, *Introduction*). Despite strong Christian influences since early childhood, Julian became an admirer of classical Greek culture and philosophy, especially after his extensive studies in the great Hellenistic centers at Pergamon, Ephesos and, later, Athens, where he apparently was initiated in the pagan religious Eleusinian Mysteries (*cf.* Chapter IV-C: Clement: Exhortation to the Greeks).

Julian was thirty years old when, on military campaign in distant Gaul and somewhat against his will, he was proclaimed Augustus (Emperor) and marched against his cousin and brother-in-law, emperor Constantius. But Constantius died on his way to defend his throne and Julian entered the capital triumphantly, to be crowned king. In the past, the last king's second wife, Eusebia, had given the young Julian much political support and also gifts of books, which he had always carried with him on his campaigns. It was from Gaul and shortly before he ascended the throne that Julian wrote an "encomium," a long letter of praise for Queen Eusebia. In this document the emperor-to-be made reference to the Lesbian poets-musicians, Terpander [*Terpandros*] and Arion (Chapter II-A) and provided a twilight illustration of the fading classical criteria for the best [*aristos*] human mode of life, which were strikingly different from the prevailing Christian notions of self-abasement, egalitarianism and humility.

> ***IN PRAISE OF EUSEBIA THE QUEEN***
> by Julianus Caesar, 331–363 A.D.
> **Oration III**
> **III.A-D.** I am thinking of the example of a highly accomplished artist, a lyre [*kithara*] singer, say, if you will, Terpandros or the one from Methymna (Arion), who was reported to have been carried safely to shore through divine providence by a dolphin that happened to enjoy his music more than did any of the men on board the ship . . . Even though he (Arion), I believe, did his best to entertain the wretched sailors with his artistic performance, they ignored that entirely and paid no attention to the music. Now, if someone could get the very best of these (Lesbian) men, cover his body with ornate clothes appropriate for an artist and present him in a theater full of men, women and children of all ages and skills, wouldn't you think the children and also the men and women of similar (childish) tastes and, in fact, most of the ignorant crowd too, would be more impressed by the clothes and the (looks of the) lyre and that the only exception would be those few able to judge the performance by the pleasure or sadness it provided? Above all among them would be a music expert who, knowing the rules of the art, would not tolerate strange combinations of melodies intended to impress and would object to the improper use of distorted modes and harmonies not conforming to the principles of true and divine music. This expert, seeing that he (the artist) was faithful to the established rules and that the enjoyment he gave the audience was not false but pure and uncontaminated, would depart praising him and appreciating his artistic performance on the stage, which in no way offended the muses.
> Quoted in Greek by Wright, 1962, Vol. I, pp. 296-298.

Julian espoused enthusiastically the intellectual refinement of the educated elite and was contemptuous of Christianity, which he called "the Galilaean faith" to stress its lowly provincial origins. In his "Hymn to Helios," written in prose because, as he indicated, poetry was by then no longer popular, the philosopher-king reflected a flicker of the mentality we encountered on Lesbos over the preceding centuries. The apostate-king defined his "intellectual god" (Wright, 1913-1969, vol. I, p. 349), Helios-Apollo, as the essence of the supreme good presiding over the intelligible world [*noetos cosmos*].

Julian was in Antioch for the fall and winter of 361–362 A.D. and there he tried to restore the neglected ancient temples. But his notion that the knowledge of god was only for philosophers, was in sharp contrast with the populist Christian doctrines. His lofty seriousness and elitism repelled the crowds and also the corrupt and pleasure-seeking officials. The "Beard-hater" was written in part as a self-critical comment but also as a semi-humorous declaration justifying the king's principles and beliefs (Wright II, 1966, *Introduction* p. 418).

> **THE BEARD-HATER [Misopogon]**
> by Julianus Caesar, 331–363 A.D.
>
> **A-B.** Anacreon, the poet, composed many delightful songs and also was granted by the fates a life of luxurious leisure. But neither Alkaios (of Lesbos), nor Arkhilohos of Paros was allowed by god to apply the muse to their own entertainment and pleasure. As they struggled one way or another, they had to rely on their music to make more tolerable what the demon (spirit) had brought upon them and did use it (their poetry) to ridicule those who had wronged them. But now in my situation I am prohibited by law to accuse by name those who try to be unfair to me, even though I have never treated them unjustly. Besides, the now prevailing system of education among freemen takes away from me music and lyrics. People consider it more degrading now to deal with music than it was in the old days to get rich dishonestly.
>
> Wright, 1962, Vol. II, pp. 420-422

The short life of Julian, the Hellenized Roman emperor of the fourth century A.D., can be related to Lesbos in more ways, besides his literary references to Lesbian poets. Julian's physician had studied in the city of Alexandria in Egypt with Aëtios of Amida, whose medical writings remained popular for centuries. More than 500 years later, the scholar and orthodox patriarch Photios (Chapters II-B and V-B) commented on the superiority of Aëtios' scientific works and added that "in view of the laziness of the present generation of doctors, who are more interested in other things than in curing the sick, this handbook ought to be studied in preference to others" (Wilson, 1983, p. 102). A namesake of this physician was Aëtios of Antioch, another contemporary of Julian, a personal friend and, later, his religious opponent. This Christian leader and "heretic" rebel had risen from extreme poverty to become the prominent proponent of the "anhomian" theological view, which considered the substance of the Son as "not-the-same" [*an-homoia*] as that of His Divine Father. Aëtios, who was later called "the atheist" by his orthodox Christian opponents, had been the spiritual counsellor of Julian's half-brother Gallus and was sent to admonish the young Julian when he, in the course of his studies at Ephesos, showed signs of becoming increasingly attracted by "Hellenism" (Wright, Vol. III, *Introduction* p. xxx). In 354 A.D., Gallus was executed by the ruling emperor Constantius, and Aëtios, as a friend of the victim and a suspected heretic, lost his position in the official church and was exiled. When Julian succeeded Constantius, he recalled his friend Aëtios from exile and honored him greatly despite their religious differences. The letter of recall has been preserved.

> **TO BISHOP AËTIOS**
> by Julianus Caesar
> **From Constantinople, January 362 A.D.**
> **404.B.** I have revoked collectively the extradition of all those who had been banished by the blessed late Constantius on account of the mindlessness of the Galilaeans. For you, however, not only I rescind that order but also, remembering our old acquaintance and life together, I issue an invitation to have you come back to us. You may use a public vehicle as far as my army headquarters with one extra horse on the side.
> Wright, 1966, Vol. III, Letter No. 15, pp. 34-35.

During his brief reign, Julian never offered Aëtios a high ecclesiastical appointment, even though earlier he had addressed him as "bishop" [*episcopos*]. He did, however, grant him a large estate on Lesbos, where Aëtios settled after the young emperor was killed in the battlefield in 363 A.D. He stayed on the island for an unknown period of time and then the restless theologian returned to the capital of Constantinople. Eventually he was made a bishop by Julian's second successor, emperor Valens (Wright, 1969, Vol. III, *Introduction*, p. xxxi). But most orthodox Christians continued to consider Aëtios an "atheist" for many centuries and all traces of his stay on Lesbos have been lost.

Barbarians through the Gates

Less than one hundred years after the transfer of the imperial government by emperor Constantine from Rome to the Greek city of Byzantium, the historic capital in Italy was sacked successively by Gothic and Vandal invaders. These and later others from the north, east and south (Reference Table K) also repeatedly attacked, ravaged, enslaved and destroyed large parts of the east Roman Byzantine territories. The invisible but at first impregnable "gates" of Hellenic culture often gave in too and only the dedication and devotion of the citizens preserved the traditions, the basic Greek speech and the newly adopted values of Christianity through the ensuing millennia.

In 395–398 A.D. king Alaric, "from the noble race of the Balti" (Gibbons, Vol. III, p. 254)—the word *baltha* meant bold—and his migrating

Visigoths, invaded Greece and captured the historic cities of Athens and Sparta. The Goths also reached the outskirts of the capital, Constantinople, and only after intricate political maneuvering Alaric was persuaded to change course and to move his people to Italy. There, after considerable deliberation and debate, they attacked and sacked Rome in 410 A.D. At that time, the crowned emperor of the east half of the Roman empire was the nine-year-old Theodosius II. He was to reign (though not to rule, because others governed for him) for over forty years, from 408 until his death following a fall from his horse in 450 A.D. The emperor has been credited for repelling the barbarian invasions, for the publication of a new imperial legal code, for the establishment of a new Greek-and-Latin university in Constantinople, and for building the new fortifications around the city. But it was his sister Pulkheria, later with the assistance of his wife, the bright, educated and independent woman from Athens, empress Athenais-Eudokia, who actually ran the state.

The marriage of Theodosius to Athenais, renamed Eudokia, took place in June 421 A.D. Years later, while the emperor and his ministers were negotiating treaties first with the Goths and then with Attila and the Huns, the queen, tired, depressed and frustrated with the course of events, with the palace intrigues and with her personal life, went on two successive trips to Jerusalem, where she eventually died in 460 A.D. surrounded by the holy men of the Orthodox Christian community there. A modern Greek biographer described evocatively the sailing of the imperial ship by Lesbos.

> **ATHENAIS AELIA EUDOKIA, AUGUSTA**
> by Jeanne Tsatsos, 1970 (pp. 103-105).
> The Athenian queen . . . follows the coastline. She looks at the distant shores of Troy . . . Sailing on . . . by Lesbos . . . Hios . . . Rhodos . . . Cyprus . . . to Antioch, that incomparable city, a favorite of the Roman emperors. Despite the warning of St. Gregory of Nyssa that "all the cities of the east, including Jerusalem, are contaminated by evil, theft, adultery, and murder" (Tsatsos, p. 117), she continued her trip by land to Jerusalem. There, the bishop offered her as a gift the holy relics of St. Stephen and the chains placed on the Apostle Peter, which the following year she brought back triumphantly to Constantinople.

Life on Lesbos at the time never approached the idyllic circumstances of "Daphnis and Chloe" (Chap. IV-B). The increasingly prevalent Christian antihedonistic fervor and the impact of the successive violent barbarian assaults on the mainland made visits to the "Grotto of the Nymphs," erotic experimentation such as was described by Longos and even the calm and pleasurable contemplation of nature, seem like remote dreams and realistically impossible. The intensity of the battles against the barbarians and the secretive mentality under the dark covers of theophobic virtuousness were reflected in the writings of a prominent historian of the sixth century, Prokopios of Caesarea. This author of the history of the wars under emperor Justinian I and his general, Belisarios, came to the capital from the port city in Palestine after completing his studies that qualified him for the legal profession. Soon after he arrived in Constantinople he impressed Belisarios, then a young army officer, and was appointed his legal adviser and private secretary. When, during the glorious reign of Justinian I, Belisarios led the "Roman" Greek-Byzantine forces in their campaigns against the Persians into Mesopotamia (527), Africa (533) and Italy (536), Prokopios was always there. So, rightfully, he could claim that he "was better qualified than anyone" (Dewing, 1954, *Introduction,* viii) to describe the events and the people. In his writings Prokopios kept referring to himself in the third person.

HISTORY OF THE WARS
by Prokopios of Caesaria [*Kaisareia*] about 500–570 A.D.

Book I.

1-3. Prokopios of Kaisareia has written about the wars that Justinian, the king of the Romans, has waged both in the east and in the west and he has described the events of each one, so that these enormous deeds may not fall into oblivion and become totally erased by the passage of long centuries for lack of documentation . . . and he has been made aware by those around him that he is especially qualified to write about these, if for no other reason than because as an adviser to the general Belisarios he had an opportunity to be an eyewitness to almost all these activities. It must be stressed that while cleverness is suitable for rhetoric and imagination for poetry, the writing of history demands adherence to truth.

Dewing, HB, Vol. I, 1954, pp. 2-4.

Book II-Section XXII

I. In the course of those years a plague occurred, which nearly wiped out all traces of human life . . .

Dewing, HB, Vol. I, 1954, p. 450.

Book III-Section I

IV. The earth, either entirely or for the most part, is surrounded by a circle of the ocean; on this our knowledge is not clear . . . It is then divided into two continents, Asia and, opposite it, Europe . . .

Dewing, HB, Vol. II, 1961, p. 2.

Prokopios went on to describe the geography around the Mediterranean Sea and then narrated in detail the victorious Byzantine campaign against the Vandal kingdom of north Africa. The historian reported and discussed the Vandal mutiny of 536 A.D., citing certain land ownership feuds first.

Book IV, Section XIV

X-XX. Another cause, not less and possibly more important (than the land feuds) prevailed in upsetting the situation in Libya. In the Roman army there happened to be no fewer than 1000 soldiers of the Arian persuasion (2) and of them the majority were barbarians . . . The Priests of the Vandals strongly urged these men to mutiny, because they were not able to worship God in their customary way and were even excluded from the sacraments and from all sacred rites. In fact, the emperor Justinian did not allow any Christian who did not espouse the Orthodox faith to take part in, or to receive baptism or any other sacrament . . .

The mutiny was suppressed and many Vandal prisoners were taken from Libya to Constantinople.

Book IV, *continued.*
Now the king had the Vandals, whom Belisarios had carried to Byzantium, placed in five cavalry squadrons in order to settle them permanently in Eastern cities. Calling them "Justinian's Vandals" he gave an order to have them carried by ship to the East. Most of these Vandal soldiers did reach the East and filling the squadrons as ordered, they have been campaigning to this day against the Persians. But others, numbering about 400, as soon as they came to Lesbos and while the sails were full, forced the sailors to submit to them and took off. They first reached Peloponnesos, then sailed down to Libya, landing at a desert place, where they abandoned their ships and went on to Mauritania . . .
Dewing, 1961, Vol. II, pgs. 330-332

A different and terribly degrading profile of the victorious Roman general, Belisarios and also of the emperor Justinian, his wife Theodora and the society around them was presented by the same historian, Prokopios, in his gossipy and scandal-mongering book that he called "Anecdota," which meant "not for publication." This volume, published in English as "A Secret History" reflected a mentality and aspects of life that might have reached the islands too, including Lesbos.

The historian-gossipist had particularly foul stories to tell about Justinian's wife, the empress Theodora, whom in his other works he had credited for saving her husband's throne against a rioting population.

"ANECDOTA" OR SECRET HISTORY
by Prokopios, c. 500-570 A.D.

Section IX.

10-12. For a time, while Theodora was not yet mature and so unable to go to bed with a man the way a woman would, she did mix with men and had a male-type of intercourse with them, even with slaves who came to the theater with their masters and took advantage of the chance to indulge in this nasty business, spending much time in the brothel with this unnatural use of the body. Then as soon as she reached puberty and her time had come, she (Theodora) joined the women on the stage and became a courtesan, of the kind people in old days used to call "pedestrian." Because she was neither a flute player nor a harpist and singer and had not even practiced dancing very much, she used to sell her youthful beauty to anyone that came along, only putting to work her own body.

Dewing, 1960, Vol. VI, p. 104

When Theodora was later given special permission by the church to marry the future emperor, Justinian, even though she had been an actress and "entertainer," she became not only a dynamic ruler but also a reformer of sinners and "fallen women." Prokopios described a characteristic incident during Theodora's reign.

Section XVII

5-6. Theodora thought of many ways and devices to take care of those immersed in the sins of the body. She gathered more than 500 prostitutes, those who were selling themselves for 3 obols—an amount barely enough to live on—in the middle of the market and she sent them across to Asia, to the so-called Convent of Repentance, where they were locked up and forced to reform and change their lives. When, however, some of them during the night jumped off the high walls, the order for the involuntary life change was cancelled.

Dewing, 1960, Vol. VI, p. 198

Besides the invasion of the Byzantine state by entire armies and foreign populations and the dynastic intrigues in the capital, the established dominance of Christianity too changed attitudes and behavior in all parts of the empire, including the islands of the Aegean Sea. John (Ioannes) Moskhos, who died in 619 A.D., was the author of popular stories about saints, monks and hermits. He wrote in the spoken Greek of his age (which reflected the changes that foreign influences and time had imposed on the classical Attic style) and his stories spread rapidly. They were translated into Latin, old Slavonic and even Arabic. In his instructive "Leimon" (meaning pasture, a grazing ground for the spirit) he compared a monk to the salt from the sea and strongly emphasized the characteristic abhorrence of sex of medieval monasticism, so contrary to the feelings of the Lesbian and Ionian poets more than one thousand years earlier.

> **LEIMON, OR PASTURE (OF THE SPIRIT)**
> by John Moskhos (died 619 A.D.)
>
> **Section 217.** The (wise) elder spoke and said "My children, the salt is taken out of the sea water and if it ever comes in contact with water again it dissolves and disappears. The same thing can happen to a monk, who is born out of a woman. If he comes near a woman again he will disintegrate and, not being a monk anymore, he will meet his end."
>
> Wilson, 1971, p. 31 (in Greek).

By the seventh century A.D., "apotheosis" was not the designation of individuals like Theophanes of Lesbos and several Hellenistic and Roman rulers in the past (Chap. IV)—as "gods," but the longing of the human soul to get closer to the divine spirit by withdrawing from, or denying any appeals of the material world. The ruination of the world, mostly by external "barbarian" onslaughts was in part the cause and in part the effect of this monastic withdrawal. Almost two centuries later, the life and death of the empress Irene "the Athenian" reflected that prevalent combination of otherworldly mystical devotion and unrestrained egocentric drives.

The Goths, the Vandals and the Huns were not the only "barbarians" who threatened to overwhelm the Eastern Roman empire and who did destroy its Western part. The greatest and nearly fatal threat to the state from the sixth to the eighth centuries A.D. were the Persians, the Slavs and the Arabs (Ref. Table K). The routes of both the aggressors and the Greek defenders often took them by Lesbos, though most historical references to the island pertain to the time when it became the place of exile of deposed rulers and other dignitaries.

After endless external and internal struggles the state was near collapse when in 610 A.D. a young general, Heraclius, Roman governor of Carthage in Africa, sailed to Constantinople, was crowned emperor and proved capable of saving the empire. He also contributed to the Hellenization of the East Roman empire by decreeing that Greek, the language of the people and of the church, should become the official state language (Norwich, p. 310). Heraclius spent almost his entire reign of over 30 years fighting the Persians along the eastern frontier of his kingdom. In one of his major expeditions, departing on Monday after Easter,

April 5, 622, he sailed on his own flagship at the head of a large war fleet through the Hellespont along the Aegean coast of the Troad and, past Lesbos, down the Ionian coast to the island of Rhodes, then east to the bay of Issus, not far from where Alexander had defeated the Persians nearly 1000 years earlier. Not until the fall of 628 A.D. the emperor was able to return victorious to his capital of Constantinople. In a triumphal parade in 630 A.D. he displayed the True Cross, which the Persians had taken from Jerusalem in 614 A.D. and which his Christian army had recaptured. But the continuous battles left both the Greeks and the Persians unprepared for the onslaught of a new enemy, the Arabs. Within ten years after the death of the prophet, Mohammed, Persia was overwhelmed and in a few years the former Greek-Byzantine provinces of Syria, Mesopotamia, Palestine and Egypt were seized by the Moslem invaders. The holy city of Jerusalem which had been retaken from the Persians also fell to the Arabs in 638 A.D.

Every year from 663 A.D. on, the Arabs expanded their conquests of Greek lands. They began successive raids north and west into Asia Minor, pillaging the country and dragging the people away to slavery (Ostrogorsky, pg. 123). After capturing the islands of the Aegean, Rhodes, Cos, Khios and raiding Lesbos too on its way north, in 670 the Arab fleet secured a base in the Sea of Marmara and in 674 it appeared before the walls of Constantinople. The emperor, Constantine IV, who had succeeded his murdered father only a few years earlier (in 668 A.D.), vigorously took up the defense and after a fifth summer of incessant Arab attacks, the Byzantines—with the help of the famous projectile "Greek fire" (3) which, thrown from the ramparts, set fire to many vessels—forced the Arab leader, Muawiya to order full retreat. Defeated and demoralized, in 679 A.D. the Arabs accepted the Byzantine terms for peace, which demanded the evacuation of the Aegean islands they had conquered, in addition to an annual tribute of 50 slaves, 50 horses and 3,000 pounds of gold (Norwich, p. 324).

Once again in August of 717 A.D., the Arab armies and fleet stood before the walls of Constantinople in a final effort to penetrate Europe. This time the siege lasted only one year. The shrewd new emperor, Leo III knew the ways and also the language of the Arabs and managed to outfox them in most of their strategic moves. Again the "Greek fire," combined with a very severe winter resulting in famine, devastated the Arab forces. A subsequent reorganization of the internal administration of the empire aimed at strengthening the defenses and included the establishment of a separate "theme" (4) of the islands of the Aegean

Sea. Then a new internal problem arose as a result of the new emperor's religious policies, the so-called iconoclastic controversy (5), which divided the state for almost 100 years and itself represented a foreign, probably semitic "invasion" of the Hellenic world and of its cult of visual images. A contemporary historian of the events of those years was Theophanes "The Confessor."

Theophanes, whose name brings to mind other men featured in this history of Lesbos (Chapters IV and VII), was a prominent religious leader of his time. He was born about 752 A.D. and died in 818 A.D. Details concerning his place of origin and his early life are not available. In late life he retired to a monastery which he had founded himself. Because of his religious orthodoxy and his opposition to the iconoclasm of emperor Leo V, he was imprisoned and then banished to the island of Samothrace (north of Lesbos) where he apparently died. Theophanes was the author of a "Chronographia" (translated as "Chronicles" or "Annals") which covers the years 284 to 813 A.D. and is "the main source for the history of the seventh and eighth centuries" (Wilson, 1971) in the East Roman Byzantine world. This history was written in the colloquial Greek of the day and remained extremely popular. Numerous Greek manuscripts survive, one dating back to the ninth century and before the end of that century the work had been translated into Latin. In describing the destructive volcanic explosion of 726 A.D., Theophanes related it to God's wrath against Leo V (813–820 A.D.), one of the last three iconoclast rulers who followed the reign of the icon-worshipping Irene the Athenian.

CHRONOGRAPHIA
by Theophanes "The Confessor," c. 752-818 A.D.

1-40. In the summer of that year of the 9th indiction—726 A.D. (6)—fumes emerged for several days from the bottom of the sea between the island of Thera and Therasia, as if from an open fire. Quickly the smoke became thicker and turned almost solid. At the peak of the fiery exhaust all the smoke looked like a flame. With the thickness of the earthy matter, the explosion sent big rocky masses all over Asia Minor and also over Lesbos and Abydos, as well as on the sea coast of Macedonia. The entire surface of the sea was full of floating masses too. In the middle of this kind of conflagration an island emerged, which was not there before and attached itself to the so-called Holy Island. The islands already mentioned, Thera and Therasia, had come out of the boiling water the same way a long time ago. So it happened also now, in the days of the God-fighting [*theomakhos*] Leo. However, presuming that the divine wrath was in his favor, he shamelessly started a war against the revered holy icons. . . . Many people were punished for their piety with amputations, whipping, exile and confiscation of their property and particularly those prominent for the nobility of their birth and for their intellect. As a result, schools were closed and the established educational system, which had lasted from the time of Constantine the Great until now, was destroyed. Whereupon, motivated by a religious zeal, many from Hellas and the Cyclades islands got together and rebelled against the emperor. They included Kosmas, whom they wanted to crown king and Agallianos . . . , who was the leader of troops and also Stephanos. But when they came near the capital the 17th of April of the 10th indiction (6), they were defeated and their ship was burned by the artificial ("Greek") fire (3) . . . Agallianos sank fully armed and drowned. Kosmas and Stephanos had their heads cut off, as the viciousness of the irreverent Leo kept increasing . . . Those going along with him then intensified the persecution of piety.

Quoted in Greek by Wilson, 1961, p.32

The Arabs remained a threat to the Byzantine empire for hundreds of years but before the end of the eighth century, while the state was ruled by an Athenian woman, another great challenge came from the West.

The horrid reign of "Saint" Irene

Irene "The Athenian," the young widow of the iconoclastic emperor Leo IV, wielded autocratic power almost continuously for 22 years (780–802 A.D.), but then she ended her life in exile on the island of Lesbos. While she ruled, this female "emperor" (she preferred the masculine title) considered marrying Charlemagne, or—it was rumored—the Arab Caliph, Harun-al-Rashid (7), in an effort to consolidate her imperial domains. She horrified the world by ordering the blinding and possibly the murder of her own son, but later she was venerated as an orthodox saint for her efforts to reinstate the worship of religious icons. Following is a translation from the medieval Greek of Theophanes' Chronicle, or "Chronography" [*Chronographia*], of the eventful last two years (800–802 A.D.) of the reign of Irene.

CHRONOGRAPHIA
by Theophanes "The Confessor," c. 752-818 A.D.

Pg. 401, C-402 A-D. In that year of the 9th indiction—800 A.D.(6)—on December 25th, Charles ['*Karoullos*"], the king of the Franks, was crowned by Pope Leo. Then, wishing to marry Irene, he dispatched delegates the following year, of the 10th indiction. In March of the 9th indiction, the pious Irene had pleased her people very much by granting the Byzantines freedom from political taxes and voiding the passage dues paid at Abydos and Hieron. In that year also Aëtios, after he had gotten rid of Stavrakios and had properly arranged his own affairs, planned in a hurry to transfer her power to his own brother (8). With that in mind he had him appointed sole army chief [*monostrategos*] . . . Humiliating the leaders then in charge, he (Aëtios) showed no consideration for anyone. The grievances of these people against him made them contemplate an uprising against the queen, which they managed to put into action. When the delegates sent to Irene by Charles and by Pope Leo arrived with a proposal for her to marry Charles in a (royal) wedding that would unite East and West, she would have accepted, were it not for Aëtios, who, as the minister close to the ruler, presented many obstacles, because he intended to usurp the power for his own brother.

In that year, on the 31st of October of the 11th indiction, on the fourth hour of Monday night before dawn, the patrician and general logothete Nikephoros staged a coup against the most pious Irene. God must have allowed this to happen because of our unspeakable crimes and innumerable sins. Nikephoros and his accomplices (nine names listed) deceived some of the leaders of the people and of the army, seized the so-called Bronze Gate and misled the guards into believing that they had been sent by the queen to proclaim Nikephoros himself as king . . . The guards did believe such a lie and joined in acclaiming the tyrant as king. So the patricians were able to come to the Great Palace and to get in. From there they sent some insignificant men and some slaves to announce the official declaration before midnight. They placed guards at the Eleutherion palace, where the queen was then staying and at dawn they had her transferred to the Great Palace and locked her there. Afterwards they went to the Great Church (St. Sophia) to have the scoundrel crowned. In the meantime a crowd of citizens had gathered and was stirring up difficulties, cursing both the one who was crowned and also the person doing the crowning. All those who had always lived piously and according to reason were puzzled by the divine judgment that allowed the woman who was a champion and a martyr of the true faith to be displaced from her throne by the vicious men of her entourage . . . who had become very rich owing to her generosity . . . Some of the people in the city could not believe what was happening and thought they were dreaming as if in a trance . . .

Pg. 403, B, C. Not to make this ugly story too long, I will just say that all the people together were gripped by a dark gloom and a most unwelcome despondency. Nature itself and the air, too, contributed heavily to the circumstances. Those days of autumn became very sullen, unlighted and persistently cold, expressing clearly the inner distress and intolerable suffering of the subjects.

C, 1-13. The following day Nikephoros took with him some noblemen and went up to the queen, who was continuously being guarded. Acting hypocritically, as he usually did, with that false virtue which had deceived most people, he apologized to her, claiming that he was elevated to the throne against his will, that he had no desire for it at all and that he was ready to curse it. In this he was acting like the treacherous Judas, who had supper with our Lord and imitating Judas he kept swearing the truth of what he had been saying. Showing to the queen the black shoes he was wearing (9) he assured her that he was her friend and truly obedient to the royal tradition. Then, still weeping falsely, he dared to swear like a slave addressing his lady master, that he would never rest until he made sure she would suffer nothing as a result of her downfall. He begged her not to hide from him anything pertaining to the royal treasures and criticized the evil passion of avarice [*philargyry*, love of silver], claiming not to be possessed by it. This way this greedy man [*pamphagos*, all-devouring] placed all his hopes on obtaining the gold. The wise and god-loving Irene, even though she ought to have been leery of his sudden transformation, being a woman, said to her servant of yesterday who today was the vicious usurper and shameless tyrant,

Pg. 404, A-B. "Oh man, I personally believe that it was God who, although I had been an orphan from an early age, elevated me and, unworthy me, raised me to the imperial throne. But I ascribe the causes of my downfall (only) to myself and to my sins. Under all manners and circumstances let the name of the Lord be blessed. Calling on the King of Kings and Master of all Masters, I also attribute the manner of your elevation to our Lord, without whom I have always believed nothing can be done" . . .

. . .

"Now I bow to you as our king, as someone presented to us by God and I request that you pity my weakness and yield to me what I have built myself, the house at Eleutherion, to lighten my soul under this incomparable disaster." He then answered, "This is to be done as you wish, just tell me frankly without hiding anything where your treasures are and I will take care of all your needs." She then took an oath saying, "I swear to the Precious and Lifegiving Woods that I will hide nothing from you not even a penny [*obolos*]." And that was exactly what she did. But as soon as he accomplished what he wanted, he had the queen exiled to Prince's island [*Prinkepos*], in the convent that she herself had built. That was even while the delegates of King Charles were still in the city and able to see what was happening. Afterwards the most greedy man [*pamphagos*] did not even try for a while to hide hypocritically his innate viciousness and rapacity. Instead, claiming that he intended to fight injustice, he set up a wicked and unfair court at the Magnaura Palace, the purpose of which, according to the tyrant, was to render justice to the poor. As things did show, however, this was a way to dishonor the rich and prominent citizens, to seize them and to transfer their wealth to himself. In fact, this was what happened. Then later, he began to notice that people were unhappy with him and feared that if they remembered the good works and kindness of the pious Irene, they would invite her to rule again. So in the month of November and under the heaviest winter weather, without feeling sorry for her, the heartless man exiled her to Lesbos, ordering that she ought to be guarded securely and not to be seen by anybody.

Pg. 405-D, 1-6. Then on the ninth day of the month of August of the 11th indiction, queen Irene ended her days in exile on the

island of Lesbos. Her body was transferred to Prince's island, to the convent which she herself had built.
>From Theophanes' *Chronographia*, a Greek-and-Latin text published in 1655 a.d. (also in *Corp. Scrpt. Hist. Byz.*)

Nothing is known about the life of another Byzantine historian, George Kedrenos (in reference texts often spelled Cedrenus, or Cedrinus). He lived in the eleventh century, may have been a monk and compiled a world history ending in the year 1057 A.D. The title of his work was *A Synopsis of History from the Creation of the World and Until the Reign of Isaac Komnenos*. The author's introduction is worth quoting.

A SYNOPSIS OF HISTORY
by George Kedrenos, eleventh century A.D.

I, 1-40. Many God-loving and history-loving [*philhistoric*] men among us have dealt with the events of history (names many and describes their work) . . . So they left for those coming after them detailed and outstanding (mental) nourishment . . . which, when memorized, feeds and expands the mind.

The events of the reigns of Irene and of her son Constantine VI in this work are described in separate paragraphs by the year of the monarchs' rule.

Pg. 385, Lines 14-21. Leo, [*Leon* IV], his (of Constantine V) son with the Khazar (princess) reigned five years . . . In the first year, as requested by the army, he crowned (as co-emperor) his son Constantine (VIth).

Lines 32-48. In the fifth year . . . the week in the middle of lent, he (King Leo IV) found under his wife's pillow two icons. After inspecting them and interrogating (the staff?), he discovered that a palace dignitary with some other officials had brought them in. Them he subjected to much torture and punishments. As for his wife Irene, he reprimanded her strongly saying "I have given an oath to my father" (not to allow icon-worship). She claimed not to have seen them (the icons) and he believed her, not knowing her well yet . . . Being extremely fond of precious stones [*lithomania*] the king happened to fall in love with the crown at the Great Church . . . which he took and wore. But the pressure caused burning sores on his head. Then he developed a high fever and in great misery he gave up his soul, an obvious example of how sacrilege is punished.

Lines 49-51. Then, in the year of the world 6288, the 780th year after the divine incarnation (6), Constantine, with his mother Irene, both orthodox (i.e. icon-worshippers), became emperors and reigned twenty-one years.
>From a Greek-and-Latin volume of "G. Cedrenos' Annales," published in 1566 (also in *Corp. Scrpt. Hist. Byz.*)

After the death of Leo IV in 780 A.D. his Athenian icon-worshipping orthodox wife Irene became the regent for their son Constantine VI, who had already been crowned when he was six years old.

A SYNOPSIS OF HISTORY
by George Kedrenos (*Cedrenos*) *continued*.

p. 386, 26-32. In the second year (of her reign), Irene sent a proposal to Charles, king of the Franks (Charles the Great, or Charlemagne) to have his daughter, named Erythro marry her son Constantine. After the agreement was made and oaths were taken, the eunuch and imperial notary, Elisaios, was assigned the task of teaching the princess the Greek letters and speech and to instruct her on the customs of the Roman kingdom.

33-38. In the third year, Irene, having made peace with the Arabs, dispatched the patrician and logothete (10) Stavrakios, against the Slavs. Descending upon them, he subdued them and made them tax paying subjects of the queen. Afterwards he went to Peloponnesos, where he took many prisoners and booty, which he carried to the queen.

39-54. In the fourth year the holy and most saintly patriarch Paul became ill and withdrew to the monastery of Floros. The queen afterwards went to him and asked him: "Why did you do this?" To which, with tears in his eyes, he replied: "I wish I had never sat on the hieratic throne of the church, which is oppressed by tyranny, is separated from the other Catholic thrones and is subject to anathema. If an ecumenical synod cannot be held to correct all the errors in our midst, you shall have no salvation." She then told him: "But why, after you were installed, did you sign (the order) not to worship the icons?" He then said: "This is why I am lamenting and seeking shelter in repentance, praying to God not to damn me for remaining silent about this until now and for not preaching the truth because I was afraid of your furor." With these words he fell asleep (passed away) in peace. From that time on began the intensive worship and support of the icons by everyone.

55-59. On the fifth year queen Irene gathered the entire senate and the people to ask them who should become the new patriarch. They all called for Tarasios and . . . he was installed as patriarch of Constantinople.

Pg.387, 14-29. On the eighth year . . . an ecumenical synod was held in Nicaea [*Nikaia*] and the Catholic church received from the most holy patriarch Tarasios and the holy and blessed fathers gathered there . . . the command to worship the icons together with the cross . . . The king and his mother also signed the document and peace prevailed in the church of our God.

30-34. On the ninth year empress Irene cancelled the contract with the Franks and brought a maid from Armenia, named Marina, whom she wedded to Constantine. He, even though unwillingly, did go through with the marriage.

35-60. On the tenth year there was a most terrible earthquake. Then some people, who were jealous of those close to Irene and wanted to take over ruling the state, prompted the mother to act against her son and convinced her to dedicate her son to God, so that she may reign alone. Being a woman, she was deceived and, given also her desire to rule, she was convinced in her own mind that it ought to be that way. But the king, now twenty years old, extremely strong and a capable warrior, could not tolerate anybody to rule and so he plotted against his mother. She, then, hearing about this from Stavrakios, put the blame on all of Constantine's staff and banned them. Her own son she repudiated strongly and placed him under a house arrest for many days. Subsequently she made the entire army and all those holding offices to take an oath pledging that "as long as you live we will not tolerate your son to rule." But the men of the Armeniac theme did not accept this and declared allegiance to both Constantine and to Irene as before . . . The members of the theme gathered at a meeting and all of them unanimously demanded that Constantine be their king. Fearing a popular uprising, Irene released him and the troops, rejecting Irene, acclaimed Constantine as emperor.

Pg. 388, lines 1-22. Coming back to the city, the king had all his father's attendants, including Stavrakios, beaten and their hair shorn, after which he exiled them. As for his mother, without any regret, [with "*apathy*"], he restrained her in the palace of Eleutherion, which she herself had built and where she had hidden much treasure. At that time also a fire broke out and the triclinon (11) of the patriarchate was burned, . . . including the chambers below, where the commentary on the scriptures, written by St. John Chrysostom, had been deposited. The flames spread . . . and burned everything . . .

The king led an expedition against the Bulgarians and came back victorious. He then left for Tarsus with a large army to campaign against the Arabs and he returned with many captives. Then, yielding to the pleas of his own mother and of many other prominent people, he quickly restored her to her position and ordered that, as originally, she ought to be acclaimed as a ruler. Everyone obeyed except the Armeniac forces, which rebelled under the leadership of Alexios Moseles. For this and also because some said he was destined to become a king, he (Constantine) had him beaten, shaved and jailed.

23-54. On the second year (of Constantine's reign) the king campaigned against the Bulgarians and confronted the Bulgarian leader Kardames . . . In the same month, prompted by the accusations of some people, he came out to the church of St. Mamas and blinded his uncles Nikephoros and Christopher, the sons of his grandfather Constantine. Another Christopher and also Niketas, Anthemios and Eudokios had their tongues cut [*glossokopsis*] and Alexios Moseles was also blinded. Divine justice however, did not appear to leave these men without revenge for very long. The king also subdued in battle the Armeniac forces and punished their leaders with ink inscriptions on their faces . . . and then banished them to Sicily and to other islands.

Since her return to power, Irene kept undermining her son's position. She not only encouraged but may have instigated his plans to send his wife to a nunnery and to marry a young woman of the court, actions which ruined his royal standing, particularly among the clergy. When Constantine led an expedition against the Arabs, his mother's own agents gave him wrong information, to make him withdraw prematurely and then accused him of cowardice (Norwich, p. 797).

A SYNOPSIS OF HISTORY
by George Kedrenos (*continued*).

Pg. 388, lines 39-54. Then the king, prompted by his own mother who still wanted to rule and aroused his hatred (towards his wife), came to dislike his wife Marina against whom he had some sinister suspicions, and forced her to become a nun. Whereupon he was engaged and married illegally to his mother's attendant, Theodote. When the patriarch Tarasios objected, Constantine declared, "If this is not accepted, I will have the churches opened to idols." The patriarch was intimidated and let him have his way, telling many people that he wanted to end his life in peace. So the king held his wedding ceremony in St. Mamas' palace. However the patriarch and also the abbot of the Studion Monastery and others, stayed away from the ceremony because of the unlawfulness of the king's marriage. The king made them be sorry for this and his mother supported him.

Pg. 389, lines 5-33. In the seventh year the king with his mother went out to Prousa to take the thermal baths. A few days later a son was born to the king, whom he named Leo. As soon as he received the news, the king left his mother, with all the royal retinue and the nobles behind, to return fast to the city. Grasping this opportunity, Irene pulled to her side the chiefs of all the regiments and planned to destroy her son and to remain the only ruler [*monocrator*]. As soon as he reached the palace and while his mother was still away, Constantine, on her command, was locked up in the Purple Room, where he had been born. There he was painfully and incurably blinded, so that, according to his mother's wishes, he could be left to die. Right then the sun was darkened and it stayed dark for seventeen days, not sending its rays down. This happened, as everyone said, because of the blinding of the king. The darkness was such that even the ships took the wrong course. As we can see, it is impossible to examine the designs of God. After fifteen years, in the same month and on the same day as when he had his uncles blinded, he too was blinded. Afterwards his mother Irene ruled alone for five years. Her husband's brothers staged a rebellion and so she had them exiled to Athens. From there they continued planning to take over the throne but they were destroyed by the local people and this way the breed of the filthy Copronymos (9) was extinguished. The day after Easter, during the traditional parade toward the Church of the Holy Apostles, the queen, riding on a golden carriage pulled by four horses and supported by noblemen, distributed gratuities among a large crowd.

34–37. On the third year Stavrakios planned to take over as dictator. Learning about this the queen ordered that no one ought to go near Stavrakios. He, overcome with grief, had blood coming up his lungs and he died.

41–59. On the fifth year the Easterners' theme [*Anatolikon*] (10) contemplated a rebellion against the ruling queen. Then arrived delegates from Charles, who had been crowned king of Rome by Pope Leo, to request the most pious Irene to join Charles in marriage and in this way to unite East and West. She was willing to accept but Aëtios (8) presented many obstacles, planning to have the state taken over by his own brother. The queen in general had governed wisely and prudently and as one would have wished. The only thing one could find against her was that she had caused the downfall and the blinding of her son. But she was noted for her religious fervor and for her orthodox faith. She was responsible for the seventh synod and for restoring the worship of the sacred icons. Her accomplishments were very many, truly a myriad. However the heavy and continuous fighting and hostility between the eunuchs, Stavrakios and Leo Klokas, undermined her rule and made it possible for Nikephoros to ascend the imperial throne . . .

From a Greek-and-Latin volume, Episcopios Br. publ. 1560.

A modern writer (Norwich, 1982, p. 20) attributed the downfall of Irene to a clique of Byzantine nobles, who traditionally considered themselves the exclusive heirs of the Roman empire, and were unable to overcome the shock of Charlemagne's coronation in Rome as Holy Roman emperor in 800 A.D. Suspecting that "the reigning empress Zoe" (*sic*—the author must have meant Irene) was seriously considering a marriage proposal of the Frankish king, in 802 A.D. they "lost no time in deposing her and banishing her, somewhat inappropriately [!] to the island of Lesbos."

The Byzantine historian Kedrenos included in this section a verbatim transcription of the history of the rebellion and of Irene's downfall, as given by Theophanes and quoted earlier in this chapter. The verbal exchange between the deposed queen and the leader of the rebels was also recorded in the same words as those of the earlier historian. The only difference, in the conclusion of this chapter, is that instead of Lesbos, Kedrenos cites Mitylene (reversing the "y" and the "i" in its spelling, as did some other late antiquity—e.g. Athenaios—and medieval writers). The last few lines of Kedrenos' story read as follows:

Pg. 390, lines 49–56. She (Irene) swore to him the truth and indicated to him (the location of) her great wealth. After he had obtained what he wanted, Nikephoros promptly exiled her to the monastery she herself had built on Prinkepos (Prince's Island). Then, when he saw that everyone felt sorry for Irene, he began to fear that considering his own greed, people would remember Irene's good works and might raise her again to the throne. So, during that most severe winter and without feeling any pity for her, he exiled her to Mitylene, where he ordered her to be under heavy guard.

From a Greek-and-Latin volume, published in 1566.

John Zonaras was another Greek Byzantine historian, active in the first half of the twelfth century A.D. He held a high office under the emperor Alexios I Komnenos and wrote a world history from the creation to the year 1118. In it he supplied valuable information and, even when copying earlier writers, he tended to view situations in an "independent way" (Ostrogorsky, p. 317). Zonaras also wrote a Lexicon and many theological treatises. In later years he became a monk and retired to "a remote island" (Encycl. Brit. Vol. 23).

HISTORY OF THE WORLD
by John [*Ioannes*] Zonaras, twelfth century A.D.

The reign of Irene and of her son Constantine

Pg. 93, 30–49. After the death of Leo, the Augusta Irene, together with her son who was in his tenth year, succeeded him to the royal position. They were both worshippers of the venerable icons but this of course antagonized many people against their rule. Some of them planned a conspiracy to have as king the Caesar (10) Nikephoros, the brother of the deceased king Leo. But the plot was discovered and the queen, to punish the conspirators, had them arrested, had their hair shorn and then had them expelled beyond the state borders. She also made arrangements to have the hair of her late husband's brothers shaved and then forced them to enter the priesthood, obliging them to distribute the holy communion to the people on the holiday of our Savior's birth. Afterwards she paraded with her son, accompanied by the armed escorts customary for royalty and when she came to the Great Church (St. Sophia) she put on the crown which her husband had taken from there. Then she went close to the people and distributed much money and jewels.

59-61. The queen, wanting to have a woman betrothed to her son, sent delegates to Charles, king of the Franks, proposing that his daughter ought to marry her own child.

Pg. 94, 1-60. Afterwards, however, due to her own love of power [*philarchy*], she abandoned the idea, fearing that her son would acquire much more power as a result of his family ties with the Franks. So instead, she brought a maiden from the east (some say from the Armenian themes, others from Paphlagonia), the daughter of Philaretos, who was famous for his charities and she had this girl married to Constantine against his will. He disliked that marriage so much that he wished he had, without formalities, abducted the daughter of Charles from her foreign lands.

Aaron (*Harun-al-Rashid*) the ruler of the Arabs (7), campaigning against the Romans, reached Chrysopolis. But Constantine sent an army and captured Lake Van. When the Arabs found this out, they asked to make peace with the Romans. The public magistrates left to go to Aaron in order to negotiate the treaty but they did not arrange to receive from him in advance the necessary hostages. So they were seized by him and put in a dungeon in chains. To save the magistrates, the rulers were then forced to agree to pay a tribute to the Arabs . . . The queen later named the patrician Elpidios as general of Sicily. But when she learned that he favored the Caesars (her brothers-in-law), she sent some of her leaders to bring him back from there. The Siceliots, however, did not allow the envoys to take Elpidios back. Irene, overwhelmed by anger, had the man's wife and children flogged instead of him and after she had their hair cut, she incarcerated them in the praetorium. Afterwards she sent an army against Elpidios, under her most faithful eunuch. There was continuous fighting and then Elpidios turned and ran away to Africa, where he joined the Arabs. They received him gladly, offered him royal decorations and were willing to proclaim him their king, even though nothing had gone for him according to his plans. After that there was peace and Irene, feeling less concerned about the Arabs, went with her son on an expedition to Thrace at the head of a large force which included a military band. They went as far as Berrhoea, where she rebuilt the fortress and renamed the city Irenopolis. Without neglecting Ankhialos, she arrived at Philippopolis and then returned. Then the patriarch felt ill and, in view of the fact that the church had reneged and had given in (5), the queen with her son went to visit him and she asked him about this change. "I wish," he answered, "that I had never sat on the archieratic throne, because the church has been under dictatorial rule and rent by divisions between it and the other Catholic thrones." Irene later sent special delegates from the senate to inquire what ought to be done to settle the situation. To this he answered, "If the mistakes cannot be corrected by a Catholic congress [*synod*] and a church union not reestablished, there will be no salvation for us." The delegates then said, "Why then, when you were installed as patriarch, you issued an order against worshipping the icons?." He then countered: "It was because of the maniacal minds of those in charge and of your own harshness; this is why I am lamenting and, through repentance, I seek shelter in God's pity, praying that I may not be judged as the head priest." Soon afterwards he (the patriarch) ended his life. The rulers then arranged to have the reverend Tarasios become patriarch and the whole population approved this.

Pg. 95, lines 13-45. Then the arch-priests and monks gathered in Nicaea [*Nikaia*] of Bithynia and the seventh ecumenical synod was held, which established that the holy icons ought to be worshipped and revered . . . And so the sacred images were restored in the holy temples and the churches were all united.

Until then all the affairs of the kingdom were directed by the queen and by those close to her. King Constantine however, was already past his childhood and as a young man of twenty years could see that his mother managed everything and that Stavrakios and the logothete (10) had the power to do everything while he could not even say a word. Discontented and burdened with worries, he plotted with some senators and with those in his service to remove Stavrakios from power and to send him beyond the frontiers. Their intentions, however, became known and the queen struck down those in the king's service who were part of the plot. After she had their hair shaved, she exiled them in different places. The members of the senate she had disgraced and ordered some of them to be deprived of their property and others to be sent away out of the state. She did not spare her own son and after reproaching and abusing him, she prohibited his public appearance and ordered the armed forces to bypass her son and, as long as she was alive, to swear an oath of allegiance only to her own imperial rule.

From a Greek-and-Latin volume, H. Wolfio, 1557.

Zonaras then went on to describe the rebellion of the Armeniac forces, the assumption by Constantine alone of the imperial power, the fire in the palace, the expedition against the Bulgarians, etc. essentially in lines taken from earlier historians. Then he arrived to the events associated with the blinding of the young king and, later, to the exile and death of Irene on the island of Lesbos.

The reign of Irene and her son Constantine
by J. Zonaras, twelfth century A.D. (*continued*)

Pg. 96, lines 55-61. The king (Constantine VI), strongly disliking his wife Marina, forced her to commit herself to a nunnery. That was done on the advice of his mother, who wanted him to be hated by all and so to have the management of all the affairs of the kingdom revert back to her. Even though they were together with her son in the royal palaces, he (Constantine) did not share any authority except in name only. She (Irene) loved to have the leadership [*philarchy*] all by herself.

Pg. 97, 1-4. So the king made his wife against her will, to replace the royal garments with the black robes of a nun. Then he brought (to his quarters) one of the queen's ladies-in-attendance, Theodote, and he married her, crowning her his empress . . .

18-31. Platon, the head of the Sakoudion monastery then sent a message to patriarch Tarasios about how intolerable it was to have him receive the king in (holy) communion, when he had rejected his own wife and against all church rules, had intercourse with another woman. Platon called that act an adultery. But the king had him brought to the palace and he locked him up there. The king's mother also reprimanded Platon for shaming and embarrassing her son. Later, while the ruler and his mother were on a trip away to

Prousa, he learned that a male child was born to him. Whereupon he left his mother and in a hurry returned to the city. She (Irene) seized that opportunity and, making gifts and promises to the offices of the regimens, convinced them to arrest her son so that she alone would maintain the absolute rule [*autarchy*] . . .

32-45. The king's newborn child, whom he had named Leo, soon died and was much mourned by his father. With the full knowledge of his (Constantine's) mother, the conspirators, worrying that with the passage of time their proposed action was going to become known, rushed and caught the king in the palace. About nine o'clock they put out his eyes in the roughest possible way, intending not only to deprive him of his eyesight but of his life as well. After that took place, for seventeen days the sun did not shine and the days became dark and without light. I do not know whether this happened by chance or it was because of the blinding of Constantine, but people considered it an indication of the wrath of the Divine Providence for what had been done by a mother to her son.

From a Greek-and-Latin text, published 1557.

Zonaras afterwards commented on the coincidence between the date and timing of the blinding of Constantine with those of the mutilation of his uncles by him. He also discussed the crowning of Charlemagne as Holy Roman Emperor by the Pope and the fact that the Franks and the Germans, long-time enemies of the Romans, had become rulers of Italy.

The reign of Irene and her son Constantine
by J. Zonaras (*continued*)

Pg. 98, 24-39. The leader of the Franks, who, as has been mentioned, was crowned by Pope Leo as the king of the Romans, sent delegates to Irene, proposing marriage and a conjugal cohabitation. She did not consider this undesirable and it would have taken place, if it were not for the eunuch Aëtios, the (imperial) ruling chief. He set every mechanism in motion to prevent this marriage. Because he was not able to be king himself (8), he planned to make his own brother Leo ascend the throne. This Leo, as had been arranged by Aëtios, had become the general of Thrace and Macedonia, while Aëtios himself controlled the eastern themes, Opsikion and Anatolikon. There, however, his disdain, contempt and false pride antagonized the officers, who therefore conspired to depose the queen and to install in her place Nikephoros, the general logothete (10).

From a Greek-and-Latin volume, I. Zonaras, publ. 1557.

As did previous historians, Zonaras wrote about the events of the officers' rebellion and how Nikephoros assumed the imperial throne. Describing the final events this author added some details to the histories of his predecessors, probably obtained from sources that have been lost.

The reign of Irene and her son Constantine *(continued)*
Pg. 99, 21-44. Nikephoros, being extremely money-hungry, greedy, unfaithful and capable of every vice, . . . killed Triphyllios with poison . . . blinded Bardanes in the monastery and . . . then claimed to have gotten hold of Irene's son Constantine and to have hypocritically convinced him to show where (more) treasures were hidden . . . Afterwards king Nikephoros began to fear that everyone was against him and that they could bring Irene back to the throne from the nearby island. So he sent her away to the less accessible island of Lesbos and installed guards to watch her. There, overwhelmed by grief, she ended her life.

The former female "emperor" of the Byzantine Roman empire died on Lesbos, in August 803, lonely and without any close supporters or friends. It was rumored that she did not even have enough food and clothing in the last year of her life and tried to make a living by taking small jobs as a seamstress or spinning wool (Head, C., 1982, p. 62). Irene may have spent the last few miserable months of her life in a small house on the outskirts of Mytilene, possibly near the existing chapel of Panayia Trouloti, the small church of "the Holy Virgin with the Dome."

Because of her efforts to restore the true faith [*orthodoxy*] and to allow again the installation and worship of holy images in Christian churches, empress Irene has been named a saint of the Greek Orthodox church. But it was not until forty years after her death, in 843 A.D., that another woman, Theodora, the widow of the emperor Theophilos, called an official synod which marked the end of iconoclasm. The extended persecution of icon-worshipping was the reason that a miraculous icon from Jerusalem was brought to Lesbos and remained there in the center of the island, attracting pilgrims and leading to the erection of a cathedral on the island. The events, from the ninth through the nineteenth century related to this icon are narrated in a relatively recent booklet written by the bishop of Mytilene.

THE HOLY VIRGIN OF AYIASOS ON LESBOS
by I. G. Kleombrotos, Bishop of Mytilene, 1982.
Agathon had been a priest in the palace of Leo IV the Isaurian (775-780 A.D.) in Constantinople, but because he opposed the iconoclast policies of the emperor, he left for Palestine, where orthodox Christianity favored the worship of icons. Twelve years later, he learned that empress Irene the Athenian, who had attempted to restore the use of the holy icons, had been deposed and exiled on Lesbos and that the faithful on that island adhered to icon worship. Then he left Jerusalem taking an ancient icon of the holy virgin holding her son Jesus in her arms and inscribed "Mother of God, Saint Scion" (12). He also carried a handwritten gospel of the

5th century A.D. and a small silver cross inlaid with precious wood from the Holy Cross. Agathon might have hoped to return to Constantinople with the queen when the iconoclast movement was suppressed.

Agathon apparently stayed on Lesbos and lived on a small uninhabited valley on the foothills of the Lesbian Mt. Olympus (13), under a huge walnut tree, which gave the spot its name, "Karya." There he built a cabin and by it he dug out a shelter, or crypt, where he hid the icon and the other items, waiting for the icon persecution to end. The place is now marked by the small chapel of the "Source of Life" [*Zoodokhos Peghe*], but the ancient icon is kept in the larger church of the Virgin, which was not built until the 12th century A.D. The original crypt and cabin gradually expanded to become a monastery with Agathon as the bishop. After Agathon's death in 830 A.D., the monks kept all the sacred objects in the crypt to protect them not only from the iconoclasts but also . . . from the increasing Saracen pirate raids of the Aegean coasts. Only after 842 A.D., when the orthodox worship of holy icons was restored under empress Theodora, were the monks able to exhibit their most holy possessions for public reverence and . . . soon people came from all over the island and from the Greek coastal cities of Asia Minor to worship.

From the Greek book of bishop Kleombrotos, 1982, pp. 9–13.

B. RUTHLESS AND ROMANTIC RULERS

The End of Iconoclasm

The modern meaning of "ruthless" and "romantic" is inevitably dependent on twentieth century conditioning and predictably may vary under different circumstances. Even for their contemporary historians, however, the extremes of cruelty, sentimentality, religiosity and erratic authoritarianism in the succession of imperial rulers of the east Roman empire seemed astounding, showing discordant trends even within one individual, king or queen. The perplexing example of Irene, a stalwart of the "true faith" and yet also the genocidal (her own genes!) destroyer of her son was cited in the preceding section. From her death in 803 A.D. to the end of Theodora, the last—also female— ruler of the Macedonian dynasty in 1056 A.D.—a period considered "the Golden Age" of the Byzantine empire (Ostrogorsky, pp. 210–315)— powerful but practically illiterate emperors were succeeded by their scholarly and sensitive sons and bright, strong, pious but also treacherous mothers and wives ran the state for their weak, inefficient or immature sons or husbands. Although Lesbos remains the primary focus of this story, a broader consideration of people and events connected at times only peripherally with the island would seem essential for the appreciation of their historical relevance. Due to the centralized autocratic structure of the medieval Byzantine State, most of the information concerning areas such as Lesbos, at some distance from the capital, came from the authorities in Constantinople. So we can focus on the island mainly through that central vantage point.

The man who took over the throne from Irene, Nikephoros I, reigned from 802-811 A.D. He may not have been as bad as the hostile icon-worshipping historians have depicted him (Ostrogorsky, p. 186). He was killed in battle fighting the Bulgarians. His son and successor was wounded mortally too at the same time. This son's widow, Theophano (an Athenian, like Irene and the earlier empress Athenais-Eudokia) came close to governing the empire but the dying king, according to Theophanes:

CHRONOGRAPHIA
... Seeing himself incurably confined, considered transferring the rule to his wife, but feared that, in addition to the preexisting evils, democracy might rise as a result.
Quoted in Greek by Ostrogorsky, p. 197.

Consequently, under joint pressure from the senate and the army, another man, Michael I (811–813 A.D.) was placed on the throne. More revolts and iconoclast-led persecutions followed. One rebel, who was eventually captured, tortured and executed, claimed to be the blinded son of Irene, Constantine VI, whose actual fate remained unknown. The name of Irene came up again when another king, Michael II "The Stammerer," forcibly married a supposed granddaughter of the savage "Saint." Near the end of the eleventh century the Greek historian John Skylitzes wrote a "Synopsis of History" dealing in detail with the rulers of the two centuries, from 811 to 1057 A.D. Skylitzes was probably born in Asia Minor and became a high imperial dignitary in Constantinople. Several manuscripts of his work exist and one, now at the National Library in Madrid, Spain, includes a total of 574 detailed illustrations, depicting events, campaigns, coronations, marriages and miracles (Grabar and Manoussacas, 1979, p. 12). This important medieval writer referred to the next-to-last iconoclast emperor with rather unflattering allusions.

SYNOPSIS OF HISTORY
by John [*Ioannis*] Skylitzes
Michael the Stammerer (820-829 A.D.).
17.77-96. When he managed to end successfully the civil wars, king Michael did not attribute the victory to God but to his own

practical wisdom and strategy. With his mind very inflated, he became unrestrained in his drives. His wife had died and so he maintained the appearance of leading the life of a widower but secretly he was sending messages to the leading assemblymen, trying to persuade them that he ought to marry another woman and threatened to use force if they did not go along with his plans . . . With skillful petitions, he then convinced the assembly and did marry a woman who had been previously committed to Christ, having espoused the monastic life since childhood. Her name was Euphrosyne and it was rumored that her father was King Constantine (VIth), who had been justly blinded by his mother for his unrestrained vices.

Corp. Font. Hist. Byz. (Beck et al., eds.), Vol. V, 1973.

Michael II, "The Stammerer" was a "rough soldier" (Ostrogorsky, p. 203) who could not even read or write, but his son Theophilos was well educated and even appreciated and emulated the Moslem culture and the art of the Arab capital, Baghdad. After the early death of Theophilos the government fell in the hands of his widow, Theodora, and her powerful and devoted minister Theoctistos. Under their leadership another ecclesiastical synod was held and the "orthodox" faith, which included the worship of icons, was finally and firmly reestablished. During that period the Arabs continued to make inroads into the Greek lands. An Arab fleet from Spain, which had failed to capture Alexandria in Egypt, turned back and landed on the island of Crete. That island remained under Moslem rule for over 150 years and became the base for frequent raids against other Aegean islands including Lesbos, as mentioned by bishop Kleombrotos in his book about Ayiasos.

A Medieval Hellenic Renaissance

The triumph of icon-worshipping over iconoclasm in the ninth century has been considered indicative of the victory of the Greek and Roman aesthetic values against a predominantly Semitic, Arab and Jewish—iconoclasm presumably was launched by Emperor Leo III under the influence of a visiting Jewish healer (Norwich, 1989, p. 355)—opposition to religious images. Even more remarkable for the history of "western" civilization was the reemergence of secular learning, a veritable renaissance of classical scholarship and rational thinking that also took place about the same time in Byzantium. A leading ninth century intellectual, a classical scholar with the broadest encyclopedic knowledge and truly a bright light of medieval wisdom, was Photios who, from a prominent learned layman was elevated, over an eight-day period of successive promotions, to become patriarch of the orthodox church in Constantinople from 858-867 A.D. and again, after being temporarily deposed by the emperor, from 877-886 A.D. In that capacity, Photios played a leading role in spreading Christianity to the Slavic nations but also in intensifying a rift with the papacy in Rome. As a scholar, Photios was responsible more than anyone of his time for the revival of education and of classical studies (Wilson, p. 40). His impressively extensive "Library" [*Bibliotheke*] was known to have consisted of 280 sections, with accounts and comments about books he had read, nearly half of them of the classical Greek literature. An example of his references to the poetry of Sappho was given in Chapter II. A "Lexicon" of Atticist Greek, compiled by Photios, was discovered as recently as 1959 (Wilson, p. 40). The introduction of paper, after the Arab conquest of Egypt had stopped the trade of papyrus, probably contributed to the expansion of private libraries during that time (Wilson, p. 65).

In the compendium entitled "Library" Photios demonstrated his knowledge of the Lesbian poetess, Sappho, whom he also quoted in his "Lexicon."

LIBRARY [*Bibliotheke*]
by Photios c. 810–891 A.D.

We read selections from the twelve books of Sopater the Sophist, . . . from "The Stories of Women Outstanding in Virtue" by Artemon of Magnesia . . . and from various others, specifically from the Eighth Compendium of Sappho.
                          Quoted by Campbell, p. 30 (Phot. Bibl. No. 161)

LEXICON
by Photios, c. 810-891 A.D.
(Word definition)

Akakos (innocent): Who has no experience of evil, not (necessarily) one of virtuous morals. This according to Sappho.
                          Quoted by Campbell, p.174 (Phot. Anec. Gr. 370)

Combined with the scholarly patriarch's religious orthodoxy was his "open-minded" attitude not only towards the ancient Greek poets and historians, but also some of the comedians as well. Next to an admiring text about Herodotos, Thucidides and Diodoros the Sicilian (see Chapters III and IV) Photios, in his writings, quoted the irreverent and almost lewd writer of comedies, Lucian [*Loukianos*], when he described one of the reading sessions of his group of intellectuals.

COMMENTARY
by Photios, ca. 810-891 A.D.

128, 1-6. What we read was the "Dialogues of the Dead" and other Companion Dialogues by Lucian, in which he made fun of practically everything Greek, the false and silly Greek gods, their unlimited uncontrolled urge for orgies and the monstrous beliefs and creations of the poets . . .

23-28. That he (Lucian) did not believe in anything is shown also by the inscription on his book, which is as follows:

I, Lucian, wrote this, knowing tales old and silly.
What to people seems wise, is in fact foolish too,
Whatever humans think they know, has no meaning
And others will laugh at what you admire.

Quoted in Greek by Wilson, 1971, pp.46-47.

A recent publication in English of fifty-two of Photios' letters includes three addressed to the bishop—"metropolitan"—of Mytilene, who had taken this patriarch's side in a dispute with the emperor and so in 870 A.D. was replaced and persecuted, when Photios was deposed and exiled.

LETTERS
by Photios, Patriarch of Constantinople

To Michael, Metropolitan of Mytilene
Other people might say that your sufferings at the hands of your persecutors are too great for any consolation. But I will say . . . that they are in fact too great for praise. Only you can now decide whether you would rather be pitied, or be considered highly blessed.

Letter No. 13, White, 1981, p. 158.

To Michael, Metropolitan of Mytilene
Someone else may want to receive your crowns without going through what you have endured and suffered for the cause of piety. For me, however, your struggles and misfortunes represent an honor, even though no one is reaching to place a crown on my head. Do not, therefore, lose heart, because the man who has become outstanding and famous for the personal risks he had taken, is enviable and blessed.

Letter No. 14, White, 1981, p. 159.

The succession of Byzantine writers, historians and commentators in the centuries following Photios owed much to the encyclopedic spirit and broad knowledge of this enlightened patriarch. One of the heirs of this intellectual tradition was the emperor himself, Constantine VII, who left for posterity extremely valuable historical writings, including a book of imperial ruling instructions for his son, the future Romanos II.

Intrigues of a scholarly king

The emperor who temporarily banished Photios was Basil I, "the Macedonian," a large, powerful and rough peasant who, through intrigues and murders, elevated himself to the throne and established the so-called "Macedonian" dynasty which lasted until 1056 A.D. The son of Basil I, Leo VI, "The Wise" [*Sophos*], created another religious scandal by marrying—against the Roman law—a fourth time, after being widowed three times in succession. On his death in 912 A.D. Leo left his wife, Zoe Carbopsina, or Carbunopsina (Jenkins, FJH, 1967, *Gen. Introduction* p. 7), i.e., the one with the coal-black eyes, as a regent for their son, Constantine VII, Porphyrogenetos (meaning "Born in the Purple," i.e., in the royal chambers during his parents' reign). The historian, educator and religious leader, Leo Grammaticos, described some of the imperial intrigues and changes at that time. Again, Lesbos was mentioned as a place of exile.

Due to internal instability and serious external—mainly Bulgarian—threats, a powerful admiral, Romanos I Lecapenos, was asked to take over. He ruled the empire while the hereditary emperor, Constantine VII, was a minor. But then continued to reign until he was deposed by his own sons and sent to a monastery in exile. Romanos' daughter Helena was the wife of the legitimate heir to the throne, Constantine VII, who for over twenty years remained in the background, writing books and allowing Romanos to govern.

> **CHRONOGRAPHIA**
> by Leo Grammaticos, 10th century A.D.
>
> **Pg. 509-C. The Imperial Rule of Constantine**
> Then Constantine, his son-in law, took over (the reign) from him (Romanos). . . . Obviously reasoning that if they did not spare their own father, they would not spare him, he (Constantine VII) began to suspect that Stephanos and his brother Constantine (his two brothers-in-law) were going to do the same thing to him. So forty days later, as they sat at the table having dinner and still with food in their mouths, he had them arrested by the so-called Tornicians, taken down from the palace and then on to the nearby islands.
>
> **510, A.** There they were confined and tonsured to become monks. After a while, they (the two brothers) requested to see their father who had been placed on the island of Prote. When they saw him clothed like a monk, they were seized by unbearable

grief. Their father, also in tears, said "I produced sons and raised them but they did me wrong." Afterwards they were exiled from there, Stephanos first to Prokonesos and later to Rhodos and then from Rhodos to Mytilene; Constantine to Tenedos and from there to Samothrace, where he tried to rebel and was slaughtered by his guards . . .

C.2-10. In December of the sixth indiction some people planned a conspiracy against King Constantine and wanted to bring Stephanos back from the island to the palace as a king. But Constantine found out about this and subjected the conspirators to intolerable beating, had the noses and the ears of many of them cut off and then had them ride on donkeys and parade through the center of the city.

From a Greek-and-Latin volume, publ. in 1655
(with Theophanes' History).

The story of the scholarly king, Constantine VII, who reigned for 46 years (913-959 A.D.), without actively ruling for the first thirty-one; of the powerful Romanos I who governed and actually sat on a throne for, or instead of him (920-944 A.D.); of the deposition of Romanos by his own sons and of the support Romanos' daughter and king Constantine's wife Helena gave her husband against her brothers—and then shared much of his power after she helped him secure his throne (Jenkins, RJH, 1967, p. 7)—was written in more detail by the eleventh century historian, John Skylitzes, who has been quoted earlier concerning emperor Michael II.

A SYNOPSIS OF HISTORY
by J. Skylitzes, late eleventh century A.D.

Constantine [*Konstantinos*] emperor again

B.320-325:1.88-113. King Constantine became an orphan at a very young age and so the state affairs were handled by his mother Zoe and her counsellors. Most influential by the queen was the chamberlain Constantine . . . who held the reins of the empire and who was definitely making plans, day and night, to transfer the royal crown to his own brother-in-law, Leo Phokas and to get rid of (the young) Constantine. But the tutor [*paedagogos*] of the Porphyrogenetos, Theodore, in a hurry summoned Romanos, the chief of the naval forces which happened to be anchored near the capital and gave him entrance to the palace, intending him to become the guardian and defender of the king. As soon as the admiral was given his chance, however, he broke his awesome oaths and declared himself to be the king. The young Porphyrogenetos suppressed his anger and actually placed the crown on the head of the usurper, who was not content to be king himself but also raised his sons Christopher and later Stephanos and also Constantine to the level of co-emperors.

One of the sons of Romanos, Christopher, died young, but the other two, after being inactive co-emperors for twenty-four years, rebelled against their father, had him seized on a cold December day and had him exiled to a monastery in the nearby island of Prote, where, against his will, he had his hair shaved and was tonsured as a monk.

> **A SYNOPSIS OF HISTORY**
> by J. Skylitzes (continued).
> **b.323-325/2.68-97.** After the fall of Romanos, Stephanos (his son) vigorously got charge of the affairs, pushing aside both his brother-in-law (the legitimate hereditary emperor Constantine) and his brother (Constantine). The two brothers soon began to disagree and to suspect each other, insulting each other continuously. While Stephanos was making a supreme effort to eliminate both his brother and his brother-in-law and to remain the only ruler, Constantine (the Porphyrogenetos) prompted steadily by his wife Helena to remove her own brothers from the throne, managed to get enough assistance and popular support and to eliminate both Stephanos and Constantine. This was accomplished on January 27 of the same third indiction (6). He put them (the brothers) on small vessels and sent them away to exile. Stephanos was carried off to Mytilene and Constantine to Samothrace. From then on Stephanos endured his misfortune with much patience and magnanimity and for nineteen years he led a simple existence on Lesbos. But Constantine was very impatient, unduly irritable and many times tried to escape. Two years after they (the brothers) lost the throne, he killed his guard and then was himself cut down by the rest of the guardsmen.

The Macedonian Dynasty ended with the daughter of Constantine VIII, who was the grandson of Constantine VII Porphyrogenetos. Already old, Constantine VIII ruled for less than three years, following the death of his powerful and heroic brother, Basil II, in 1025 A.D. These two brothers were young children when their father, Romanos II (the son of Constantine VII and of the daughter of Romanos I, Helena) died. Two brilliant generals, Nikephoros II and John I Tzimiskes held the scepter in succession until Basil II became eighteen years old.

> **A SYNOPSIS OF HISTORY**
> by J. Skylitzes, late eleventh century A.D.
> **b.379,1.93.** John Tzimiskes assumed the responsibility of ruling the Romans, keeping as co-emperors Basil and Constantine, sons of Romanos. Basil was seven and Constantine five years old . . . As soon as he took over, he dismissed those who were influential under Nikephoros and placed the chief chamberlain, Leo the kouropalates (10), under house arrest on Lesbos.

Leo the Deacon [*Leon Diakonos*], in his ten-book history of the period from 959 to 976 A.D. (Gibbon, E., Vol. V, p. 535; Ostrogorsky, G., 1969, p. 211) provided additional contemporary details of how John Tzimiskes safeguarded his throne (which he had obtained with the assassination of his predecessor, Nikephoros Phokas) by using Lesbos as a place of exile for his foes.

NIKEPHOROS PHOKAS AND JOHN [IOANNES] TZIMISKES
by Leo Diakonos, b. 950 A.D.

Book VII

95-96 . . . Well before the rays of the sun shone upon the earth . . . all of Nikephoros' people were expelled from their posts and the highest offices of the State were taken over by men trusted by John (Tzimiskes). In addition, he (John) ordered the blood relatives of Nikephoros to withdraw to their estates and to confine themselves there. He also had the kouropalates Leo, brother of emperor Nikephoros, and also Leo's son, the patrician Nikephoros, banished to Methymna, a city on the island of Lesbos, after he had provided guarantees for their personal safety.

112-114. While emperor John was busily making preparations for a war against the Russians, duke Bardas, a son of the kouropalates Leo and nephew of the (murdered) emperor Nikephoros . . . (and others) . . . secretly came back from Amaseia, where they had fled, and began planning an uprising . . . Among them was someone named Symeon, who, after his occupation, was called Ampelas ("The Vineyard-owner," or "Vintner"). He was a man of low class, but had the courage and the power to claim the crown . . . When Bardas saw that the group gathered around him (Ampelas) was quite large . . . he joined the camp of rebels . . . Also the father of Bardas, the kouropalates Leo, became involved in the insurrection. He still lived in exile on the island of Lesbos, but through the bishop of Abydos, Stephanos, he promised the Macedonians money and positions. He also offered to join them against the emperor John, as soon as he could leave the island . . . But the conspiracy came to light and . . . the emperor brought bishop Stephanos to a church tribunal [synod], which deprived him of his position. The kouropalates Leo and his son Nikephoros were sentenced to death by the judges but, he (emperor John) spared them from execution and ordered (instead) to have them blinded and banished (again) to Lesbos.

Loretto, F., 1961, (in German translation from
the original Greek), p. 90 and pp. 105-106.

Although he relied on some of the same chronicles of the times as Leo the Deacon (Ostrogorsky, G., 1969, p. 211) the historian John Skylitzes gave this episode a slightly less gory conclusion.

A SYNOPSIS OF HISTORY
by J. Skylitzes (continued)

b.388-390, 7.14-20 . . . Symeon Ampelas, placing a crown on his head and assuming all other signs of royalty, started an uprising against the king. His father, Leo the kouropalates, tried to gain support with generous gifts to some people and promises of offices and property to others, using for this purpose the services of the bishop of Abydos. He also wanted to escape secretly from Lesbos himself and with his son Nikephoros to cross over to the region of Thrace. But the king found that out after the bishop was caught and, having no way of evading the interrogation, clearly admitted everything. The kouropalates was surrendered to the judges and they all were in favor of a death sentence for him and for his son. But the king was more lenient and ordered to have only the eyes of both burned out. In fact they say that secretly he asked the executioners not to mutilate their faces in any way and to spare their eyesight, but not to reveal that it was a royal order and instead to make it seem that it was their own philanthropic doing.

After a fifty-year reign, the childless Basil II was succeeded by his brother Constantine VIII who only became aware of the problem of succession when he was dying, in 1028 A.D. He had three daughters, the oldest of whom had become a nun and the youngest was withdrawn and relatively unattractive. It was then decided that the second daughter, Zoe, had to marry quickly to provide a male ruler for the kingdom. She must then have been over 45 years old and the husband chosen for her by her father was the mayor of the city and was married. The man's wife had to be forced to enter a nunnery and he ruled, as Romanos III, for six years, until he too died, under circumstances suggesting that he was either poisoned or drowned by his staff, or both. Two other rulers followed. Both were launched on their imperial destinies by their powerful relative, the court eunuch John "The Orphans' Guardian" [*orphanotrophos*, orphans' feeder], who later was to be put to death in exile on Lesbos. The first to succeed Romanos as the new husband of Zoe was the eunuch's brother, Michael IV the "Paphlagonian" (from Paphlagonia, in northwestern Asia Minor).

CHRONOGRAPHIA
by Michael Psellos, eleventh century A.D.

Among the emperor's staff . . . there was a eunuch, a mean and despicable person but gifted with a very astute and inventive mind . . . The eunuch had a brother . . . a young man . . . as fresh as a flower, clear-eyed and, truly, "red-cheeked."

The moment this eunuch's brother Michael was shrewdly presented to her by his uncle, Zoe fell in love with him. She married him immediately following the death of her first husband, which the two lovers were suspected of having implemented. After a reign of barely six years (1034-1041) Michael IV died in an epileptic attack and was succeeded by his nephew who, again thanks to the intrigues of the other uncle, the orphanotrophos John, had become the adopted son of the empress Zoe. He reigned less than two years as Michael V. His arrogant and cruel behavior eventually caused an uprising. He was seized by a rebellious crowd, was publicly blinded and then sent to a distant monastery. Then came the turn of a nobleman, who had been living in exile on Lesbos for seven years, to become the third husband of the sixty-two year old Zoe—she was born in 980 A.D. (Sewter, 1984, p. 65)—and the next emperor (1042–55 A.D.) of the Byzantine State.

An imperial erotic triangle

A nobleman of the Monomakhos (14) family, who had been exiled on Lesbos because he was suspected of political maneuvering against Michael IV, was chosen to become Zoe's third husband and to reign as Constantine IX.

A glorious future for the exiled aristocrat had been foretold by three religious hermits from the nearby island of Khios [*Hios*]. They saw a vision of the virgin Mary near their mountain cave and were told by Her that Constantine was destined to become emperor of Byzantium. Crossing over to Lesbos, they had given Monomakhos the Divine good tidings and he, in turn, promised that if he ever became king, he would fund the building of a large church and monastery on the spot where the Virgin had appeared to the hermits. True to his word, Constantine IX later ordered the construction of the magnificent New Monastery [*Nea Moni*] on Hios. When it was completed twelve years later, Constantine had just died, but some of his original sealed decrees, as well as records of the hermits' role are still preserved in the archives of the monastery (Axiotakis, A.S. 1982, pp. 10-13).

The eleventh century historians John Skylitzes and George Kedrenos and also the scholar, philosopher, administrator and educator, Michael Psellos, recorded the events of Constantine Monomakhos' reign and of the intriguing imperial erotic triangle of his court.

A SYNOPSIS OF HISTORY
by J. Skylitzes, late eleventh century A.D.

Constantine Monomakhos

1.9-48. Again the ruling power returned to Zoe who had to reign, against her will, together with her sister Theodora . . . As the senate proposed to find a king, a lawful husband for Zoe, she rushed to invite Constantine (Kavasilas) . . . who was a very dignified person and was reported to have approached Zoe secretly. But his wife caused him to end his life with poison, not because she did not love him but because she feared she was going to part from him while she was still alive. So when the queen missed her aim, she recalled from exile Constantine Monomakhos, who . . . had been sentenced to live on Mytilene because of rumors that he was destined to become king . . . Although she wanted the other Constantine, after he, as mentioned, was destroyed by poison, the said Monomakhos, a namesake of the dead Constantine, in some way was brought to the attention of the queen . . . So Stephanos, one of the eunuchs and chamberlain of the queen, was sent to him and after making him replace his ordinary clothes with the royal purple, boarded him on a fast ship and carried him to the capital. There, as soon as he arrived, the queen took him in marital communion. The secret church service was performed by the first presbyter, Stypes, on June 11 of the year 6550 (1042 A.D.) and the following day he was crowned by the patriarch.

George Kedrenos' history was almost a verbatim duplicate of Skylitzes' text but it included some further details.

A SYNOPSIS OF HISTORY
by George Kedrenos

p. 621-2, lines 56-60 and 1-12 . . . Then the Queen . . . recalled from exile Constantine Monomakhos, who had been condemned by the orphanotrophos to live on Mitylene island because it had been rumored that he was destined to rule the kingdom. Wanting to elevate this other Constantine to the throne, she first appointed him a governor [dikastes, literally a judge] in Greece. Because as we indicated, the first one—Constantine Kabasilas—had been destroyed by poison, the said Monomakhos, the dead man's namesake, was taken to the queen and this is how it was done. He was carried to the leading general's headquarters . . . and one of the queen's attendants, Stephanos Pergamenos, was dispatched there, had him (Constantine) remove his ordinary clothes and had him dressed in the royal purple. Then he had him board a cruiser [*dromon*] and transported to the royal domains . . .

A SYNOPSIS OF HISTORY
by J. Skylitzes

2.49-55. Now that he held the royal scepter, Constantine granted promotions to the officers and gained the favor of the crowds with distributions of money. He sent messages to all the provinces about his enthronement, declaring all good will for the virtuous and the elimination of all evil. He transferred John Orphanotrophos (15) . . . to the island of Lesbos . . .

Greek text, edited by H.G. Beck et al.,
Corp. Font. Hist. Byz., Vol. V, 1973, pp. 422-423.

The historian George Kedrenos (Cedrenos) had more to say about the fate of John "The Orphans' Guardian" (10, 15).

A SYNOPSIS OF HISTORY
by George Kedrenos, eleventh century A.D.

749D. p. 535 ... In fact he (Constantine IX) banished him (John, the Orphanotrophos) to a place reserved for convicted pirates ... So John departed ... destined to suffer one misfortune after another ... Evil followed evil until finally Fate deprived him of his eyes and then, awfully fast, the executioner's hand inflicted on him a most violent death.

John was blinded in 1043 by order of his unforgiving enemy, the new patriarch Michael Kerularios (16). Constantine IX, evidently considering the eunuch still a threat, banished him to Mytilene, where later he had him put to death.

A SYNOPSIS OF HISTORY
by J. Skylitzes

Constantine Monomakhos, *continued.*

2. ... on October 6 of the next year (1043. A.D.), a comet appeared in the sky from the east going west and was seen shining all that month. This was thought to be announcing the forthcoming world disasters.

. . . .

3.60-66. After the scepter of the Romans went to Constantine Monomakhos, Skleros was very fortunate because his sister was Monomakhos' mistress. He received the honor of being appointed a magistrate and protostator.

29 ... The king had a monastery built on the place called Mangana, in the name of the great martyr St. George. Spending the public funds without restraint for its edifices, now building, now demolishing, he came to great straits. Consequently he had to devise all kinds of extortions and to invent improper and intricate ways to raise money. He thought of many other wicked and illegal methods to increase the revenues, which even to list would be shameful. One thing I must say is that from this king on and from his prodigal ways began the decline of the Roman affairs ... While he crudely pursued liberal policies, he carried on with his prodigal ways to the extreme. Yet he did not totally miss doing some good and some works of his deserve to be described in this history. In the monastery already mentioned, there were accommodations for old people, guest quarters and facilities for the indigent which are worth much praise.

. . . .

30 ... But then an epidemic disease hit the royal capital and there were no people left with any strength among the living to carry away the dead. On top of this a hailstorm fell that summer and destroyed not only many animals but people too. As for the emperor, afflicted by his chronic disease, podagra (gout), he was bedridden in the newly built monastery of Mangana. As the symptoms multiplied and death already was near, the top dignitaries began to think of possible successors. They considered

Nikephoros Protenon as the most capable candidate and sent a messenger to bring him back from Bulgaria where was then. But those in the service of queen Theodora (Zoe, her sister, had already died), put her on a galley and brought her to the palace where she was acclaimed queen. The emperor died in Mangana and received only an ordinary burial.

Corp. Font. Hist. Byz. Vol. V, 1973.

No better, more realistic, reliable and also very readable and entertaining description of the major events around the year 1000 (more precisely from 976–1078 A.D., covering the reigns of fourteen Byzantine rulers) can be found than the *Chronicle [Chronographia]* written by "the intellectual giant" (Sewter, 1966, editor's note) on the scene, Michael Psellos. According to the modern English scholar and translator of his work, Psellos (originally christened Constantine, he changed his name to Michael when for a short time he withdrew to a monastery) was a child prodigy from a prominent but not rich or powerful family (Sewter, 1953-84, *Introduction*, p. 13). He was so bright, well learned and eloquent that he eventually dominated the political and intellectual scene in the capital of Constantinople. His words were "honey" and "nectar" (Sewter, *Introduction*, p. 14) for the sophisticated nobility and for the kings and queens he served. His writings were read and quoted by generations of Greek Byzantines and, besides his powerful palace intrigues—some beneficial, others disastrous—he can be credited for his role in establishing the free University of Constantinople (in 1045 A.D.), which opened the doors to a "renaissance of learning" (Sewter, p. 13), without prejudice, to anyone with a recognized ability.

Michael Psellos

The Greek text of the *Chronographia* is often rhetorical in style, but is also full of lively personal profiles and comments. The English translation of the section concerning the romantic aristocrats exiled on Lesbos and their subsequent lives, is from the Greek text edited by Sathas (1899) and by Renauld (1926). The French translation of the latter and the modern English rendering by Sewter (originally published in 1953, revised 1966 and reprinted 1979-84) have been useful guiding references.

CHRONOGRAPHIA
by Michael Psellos, 1018–96 A.D.

Volume VI
Zoe and Theodora—Constantine IX

I. So the reign reverted to the two sisters and then, for the first time our era saw the women's quarters [gynaikonitis] transformed into a royal council chamber . . .

Psellos went on to describe the palace protocol, the government functions, the royal sisters' physical appearance, characters and habits, with their striking differences. He bitterly commented on their mismanagement of the state affairs and funds.

> **IV.** To describe the personality of the queens, for those who did not know them, I must indicate that Zoe, the older one, had a greater readiness of mind for understanding, but her tongue was slower in expressing her thoughts. Theodora was the reverse in both, not very quick in her judgement but, once she launched into a conversation, she chatted with a skillful and excited voice. Zoe, on her part, tended to rush towards anything she desired and showed an equally sharp trend towards two things, I mean life and death, being like the waves of the sea that raise a boat up and then immediately sink it low. Theodora, however, showed no such character trait and her mood was steady and even, although, if I may say so, also a little dull.
> . . .
>
> **VIII.** The soldiers' compensation and the funds designed for the military were needlessly diverted and placed at the disposal of others, the crowds of flatterers and similar imperial escorts, as if the royal treasures of emperor Basil had been reserved for such individuals.
>
> **IX.** Most people think that only now, for the first time, the nations around us have thrown themselves against the Romans and that unexpectedly have massively penetrated our borders. But I believe that a building falls apart whenever the bonds that hold it together are dissolved. Even though the majority had not sensed the beginning of the disaster, it did develop out of these original conditions and it was the gathering of those clouds that precipitated the present great deluge.
> . . . .
>
> **XIV.** So Constantine, the son of Theodosios and last scion of the ancient tree of the Monomakhos family, was the one destined to hold the scepter next. He reigned longer than any of the rulers after Basil and did more than the others, some things better but some much worse. I have served him in everything from the start and was promoted to the highest ranks, being entrusted with the most important matters, so there was nothing I did not know, whether overt or secret.
> . . . .

On How and by What Means King Constantine Was Raised by the Augusta to the Royalty

XV. . . . This man, due to his family background, was entitled to the highest ranks in the empire. Privileged with great wealth and remarkable for his handsome looks, he seemed undeniably suitable for an alliance with the noblest families. He was initially joined with a most notable person and quickly after a disease caused the death of his wife, he was linked to another marriage . . . It was to the daughter of (the future) king Romanos' sister, Pulkheria, who, in the past had been married to Basil Skleros—fate later deprived him of his eyesight (17)—and she was the mother of this only daughter. Married to her and also because of his background, Constantine could shine above all others, yet he was not granted any prominent positions. Those around emperor Basil hated him because they hated his father, who had been caught in a conspiracy and then gave the royal hatred as an inheritance to his son.

XVI. Nor did Romanos, when he became king, try anything special for Constantine . . .

XVII. He (Constantine) still continued to seem like a possible competitor for the throne and so Michael too, when he took over from Romanos, was suspicious of him . . . He set up some false witnesses against him and drove him away from the City, committing him within certain restricted bounds. These bounds were on the island of Mytilene, where Constantine spent seven miserable years, the entire duration of Michael's reign. The hatred against him was then inherited by the second Michael too.

XVIII. When the power returned to the noble queen . . . she began to think of Constantine. She openly talked about him to her entourage and house staff and when she saw that all, as if on a signal, were voting in favor of him assuming the royal power, she announced her wishes to the senate. The decision appeared to them godsent and so Constantine was recalled from his exile and departed from there in no spectacular way (at first).

XIX. But as soon as he approached the City a much more luxurious lodging was prepared for him and a royal tent was erected with the imperial guard around it. In front of the palace a spectacular magnificence was awaiting the man. People of all ages and conditions, others on top of others, ran towards him and loudly acclaimed him . . . The City crowd poured well beyond the City walls and there were celebrations and speeches. When everything was ready and the entrance arrangements were completed, the signal was given and with a spectacular parade Constantine entered the inner court of the palace.

XX. Because it was necessary to circumvent the existing marriage laws, the patriarch Alexios, after respectful consideration allowed an exception due to the circumstances and bowing as can be said, to the will of God. He did not place the wreaths on the couple with his own hands but after they were married and crowned, he embraced them. I cannot tell whether this was the act of a priest or a flatterer, or one adapting himself to the occasion.

XXI. . . . That was the beginning of the establishment of the reign of Constantine Monomakhos. They (the two queens) gave up their power, having ruled together for three months . . .

. . . .

XXIV. . . . What I want is neither to refer to him (Constantine IX) with the best possible words, nor to be silent concerning his deeds that deviated from the best principles. If . . . I appeared to recollect only the worst affairs, I would be as vicious as the son of Lyxos (the historian Herodotos), who included in his History the worst actions of the Greeks (18).

. . . .

XXVII. Most historical writers about kings have expressed wonder that none of them withstood the test, well until the end. For some (kings) the early years were the best, while the life of others was better close to the end. Some chose a life of pleasures, while others seemed concerned with philosophy and then, confusing their inclinations without any order, have conducted their lives most inappropriately. I do not find this strange however and the opposite would surprise me, if it ever happened. It would be truly unique to find a life that has been directed by one and the same line of conduct from the early beginning until the very end . . .

. . . .

XLVII. This emperor did not comprehend at all the nature of royalty, neither that it is a function aiming at serving the people, nor that it requires a mind constantly alert for the best administration of the state affairs. Instead, he considered his reign as an opportunity to rest from his toils, to satisfy his desires and to relax his spirit. So, as if he had sailed into it not to take over the government, but to enjoy the advantages of tranquility, he delegated to others the attention to public affairs, the privileges of delivering justice and the supervision of the military organization, keeping for himself only a small part. What he reserved for himself was the life of voluptuousness and pleasures, as if it belonged to him naturally . . .

XLVIII. Like a robust animal, strong in every aspect, may not be changed rapidly by the onset of future disease, so under this ruler also, there was no sign of an unhappy end for the kingdom. Because the state still had spirit and strength, only a trace of a decline was apparent, until gradually the evil grew and, reaching a peak, toppled and confused everything.

XLIX. Not a small part of the king's lack of restraint was due to the undisciplined habits of the queens and to his desire to indulge with them in leisurely pursuits and laughter. This sharing of pleasures he called "care" [therapy] and did not wish to oppose them (the royal sisters) in anything. Instead, he brought them every possible amusement [*glykythymia*, i.e. mood sweetener]. But when a certain trouble developed, an immediate clash with them would have occurred if his spouse had not gone along with him, either hiding her jealousy, or not feeling any because of her age.

How and by what means the honorable Skleraina was introduced to the reigning queen

L. What happened was this. After the death of his second wife, who was a descendent of the most illustrious Skleros family, the king, being still a private citizen at that time, was not at liberty to show an interest in a third marriage, because this would not have conformed to the laws of the Romans. Consequently he chose a much worse solution, which anyone would have preferred to keep secret. In a most unlawful cohabitation arrangement, he shared his life with the niece of his deceased wife, a beautiful and otherwise thoughtful person, either persuading her with gifts, or charming her with words of love, or using for this purpose some different powerful means.

LI. To such a degree they were bound by love, that neither wanted to be deprived of the other, not even when they were going through the most unhappy circumstances. And when the king had to go to exile, as mentioned before, the woman was by him. She took care of everything to the extreme, placed all her belongings at his disposal and in every way she comforted him and relieved him of most of the burden of his misfortune. She did, in fact, nourish hopes of becoming queen and she put everything in second place behind her expectation of a joint reign. She believed that their marriage would take place and all their wishes would be realized when he, as the ruler, would be able to change the state laws for that purpose. But when only one of their expectations did materialize—I mean that Constantine became king—yet the other seemed impossible because of the situation and because queen Zoe had retained all authority, she (Skleraina) began to totally despair, not only for her dearest hopes, but also for her own survival. She believed that the queen was very angry with her and so she was terribly afraid of her.

LII. But the emperor never forgot his woman, even after he ascended the royal throne. On the contrary, while he looked at the queen with his physical eyes, with those of his mind he visualized and contemplated her form and when he held the first one in his arms, in his soul he embraced the other. He was not afraid either of the circumstances or of the queen's jealousy and he was not influenced by anybody's advice and all counsel took second place to his desires. He even disregarded the advice of his sister Euprepia, one of the wisest women of our times, who opposed him and tried to arouse his conscience. Constantine dismissed all this and even at their first encounter he spoke to the queen about this woman, not as if she were a spouse or a possible mistress, but as a person who had suffered much because of her family and also for his sake. He proposed that she deserved to be recalled and to be granted some modest recognition.

LIII. The queen was thus promptly persuaded. She did not nourish any jealousy, having suffered many misfortunes and having reached an age that does not sustain such feelings. While the young woman (Skleraina) expected the worst to befall on her, suddenly arrived the messengers with their imperial escorts, inviting her back to Byzantium. They presented to her letters, both from the emperor and from the queen herself, assuring her of their kindest disposition and encouraging her to come. And this was how she arrived in the queen of the cities.

LIV. At first she was awarded a relatively modest lodging and a retinue not at all spectacular. In order to have an excuse to spend more time there, the king made that building his own home, and to make it more impressive and suitable for imperial visitations, he placed a larger foundation outside of it and made it become a more spectacular edifice.

LV. So then, time after time, he found a pretext of a construction problem and many times each month he went there, claiming that he had to see what was going on but, in reality, to get together with this woman. Because he was escorted also by people from the other (the queen's) side, to prevent any indiscretions he arranged for them a luxurious outdoor table and was treating them to a banquet, where they were receiving anything they had previously requested. They, well aware of what was going on, worried less about their queen and were more preoccupied with their own enjoyment and with obtaining what they had in mind. Even when, at times, they noticed that the emperor was squirming to get there, but was hesitant and often embarrassed to proceed, each one of them found a different excuse to smooth his way to his beloved and, by doing this, obtained the king's greatest favors.

LVI. That was how, at first, the emperor covered up his relationship with the woman and his love affair was not originally without some embarrassment. Gradually however, he discarded all prudence and unveiling all his designs he eliminated every cover. Whenever he wanted he was with her and by her in the open. To anticipate my whole story about her, what people saw and heard seemed incredible. In fact, the king was not with her as with a mistress, but clearly as with a spouse.

LVII. For her sake he exhausted the imperial treasury giving her everything she wanted. He had found in the palace a copper coffer, covered with designs and sculptured reliefs and, filling it with money, he sent it to the woman. He did such things not at long intervals but constantly he had more and more carried to his beloved.

On how the "Sebaste"—Venerable lady (10)—entered the royal palace

LVIII. For a while, this amorous exchange had gone on half-seen. But as the passage of time kept revealing little by little what was formerly hidden, he made his love prominently public and after a delicate conversation with his queen, he convinced her to favor living together with that woman. Once he had her consent, his soul's desires did not stop there, but he also prepared a written declaration of friendship and made royal protocol arrangements, according to which they (he and the two women) would be seated (at ceremonies) in the front row. The councilmen, while complying with the new rules, kept blushing and whispering a lot, yet they praised the edict as if it were a message from heaven and called it a cup of friendship and other such sweet names, which customarily flatter or deceive a flighty and vacant soul.

LIX. When this ruling was established and the oaths performed, the former mistress was introduced into the exclusive royal chambers, no more being called by that name but, instead, a sovereign and a queen. Most amazing was the fact that while the spirits of the majority of the people were hurt because their queen had been cheated, disregarded and humiliated, she showed no change herself and was seen smiling to everyone and delighted with the situation. Very often she kissed profusely and affectionately the woman that shared her power and both of them stood helpfully by the king and assisted in handling his affairs. He, in turn, kept a similar balance between the two of them in weighing their advice, even though at times he paid more attention to the second queen.

From a Greek-and-French edition by E. Renauld, Vol. I, 1967.

Although the courtiers in the palace tried to accept the imperial *ménage-à-trois*, the people were shocked and angry to have the young woman share the throne. The historian Kedrenos described a riot that almost cost Constantine his life.

A SYNOPSIS OF HISTORY
by George Kedrenos

... In the month of March of that year (1044 A.D.), during the holiday festivities of the Forty Holy Martyrs, as the king was about to begin with the Saints' public procession, he was faced with a revolt of the people. As he walked out of the palace with a large retinue and applause and was about to mount his horse ... a voice came suddenly from among the crowd: "We do not want Skleraina as our queen, or to see our ladies [*manai* = mothers] Zoe and Theodora, who were born in the purple, perish because of her." There was instantly total confusion, the crowd was seized by a great turmoil and tried to get hold of the king. If the queens had not come quickly out from above and quieted the crowd, not a few people would have died, including possibly the king himself. Even though, however, the disturbance was over, they (the royal assembly) cancelled the parade of the martyrs and returned to the imperial residence.

From a Greek-and-Latin edition, published in 1566
(p.628, lines 8-30).

M. Psellos continued the biography of Constantine and his women with a personal profile of the king's young paramour, the "Sebaste"—Venerable (10)—Skleraina.

CHRONOGRAPHIA
by Michael Psellos, *continued*.

LX. Although her physical appearance was not entirely marvelous, it did not in the least invite any down-grading and offensive comment. Then, concerning her personality and her intellectual aptitudes, with the former she could delight even rocks and was most capable to control and dominate circumstances. But it was her speech that had no equal, for it was refined, embellished and with a sophisticated rhythmical quality. Along with her tongue there ran a spontaneous verbal sweetness and when she told a story it sounded with an indescribable charm spreading all over. She used to delight me, often questioning me repeatedly about Greek myths and adding herself what she might have heard from some other expert authority on these matters. She was a good listener too, more so than any other woman (which, I guess, did not come naturally but was acquired because she knew all tongues were aiming at her) and even someone's mumble between the teeth she turned into a clear sentence for her and she could liken a whisper to an expression with meaning.

LXI. One time, when we and other secretaries were gathered, a procession of the queen and her retinue happened to come by. Leading were the queen herself and her sister Theodora and right behind them the sebaste (this was in fact her new title, with which the reigning sisters had honored her, according to the wishes of the emperor). Then, as they proceeded going towards the theater and many in the crowd were seeing her for the first time accompanying the queens, someone expert in flattery quietly recited the poetic line "You can't blame . . . " (19) without going any further into the epic lines. At that moment she showed no sign of response to his words, but when the procession had ended, she sought out the man who had spoken and questioned him about that expression, not mispronouncing anything but very precisely sounding the words. After the speaker of those words told the full story with perfect exactness and the many people around nodded approving the explanation, she was instantly filled with pride and rewarded the author of the compliment not with few and worthless gifts but with presents of the kind she had been accustomed giving and receiving. Indeed, in order that all others and particularly the queens were motivated by the best feelings towards her, the emperor had provided the sebaste with her own special funds to distribute to each man or woman what was appropriate.

LXII. Seeing that from the two sisters, the one felt a need for more gold, not for the sake of possession or accumulation but to have it redirected towards others and she also loved perfumes of exquisite Indian origin and aromatic woods that had not lost their natural sap, tiny olives and the whitest laurel berries and that the other, the youngest one, felt daily pleasure with her thousands of daric coins, for which she had made bronze coffers, the sebaste distributed to each one of them what she believed would be most suitable. In fact, the first one, the queen, having put aside any jealousy due to her age, felt no resentment towards the sebaste and, dragged down by the weight of her years, bore the burden without anger. As for her sister, as long as she got what she wanted, she cared even less than Zoe about the situation.

LXIII. As a result, everything that king Basil (Basil II, 976-1025 A.D.) had accumulated in the imperial treasury with so much sweat and struggle, was before these ladies like a joyful light game. More and more, they were rewarding themselves, or giving each other and more they were providing for others, so that in a short time everything was spent and wasted . . . Now when it came to the assignment of residential quarters, the king occupied the central part among the three and they (the two women) were lodged on the sides, with the innermost chamber belonging to the sebaste. The queen, in fact, in no way ever approached the emperor without first trying to find out whether he was in his chambers by himself and away from his beloved. If this were not the case, she kept busy with her own affairs.

The author went on to describe many strange hobbies and activities of the queen, particularly her preoccupation with an image of Christ, which she had made herself.

CHRONOGRAPHIA
by Michael Psellos, *continued.*

LXVIII. Having talked so far much about the queen, let us return to the sebaste and to the emperor and, if it seems right, let us talk about them separately.

About the Death of the Augusta

LXIX. Perhaps the emperor (according to much widespread talk about this) was planning a future kingdom destined for her. I have no idea how this was to be accomplished but he did indulge himself in the prospect with pleasure. However his proposed projects and her hopes were cut short, because she was suddenly taken away by an illness resistant to any medical art and any remedy. Not responding to any of the treatments applied, she suffered chest pains and was terribly sick with asthma. So the young woman who had visualized the greatest things for herself, was prematurely deprived of all her hopes and expectations.

LXX. I could have omitted from the main text of my history everything the emperor did upon her death, his crying and lamentations, the acts he performed and the sobs of deep distress in which he indulged in his suffering . . . Petty talk and discussion of minor details are not appropriate for an historian . . . Yet I have such a style in some spots myself . . . because the rules of history are not rigid and do not require us to abstain from occasional side trips and digressions . . .

From a Greek-and-French edition
by E. Renauld, Vol. I, 1967.

Skleraina, the "sebaste" and mistress of Constantine IX, was buried in a beautiful site at the monastery of Mangana, next to the spot the emperor had reserved for himself. When he died, about ten years later, Constantine IX was buried next to his beloved niece and not near his wife, empress Zoe, who had predeceased him. In the last years of his reign, Constantine IX showed sudden changes in his favors and began to dislike or hate a number of his associates and former friends. Michael Psellos and other scholars of that circle, prudently left the court and retired temporarily to a monastery on the mainland of Greece. When he was writing his history, after he had returned to the court to serve as an intimate adviser of the next two kings, Psellos reported that Constantine IX had missed him.

CHRONOGRAPHIA
by Michael Psellos, *continued.*

CCI. After he was deprived of our guidance and received no more the grace of the lyre of reason, he (the king) ran again into the shelter of sensual attractions. In the middle of an orchard, full of all kinds of fruit, he had excavated a deep swimming pool, had the ground around it all leveled and then had it filled with running water. If then someone, not aware of the excavation in the middle of the orchard, suddenly reached for an apple or a pear, he promptly fell in the water, sinking down to the bottom, before he struggled to swim back on the surface. All this seemed very amusing to the emperor. Not to limit his games to the swimming pool, he also had built a charming pavilion with magnificent landscaping around it. Sometime later, however, swimming in the warm water many times daily and going in and out, he (the king) was affected by the wind and suffered a sort of pleurisy. At first this did not seem to have hurt him, but afterwards, the virus extended to his insides and involved the inner tissues and membranes.

CCII. Despairing about his survival, he lay in bed like a sacrificial victim, in the worst mood about dying, without any thought of transferring the royal power to queen Theodora, but hiding his intentions concerning her, he was secretly searching for a royal successor. As it was impossible not to detect his intentions, his plans were communicated to Theodora. She promptly boarded an imperial vessel with the best of her entourage and, as if borne by the waves, she was carried to the royal courts. Once there, she had the entire staff come to her. The fact that she had been born in the (royal) purple, the gentleness of her soul and the sufferings of her earlier life had an overwhelming effect on everyone. The king was very disturbed hearing about these events and that added to his pains. As it did not seem possible either to cure his illness or to come to a wise decision, he quickly suppressed his reasoning, closed his eyes and allowed his thoughts and his tongue to wander. Then, for a short while, he regained consciousness and recognizing the gravity of his affliction, grudgingly gave up the spirit.

XXIII. So this was how the emperor Constantine Monomakhos ended his life, after he had reigned twelve years, mostly having done well in his public works and having left with his character not a small example for those who desire to live the best life. If, in fact, we were to dismiss his tendency for acute sudden fits of anger, he was otherwise the kindest of all men. His history seems somewhat erratic due to his moodiness. The change in himself and the different phases of his personality were reflected in the course of his reign. My narrative is not a rhetorical exercise but the true record, a sympathetic description of the emperor as he really was.

Death and tenderness in Constantinople

The aging princess Theodora, Zoe's unmarried sister, reigned for a year after the death of her brother-in-law Constantine IX. The almost cynical description of Theodora's death by the contemporary historian M. Psellos presented a striking contrast to the sensitive lines of a dignitary from Lesbos, who also lived in Constantinople at that time and wrote a tender poem on the death of his young sister.

> **THE REIGN OF THE EMPRESS THEODORA**
> (1055-1056 A.D.)
>
> **I.** When he (Constantine IX) died, the supreme rule passed into the hands of Theodora, the daughter of Constantine (VIII). It was generally expected that she would entrust the government to one of the prominent noblemen, yet, against all expectations and beliefs, she assumed herself the duties of a Roman sovereign.
>
> . . . .
>
> **XVII.** The Ecumenical Patriarch was then Michael—Kerularios (16)—   . . . Although she had been very friendly to him before she became empress, . . . once she was well established in power, she began to hate the man, and refused even to meet with him. There was a reason for this: the patriarch was very upset because the Roman Empire was under the rule of a woman . . . and he spoke his mind freely . . .
>
> **XVIII.** There were people (who influenced the empress) . . . who acted like angelic creatures . . . but were at heart hypocrites . . . They behaved as if they were demi-gods . . . uttered prophecies with the assurance of an oracle and (some) professed to change the laws of nature. They claimed to make immortal the perishable human body and to arrest the natural changes which affect it. It was told that they always carried arms, like the ancient Acarnanians (20) . . . Well, these were the men who led the empress astray, telling her that she would live forever and with their deceit very nearly ruined her and destroyed the entire state too.
>
> . . . .

XIX-XXI. The fact was that she was afflicted by a very serious illness. Her excretory process broke down, she lost all appetite, started to vomit and then suffered with violent diarrhea. An almost total emptying of her intestines left her at death's door. . . . When it appeared that she was about to die, the counsellors chose . . . a successor, who might have been the best candidate, except that he was the type to be ruled by others rather than to rule, . . . verging on old age and with his hair almost all white . . . Without hesitation she crowned him as her successor, then lingered on for a while and died, four months before the year's end (1056 A.D.).

From a Greek-and-French edition by E. Renauld, Vol. II, 1967.

More personal and much more common than the historical texts about royalty and wars in the medieval Greek world were writings of church hymns, oratory and short epigrammatic verses on a variety of subjects. A native of Lesbos, Christophoros of Mytilene (about 1000–1050 A.D.), who served as a proconsul, a "patrikios" of the Byzantine State and as a judge in Paphlagonia, composed religious poems in ancient meters and may have been the originator of verse calendars, dry ritualistic couplets commemorating saints, holy martyrs and various feasts for every day of each month (Trypanis, 1981, p. 459). Christophoros also wrote numerous iambic verses praising kings, congratulating church leaders, expressing sympathy, or giving advice and is considered "a major epigrammatist" of the eleventh century (Trypanis, 1981, p. 474). Nearly 150 of these short poems have survived and they include inscriptions [*epigrams* in the literal sense] for public art works and for religious images. The poem on the death of his sister Anastasia is "truly moving" (*ibid.* p. 474).

On the death of Anastasia
by Christophoros of Mytilene, c. 1000-1050 A.D.
Black death has now taken a rose-like young woman
She lies on her bed like a sapling cut down
Resting all wrapped with virtue's tight wreath
She brilliantly shines even though lying dead.
Rain-bearing clouds come shed your wet tears
for the light of the liveliest maiden is suddenly gone
Let all eyes weep for her with compassion
All mouths be ready to tell of her virtues
In my heart, I, your brother, grieve for you, oh, my sweetest.
Like a cypress inside here you lie,
My own dearest sister, having left us in deep sorrow.
Sound the lyres of good words, all you lovers of learning.
With phrases of praise crown this exquisite maid.
. . . .
. . . .
As your bier is being raised I sorely lament
For they carry you to your grave, maid with the liveliest complexion.
    Translated from the Greek in Trypanis, 1981, pp. 439-440.

Christophoros' riddle-like epigram on *The Hours* reflects the lighter and more sparkling style of this Byzantine dignitary from Lesbos. Its seven lines may meaningfully conclude the second millennium of the island's three-thousand-year history.

> **The Hours**
> by Christophoros of Mytilene, 1000-1050 A.D.
> We are true sisters with no life in us
> each one older than another
> yet we are all equal as the time goes on.
> We regularly call never opening one mouth
> and keep marching on though we do not have legs
> You can see we are here now speaking to you,
> but were you to look, you could find us all over.
> Translated from the Greek in Trypanis, 1981, p. 441.

The secular poems of Christophoros, which are regarded as "a relief... after the soulless verse" of Byzantine literature and comparable to those of "the best epigrammatists of antiquity... with their wit, elegance and delicacy of feeling" (Trypanis, 1981, p. 474) sensitively reflect the sparkle and the sadness in the Greek world at the beginning of the new millennium.

Chapter VI

COLLAPSING FENCES AND DEFENSES

A. Agony and progeny
   The "first woman historian": Anna Komnena
   A Turkish rebel on Lesbos
   The crossing of the crusaders

B. Fatal family feuds
   Byzantine civil wars
   Latins in the Levant
   Lesbos Genoese

C. The Ottoman conquest
   The Turks in Europe
   The fall of Lesbos, 1462 A.D.

Audience in the court of the Turkish sultan, Suleiman "The Magnificent," Constantinople, sixteenth century A.D., from the Topkapi Palace Museum.

Overleaf: Mohammed II (also written *Mehmed*), "the Conqueror," 1430–1481, Ottoman Turkish sultan who captured Constantinople and destroyed the Byzantine State; in Ridpath 1885, p. 934.

A. AGONY AND PROGENY

In the second half of the eleventh century there was a breakdown of the fences that presumably marked and safeguarded the boundaries of the East Roman Empire. People and patterns of integrated social living moved across the lines of Byzantine culture both in the direction of expansion—as was the spread of Christianity to the northern Slavic nations—and also of infiltration, when much of what was Greek-Byzantine Asia Minor was gradually conquered by invading Turkish tribes. The central government in Constantinople changed hands and policies repeatedly and there were disastrous deficiencies in its organization and function. In the twenty-five years after the death of empress Theodora in 1056 A.D., the throne was occupied by six successive rulers, including one more woman, the clever and ambitious young widow of Constantine X, Eudokia. Another widowed empress, the exotically beautiful Maria of Alania (1) was also for a while left in the palace alone and was in part responsible for the end of the imperial instability, when she helped the young general, Alexios Komnenos (often transliterated Comnenus) stage a coup and ascend the throne, in 1081 A.D.

It took a few years but eventually Alexios consolidated his position on the throne and also repulsed foreign attacks and recaptured much territory after fighting successfully against the invading Slavs, Normans and Turks (Table K). Imperial strategy also saved Lesbos from an aggressive Turkish lord, the rebellious emir of Smyrna. The Komnenos royal dynasty established by Alexios I lasted for over one hundred years, a period of great dangers, military triumphs and setbacks, but also of high learning and cultural ferment anticipating by hundreds of years the Italian Renaissance.

The "first woman historian": Anna Komnena

The rise of Alexios, his ascent to the Byzantine throne and his struggles against internal foes and foreign invaders were narrated in captivating detail by his own daughter, Anna Komnena (2). Anna was born on December 2, 1083, during the second year of her father's reign, so she was a *porphyrogeneta* (cf. Chapter V), "born in the purple." This "first woman historian" (Dalven, 1972, *Introduction*) included in her book a note about her own birth, as the first child of the royal couple, Irene and Alexios.

THE ALEXIAD
by Anna Komnena, 1083–1153/55 A.D.
Book VI
8. Then the king . . . carrying the laurels of victory returned to the queen of the cities . . . the first of December of the seventh

indiction (3) and found the queen in labor pains, in the chamber designated from old times for the confinement of empresses. Traditionally this had been called the purple room and from it the name "born-in-the-purple" [*porphyrogenetos*] has been adopted throughout the world. About early dawn (it was Saturday) a female child was born to them, who, as they said, looked very much like her father. I was that baby.
Translated from the Greek in Leib, Vol. II, 1967, pp.60-61.

After a life of intense personal involvement with political events and palace plots (she conspired to eliminate her brother and to obtain the throne for her husband and herself), Anna died in 1153—or 1155?—in the relative isolation of the convent of The Most Gracious Mother of God, which had been built by her mother.

Anna probably completed the history of her father's reign about 1148 A.D. The title "The Alexiad" was chosen to reflect the epic proportions of the accomplishments of emperor Alexios, to be compared to those described by Homer in the Iliad. The king's daughter was indeed very familiar with ancient Greek as well as with Christian literature and quoted both abundantly in her work. This unique and extremely valuable record of the history of the "Roman" (1) state during the last quarter of the eleventh and the first part of the twelfth centuries remained virtually unknown for over 400 years (Dalven, 1972, Preface). A manuscript bought in Munich was abridged and published in 1618 and 30 years later a translation of it appeared in French. The Greek text with a Latin translation was published later in the same century. A twelfth century manuscript found in Florence, Italy, was the basis for a three-volume bilingual publication in Greek and French by B. Leib (1937–45). This has been the primary text for the present English version. Complete translations in English previously have been made by Elizabeth Dawn in 1928 and by E.R.A. Sewter in 1969. The frequently reprinted work of this British authority has been a valuable reference for ren-

Emperor Alexios I.
Vatican Library, Greek manuscript.

dering the lively though somewhat archaic Greek of Anna Komnena into English in this volume.

The first two chapters or "books" (*biblia* in the original Greek) of the Alexiad covered the early exploits of general Alexios Komnenos, from his volunteering, at age 14, to join the military campaign against the Turks, to his clever and shrewd dealings with his numerous internal and external (Turks, Normans, Franks, Slavs, etc.) foes. The princess-historian described the plots and intrigues in and near the Byzantine capital, Constantinople, which forced the abdication of emperor Nikephoros Botaneiates in 1081 A.D. Book III provided vivid personal portraits of Alexios, of his wife Irene, and of members of their families. Books IV, V and VI were primarily concerned with the series of battles of the general and, later, emperor Alexios, against the Normans, who had invaded the western Greek mainland from Sicily, against the "Scythian" (1) aggressors from the north, and also against the Seljuk Turks in Asia Minor. Also narrated were the internal conflicts with fanatical Christian "heretics" and other religious and military factions. Book VII continued with the wars in the Balkans against the Scythians and described their crushing defeat by the "Roman" (1) armies of Alexios. It then switched to the Turkish provincial lord from the Greek city of Smyrna (modern Turkish *Ismir*) who had attacked Lesbos as part of his plan to take over the entire Byzantine state.

A Turkish rebel on Lesbos

The name of the aggressive lord—*emir*—of Smyrna was Tzakhas, which according to Anna's writing was to be pronounced Tzahas. It is spelled *Chaka* in recent English publications, possibly to approximate the original Turkish phonetics (Runciman, 1957, pp. 65, 72, 182, 194). Tzakhas was one of the regional Seljuk chiefs (4) who had taken advantage of the Turkish penetration into Asia Minor. He had spent much of his youth as a hostage in Constantinople and there he had learned the manners and military tactics of the Greeks. "More ambitious than most of his compatriots" (Runciman, 1957, pp. 77-78), Tzakhas tried to form a Turkish alliance against the Greeks and for this purpose he had even arranged for his daughter to marry the powerful young Turk, Kilij Arslan, the sultan established in Nicaea [*Nikaia*], closer to the Byzantine capital. He also built a large fleet, and for greater efficiency hired many Greek sailors in preference to Turks (Runciman, 1957, p. 77). Between 1080 and 1090 A.D. Tzakhas managed to conquer most of the Aegean coast of western Asia Minor and also invaded the islands of Lesbos, Khios

[*Hios*], Samos and Rhodos. In the spring of 1088 (3) the elite Byzantine army of Alexios, with Latin cavalry and knights from Flanders had to rush to Asia Minor after a successful campaign against the Scythians in the north, to defend the remaining Greek territories against another Turkish attack.

THE ALEXIAD
by Anna Komnena, 1083–1153/55 A.D.
Book VII
8, 1-3. At that time Tzakhas, certainly aware of the king's many troubles in the west and his frequent wars with the Patzinaks (4), seized the opportunity and decided that he needed to build a fleet. He found someone from Smyrna who had much experience with such projects and assigned to him the construction of the pirate vessels. When this man had built for him a large number of ships, including forty decked ships of chase, he manned them with experienced crews and sailed to attack Klazomenai, which he stormed and conquered. Then he left for Phokaia, which he also attacked and captured. From there he sent a messenger to Alopos, the curator entrusted to govern Mitylene (5) threatening him with terrible treatment if he did not leave from there immediately. Pretending that it was out of concern for him personally, he warned him about the awful fate that awaited him if he did not get away. Terrified by Tzakhas' threats, the man boarded a ship at night and left Mitylene for the capital. Upon learning this, Tzakhas took off without delay and captured it. But the city of Methymna, which is located on a promontory at the other end of the island, did not submit to Tzakhas and the king, informed about this, promptly dispatched a mighty force on ships and built its defenses. Tzakhas, however, made no plans against Methymna and, instead, departed for Khios, which he stormed and subdued. Upon hearing this, the emperor sent against him a fleet with a good number of able soldiers and made Niketas Kastamonitis their leader. This man then took off but upon encountering Tzakhas in battle he was defeated and Tzakhas took from him the ships under his command. When the king was informed what had happened to Kastamonitis, he equipped another fleet and placed it under the command of Constantine Dalassenos, a most capable warrior who was also related to him on the maternal side. Then he, upon reaching the coast of Khios, began the siege, eager for battle and hurrying to capture the city before Tzakhas caught up with him from Smyrna.

Leib, Vol. II, 1967, pp. 110–111.

After describing in detail the maneuvers of Tzakhas' forces and those of the Greeks or "Romans" under Dalassenos on and around the island of Khios and on the mainland, Anna concluded this story with a report about the attempts to negotiate peace and the subsequent return of the victorious Byzantine navy to Lesbos.

THE ALEXIAD
by Anna Komnena, (continued)
Book VII
8, 5-9. Tzakhas . . . sent a proposal to Dalassenos, pretending that he wanted to talk about peace. The latter made it known to Tzakhas that he would come out to the end of the camp to listen and to talk about anything, so that they both could reach an agreement. The barbarian did not easily consent to that, but the next morning both he and the general went for that meeting. Tzakhas started the talk, addressing him (Dalassenos) by name: "You must know that I am that young guy who was chasing all over Asia and fighting bravely but due to his inexperience he was misdirected and was captured by that (general) Alexios Kabalikas. From there, I was taken by him prisoner to the emperor, Nikephoros Botaneiates. Soon I was honored by him with the title of protonobilissimos (6) and after I received generous grants, I promised to serve him well. However, since the reins of the kingdom were taken over by Alexios Komnenos, everything fell apart. So I came here to present to you the causes of my hostility. Let the emperor too know about this and if he wishes to erase the enmity that has erupted, let him render to me everything that has been due and has been withheld from me. Moreover, if it seems right for you also to have our children joined in marriage, let a contract between us be prepared in writing, as is the custom of the Romans and of us barbarians too. If everything I have outlined is accomplished, I will return all the islands that I have raided and taken from the Roman authorities, through you to the emperor and when I finalize my treaty with him I will go back to my home country." Dalassenos, having known for a long time the deceitful mentality of the Turks, considered all that as false pretenses. So he deferred any action on the proposal, while he tried to expose what hidden understanding he had concerning his opponent by answering him this way: "You will neither return the islands to me as you just said, nor will I be able to act as you requested, without knowing the wishes of the emperor. But now that the grand duke John [*Ioannis*], the emperor's brother-in-law, is on his way with all the navy and is coming down having gathered all his men and his naval force, let him listen to what you have to say. You know well that only this way, only if he is the peace negotiator, the treaty with the emperor will be concluded."

. . . This John Doukas had spent eleven years fighting near Dyrrhakhion (7) . . . He was a most capable warrior . . . and never disobeyed orders so the emperor decided to send him against Tzakhas . . . Because he was expecting him at the time of his talk with Tzakhas, Dalassenos made it clear that all decisions were to be referred to the arriving Doukas. On his side, Tzakhas seemed to be acting according to the line in the Homeric epic poem: "The night has already fallen and it is good to let the night prevail" (8). He promised to bring many of the needed provisions when day broke. But it was all treachery and deceit and Dalassenos never deviated from his own goals. In fact, in early dawn Tzakhas stealthily sailed down the coast of Khios and, catching a favorable wind, reached

Smyrna to gather more forces and to return immediately to the conquest of Khios. But Dalassenos never showed himself inferior to Tzakhas' machinations. He boarded the available ships with the men under him and got control of Bolissos. He left the ships well-equipped, set up more siege machines and after he allowed his soldiers some rest and added more to his forces, he returned where he had started. Then he engaged in a fierce battle against the barbarians and after he demolished the walls, he got hold of the city, while Tzakhas was still back in Smyrna. Afterwards, finding the sea calm and without waves, he sailed smoothly with his entire fleet and reached directly Mitylene.

9, 1. The emperor had thus taken care of his conflict with Tzakhas when he learned that the Scythians were marching against Rousion.

Leib, Vol.II, 1967, pp. 113-116.

More wars and attempted revolts occupied Chapter VIII of the Alexiad. The emperor had barely succeeded in defending his western front against the Norman invasion when the Patzinaks (4)—or Pechenegs—attacked from the north. In a combined strategy with Tzakhas, they reached Constantinople in the winter of 1090–91 and lay siege to the capital (Ostrogorsky, 1965, p. 360). Alexios was able to reverse the critical situation only by inciting another "barbarian" Turkic group (4) the Cumans, or Komans (Enc. Brit. Vol. 13) to attack the Patzinaks from behind. That enabled the desperately fighting Byzantines, Anna's "Romans," to defeat the invaders and, in April 1091 to finish them as a distinct ethnic population.

THE ALEXIAD
by Anna Komnena, (continued)
Book VIII
5, 2. . . . seeing the Romans terrified, God unexpectedly granted them the victory, even when they had lost all hope for survival. They captured, slaughtered, or enslaved the Scythians to the point that their entire nation, tens of thousands of people, became extinct in only one day.

Leib, Vol. II, 1967, pp. 143-44.

According to Anna, when her father Alexios was asked to have all the prisoners killed too, for fear that the other barbarians, the Cumans, might change sides and free them, the victorious king replied:

Book VIII
6, 1. "They may be Scythians but they are still human; even though they are our enemies, they are entitled to our mercy."

Leib, Vol. II, 1967, p. 144

Consequently, the captives were kept as slaves (9) and most of them were put to serve at Byzantine military outposts.

The military and diplomatic strategy of emperor Alexios stopped the barbarian threat against his capital but the Turkish menace to the Greeks of the eastern Aegean did not end until 1092, when Tzakhas was murdered by his dinner host and son-in-law, Kilij Arslan, who had been induced by a personal note from emperor Alexios to believe that his own safety and survival made this killing necessary.

THE ALEXIAD
by Anna Komnena, (continued)
Book IX
1, 2-9. . . . Not much time passed and the emperor received more precise information about the activities of Tzakhas. Nothing that had happened to him at sea and on the land had made that man give up his original intentions. On the contrary, he began to wear the insignia befitting royalty, calling himself king and establishing himself in Smyrna as if it were his kingdom. Again he got a fleet ready with which he could ravage the islands and reach Byzantium itself, so that, if it were possible, he might attain the supreme royal position. The emperor kept receiving every day confirmation of these actions and knew that there ought to be no relaxation of effort and no weakening of purpose. Between the end of that spring (3) and the following winter he would have to make preparations so that by the following spring he could launch a vigorous attack against Tzakhas, not only to prove, by all means, that all his projects, expectations and exploits were purposeless, but also to expel him from Smyrna itself and to take back from him everything he had managed to seize. Then, after the winter had passed and the smiling spring had arrived, the king recalled from Epidamnos (7) his brother-in-law, John Doukas and appointed him grand-duke of the navy. He gave him an army of select continental troops and ordered him to cross over by land and to move against Tzakhas. He directed him to delegate the command of the fleet to Constantine Dalassenos, who was to sail down along the coast, so they would arrive in Mitylene at the same time by sea and over land, to engage Tzakhas in battle. As soon as he reached Mitylene, Doukas erected wooden towers in a hurry and, using these as his base of operations, organized a forceful campaign against the barbarians. Initially, Tzakhas had entrusted the defense of Mitylene to his brother Galabatzes, but when he realized that the man was not an adequate match to fight such an opponent, he rushed back himself, formed a battle line and engaged Doukas. The fight was still going strong when nightfall put an end to it. From then on and during three mooncycles Doukas did not relent but attacked the walls of Mitylene every day and engaged Tzakhas in brilliant combat from sunrise to sunset. Despite all efforts, however, Doukas accomplished nothing and the emperor, informed about this, was disturbed and worried. One day he questioned a soldier who had come from

there and when he learned that Doukas did nothing else but fight and make war, he inquired about the circumstances and the timing of the battle against Tzakhas. When that man said that they started as soon as the sun rose, the king promptly asked: "Which of the combatants faces east?" and the soldier answered: "Our armies." Whereupon, the king recognized the problem and always quick to realize what had to be done, he drafted a letter to Doukas, advising him to stop attacking Tzakhas at dawn, to avoid this way being one fighting against two, meaning against Tzakhas and also the rays of the sun; instead, he was to attack the enemy at noon, when the sun had crossed the meridian line towards the west. He handed the letter to the soldier with repeated orders about this and finally he declared emphatically: "If you attack the enemy when the sun begins to set, you will quickly be victorious." Doukas received this message from the soldier and, as he had never disregarded any advice from the emperor, when the next day the barbarians as usual were armed and ready, none of their adversaries appeared (because the Roman units kept quiet, as the emperor had admonished them). Not expecting to fight that day, they put down their arms and stayed where they were. But Doukas did not keep quiet; by the time the sun reached the zenith, he and all his forces were fully armed. And when the sun began to go down, they suddenly fell upon the barbarians in battle line formation and with war cries and roar. Yet Tzakhas did not seem to have been unprepared and his men, armed powerfully, engaged the Roman units promptly in battle. A strong wind then began to blow and as the battle reached its peak, the dust rose up to the sky. With the sun shining against their faces and their sight in a way blocked by the dust while the Romans attacked more strongly than ever, the barbarians turned back and were defeated. Thus, eventually, Tzakhas, not able to withstand the siege anymore and not equipped for continuous battle, sued for peace, requesting only to be allowed to sail away without harm to Smyrna. Doukas was persuaded after he received as hostages two of the highest officers [*satraps*]. On his side, Tzakhas also asked Doukas for guarantees. On condition that noone in Mitylene was to be treated badly or be carried away as they sailed to Smyrna, he (Doukas) gave him Alexander Euphorbenos and Manuel Boutoumites, both of them seasoned and brave warriors. Having thus received each other's assurances, they felt no more concern, the one about Tzakhas causing harm to the people of Mitylene as he left and he, in turn, about being ill-treated by the Roman fleet as he crossed the sea. But the crab has never learned to walk straight and neither did Tzakhas ever give up his original wickedness. So he did try to carry away with him all the people of Mitylene, with women and children. While this was happening, Constantine Dalassenos, who was the admiral of the fleet and had not yet arrived but following the orders he had received from Doukas had anchored his ships by a promontory, the moment he heard about that, came and requested from Doukas to be allowed to engage Tzakhas in battle. Honoring his oath, Doukas initially deferred any action. But Dalassenos persisted, saying something like this: "You have sworn but I was not present. So you may keep unbroken the assurances you gave, but as I was not there, I did not take an oath and did not even know what was the agreement between you two, I can let myself go and make war against Tzakhas." So when Tzakhas had raised anchor and with everything he had was sailing away straight for Smyrna, Dalassenos caught up with him faster than it could be told and immediately attacked and pursued him. But Doukas also, catching up with the rest of Tzakhas' fleet as it raised anchor, captured the ships and freed all the prisoners of war and all the other bound captives from the barbarians' hands. Dalassenos also seized many of Tzakhas' pirate ships and ordered the extermination of all on board, including the rowing crews. Tzakhas himself would have been captured if he were not that tricky and, sensing what was about to happen, had not moved to one of the lighter ships and without being detected had escaped and saved himself. In fact, suspecting what might happen to him, he had placed Turks on a promontory to stand and watch until either he reached safely Smyrna or, if he had any encounter with his enemy, he could dock his ship near there and find shelter. His aim was not off the mark and he did reach the coast near there and after he joined the Turks who received him, made his way to Smyrna and finally arrived there. Dalassenos returned victorious and joined the Grand Duke. Doukas then fortified Mitylene and after Dalassenos returned, he detached a major part of the fleet and sent it against the possessions of Tzakhas (who had captured a good number of islands). Then, after he attacked and conquered Samos and some other islands, he returned to the capital.

Leib, Vol. II, 1967, pp. 157-162.

The next section of Book IX was devoted to the imperial campaign against rebels on the islands of Cyprus and Crete. Then it returned to the story of Tzakhas and to the end of this aggressive Turk at the hands of his son-in-law in 1092 A.D.

THE ALEXIAD
by Anna Komnena
Book IX
3, 1-4. These were the events on the islands and here I am talking about Cyprus and Crete. Then Tzakhas, warlike [*philopolemos*] as he was, would not allow his enterprising activity to quiet down and not long afterwards descended upon Smyrna and occupied it again. Immediately he began with great care to build pirate ships, fast cruisers, diremes and triremes and also other lighter boats, still possessed by his own original plans. As soon as the emperor learned about this, without being discouraged, he did not tarry one moment but rushed to oppose him both by sea and by land. He appointed Constantine Dalassenos as chief admiral and sent him with the entire navy against Tzakhas. He also considered it to his advantage to stir the sultan against him (Tzakhas) and sent to the former a letter like this: "You know, most

distinguished sultan Klitziasthlan (Anna's spelling for Kilij Arslan II, the Turkish "Sultan of Rum" from Iconium, 1156-92 A.D.; cf. notes 17 and 20) that this dignified royal position belongs to you from your fathers. But your father-in-law, although he appears to arm himself against the Roman kingdom and calls himself king, is doing this clearly as a pretext. With his experience and thorough knowledge, he cannot ignore the fact that the Roman kingdom is not for him and that it will be impossible for him to seize that power. The whole vicious machination is prepared against you. You must not therefore tolerate this nor feel intimidated, but must be on the alert, so that you may not be deposed from your royal power. I, with the help of God, will chase him out of the Roman kingdom's borders. But I worry about you and warn you to take care of your own power and position and, whether peacefully or, if he does not comply, with the sword, to hurry and subdue him." While the king was taking these steps, Tzakhas with his forces reached Abydos by land and surrounded to it with siege machines and all kinds of rock-throwing equipment. The pirate ships were not ready yet and were not with him. In the meantime Dalassenos, a very high-spirited man who loved danger, steered with his forces towards Abydos. The sultan Klitziasthlan on his part, after receiving the king's message, acted immediately and took the road against Tzakhas, to engage him with all his army. This is how the barbarians are, always ready for slaughter and war. When the sultan came quite near and Tzakhas saw his enemies attacking from the land and the sea, while none of his ships still under construction were there and his forces inadequate to fight both against the Romans and his relative Klitziasthlan, he was at a loss. Fearing also the people and the soldiers of Abydos, he decided to go to the sultan, not knowing the plot fomented against him by the emperor. Seeing him, the sultan showed a smiling face and received him gladly. As customary, a table was prepared and as they dined together, he forced Tzakhas to drink more and more heavily. When he noticed that the man was loaded with wine, he (the sultan) pulled his sword and plunged it into his flank. Tzakhas fell dead on the spot. Then the sultan sent delegates to the emperor to settle in peace and they did not fail in their goal. The emperor accepted this request and after the peace treaty was concluded according to custom, stability was restored in the provinces along the sea coast.

Leib, Vol. II, 1967, pp. 164-166.

The name of Tzakhas appeared again in Anna's "Alexiad" as it did also in Runciman's "History of the Crusades," in connection with the siege by the western crusaders of the city of Nicaea [*Nikaia*] and its capture by the Byzantines (Runciman, p. 182). This Turkish emir was probably the son and successor of the earlier ruler of Smyrna. The release of the sultan's captive sister, his wife (the daughter of Tzakhas) and children by the Greeks without ransom may have shown that "Alexios was a kindly man, and he well knew the values of courtesy to a defeated enemy," but it made the crusaders consider him "double-faced and disloyal" (Runciman, p. 182).

After capturing and refortifying Nicaea, emperor Alexios sent his brother-in-law, John Doukas, to reconquer Ionia and Phrygia. In his final thrust to liberate Smyrna and the islands of Lesbos, Khios and Samos, Doukas, to intimidate the Turks, carried with him the captive Sultana, daughter of the older and probably sister of the younger Tzakhas. When, after a successful combined land and sea attack, the young Tzakhas surrendered to the Greeks, he was allowed to take the captives with him and to withdraw to the inner land of eastern Anatolia (Runciman, p. 194). By 1097 A.D., the great cities of Philadelphia and Sardis with all the region of Lydia were again in Greek hands.

The last six chapters of "The Alexiad" (Books X–XV) continued with descriptions of battles against Turks, Normans and others and devoted considerable attention to the crossing through the empire of the first crusade, 1097–1104 A.D. Domestic troubles, conspiracies and heresies were also treated in much detail. Along with all these were comments about the educational standards and the flourishing Greek culture, especially in the capital of Constantinople. The final illness of Alexios I Komnenos and his death, in 1118, were given in detail in the last several pages of his daughter's history book.

The Crossing of the Crusades

The same year of Alexios' death, 1118, the doge of Venice, Ordelafo Falier (9) was killed in battle, after a sixteen-year rule (Norwich, 1982, p. 86). Under the next doge, Domenico Michiel (1118-1130), and the heir of Alexios, John II Komnenos (1118-1143), there was an escalation of the friction and renewed hostilities between Byzantium and the Venetian Republic. When their commercial privileges—granted by Alexios—were terminated by the new Byzantine king, the Venetians diverted the course of their large fleet "with over seventy men-of-war" (Chalandon, Vol. II (1), p. 157; Norwich, 1982, p. 88) and sailed north across the Aegean sea. They "raided and plundered Lesbos and Khios . . . before dropping anchor, in the end of May 1123, in the port of Acre" their original goal in Palestine (Norwich, 1982, p. 88).

The second (1147–1149) and third (1189–1192) crusades (Table VI-1) again harassed the Greek Orthodox populations of Asia Minor and the Near East. Even though some farmers and traders profited, most of the people felt mistreated and were actually vandalized. The French king spent much of his campaign budget paying (at times overpaying) for the damages inflicted by the crusading armies on their fellow Christians of the East. In November 1147, the crusading French and German kings, Louis VII and Conrad III, on their way to liberate Jerusalem, took their forces across the Bosphorus and along the western coast of Asia Minor, to avoid the dangerous central mountainous region, to ensure better availability of supplies and to remain in touch with the Byzantine fleet. Louis and his wife, Eleanor of Aquitaine, with many couples of the French nobility and their troupes, passed through Adramyttium [*Adramyttion*] across the narrow strait from Lesbos. Then, about one day ahead of the Germans, they marched down to Ephesus [*Ephesos*], where the French royal couple spent four days before proceeding on their disastrous expedition to the Holy Land (Runciman, S.: 1951/90, Vol. II, p. 269).

Table VI-1
THE FIRST FOUR CRUSADES CROSSING GREEK TERRITORIES

I.	1095–99 A.D.	Following the first disorganized crowds, western crusading armies crossed the Balkans, reached Constantinople and with Byzantine help sailed across to Asia Minor, ravaging the countryside on the way to the Holy Land. After many disasters the crusaders captured Jerusalem in June 1099 and formed Latin States in Palestine and Syria. A rich Lesbian eunuch left Constantinople and stayed for a while in Palestine to avoid problems with the authorities in the capital.
II.	1147–49	Christian armies were defeated by the Turks in Asia Minor. The French king Louis VII and his wife, Eleanor of Aquitaine, stopped at Adramyttion, across the straits from Lesbos, on their way to Antioch and to the Holy Land. The German king Conrad III followed, but fell ill and returned to Constantinople, later sailing south by Lesbos to fight the Moslems at Acre.
III.	1189–92	The French and English kings Phillip II and Richard I tried unsuccessfully to recapture Jerusalem and Acre, sailing south of the Aegean Sea on their way. The German Holy Roman emperor Frederick I led his armies though western Asia Minor, not far inland from Lesbos, but drowned crossing a river.
IV.	1203–04	Led by the Venetian doge Enrico Dandolo, crusaders on Venitian ships sailed past Lesbos, went through the Hellespont and, in collusion with the deposed Byzantine king, attacked and captured Constantinople. Thus was established the short-lived Eastern Latin Empire, which included Lesbos.

The Greek historian of the years 1118–76 following the death of Alexios I, was John Cinnamus [*Ioannes Kinnamos*], who was born "sometime after 1143 of distinguished parents" (Ostrogorsky, p. 352), served as imperial secretary of king Manuel I Komnenos (the son and successor of John II) and was "probably an eyewitness" (*Encycl. Brit.*, Vol. V) of the events in the last decade of his historical work, which ends abruptly, possibly due to the mutilation of the last part of the single surviving thirteenth century manuscript. Another Greek historian of that period (1118-1207), Niketas Choniates [*Khoniates*], made no mention of the work of Cinnamus, probably because "it was an unpublished manuscript known only to the imperial secretaries" (Magoulias, HR, 1984, *Introduction*, p. xvii). *Cinnamus' History* was first edited and published in France under the patronage of king Louis XIV, by Charles Du Fresne (1610-88), "the real founder of Byzantine studies" (Ostrogorsky, p. 4). Following a brief report of the contacts between the Latin king from Jerusalem and the Byzantine emperor in Constantinople, Cinnamus went on to bemoan the problems of the Greeks with the Venetian intruders.

HISTORY
by John Cinnamus [*I. Kinnamos*], twelfth century A.D.
Section L.VI (p. 164), 10, A-C
In the interval the king of Palestine (10) came to Byzantium to plead with the king for what was necessary. Having received what he needed, he pledged all kinds of things and above all service to the king. Also during that time, the king sent government inspectors to obtain a public record of the properties of all Venetians living in Byzantium (11) and anywhere else on Roman land . . . This race (the Venetians) is corrupt, foul-mouthed and niggardly, also being replete with the vulgarity of sailors. These people, after they aligned themselves with king Alexios . . . got immeasurably rich with their trading and this quickly led them to become very arrogant. They behaved towards the citizens, not only the ordinary crowd but even more so towards those who were most prominent, honored and respected among the Romans, as if these were lowly servants. Whereupon King John, extremely disturbed, ordered them expelled from the Roman territories. So they were thinking of ways to defend themselves against the Romans. Having a fleet, they took their ships against the land; they seized Khios and Rhodos and Lesbos, all of them well-known islands. Then they proceeded to conquer the land of Palestine and after laying siege to Tyre, they subdued it and, the evil demons, carried all their loot off by sea sparing noone. After all that, the king was induced to reconsider his previous order, which made them (the Venetians) even more arrogant and disdainful than before.

D. They did not act any better at all in the years of king Manuel, settling themselves with their wives next to the Romans and then coming like the rest of the Romans to make their homes outside the quarters assigned to them by the king.

Corp. Script. Hist. Byz., 1836, pp. 280-281.

A series of naval battles between the Byzantines—"Romans"—and the Venetians ensued and finally the Venetian fleet was forced to leave the area. Cinnamus referred to an imperial messenger who had originated from the island of Lesbos.

Section L.VI. (p. 166).10 C
At dawn the Roman fleet came to Lesbos but as soon as they heard the news (of the Venetian fleet leaving Khios) they chased after them . . .

. . . .

Section L.VII (p .135), 2,A-C
. . . Michael Gavras (12) with his army came to Amasia and asked those in the city to surrender it right away . . . The king, still fighting around Dorylaion, sent Thomas, the eunuch . . . to Amasia with a message, demanding an oath of allegiance . . . and threatening to come before long and punish them if they did not refrain from offending the Romans. Who was that Thomas I will now make clear. He came from Lesbos, from an obscure home and, having no worthwhile skills, after he went to Byzantium he engaged in cutting people's veins and that is how he made a living. But it seems that nobody can ever guess what fate is willing to bring our way. Thomas, even though characterized by the worst kind of vulgarity, with his lowly art he became one of the biggest men in the kingdom, made a great deal of money in a short time and with that he later departed for Palestine. There, however, he had a disagreement with the people and he soon came to present himself to the king. Though he was fortunate to receive his kind consideration, he soon turned out to be ill-tempered and was then taken to the palace guard, which by custom is called Elephantine and there he ended his life. But more about this later. After he presented himself to the sultan, as we were saying, he found that he (the Turkish ruler) was not willing to comply in any way and so he returned to the king without accomplishing anything and even barely escaped being murdered by the Persians (the author meant Turks) who laid an ambush by the roadside.

Corp. Script. Hist. Byz. pp. 284 and 296-297.

As the Greek historian indicated, the privileges of Venetian merchants throughout the Byzantine state were restored and near the end of the reign of King Manuel I, it was obvious that they were ruining the Byzantine economy and the people. The emperor tried to control the Venetians by concluding alliances with their Italian rivals, Genoa in 1169 and Pisa in 1170. That led to open conflict with Venice and in March 1171 all Venetians in the Byzantine empire were arrested and their properties confiscated. In retaliation, a strong Venetian fleet attacked coastal cities and (again) sacked the islands of Khios and Lesbos. Then the Venetians settled on Khios waiting for the outcome of new negotiations in

Constantinople. While they were camped on that island, a terrible plague decimated most of the Venetian forces and several encounters with the Byzantine navy resulted in more losses. The survivors of the failed expedition eventually made their way back to Venice (Norwich, 1982, p. 106). Relations between Venice and Byzantium were not resumed until ten years later, by the next emperor, Andronikos I (Ostrogorsky, p. 389).

The Byzantine State in the twelfth century continued to be convulsed by internal religious conflicts and "heresies." Reference to Lesbos during the reigns of John II and Manuel I was made repeatedly in connection with theological controversies requiring the attendance of Lesbian church officials at the special councils in Constantinople. From the beginning of his reign (1143-1180 A.D.) Manuel was heavily involved in religious affairs. He had to select immediately a successor to the patriarch, who had just died, so that he could be crowned by the new head of the Orthodox Church. That same year the new emperor was confronted by the reemergence and spread of the heretical sect of the Bogomils. This religious movement, which had started in the tenth century in Bulgaria, was radically opposed to all established authority and was against all ecclesiastical ritual, against all rulers, against the powerful and the wealthy. The Bogomils believed that the visible world was the work of Satan and that everything happening on earth resulted from the conflict between Good (God) and Evil (Satan). A fanatical monk, Niphon, preached the Bogomil faith, or "heresy," in the capital and even the patriarch in Constantinople, possibly in collusion with the emperor's brother, Isaac Komnenos (who may have been using the movement in a plot to replace the king) seemed sympathetic to it. The emperor found it necessary to convene major Church councils of all the regional high-priests, to defend orthodoxy—and his throne?—and to condemn the monk Niphon and the new heresy. Of the two twelfth century Greek historians who described the proceedings, one, N. Khoniates (Choniates), presented the "official version" (Chalandon, V. II-2, p. 636) while the other, G. Kinnamos, (Cinnamus), tended to favor the Bogomil cause and the patriarch Kosmas, who was accused of accepting it.

Attending the council [*synod*] meeting in 1147 to condemn the Bogomil heresy and to depose patriarch Kosmas, were several members of the imperial family—including Alexios, the son of Anna Komnena— and over twenty bishops and other church leaders. Among them was George, metropolitan of Methymna on Lesbos. A later church council, called by Manuel in Constantinople in 1157 to debate a new controversy concerning the sacrifice on the cross—whether it was for the Father and for the Holy Spirit only, or also for the Word [*Logos*]—likewise had among the participants the metropolitan of Methymna. Two other high church dignitaries from Lesbos, Pothos of Mytilene and Nicholas of Methymna, took part in the ecclesiastical council of 1166, which met in Constantinople, in the palace of Blakhernai "whose walls sparkled with gold and mosaics" (Khoniates, quoted by Chalandon, V. II-2, p. 648). The majority of the church fathers supported the emperor's theological views concerning the equality of the Father and the Son and his argument against a postulated inferior "human nature" of Christ (Chalandon, Vol. II-2, pp. 644-646). Obviously, both the emperor and the bishops delved enthusiastically in abstract theological debates. Manuel, however, tried to prevent the church officials from staying in the capital too long. The city had already many bishops and priests living there after they had been expelled from their homes by the Turks. So all those from a still free region were sent back expeditiously. Despite his profound religiosity, the king also "got rid of the pest . . . of the itinerant—vagabond—monks" (Chalandon, Vol. II(2), p. 633) that infested the attractive and seductive city of Constantinople.

As a direct result of the military buildup and the renewed strength under the Komnenos dynasty, the danger of piratical raids against the coastal areas was much diminished. By 1170 A.D. the people on Lesbos felt secure enough to begin building a new and magnificent cathedral dedicated to the ancient icon of the Holy Virgin, which the monk Agathon had brought from Jerusalem almost 400 years earlier (Chapter V). They selected a new site, not where the old monastery was but above it, away from the winter torrents that flooded the valley next to Mount Olympus. The place has since been called Ayiasos, after Holy Sion, (13) *Ayia Sion* in Greek. The Byzantine governor of Lesbos, Konstantine Valerios, granted a written permission, which read:

> As authorized by the glorious, virtuous and superior to all earthy worldliness, the great emperor of the entire Byzantine State,
> I, Konstantine Valerios, lord of all Lesbos headquartered at Mytilene,
>
> Cognizant of the prayers of the Christians residing in the area around a place called "Karya," where in a sacred shelter is enthroned an icon of the Most Holy Mother of God that came from Holy Sion, the possession of the faithful and obedient subjects of our glorious and world-ruling empire,
>
> I grant them freedom to build a House of God in the name and memory of our Most Holy Virgin, Mother-of-God on the site of the tomb of the monk-priest Agathon of Ephesos, who brought the holy icon here.

> VALERIOS, KONSTANTINOS
> Governor of all Lesbos
> From the Governor's Mansion, August 17, 1170.
> Copies of a manuscript found in Constantinople and taken to Lesbos in 1704.
> Quoted by Kleombrotos, I.G., 1982, pp. 12-13.

The church was completed in three years. It was smaller than the present building, but beautiful and imposing. Over the entrance was placed the following inscription:

> DURING THE REIGN OF EMPEROR MANUEL KOMNENOS
> AND WITH VALERIOS, KONSTANTINOS, AS GOVERNOR OF LESBOS
> THIS CHURCH OF THE MOST HOLY MOTHER-OF-GOD WAS ERECTED
> WITH THE EFFORTS OF THE FAITHFUL CHRISTIANS
> IN MEMORY OF AGATHON THE EPHESIAN
> REVERED HOLY MAN BEARER OF THE SACRED ICON
> AUGUST 15, 1173

Outside the church the monks built cells in which they settled and also a guest house for the pilgrims, with the following sign on its façade:

> WE KINDLY WELCOME WITH ALL OUR HEART
> THE PILGRIMS COMING TO HOLY SION

A good-size community was established around the religious complex and was called Ayiasos, after the Greek Ayia—or Aghia-Sion (13). The original church lasted 636 years. About 1783 the monastery was disbanded... the building was about to collapse. In 1806, with the initiative of the bishop of Mytilene Jeremy and of civic leaders in Ayiasos, it was demolished and a new church was built, larger than before even though the Turkish authorities had given strict orders to erect it on the foundation of the old one (Kleombrotos, 1982, pp. 11-14).

B. FATAL FAMILY FEUDS

Byzantine civil wars

When the pro-Latin king Manuel I died in 1180 A.D. his son, Alexios II, who succeeded him, was only twelve years old. His sixty-five-year-old popular, adventuresome and anti-Western uncle (Manuel's cousin), Andronikos Komnenos, marched on Constantinople, replaced the regent and within months became co-emperor. The rioting Greeks of the capital massacred all the Latins they could find and destroyed their property.

Andronikos had his nephew sign the death warrant of his widowed mother, empress Mary of Antioch and soon afterwards had the youngster murdered also. To make his position seem legitimate, the aging usurper married Alexios' thirteen-year-old child bride (the daughter of king Louis VII of France) and had himself crowned emperor as Andronikos I. His cruelty and ruthless taxation, however, turned his popular appeal into hatred and in 1185 he was savagely attacked by the rioting crowd, publicly mutilated and killed. The struggles for his succession encouraged an even greater penetration of Latins—"Franks"—into Byzantine territories.

After the violent death of Andronikos I marked the end of the Komnenos dynasty, members of the Angelos family (related to Komnenos on their grandmother's side) feuded for the throne. Under the leadership of the aggressively ambitious Venetians the forces of the fourth crusade changed course presumably to support the claimant to the throne. Instead of sailing as planned for the Holy Land, they attacked Constantinople, which they captured in 1204 A.D. After widespread looting and massacre, the crusaders established a Latin empire in formerly Byzantine lands. The Latin emperor, Baldwin I of Flanders, was installed in Constantinople and was also granted jurisdiction over several Greek islands in the Aegean, including Lesboš, Khios and Samos (Ostrogorsky, p. 423). Years later, after a series of military setbacks fighting the Greeks and also the Bulgarians and others from the north, the Latins, by 1225 A.D. lost their lands in Asia Minor and the Greek fleet reconquered Lesbos and the other islands (Ostrogorsky, p. 435). Constantinople itself was regained by the Greeks in 1261 A.D.

The Greek-Byzantine "Roman" Empire was partially restored under the emperor Michael VIII Palaiologos (1259-82), founder of the last imperial Byzantine dynasty. But even though Constantinople again became the capital, the economy had been ruined, the army could not be supported adequately and so the state was not able to defend its borders against the numerous invaders, Turks, Slavs and Franks. By the year 1300, during the reign of Michael's son Andronikos II (1282-1328) almost all of Asia Minor had been captured by the Ottoman Turks. Another Turkish group, the Seljuks—also written Seljuqs (4, 17)—who "hated the Ottomans and the Latins as much as did the Byzantines" (Ostrogorsky, p. 507), pushed to the southwest of Asia Minor. There, early in the reign of Andronikos III (1328-41), they helped the Greeks expel the Latins who had remained on the Aegean coast. With Seljuk support the young emperor also "finally rescued Lesbos from its attempted conquest by the Western powers" (Ostrogorsky, p. 507).

Recurrent civil wars, or, more precisely, "family wars," further weakened the empire and precipitated its final collapse. Soon after the early death of his son and co-emperor Michael, king Andronikos II disinherited his grandson, also named Andronikos, who was "frivolous," "dissipated" and was implicated in the accidental murder of his own brother in connection with "one of his love affairs" (Ostrogorsky, p. 499). The young Andronikos rebelled and a series of armed conflicts followed. In his eventual ascent to the throne as Andronikos III, the young king was guided by the ambitious nobleman, John Kantakouzenos. When Andronikos III (1328-41) died, his son John V was nine years old and John Kantakouzenos "who had been the real ruler even during Andronikos III lifetime . . . asserted his claim to the regency" (Ostrogorsky, p. 510). Strong opposition and intrigues in the court and especially by Andronikos' widow, John's mother, the Latin Anna of Savoy, led to the massacre of the pretender's supporters and the destruction of his property. This prompted Kantakouzenos, who was then campaigning in Thrace, to declare himself emperor, as John VI (1347-54). The struggle of John V (who had become the son-in-law of John VI) to regain his throne -which he occupied intermittently for fifty years from 1341 to 1391—involved Lesbos. It was in 1355 that "the strife between John Cantacuzene [*Kantakouzenos*] and John V Palaiologos for the throne of Byzantium enabled a daring Genoese, Francesco Gattilusio, to found a dynasty on Lesbos . . . " (Miller, 1921, p. 313).

Latins in the Levant

Francesco Gattilusio has been described by some of his contemporary Greek writers as a "pirate" [*peirates*, which in Greek means the one who tries, challenges, attacks] and by twentieth century historians as a "Genoese corsair" (Ostrogorsky, p. 531), but he was in fact a member of a family prominent for over two hundred years. Among his ancestors were several members of the Great Council of Genoa and his grandfather, a "troubadour and a man of affairs" (Miller, 1921, p. 314) was a council member and envoy to the pope. Some relatives were Genoese colonists at Pera across from Constantinople and an uncle was an ambassador who concluded the treaty between the Republic of Genoa and the Byzantine regent for John V, queen Anne of Savoy (Miller, p. 314). As a husband of a Greek princess, Francesco was well accepted on Lesbos. He learned to speak Greek and, although he installed Catholic bishops, he kept the Orthodox clergy (his wife Maria remained a faithful Greek Orthodox) including the bishops [*metropolites*] of Mytilene and, later, Methymna.

Existing letters in Greek by the later Gattilusi, Dorino I and Domenico demonstrate their familiarity with the tongue of their people, who, however, never stopped to view them as foreigners (Miller 1921, p. 352).

Francesco Gattilusio, being older and considerably wiser than his brother-in-law, emperor John V, advised him on diplomatic, military and even family matters, including the incidents of his confrontation with his other brother-in-law, Matthew Kantakouzenos, son of the deposed John VI and brother of Helena, the reigning queen and wife of John V. Matthew had been named co-emperor during his father's seven-year reign and did not relinquish his title after his brother-in-law, John V, recaptured the throne but maintained independent control over the mountainous area of Thrace. There, however, he was captured in battle by the neighboring Serbs and was turned over to John V, who forced him to renounce any claims to the throne (1357). For added security, Matthew and his family were sent to a guarded exile on the island of Tenedos. Later their children were transferred to the care of their relatives on Lesbos (Table VI-2).

Gattilusio, Genoese Lord of Lesbos, ca. 1400 A.D. Gold ducat from the author's collection

Francesco Gattilusio was considered an important intermediary in the attempts to reunite the Eastern Orthodox and the Catholic Christian churches. In 1369 he even went to Rome with his brother-in-law, John V, and signed as a witness before the pope the "confession of the Catholic faith," which, they hoped, could unite (it never did) all the Christians against the expanding Turkish threat.

The Genoese of Lesbos tried to deal peacefully both with their native republic of Genoa and with its competitor, Venice. But when in 1377 the two of them went to war over the possession of the Greek island of Tenedos—which at the time was held by the Venetians and the rumor had spread that if it became Genoese all the Venetians there would "be forced to turn Jews or emigrate" (Miller, p. 317)—Francesco helped supply the Venetian fleet instead of his own Genoese people. Despite all warnings and threats from Genoa, the new Latin ruler of Lesbos began minting gold coins that looked like Venetian ducats with added Byzantine imperial insignia. The practice continued for at least four generations of the Gattilusio rule on Lesbos and the abundance of gold coins minted by the Genoese lords of the island reflected their wealth and prosperity. Their life style and cultural efforts were described by a knowledgeable contemporary, Leonardo of Chios [*Hios*]. In 1446 he wrote his "Treatise Concerning True Nobility" and in the course of a Platonic type dialogue he reported that "the prince . . . protects religion; his senate is wise . . . and he lives in splendid state among his lovely halls, his gardens, his fish-ponds and his groves" (quoted by Miller, 1921, p. 352).

Table VI-2
GENOESE RULERS AND MAJOR EVENTS ON LESBOS 1355–1462 A.D.

Gattilusio Ruler	*Years of Rule*	*Family Connections and Events*
Francesco I	1355–84	Married Maria, sister of emperor John V and received Lesbos as her dowry. Accompanied John V (1369) to Rome to sign "confession of faith" before the pope. Died under his collapsing castle during an earthquake.
Francesco II	1384–1404	Helped the Genoese of Constantinople and Pera to repel Turkish attacks. Daughter Eugenia married John Palaiologos, nephew of emperor Manuel II and with her husband assumed imperial duties during Manuel's long trip through Europe. Many foreign missions, including embassies from France and Castile, visted Lesbos.
Jacopo	1404–26	Joined anti-Turkish league (1415). Lesbian ships attacked Saracens provoking reprisals against Genoese and Venetian subjects. Lesbos prospered.
Dorino	1426–55	Involved in peace treaty (1429) between Genoa and Aragon. Daughter Maria married Alexander, son of the Greek emperor of Trebizond. Daughter Catherine married Constantine Palaiologos (who later, as the last emperor, was killed in Constantinople fighting the Turks). She died after a miscarriage during the Turkish attack on Lemnos (1442). In 1450 the Turks ravaged parts of Lesbos but "The Lady of Lesbos" Orietta d'Oria saved Molyvos [*Methymna*] when in full armor she led the people against the attackers.
Domenico [*Kyriakos*]	1455–58	Governed Lesbos since 1449 for his bedridden father Dorino. Sent his secretary and historian Doukas with annual tribute-paying missions to the Turkish sultans. Pleaded to Genoa for help against the Ottomans. Imprisoned and strangled by his brother Nicolo.
Nicolo [*Nikorezo*]	1458–62	Disliked by Lesbian people. In 1462 Mytilene surrendered after a long Turkish siege and over 10,000 taken to Constantinople as slaves, including Dorino's daughter, Maria, the widow of Alexander of Trebizond, and their only son, who became one of the sultan's favorite pages. Nicolo was jailed in Constantinople and later strangled there.

Francesco's tragic death under the ruins of his castle was said to have been prophecized by a Lesbian monk (Miller, p. 318). On August 6, 1384 a terrible earthquake demolished the palace which he had built and "after a painful search" (Miller, p. 319) his body and those of two of his sons were found under the wreckage. A third son, Jacopo, supposedly also had been in the castle sleeping near his brothers but by some "miracle" he was found, alive and alert, outside the fortress in a vineyard. Changing his name to Francesco to honor and preserve that of his father, he took the oath as the next lord of Lesbos. Because he was a minor his uncle Nicolo shared the authority of governing Lesbos for the first three years, until a feud with his nephew forced him to leave for the mainland on Thrace, where he was in charge of his own domains.

In April, 1387, the co-emperor, Manuel II, giving up all hope of defending Thessaloniki (Salonika) against the Turks, sailed to Lesbos (Ostrogorsky, p. 546) and stayed there "for a few months" as guest of Francesco Gattilusio (*Kathemerini*, "The Daily" Athenian newspaper, 8/1/64). The imperial monogram still to be seen on the walls of a small chapel, was probably taken from a nearby castle, where the emperor stayed, in the neighborhood of Lisvori. The name of the village, Vasilika, or Basilika, meaning "Royal," supports the view that imperial visitors, from the Roman Diocletian (245–316 A.D.) to the Byzantines Manuel II and John VII, often came here for summer vacations. The ruins of a Frankish church (the Gattilusio private chapel?) also exist as a reminder of a "Frankish village" in the area (14).

Recognizing the growing danger of a Turkish attack, Francesco II in 1388 joined the defensive Christian league of the Knights of Rhodes, of the Genoese Commune of Pera in Constantinople and others. In 1396 he helped defend the capital against the forces of the Ottoman sultan. The same year he interceded on behalf of the French and other prisoners taken by the Turks and as a result "Lesbos emerged into prominence throughout the French-speaking world" (Miller, p. 320).

From his island domains Francesco II had to exercise delicate international and personal diplomacy between the Greeks, the Latins and the Turks and also among members of his extended family. In the summer of 1399 the French marshal Boucicault (who had been one of the prisoners taken by the Turks in 1396 and later freed with the intervention and large ransom paid by Francesco) arrived on Lesbos, sent by the French king Charles VI to help emperor Manuel II defend Constantinople against the Turks. This time the Frenchman placed Francesco in a very difficult position because the Lesbian ruler was under obligation to report to the Turks any movements against them. Besides, his son-in-law, John Palaiologos, who had been spending much time on Lesbos, had received Turkish help against his own uncle, emperor Manuel II, whom he had tried to overthrow. Eventually it was the visiting Frenchman, Boucicault, who achieved the reconciliation of emperor Manuel and his nephew John. In a marked reversal of their relationships, John with his wife Eugenia (daughter of Francesco Gattilusio), sat on the Byzantine throne and ruled in Manuel's place while the emperor, escorted by Boucicault, left for an extended three-year mission to Europe seeking desperately help to survive the Turkish onslaught. When Manuel II returned in 1403, he failed to honor his promises of land grants to John and hostilities were resumed. Francesco II of Lesbos sailed with five ships to the coast of Macedonia to support his son-in-law, who finally obtained what he wanted.

In the fall of 1403 a Spanish mission stopped on Lesbos. It had been sent by Enrique III of Castille to the Mongol king Timur, who had come down from his capital, Samarkand, and had totally defeated the Turks in Asia Minor. The Castillian ambassador, Ruy Gonzalez de Clavigo, wrote a descriptive account of Lesbos as he saw it during the rule of Francesco II. He described the capital as "built on a high hill near the sea . . . surrounded by a wall with many towers" with a "large suburb" outside it. The area around the city was well-cultivated and full of gardens and vineyards. There were "very large houses and churches" (that must have been before the great earthquake) and also "ruins of great—ancient - palaces and in the middle of these ruins about forty blocks of white marble." The envoys stayed on Lesbos five days and had an opportunity to meet there John Palaiologos, the Gattilusio's imperial son-in-law (Miller, W. 1921, p. 323).

Francesco II died in 1404, also accidentally, under a collapsing building, according to a Greek historian. He had ruled eventfully for twenty years (Table VI-2). His son Jacopo (cf. note 2, Ch. VII) succeeded him, first as a minor with Nicolo again as a regent and then, since 1409, alone. He, as well as his father and grandfather, have been credited by Greek historians for "wisdom, . . . education, courage and physical gifts" (Miller, p. 325) and for extending Lesbian-Genoese ventures, including some daring raids, to Syria, Egypt and Libya. As a descendent of "the famous house of Byzantium and Savoy and connected with that of Austria, the lord of Mytilene . . . was regarded by western visitors as a great baron" (Miller, p. 323). A seal of pope Eugene IV (1431–47), recently discovered near the village of Lisvori in central Lesbos, has been viewed as an additional evidence of the energetic exchange between the Genoese lords of Lesbos and the Roman Catholic hierarchy towards the goal of Church Union.

Lesbos Genoese

The principal Greek historian of the years 1204–1359 was Nicephorus [*Nikephoros*] Gregoras (1290/91–1360), "one of the most remarkable and prolific scholars of Byzantium, who wrote on all aspects of contemporary knowledge" (Ostrogorsky, p. 466). As an influential favorite of Andronikos II (1288–1328), Gregoras was among the losers when that aging ruler was overthrown by his grandson, the rebel Andronikos III (1328-41). Later, during the second "civil war" of that century for the throne of Byzantium, Gregoras was imprisoned by emperor John VI Kantakouzenos (1347-54), former counselor for Andronikos III and usurper of the throne of his son-in-law, John V, for having supported the hereditary claimant, John V Palaiologos against his father-in-law. When John V regained the throne in 1355 and forced John VI to enter a monastery, Gregoras was freed and honored. Besides his "Roman History," which is "graphic and generally reliable" (Ostrogorsky, p. 466), Gregoras wrote extensively on philosophical and religious subjects, especially opposing the "hesychast" (15) movement. Among other concerns, he proposed a reform of the traditional Julian calendar, more than 200 years before that was officially done (1582) by Pope Gregory XIII (Encycl. Brit., Vol. 10). Parts of Gregoras' *History* were published in Germany (along with the *Chronicle* of John Zonaras and the *History* of Niketas Khoniates) by Hieronymus Wolf (1516-80), the "first scholar to appreciate Byzantine history" (Ostrogorsky, p. 2).

ROMAN HISTORY
by Nikephoros Gregoras, 1290/91-1360 A.D.
Book XXIX
5. Before long the winter winds from wild became mild and at the same time the waves gently made peace on the shores. The spring season seemed to invite the days to open their gates to the sun and to overtake the nights in their contest. So then the merchant ships too, getting bolder, began to leave port and the triremes got the blades ready and lifted the oars. King John Palaiologos raised anchor from Thessaloniki with four triremes and diremes and many monoremes. After stopping at Lemnos and from there passing by Samothrace and Imbros, he reached Lesbos. With his presence there he reassured and emboldened those who were previously ambivalent in their reliance on him. Then finally he dropped anchor in a harbor at Tenedos. After learning there that for some time the emperor, his father-in-law (Ref. Table K) had been getting ready eleven triremes to fight him,

he decided to stay on the island and to wait for the naval expedition with every bit of his thoughts and of his mental resolve.

. . . .

27. The fall season was already coming close to its end when suddenly in the middle of one night—November, 1354 (Ostrogorsky, p. 531)—the news spread all around Byzantium that the young king Palaiologos was inside the walls, having arrived from the island of Tenedos with all his foreign allies. Without anybody noticing it, he had sneaked through the eastern harbor and the boat yards, sailing with two very large triremes and sixteen monoremes. Some of these had been built earlier in the City and the others had been recruited from Tenedos and from Lesbos and Lemnos . . . When Kantakouzenos heard what was happening, he couldn't think of a way to break away and he feared the violence of the Byzantines, who for a long time had been strongly agitated against him because . . . he had trampled on the respected traditional laws and has deprived the Romans of whatever freedom they had left, by forcing them to work for barbarians and for dishonorable enemies . . . To further complicate matters there were hardly any flour mills and no flour or bread had been kept in storage because the disaster had not been expected. But the crowd in the city demanded food distributions as needed and so the complaints and insults against Kantakouzenos kept increasing. That forced him to hurry to his son-in-law king Palaiologos and to come to terms before he suffered something intolerable . . . Consequently before not many days he left the palace during the night dressed in a monk's habit, together with his wife. Changing his name to Ioasaph, he entered the monastery of Mangana and she, renamed Eugenia, went to the one called Martha's. However they took with them not only what they needed to live but everything they had accumulated in the royal coffers.

. . . .

43. While all this was going on queen Helena came to Byzantium from Tenedos and restrained the impulses of her husband king Palaiologos, not wanting by any means to become a witness to the disgrace of her father Kantakouzenos.

. . . .

XXXVI.3. That winter turned out to be most bitter, with heavy and frequent snowfalls almost covering all the houses. All this time the king remained on Tenedos, managing his affairs but most of all showing great care in guarding Matthew, who was the king's brother-in-law. He (the king) then decided to send him to Mitylene to have him guarded by the Latin Katalouzo (16) who, as the king's brother-in-law for having married his sister, was ruling Lesbos. When that was done the king left for Phokaia going after the son of Hyrkan (17) but returned without accomplishing anything of what he had wanted. Before long winter was over and at the beginning of spring the king returned to Byzantium.

. . . .

XXXVII.45. And that is how things took place, some of which I will now recapitulate . . . That was how during a short time, driven by irrational impulses and a strange destiny they found the opportunity to move against each other. By this I mean (first) the conflict between the two Andronikos kings, or more correctly the rebellion of the young one against his own grandfather. And in the second case, after these two had died, how Kantakouzenos moved against the young king and the young man's mother and with all kinds of various intrigues . . . promises to some and generous bribes to others he deceived everyone . . .

. . . .

Given the opportunity of the fight of Kantakouzenos for the monarchy, many people came to the young man in his exile on Tenedos and with oaths and written statements . . . expressed their desire to contribute arms and money to his cause. Not only they but also another Latin, of the same mind as they, with only one trireme and after living the life of a pirate and having become rich with that . . . also came by the king on the island of Tenedos. Subsequently, when the young man regained his throne, they all received what was promised to them, the first ones the fortress . . . and the other one, after he became brother-in-law of the king by marrying his sister, taking the island of Lesbos for a dowry.

. . .

XXXVII.64-65. . . . The summer was already at its height and the wheat was calling to be harvested when Matthew, the co-emperor and son of Kantakouzenos got hold of 4,000 barbarian warriors on horses, sent to him by his brother-in-law, Hyrkan (17), and, along with those Roman soldiers under his command . . . raided the towns surrounding Philippi . . . But armed vigilance was strong and Matthew the king was defeated overwhelmingly. He was captured alive and so were almost all his men, those who were not put to death by the sword. When the king (John V) heard that, he took off from Lesbos, where he had given his navy an opportunity to rest . . . and sailed toward Abdera. He then sent delegates to Tribeallos, who was holding Matthew captive and, after giving and receiving pledges of friendship and offering him gifts not small at all, he took Matthew prisoner along with his wife to the island of Tenedos. Their children he sent to have them guarded by his Latin brother-in-law on his sister's side, who at that time was ruling Lesbos.

The Greek-Byzantine historian, Michael Doukas—also spelled Ducas (18)—lived on Lesbos and represented the island's lords in delegations to the Turkish rulers before the capital of the state, Constantinople, was captured (1453) and also afterwards until Lesbos too fell to the Turks in 1462 A.D. Preceding his detailed description of these terminal events—at which time the author himself most likely perished (Margoulias, 1975, *Introduction*)—Doukas wrote a synopsis of world history, beginning with the biblical description of the creation of the world.

BYZANTINE HISTORY
by M. Doukas, fifteenth century A.D.

I.6. . . . From the creation of the world to Doukas (emperor Alexios V) under whose reign Constantinople was captured by the Latins (1204 A.D.) had elapsed 6,712 years . . .

. . . .

II.1. After the fall of the City, Theodore Laskaris reigned in Nikaia (Nicaea) for eighteen years . . .

4. . . . Andronikos . . . "the Younger" (the IIIrd) . . . reigned thirteen years (1328-1341) . . . and was succeeded by his son, John Palaiologos (the Vth, on the throne 1341-54, 1355-76 and 1379-91) who, due to his young age, was placed under the guardianship of lord John Kantakouzenos (co-emperor, 1347-54, as John VI).

. . . .

V.1. . . . In emperor John's youth . . . lord John Kantakouzenos, a wise man, very experienced in military affairs and, one might say, a glorious flower . . . from the nobility, governed as regent.

While Kantakouzenos was away on a military campaign, a palace coup, instigated by the widowed empress Anna, the German-born mother of John V, resulted in a massive slaughter of the regent's supporters.

V.5. . . . They slaughtered everyone except for six . . . one of whom was my grandfather Michael Doukas . . . He was very learned, master of all secular wisdom . . . My grandfather fled to Asia . . . and was welcomed by Isa, the son of Aydin (17) . . . The (Turkish) ruler granted him all kinds of privileges and . . . settled him in Ephesos.

. . . .

VII.1. One of Aydin's sons, Umur by name (17) . . . ruler of Smyrna . . . built a large number of diremes and triremes for piratical purposes. With these he raided the nearby cities and islands, Mitylene and all of Lesbos and also Khios, Samos, Naxos and all the surrounding islands.

. . . .

IX.1. Then Kantakouzenos, . . . when he was expelled from the regency and made a fugitive after the Romans had murdered his relatives, sent ambassadors to Orkhan (17) asking for help and promising his own daughter in marriage, with many treasures for dowry . . . As he listened, Orkhan was . . . like a bull . . . These Turks are lustful, shameless and lecherous, having intercourse both natural and unnatural, with females, males and with animals . . . A Greek, or Italian woman . . . they embrace as if she were Aphrodite, but a woman of their own nation . . . they loathe as much as they would a bear . . . The abominable marriage took place in January of that year (1346).

2. . . . Taking with him many Turkish troops, Kantakouzenos . . . entered the City . . .

X.1. . . . He . . . kissed the youth's hand and . . . he addressed empress Anna and her son John as "emperor and empress of the Romans." . . .

3. He appeased the empress with sweet words and well-planned measures and persuaded her to take his daughter Helena as a bride for her son John Palaiologos . . . The sacred ceremony of the wedding and the coronation took place together . . . John Kantakouzenos, father-in-law of the king, was also crowned and acclaimed as emperor of the Romans . . .

4. Emperor John was in the early blossoming of his manhood and empress Helena was thirteen-years-old . . . As emperor John grew older, he became very irresponsible and indulged in . . . lascivious and promiscuous intercourse . . .

XI.1. Seeing the Roman State in an extremely difficult situation and his son-in-law and co-emperor John wasting his time in debauchery and drunkenness, Kantakouzenos could not contain himself any longer . . . One day he publicly chastised John, who then left the city with two triremes and went to Italy.

2. Emperor John spent two years in Italy and Germany . . . and then came back. When he reached the island of Tenedos . . . he anxiously tried to find out how his father-in-law, the emperor, might receive him . . .

3. A nobleman from Genoa, sailing with two triremes towards the Hellespont, stopped on his way and met with the emperor . . . who found him willing and ready to provide all possible assistance. The emperor asked him even to risk his life in an attempt to wrest the city from the control of Kantakouzenos and to restore him as the sole emperor of the Romans . . . That man was Francesco, surnamed Gattilusio (16). The emperor made a promise: "If, with the help of God, this is done and with you as my ally I recover my imperial throne, I will make you my brother-in-law by giving you my sister Maria as your wife."

4. Satisfied with their pledges, the two men sailed through the Hellespont . . . reached the City and with two thousand fully armed men gained entrance . . .

5. Emperor Kantakouzenos asked permission from the emperor to withdraw from Constantinople and to be able to depart for the Holy Mountain (Mount Athos) and he lived there as a monk (November 1354) . . .

XII.5. To Francesco Gattilusio, his good and faithful friend, the emperor gave his sister in marriage and the island of Lesbos for a dowry. They celebrated the wedding and then sailed to establish themselves in Mitylene. Members of their family in succession have continued to rule the island up to the present times (Table VI-2).

Orig. Greek in *Michaelis Nepotis Ducae Historia Byzantina*, Imm. Bekker, editor and transl. in Latin, Bonn, 1834; also Engl. trans. by H.J. Magoulias, 1975, pp. 58-78.

The year 1354 A.D. (ninety-nine years before the fall of Constantinople to the Turks) was critical for the Roman State in many respects. A violent earthquake, torrential rains and heavy storms devastated the northern Aegean coastal areas and caused a large number of deaths. Many of the survivors were subsequently taken captive and enslaved by the invading Turks. In the spring of the following year the son of John VI, Matthew Kantakouzenos fought and lost a battle against his brother-in-law, emperor John V. In 1356, with Turkish help, Matthew again tried to move against the emperor but he was captured by the Serbs and handed over to emperor John V, who exiled him to Lesbos (Magoulias, 1975, pp. 274-5; note 56).

At the beginning of the next century, the populations of Asia Minor as far as the eastern Aegean coast and also the Latin rulers of these lands and even more so, the Turkish conquerors, were confronted and temporarily overwhelmed by the invading Mongols under the savage and ruthless Timur Lane or Tamerlane. The fifteenth century Greek historian, Doukas, provided a record of an exchange between the invading Mongol leaders and the lords of Lesbos.

BYZANTINE HISTORY
by M. Doukas, fifteenth century A.D.
XVII.1. . . . Timur came to Prusa spreading destruction, capturing slaves and looting every treasure he discovered after torturing or variously penalizing people . . . He moved on in Asia and after he passed through Adramyttion and Assos he reached Pergamon . . .
5. The cities of Old and New Phokaia (19) sent ambassadors to Timur before he got there . . . and declared their submission, with many gifts. New Phokaia belonged to the Genoese and Old Phokaia was ruled by the lord of Mitylene. After Timur came to Smyrna he sent his grandson to explore Old and New Phokaia. When the lord of Lesbos heard this, he boarded a trireme and sailed to Old Phokaia and there he entertained Timur's grandson lavishly. After they ate, drank and partied together, he (the Lesbian lord) gave him many gifts and bid him farewell. The grandson of Timur in turn gave him a scepter as proof of friendship and they embraced . . .
. . . .

After a year outside Persia, Timur returned . . . carrying back more treasures and booty than any Persian ruler before him.
Magoulias, 1975, pp. 99-100.

In June 1403 emperor Manuel II returned to the Byzantine capital after traveling west for three years—including lengthy stays in northern Italy, Paris and London—in search of help to defend what remained of his empire against the Turks. Manuel's nephew, John VII, who ruled in his absence had shown a pro-Turkish policy (Magoulias, 1975, p. 285, note no. 104) and for that reason he was banished to the island of Lemnos. But instead of going there, John VII sailed to Lesbos to seek aid from his father-in-law, Francesco II Gattilusio, for a proposed attack against the Turks in Thessaloniki. The young pretender also made an attempt to sell his claim to the throne to the French king, in exchange for an estate in France (Ostrogorski p. 554). But he never carried out any of his plans and after becoming a monk (as his grandfather John VI Kantakouzenos had done before) he died young in 1408.

C. THE OTTOMAN CONQUEST

The Turks in Europe

Under sultan Murad II (1404-1451 A.D.; reigned 1421-51) the Ottoman Turks became masters of almost the entire Balkan peninsula. After their decisive victory against the Hungarians and their western European allies in the battle of Varna in 1444, Murad and his Serbian wife, sultana Mara, dominated the course of events both in southeastern Europe and in Asia Minor and the Middle East. The Byzantine capital, however, remained in Greek hands. It was left for their son and successor to complete the Ottoman conquest, both of Constantinople, the "City of Cities" and also of the Aegean islands, including Lesbos.

Mehmed II—also spelled Mahmoud (20) or Mohammed (Encyc. Brit., Vol. 15), surnamed "the conqueror" [*Porthetes* in Greek, *Fatih* in Turkish]—was nineteen years old when his father died in Adrianople [the Greek *Adrianoupolis*, *Edirne* in Turkish], which was the temporary European capital of the Ottoman Turks. Mehmed II had made treaties with the Hungarians and the Serbians and "he had expressed good will . . . to the Genoese lords of Khios and Lesbos" (Nicol 1972, p. 395). A contemporary Greek historian, George Sphrantzes, recorded the events during the reigns of Murad and Mehmed. Information about the author's personal life (Philippides, 1980) illustrates more intimately the upheavals in the Greek and Byzantine world of those times.

Sphrantzes was apparently born in Peloponnesos but his grandfather came from Lemnos, an island not far from the northwestern coast of Lesbos. The original family name might have been Frantzes, possibly a Greek version of Francis (Philippides, 1980, p. 10). At the age of seventeen George Sphrantzes was appointed attendant to emperor Manuel II (1391-1425) and about ten years later he was sent to sultan Murad II as an ambassador. A year later, in 1430, he was captured by Catalan pirates, who roamed the Greek waters and was sold for a ransom. In 1440 Sphrantzes was responsible for negotiating the marriage of the future emperor Constantine XI and the daughter of Dorino Gattilusio, the Genoese lord of Lesbos. After the battle of Varna in 1444, Sphrantzes travelled to the court of sultan Murad II again as an ambassador. In 1449 the Byzantine dignitary and historian travelled to the eastern shores of the Black Sea, to Georgia and Trebizond in search of a second wife and possible marriage alliance for the last Byzantine emperor Constantine XI Palaiologos. When Constantinople was sacked by sultan Mehmed II (20) in 1453, Sphrantzes was captured and became a slave but he was ransomed four months later and went back to Peloponnesos. He travelled to Italy twice, in 1455 and again 1466. After becoming a monk in 1472, he lived on the island of Corfu [*Kerkyra*] and died there in 1477, at the age of 76. His children had predeceased him under tragic circumstances. Sphrantzes' work, known as the *"Chronicon Minus,"* the *Minor Chronicle*, has recently been translated and published in English under the title "The Fall of the Byzantine Empire" (Philippides, 1980).

MINOR CHRONICLE
by George Sphrantzes, 1401-1477 A.D.

XXIV 7. On December 6, 6949 (1440 A.D.), I was sent to the island of Lesbos and arranged the betrothal and marriage of lord Constantine and Catherine, the daughter of the lord of Mitylene and of the surrounding areas, Dorino Gattilusio-Palaiologos.
. . . .

11. In September 6950 (1441 A.D.), lord Constantine left his wife and queen in the care of her father and sailed to the Morea [*Peloponnesos*] on the same imperial vessel, which was accompanied by one other ship from Mitylene.

Section XXV.
4. In July of the same year (1442) my lord and master, on his way to the aid of the City (Constantinople), stopped at Mitylene, took his wife the queen and then came to the island of Lemnos. Caught there, he was besieged . . . by the whole Turkish fleet for many days. With God's help the Turks failed and were forced to withdraw. However the queen fell ill under such circumstances, suffered a miscarriage in August of the same year and passed away . . . on that same island of Lemnos and she was buried there.

9. On Tuesday May 29 (1453), early in the day, the sultan took possession of our City. At the time of this conquest my late master and emperor, lord Constantine, was killed.
. . . .

11. I was taken prisoner and suffered the evils of miserable slavery. Finally I was ransomed . . . and departed for Mistra. My wife and children had passed into the possession of some elderly

Turks, who did not treat them badly. Then they were sold to the sultan's Cavalry Master, who accumulated a great fortune by selling many other beautiful noble ladies.

12. My children's beauty and proper upbringing could not be concealed; so the sultan found out and bought my children from his Cavalry Master . . . Their wretched mother was left all alone in the company of a single nurse . . .

XXXVII.9. In September 6964 [1455 A.D.], my beautiful daughter Thamar died of an infectious disease in the sultan's palace. Miserable me, her unfortunate father!, she was fourteen years and five months old.

10. As I, her miserable father, did not know about her death, I went as an ambassador to the Venetian senate and their doge, Francesco Foscari, on October 25th.

XLII.8. In the year 6972 [September 1463—September 1464], the Venetians took control of Monembasia (on the Peloponnesos) . . . and also the castle of Lemnos . . .

9. The Venetian admiral proceeded to Lesbos, fought but failed to capture the island so he departed empty handed.

Adapted from Philippides, 1980, pp. 52-86.

The fall of Lesbos, 1462 A.D.

While George Sphrantzes was a typical Greek Byzantine dignitary and diplomat struggling for the survival of his state, two other contemporary historians of the downfall represented distinctly different points of view. The work of Doukas—whose last name, with the long Greek *oo*, or *ou*, is at times transliterated as Ducas and his first name, though not in the text, was presumably Michael, after his grandfather (Magoulias, 1975, p. 26)—covered in detail the period from 1389-1462 in an "exciting journalistic style" (Magoulias, 1975, p. 40) "characterized by reliability and vivid description" (Ostrogorsky, 1969, p. 468). Doukas had been in the service of the Genoese of Lesbos for many years and represented these island lords in negotiations with the Turks. In contrast to other writers, who cultivated an antiquated classical "Atticist" Greek, Doukas wrote in the spoken vernacular language of his day. As an eyewitness, he described events "soberly and objectively" (Pappageotes, 1977, p. 43). The existing Greek text ends abruptly in mid-sentence with the Turkish conquest of Mytilene, but an Italian edition fills in some of the missing parts of the story. Doukas' history, in Greek, is part of the series *Corpus Scriptorum Historiae Byzantinae* (CSHB), edited by I. Bekker under the supervision of B. G. Niebuhr. It was published in Bonn, Germany in 1834. The title of this work was given as "Byzantine History" and the author's name as Michael Ducas. The lower part of each page included a

Latin translation by Immanuel Bekker. An annotated translation in English by H.J. Magoulias—who cites the original Doukas title as "Historia Turco-Byzantina"—was published in the U.S.A. in 1975 under the title "Decline and Fall of Byzantium to the Ottoman Turks."

BYZANTINE HISTORY
by M. Doukas, fifteenth century A.D.

XLII.1. Three days after the fall (of the city of Constantinople) Mehmed let his ships go, to sail back to their own lands and cities. These carried so much booty that they almost sank from the weight . . . Countless books were loaded too and were scattered over all east and west. Ten books were sold for one single gold coin . . . the works of Aristotle and Plato, religious and a variety of other volumes . . .

. . . The holy icons were thrown to the flames and over that fire they (the Turkish conquerors) roasted their meat to eat . . .

. . . .

4. He left the city on the eighteenth day of June . . . and . . .

5. Made a majestic entry back into Adrianople, where the Christian governors and rulers lined up to greet him . . . and to declare their submission.

6. . . . The lord of Khios was to pay a tribute of 6,000 gold coins and the lord of Mitylene 3,000 each year . . .

XLIV.1. (CSHB:D 44). In that year, on June 30 of 6963 (1455 A.D.) the ruling lord of the island of Lesbos, Dorino Gateluzio (16) died. On August 1, I was sent by the new lord, his son Domenico Gateluzio, to Adrianople in order to deliver the expected annual tribute, 3,000 gold coins for the island of Lesbos and 2,325 coins for the island of Lemnos, which had been assigned by the tyrant to the lord of Lesbos, to collect each year the prescribed tax. As I walked in, I bowed to the (Turkish) lord, kissed his hand and sat before him until he had finished eating his dinner. Then, bowing again, I left. The next day I took the gold and delivered that into the hands of the viziers. After they received the tribute, they spoke and asked me: "How is the lord of Mitylene? Is he doing well?" And I responded: "He is well and sends you his regards." Then they said: "We are inquiring about the old man, the overall [*catholic*] ruler." And my answer was: "That prince died, it will be forty days today. The one now ruling, his son, has been in charge for six years. The father, being bedridden and ailing, had granted the governorship to his son, who has come to pay his respects, not only once but twice and has made solicitous presentations to the Great Lord."

But they retorted: "Stop all this talk. Only as of today he may become the ruler and he cannot be called the lord of Lesbos unless he comes here to receive the authority from our Highest Chief. Go on now, take him with you and come back with him. Otherwise he should know what his future will be." So I went back to Mitylene, took the ruling prince and a few leading Latins and

Romans (1) with me and, entrusting our hopes in God, we left the island and, crossing through Chersonese, we arrived in the city of Adrian. But the (Turkish) Lord had been moving from place to place because of the scourge of the plague (there was, in fact, in the Chersonese and all over Thrace such a pestilence that many unburied bodies were thrown at the crossroads) and after learning that he was staying in Philippopolis, we went there ourselves. There we found out that he had left two days before (because the dreaded disease had gotten there too) and that he was in camp in the area of Sophia. So we too left the City of Philippos and going over almost impassable mountains, we came on the third day to a Bulgarian village called Izlati. That was where the camp was and the tyrant was there too. After we arrived, carrying numerous gifts, we presented ourselves to the courtiers, including Mahmud Pasha and Said Ahmad Pasha. The next day we appeared before their leader and after the lord of Mitylene kissed the hand of the tyrant, we walked out. The following day a message came through the courtiers to our own lord, that the tyrant wanted the island of Thasos and demanded that he (our lord) was to offer it to him as a gift. The lord of Lesbos, unable to argue or to speak, gave away the island. Then, the following day, there was another message, that he (the Turk) wanted to double the taxes he had been getting every year. The lord of Mitylene was very upset with that and protested that "if he (the Turk) wants to own all of Lesbos, that is in his power, but what he asks is above my control. So I beg you, my lord, to lend me a hand of assistance." Whereupon, the middle-man pleaded with the tyrant and so he added 1,000 pieces of gold and no more. The annual tribute had been 3,000 coins and it became 4,000. Later, they dressed him (Domenico) in a gold-embroidered gown and us in robes of silk and, after we had made our written pledges, we departed. In thirteen days we reached the island of Lesbos, all of us praising God who had saved us from the hands of the relentless conqueror.

While we were still in Philippopolis, the tyrant, as already mentioned, had assembled a small fleet, with ten triremes and another ten diremes, under the command of someone named Yenouz (17), a good-looking young man, whom he also had appointed district governor of Kallipolis (Gallipoli) and grand admiral of the fleet. Taking off from Hellespont (the Dardanelles) he went navigating towards Khios. When they were near the region of Troy and as they started from there hoisting their sails, a heavy storm arose, with howling winds blowing violently and stirring up the sea ... Before they had a chance to change course, five of the twenty ships sank and two were crushed on the coast. Then the navigator of admiral Yenouz, an expert hand in such violent tempests and rough seas (he was originally a Latin from Spain) turned his bow and after skillfully crossing without much trouble the crests of the waves, sailed out to the open sea ... During the night calm returned and when morning arrived they approached Khios from the east ... addressing songs of thanks to their god and their prophet Mohammed. Truly unfathomable is the will of God. How was it in such a violent sea storm, that the ship did not sink? The tyrants' officer was saved due to our sins. In fact, the trireme of Yenouz was the only one that went off course. The rest that had survived sailed into the harbor of Mitylene. When they inquired about their leader and learned that he had been seen in those parts, they became very anxious and impatient. It was already the evening of that day when a direme was seen sailing in. That was a ship of Mitylene which had been dispatched to Khios by the lord's brother, to check whether Catalan pirate ships might have come there, so that they might notify the Turks of the area to be on guard. Such messages were an obligatory service forced upon the Lesbians, because if they failed to carry the word that the pirates were about to attack, any losses the Turks might suffer had then to be replaced by the Lesbians themselves. The boundaries of this bondage extended from the river Pergamon to the town of Assos, which is now called Makhran (21).

When the direme entered the port, another sailboat was sighted and when they noted the large and red colored sails, they assumed that it was that of their admiral and rejoiced. So they docked, disembarked and pitched a tent on dry land, to rest from the storm and the bouncing turbulence. The brother of our lord, master [syr, in the Greek text] Nicolo Gatilusio (16), organized a grand reception and came down from the castle to the tent, stayed there for a short time and then went back. Whereupon, the disciple of the cunning conqueror weaved a plot against him saying: "The direme that I have forced to come here after a chase belongs to me, the boat and everything in it." It so happened that inside the boat was the most prominent wife of one of the lords and with her she had much gold and silver. "If you are a friend of my chief, you will have to deliver her to me. If not, I am going to write about this to the grand emir right this minute." He then answered: "I don't know what you are talking about. That direme was sent to Khios for a special mission. The noblewoman you mentioned has been here for a long time." She was in fact the mother-in-law of the ruler . . . and that was the truth. But the admiral did not believe what he heard and wrote to the emir whatever he wanted . . .

The Turks then sailed to New Phokaia and when they subdued the city they took much booty and enslaved many people, with many Genoese merchants among them.

(CSHB:P. 189-14). When the lord of Lesbos came to Mitylene and learned from his own brother what had happened and that the Turkish admiral wanted his mother-in-law as one of the noblewomen from Khios . . . he sent me to explain and to give an account of that affair. When I arrived in Constantinople, I presented myself in front of the viziers together with General Yanuz and told all the truth under oath. And Yanuz also under oath told every lie. But the judgment was in his favor and I received the blame. So the ruler ordered me to choose one of two things, either to bring him 10,000 coins of gold, or to prepare for battle. When I protested against such an injustice, he, without anybody knowing it, sent one of his slaves and subdued the city of Old Phokaia, which had been under the jurisdiction of the Lord of Lesbos. That happened on the 24th of December of the year 6964 (1455 A.D.). After the tyrant learned about the capture of Phokaia he released me and terminated the hearings.

XLV.1. With the beginning of spring the tyrant assembled a large fleet and ordered it against Khios. The people of Khios paid dearly and promised an annual tribute to avoid the onslaught. The island of Lemnos at that same time was about to surrender to the Turks...

3. While all this was going on, the lord of Lesbos sent one of his diremes with over 100 men to Lemnos... and commanded them either to make the Lemnian people change their minds and, treating them kindly, with sweet words and promises to make them place the island back under him, or to return to Lesbos bringing back with them his brother, Nicolo, who was there in the Old Castle holding court. Instead of that, however, these people landed and started an armed combat, whereupon the Lemnians, about 500 of them, came out riding on horses and overwhelmed them (the people from Lesbos) slaughtering some, chasing others down to the sea where they drowned and capturing about forty of them. Those who were left on the direme sailed back to Lesbos, taking Nicolo with them. Three days later Ismail arrived on Lemnos and when he heard what had happened, he praised the Lemnians and taking the captive Lesbians with him, in the month of May of the year 6964 (1455 A.D.) he returned to Kallipolis.

XLV.7. (CSHB:P. 191, 17-24). In the month of August I was sent to deliver the annual tribute from the lord of Lesbos. After I presented that, I requested to take back the men whom the Lemnians had turned over (to the Turks) for insubordination, but he—the sultan, or "tyrant"—not only refused to release them, but instead he ordered to have their heads cut off; they were all his prisoners in Adrianople. But as they were taking them to the place of execution, the tyrant changed his mind and ordered to have them ransomed, so they were sold for 1,000 coins.

8. In the year 6965 (1456 A.D.) eleven triremes came from Rome under the leadership of the patriarch of Aquilia, sent by pope Callistus to aid the islands close to the Turks, Rhodos, Khios, Lesbos, Lemnos, Imbros, Samothrace and Thasos. They reached Rhodos, which was under the control of the pope and urged the people not to pay taxes to the Turks but to decide to fight instead... They did that on Lesbos too... And from Lesbos all the pope's ships and the Catalans and other pirate ships numbering up to forty sailed to Lemnos and after they captured it... they made it to Thasos. There they installed a guard and then returned to Rhodos. Learning what was happening, the pirate blamed it all on the lord of Lesbos and organized a ferocious attack against him. He assembled a mighty fleet and in March he sent it against Lesbos under the leadership of Ismael. He reached Methymna, but despite the use of all kinds of methods, mechanical devices, stone throwing machines and ladders, he was unable to subdue it. On the contrary, he lost many of his own forces so he turned back without accomplishing anything.

23. In the year 6971 (1462 A.D.) after he had assembled a fleet of sixty triremes and diremes, plus seven other vessels, he—the "tyrant"—in the month of September, descended upon Lesbos. He came himself down by land with his forces and then demanded the surrender of the island from the ruler, Nicolo Gatelusio. He was the brother of the previous ruler, Domenico, whom, they said, Nicolo had overthrown from his position and had him strangled. He then became lord of Lesbos and that was the fourth year of his rule. Nicolo had made Mitylene secure with military preparations and abundance of armaments, deep trenches and the construction of earth mounds and had placed himself in the middle of a large number, over 5000, of fighting men. There was also a crowd of over 20,000 people, counting the women and children. When the tyrant crossed over . . . and demanded the city and the whole island, Nicolo answered: "It is not possible to surrender the city and the island without first fighting to death according to military standards." Then again the tyrant crossed the water passage and left his vizier, Mahmud to lay siege to Mitylene. He then arranged his rock throwing machines against it and bombarding with rocks that part of the city called Melanoudion, he demolished it. Then he did the same from other sides against the ramparts and the towers. Those inside, seeing . . .

Bekker, I. Greek and Latin text, CSHB, 1834, pp. 328-346.

The Greek text of Doukas' manuscript stopped in mid-sentence. The author may have been killed, or taken to slavery (Magoulias, 1975, p. 29). An anonymous Italian translator recorded the final tragedy of the beleaguered city, possibly adding his own concluding notes (Magoulias, 1975, p. 41). A Turkish fleet under Mehmed, or Mahmud (20), a Greek Moslem convert, dropped anchor in the harbor of St. George, while six large Turkish canons, shooting balls over 600 pounds each, continued to wreck the city walls. The lower castle, Melanoudi, was stormed by 20,000 Turks and the defenders, left without a trusted leader, fled the enemy and attacked the stores of food and wine. Nicolo Gattilusio surrendered to Mehmed, kissing his feet and presenting to him the key of the city. The remaining houses of Melanoudion were razed to the ground and 300 defenders, including Catalan mercenaries and seventy knights from Rhodos, were sawed to pieces. Of the people of Mytilene, about 10,000 were carried to Constantinople and when many of them died on the way, their right ear was cut off and taken to the capital as proof of their capture. The rest of the citizens were sold locally to slavery at a public auction. Only the old, sick and "worthless" remained. For his own pleasure, Mehmed kept the loveliest maidens and a few hundred young boys. The last Genoese lord of Lesbos, Nicolo Gattilusio with his family and also the

Catholic archbishop of Lesbos were taken prisoner to Constantinople. To save their lives, Nicolo and his brother converted to Mohammedanism and had to be circumcised. Later, however, Nicolo was again thrown in jail and there he was strangled with a bow string, exactly the way he had murdered his brother Domenico, when in 1458 he displaced him as the last Latin ruler of Lesbos (Miller, E.L.O., pp. 345-58; Magoulias, H.J., 1975, pp. 322-323).

A modern introductory booklet about Lesbos contained a few details about that final battle for Mytilene.

LESBOS: THE ISLAND OF HARMONY
by M. Kh. Eleftheriadis, 1981.

In 1462, after a stubborn and hard resistance, Lesbos was subdued by the Turks. One of the heroines in that battle, according to the records, was the daughter of a priest, Arianne, who repeatedly pursued the Turks down to their boats.

Mytilene was looted with an unheard-of fury, never seen before. Its young people were decimated and young Lesbian maidens were sent to the harems of The City (Constantinople).

Eleftheriadis, 1981, p. 10.

Another late Byzantine historian, Michael Kritoboulos of Imbros (a smaller island, northwest of Lesbos) viewed the collapse of the Greek state and the enslavement of its people in a more detached and tolerant manner, with less of the anger and despair of his contemporary writers. His "eulogistic" (Pappageotes, 1977, p. 43) approach may have been mainly due to his intention to write a relatively complimentary history of the exploits and conquests of sultan Mehmed II (Fig. VI-9) and so to attract his attention, to please him and to receive a generous reward. A certain recognition may have been granted to Kritoboulos when he was appointed by the Turks as governor of his island of Imbros but he was denied the laurels of official royal historian (Magoulias, 1975, p. 25).

Kritoboulos was born about 1400-1410 A.D. and he probably completed his "historical writings" around 1467-68, soon after Lesbos was conquered by the Turks (Reinsch, 1983). It is not known what happened to Kritoboulos after 1468. The author/governor had many personal contacts with prominent Turks and also with the Genoese Lords of Lesbos. He wrote in Greek, even though under Turkish occupation, because that was the predominant written language of that region in those times. The manuscript found in the Library of the Old Palace, the

Topkapi serai (Turk. *saray*) in Constantinople (Turkish Istambul) has been the basis for a recent publication of the Greek text with a forward and critical notes in German (Reinsch, D.R., 1983), in the series of *Corpus Fontium Historiae Byzantinae* (CFHB).

HISTORICAL WRITINGS
by Kritoboulos of Imbros, c. 1400-1468 (?) A.D.

Letter to his imperial majesty

(This) contains . . . an outline of the history included in this book and a declaration of the purpose of this writing.

(To) His imperial majesty, the king of kings Mehmed, most fortunate, victorious . . . triumphant, invincible master of both land and sea by the will of God, from Kritoboulos, the humble servant.

. . . .

Part A

A meditation of the futility of human affairs, the instability of the present existence and on how nothing in it is permanent or certain.

69.3. Nothing in human affairs is steadfast or certain but everything . . . moves up and down and the sharp turns of life make full circles . . . So it was that Constantine, the son of Helen, was a fortunate king and raised the City (Constantinople) to the extremes of prosperity and good luck and now under another Constantine, an unfortunate king—also the son of a Helen—it (the same City) was conquered and brought down to an ultimate wretchedness and slavery.

74.1. . . . When the king returned to Adrianople in the summer, he received there delegations from . . . Illyria and Peloponnesos and also from Mitylene and Khios and from many other places. He treated all of them very kindly . . . giving and receiving assurances from some, to others giving appropriate gifts and for others waving the taxes due, or doing something else good for them and to all of them speaking in peaceful terms.

75.1. In those same days arrived also an embassy from the islands, sent by Kritoboulos of Lesbos, the present writer . . . **4.** The king also received them very kindly and granted what had been requested, giving the islands—the way they had been assigned under the previous (Byzantine) king—of Lemnos and Thasos to Dorino, lord of Mitylene . . .

Part C

9.10. . . . The king reached Adrianople in mid-autumn.

10.1. After he arrived there, he immediately dispatched Ismael, the district governor of Kallipolis and chief of the entire navy, with orders to equip a fleet of 150 ships the soonest possible and to sail against Lesbos and Mitylene and to attack all of it, to ravage, plunder and destroy it thoroughly.

2. The two sons of Lesbos' lord Dorino, finding themselves heirs to the whole island and its government, staged a revolt . . . They concluded a treaty with Lodovico, the admiral of a thirty-trireme fleet sent by the high priest in Rome and so broke the contract with the king (the Turkish sultan) and refused to deliver to him the usual tax obligation, which had been paid annually. Not only that, but in that connection they provided landing places for the pirate ships and secretly granted them allowances. Then they ravaged all the nearby coast and raided any merchant ships sailing by.

3. Angry at them for these actions, the king sent his navy against them.

The sailing of the royal navy against Lesbos and Mitylene, the invasion of the island and its ravaging with the taking of much booty.

As quickly as possible, Ismael equipped 150 ships and loaded them with arms and machines and with well-trained soldiers, plus horses on the horse-carrying ships and gathered all other necessary preparations and supplies and then, boarding his ship, he took off from Kallipolis and in three days he reached Lesbos. He landed in the small coastal town called Molyvos and first he cut down all the surrounding area and ravaged it. Afterwards he surrounded the city and encircled it with his army and his war machines, to begin the siege.

4. On Lesbos at that time happened to be present twenty triremes, as provided by the alliance with Ludovico. They were under the command of Sergios and had been sent in advance to Ludovico to help Mitylene in case (as had been rumored) the sultan's navy sailed against it. When they received early warning that the sultan's fleet was coming, they were frightened and promptly sailed away to Khios and stayed there waiting.

5. When, after a ten-day siege of the city, Ismael accomplished nothing, he set fire to the houses in the outskirts of the city and after he raided a good part of Lesbos and ravaged and looted the villages, taking much booty with him, he sailed away home to Kallipolis and there he released his fleet.

6. When Sergios with his twenty ships learned that the fleet had left Lesbos, he returned to Mitylene. There he was put to great shame and received much blame by the city leaders because, despite the alliance and the promises of help, he left the city with empty hopes in times of need and ran away. So quite disturbed, or rather embarrassed, Sergios left for Lemnos and later went to Rhodos to be near Ludovico.

7. The people of Mitylene, feeling hurt like children, recovered their senses and, after these events, sent their delegates to the king to apologize and to defend themselves against the charges, to pay the tribute which they owed and to beg for an amiable consideration and for peace from then on. And that was how it was done after they were received by the king.

8. Later on, the people of Khios and Naxos did the same thing, fearful that they might suffer the way the people of Mitylene had.

COLLAPSING FENCES AND DEFENSES 313

They sent ambassadors to pay the tribute they owed and they renewed their treaties with the king.

. . . .

Part D

10.10. Again the king . . . crossed the Istros (the Danube river) and reached Adrianople, where he gave his army some rest. Soon afterwards, he summoned the leaders of the fleet and ordered them to prepare 200 new ships for (the attack against) Lesbos.

Sample page from the original fifteenth century manuscript found in the Library of the Topkapi Palace in Constantinople (Istanbul). From D.R. Reinsch, 1983.

Remarks about the causes of the king's campaign against Lesbos and Mitylene.

11.1. Nicorezo (16), the son and with his brother Dominico, heir of Dorino (Gattilusio), took over the paternal rule after their father's death and that included the treaties with the king and the obligation to pay tribute to him. However Nicorezo demonstrated his evil intentions with an unholy act. He seized his brother, imprisoned him and treacherously killed him. After that, he neither paid readily the tribute to the king, nor did he comply honestly with the treaties. Instead, he made secret contacts with the Italians and reached an agreement with them, as I mentioned earlier. He kept breaking his treaties with the king in many and different ways, yielding landing privileges to the pirate ships, adding to them his own and granting them control over the land and the harbors, bespoiling all the king's coast close to Lesbos and not only there but going beyond to Thrace and Macedonia.

2. Being informed about these actions repeatedly, the king sent a message and ordered him (Nicorezo) to stop behaving this way and to observe honestly the treaties, to maintain peace and also to pay promptly the tribute. Otherwise he was going to make war against him.

3. But he (Nicorezo) refused to comply and thinking that he was acting secretly, he ignored the king's warning and placed his vain hopes on the Italians. On his side and after many threats, the king did send a fleet to raid parts of Lesbos and this way to bring some sense to him (Nicorezo). But he was not intimidated and only for a short time he appeared to refrain from attacks, due to fear. Not much later, he again pursued his (aggressive) activities.

Expedition of the king against Lesbos by land and sea

4. Furious about all that, the king organized an expedition against him (Nicorezo). He prepared the navy as quickly as possible, arming it well and boarding many soldiers and all kinds of weaponry on the ships, including rock throwing machines and launches. He appointed Mahmud Pasha as the admiral and plenipotentiary chief of the fleet and sent it on its way. He (the sultan) then crossed with his army the Hellespont and marched by land through lower Phrygia.

Remarks on how the king made a historical notice of the heroes' graves when he crossed Troy and how he praised them and thought them blessed.

5. When he arrived at Ilium, he surveyed its ruins and the traces of the old city of Troy . . . and remarked on the history of the heroes' tombs, that of Achilles, of Ajax and the others and he praised them and thought them blessed, both because of the memory of their deeds and also because they had the good fortune of being extolled by the poet Homer . . .

12.1. From Troy he rushed to Lekton and moving from there he set camp on the continent facing Lesbos, right opposite Mitylene. On his part, Mahmud, coming from Kallipolis with all his fleet of 200 ships, reached Mitylene and had his army disembark and camp not far from the city.

The siege of Mitylene

2. Initially the people of Mitylene made a sortie but accomplished nothing, overwhelmed by the soldiers' force and so went back to their city, where they remained, closing all gates. At first, Mahmud sent word to them with an offer to them and to their ruler to come to an understanding with the king after surrendering themselves and the city to him. Unable to persuade them, he started to destroy and to loot everything in the outskirts and then lay siege to the city, encircling it with his army and installing his machines all around it. In six or seven days he shook and demolished with his machines not a small part of the walls.

3. Those in the city, seeing the walls collapsing, carried big logs and crossed the fortifications with them, inside and outside all around and also piled much dirt and other material from the inside, then fought on these.

4. Then the king, watching what was happening from the distance of his camp, could not wait anymore . . . but readied all his army and all his forces for an attack on the city, to capture it with one thunderous onslaught. And right away he ordered the army and all the military equipment to be transported to the island the soonest possible. So they all sailed across.

The king's crossing to Lesbos

5. The king himself boarded a trireme and reached Lesbos, where he joined Mahmud and was informed about everything. Afterwards, riding around it on a horse, he inspected the city and its fortifications, the nearest and the far away spots, from the land and from the sea. Then he ordered his army to spread out and the triremes to be combat-ready for an attack on the harbor.

Fall of Mitylene and surrender of all Lesbos

6. Whereupon, those in the city and their ruler, seeing that the king had come across and that his armies by land and sea were getting ready for the attack, were very fearful that they would be forced to drop their arms and be captured. They could see their walls collapsing under the enemy's bombardment, the endless crowd, the vigor and the full armor of the soldiers and realized that the onslaught of the king would be unstoppable and that he could overrun the whole island, if not destroy it totally. So they sent a messenger, surrendering themselves and the city to the king and also begging to be forgiven for not yielding promptly when they were called to do so.

7. The king received them and granted a pledge of good faith. Thus, the people of Mitylene with their ruler came out of the city and, bowing to the king, they surrendered it to him. He welcomed them kindly and rewarded them honorably. Afterwards he entered the city and inspected all well, judging it to be excellent and most beautiful. Then came the people from other fortresses and settlements to give themselves and their castles up.

8. The king spent altogether four days on the island and viewed it and everything on it, admiring its size, its beauty and all the other qualities of its soil and its structures. Then he boarded a trireme and crossed to his camp, leaving Mahmud to dispose of the affairs of the city and of the island as preordained.

9. He then gathered all the people in the city, by which I mean men, women and children and divided them into three lots. The first one he allowed to remain in the city and to live there, keeping and working their own lots and paying the customary annual dues. The second group he transferred to Constantinople to be settled there and of the third lot he made slaves to be distributed among his soldiers. But anyone he found that had been mercenary of the Italians he had them all put to death.

10. The other forts and settlements on the island he let them be and that's how they were for the time. Later he demolished some of them and dug them up, resettling the men, children and women to Constantinople.

11. After he disposed of those things in Mitylene and in all of Lesbos, Mahmud left to join the king, installing a strong guard in the city and in the other forts and leaving in charge as satrap (governor) a man named Samian Ali, who was renowned among them (the Turks) and well-known for his courage, military skills and his other qualities.

12. The head of the navy then took with him the lord of the Lesbians and all his entourage, men, boys and women, for the purpose of settling them in the City [Constantinople (11)]. Loading their ships with all kinds of booty, they sailed off for home, whether Kallipolis or Byzantium. Then he (the admiral) disbanded the fleet.

13. After dismissing his troops, the king himself and his personal attendants arrived in Byzantium. That was near the end of autumn of the year 6971 (1462 A.D.), the twelfth year of the king's reign.

13.1. That was how Lesbos and Mitylene were conquered by the king, after prospering in our own times, rising to great prominence, power and wealth for 150 years, from the time it was given by the king of the Romans to Nicorezo, the first of the Gateliusos, a man among the well-born from Italy.

. . . .

14.1. After the king returned to Constantinople, he settled the Mityleneans in one part of the City and gave to some of them houses, to others land to build a home and to the rest whatever they needed. However he locked their ruler, Nicorezo in prison and shortly afterwards he had him executed for good reason . . .

Part E

Campaign of the Venetians with seventy ships against Lesbos

7.1. That same summer the Venetians led an expedition against Lesbos and Mitylene with 70 triremes, large merchant ships in tow and 3,000 soldiers on board. They also had many arms on the merchant ships and stone-throwing machines and launchers, ladders and all other equipment required for storming walls.

2. When they arrived on Lesbos they settled in the harbor of Mitylene and after they disembarked they set up camp facing the city and then sent a message to those in the city requesting their surrender and that of the city. They, however, refused; there were at that time in the city 400 guards in full armor, from the royal court.

3. The Venetians first ravaged part of the land (they did not want to ruin it completely because they expected to capture it) and afterwards they surrounded the entire city, forming a circle with their army from the land and from the sea with the navy and, setting up their machines, they lay siege.

4. During the day they shook the walls with their machines and caused small parts to fall, but the people inside the city built those up during the night and further strengthened the walls with stones and wood and dirt. They also brought some large beams and crossed the walls with them . . .

5. Every day, the king's men made some sorties too, attacking the Venetians. Only a few of them died but many were wounded. The Venetians tried to dig tunnels under the walls and also erected some ladders and set up all kinds of machines.

6. Then came over to them two of the other settlements, so they already had great hopes to capture Mitylene and to get hold and control the rest of all Lesbos . . .

The king's navy sails off against the fleet of the Venetians in Lesbos

7. When the king learned about the attack of the Venetian fleet against Mitylene and its siege and that the city was in danger of being captured if it did not receive help very quickly, faster than words can tell, he equipped 110 triremes, boarded a large number of soldiers and a large number of arms and launching machines on them . . . and, assigning the leadership of his forces to Mahmud Pasha, he ordered the fleet to sail as fast as possible and to engage the enemy ships wherever they happened to be.

8. Leaving Byzantium, Mahmud sailed down the Hellespont and . . . beyond Kallipolis spotted four enemy triremes scouting around the port of Tenedos. During the night, they turned around and escaped and Mahmud, not to be seen humiliated took advantage of the right wind and next day reached Tenedos.

Capture of two Venetian scout triremes in Tenedos

9. There, in front of the harbor, he seized two of the triremes with all men on board, as they were trying to sail away. But the other two were already ahead and were just able to escape . . . These arrived in Mitylene and announced to their generals the approach of the king's fleet and the capture of the two ships.

Disorderly flight of the Venetian fleet from upon the approach of the royal navy

10. When they heard the news, which hit them like a thunderbolt, the Venetians abandoned everything there, the machines, the arms and all other equipment and boarded the triremes in disorder without any plan or logic. They took with them the men, women and children from the forts that had come over to them and were out in the open sea before the king's fleet arrived. That was to be expected, they said, in about eight hours.

11. When he came to Mitylene and found out that the Venetians had just departed, Mahmud began the chase in a hurry . . . Out in the open, he could barely see them approaching Lemnos, so despairing about his chances of catching up with them, he returned to Mitylene. He stayed there four days, settled all his affairs well and leaving a strong guard, with arms, much grain and all other necessities, he sailed back to Byzantium near the end of the fall season and there he disbanded his fleet. When he had finished with everything it was the year 6972 (1464 A.D.), and that was the 14th year of the king's rule.

Reinsch, D. R., 1983, pp. 79-192.

Lesbos remained under the domination of the Ottoman Turkish sultans for four-and-one-half centuries, from 1462 to 1912.

Chapter VII

ON THE VERGE OF FREEDOM

A. **On the verge of extinction**
   Under the "Franks" and the Turks
   A painful coexistence
   Aeolian "enlightenment"
   Free at last!

B. **Liberation and literary ferment**
   Ethnic re-awakening
   Some ordinary people
   The novels of S. Myrivilis: *Daskala*; *Mermaid Madonna*

C. **Now—and then . . .**
   Lesbos now
   A Lesbian-French art connection
   The Nobel-laureate poet from Lesbos
   Recycling the past

Peasant couple from Mytilene, Lesbos, painting by the folk artist M. Theophilos, 1931, Theophilos Museum, Varia, Lesbos.

Overleaf: Sketch of A. Eftaliotis, twentieth century businessman and poet from Lesbos, in G. Valatas' *Aeolic Bibliography 1566–1939*, Mytilene, Lesbos, 1939.

A. ON THE VERGE OF EXTINCTION

After belonging for 107 years to the Genoese Gattilusio family, Lesbos remained under the foreign and cruel domination of the Turkish sultans for 450 years, from 1462 to 1912. Amazingly and to the credit to both the conquered and the conquerors, the Greek language and traditions, the Christian Orthodox religion and the deeply rooted ethnic identity of the islanders persisted practically unchanged. In fact, near the end of the Ottoman rule, many among the Turkish elite seemed eager to adopt the Hellenic culture, mentality and habits. The last Turkish governor of the "Archipelago" (including Lesbos) in the first decade of the twentieth century, Abedin Pasha, or "Dino," had attended one of the better Greek schools on the mainland, spoke Greek well and was distinctly philhellenic (Karayiannis and Molinos, 1984, p. 35). In general, however, the ethnic and religious divisions and hostility persisted. Even in the mid-twentieth century, Greek writers, official proclamations and reports, while somewhat ambivalent concerning the Latin, or "Frank" (1) intruders, stressed consistently the horrors of slavery and the savagery of the Moslem masters. Enthusiastic philhellenes extolled the heroic Greek struggles for freedom and only an exceptional inquisitive historian delineated the gradual reversal of roles and the adaptability of both the Turks and the Greeks to the need for some stability, economic cooperation and survival (St. Clair, 1972, pp. 3–4, 7–10).

Abedin Pasha, the last Turkish governor of Lesbos (Karayiannis & Molinos 1984)

Under the "Franks" and the Turks

A twentieth century Greek travelogue referred to the impression of an Italian who saw the Aegean islands soon after the Turkish conquest.

> **A TOUR AROUND GREECE**
> by Chr. P. Zalokostas, 1940
>
> A Florentine, father Delmonte, . . . described vividly how he found the islands soon after the conquest by Mehmed. The men had vanished, the few women lived . . . "like animals," eating acorns and wild grass . . . The donkeys had become wild for lack

of masters . . . Those who had never been happy with the Byzantine rule were now saying "when we thought we had the worst we were better off" . . . (pp. 154-155)

The modern Greek novelist, historian, folklorist and neo-Byzantine painter, Photis Kontoglou, a refugee from the Aeolian lands of Asia Minor, wrote a series of articles in 1961 on the "Genoese on Lesbos," more concerned with stylistic mood than with historical facts (cf. Ch. VI, Table 1 and note 3). Subsequently these became part of a book, *The Suffering Greek People,* or *The Tormented Roman Folk* [*Ponemeni Romiosyni*], published in 1963 and reprinted many times since. The author borrowed much from the late Byzantine historical writers of the fourteenth and fifteenth centuries but also he reflected the deep emotions of the displaced Greeks of the twentieth century.

THE SUFFERING GREEK PEOPLE
by Photis Kontoglou, 1963
Mytilene under the Genoese and the Turks (5th printing, 1980, pp. 171-172).
This great island has been called Lesbos since ancient times and Mytilene has been its capital.

. . . .

Like all things in this unstable world, Mytilene also declined. . . . In Byzantine times, they exiled to Mytilene those condemned to this kind of punishment.

After 1000 A.D., however, this neglected island began to revive and that was done by some Italian merchants who settled there . . .

In 1330 a large fleet of Frankish ships arrived to fight the Turks. It was sent by the pope, the Venetians, the kings of France, of Naples and of Cyprus, by the knights of Rhodes and the lords of Naxos and Phokaia. After beating the Turks several times they returned to their home countries. Then the Genoese lord of Phokaia, Domenico Cataneo, the lord of Naxos . . . and the knights of Rhodes joined their naval forces and sailed to Mytilene to capture it, because the army that the king of The City (2a) had placed there was very small. In fact, they easily took most of the island forts, those of Kalloni, of Gera, of Petra, and of Saint Theodore, except for two strong forts, those of Molyvos and of Eresos, which remained faithful to the Greek king of The City. When the king, Andronikos Palaiologos, learned that the Franks had taken Mytilene, he set fire to their towers on Galata (2b) to punish the Genoese. Afterwards, within twenty days, he equipped 84 warships and in June 1334 went for Mytilene.

First he went to Molyvos, the ancient Methymna, and then to Eresos, to thank the people there for remaining faithful to him and to give them courage and support. In the meantime, however, Cataneo took time to fortify his garrisons in Mytilene and in Phokaia.

> The royal ships then went to Kalloni, where they killed a number of Genoese and took others prisoner. Later the king went to Hios . . . leaving in Mytilene his uncle Alexios . . . who was a brave and experienced general. In a short time he captured all the forts on Lesbos except for the capital, which took him more time to conquer.
>
> In 1354 the Genoese, Francisco Kateliuso (3), arrived in the waters of the East.

The author outlined the conflict between the son and successor of king Andronikos, John V, and his counsellor, presumed guardian and usurper of the throne, John VI Kantakouzenos. With the help of Gattilusio (or, for Kontoglou, *Kateliuso*), John V recaptured his throne and granted the Genoese the promised reward, which included his sister for a bride and the island of Lesbos for dowry.

> ### Mytilene under the Genoese and the Turks
> (cont., pp. 173–177)
>
> The next year, that is 1355, took place the marriage of the king's sister to Francesco Kateliuso and in a few days they landed on Lesbos, which the clever Genoese had received as dowry.
>
> The people of Mytilene did not resist the Frankish (1) lord because they did not see him as an alien but as the brother-in-law of the king and as one of their own, considering that he even minted money with the Palaiologos' insignia. Even so, Kateliuso never stopped being a Frank, in other words subservient to the pope . . . and did everything to have the patriarch and all the clergy recognize the primacy of the pope (of Rome) . . . The union they wanted with the orthodox was that of a wolf that is united with the lamb after eating it . . . But despite all the base and vicious efforts, the people of Mytilene remained unshaken in their faith. Even Francesco's wife was never attracted to her husband's religion and remained faithful to orthodoxy . . . In all the years that the Franks ruled Lesbos, the two orthodox sees [*thrones*] of Mytilene and Methymna never ceased to exist.
>
> The truth is that Francesco did much for the island's progress and put things in order as much as he could. He asked the knights of Rhodes to take to the island of Kos the many Armenians who were often creating disturbances and that brought peace to Mytilene. He repaired and fortified the island's forts and castles, he governed well and the people became fond of him. He died about 1376.
>
> After him ruled his son Jacopo, a lad of twenty years (Ch. VI, Table 1) In his time there was a conflict between Genoa and Venice ("two asses fighting in someone else's barn"). Mytilene however was not damaged . . . In the years of Jacopo's rule the island was fortunate. The commerce blossomed much more, many people became rich and Jacopo was loved by the Greeks. He died in 1397 and was buried with great honors. After him, lord of Lesbos became Francesco II (3), who departed early from this world. He was killed in a great earthquake which destroyed his palace and

ruined all the islands. In his years Mytilene began to pay tribute to the sultan. When Francesco II died in 1401 his brother Dorino succeeded him but because he was a minor, his uncle Nicolo governed for him. He died in 1409 and Dorino took over the government . . . Dorino made Constantine Palaiologos (who was to be the last king of The City) his son-in-law, by having him marry his daughter Katherine [*Aikaterina*].

. . . .

In 1442 the Turkish fleet . . . attacked the strong fortress of Molyvos. But the few fighters in it resisted strongly and the Turks left in shame.

In 1445 another robber landed on Lesbos, a Bulgarian turned Turk called Paitoglou, and he ravaged it. He totally demolished Kalloni, down to its foundations.

In 1449 old Dorino handed over the government of the island to his son Domenico. Those were hard years. The Turks had become wild and the Franks, fearing them, were very careful not to provoke them at all . . . But Domenico, being a thoughtless youth with boiling blood, did not wait for a Turkish challenge and decided to launch an expedition against the Turkish territories. He equipped many ships and as the new year 1452 began, he left the port of Mytilene and sailed against the opposite coast, which was held by the Turks and was rich with all kinds of produce and livestock. He captured a lot of that and took everything over to Lesbos . . .

. . . But the son and successor of Murad, Mehmed II, a 20-year-old Turkish youth, was like a mad dog . . . waiting for the hour of revenge.

Domenico did not understand his miscalculations . . . until a year later, after the Turks had captured The City and he saw with horror some boats coming to Mytilene with half-dead refugees fleeing the massacre . . . To appease the sultan, when the Turkish fleet was passing the straits between Lesbos and Asia Minor to attack Rhodes, Domenico sent to the admiral, Hamza Bey . . . expensive gifts: eight silk coats, 6,000 gold coins, 20 bulls, 500 sheep, 800 "measures" of wine, two "modes" of special cookies [*paximadia*], bread and cheeses . . . When Hamza once more anchored by Mytilene on the way back, Domenico again sent him many gifts and even went to the admiral's ship to dine with Hamza at a rich banquet which he had provided himself.

This story of Lesbos under the Genoese and the Turks continued with the description of the embassy headed by Doukas and the payment of annual tributes to the Turkish king. It described the siege and capture of Mytilene by the Turks, with reference to the fifteenth century Greek texts, which have been quoted in translation in Chapter VI. Then the modern Greek writer went on with more personal and emotional accounts of the suffering of Lesbos under the Turks.

Mytilene under the Genoese and the Turks
(cont., pp. 184-186)

Two days after the capture of Mytilene, sultan Mehmed sat on a high throne which had been placed near the North Harbor and ordered to have brought before him all the people of the city, young and old, men and women, to be listed by his scribes. Like a frightened herd, they were all pushed in front of the sultan and their wailing and lamentations reached the sky. With one nod from the sultan, 500 young men and girls were seized by his men for their master's harem . . . They did not even dare to cry freely . . . because those who did had their heads cut off . . . The sultan ordered all the prominent and wealthy people of Mytilene to be loaded on his ships. Only the poor were left . . . Some of the prisoners, about 10,000, reached The City alive. Some of them the sultan gave to his pashas, others he sold to slavery and the young and strong he placed in his army. Very few were ransomed by the pope and one of those was bishop Leonardo, who also wrote a history of the siege.

On the boats carrying the slaves to The City was also the ruler, Nicolo Kateliuso . . . After unbearable suffering . . . and because he had been accustomed to a good life, he gave up his faith and became a Moslem. But soon after his circumcision wounds healed, he was ordered by the sultan back in prison and later hanged on a bow string. So he died the same death he had inflicted on (his brother) the luckless Domenico.

The death of Nicolo was the end of the Kateluizi who ruled Mytilene for 107 years. Even though they were Franks (1), the truth is that they did not show the fanaticism and the conversion-mania typical of the Latins . . . Dorino loved Greek learning and took great care to preserve the antiquities on the island. All the Kateluizi, some more and some less, were among the better educated people of their times and wanted their land to prosper and to live in peace.

According to more recent commentaries (personal communications) the Genoese were not very kind to the islanders. They confiscated all the better farmlands and forced the former owners to work there as laborers. The Gattilusio lords only granted some favors to a few prominent Lesbian families, to gain their support and thus make their own position more secure. When the Turks came, they took many of the largest farms for themselves, but gave others back to the families of the original owners.

Mytilene under the Genoese and the Turks
(cont., pp. 186-189)

After it fell in the hands of the Turks, Lesbos withered. From 100,000 during the Kateluiso rule, the island population dropped to 30 or 40,000. Hunger and misery spread everywhere . . . During the first one hundred years of slavery one could not find a single literate person because the Turks had destroyed all the monasteries (4). Lesbos began to revive from that spiritual death only after 1700. Slowly the people of Mytilene started to engage in some commerce and many merchants settled in The City (Constantinople) and in Smyrna and became prominent. Others went over to the fertile areas of Asia Minor across the sea . . . and became rich. The Turks, as was their habit, after they took Mytilene, engaged in all kinds of barbarism. They looted, slaughtered, raped women, beat and tortured without cause . . . following the example of the heartless, cruel and bloodthirsty sultan Mehmed.

With such monsters . . . even the quietest people went wild with despair. Many Christians armed themselves and took to the mountains. A few of these armed rebels were in the area of Therme and apparently they were supported by the monks of the monastery of Karya, the abbott of which was Saint Raphael. Before he became a monk, Saint Raphael (who was made a saint after his martyrdom) must have been an army officer and probably one of the last Greek fighters that survived the fall of Constantinople . . . Besides the monks, the president of the village, Basil, and the teacher, Theodore, were among those who supported the rebels with food and ammunition and also warned them about approaching Turks.

. . . .

After the rebels took to the mountains, the Turks, like mad dogs, arrested the village president and the teacher and took them to the monastery to make them reveal, along with the monks, where the rebels were. To make the village president talk, the monsters tortured his little girl Irene in front of him, pouring boiling water down her throat. Finally they beheaded Saint Raphael and the teacher and they burned Irene in a big cauldron.

. . . .

The next day, the Turks, from what we know, demolished the church (of the monastery), took many of the pieces of marble away and then set the monastery on fire. The Turks cut down all the walnut trees around the monastery, which had given the place the name Karya and with the passage of time everything was buried under the dirt brought down by the running waters. On the resulting dirt hill later the Christians planted olive trees like we see them today.

. . . For five hundred years this story of the monastery of Karya remained completely forgotten, as if its awful secret was covered by a silent tombstone. Suddenly after all these years "the earth opened" as if by a signal and the dead jumped out and began to speak to the people around and to reveal all these things that had been forgotten for centuries . . .

. . . .

One would think that the words of the prophet Solomon were written for such a newly-revealed [*neophaneromene*] story, which had been buried for 500 years, saying that "the time will come for them to shine above all and to lead the path like the sparks of a torch." That demon-minded [*daimonopsychos*] sultan Mehmed, however, who terrorized the world and killed thousands like the holy martyrs of Therme, one wonders, where is he today? Who remembers him?

Despite the enduring mutual hatred and distrust, the subjugated Greeks were allowed a limited degree of self-rule at the local level. Higher up there was almost always a Moslem governor, a Turkish pasha, or military commander. One rare exception, cited recently by an historical researcher, professor Zwi Ancasi, was the appointment by sultan Selim II (1566–74) of a Turkish Jew, Don Solomon Yais (5) as governor, or "duke" of Lesbos. Jewish communities evidently had existed on Lesbos for hundreds of years. The twelfth century Spanish rabbi Benjamin of Tudella, on his extensive travels visited Lesbos—probably in 1169 A.D.—and noted that "on the island of Mitylene [*Mitali* may be phonetically closer to the Hebrew text; S. Ward, personal communication] ... there are ten Jewish synagogues in ten locations on the island" (*Jewish Quart. Review*, Vol. 16, p. 730, 1904; also reported in the Greek newspaper *Eleutheria*—"Freedom"—on Sept. 1, 1967).

A painful coexistence

Examples of Turkish-Greek interactions, ranging from brutal oppression and murderous revolts to business transactions and cooperative building are part of the history of those "dark" centuries. In a series of newspaper articles, another prominent modern Greek novelist, Elias Venezis, also a refugee from Aeolian Asia Minor and later a member of the National Academy of Athens, described a number of characteristic incidents. Venezis spent many years on Lesbos after the Greek military disaster of 1922 and the forced exchange of Greek and Turkish populations, which the two governments agreed to undertake in order to minimize regional ethnic diversity. Venezis was buried in the cemetery of Molyvos [*Methymna*], according to his wishes.

> **THE HOLY VIRGIN [PANAYIA] OF PETRA**
> by Elias Venezis, 1968.
> Petra, on the north side of Lesbos facing Molyvos, is one of the most picturesque villages of the Archipelago. It has a marvelous sandy beach, has been privileged to produce people dedicated to learning, literature and the arts and it also has its own chapel of the Virgin Mary on a rock, which dominates the little town, protects it and grants it beauty and charm.
> ... We climbed the steep steps, carved on the rock, again after so many years had passed since our youth ... The reverend priest spoke to us about the chapel's story, ... the miracles performed during the years of the Turkish rule ... He showed us the imperial

decree [*firmani*, in Turkish/Greek] of the year 1255 (Islamic year of the Hegira, corresponding to 1877 A.D.), in which the sultan permitted the rebuilding of the chapel "not one finger larger than the original," not so much to preserve Christian architectural tradition . . . but to prevent the temples of the infidel slaves from standing out.
>> Newspaper "Acropolis," Sept. 1, 1968, p. 5 (in Greek).

Compromise and submission among the enslaved Greeks were punctuated by acts of unrestrained provocation and challenge. A vivid and intense characterization of Christian self-denial and sacrifice, not much different from those of the first centuries of our era, was the life and martyrdom of Saint Theodore, the patron saint of Mytilene. His life and sacrifice were described in a booklet by the theologian and educator George Soteriou. The same author has published (1958) a *Lesbian Hagiology* about the lives, works and monuments of the saints on Lesbos, a booklet on *Actor-mania: A disease of our times* (1961) and, in 1989, a 150-page volume entitled *Hold on to the Truth*, extolling Orthodox Christianity against the errors and misdeeds of catholics and protestants.

SAINT THEODORE OF BYZANTIUM—PROTECTOR OF MYTILENE by George Soteriou, 6th edition, 1991 (in Greek)

The martyrdom of the neomartyr Saint Theodore of Byzantium (pp. 7–28)

In the holy series of new martyrs [*neomartyrs*] belongs also Saint Theodore, whose revered remains are guarded and honored as a precious treasure by the island of Lesbos. Like all the holy neomartyrs he too brightened with his faith and his martyrdom the somber years of slavery. He was born in 1774, in Neokhorion ("*New Village*") of Byzantium. His father's name was Anastasios and his mother's Smaragdee.

. . . .

To learn a trade, Theodore was placed beside a Christian painter, who worked in the palace of the sultan. How sad! . . . His daily contacts with the Moslems and his inexperienced and unstable youth contributed to a denial of his faith and his conversion . . . to the mohammedan religion.

The Divine Grace, however, at times descends upon men with the yardstick of a trial. Three years had passed and the terrible malady of the plague began to strike the area of Byzantium. The sickle of death was reaping daily dozens of both the rich and the poor. It was then that Theodore realized how fleeting is everything on earth . . . and sought the support of prayer . . . A feeling of remorse and repentance possessed his soul. Day and night only one thought prevailed in his mind: to find a way to escape the satanic environment of the infidels and to return to his own faith.

. . . After a first failure . . . a friend . . . helped him find a sailor's uniform, which would make it impossible for the Turks to recognize him. He put it on, painted his face darker . . . and carrying a pitcher, he made the sign of the cross . . . and ran away . . . After great pains and dangers he managed to reach the island of Khios.

He remained on Khios, fasting and praying and reading the Holy Scriptures and other religious books, among which the stories of martyrs, old and new, impressed him greatly . . . He admired their virtues and zeal and meditated deeply about their suffering and death for the love of Christ. Guided by his spiritual father, a good monk with whom he shared a hermit's life in a remote isolated spot, he prayed constantly to God, to give him strength. History has preserved the prayers written by that good monk, which Theodore learned and recited. Here is one prayer:

> "Lord Jesus Christ, healer of my miserable soul, do not disdain me the sinner but strengthen my weak and corroded heart and warm it up with the love of martyrdom for thy sake. It is through your grace that, after I denied you, my creator and benefactor . . . and became a servant of the filthy devil and a plaything of the demons, I may now, miserable and worthless that I am, with your unsurpassed tolerance and good will, which helped me escape their traps, become worthy of the Christian calling and of eternal blessing . . ."

. . . .

The strong desire for martyrdom led Theodore to Mytilene, where in front of higher Turkish authorities, he could present himself and declare his faith . . . The devout monk went with him to Mytilene, encouraging him and praying together with him.

The body of the martyr had become exceedingly thin from exertion and agony. Theodore took very little food saying "I cannot eat but must hurry towards my goal."

. . . After four days' stay in Mytilene, the monk met two Christians coming from the castle, who, after he questioned them, said: "Father, today we saw a young man named Theodore, who died in martyrdom for the faith of our Christ; he was hanging on the gallows and a crowd of people in awe admired his courage and the steady faith of this youth. He was about twenty years old."

The devout brother shed tears of joy and when they asked him why, he answered: "I heard something I never hoped to hear and that is to learn that someone suffered martyrdom for Christ in these times when evil has multiplied so much!" Then they started to tell him one-by-one the details of the full ordeal of the martyred Theodore . . . which were as follows:

On the fifth day of the first week of the Great Lent the martyr Theodore appeared before the judge of Mytilene . . . and bravely said: "I am an Orthodox, the Christian Theodore who ten years ago was led astray but later escaped your false and filthy Ottoman religion. I came to throw it back at you and recover my own faith" . . . Startled by the young man's temerity the judge asked those present who he was. They said that he was mentally deranged. The martyr interrupted them and said that he was not at all crazy but of a sane mind; he was an orthodox Christian, born a Christian and remaining and ready to die a Christian . . .

Getting angry, the Ottoman dignitaries present sent him away, pushing and whipping him mercilessly . . .

The next day, Friday of the same week, at 6 o'clock in the afternoon, they forcibly brought back the martyr for questioning and promised to give him many and large gifts and any other valuable things he wanted, if he would come to his right mind and stick to their religion. But the martyr answered: "I have a sound mind and also a steady and unshakable commitment to my faith. It is you who are moronic and mindless . . . I offer my life and despise all else for the love of my Christ. . . ."

To stop him from challenging them anymore, the chief of the military guard then ordered to have the martyr whipped and beaten and then taken to jail, where they tied him up. After he suffered three hundred lashes on his feet, they allowed any other Ottoman subject to come in and whip him. Fifteen other Ottoman Turks whipped him indiscriminately on both sides and rolled him on the ground like a sack . . . Afterwards they put two pieces of tile on the sides of his head and fastened them so tightly with a rope that his eyes bulged out of their sockets and his head was turned backwards. Yet the soldier of Christ kept saying "I am a Christian, Christian, Christian." So the ferocious Ottomans, to make him keep quiet, put a stick in his mouth, pressed hard on his jaw and pulling the stick back forcibly, broke several of his teeth and left him half dead in the jail.

Saturday morning . . . one of the Ottomans . . . put tobacco smoke under his (Theodore's) nose and placed a burning ashtray on the back of his neck saying "This is what you get for cursing our faith."
. . . .

In the meantime the rumor spread that . . . they were going to cut the martyr's legs from the knees down. But, hearing this, the local chief sent a message to the Ottoman judge, blaming him for not knowing the laws that required him to condemn the martyr to death promptly after he had uttered blasphemies against Mohammed . . . So the infidels put a rope around his neck but when they pulled it, it broke and the martyr fell to the ground and wounded his knee, from which ran much blood. In that condition, the infidel Turks pulled him up again and placing another rope around his neck they hung him. It was this way that the blessed man was given the wreath of martyrdom he desired. Blood dripped from the knee of his tormented and martyred body for three days without stop. Christians came from everywhere after he was dead and with the greatest reverence approached the body of the martyr and each one cut a piece of his coat, dipped it in the blood of his martyrdom and guarded it safely in their homes as a sacred benediction. Many among them declared and vowed that after they drank from a distillate of that blood and in deep devotion called upon the saint's recognition, they were cured from their ailments.

With the grace of God, the revered remains of the saint were found intact after the passing of three years. In 1798 the body was secretly, without the knowledge of the Turkish rulers, taken to the cathedral, where it was deposited . . .

Saint Theodore saves the people of the city from the plague (pp. 39–42)
... In the year 1832, a terrible plague struck Mytilene ... and led dozens of Turks and Christians, regardless of class and age, to their graves ... But the neomartyr Theodore's mediation by the Lord managed to accomplish what the numerous medical teams and medications could not ... A permission was granted ... for a procession of the saint's body ... and from that moment no other deaths were noted ... Since then Saint Theodore had been revered as the patron saint of Lesbos.

Saint Theodore (cont., p. 44)
When during the bitter days of the last war (World War II) the city and the island remained "unshaken, not-burned and bloodless" as written in the ancient prayer book, ... the pious population of Lesbos attributed the protection of the island ... to Saint Theodore's mediation by the Lord and that strengthened everyone's faith. This is shown in many ways and particularly during the day of the Saint's community-wide religious procession.

The cathedral of Mytilene is the church of Saint Athanasios, located at the north end of the commercial district and near the old Turkish neighborhood. Records of repairs and additions dated from 1706-07 indicate that the main building of the church was there at the beginning of the eighteenth century (Soteriou, 1991, p. 68). Under the glass cover of a heavy wooden coffin one can still see today the white skull of Saint Theodore, partly covered by a heavy ornate crown.

Massive slaughter of Christians took place on Lesbos from 1769 to 1774 during the war between Turkey and Russia. The island was part of the Ottoman line for the defense of the Hellespont (the Dardanelles) but irregular bandits accompanying the Russians managed to land on Lesbos and looted Turkish properties. In revenge the Turks massacred many Greeks indiscriminately. A particularly heavy slaughter of Christians took place in 1771, when the Russian navy burned two Turkish warships in the harbor of Mytilene. The Turks also mistreated and abused the orthodox patriarch Meletios, who happened to be on Lesbos, exiled from Constantinople. After the war, however, under the treaty which provided for greater religious freedom for the subjugated Greeks and gave the Russians the right to intervene to protect them, there was a period of increased security and prosperity for the natives of Lesbos. Before long, the stirrings of a Greek independence movement were beginning to be felt.

LESBOS—THE ISLAND OF HARMONY
by M.H. Eleftheriadis, 1981.
The flame of national pride always burned strongly in the hearts of the enslaved people of Lesbos. In 1817 came from the Black

Sea to Mytilene two Lesbians, Palaiologos and George Lemonis. They had been initiated in the secret "Society of Friends" [*Philiki Hetereia*] and they returned to begin spreading the word about the revolution to shake off the Turkish yoke. Besides the Lemonis brothers, other members of the *Philiki* society were the scholar Benjamin the Lesbian from Plomari and the Metropolitan of Hungary-and-Wallachia [*Vlakhia*] Ignatios.

In 1824, while the war of independence against the Turks was expanding on the mainland of Greece, an uprising was attempted also on Lesbos but it was bloodily suppressed. Two years later, however, in 1826, Greek revolutionary naval forces under captain Miaoulis defeated the Turkish fleet in the straits off Mytilene and chased it as far as Smyrna (Elef. p. 12). Lesbos, however, remained in Turkish hands until 1912.

Aeolian "enlightenment"

An abundant literature in modern Greek, both in the "purist" style observing ancient linguistic forms and in the "demotic" (6) everyday language of the people, reflected eloquently—sometimes too eloquently, in flowery and pompous terms—the aspirations and ideals of the Greek population of Lesbos. These are included in two extensive publication lists of *Aeolian Bibliography* which appeared in 1939–40. The first ("A") by G. Valetas was sub-titled "1566-1939: Printed books and other published matter on Lesbos and its Aeolian district; printed books and other matter written by Lesbians and Adramytians" (*sic*, with one "t") . It contained an impressive list of 1,374 items, most of them books and journals in Greek. History and current affairs, literature, education and religion were the prevalent topics. Publications by Lesbians in foreign languages (mostly French and German) dealt mainly with medicine, biology and chemistry. "A contribution to Aeolian bibliography" by K.M. Michaelides ("B"), published soon after the first one in 1940, covered the years 1820–1939 and, following an introductory critique of the first compendium, it listed 602 works, including (according to the subject index) 98 on modern Greek literature and folklore, 75 on education and 151 on medical matters. Of special interest were some Greek books published in the U.S.A. such as (list "A," No. 597, 600) "Ruined altars—songs of love and emigration" by G. Semeriotis, New York, Divry Publ. 1912; "Songs of emigration" by D.E. Valakos, New York, Divry Publ. 1912 (?) and (list "B" No. 223) "A father's love—a drama in three acts" by John P. Palaiologos, New York, Kosmos Publ. 1914. On list "B," No. 342 was a "Commemorative Album" dedicated to the nineteenth century Lesbian poet and scholar D.N. Vernardakis, published in 1929 in Newark, New Jersey, on the occasion of the annual ball of the Panlesbian Society of America. It included photographs and original poems. Earlier works in Greek from the 16th-18th centuries, when an independent Greek state did not exist, were published in Austria, England, France, Germany, Italy and Russia. A Dutch translation in 1918, of a much appreciated work by the turn-of-the-century Lesbian writer, A. Eftaliotis, his "Island Stories," was also cited (list "B," No. 246). A new compendium (6) listed 2,094 more works by 365 Lesbian authors published in the last fifty years (Missios, K.G.: *The Books of Mytilenean Authors*—from Jan. 1, 1940 to Aug. 31, 1989, Mytilene, 1989). These pertain mostly to literature, history, education and theology, but also include archeology, art criticism, folklore, medicine, philosophy and children's books.

Of the few works that can be mentioned in this 3,000 year history, several reflected the emphasis placed by the Lesbian society of 100 or 150 years ago on Hellenic culture and education. The Vernardakis family included several members prominent in literature, education and the social sciences. The elder Vernardakis, Demetrios N., wrote pioneer texts on Greek grammar (list "A," No. 132, of 1868, with several subsequent editions) and later Gregory N. Vernardakis published books on "Syntax and hermeneutics" (list "B," No. 182, 1907) and "A lexicon of the most famous Greek poets and writers" (list "B," No. 184, 1907). Several scholarly women of Lesbian background wrote books for children or on children's education. Such were the illustrated "A children's calendar," by Polyxene Melandinos (list "A," no. 358, Constantinople, 1896) and three works by this author and her sister Harikleia, with the title "A girl's reader," published between 1902 and 1904 and reprinted often afterwards (list "A," Nos. 432, 433, 447 and 454). Harikleia Melandinos also published a three-part writing manual for school children entitled "Compositions" and published in Constantinople in 1905 (list "A," nos. 466–468).

The "Aeolian Bibliography" also listed the impressive publications by secondary school students, such as the one on "Our Art" [*Tekhne*]— No. 960 on list "A." These were mostly periodical publications, some of which appeared in only one or two issues and others continued publication for several years and demonstrated the enthusiasm and literary productivity of the young islanders in the past 150 years. It must be noted that during most of this time Lesbos was not part of Greece but remained under Turkish domination.

LESBOS—THE ISLAND OF HARMONY
by M.H. Eleftheriadis, 1981, (p. 10).
After the new Greek State was founded (7) Lesbos remained

outside its borders until 1912, when . . . it was liberated by Paul Kountouriotis. The island became officially part of Greece by the treaties of London and of Athens in 1914. The rights of the Greeks on Lesbos were recognized by the treaties of Sevres and Lausanne in 1923, at which time, with the population exchange (7) the remaining Ottomans left the island.

The conditions on Lesbos in the early twentieth century, the historical events associated with the liberation from the Turks, the news coverage, the military and other official proclamations were contained in a special commemorative edition of 1984.

MYTILENE, 1912
by V. Karayiannis and S. Molinos, 1984.

Introductory notes (p. 6–8, in Greek)

In the beginning of our century, the Turkish presence on Lesbos—of about 450 years—still cast its heavy shadow over this gentle land. On the island, so blessed by nature, lived about 20,000 Turks, who, however, were financially dominated by five times their number of Greeks, most of them Ottoman subjects.

The Lesbians cleverly maintained their own special policies regarding everyone's interest and welfare . . . They gave the appearance of accepting the Turkish rule even though in reality they undermined it . . . The conqueror, dispirited and lazy by nature, became financially dependent on the banker who was his lender. Gradually

Facing page: Postcards with view of the port of Mytilene on Lesbos, and view of the quay near the garden in Mytilene (note French spelling, *Métélin*, Turkish postage stamp). *Above:* Postcard with view of the *Gymnasium* (high school) in Mytilene. Greek army on Lesbos, 1912 (in Karayiannis & Molinos 1984).

and stealthily, the people of Mytilene (8) bought back for a loaf of bread the Lesbian farmland that had been seized by the Turkish lords ... and they held all business in their own hands.

The privileges granted from time to time to the Christians by the sultans, whether because they feared their rebellion or because they wanted to prevent the emigration of the educated class, contributed to the intellectual ascent of the Greek element and the preservation of the ethnic identity of the enslaved population.

At the time (the beginning of the twentieth century) there were in Mytilene literary groups and clubs, printing shops, libraries, reading rooms and banks. Newspapers and periodicals of enviable quality were published, lectures and artistic performances were held, which naturally raised the cultural level of the people and bolstered their morale ... The island blossomed. It was called by the Turks *Altin adasi*, which meant the Golden Island. Olive oil was the local gold. The harbor rang with activity. Many industries, flour mills, oil presses, soap factories, tobacco handlers, textile mills ... machine shops, were all incessantly busy.

... Confronted by the specter of the conqueror, our people established athletic clubs, where in addition to gymnastics, they cultivated their members' national awareness, organized quasi-military exercises and provocative parades in special uniforms, with trumpets and drums that stirred the subjugated Greeks [*rayias*] ...

It seemed hard to believe, but in 1908, when the sultan consented to grant a constitution, the representatives from Mytilene, chosen by the first election, were all Greek. This was not seen anywhere else in the occupied lands.

Around 1910 the surrounding islands were part of the department [*Vilayet*, in Turkish] of the Archipelago ... This was divided into four districts ... and the Muscat Islands of Adramytion Bay belonged to the district of Lesbos. The military guard of Mytilene had its barracks inside the fort [*kastro*] ... The duties of the gendarmes were minimal ... Armed irregulars [*basibuzuk*, meaning free agents in Turkish], however, irresponsible and unrestrained, were everywhere and, always undisciplined, had constantly their minds on looting. The Turkish families in Mytilene lived in their own district on the Upper Harbor, the *Skala*, by the Northern Bay. Their houses there, in the middle of mosques and bathhouses [*hamam*, in Turkish] were poor and dilapidated, with some exceptions of a few lordly mansions. There were also some Turkish homes inside the Fort, for the greater security of those who feared a sudden rebellion of the subjugated Greeks.

The Christian neighborhoods were concentrated in the middle of town and on the hills, stretching toward the Long Beach [*Makry Yialo*] and the surrounding countryside, where most of the mansions were built. Churches and small countryside chapels [*exocclesia*] were everywhere. People were very religious ... and seemed to feel protected being close to the saints.

Free at last!

The commemorative volume on the liberation of Lesbos continued with the description of events, with photographs and verbatim quotations of official proclamations and orders.

MYTILENE, 1912
by V. Karayiannis and S. Molinos, 1984, cont. (pp. 54-118).

In the fall of 1912 much tension was in the air on the island and especially its capital, Mytilene . . . Early in October, the first Balkan war was declared against Turkey, which then lost one after another its occupied lands. The enslaved population started to dream about the hour of their island's liberation, while the Turks became increasingly suspicious and violent . . . The Greek navy controlled the Aegean and challenged the Turks . . .

. . . Religious leaders on both sides adopted a diplomatic and tactful tone in their speeches and publications. Metropolitan Kyrillos advised the Christians "in those extraordinary and difficult circumstances to establish closer ties of brotherly love and compassion with the Moslems and not to indulge in the slightest act of provocation . . . " The Turkish *mufti* (religious counsellor) went along and counselled calm and "to trust their Christian compatriots." But it was generally believed that the remaining days of the Turkish occupation were very few . . . The Greek army . . . planned to finish the campaign in Macedonia and . . . afterwards to turn to the Aegean islands. The final decision was to reach Lesbos on November 8, 1912.

We expected their arrival . . . like slaves waiting to be freed.

. . . About 10:30 P.M. the destroyer "Arrow" [*Velos*] docked by the tanneries and a messenger disembarked and carried the announcement to the cathedral and to the few of our citizens . . . that the reinforced fleet would sail into Mytilene at about 4:30 P.M.

From the newspaper "Popular Strife," Nov. 9, 1912
(quoted in Greek, p. 56).

Declaration (p. 75)

**IN THE NAME OF
HIS MAJESTY, THE KING OF THE GREEKS
GEORGE I**
I, vice admiral Paul Kountouriotis
Chief of the Aegean fleet
TO THE RESIDENTS OF MYTILENE ISLAND

I declare and order:

1. The island of Mytilene (8) with all the towns, villages and communities on it, with its harbors and seashores has been taken by us and remains from now on in our possession.

2. The Ottoman authorities on the island, except for local government clerks, are to step down and their authority is to be

assumed by the Commander of the occupation forces, captain Manousakas, whom we appoint as general supervisor. The entire island is declared to be in a state of siege . . . and a special military court is being established in the city of Mytilene, with authority over the entire island.

3. The general supervisor has the authority to employ for the administration of the island the existing Ottoman subjects, but he may replace them in accordance with the needs and best interests of the services.

. . . .

11. Any act or attempted act that endangers the security of the occupation army, the navy and/or in general the best interests of Greece, will be handled by the military court as a crime of high treason and will be punished by death 24 hours after judgment is rendered.

. . . .

In sight of Mytilene and from the battleship "G. Averoff."
Nov. 8, 1912
The vice admiral and chief of the navy.
Paul Kountouriotis

The first military circular of the Commander of the Occupation Army read as follows (Karayiannis/Molinos, 1984, p. 97):

The Commander
of the Occupation Army
To the Communities
and the Religious Authorities of Mytilene

We command you, in joint and harmonious cooperation and under the protection of the Greek Laws, to continue peacefully your work and to protect the life, honor and property and the family security of all citizens without exception and regardless of religion.

You must report to us directly the unlawful act of anyone who disturbs or in any way oppresses any peace-loving citizen.

You must recommend and maintain a concordant spirit between Christians and Ottomans and must explain to them that under Greek law they are all equal.

Finally you must counsel everyone to disarm and you must collect all arms and ammunition, allowing to bear arms only the civilian guards appointed by you, whom you must provide with a written permit, duly signed by you.

Anyone not complying immediately with these orders of ours will be arrested and taken to the military court to be tried according to the Military Law.

In Mytilene, Nov. 20, 1912
The Commander of the Occupation Army
A. Manousakas

The Protocol of (the Turkish) Surrender

Captain Const. Melas

The following protocol of surrender was contracted between the navy captain K. Melas, military commander of Mytilene and army captain Eleftherios Vernardos, chief of staff of the occupation army, as representatives of the overall chief of the army of occupation on one side and on the other of Mssrs. Ahmet Ikhsan Bey, military doctor and of Kemal Bey, vice-commander of the gendarmerie, as representatives of the Ottoman army of Mytilene.

1. The officers of the defense forces of the Ottoman army are allowed to go free on the island of Mytilene, keeping their swords upon their word of honor that they will no more take up their arms against Greece or against the allies.

2. The captured Turkish army, whatever their number might be, will surrender its arms and ammunition and all material considered as spoils of war and will be fed and maintained at the expense of the Greek government.

3. The defendant army must gather in the fortress of the city of Mytilene under the supervision of the Greek army. After order has been established, any local draftees may return to their villages by special permission of the military commander.

4. The occupation army will by in charge of the medical care of the wounded Turkish men who, after they recover, must gather in the fort.

5. The families of the officers will be free to go anywhere they wish.

6. The details of the transport of the prisoners, of the arms and of all other material to Mytilene will be settled by special order of the commander.

The present protocol, written in duplicate, one in Greek and the other in Turkish, has been signed by all the representatives ...

Saturday, December 8, 1912, 11 A.M.
Signed: Melas, Bernardos, Dr. Ikhsan, Kemalbey

Ibid., p. 111.

. . . .

(From the report of the Army General Staff).

Thus terminated the expedition of Lesbos, with total losses:
    One officer dead, . . . and eight soldiers.
    One officer wounded, . . . and eighty soldiers.
(From the report of the general staff).

Ibid., p. 113.

. . . .

The verses of the Lesbian poet Argyris Eftaliotis were quoted in the speech of B.P. Alvanos, welcoming the victorious troops.

> A fire your eyes now thrust, a fire scorching lands,
> A fire that frightens all your foes and bolsters all your friends,
> So now again you have spread the greenery of freedom
> On our deserted dry hills and our withered fields.
>
> *Ibid.,* p. 118

Lesbos officially became part of Greece by the treaties of London and of Athens in 1914. After the Greek military disaster of 1922, a population exchange was arranged (7), and thousands of refugees from Asia Minor came to the island as they also migrated to other parts of Greece. The Turks left Lesbos to relocate in what had become the new Republic of Turkey. During World War II Lesbos again lost its independence. It was occupied by the German army from May 14, 1941 to September 10, 1944. The privations and armed guerilla movements encountered in the rest of occupied Greece were also seen on the island but to a much lesser degree.

B. LIBERATION AND LITERARY FERMENT

Ethnic re-awakening

A current booklet on the "history-folklore-archeological interest-tourism" of Lesbos outlined the course of the Hellenic Renaissance on the island prior to the 1912 day of liberation from the Turks.

> **LESBOS—THE ISLAND OF HARMONY**
> by M.H. Eleftheriadis, (p. 11).
> During the Turkish occupation all cultural and intellectual activities on the island were dead. The first official school appeared in 1774. In 1864 were published the Regulations of the Gymnasium (High School or Lyceum) in Mytilene. The foundations of education were then established. An intellectual rebirth began in the last quarter of the 18th century. The introduction of printing presses on the island contributed to that. In 1881 the periodical "Sappho" began its publication. The first newspaper . . . "The Trumpet" [*Salpinx*] started publication in 1909.

The educational activities in the Turkish-occupied Greek lands were described in much detail in an 1867 book published in the then-Turkish capital, Constantinople, in Greek.

> **A Sketch of the Status of Education Among the Greek People [*Ethnos*] From the Fall of Constantinople**

(1453 A.D.) to the Beginnings of the Present (Nineteenth) Century
by Matthew K. Paranikas, 1867.
Chapter III (p. 173)

. . . .

In Mytilene, in 1757, there was a record of an already existing School; out of it came, besides Dorotheos the Lesbian and Ioannis—John, also called Tzanis—who were schoolmasters at the Patriarchal School (1726-1744), . . . the scholar Serapheim (1703), a monk-priest who corrected the first translation of the New Testament in our common current [koine] language; Anthony Palladokles (1770), a scholar who lived in Russia and composed songs in Greek, in iambic, sapphic and heroic meters, . . . Theodosios the Lesbian (1807), who published "The Elements of Navigation" and others. The School of Mytilene has been maintained ever since and now it has been converted into a Gymnasium (High School).

Among the many works by Lesbian authors published in the 50 or 75 years before liberation were several ambitious theatrical pieces on ancient or revolutionary heroic themes. *Merope* was a five-act tragedy by D.N. Vernardakis (1866); *The Death of Markos Botsaris* (a revolutionary fighter against the Turks), a tragedy in three acts by Theo. Alkaios (1876); *Belisarios* (sixth century Byzantine general) a tragedy in five acts, by K.P. Yakinthos (1877); *Nikephoros Phokas* (tenth century Byzantine emperor), a drama in five acts (1905), etc. Of greater and longer-lasting impact was the full series of publications by the succession of men in the Vermardakis family and then the stories and poems by the Lesbian emigré and international businessman A. Eftaliotis. *Argyris Eftaliotis* was the pen-name of Kleanthes Michaelidis (1849–1923), which he chose to refer to his native village of Eftalou on the north shore of Lesbos. As a writer, Eftaliotis was an "influential figure" in promoting the use of the "demotic," or (common) people's language in literature and he retained his "intransigent linguistic views to the end, as only men living abroad and away from the realities of Greek life could afford to do" (Trypanis, 1981, p. 664). This meant that Eftaliotis, an independent and successful businessman in England and in India, did not have to fear ridicule and to worry about losing his job if he opposed the conservative officially imposed "purist" language style approximating the Greek of antiquity. Evidently multilingual (his business was in England and in India and in later years he lived—and died—in France), Eftaliotis wrote abundantly in modern Greek with an extraordinary feeling for the warmth, the musicality, the plasticity (he created new words himself when needed) and the lyrical qualities of the living language. His translation of Homer's *Odyssey* (Kollaros & Co., Athens, 1932) is a literary tour de force unequalled among modern translations and truly a marvelous work of art, which regrettably cannot be appreciated by those not familiar with the nuances and the pulse of contemporary Greek poetry. Curiously, at present even in Greece the works of Eftaliotis receive relatively little attention. His *Complete Works* [*Apanta*] were published (some only posthumously) in Athens in three volumes, between 1952 and 1973. Yet currently (1992) no bookstore in Athens, nor in Mytilene, could be found to carry his once internationally recognized *Island Stories* [*Nesiotikes Istories*], which were published originally in 1894, with second and third editions in 1911 and 1975 and several foreign language translations in the interim.

A modern Greek anthology of poetry contained four poems by Argyris Eftaliotis.

> **Anthology** 1708–1952
> by H.N. Apostolidis, 1954.
>
> A. Eftaliotis (p. 201–202)
> *From* **The Mother The Child** (9)
>> From the mother comes the babe
>>   from the earth spring all the flowers
>> from a well we get the water
>>   and from love is born a song
>> But that song no matter how sweet
>>   how joyfully it comes to be
>> holds a deep bewitching magic
>>   and you are left forever sad.

Also in the *Anthology* of 1954 were the poems "A Tavern Song," "Promenade" and "Song of the Loom." The last one was set to music and became a popular song in the 1930s (Keeley and Bien, 1972, p. 196).

> **Song of the Loom**
>> Weave now fast my shuttle through,
>>   the finest silk arrange
>> My beau will come on Easter Day,
>>   in golden clothes to change
>> (tack-o-tack my loom is humming
>>   tack and lo!, my beau is coming!)
>> . . . .
>> I'll become the warp myself
>>   and he shall be the weft
>> To get enmeshed in the cloth
>>   never to have me left
>> (tack, he'll come, can never miss
>>   for wedding wreaths and also a kiss).

Eftaliotis died in Antibes, on the French Riviera in 1923. In 1974 his remains were brought to Lesbos and buried by the beach in Eftalou.

Some ordinary people

The emphasis on "lofty" literature and international politics may be balanced by some consideration of simple, "lowly" trades and occupations. In a nostalgic and picturesque description of now almost extinct types of work in the village of Kalloni on Lesbos, a dedicated Lesbian folklorist and social worker by profession has listed 51 old trades that modern developments made disappear. He also outlined some major demographic changes on the island—particularly since the arrival of thousands of refugees from Turkey in 1922–23—and gave lively profiles of individual tradesmen and women.

> **GONE BUT NOT FORGOTTEN: ANCIENT OCCUPATIONS AND TRADES IN KALLONI OF LESBOS**
> by Chr. I. Tragellis, 1986
>
> **The town crier** (*telalis*)
> One of the most picturesque professions in those days . . . which adorned and embellished the then peaceful life in Kalloni was the *telalis*. He was a distinct personality, a man with something unique, considering that his fellow villagers counted on him for learning about important events, for any announcements from the community office and about public auctions. He also brought to the people current news about the arrival of various merchants for the purchase of tobacco, grapes, figs, wheat, etc.
>
> The *telalis* was appointed by the community office . . . Each man had his own peculiar way of calling his messages but they all had a characteristic thundering voice. They stood firm with legs apart and placed their hands on their waist . . . in a position to make their voice as loud as possible.
>
> Many years ago, when the maestro Myrojiannis came to Kalloni of Lesbos with his two brothers . . . for a musical performance, the *telalis* advertised it this way: "Hear, hear, now came the Myrojiannelises and brought with them some special table. When you strike this it sounds glan . . . glan!" That "table" was a piano . . . (pp. 60–63).

The author went on with sketches of three known town criers and stories about them.

> **Candle makers**
> The only family involved for many years in the manufacture and sale of candles in Kalloni was that of Michael Konstantellis . . . That was not the only business activity of that family. Michael . . . was the most progressive and inventive merchant in Kalloni. He

started his business around 1910–13 at the age of twenty years and kept working between Kalloni and Egypt. In 1913 he opened in his own building in the market a store selling only wedding and baptism supplies. At the same time he operated a soap-making factory in the backyard of his home . . . In 1914 he followed the trend of his times and left with others from Kalloni for America, letting his brother Demetrios manage his affairs. When he returned from America in 1924, enriched by the experience in the New World, he expanded his business activities and established a kind of home-industry, working with his brother and his two sisters, one of whom left a wealth of folklore material, later recorded by a folklorist . . . He organized the soap factory and started making aromatic soaps on which he imprinted his seal . . . Along with all this he created a candle factory . . . which made the most beautiful kinds of large candle [*lambada*] decorated with ribbons, etc. He even improved the manufacture of wedding items, wreaths, garlands etc. and also of christening supplies. All these items they made themselves at home. They also built there beautiful boxes to put their merchandise in.

On their own they also made different kinds of incense, into which they mixed many aromatic plants. Finally, in the backyard of their home there was a full set-up to make wine, ouzo, brandy and various liqueurs like menthe and cherry. . . . We must also mention that Michael Konstantellis was fairly well educated . . . and was intensely involved in various cultural activities. Thanks to his initiative, the Amateur Club of Kalloni was founded in 1913 and it continued theatrical performances. Any proceeds were contributed to philanthropy (pp. 105–106).

"Goat-love dealers"

This is how I decided to call those tradesmen who maintained their billy goat to make him available to those . . . who kept goats at home. From August 1 until the end of November . . . that owner would bring his goat to the billy goat to "alter" her, meaning to make her pregnant. Pregnancy was confirmed in 8–15 days with another visit to the billy goat. He then would approach and smell her and if in this way he detected that she was pregnant, he would avoid her. Her owner then paid whatever the billy goat love was worth and took her back . . .

During the time the billy goat was "busy," the whole surrounding area smelled very bad . . . This business slowly began to disappear because very few people kept goats at home anymore (pp. 166–168).

The names and personal stories of five men and one woman "goat love merchants" followed, with graphic details of their work.

A very different and broader perspective of the Lesbian scene in the past 100–200 years was provided by another recent publication entitled *Travelers' accounts about Lesbos*, by P.S. Paraskevaidis (2nd ed., Athens, 1983). It included general impressions and regional details noted by foreign visitors to the island (quoted by Tragellis, 1986, p. 158). Those rare and perceptive guests have now been followed by crowds of poorly discriminating tourists.

The novels of Stratis Myrivilis

The feelings and frustrations of the people on Lesbos after their independence from Turkish rule have been vividly described by a writer, whose own life reflected the longings, hopes and despair of that generation on the island in the aftermath of World War I and following the catastrophic collapse of the Greek struggles for the revival of the Hellenic world in the Eastern Aegean shores. The author, Stratis Myrivilis who has been called "the originator of the Lesbian Spring" (Annotations, pp. 92 and 184), was born in 1892, in the village of Sykamia (probably from the word *syko*, meaning "fig" in Greek), also written Skamnia (Annotations, pp. 89, 183) in north Lesbos. His family name was Stamatopoulos and his father was a merchant who, in later years (after the eastern markets were lost to the Greeks) stayed home to cultivate his own lands. Stratis attended school in Mytilene and, when he failed to complete the third grade of the local gymnasium (equivalent to ninth grade U.S.A.), because "his mind wandered," or because he disliked the teachers (*Annotations,* 1987, p. 183), he was sent to a Greek school across the sea in Asia Minor. In 1910 he was appointed school teacher on Lesbos and started to write, using the pen name Myrivilis, after the name of a local mountain peak (derived from the Byzantine word "hemeroviglion," meaning a day-watchpoint). In a literary contest sponsored by the Greek journal "Youth" [*Neotes*] of Smyrna, Myrivilis won first prize. In 1912 he and other young men from Lesbos volunteered to serve in the Greek army fighting the Turks, even though they were officially Turkish subjects, because the island still belonged to Turkey. Wounded in the leg by two bullets, he was recuperating in the hospital when he heard that Lesbos had been liberated by the Greek navy. He sold his watch to treat friends to dinner and celebrate. In 1914–16 he was the editor-in-chief of the largest Lesbian newspaper, "The Trumpet" [*Salpinx*], but then again, in 1918, he found himself in the army in Macedonia, after Greece had entered the war on the side of the Allies. The Greeks continued the war

S. Myrivilis. *Commentaries,* 1987

against Turkey and advanced deeply into Asia Minor. Myrivilis was near the front when the expedition ended with the military catastrophe of 1922 and with the flight of as many Greeks as could escape from the ancient Aeolian and Ionian coasts. The following two decades were Myrivilis' most productive years. From 1936 to 1951 he was General Program Director of the Greek National Broadcasting Institute (Gianos, 1969, p. 192), in part under a right wing dictatorial government. In 1945 he resigned from the Hellenic Literary Society because of its strong leftist orientation. An insightful travelogue *Around Greece* was published in 1954. Later, in 1958 he was elected member of the prestigious National Academy of Athens. He died in Athens in 1969.

The work of Myrivilis included editorials, reportage, short stories and a late collection of poems with the title *Little Fires*. He has been "widely translated" (Gianos, 1969, p. 192) into French, German and English. Best known are his three long novels, all related to World War I or its aftermaths. Two of them describe people and events on the island of Lesbos.

The first major novel, *Life in the Grave* (the Greek title *Zoe en Tapho* is a line from the Good Friday liturgy referring to the entombment of Jesus Christ) is about the fighting of Greek and French forces against the Bulgarians on the Macedonian front during World War I. It was first published in 1924 in Mytilene, in rough pocketbook form. In 1930, a standard edition in Athens was a literary sensation and broke a circulation record. The book has been fairly assessed as a significant landmark in anti-war prose and (Gallos, K., Annotations 1987, p. 130) "a title of honor for Greek literature and particularly that of this area (Lesbos)." A recent reviewer (Athanasiades, Annotations, 1987, p. 24) quoted the *French Encyclopedia*, Volume 17 (year not indicated), according to which *Life in the Grave* represented "a startling, most remarkable book," admirable "for the extraordinary excitement of everyday life on Lesbos.... The heart-rending pathos in episodes narrated so simply, ... the overflowing richness of the language..." The anti-war theme continued in the first quarter of Myrivilis' next large novel, *The golden-eyed teacher,* first published in 1933 in Athens. The rest of the story took place after the war on Lesbos. There, a surviving warrior fell in love with the widow—a *daskala* (Ref. Table L), schoolteacher—of his dead comrade and after much hesitation, misunderstandings and ambivalence, they consummated their mutual love.

The Golden-eyed Teacher [*Daskala*]
by Stratis Myrivilis, 1892-1969.
A modern Greek novel, first published in 1933.
Selections and summaries.

Chapter 1.

So many years! How he longed for and dreamt about this solemn hour of homecoming! Inside the trenches, in the hospital, on the marches. It must have been summertime on the island. A Resurrection of Nature and of the Spirit. The pots would have been planted with carnations, capers in bloom and daisies would be growing along the lonely walks. All would be so festive . . . He wished he could have been a tiny shell in the sand of a Lesbian beach. To be able to go back! To be there! To the shores of his island, under the island's sun, wet by its sea, frosted by the silvery salt-spray of the island.

But how different was everything now.

With tears in his eyes, the hero, Leonis (short for Leonidas) boarded a dark-maroon rowboat which took him from the steamship to the dock. Everything on the land, the Venetian castle, the pine woods, the poplars in the Public Gardens were all in order, yet that was not the return he had expected. He felt like a lone survivor from an enormous shipwreck. A strange, bitter silence awaited him at home. With tears and sobs, his sister Adrianne told him that their mother had died two months before (she had written to him, she said).

Settling down with difficulty, Leonis picked up his stiff dry paint brushes and began stubbornly to work again on his art, forcing himself to paint joyful scenes, with smiling playful children . . .

In Chapter 2 a note from the district army office, asking for papers to prove his war service and his official discharge, started Leonis on a series of reminiscences (continued in Chapters 3 and 4), with flashbacks of battles, marches and retreats in the blistering summer heat of Phrygia. Leonis recalled how another officer and recruit from Lesbos, second lieutenant Stratis Vranas, dying after weeks in the military hospital with a spreading gangrene of his fractured thigh, had told him, between hallucinations, about his beautiful wife Sappho, a schoolteacher on their island. Stratis gave Leonis her small photograph, a piece of shrapnel from the bomb that was taken out of his leg, his wedding ring and also his wristwatch still stopped at 4:30, the time before dawn that the bomb had exploded near him. Vranas expired a few days before the front collapsed, the army fled and the massacre of thousands of Greek civilians and soldiers ended the millennia of the Hellenic presence in western Asia Minor.

Leonis and Adrianne later left the city (Chapter 7) to pass the hot summer days in their small family home in the country, where they had spent many summers as children.

Chapter 7 (pp. 92-93)

Leonis had heard . . . that the widow of Vranas had been appointed elementary school teacher . . . He felt a strange respect for this unknown woman, who had launched courageously on a brave effort to be self-supporting . . . Many times he thought of going to pay her that mournful visit, to bring to a fulfillment his secret mission. But he always hesitated and twice, when he came in front of her house, he turned the other way . . .

One day, quite unexpectedly, he found himself face-to-face with the teacher. He was going up the hill to the Genoese castle still standing near the edge of the village . . . Turning along one of the climbing tortuous narrow paths, he heard many children's voices coming out of wide open windows . . .

An old woman, spinning her yarn on her front porch, informed him that he was in front of the school where Sappho Vranas taught.

Once more he hesitated . . . then knocked . . . and a woman's voice answered:

"Come in."

He turned the doorknob and walked in, taking off his hat. The children, about fifty of them, noisily stood up in front of their desks and gave him a military salute . . . That seemed for them to be a ritualistic game they enjoyed . . . Somewhat puzzled by the unusual reception, he bowed and walked ahead.

"Sit down" he said to them . . .

He offered her his hand.

"Allow me madam (10). I am the second lieutenant Leonis Drivas. Stratis Vranas was my close friend and colleague . . . I came . . ."

"Please sit down," she interrupted . . . "You were his friend?"

Her voice was clear, steady and melodious. He tried to make his also steadier.

"Yes . . . This is a sad assignment, given to me by the departed of blessed memory [*makarites*] . . . And . . . now that I have been released and came here with my family—we have, as you know, a home and some land here . . ."

"I know, . . . the Drivas Castle, by the sea . . ."

. . . .

"I brought you some memorabilia your husband gave me for you. He handed them to me in his last moments . . ."

Searching his pockets, Leonis realized that he had changed coats and did not have them with him.

"You know," he tried to explain, very embarrassed. "I came here by chance, when I heard the children. I planned to bring them to your home."

"Don't worry" she said politely. "That would be better anyway. Why don't you come to my house this afternoon?"

> . . . .
> Red-faced with embarrassment he sort of adjusted his hat and left in a hurry. "How could I be so ridiculous?" he thought. "And that word, *makarites* (of blessed memory) left such a ludicrous impression . . ."
>
> **Chapter 8** (p. 102)
> He knocked on the brass door knob and . . . an older woman, about fifty years old, opened the door. Her head was covered with a black kerchief.
> "Mrs. Vranas?" he inquired.
> The woman nodded "yes."

He was seated and, overwhelmed by sudden emotion, gave the teacher the photographs, the watch, the bomb fragment and also the wedding ring. Later, after he left the house of the "daskala," he learned that the Vranas' three-year-old child had severe cerebral palsy and also that the old woman was a refugee from Asia Minor who had lost all her family in the massacre and herself had been tortured and had her tongue cut off by the Turks.

One Sunday afternoon (Chapter 11) a memorial service was held by the Veterans Association of the district, with eighty-two candles and eighty-two dishes of *kolyva* (Ref. Table L) for the eighty-two local sons killed in the war. There was also one more, a large memorial candle set up by the Refugees' Union, for the slaughtered women and children and for those martyred in captivity. After the church services and the lengthy speeches, Leonis rushed to the podium.

> **Chapter 11** (pp. 132-136)
> He asked to be excused by his comrades and by the bishop and the Union for standing up to speak without permission. But, he said, the comrade who had just finished speaking had not fully expressed what had to be said on this mournful occasion . . . In front of the flames of the eighty-three candles, Truth and Love should be the only ones to be heard . . . It is not true that the dead want revenge, more killings, more monstrous acts . . . With their flesh now gone, they lost all craving for more blood . . . If they could speak, their pale lips would only move to sound the great words of Christ: "Love each other . . . Peace unto you."
>
> The passion was shining in his eyes . . . But as he stepped down and pushed his way through the crowd, he already regretted what he had done . . . He spent the evening with a large group of prominent villagers in the cafe . . . They seemed to approve what he had said. Very late he walked slowly home, his steps heavy on the pure sand . . . as he listened to the sweet and sad song of the sea . . .

Chapter 12 (pg.147-153)
The school year was almost over. The village mayor gave a dinner for all the teaching staff, as he did every year . . . Drivas, his sister, the village doctor and some businessmen from the city were also invited . . . Leonis could not stop looking at Sappho . . . who was wearing a subtle silk dress with a white collar, modest but coquettish, poured over her marvelously shaped body, which moved as if only to enjoy its own svelte voluptuousness . . . Her abundant wavy hair formed warm shadows, sparkling like brass. She talked with Adrianne, perhaps about him, because once or twice they both raised their eyes to look at him . . . For the first time, under the strong light bulb, Leonis could notice the strange color of the teacher's eyes. They were pale-chestnut but under the light they became golden, bright-gold like the eyes in the statue of some divinity . . . They reminded him of the eyes of a wild animal he had seen, in front of the headlights of an automobile. She was a woman with golden eyes!

Continuing to consume the variety of delicacies and wines on the big outdoor table, the rather disparate group became louder and somewhat silly. The newly-arrived village doctor started a long story about his internship in Paris during the (first) World War, about all the wounded, the amputees, the bombing of the city. Others added their experiences of suffering and horror as the Greek forces retreated from Asia Minor. Emptying another glass of wine Leonis made some cynical remarks about the wars and then started to laugh, sarcastically, uncontrollably, all the time looking harshly at Sappho, whose golden eyes seemed to him to get bigger and bigger, until they filled the whole wall behind her. Later on, following some provocative remarks, the conversation switched from death to love-making and to the science fiction of test-tube insemination and mail-order pregnancies. Past midnight, as they were walking home, Adrienne chided her brother:

Chapter 12 *cont.* (p. 164)
"Do you realize you behaved very badly in front of Mrs. Sappho?"
"I know" he said, "I was . . . rude . . . I think I was a little drunk."
"One would believe that you hate her . . ."
"Maybe I do," he said pensively, "There are many confused thoughts in my mind about her . . ."
. . . .

Chapter 13 (pp. 165–169)
One afternoon (chapter 13) the *daskala* went to see Adrianne . . . They opened their hearts to each other . . . and talked like friends of many years. Just then Leonis came, carrying his straw hat full of figs . . . and his wet swimming trunks.

The teacher was talking about the memorial services . . . and one's own people who never came back . . .

. . . The painter gave her a serious look, the way he would for a man he began to respect.

"I volunteered for the war myself . . . I believed in the war and its moral purposes. So . . . I believed in its justice, . . . the shooting of the frightened soldiers who tried to desert . . . , the burning of the villages . . . I excused everything, because there was no love in me."

"Love," repeated the teacher in a low voice. "What love?"

"Love for one human being or for humanity in general . . ."

He looked at her straight in the eyes, almost hard and added:

"The kind of love you probably never felt. You did not love your husband!"

"I did not love him," admitted the teacher, blushing deeply up to her ears . . .

It was an abrupt, almost stubborn confession that jumped suddenly, rushing as if it had remained suppressed for a long time. Brother and sister looked at each other . . .

"I think," she continued, "that I can talk to you this way . . . In four months I will be twenty-two years old . . . and this is the first time, in twenty-two years, that I open my heart to anyone . . . I must tell you everything, from the beginning . . . I lost my mother when I was 12 years old. An old aunt of mine . . . took me with her. She was the only one I had in the world . . . She sent me to school in the city . . . She wanted me to get married before she died. The teacher, Vranas, asked me. I said 'yes,' without knowing . . . His love was hitting me like a rock. It felt heavy, barbaric . . . I tried to love him. He always felt I did not love him. I did not want him . . . He began to feel jealous. One day he raised his hand to hit me . . ."

Drivas was listening puzzled and confused.

"Did he do that?"

She shook her head.

"Yes. He beat me often . . . Then felt sorry . . . and wept like a baby . . . Like the child now, so it was with the father. I felt sorry for them . . . I never loved . . . I often wanted to leave everything behind . . . The child, the villagers whom I hate . . ."

Chapter 19 (p. 242–244)

One day the mail from Athens brought Drivas a great joy. A large exhibit of the "Free Artists" had opened and all the newspapers wrote about it and also about his five works there.

A reporter friend of his sent him a package of newspapers with a wordy letter, the most important part of which was the post-script.

"P.S. All five were sold . . ."

He felt the profound pleasure of victory, the incense of triumph . . . a victory almost against his own self . . .

... The thing made a sensation in the local club "Arion." The village folk bragged that . . . they had sensed the talent of "the lad" . . .

Chapter 23 (p. 292)
Often Leonis felt exhausted by the stubborn arguments he had with himself. Those were taking place mostly at night until he finally could fall asleep. For the first time love was opening its flaming flower right in front of his bewildered eyes. Why did he not have the right to extend bravely his arms for it? Against whom was he set for battle? Was it against the dead husband or against his own conscience? . . . That law, inside his own soul, created by old customs, old prejudices, old traditions . . . It was about time to push aside the hollow ghosts that blocked his way . . . Sappho had to be his, because he was in love with her.

Chapter 24 (pp. 295–315)
One afternoon, Drivas was in the yard under the climbing grape vine, lying on his hammock and reading, when he saw Sappho coming. He had not seen her for three whole days and his heart beat faster as she came closer . . . When she learned Adrianne was not there . . . she debated (to stay? to leave?).

. . . "You were reading. I interrupted you . . . "

"I read when I have nothing better to do . . . Your company gives me great pleasure."

"This tells me that you avoid great pleasures these days . . . "

For a moment he was ready to tell her everything, to be stuck in the shallow waters of a declaration of love . . . But he talked about anything else, such as his work, that could keep him away from any sentimental rough road . . .

"Yes," commented the teacher seriously, "Work is a good shelter. It sustains the spirit and the heart. This is what saved me . . . "

". . . That is right," Drivas agreed with a sense of relief. "Man can be liberated only when able to make work a labor of joy . . . "

. . . .

He often went to gather wild flowers for Sappho, knowing well that he was never going to send them to her . . .

He ought to get away . . . There was no other way out.

Chapter 27 (pg. 326)
When Adrianne told her that they were leaving, Sappho felt an irresistible urge to . . . shut herself in her house, to be left alone, alone with herself . . . Now, again, she was going to be by herself, with her dead hero and the savage villagers . . .

Chapter 28 (pp. 329-339)
Brother and sister began their farewell visits . . . Leonis was lately getting more and more irritated with such formalities. He hated it even more when at the mayor's "family circle" dinner Sappho was not invited . . .

. . . .

"They are jealous of this girl . . ." Adrianne said to him.

"Maybe you made your preference for her quite obvious," he commented, as he smoked without showing any interest.

. . . .

The dinner was as depressing as could be, until about 10 P.M., when there was a surprise. An older villager, a Mr. Kyryiannakis, arrived uninvited, bringing with him a visiting hypnotist from Athens . . . Everyone was intrigued, because of the controversy around his name . . . Kyryiannakis became the subject of the hypnotist . . . and at first he made the company laugh a lot, . . . when, in a trance, . . . he put salt (which was presented to him as sugar) in his coffee and drank it with delight.

. . . .

"Would you like to try an experiment in hypnosis?" asked the hypnotist. "We could communicate with the spirit of some dead person you knew."

"One of the boys that fell in the war" a woman said.

"Let's try Vranas" the hostess proposed, looking around. They all nodded "yes, yes."

. . . The hypnotist asked with much respect: "Lieutenant Vranas, do you have anything to say?"

"Oh, yes! . . . My beloved little boy. My wife . . . "

The medium sobbed quietly, as if tormented by the strange spirit . . .

"Go on! Speak in the spirit of peace."

. . . .

"Sappho . . . I love you deeply Sappho. Our child . . . Drivas my friend, I thank you . . . My friend . . ."

The hypnotized old man moaned and breathed hard . . . All the women were crying.

"For God's sake, wake him up" begged the hostess, her hands trembling . . .

. . . .

A large round moon was shining above the olive trees as brother and sister were leaving for home. After a long silence Adrianne asked:

" . . . Do you truly believe that the dead can speak to us this way? That would be frightening."

Drivas tried to sound humorous.

"Not frightening, really. It might be rather strange. Can you imagine Kyryiannakis being like a telephone between the Underworld and the World Above? But we are such powerless, weak creatures," he continued, "capable of all kinds of crazy things."

. . . .

Back in his room alone, Leonis stood by his open window. Facing him was a brilliant moon, God's imperial gold seal on the endless work of His Creation. Immersed in the infinite calm of the silent sea and the proud glory of the sky, he heard again the fading distant voice of his dead friend:

"I thank you, my friend . . . My friend."

He lowered his head and deeply inside himself felt the tragic battle . . . He went to sleep calmer, with a sad contentment settled inside him . . .

Chapter 29 (pg. 340-357)

That morning, when the three of them, brother, sister and Sappho, started on their day-long excursion, Leonis felt the saddening pressure of next day's departure weighing on the small party, although no one wanted to admit it. At the same time, however, he felt a sort of relief, as if he had some burden lifted off him and now, light-footed, he could walk on his way ahead.

Hiking through the open green countryside . . . Adrianne stopped, deeply moved.

"What beauty," she whispered. "I don't know if anyone can find such charm in nature anywhere else."

Leonis was ready to declare that this was the untamed erotic breath coming from within the island's soil, from the time of the ancient Sappho until now . . . But he said nothing that might have had a double meaning in the teacher's, or also in his own mind. He stepped lightly toward a wide old olive tree and caught a cricket that was filling the world with his noise. He was tempted to drop it down Adrianne's bosom, or do the same as innocently down the open decolleté of Sappho, just as it was done in the story of Daphnis and Chloe. He was about to remind Adrianne that this was the landscape of the idyll by Longos (cf. Chapter IV), the most erotic in the world . . .

. . . .

They came across a pear tree and Leonis' eye caught one lonely pear, ripe-yellow like a gold coin hanging at its top . . . He climbed through the fresh foliage . . . pulled the branch and cut it . . . With a voice echoing across the valley, he recited loudly the ancient Lesbian verses

> Like the sweet apple, turning red, up at the very end
> Of the highest branch, missed by the fruit pickers;

The *daskala*, from the ground below, completed the lines and in her rhythmical voice there was a slightly trembling tone.

> But no, they did not overlook it, they were unable to reach!

(Quoted by Myrivilis in the original Aeolic Greek. Cf. *Sappho*, Ch. II-A).

Just then the gardener came back. He brought them marvelous ripe fruit . . . and frothing fresh milk . . .

. . . .

Adrianne had an idea.

"Let's go to the creek . . . to look for crabs. There are so many there . . ." she remembered from childhood.

The girls screamed with every new discovery along the creek . . . Hanging vines, wild flowers, rocks, caverns . . . They even found a hidden fig tree, growing through the shade, with a few late-ripening figs.

Coming upon a thick laurel bush, Leonis, filled with childhood memories by its odor, . . . cut two thin branches and made a wreath for his sister . . .

"The laurel of Apollo," he said . . . "suitable for heroes and also for rabbits" (11).

. . . .

Carrying a kerchief with the crabs they had caught, Sappho tried to step down a steep slippery rock, holding onto the branch of a wild fig tree.

. . . .

"Stop, you will fall!" shouted Leonis.

"What, don't you think a village-girl can climb down as well as a city boy?"

. . . She then lost her footing, still hanging from the fig tree and holding the crabs with the other hand . . .

"Come, come lean on me" . . .

She let herself fall in his arms . . . slowly letting go of the fig tree branch . . . under a shower of falling leaves . . . Overwhelmed, as if by a wave of fire, . . . he felt her warm body tightly clinging to him, like ivy . . . Her heart, beating under her delicate blouse, seemed to be his own. Their blood rushed . . . as if their arteries had been joined together.

As she stepped down, he did not let go of her . . . but put his other arm also around her body . . . holding her . . . like a booty. He leaned over her face . . . bending over her golden eyes . . . His glance pierced through her, masculine and barbaric . . . A sweet chill totally overcame her and she squeezed herself onto him with all her being. He turned his eye around like a wild beast looking for a shelter to slaughter his prey. He saw the dense tufts of fern and hurriedly carried her there, placed her gently on the thick mattress of greenery, crushing it under his knees and there . . . he made her his own in a violent, almost hostile way. Her eyes sank under the heavy eyelids and her fingers slowly let go the kerchief with the crabs. They quickly ran free and scattered with a joyful crackle through the grass and the rocks . . . rushing back with their claws erect, to find their waterbed.

I.D. Kollaros and Co., publishers, Athens, Greece,
21st printing, 1986.

Myrivilis' third major novel, *The Mermaid Madonna—The Holy Virgin [Panayia] the Mermaid* ["Gorgona"—Ref. Table L], published in 1949, has been thought to reflect "perhaps the best spiritual moment . . . of the mature . . . writer from Lesbos" (Korsos, in Annotations, 1987, p. 16). The story also takes place on Lesbos, on one of the remote shores of the island, where a group of refugees from Asia Minor after the 1922 military catastrophe, has started a new life. Among them a beautiful girl, of unknown parents, growing up confronts them with the problems of her extraordinary feelings and behavior. Her godfather [*nonos*—Ref. Table L] presented "a satire of modern technology . . . as an immigrant returning after six years in America to his home on Lesbos." (Kobaios, Annotations, 1987, p. 136). The most outstanding feature of the book is the absolute erotic fixation of the young heroine to her godfather's son ("brother-of-the-cross"), only after his death and her subsequent dedication to the monastic worship of the Virgin.

THE MERMAID MADONNA
by Stratis Myrivilis, 1892-1969.

A modern Greek novel, first published in 1949. Selections and abstracts.

Chapter 1 (pg. 9-16)
Right in front of the fishing harbor, smack in the eye of the *ponente* (west wind), on top of a huge rock, stands the little chapel of the Holy Virgin the Mermaid . . . This is not the kind of building we could call ancient, not like the tiny masterpieces . . . of Byzantine architecture . . . It is a solid square, built with much piety but little taste by some god-fearing masons and sailors about 70–80 years ago.

It has a small bell hanging from an iron arch . . . It also has a tall flagpole . . . After the battleship "Averoff" liberated the island, they set it up there and every Sunday they raised the blue-and-white national flag, to watch it and to feel proud.

Later, however, came bad and unlucky ("leap") years . . . The winds tore up the flag, wars, poverty and the politicians destroyed the people's enthusiasm and nobody felt any urge to look for another flag. So the tall mast was left there warping and its paint fading with the sun and the storms.

A mysterious old man, Captain Lias, lived there for years and even after he left nobody could tell who he was and from where he came. What remained behind was only his name and a strange painting he had hung on the wall of the little church. It still stands there today, half-faded from the wind and the salt of the sea. It is of the Holy Virgin [*Panayia*], the strangest one in all Greece and in the whole world of Christianity. Her head is just as we know it from the murals of the Madonna . . . only that her eyes are green and unnaturally wide. From the waist down, however, she's a fish. In one hand she holds a boat and the other a trident like that . . . of the ancient god Poseidon . . .

When the fishermen and the villagers saw this icon for the first time, they admired it but were not startled. The women came to worship and burned their incense for it as they did for all other icons. They all called it "The Mermaid Madonna" [*Panayia-*

Gorgona] . . . and from it took its name the chapel and also the harbor . . .

. . . .

The beauty in the nature of this place all around is such that seeing it you marvel at the generous heart of God. This Aeolian seashore manages not to lose its charm and joy, even when August is burning the whole world or when the winter hits it hard . . . On this island Greece and the East mingle their flavors and match the grace and the meaning of their lands . . .

Chapter 2 (pp. 24-33)

Until the great catastrophe in the East, Captain Lias was the only outsider among the few local folk . . . The people who fill the seaside these days with their families and their boats . . . they all came from across the sea after the disaster (1922) . . . They are not at all like the lordly old local captains, who went up and down in the peaceful days of the past with their tall . . . fezes, . . . and their silk tassels . . . Those were different years, the wars had not yet started to upset populations and to raise one against the other. People here knew the opposite coast of the East like their own . . . They would say "We are going across," take their colorful handwoven blankets, put some food in the basket, go in their *kaiki* (Ref. Table L) and sail east . . .

The place had much give-and-take with Turkey . . . They sent oil and soap to The City (2a) to the Black Sea, to the *Vlach* country (12) . . . and all the way down to Egypt.

. . . .

Then suddenly, one day, the blessed mainland was cut off and became very, very distant. It seemed so far from Skala (the little port) that people saw it as a foreign land, say like America.

. . . .

They came from the coast across, all these fishermen and sailors one bitter poisoned day . . . They came rowing and sailing in some old fishing boats . . . A loud murmur echoed among the crowd standing on the shore:

"The refugees! . . . "

. . . .

The natives made much ado, eager to help those coming persecuted . . . The island women cried . . . and even the doctor came from the upper village with his bag and his medicines.

They took those who had died on the way up to the cemetery of Mouria (the village up the hill) . . . The whole village went for the services . . . The local women, who had lost children in the war and in captivity, felt their sorrows return and standing near the graves of relatives wept loudly and mourned the unburied victims left in Anatolia (13).

Chapter 3 (pg. 34-39)

So they settled in the Skala (port—Ref. Table L) of Mouria, all those dispossessed families and day-by-day struggled to feel more at home with the people, the place and the things.

As the days went by, the bitterness of their uprooting lessened, their battered spirits quieted down. That is how man has been made, to go along with whatever happens, good or bad. If this was not so, the whole world would be going crazy with all the unexpected turns that we have to face time and again.

The new residents of Skala slowly began to realize that fate had thrown them as softly as one might expect to be shipwrecked . . . They began more or less to recover . . . and got to work . . . They repaired and repainted their boats . . . So the harbor of the Holy Virgin was full of the working men's knocks and bangs and voices. As soon as they had a roof over their heads, they began to marry and to have babies . . . Coming down to Skala, you could not see a refugee woman without a baby in her arms and another in her belly.

. . . .

Then one day came the Housing Committee . . .

Chapter 4 (pp. 41-46)

The bishop from the city had heard of the crowding and poor living conditions and sent the Housing Committee. He was himself a refugee from the same land . . .

They got organized . . . and started a fund. Already they began to talk seriously about a housing project. After endless arguments and misunderstandings they elected Varouhos, one of the fishermen, as a president.

. . . .

Most serious discussions were taking place at the coffee shop of Fordis, "The Sycamore." The enormous wild sycamore in front of it was always full of birds . . . When his wife was still alive (she had died with her second childbirth), Fordis had taken their only son, Lambis and, showing him the stork's nest on the tree, had said:

"See that, kid? It is from there that you came to this world."

Chapter 5 (pp. 47-50)

There were one or two other coffee shops in Skala but then everybody . . . preferred Fordis' cafe . . . for his pure coffee, the best *raki* (Ref. Table L) . . . and they loved to hear his spicy stories . . . about . . . his travels in America . . . where he had spent six years at Ford's auto works (hence his nickname Fordis), hitting screws on the head . . . until one day, a screw popped up and destroyed one of his eyes. They took him to the hospital, removed the screw and after he healed they gave him $500 and dismissed him.

. . . .

He took the money, withdrew his savings . . . and returned home. He bought a house and some farmland, opened a coffee shop and married a good-looking village girl . . . rosy-cheeked and cheerful . . . But it was not meant for him to enjoy her company for very long.

. . . .

When he was in America his mind always turned to this seashore. Now that he had settled here, his soul could not detach itself from

America . . . In the shop, next to the counter, he had three pictures hanging in their frames, one was Venizelos (14), the other patriarch Ioakeim (14) and in the middle was Ford with a face wrinkled like a raisin. "My holy trinity" he kept saying.

Chapter 10 (pg. 104)

Varouhos, the fisherman, returning at dawn to the Skala, tired and half asleep, heard the cry of a baby from a basket under the boat deck. He quickly realized that he was not dreaming . . .

Chapter 11 (pp. 107-111)

He tied up his boat, took the basket with the baby . . . and rushed home . . .

"What will my wife, what will Nerantzee say?"

. . . .

How did all these people smell his secret was a mystery . . . They all gathered . . . the neighbors . . . even Fordis came up . . . They admired the baby's fancy clothes, special diapers . . . , expensive blanket, all white in this household dressed in black (mourning for their daughter).

The blondish blue-eyed baby was breast fed by a nursing mother, then became very playful.

"What a *kefi* (Ref. Table L) he has the bastard" said the fisherman.

"It is a girl," his wife Nerantzee corrected, without lifting her head.

Fordis . . . came back with a bucket of fresh milk.

"My goat, Garbo, sends this" he declared.

The teacher was asked to read a note pinned on the blanket, which only said, "Not baptized."

. . . .

Fordis touched his bald head.

"By law you must report it and send the baby to the city orphanage."

"God forbid . . ." clipped Nerantzee, "she was sent to us by the Mermaid Holy Virgin and *Panayia* will help us raise her."

Chapter 13 (pg. 117)

Varouhos really meant it. With that little girl joy came to the house. The miracle started with Nerantzee . . . who for almost two years had sipped with a strange pleasure the same bitter drink of their daughter's death . . .

Chapter 14 (pg. 123)

When the two full years of mourning were over, they held one Sunday the baptism up in the chapel of the Mermaid Madonna. They named the baby Smaragdee (Emerald), after the color of her eyes, as the godfather, Fordis, wanted . . .

Chapter 18 (pg. 156)

The home of Varouhos soon stood out among the little houses of the maritime community. Nerantzee had planted a climbing vine by the front door porch . . . and had flower pots placed by the windows.

Chapter 19 (pg. 162)

Years passed and one day Smaragdee showed up among the fishermen's kids that crowded themselves in the village school . . . She wore new sandals and a sky blue ribbon with a bow on her well-combed hair . . .

"Will you wear these every day?" asked a barefoot little girl . . .

. . . .

"Then what will you wear for Easter?"

Chapter 22 (pg. 188-189)

Smaragdee was unable to fully comprehend the disaster in all its gravity . . . She listened without understanding, the explanation that the daughter of Lathios gave to Varouhos. It was that her beloved step-mother Nerantzee had gone to gather figs and then had slipped from the tree and was found on the ground gasping her last breath . . .

. . . .

"She's gone" Lathios' daughter had said.

Chapter 23 (pg. 202-208)

One morning Varouhos went down and found Smaragdee on the boat, washing the deck. Taking another sip of coffee he suddenly said:

"You slept away from home last night."

"I slept at Lathios' . . . "

"I know . . . It was my fault . . . It is that drinking . . . "

. . . .

"When drunk" he continued "one can do all kinds of things . . . can hit someone."

Her voice was tender but firm:

"If you raise your hand to hit me, father, I will leave this house."

. . . .

"Stop drinking, father. The drink will ruin you."

"I will . . . Now go to sleep. We have to work tomorrow."

He said that with determination, but it did not last . . .

There were times when Varouhos disappeared from the coffee shop and Fordis knew that his *koumparo* (Ref. Table L) had gone again to drink . . . At times they carried him home lifting him from the arms. Those nights were for Smaragdee a nightmare.

. . . .

Fordis followed the drama of the girl and one day, when Varouhos was in a good mood, he took him to the back of the coffee shop and lectured him.

" . . . You were the wisest one among the fisherman . . . everyone respected you when Nerantzee was alive . . . Now they all laugh at you . . . They carry you home at midnight and call "Come down, Smaragdee, come to get your old man . . . "

Chapter 26 (pg. 242)

Tired from work, Smaragdee gave up waiting for her father who was not showing up (again getting drunk) . . . Half undressed the young woman went to bed with the moonlight shining in her room.

. . . .

Varouhos came in and leaned against the wall, dizzy and out of his mind . . . Suddenly he unglued himself from the wall and moving close to the sleeping girl he rushed and grabbed her body like a hungry beast . . . his face distorted in an ugly spasm.

Smaragdee woke up with a horrible feeling of terror, suffocation, pain and disgust . . . Overwhelmed, she began to scream . . . Soon the room was full of the neighbors . . . Some grabbed Varouhos, dragged him on the floor and began to beat him and kick him.

Chapter 27 (pp. 245-259)

When God began the new day, the whole settlement echoed with the rumors and the gossip . . . But nobody talked about calling the police. These folks, who had run away from under a foreign yoke, always saw the police as an enemy . . . even among the locals.

. . . .

The erotic torment which afflicted all these people their entire lives and had remained buried in their hearts . . . now found the opportunity to spring loose with loud noises in the narrow streets. Under the banner of morality they got their revenge against the miserable old man who dared break the law that oppressed all of them . . . and allowed no exceptions . . .

. . . .

Fordis made them shut up.

"I am telling you the man is not well . . . "

He took some iodine, cotton and bandages . . . and dressed Varouhos' wounds.

Chapter 28 (pg. 253)

After that night Smaragdee moved to her own little house . . . In the daytime, after she had finished her housework, she would go fishing with Lathios (a neighbor) . . . The fisherman was amazed:

"This girl," he kept telling Fordis, "your godchild my friend Komnenos (15), is a perfect fisherman . . . "

Chapter 29 (pp. 261-265)

Some months later, Fordis took Lathios aside, treated him to a cup of coffee and asked:

"How is the little one? Has Smaragdee learned more of the tricks of fishing? I heard from the city that her boat we had ordered is ready."

. . . .

Two boats were seen to arrive . . . One was Lathios' and the other, painted bright red and pale blue, adorned with flags and lanterns, was the new one for Smaragdee.

Chapter 30 (pp. 272-274)

Her godfather loved big parties and festivities.

"We will have a christening for your new boat" said Fordis "to name her *Nerantzee* and to pray for good luck . . . "

. . . .

Lambis, the young son of Fordis, was holding the bowl with the holy water . . .

"Come and kiss your godsister," said the *kafetzis* (Ref. Table L).

The boy suddenly turned red. He tried to smile but his lips were trembling . . . He jumped lightly off the boat deck without a word and went away.

"Don't pay attention to him, he is a bit wild and uncouth" laughed Fordis.

Chapter 32 (pg. 283)

As time passed and her body was getting full and mature, Smaragdee felt more constrictive around her the male desires . . .

The villagers used to see a woman as a helpless prey, without any means of her own to safeguard her feminine treasures. That was the job of a parent, brother or husband, standing by her. When these natural protectors were missing, others began to see that woman as an unfenced property. In the case of Smaragdee, the incident with Varouhos further inflamed their imagination and sharpened their tongues . . .

Chapter 33 (pp. 285–291)

One afternoon Smaragdee sitting on the boat's deck, was chatting with Vatis, the younger Lathios boy . . . He suddenly said: "What do you think? Are there any mermaids in the sea?"

Smaragdee smiled:

"If your grandmother seems to be sure that I am the child of a mermaid, then it can't be that there aren't any."

"But you don't know who your mother was" . . .

"There is nobody else but Nerantzee. If someone, human or mermaid, came and told me she was the one that gave birth to me, I wouldn't want to know her, even if she were a queen" . . .

. . . .

"When I grow up and I am twenty-five years old I will marry a mermaid."

"Why twenty-five?"

"My brother, Manolis, told the old man he wants to get married and our father cut him short: Marriage needs brains. When you are twenty-five you may marry, he said."

 . . . "It's you that Manolis wants to marry . . . "

. . . .

"If that's what worries you, calm down. I will marry no one."

They talked about other, unrelated things and as they were finishing their work, Vatis suddenly said:

"You should know that Lambis loves you too. Lambis, the son of Fordis. He is a year older than you and he loves you . . . "

"Stop that again . . . How do you know? Do you ever talk about such nonsense?"

. . . .

When she was left alone, she went into a deep meditation about what the lad had let slip through his tongue.

. . . .

She had felt warmly at home by the Lathios family . . . Vatis was now coming to spoil that . . . if it was true that the other two boys in the family saw her from an erotic angle without revealing it . . . Did she now have to be on guard even in her godfather's home because of Lambis? No, she couldn't take Vatis' childish talk seriously . . . Staying away from the Lathios' family would be like being orphaned a third time . . .

Chapter 38 (pp. 324–333)

The autumn nights wrap the Aegean islands with a pale blue darkness. One such night, under the full moon, Smaragdee rowed along the coast, anchored under the shadow of the rocks, took off her clothes and jumped in the water, swimming along the golden carpet of the moon's reflection.

. . . .

Suddenly, on the sparkling interplay of moonlight and water she thought she saw a long dark shadow . . . Instantly she froze and her swimming strokes became spasmodic, crazy . . .

"Come! Come help me!"

A man jumped from above, grabbed her and pulled her to shallow waters. The tight contact of her nakedness against the stranger's flesh made her quickly come to her senses in the ugliest way.

"Go away" she gasped.

In the moonlight . . . she recognized Lambis, the son of Fordis.

"It's you" she screamed, alarmed, with a savage voice.

He nodded "yes" and stood there unsure whether to go back or forward. He then started to move away.

"Stop" Smaragdee said, "You are bleeding."

She washed the blood from his arm and bandaged it with her mantilla, red with white polka dots.

"Go now" she told him. "If I catch you again spying on me I will break your head . . . and will report you to my god-father."

She rowed back, a girl alone under the big sky on the wide sea . . .

Chapter 48 (pgs.429–431)

It was a night in heavy winter, thundering with the wild wind that rattled the windows and made the boats' ropes ring without stop . . . All of a sudden there were screams, yelling and cursing. The settlement was all sounding with the big trouble that broke out in front of the house of the Gatzalis. The whole Gatzalis clan, men and women, were cursing and throwing rocks.

A shrill woman's voice cried:

"Here's where the rascal jumped . . . block his way."

Smaragdee was undressing to go to bed . . . She put on some clothes and opened a window . . .

"Here we caught him" called an old man.

They started hitting blindly with sticks and broken oars. There were suppressed moans but no voice . . . When they lowered their torches . . . they recognized Lambis.

They dragged him all muddy, bleeding . . . they spat on him and slapped his face. The neighbors turned off their lights to avoid being called as witnesses in court . . . Only from Lathios' came Manolis and Vatis with a lighted torch. Smaragdee took courage seeing them and came out . . . She saw Lambis kneeling in the mud, being kicked, his hair pulled, his back beaten with an oar . . .

"You will kill him" she screamed in despair . . .

Lambis heard her voice . . . and raised his eyes to look at her. Only then he let a loud sad scream . . . like a wild beast . . . He jumped . . . walking a like a drunk, rushed away as if blindly looking for an escape and disappeared in the darkness . . .

"We caught him climbed on a tree, watching the girl undress . . . " someone explained. "He comes every night to ambush . . . "

That night Fordis waited in bed in vain to hear the footsteps of his son.

Chapter 49 (pgs 434–440)

Three days passed . . . and Lambis did not show up in his workshop. Three nights and he did not go to his father's home.

"He's ashamed of what happened" someone consoled Fordis. "Let's wait."

Days and nights they waited. Nothing!

. . . .

A fine cold rain had been falling for days. One day God brought them better weather and the waters were clear. Boats went to look for Lambis along the coast . . .

Looking through a glass-bottom barrel, Manolis suddenly raised his hands.

"Stop" . . . "Here he is . . . stuck on the rocks, on the bottom . . . Something's holding him on the bottom."

"His neck is tied to . . . an anchor. Pull and he will come up . . . "

Lambis was fully dressed and around his neck was a red mantilla. When Smaragdee saw it her knees gave in and she bit her lip hard. That was the mantilla she had used to bandage his scratched arm that night under the moonlight.

Chapter 50 (pp. 443–447)

It was getting dark when Lathios with his wife and Smaragdee took the boat and went to light a candle on the remains of Lambis. Vatis jumped in too at the last minute . . .

Smaragdee was unable to cry. She felt a deep inner emotion much more disturbing than the quiet wailing of Lathios' wife.

. . . .

One thousand things crossed her mind continuously. Lambis' words and movements . . . More than anything she was overwhelmed by a deep grief for Fordis . . .

It started to rain. A freezing rain that hit the windows like hail. Smaragdee felt a bitter sadness filling her . . . With the thought that the same rain was falling on the dead lad . . .

There was talk about getting rid of the refugees, the "murderers," who had contaminated the peaceful spot with their thefts, their immorality and their crimes . . .

"I will sell all my property, get rid of the coffee shop to take you to court . . . to wipe you out of this world, seeds of the Turks" Fordis was saying, "The way you wiped me out."

. . . .

The court found the Gatzalis not guilty for the death. They only got a few days in jail for beating the kid. So they came back to Skala more insolent than ever.

Chapter 51 (pg. 452)

On the Aegean shores spring erupts from the sea . . . like Aphrodite . . .

. . . .

Smaragdee listened to youth singing inside her bosom, a sparkling fountain rushing onto crystal-clear pebbles . . . A song came up her lips . . . It had been a long time she had not sung . . .

Chapter 52 (pp. 460–465)

. . . That evening she went to the "Sycamore" cafe to see Fordis. After the disaster of the fatal accident she often went to keep him company . . . struggling to give him some moral support . . . She walked directly behind the tall counter where Fordis was sitting, away from the parties, trying to avoid having to talk.

. . . .

"Wait for me at home" he told her as she got up to leave. "I must talk to you."

After she left, someone said:

"Be happy with your goddaughter, uncle Komnenos (15). She's like a bright shining sun."

"Yes, she's a perfectly pure sun" said Fordis after some hesitation, looking at him very kindly.

Very late . . . Fordis walked towards the housing project. Smaragdee was waiting . . . They sat facing each other, knees against knees.

"See" said Fordis, "I was once a father myself. Now I have nobody . . . but two things sustain me. One is God . . . When we were young Uncle Lias was telling us not to get far from God because we would want to lean on His staff someday. The other is you Smaragdee . . . "

Very moved . . . she put her arm against the bony hand of the old man.

"God bless you nono" she said.

. . . .

"I worry about you. I don't want to die before I see you married . . . I know Manolis wants you . . . "

"No, my nono," Smaragdee replied weeping . . .

"Why not?" . . .

She tried to explain . . . that she had made up her mind never to marry . . . Her freedom was too dear to her . . .

. . . .

Fordis left worried, his head down. Nothing made sense . . .

"To love them, to adore them, yet not to know their language . . . and find them unable to understand yours. That is the biggest bitterness."

Chapter 53 (pp. 471-481)

Everytime the divers returned from sponge-gathering they brought some small souvenirs for Smaragdee, a rare shell, a coral branch, or a petrified little tree, all from the bottom of the sea, just for her. She felt a strange joy to see that they thought of her, those hard-working men, beneath the waves of the sea. Among them was Achilles. He treated her often as if he was dealing with a little girl.

. . . .

Vatis one day, as he was polishing a soft rock, told Smaragdee:

"Stratis does not love you anymore . . . He thinks your boat has gone to your head and that's why you refuse to place the wedding wreath on it . . . "

"You're a child, full of imagination" she interrupted him angrily.

"Not at all" he replied stubbornly . . . "Nobody knows that Achilles loves you too. But I know it . . . No one also knows as much as I do about the Lambis affair . . . "

"Of Lambis?" she said startled.

. . . .

"Here it is: Lambis fell in the water and drowned himself out of self-pride and his love for you . . . "

"Nonsense" argued Smaragdee. "The Gatzalis clan beat him up because he loved to peek at their daughter Jeanne . . . "

"Not so, my lady. Lambis only loved *you*. It was for you that he fell and drowned."

"Lies!" She grabbed him from the sleeve. Her voice broke. She was shaking all over.

"Listen, Smaragdee . . . the Gatzalis boys were wrong thinking that he was after their sister. Lambis came at night waiting to see you . . . He often crept through the grass to see you go by on your boat . . . Oh! how he loved you."

There was silence. Then suddenly she asked:

"And how do you know all this? Did he tell you himself?"

"You didn't know Lambis. He never talked. He was a man! . . . I followed him . . . His greatest humiliation was that he was caught in front of your eyes . . . "

She listened, awfully upset.

"Then he ran away, he kept running all night. I ran after him. He sat by the beach, crying like a baby. Afterwards he saw the broken anchor . . . took it on his shoulder . . . I saw him standing at the end of the rock. Then it dawned on me. 'Lambis!' I cried. And he . . . jumped . . . "

"You . . . why did you follow his steps?"

Vatis was silent.

"I asked you why" she repeated. "Why don't you talk?"

He raised his head and whispered:

"You told me never to talk again about *that*."

She got up and left, all mixed up . . . She cried all night, sleepless . . . In the morning she went to Fordis'. He was startled . . .

"You didn't sleep?" he asked. "Are you sick? Were you crying?"

Smaragdee sighed.

"I came to stay with you nono. I have been thinking that you . . . and I are alone. I will come near you to take care of you. I will never leave you, nono."

"Good" he said emotionally. "My daughter, have you thought again about what I had said to you?"

"That . . . and much else. I will give up my house . . . and my boat . . . I will give it as a gift to Manolis . . . "

Now the old man was puzzled . . .

"What is the matter Smaragdee?" he anxiously inquired. "What happened?"

"Nothing" she said . . . To hide her emotion she started walking through the rooms and rearranging them.

"Here is his room" said the *kafetzis*. "It is the way he left it that night, when he never came back to me."

"Nono" said the girl. "Do you want this to be my room? Now I will be your own child and will double my love for you."

She threw herself in his arms and they cried together.

Chapter 54 (pp. 482-487)

That night she turned on the lamp and kept meditating . . . She looked through the pile of Fordis' American magazines, . . . with the beautiful girls jumping in the air, with their naked arms open like wings, their hair flying . . . They seemed happy, . . . their wings wide open . . .

. . . Her wings were now paralyzed, broken forever . . .

Then she saw Lambis' old school books and, among them, some unfinished notebooks. She read:

"She was drowning. I saved her. I took her in my arms and saved her. I wish I had instantly died that moment . . . She yelled at me . . . but gave me her red mantilla. I sleep on it every night."

"Today I saw her again . . . I wish I could go near her."

" . . . They say that brother and sister of the cross (christened by the other one's father) are not allowed to marry."

She started to cry . . . and cried even after she had fallen asleep.

Slowly, the face of Lambis appeared to her totally different from what she remembered until she had that revelation . . . That was not sorrow, it was love, true and great love that exploded triumphant and violent, the unique and unbeatable goal of her entire life . . . Nobody . . . would ever know about it. Now only she and her dead lover were there. He would never disappoint her, would never touch her . . .

She felt an uncontrollable disgust for the sea. She would never dare look into the sparkling waters, where the brown and golden seaweeds on the rocks at the bottom wave like the hair of drowned young men . . .

She put on again all black clothes, which she was never going to change . . .

"What are you doing?" the old man asked. "You are still a child and you are letting yourself wither like a widowed woman."

She liked those words. She did not answer right away but she treasured that like a precious discovery: "A widowed woman."

Later she said with a serious, calm and determined voice:

"It is because I pledged myself to the Virgin, nono."

Fordis knew her well and never spoke again about that.

Every day she would go to take care of the little chapel on the rock, to light the candles and to pray in front of the strange icon. And the Holy Virgin, the Mermaid Madonna looked at her with her slanted almond eyes, motionless, wrapped in her mystery and her silence . . .

I.D. Kollaros & Co., Athens 1958.

NOW—AND THEN . . .

Lesbos now

The island of Lesbos *now* is described and often "promoted" in current booklets and brochures intended mainly for tourists and other visitors. Some of these publications are available in several languages. Translations from the original modern Greek texts and also of selections from recent articles in daily newspapers, periodicals and books, may provide the necessary basic data, facts and findings to connect the changing present with the immutable and ever-receding past.

LESBOS: THE ISLAND OF HARMONY
by M. H. Eleftheriadis, 1981 (pp. 5-6).
Getting acquainted with the island (pp. 5-9)
Lesbos is . . . the fourth largest Greek island (Fig. VII-5). It is northeast of Athens . . . at 39 21' 20" to 38 37' 30" north of the equator and 25 49' 30" to 26 38' east of Greenwich . . . Mytilene, the capital of Lesbos is at a distance of 188 miles from (the port of) Pireus. The ships of the (regular) lines cover the distance, with one stop, . . . in 15 hours and the airplanes of Olympic in 30 minutes. On the east side Lesbos is 6–10 miles off the Turkish coast and on its north side 5–6 miles.

. . . The length of Lesbos is 70 km. (43.4 mi.) and its width is 45 km. (27.9 mi.). The perimeter of its coastline is 99 miles and its surface covers 1,612 km (622 sq. mi.). Of this about 200,000 acres are olive groves, 160,000 forest, 220,000 grazing pastures, 12,000 vineyards, 7,000 fruit orchards, 11,000 vegetable gardens . . . The population . . . in 1971 was 97,013 . . . The climate is mild, Mediterranean. Average annual rainfall is 600-650 mm. (23.4-25.35 inches). Average annual temperature is 18°C (68°F) with summer peaks of 25-38°C (80-102°F) and winter lows of 1.2-0.8°C (40-33°F).

This section continues with details about the geography, mineral wealth, vegetation (including aromatic and medicinal plants), roads, etc. It is followed by a summary of Lesbian history and culture. Maps and illustrations, lists of hotels, museums, airlines, etc. are included, along with a number of advertisements.

The present citations of sites, people and events on "Lesbos Now" pertain to the three-thousand year history of the island and stress the prototypical uniqueness of human expressions and experiences. Important modern population centers and activities not integrally part of this narrative, are more appropriately considered in the current travel guides and reference texts available in several languages, such as "Lesvos" in English (Toubis publications, Athens, 1986).

Mytilene—also in current texts and in road signs spelled Mitilini—now is a city of about 25,000 people. Here, as elsewhere in the area, a severe earthquake in 1867 caused widespread destruction and many deaths. The mansions that now stand in the outskirts of Mytilene are mostly from the late nineteenth century. Near or next to them are several public buildings of respectable size and a growing number of multistory condominium apartment complexes of almost uniform rectangular modern style.

In the center of town, the rather narrow main business street appropriately named after Hermes, the ancient god of communications and commerce is dotted with small thriving shops that sell everything, from several brands of the local ouzo (among the best in Greece and still flavored with the same species of herbs that Sappho's girls used to make wreaths for their heads) to exotic liqueurs (some actually produced locally) to imported watches and electronics. Between butcher shops and fish mongers are also some poorly lighted old book stores with ceiling-high hard-to-reach dusty shelves. The ubiquitous sounds of spoken modern Greek—a language not much removed from the ancient idioms despite the sporadic additions brought by invaders, refugees and more recently trade and tourists—are often intermingled with the sounds of recorded music, traditional popular or the latest rock, that come from a constantly increasing number of American-style fast food establishments and, recurrently, with the clang of church bells signalling the time for vespers or other mid-day services. On top of these, noises of cars, the multitude of motorcycles and some endless construction activity abound.

Part of Hermes Street runs almost parallel to the broad boulevard along the harbor, which is crowded with buses, trucks and, among the throng of motorcycles and cars, an occasional cart drawn by a donkey. A row of taverns, coffee shops, restaurants and pastry or ice cream parlors thrived until recently between the harbor and Hermes Street and could be entered from either side. They are gradually being replaced by hamburger, hot dog and pizza places and the famous dishes, especially the variety of *mezedes* (Ref. Table L) they used to serve, can best now be found outside the city, often by a beach or a bay, five or ten miles away. Fortunately, the great art of hors d'oeuvres, also called *orectica* (i.e. appetizers) or in Hellenized Turkish *mezedes*, has not perished and may even be expanding, as shown by the long list of selections in the menus of outstanding establishments in Mytilene and also the surrounding areas of the Bay of Yera and the suburb of Therme on the north. Equal and perhaps superior to these Lesbian eating places are their transplants thriving right in the center of Athens, such as the unique taverna-ouzeri (Ref. Table L) "Mytilene" off the crowded Omonoia (Concord) square, where the culinary art is unquestionably no less meritorious than the poetry of Elytis and Sappho, or the science and philosophy of Theophrastos and of the epicureans of antiquity.

A short walk from the harbor, at the center of town, is the large church of St. Therapon (Holy Healer). Its huge dome can be seen dominating the city skyline from any boat approaching the harbor. The church in "neo-Byzantine style" was designed by the Lesbian architect Argyris Adalis and was completed in 1860. As suggested by its name, St. Therapon could well represent a continuation of the ancient function of the site, where according to recent archeological findings there was a temple of Apollo, or possibly of Asklepios (Latin *Aesculapius*), the god of healing. The existence of mineral springs nearby might have promoted healing practices on this location. Interesting mosaics from the 4th century A.D. have been excavated in the area and can now be seen in the city archeological museum. They represent scenes from the comedies of Menander [*Menandros*, 342/1—293/89 B.C.], and also presumably the portrait of the author himself. A Roman aqueduct has been located nearby. In front of the church stands the bust of the prominent church leader, educator and philosopher, Bishop Ignatios of Hungary-and-Wallachia (12) who was born on Lesbos and, after a prominent career in central Europe, in 1828 died in Pisa, Italy and was buried there. His remains were transferred back to his native island in 1965 and deposited on the grounds of St. Therapon in the center of Mytilene.

Modern scholars also believe that the gathering place of Sappho and her "school" of girls in antiquity was also where St. Therapon is now. Back towards the harbor on a small square and facing the sea, is a nearly life-size marble statue of the famous Lesbian poetess, carved by the twentieth century Greek sculptor G. Lemnaios. It was unveiled in 1965, a gift to the city of Mytilene by the English writer Rose Macauley (Emery, J. 1991). As in the case of ancient portraits of Sappho, this modern statue in no way can be thought to approximate the physical appearance or even the spirit of the "*melopoios*" (Ref. Table E) Sappho.

Closer to where the big passenger ships dock on the north side of the harbor is another modern sculpture, the bust of Admiral G. Kountouriotis, who, in 1912, led the forces that liberated Lesbos from the Turkish rule. The bust of the outstanding Lesbian novelist, Stratis Myrivilis, is further inland on the public square. Another sculpture worth noting in modern Mytilene is the full-sized Statue of Liberty, designed by the renowned nineteenth century Lesbian artist, George Iakovidis, and cast by the sculptor G. Zevgolis. Standing on the rocky coast north of the harbor, it has a much freer, nobler and more "liberated" romantic expression than the famous, oversized but lifeless statue in New York harbor, U.S.A. Above and behind the Lesbian Statue of Liberty is the old fort [*kastro*, meaning castle and also fortress], a Byzantine-Genoese-Turkish structure built on what is now and extension of the mainland. Formerly this was the small island that divided the port into a northern and a southern part and where the original settlement of Mytilene was established. Over one of the main gates, a sculptured relief of the Byzantine imperial emblem of the Palaiologos royal family, and next to it the insignia of the Genoese Gattelusi, reflects the sequence of powers dominant on the island. Inside the *kastro* are the ruins of the palace of the Byzantine bride, princess Maria Palaiologos, who was given to the Genoese adventurer by her royal brother, Emperor John V as a reward for his services. The still impressive walls and ramparts of the *kastro* are an enduring monument of agonizing freedom fighting and of oppressive rule.

A little further inland from the castle on the crest of a hill stood the walls protecting the ancient Aeolian city of Mytilene [*Mytilana* in their Aeolic dialect]. Just below these was built the Hellenistic theater, which so impressed the visiting Roman general Pompey the Great—when he was glorified there with recitations about his deeds after his victories in Asia Minor—that he ordered a large size replica of it to be constructed in Rome. Most of the marble seating of the theater is gone, whether to be used as a building material for nearby structures, or piled nearby for possible future restoration. The excavated semi-circular slope, however, maintains the marvelous acoustics, enhanced by the breeze ascending from the seaside in the evening. The close to 15,000 spectators in ancient times could see, beyond the stage, the Acropolis of Mytilene, the two harbors and the Aeolian coast of Asia Minor across the sea. A marble throne, now in the archeological museum in Mytilene, bears an inscription assigning it to the rhetorician and ambassador to Rome, Potamon (75 B.C.–15 A.D.), son of the philosopher Lesbonax, but its style indicates that it dates from about 300 years earlier and probably was the throne reserved for the priest of Apollo.

The north side of Mytilene is where most of the Turks and in earlier times the Romans had their homes. The moslem "New Mosque" [Turk. *yeni cami*, pronounced *jami*] built in 1823–28 (with notable Greek influences) has been viewed by the prominent Lesbian-French art connoisseur, S. Teriade as an architectural masterpiece. A traditional Turkish bath house still exists next to the mosque.

The ancient city of Methymna (pop. 1600), now commonly called by its medieval name of Molybos, is about 62 km. northwest of Mytilene on a well-paved highway crossing the island. A longer and slower road along the northern coast of Lesbos passes through the village of Therme, named after its hot mineral baths. Prehistoric artifacts have been unearthed in this area by the British archeologist Winifred Lamb (Chapter I). The foundations of an ancient temple of Artemis can still be seen next to a sunken chamber for bathing and healing. Possibly this area was also where Achilles landed to loot the island on his way to the Trojan war. A small chapel, that of the Virgin-with-a-Dome [*Panayia Trouloti*] contrasts, in its impoverished appearance, with the aristocratic country homes of Lesbians who prospered even under Turkish rule. Some believe that empress Irene may have lived in this area in exile for a few months before she died in 802 A.D. (Chapter V). Closer to Methymna the coastal road crosses Sykamia—also known as Sykaminia, or Skamia—the birthplace of the twentieth century novelist Myrivilis. His story of "the Mermaid Madonna" was about people and a little chapel down the hill by the seashore. Four kilometers before Methymna is the village of Eftalou, birthplace of the businessman-poet A. Eftaliotis. Inland between Sykamia and Eftalou is Mountain Myrivili. Its name was adopted by the prominent Lesbian novelist. South of it is the higher (968 m./3175 ft.) Lepetynmos mountain on the slopes of which (at 400 m./1312 ft.) is the village of Pelopi. It may be far-fetched to trace the name of Pelopi to the landing on Lesbos of the mythical winged chariot of Pelops nearly 3000 years ago. The village became internationally known (*Time*, May 2, 1988, p. 30) during the campaign of the USA presidential candidate Michael Dukakis, who is the son of a Pelopi native. In the fall of 1988 large portraits of the candidate were posted on the walls and windows of tavernas, shops and houses of Pelopi.

The population of Molyvos/Methymna, much reduced in the medieval period, clustered inside their fort [*kastro*]. The town began to thrive again after the Genoese took over the island (1355-1462) and further fortified that growing commercial center. By the eighteenth century local Greek merchants gradually recaptured some of the trade from the Turks and started building large traditional homes between the kastro and the sea. One of the still-standing mansions has been converted into a university level—"superior"—School of Fine Arts, for students from many nations, to study and work. Exhibits are held in the Community Art Museum, which is the converted home of the poet A. Eftaliotis. A bronze bust of Eftaliotis stands in front of his two-story old house on the hill. Among other honored Lesbian natives, whose remains were brought back to the island in recent years was a woman, St. Theoktiste, who died on the island of Paros in 879 A.D. She spent about forty years there serving the churches, after she managed to escape from the Saracen pirates who had kidnapped her from Lesbos. In 1960 her remains were brought back and interred by a chapel in Molyvos named in her honor.

Ancient Antissa—the birthplace of Terpandros (Chapter II-A)—was an estimated 12 km. northeast of the present hillside (elev. 300 m.) community of about 1900 people that bears the same name. Directly south of Antissa, across west-central Lesbos is Eresos (pop. 1800), the birthplace of the philosophers Theophrastos and Phainias (Chapter IV) and also probably of Sappho. Off the road leading there, against the mountains, is the small village of Khydera, birthplace of the prominent nineteenth century painter Iakovidis. That is also the site—one of many all over Greece—of an August 15 festival honoring the assumption of the virgin Mary, at which the fattest lambs are offered for auction and the proceeds are donated to the church. Nearby there are traces of pre-Hellenic Pelasgian walls (Elef. p. 53). In the small town of Eresos too, there are ruins of the ancient walls that surrounded the city and of its acropolis and also of a medieval Genoese tower (Elef. p. 17). Ancient coins of the city-state of Eresos, many of them honoring Sappho, can be found in numismatic collections scattered throughout the world. A remarkable medieval monument in Eresos was the Basilica of St. Andrew, dating from the fifth century A.D. The mosaics of the floor, still in fairly good state of preservation, depicted peacocks, symbols of immortality.

East of Eresos, on a small promontory on the south coast of Lesbos, is a practically deserted little church [*heremoclesi*], in the name of St. Phokas. The few scattered ancient marbles around it probably belonged to the temple of Dionysos Bresagenes, a prominent deity on the island (Chapter I), but some modern scholars consider this the location of the large communal or island-wide sanctuary of the triple deity, Zeus, Hera and Dionysos (Quinn, 1961). Turning toward the center of Lesbos along the east coast of the Gulf of Kalloni, one passes by the village of Lisvori, where the recent discovery of a papal seal indicated that this was probably where, in the fourteenth century, Catholic representatives of the Pope from Rome and a Greek Orthodox delegation debated the possible union of the two Christian churches that had been split since the middle of the eleventh century. The nearby village of Vasilika (meaning "Royal"), 38 km. from Mytilene, may owe its name to its association with empress Irene's residence in exile (Eleftheriadis, p. 70), or to the fact that kings and nobles in the middle ages vacationed here. In the course of his travels, in 52 A.D., Saint Paul may have landed below Vasilika, near the entrance of the gulf of Kalloni (Eleftheriadis, p. 70).

Higher up (elev. 475 m.), by the foothills of the Lesbian Mt. Olympos, is the historical town of Ayiasos (pop. 3900), where a monk from Jerusalem in the ninth century brought the holy icon of the Virgin and Child reportedly painted by St. Luke himself (Chapter V). In 1701, after the local Turkish governor was cured from some chronic disease by a miracle attributed to the Virgin, Ayiasos was declared a tax-free district by the Ottoman sultan. This made many people move to the area and that continued until the decree was rescinded in 1783. In the courtyard of the baroque-style new church, erected in 1814, are the modest quarters of the monks and, upstairs, a small museum containing many valuable religious and historical items. The town of Ayiasos overflows with pilgrims and other visitors during the religious festivities and colorful popular celebrations for the August fifteenth east of the assumption of the Virgin Mary. The 40 km. ride from the curving north end of the gulf of Kalloni back to the capital of Mytilene may complete a rapid tour of the island, as it also traverses a full cycle of Lesbian history. A short distance north of Lisvori is the site of ancient Pyrrha, one of the five great city-states [*pentapolis*] of ancient Lesbos. Some walls and harbor structures can be seen on the bottom of the sea by the coast, sunken under water after one of the recurring earthquakes centuries ago. Further inland and to the north, by a spot called "Mesa" are the ruins of a large third century B.C. temple which might have been dedicated to the Lesbian worship of the three gods (trinity?), Zeus, Hera and Dionysos. Higher up and past the medieval "Hanging Bridge" of "*Kremasti*" is the town of St. Paraskevi (meaning preparation or "Friday"), where every year the last weekend of May the large and picturesque festival of the Bull [*Tavros*] represents ancient pagan, Christian and also relatively recent customs (Elef. p. 18). On a nearby hill is a war memorial honoring those fallen in 1912, when Greek military forces landed on Lesbos to expel the Turks. Returning towards Mytilene the road passes by pine forests (no longer tapped for their resin), olive groves and small industrial plants. A well-preserved Roman aqueduct closer to the city is a high-standing reminder of the centuries of Roman rule. In the outskirts of the Lesbian capital, the Moslem mosque on the north side still signals the past five hundred years of Turkish rule. Then, on the opposite side to the south, the airport may be considered as an indication of new developments, current and future.

A Lesbian-French art connection

One of the most prominent proponents of modern art, a connoisseur and pioneer publisher of art books in France, known generally by the French version of his name, *Teriade*, came from Lesbos. An impressive introduction to his life and work [*oeuvre*], with excellent illustrations was published in French in 1987, and in English in 1988. This 397-page large volume contains reproductions and articles from the outstanding art journal *Verve*, which was one of Teriade's major publishing achievements in Paris.

Verve—The Ultimate Review of Art and Literature
(1937-1960)

An Album and Review of its contents edited and annotated by Michel Anthonioz, 1988.

Teriade's oeuvre

Lesbos (1897-1915)

Efstratios Eleftheriades was born May 2, 1897 in Varia, a small village on the outskirts of Mytilene, "capital" of Lesbos. *Teriade* (the name he adopted once he had settled permanently in France) was the only son of one of Mytilene's leading citizens. His father owned a small factory that made soap from olive oil, the island's chief natural resource . . .

E, Eleftheriades (Teriade), in Antonioz 1988

Young Efstratios—*Stratis* (16)—was brought up in a cosmopolitan milieu that looked to France as its sole cultural polestar . . . The upper classes of Mytilene . . . travelled widely and were more interested in the latest news from Paris than in anything from Athens . . . Teriade spent his early boyhood in the country, in a square house at the edge of a wonderful olive grove, a patrician two-story house. On the ground floor was a sitting room (with) . . . long, low benches, ready to receive chance visitors who might step in for some conversation over the traditional sweet and glass of water. In front of the house and shaded by a trellised vine, the terrace was natural extension of the sitting room. At dusk, the family would gather to dine there, lingering outdoors for hours on end . . . The house Teriade and his wife would choose years later on the French Riviera . . . , their "Villa Natacha" . . . was very reminiscent of his house on Lesbos and the couple would continue there . . . the tradition of unstinting hospitality . . . with the leading artists and writers of the day as their guests (Anthonioz, 1988, p. 11).

In 1915, after finishing secondary school, young Stratis was sent to Paris to study law. He arrived in France "dressed in the stiff collar and tailored coat typical of a young man from a respectable family" (Anthonioz, 1988, p. 15) and was shocked by the confusion there of the first year of the war. The study of law bored him and he spent hours in cafes, developing the habit of drinking coffee cold. He never forgot his early contacts there and eventually his close friendships with the leading twentieth century painters, Matisse, Picasso, Braque, Chagall, Léger, Miró. Although he had done some painting himself back on Lesbos, it was art appreciation and criticism that aroused his enthusiasm. In 1926 he joined an older fellow Greek, Christian Zervos to publish *Cahiers d'Art*, writing 42 articles for the magazine himself during the next five years. After 1928, he also became a regular contributor to the "chic" Parisian newspaper, *L'Intransigeant*. From 1931-1937 Teriade worked with the prominent art book publisher Albert Skira and jointly in 1932 they started publication of the *Minotaure*, a major medium for carrying the message of surrealist art. For their seventh issue of *Minotaure*, Teriade wrote a "most probing," "clear and forceful" (Anthonioz, 1988, pp. 21–22) metaphor on art, comparing it to the skin "clothing itself" in Renaissance, "crushed" in Baroque art, gracefully "powdered" in Rococo and rising up "for the flight . . . of romanticism." With modern painting the skin was "split open, to reveal the structure and the intimate details of the body within it." Another forum for the aesthetic views of the Lesbian connoisseur was the equally revolutionary art publication, *La Bête Noire*.

Verve—The Review of Art and Literature (1937-1960)
Notes by M. Anthonioz, continued.

The first issue of *Verve* appeared in December 1937. Teriade was to channel most of his energy into *Verve*, which was first a magazine and later a publishing house. He had left *Minotaure* the year before and now—after a brief excursion to his native Greece—he started alone down a road on which many before and after him have come to grief: The foundation of a major, ambitious and free-spirited publication focusing on art and literature.

. . . .

. . . Documents and art works speak for themselves . . . However, these . . . would not have succeeded . . . had Teriade not insisted on reproductions of the highest quality . . . As the following statement from the opening page of the English-language version of *Verve* No. 1 indicates, this was always a priority.

Verve proposes to present art as intimately mingled with the life of each period and to furnish testimony of the participation by artists in the essential events of their time.

. . . .

It will present documents as they are, without any arrangement which might detract from their naturalness . . .

. . . .

The luxuriousness of *Verve* will consist in the publication of documents as fully and as perfectly as possible.

Despite the difficulties in getting from one place to another, the rationing of paper, and other handicaps, six issues of *Verve* managed to emerge between 1940 and 1945.

What made *Verve* such a momentous phenomenon was that it brought together traditionally segregated fields of artistic and literary endeavor at a special moment in history . . .

. . . .

After the war, there were few "general" issues and more special issues devoted to the work of an individual artist. Time and again, three geniuses—Matisse, Chagall, and Picasso—treated readers of *Verve* to dazzling displays of "creation-in-progress."

. . . .

In 1973 . . . the National Center for Contemporary Art organized an exhibition entitled *Hommage à Teriade*. The significance of this richly deserved tribute was not lost on Teriade. There, on the walls of the Grand Palais (Paris), near the gardens of the most beautiful avenue on earth, the pages that had been created by this wizard were displayed for all to see—a dazzling spectacle.

For a Greek, enthralled by beauty, who had arrived in Paris sixty years earlier without credentials or connections, France's tribute meant more than any words could say. Paris—the city of light that owes so much of its brilliance to artists—had acclaimed Teriade, the publisher of what had indeed turned out to be "the most beautiful magazine on earth."

Anthonioz, M., 1988, pp. 25-27.

In 1969, at the time freedom in Greece had been suppressed by the dictatorial junta (1967-73) the Greek poet Odysseas Elytis, on his way to a two-year self-exile in France, stopped in the French Riviera to visit his friend and Lesbian compatriot, Stratis Teriade and his wife at their "Villa Natacha." On that occasion the poet, in his characteristic semi-surrealist way, wrote a short poem in Greek, which has recently appeared in an English version (Keeley and Sherrard, 1981, p. 98) and also in a bilingual, Greek-and-English publication (Broumas, 1986, pp. 32-33).

Villa Natacha
by Odysseas Elytis, 1969.
I have something to say, lucid and unfathomable
Like the song of a bird in time of war
Here as I sat in a corner
To smoke my first cigarette, free (17)
Awkward in the middle of good fortune I tremble
Fearing I might break a blossom, disturb a bird . . .

. . . .

And yet they all listen to me
   . . . and the garden's entire firmament
Reflected in my mind.

. . . .

   . . . and all the designs
Clearly drawn among the fruit: the circle, the square,
   the triangle and the diamond [*rhombus*].
As seen by the birds the world becomes much simpler.
A drawing by Picasso
With a woman, a little child and a seahorse.

. . . .

I say: this too will come. And other things shall pass

The world does not need very much. Only a little.
The slightest thing. Like a wrong turn before the accident
But
Exactly
In
The opposite direction.
. . . .

In Broumas, 1986 (in Greek), p. 31.
(Other English translations in Keeley & Sherrard, 1981, p. 98;
Broumas, 1986, p. 32)

Teriade lived and died in France but almost every summer he spent some time in his paternal home at Varia on Lesbos. There he was often joined by his younger friend, the poet Odysseas Elytis. In 1972, with Teriade's initiative and funds, a two-story museum with a library was established in the midst of an ancient olive grove up the hill about 4 km. south of Mytilene. In that all-white classically simple structure (with floors of dark gray Lesbian marble dotted with characteristic reddish and yellow spots) the pioneer art connoisseur offered for permanent display most of his collection and books. Among these were the complete series of illustrations by the Russian-French painter Marc Chagall for the unique publication, commissioned by Teriade, of the romantic pastoral story of "Daphnis and Chloe" by the fourth century Greek author, Longos (Chapter IV). Numerous issues of Teriade's art journals, *Minotaure* and *Verve* were also donated for exhibit. On the main floor of the museum, paintings were hung by prominent international and modern Greek artists, including paintings by Yiannis Tsaroukhis. Some forty works by the folk artist, Theophilos, whose talent was first recognized by Teriade, were included.

Next to the Teriade museum a separate building was erected, dedicated to Theophilos and that also was made possible with Teriade's support. This "Theophilos museum" houses over eighty paintings by this self-taught "primitive" artist, who was born at Varia in 1873. Almost totally ignored during his relatively short life (he died in 1934 of food

M. Theophilos, Lesbian folk-artist
Theophilos Museum, 1990

poisoning), Theophilos painted without stop, often on walls, doors and windows of buildings that since then have been demolished. Mainly thanks to his compatriot Teriade, now the talent of Theophilos is widely appreciated. According to the Lesbian poet O. Elytis, Theophilos "put Art back on its original foundation, Nature" and, significantly, that happened "nowhere else but on Lesbos, an island (of) . . . rich and ancient nature-oriented [*physiocratic*] tradition" (Introduction, in *Theophilos—Paintings*, Theophilos Museum Publ. 3rd edition, 1990).

A small third structure built thanks to Teriade on the hill at Varia was the chapel of St. Paraskevee (a name that means Preparedness and so is also the Greek word for Friday), with iconography by the painter Yiannis Tsaroukhis, a friend of Teriade's and widely recognized in Greece for his diverse works. Included among these is the jacket for the phonograph album of the oratorio "*Axion Esti*" by M. Theodorakis, based on a long poem by Odysseas Elytis.

The Nobel Laureate poet from Lesbos

O. Elytis, from Broumas 1986

The road down the hill from the Teriade and the Theophilos museums returns to the narrow coastal highway which leads to Mytilene. At the southern outskirts of the city, among a row of mostly neoclassical two- or three-story mansions, is the villa of the modern Greek poet, Odysseas (at times written the classical way, Odysseus) Elytis. The poet's family name was Alepoudelis [*alepou* means fox in modern Greek]. Odysseas' father, the son of a wealthy landowner (Friar, 1974, p. 3) left Lesbos young to go to Crete, where he established a thriving soap manufacturing business. He returned to Lesbos to marry a young woman from his own island and the couple went back to Crete (18), where Odysseas was born in 1911, the youngest of six children. Just before the first World War in 1914, the family moved permanently to Athens, the capital of modern Greece, where Elytis had his education. After he started his literary career and perhaps "to disassociate himself from industrial connotations" (Friar, 1974, p. 3) the young man chose the surname Elytis, presumably to evoke the EL of hope [*elpida*, in Greek], freedom [*eleutheria*], Greece [*Ellas*, or *Hellas*] and of the beautiful Helen [*Eleni*, in modern Greek] of Troy. From a different perspective one may think of the poet's adopted name as, perhaps unconsciously, indicative of a *lytis* (the one who solves a problem, or a solution-bearer), of the *elite*, or simply an expansion of the dominant Lesbian eponymic suffix—*elis* (19).

After extensive reading during an early youth of rather poor health—"a glandular illness" (Friar, 1974, p. 4)—Odysseas' search for "inner validity" (*ibid.*, p. 4) persisted until, at the age of eighteen, he reportedly felt "liberated" (*ibid.*, p. 5) when he read the French surrealist poetry of Paul Eluard. While attending law school at the University of Athens (which he never finished) in 1930–35, Elytis had a series of poems published in the avant-garde Greek literary journal "New Letters" [*Nea Grammata*]. In later years, his adaptation of surrealism was to influence greatly the course of poetry in Greece (*ibid.*, p. 7). In 1943 appeared Elytis' prize-winning "Sun the First," with the verses that "confronted and transfigured . . . the despair and darkness" of the war years (Friar, 1974, p. 13). As a reserve officer in the Greek army, Elytis had been a second lieutenant during the 1940-41 war, when the Greek forces repulsed an Italian fascist invasion through Albania. His experiences were reflected in a collection of poems. A major work, the award-winning "*Axion Esti*" (translatable as "It is Worthy"—Ref. Table M) was published in 1959. Later the poem was set to music in the form of a modern oratorio, by M. Theodorakis (Friar, 1974, p. 42). Besides its metaphysical connotations and poetic symbolism, the work is considered "a rich treasure of the Greek tongue" (Friar, 1974, p. 28). The year he began "*Axion Esti*," 1956, Elytis also wrote poems such as "The Other Noah" and "Laconic" (Friar, 1974, p. 23). This latter will be cited in English translation, for the purpose also of allowing a comparison with the more vigorous, concise and playfully cosmopolitan 1972 "Laconic" by the Greek-born U.S.A. physician, Inos Phos (20), a K.I. Fallieros alias.

In 1961, invited by the U.S. State Department, Elytis spent over three months in North America, visiting Washington, New York, Chicago, New Orleans and Santa Fe. The next year he also accepted an invitation to visit the U.S.S.R. In the following years he worked on the long poetic "double monologue" of a young woman and a poet, "Maria Nephele," which contained images referring mostly to city life.

After the 1967 military coup of the dictatorial junta in Greece, Elytis lived in France for over two years, 1969–71. One of the poems he wrote during that period was on the occasion of his visit to the "Villa Natacha" of his friend and compatriot from Lesbos, Stratis Teriade on the French

Riviera. Elytis received a Ford Foundation award in 1972 and in 1979, following the publication of his *Maria Nephele*, he was awarded the Nobel Prize for Literature. That was sixteen years after the same recognition had been bestowed upon another Greek poet from the eastern Aegean shores, George Sepheris (Keeley and Sherrard, 1981, Introduction, ix).

In an interview for *World Literature Today* in 1975, Elytis pointed out the need of modern Greek writers "to destroy the tradition of rationality which lay heavily on the Western World" and "to regard Greek reality without the prejudices that have reigned since the Renaissance" (Keeley and Sherrard, 1981, Introduction, x). Decidedly, what is reality and what exists or "ought to be" and whether intense emotion, such as love, must be viewed as irrational, are matters of individual mentality and speculation. Writing about love, Elytis tried to give his poem "a bone structure that firmly encases and holds upright its pulsing heart" (Friar, 1974, p. 39). This comment is from the forty-four page introduction to the English translation of *The Sovereign Sun*, a "charming bittersweet song" based on folk songs and intended—before it developed into "self-sustained poetry" and "a coda to all of Elytis' compositions on the sun" (Friar, 1974, p. 42)—to provide the lyrics for songs by Manos Hadzidakis, the modern Greek composer better known internationally for his music for the movie *Never on Sunday*.

Already by 1954, the sixth edition of an *Anthology* of Greek poetry from the nearly 250-year period, 1708–1952, included—among the works of 359 poets—27 selections of poems by Odysseas Elytis. In the present translation of some of these and also of the extended works that followed them, choices had to be made among several possible English equivalent terms, due to the relatively broad range of meanings of the original Greek. An indication of these choices and of some different preferences shown by other translators is given in Ref. Table M, with a numerical signal (e.g., M.1, 2, etc.) next to each word in question.

> ***Anthology***, 1708-1952
> by H. N. Apostolidis, (6th Ed.), 1954 (in Greek)
> **Odysseas Elytis** (pp. 176-197)
> **The Birth of the Day**
> When the day stretches from its twig and spreads
> All the colors upon the earth
> When from the voice in one mouth the stalagmite cracks
> When the sun swims like a river through an unharvested field
> And a sail, shepherd boy of the winds runs far
> Your dress is always the dress of the island,
> A windmill that turns the years in reverse

.... (28 lines skipped)
You know every voyage is open to the pigeons
The whole world leans on the sea and the land
—we'll catch the cloud, get out of the disaster of time
From the other side of misfortune,
We'll play with the sun in our fingers
In the countryside of the open heart
We'll see the world being born again!

The Crazy Pomegranate Tree (Ref. Table M-1, M-2)
In those stark-white courtyards, where the south wind blows
Whistling through arched porches, tell me, is she (M-2) crazy, the pomegranate tree
That quivers in the light, spreading her fruit-bearing laughter,
With the stubbornness of the wind and with whispers—tell me is she crazy, the pomegranate tree
That shakes with newborn foliage at dawn
Spreading out all colors with a shiver of triumph?
.... (30 lines omitted)
(Cf. English translations in K. Friar, 1973, p. 592).

Variations on a Sunbeam
I. Red
The mouth that is a demon, a conversation, a crater
The wild poppy's nourishment and blood for passionate longing
 . . . your mouth talks with four hundred roses
It beats the trees, it melts the whole earth
And pours inside the body the first most tender quiver
.... (7 lines)
Caves of wholesomeness will drink to the good health of the sun
This must be what the world is, or a total loss, or the double voyage, here, on the wind's sheet, there, with a view to infinity.
.... (4 lines)

The sea, particularly the Aegean Sea, competes with the sun for primacy in the poetry of Elytis.

Orientations, 1940

On the Aegean—I

Love
The island cluster
And the bow of its white caps
And the seagulls of its dream
On the tallest mast a sailor waves
A song

Love
Its song
And the horizons of its voyage
And the echo of its longing
On the wettest rock of love, the bride
Is waiting for a boat.

Love
Its boat
And the carefree spirit of its yearly winds
And the jibsail of its expectations
On the highest wavecrest an island
Welcomes the homecoming.
   (Also in English by E. Keeley and Ph. Sherrard, 1981, p.4)

In 1959 was published Elytis' award-winning *"Axion Esti"*—"Worthy (M-3) It Is." In this major work of his, the poet was seen "translating his early surrealist mode into a new style ... more subtle ... more controlled ... that still retains a lyrical vitality and a cunning arrangement of evocative images." (Keeley, 1983, p. 137). As noted (*ibid*. p. 136), Elytis had spoken "specifically of his interest in combining the surrealist belief in the value of the senses with the Christian notion of sanctity ..." (Keeley, 1983, p. 136). The title of this long poem, from the Greek Orthodox divine liturgy, revealed the trend of " ... some of the best poets ... in modern Greece" to experience "a kinship with their medieval Byzantine heritage and the Christian tradition" as much as "with its pagan antecedents or the subsequent incursion of Renaissance influences from the West ..." (Keeley, 1983, p. 130).

Axion Esti (Worthy It Is)
by Odysseas Elytis, fifteenth edition, 1989
Genesis (pp. 11-24)
In the beginning the light And the first hour
   when the lips still in clay
   try and test the things of the world
. . . .
The line of the horizon did shine
visible and thick and impassable
   THIS the first hymn.
AND THE ONE I truly was The one of centuries ago
Still tender-green inside the fire The One Not-Made-by-Hand (M-4)
   with his fingers drew the distant
   lines.

One moment when he stopped to consider
   something hard or something high:
. . . .
And becoming aware how beautiful 't is to be in the arms of each
  other
   The big ponds all filled with love ...
. . . .
  . . . . with open hands he sowed
   daisies, crocuses, blue-bells
   all kinds of stars from the earth ...

. . . .
                        Then before I heard the wind or music
                As I moved to get out through an opening
(climbing upon an endless red sand and
erasing History with my heel)
      I struggled with my bedsheets
      That was what I was looking for
      innocent and tremulous like a vineyard
      as deep and unetched as the other side of heaven
. . . .
THIS ONE
the world, so small, so great! (M-5)
And the Scale (M-6) that, opening my hands, seemed
to weigh the light and the instinct was
                THIS ONE
                the world, the small, the great!
. . . .
And much deeper behind the waves
on the Island with the bays of olive-tree groves
For a moment I thought I beheld Him
who gave his blood for me to be flesh
ascending the rough road of a Saint
                one more time
                One more time
on the waters of Yera to touch his fingers
and light up the five villages (M-7) . . .
. . . .
Still tender-green inside the fire Uncut from the sky
                Went through me He became
                The one I am.
. . . .
The Sun got a face The Archangel on my right forever.
                THIS ONE then I
                and the world the small the great!

The Passion (pp. 27–28)

A.   HERE then I am,
created for the little Maidens [*Kores*] and the Aegean islands;
. . . .
B.   THE TONGUE they gave me the Hellenic
the humble home by the beaches of Homer.
       My only concern my tongue on the beaches of Homer.
. . . .

N.	(j) *Blood of LOVE*	*	*Coated me in purple*
	And joys unseen	*	*cast a shadow on me*
	I was oxidized (M-8)	*	*in the southern wind*
		*	*of mankind*
	Faraway Mother	*	*My Everlasting Rose*

R.   To a land faraway and unwrinkled now I march.
Now the hand of Death
     is the one giving Life

and sleep does not exist.
>   The bell of midday rings
and slowly on the heated stones engraved are the letters:
>   NOW and FOREVER and WORTHY IT IS.
Forever forever and now and now the birds are singing
>   WORTHY IT IS the prize (M-9).

Gloria (pp. 73–88)
>   WORTHY IT IS the light and the first
wish of mankind engraved in stone
>   the vigor in the beast that leads to the sun
the plant that sang and the day broke

. . . .
>   WORTHY IT IS to celebrate the memory

. . . .
>   REJOICE you who are Burning and you Tender-green
Rejoice the Unrepenting with the sword on the bow

. . . .
>   Rejoice, you the modest one with the precious sword
Rejoice, you the prophetic and Daedalic (M-10)
>   WORTHY IT IS the earth that lets up
a smell of thunder . . .

. . . .
>   WORTHY IT IS the distant song

. . . .
>   WORTHY IT IS the hand that returns
from horrible murder and now knows
>   which world truly dominates
which is the "now" and which the "forever" of the world:

. . . .
>   Now the wrap of the Earth and the Authority
Forever the consumption of the Soul and the quintessence

. . . .
>   Now the humbling of the Gods Now the ashes of Man
Now Now the Null (M-11)
>   and Forever the small the Great world!

While working on the "Axion Esti," Elytis wrote several shorter poems, which were published subsequently.

Six and One Pangs of Conscience For the Sky, 1960
Laconic (22)
So much it burned me, the longing of death,
  that my bright spirit went back to the sun
Who now dispatches me into the perfect syntax of rock and air
So I am the one that I have sought.
Oh, straw-colored summer, reticent fall,
Most humble winter,
Life yields its mites, the leaf of the olive tree

And in one night of dullness with little crickets
It vindicates again the claim of the unpredictable.
> (also, in English translations, in K. Friar, 1973, p. 606;
> and Keeley and Sherrard, 1981, p. 69).

An intricate and intriguing collection of forty-five poems, written over nearly twenty years, was published in 1978, in Athens and it "enjoyed an unprecedented success" (Anagnostopoulos, *Introduction*, 1981, p. vii). The title *Maria Nephele* (M-12) may be "laden with mythologic significance," Maria being the name of the mother of Christ and *Nephele* referring to the ancient Greek imagery for "natural deities" representing "new trends in education, cultural and philosophical thought" (Anagnostopoulos, 1981, *Introduction*, p. vii). Maria is also a very common girl's name and in these double poetic "parallel monologues" (*ibid.* viii) the young woman, "real and mythical" (*ibid.* vii) speaks of her world, "that of the young generation of today" (*ibid.* vii), while the respondent [*antiphonist*] is the poet himself. With her "indomitable spirit in . . . search for self-knowledge and her pursuit of justice," Maria Nephele is ready "to restore the dignity of life to its original unadulterated state" (*ibid.* viii). She represents "both divine grace and change" (*ibid.* ix) and with her as a guide, the poet "abandons his seclusion" (*ibid.* ix). He is not "an intellectual removed from reality" but becomes the Homeric Cloud-Gathering [*nephelegeretes*] Zeus and "the captive of her dreams" (*ibid.* x), who "knows how to reveal the hidden dimensions of reality" and to "cross over to the other side" (*ibid.* x). The admittedly somewhat pompous and inflated claims—consistently reflecting also the poet's own pontificating self-assessment—seem to be compounded by a mystical preoccupation with "magical . . . numbers" in a "mathematical structure . . . in accord with the tendency towards forces that transcend man" (*ibid.* xi). Pairs of poems, for instance, designated by the number four deal with "beauty, purity, justice," etc.; those by the number seven "refer to significant . . . events" (*ibid.* xi), such as the "Trojan War or . . . Stalin." Epigrammatic statements, or oracular responses—e.g., the unimpressive "it is bigamy to love and to dream" (*ibid.*, p. 11)—stand apart at the end of each poem.

> ***Maria Nephele: A Poem In Two Voices***
> by O. Elytis, 1978
> . . . .
> Nephele:
> I live day by day—who knows what tomorrow will bring.
> My one hand crumbles the money and the other smoothes it over.
> . . . .

Other people see you as an intellectual
And only I, who love you: as a captive of my dreams.
. . . .

The Cloud-Gatherer [*Nephelegeretes*]:
Ah, how beautiful to be a Nephelegeretes
To write epic poems like Homer and not to care
Not bother whether you're liked or not
. . . .
You undress as those who understand the stars undress
And with sweeping strokes you head for the open sea to
 weep
Freely . . .

> (translated by Anagnostopoulos, 1981, pp. 10-11:
> also in Keeley and Sherrard, 1981, pp. 102-3,
> as "The Cloud" and "The Cloudgatherer"

. . . .

Maria Nephele: "Patmos"
So it is, before you even know him,
That death alters and distorts you;
From living with his finger marks upon us
Half-savage, with our hair dishevelled, we bow
Gesticulating on harps that make no sense. But
The world is fleeing
Ay, ay, the beauty does not come twice and neither does love.
Pity, it's a pity, oh world,
that you are ruled by those meant to die
. . . .
To go there, there on that stone-covered island which the sun hits
sideways like a crab's walk
. . . .
Fully equipped . . . with sleeping bags and maps, . . . telephoto
lenses
and cartons of mineral water,
I set out—for a second time—and nothing
. . . .
By nine o'clock already, on the Mykonos dock,
I faded out over ouzo and much talk in English,
Customer of a weightless sky where all
Things weigh twice their own weight.
While the umbilical cord stretches from the stars
To the breaking point and you are lost . . .
. . . .

> From the Greek text in Broumas, 1986, pp. 74-76;
> other English translations in Anagnostopoulos 1981, p. 12;
> Broumas, 1986, pp. 75-77).

A characterization of "the girl" Maria Nephele is given in an earlier section of Elytis' prize winning long poetic "double monologue."

The Song of Maria Nephele
"What a pity (M-13) is this girl"
So they say in a mournful tone
They shake their heads, false tears unfurl
Can't they leave me alone!
Through the clouds my rounds I make
Like a lightning that brightly burns
And whatever I give and take
Quickly to rain it turns.
Joy I have never known
And on sorrow I tread unseen
Like an angel I have flown
Over the ravine.

(Greek text in Broumas, 1981, p. 62;
other English translations
by Broumas, 1981, p. 63).

One of the most recent works of Odysseas Elytis was about *"The Little Mariner,"* the sailing spirit evocatively called by the archaic Greek word for voyager, "Nautilos."

The Little Mariner [*Nautilos*], 1985
No. 15
This marble head, these cracked flower pots,
Setting like the sun at the time of watering,
In Aegina or Mytilene—this fragrance
Of jasmine, lemon balm and hyssop,
Holding the sky at a distance.
If you really are the one
That instant passing high over the rooftops
Just like a schooner with open sail
. . . .

(other English translations by Broumas, 1988, p. 93)

Many translations of Elytis' poetry have appeared, in several languages. Between 1973 and 1988 at least six books with selections from his poems and also some complete works have been published in English translations (Keeley, 1974; Friar, 1974; Keeley and Sherrard, 1981; Anagnostopoulos, 1981; Broumas, 1988). At least two of these included bilingual, Greek and English texts (Keeley, 1974; Broumas, 1986). In turn, Elytis has been the translator of significant literary works from other languages into modern Greek. His translation of "The Caucasian Chalk Circle" [*Der kaukasische Kreidekreis*] from the German of Bertolt Brecht, provided the lyrics for four songs by the composer Manos Hatzidakis (Keeley and Bien, 1972, pp. 194, 203).

Recycling the past

Segments of Elytis' philological commentaries and literary criticism, including self-assessments, have been interspersed in the present notes, frequently quoting quotes from other recent texts. In his review and reprinting of selected material from the great turn-of-the-century Greek novelist, A. Papadiamantis, the poet included passages referring to the ancient Lesbian poetess, Sappho.

> **THE MAGIC (M-14) OF PAPADIAMANTIS (23)**
> by Odysseas Elytis, 1976/89
> **Introduction**
> ... If nobody climbs on Mount Olympos, that does not mean that Olympos does not exist. What we call "poetic truth" is self-validating *(Introduction,* 4th printing, 1989).
> **Anthology**
> The moon was up, at midnight. Old Parthenis ... had enough sleep and stepped out of his little hut.
> ... He heard a whisper ... there stood three figures ... three women, naked like their fore-mother Eve ...
> . . . .
> ... Magic is dissolved only by magic ...
> ... The third didn't want to say what she desired ...
> was she trying to concoct a potion under the mellow moonlight, to turn his mind to her? "She may not love now but soon she will be in love." Sing, sweet Sappho, to comfort your own sex [*homophyle*] ...
>
> Quoted by Elytis, 1989, pp. 93-96 (in Greek).

A luxurious second edition of Elytis' translations of the poems of Sappho (Chapter II and Ref. Table H) in modern Greek appeared in 1985. The introduction was a revelation and a link of the "Now and Then," a closing of a loop, a convergence towards a center of unending inspiration and sensuous spirituality.

> **SAPPHO: RECOMPOSITION AND RENDERING**
> by Odysseas Elytis, 7th ed., 1985 (in Greek)
> Back two-and-a-half-thousand years, in Mytilene, I still see Sappho like a distant cousin with whom we played together around the same gardens, around the same pomegranate trees ... A little older than me ... with a secret notebook full of verses that she never let me touch.
> Of course that may be because we have lived on the same island. We had the same sensations of the physical world ... of Aeolis. But above all, it is because we have worked ... with the same concept, concerns (M-15), not to say almost the same words: with the sky and the sea, the sun and the moon, the vegetation, the

girls and love . . . So let me be forgiven if I speak about Sappho as my contemporary. In poetry, as in dreaming, one does not age (pp. 9-10).

. . . .

Certainly her home must have been somewhat comparable to the "literary salons" of pre-war Europe . . . where the more advanced girls of the island had an opportunity to achieve perfection in dance, in singing, in poetry, and in refined manners. It was destined that some of them, Atthis, Anactoria, Gongyla, Gyrinno, Mnasidika, should reach us wrapped in a golden cloud of astonishment and beauty.

. . . .

It was this smallish, dark-skinned girl . . . that proved capable to subdue a rose, to interpret a wave or a nightingale and by saying "I love you" to move the whole world (pp. 13–15).

In the summer of 1992 the small Modern Art Museum on the island of Andros (one of the Cyclades in the Aegean sea) organized an exhibit of semi-abstract paintings and collages by Elytis. A booklet (Elytis, O., Andros, 1992) was published with illustrations of these, accompanied by lines of verses and prose by the eighty-one-year-old poet and artist. On the first page, over a background of softly geometric shaded contours, three lines again referred to Sappho:

The pure truth
Seven transparencies
for Sappho.

Even those unimpressed by the poetry and the art of Elytis, who may actually disagree with the Nobel prize committee and do not feel the need to glorify certain human beings, should recognize that not so much the imperfect persons,—whether Sappho, Aristotle, or Elytis— but their *Words*, such as *pure, truth, love,* are the links of beauty and ideas that make the 3000-year history of Lesbos worth noting.

Daphnis and Chloë, etching by J. Miró, 1933, *Encyclopedia of World Art*, Vol. XI, Pl. 333, 1966.

APPENDIX

THE SHAPES AND SOUNDS OF THE GREEK ALPHABET

A, α	alpha, as in āllergy
B, β	veta, soft sound as in varvaros (barbarian!)
Γ, γ	gamma, softer than gh, at times y, as in yes
Δ, δ *	delta, softer than d, usually th, as in then
E, ε *	epsilon, as in energy (ΕΝΕΡΓΕΙΑ)
Z, ζ	zeta, as in zoo, etc.
H, η *	eta, long ē, as in Electra (ΗΛΕΚΤΡΑ)
Θ, θ *	theta, th as in Theos (ΘΕΟΣ)
I, ι	iota, short i, as in idiom, if.
K, κ	kappa, usual k, as in kinetics
Λ, λ	lambda, usual l, as in lexicon (lexis = word)
M, μ	mu, e.g., mega- (ΜΕΓΑ), micro- (ΜΙΚΡΟ)
N, ν	nu, as in neon, neologism
Ξ, ξ	xi, the equivalent of x, e.g., xenon (ΞΕΝΟΝ)
O, ο	omicron (small "o"), as in oligo = little
Π, π	pi, as in petroleum (ΠΕΤΡΕΛΑΙΟ)
P, ρ	rho, as in rheumatic (ΡΕΥΜΑΤΙΚΟ)
Σ, σ, ς	sigma, as in symbol (ΣΥΜΒΟΛΟ)
T, τ	tau, as in tria = 3, telos = end
Y, υ	upsilon, in modern Greek the same ē sound as H and I
Φ, φ	phi, as in philosophy and Fallieros (ΦΑΛΛΙΕΡΟΣ)
X, χ	chi, a soft "h" as in he; or hard as in chronos
Ψ, ψ	psi, as in psychology (ΨΥΧΟΛΟΓΙΑ)
Ω, ω	omega ("big" O), now sounds the same as omicron

Diphthongs

αι = ay; οι = ēe; αυ, ευ = af, ef; ου = ōo; (as in ōozo, ouzo)

---

*Problems related to the rendering of both epsilon and eta with "e," both delta and theta with "th," etc., are discussed in the Introduction.

NOTES

Chapter I

1. Many neolithic objects have been unearthed on the east coast of Lesbos by the dedicated British archeologist Winifred Lamb who, in the 1930s, sold her property in England to finance her studies on Lesbos.
2. Pitane, in Aeolis facing Lesbos, was where the Platonist philosopher Arkesilaos was born in the fourth century B.C. (Chapter III-C and Notes III, no. 14 & 18).
3. Macareus and Macar were two different persons, but the names are often confused (Oxf. Class. Dict. p. 633; Dict. Class. Myth. p. 268).
4. More than 1000 years later, Pompey was to suffer in Thessaly his final defeat by the armies of Julius Caesar (Chapter IV-A and Note IV, no. 6).
5. Another tradition mentions Mytilene as the wife of Lesbos.
6. The mountain village of *Pelopi* (home of the father of the USA 1988 presidential candidate, Massachusetts Governor Michael Dukakis) might be deriving its name from Pelops' landing.
7. The ancient *kithara* was a type of hand-held harp, but the modern words *guitar* and *zither* derive from this, which also means guitar in modern Greek.
8. *Siren* is still the word for a dangerously seductive female; it is not clear why it also indicates a device for a sound alert and is also the name for an eel-like salamander.
9. Although the serene clear light of the Apollonian spirit has been contrasted to the orgiastic intoxicated rambunctiousness of Dionysiac bacchanals, in ancient and in modern times (especially since F. Nietzsche), both Greek Gods have been associated with the mystical worship of "ecstasy" [*ek-sta-sis*], getting out of one's self.
10. *Eleusis*, meaning arrival, is a now neglected ancient spot near Athens, renowned in antiquity for its temples and rites of mystical worship.
11. Besides the twelve Olympian Gods (Ref. Table B), the ancient Greek Pantheon included several other major deities, such as Dionysos, Dios' [*Zeus*]

son, taken from his mother's womb when she died after seeing Zeus in all his glory and implanted into his father's calf, from where he was born a second time. Among the many secondary but very important "immortals" were Eros (Cupid, Love) and Pan, the horned, goat-footed mischievous little god of the woods and fields.

12. The companions of Dionysos were the nine Muses (note 14).
13. Volumes have been written about the concept of *salvation*—"soteriology"—and the appeal to Zeus the Savior, or, in this hymn the call to Apollo, to "save" the initiated, shows how profound is the urge to be released from the confines of the tormented *self*.
14. The traditional *Nine Muses* and their artistic domains are listed in Reference Table D. The brilliantly enduring Greek words in this hymn to the Muses are included in Ref. Table E.

Chapter II

1. *Coins* (the word means corner, wedge), standardized flattened metal pieces issued and guaranteed by a ruling authority, began to replace animals, grain, axes, pots and tripods as means of commercial exchange about the middle of the seventh century B.C. The early coins of Lydia, including those of king Croesus [*Kroisos*], were of "electron" (the Greek word for amber from which derives the term for electricity), an amber-colored mixture of gold and silver (Oxf. Class. Dict. p. 258-161; Encycl. World Art, Vol. III, p. 699-715).
2. The earliest known examples of Greek writing date from the second half of the eighth century B.C. Like other Semitic scripts, the Phoenician (introduced by Cadmos, who came looking for his sister Europe) had only consonants, so the Greeks turned some of them into vowels starting with *aleph*, which became *alpha*—and added some new letters.
3. **a.** The Parian Marble [*Marmor Parium*] is a tall (about 2 m./6 ½ ft.) plaque inscribed with over 100 entries on historical and literary events from the earliest Greek antiquity to 264/63 B.C. One piece was taken from Turkey to London in 1627 and the other was found on the island of Paros in 1897 and is in the Museum there.
   b. According to the chronology of the Parian Marble, the Greeks [*Graikoi*, Graecians, i.e., worshippers of the Grey Old—"*Graia*"— Goddess] began to be called "*Hellenes*" about 1521 B.C. (Graves, 1957, Vol. I, p. 161).
4. *Dithyramb*[*os*], a word possibly of non-Greek origin (although some interpret it as meaning "double doors" and referring to the double entrance, or birth, of Dionysos) applied to wild, orgiastic choral songs celebrating Dionysos and sung under the influence of wine. Dithyramb competition festivals were held in later Greek antiquity for several hundred years.
5. *Stadion* (pl. *stadia*, Lat. *stadium*) was a standard of Greek length measure of about 185 m. or 606 ft. Since the race-course in ancient Olympia was exactly one stadion long the word has continued to indicate a facility for

athletic competition. The *cubit* was another ancient measurement based on the length of the forearm (Lat. *cubitum*, elbow) about 45–50 cm. or 18–20 inches long.

6. Evidently by Strabon's time it was common to spell the name of the principal city on Lesbos *Mitylene* (cf. note II-11 and notes Chap. V and VI). Strabon also spelled *Eressos* with a double "s."
7. *Solon* (about 638-558 B.C.) was an Athenian statesman and law-maker who also wrote poems. His "learn and die" appreciation of Sappho's song can be compared to other unique life's experiences, after which a person is "ready" for death, such as the Biblical Simeon after he beheld the newborn Jesus.
8. *Cicero* (106-43 B.C.), Roman statesman and author, had studied philosophy and oratory both in Rome and in Greece and knew the Greek language and culture very well.
9. Plutarch's Greek words for *envy, viciousness* and (no single word in English) *vicarious enjoyment for the misfortunes of others*, are included in Ref. Table E.
10. The original text or Herodotos is quoted, in English, in Chapter II-B, about Alkaios (*ms*. p. II-47).
11. The Greek text of Athenaios in the Harvard series has the name of the city on Lesbos spelled mostly Mitylene but elsewhere it appears as the more traditional Mytilene (e.g. vol. IV, p. 424). This probably indicates that for Athenaios (cf. note no. 6) phonetically "y" and "i" sounded the same (as they do now).
12. *Archilochos* [*Arkhilokhos*] was an elegiac poet from Paros, at least one generation older than Sappho. *Hipponax*, an Ionian satirical poet, was about one generation younger than the Lesbian poetess.
13. The English translation of this fragment, rendering the line as "playing in country quiet, country games" (Davenport, 1981) seems to confuse the Greek word for child-play [*paidia*] with that for education and learning [*paideia*].
14. The poem used the word meaning sparrows, presumed to be birds bringing fertility, but translators have argued that it may have meant swans or other avian species.
15. The Greek adjective for *unwilling*, in feminine, is the only indication of the sex of the beloved person.
16. Sappho's *EPEA ANEMOENTA* (words of the wind, or songs in the air, or *windy words*) are very close to one of Homer's favorite expressions, *EPEA PTEROENTA* (words with wings, flying words), as in the *Odyssey*, X-418, X-430, XI-209 (Murray, 1984).
17. The Greek words for desire, passion, longing, sexy, courtesan—not the same as *porne*, a prostitute—etc. are presented in Ref. Table E.
18. *Poseidippos* (Posidippus), an epigrammatic poet in the first half of the third century B.C. lived on Samos and later in Alexandria, Egypt.

19. *Kallisteion* [neut., plural *kallisteia*] a beauty contest and also the prize, from *kallos*, beauty, *kallistos* (masc.) the most beautiful. Other derivatives (not listed on Ref. Table E) include—besides calligraphy and calisthenics— *kalligamos* (masc.), beautifully married; *kallilogos*, beautifully worded; *kallipolis*, beautiful city (Liddell, Scott: Lexicon) and *kallichoros*, of the beautiful dance (Barnard 1958, p. 97).
20. *Atreid*, a descendant of *Atreus*, king of Mycenae, son of Pelops (cf. Ch. I), father of the Trojan heroes Agamemnon and Menelaos and ancestor of the noble first settlers on Lesbos.
21. *Sisyphos*, mythological son of *Aeolus* [*Aiolos*] and so grandson of the hero *Hellen* (Chapter I, Table 1), reported to have been the most cunning of mortals (Dict. Class. Myth., p. 422). He was able to chain Death [*Thanatos*] so that no mortal would die and later, after Zeus freed Thanatos, Sisyphos still effectively maneuvered to avoid the Underworld [*Hades*]. When finally he died and "crossed the Aheron" a second time, he was condemned to roll a heavy rock uphill forever (Graves, 1957, Chapt. 67).
22. *Photios*, a medieval Byzantine Greek scholar, served as Ecumenical Patriarch of the Orthodox Church twice, from 858–67 and 878–86 A.D. and was instrumental in sending Christian missions to the Slavic peoples. Photios assembled, or wrote himself "a monument of erudition" (Gibbons, quoted by Oxf. Class. Dict. p. 828) called the "*Myriobiblion*" (meaning 10,000 books) and also an extensive *Lexicon*.
23. A search for translations of Lesbian and other Greek lyrical poetry into Slavic, Oriental and other non-European languages had not been completed at the time this volume was ready for publication.

Chapter III

1. An impressive positive interaction between politics, poetry and philosophy was common in the Greek world of the seventh and sixty centuries B.C. In addition to the "Seven Sages" (often ruthless rulers, but respected for their laws and literary legacy) such as Pittakos, Periander [*Periandros*] and Solon—Ref. Table F—other prominent philosophers-poets ruled their cities, among them the famous Pythagoras (Chapter II-A) and Parmenides. Herakleitos too was concerned with politics, but in a negative, rejecting way.
2. *Diogenes Laertios* (called *Laertes* by some ancient authors) left a valuable record of the lives and opinions [the Greek word of his title, *gnome*, means knowledgeable opinion, which differs from *doxa*—cf. *dogma*—the word for belief] of a total of eighty-two ancient Greeks, who had "done well" [*eudokimesan*] in philosophy. The tenth book ends the series with Epikuros, of the third century B.C. The biographical details, interesting quotations and often gossipy style make the books quite readable even today.
3. *Croesus* [*Kroisos*], last king of Lydia (560–546 B.C.) famous for his wealth. He was visited by many prominent Greeks and himself made generous

offerings to Hellenic shrines, especially Delphi. Croesus was overthrown and probably died on a pyre when his capital, Sardis, and the kingdom of Lydia, were conquered by the expanding Persian empire.

4. *Aristotle* [*Aristoteles*], a most prominent philosopher of the fourth century (384–322) B.C., founder of the Lyceum [*Lykeion*] in Athens (Chapter III-C) and author of books (many compiled by Theophrastos of Lesbos) on *Politics, Ethics, Poetics, Logic, Metaphysics,* as well as the *Natural Sciences* and practically every field of knowledge.

5. *Diodoros of Sicily* [*Diodoros the Sikeliot,* or *Diodorus Siculus*] was active in Roman times under Caesar and Augustus until about 21 B.C. and composed a forty-volume "Library of History" (he called it *"Bibliotheke"*, a book-shelf compilation of history) starting from the earliest, mythical times and ending with Caesar's Gallic War.

6. *Pherekydes* of Syros was classified by Aristotle as a "mixed" type of philosopher, one who combined in his cosmogony rationalism and myth. Mathematics took basically the place of myth in the world-view of *Pythagoras*, who remained with Pherekydes on Lesbos for more than ten years, until this pioneer philosophy teacher died. He was said to have been buried by his student, Pythagoras himself. The student-teacher bond was uniquely intense in Greek antiquity, as reported in more detail in Chapter III-C.

7. The laws of *Solon* (see also note No. 7, Chapter II), besides imposing on the Athenians a property tax—as reported by Herodotos—consisted of a new constitution and economic reforms, which waived much of the public debt and restored their lands to farmers who were about to lose them and to become serfs, being unable to repay their loans.

8. The word "barbarian" [Gk. *barbaros*] did not necessarily mean cruel and barbarous, but simply a person or nation speaking a non-Greek language, sounding "bar-bar" (not unlike "blah-blah").

9. Sadly, the Greek tribes that fled east from Greece to Asia Minor due to the Dorian invasion from the north, failed to unite against the Persian conquest and many had to migrate again, north or west. Some members of the Hellenic ruling classes, however, welcomed Persian support of their authoritarian oligarchic rules, against the popular democratic movements which threatened them.

10. *Delos*, a small island in the center of the Cyclades (more about it in the forthcoming book on *Paros: 3000 Years in the Center of the Cyclades*) revered as the birthplace of Apollo and Artemis, son and daughter of Leto. The Greek alliance, later called the Delian league, was initially headquartered on the island. Although Lesbos took a major initiative in forming the league and provided ships for the allied fleet, subsequent disappointments prompted several attempts to withdraw (Oxf. Class. Dict., pp. 319–322).

11. Other historical data suggest that 1000 is an exaggeration and that only about 30 Lesbians were executed (Bury, 1912, p. 400).

NOTES 399

12. Syracuse and Sparta were both Dorian city-states and military allies. The Spartans contributed to the military defeat of the Athenian expeditionary force in Sicily. Their victorious general started his speech with an apology for the proverbial short and to the point and not always explicit manner of speaking, common in Laconia (where Sparta is located), which continues to be called "laconic" (cf. note VII-21).
13. *Mna*, a relatively large sum of money [Latin *mina*] amounting to 100 drachmas [*drakhmai*]. Sixty *mnae* [*mnai*] made one *talent* [*talanton*], estimated to have been worth more than 1,000 (1990) US dollars.
14. *Arginousai* (plural, also *Arginusae*): cluster of small islands between Lesbos and the coast of Asia Minor. The relationship of the name to the—also very small—*Oinousai* islands (home of prominent twentieth-century Greek ship-owner families) a little to the south near Hios, is not clear.
15. *Kyme*, or *Cyme* (pronounced Keeme), named after an Amazon (Chapter I-A) was the largest and strongest of the Aeolian cities on the western coast of Asia Minor, facing north-west towards Lesbos. The people of Kyme had a reputation for their relaxed and pleasurable life-style. Like *Kyme*, *Pitane* was a coastal city in Aeolis also named after a mythical Amazon.
16. *Euripides* (about 485–406 B.C.), Athenian playwright, who wrote ninety-two plays, of which eighty titles are known and nineteen have been preserved. The tragedies mentioned by Diodoros, "The Phoenician Women" [*Phoinissai*] and "The Suppliants" [*Iketides*] are among those still extant and performed on stage. "Cadmean" victory refers to Cadmus [*Kadmos*], founder of the city of Thebes, where the action of many of the dramas took place.
17. *Pericles* (495–429 B.C.) Athenian statesman, influential and effective leader, despite his aloof and proud demeanor. The "Golden Age" of the fifth century in Greece has been associated with Pericles' government in Athens.
18. Another version is that of *Xenophon*, who wrote (*Hellenika*, 1.6.33, cited by Oldfather, 1968) that Callicratidas "fell overboard and disappeared."
19. In translating Diogenes from the Greek, the words "gay" and "fag" are used to convey the author's—and Greek society's—disgust with a man's affected effeminate behavior, which could be contrasted to a generally high regard for men who loved each other without diminishing their masculinity.
20. *Phanias* was apparently not an uncommon name in the area. The father-in-law of Aristotle was Phanias, ruler of Assos. The Phanias quoted by Parthenios may have been the same Phanias, an author and philosopher, mentioned by Strabon (Chaps. II-B and III-C) as a native of Eresos on Lesbos and probably the Ph*ai*nias often quoted by Athenaios (Chapters III and IV-A).
21. *Pamphile* (*Pamphila* in Latin) of Epidauros, was a Greek scholar and historian in Nero's imperial Rome. Her principal work, "*Collected Historical Memoranda*" is cited by Diogenes in his "*Lives and Opinions*" at least nine times.

22. The *Introduction* to Theophrastos' *"Characters"*, as appropriate and meaningful as it is, may not be the philosopher's work but a much later Byzantine interpolation (Edmonds, 1946).
23. Obviously these were the girls' nicknames, appropriate for *heterai*, or courtesans. They refer to breasts [*Mammarion*], voluptuousness [*Hedeia*], cupid-love [*Erotion*] and most are of the neutral gender ("it"), as diminutive as for instance the German *Mädchen*.
24. Reference to *logos*—"The Word"—in the Gospel of Saint John is an example of undigested philosophical terminology used to impress with no intention to explain or to comprehend.

Chapter IV

1. *Caria* [*Karia*], a region in the southwestern corner of Asia Minor—facing the islands of Rhodos, Kos, etc.—was Hellenized beginning about 1000 B.C. (Grant, 1987) by Ionians (on the north side) and then by Dorians, who intermarried with the native Carians. The area subsequently became part of the Persian empire, ruled by a satrap. Later it was incorporated into the Greek-Macedonian domain of Alexander and his successors. The city of Cnidus [*Knidos*] in Caria was famous for its medical facilities and also for the exquisite statue of Aphrodite by Praxiteles. Evidently the worship of this Goddess of Love did not discourage politically advantageous marriage contracts, such as the one proposed by the satrap.
2. "In his right mind" is the closest rendition in English of Plutarch's Greek word *"phreneres"*, from *"phren"*, mind or spirit (Ref. Table E) and *-eres*, well-put together, tightly joined.
3. *Bactria*, the region in Central Asia covering and extending beyond the present state of Afghanistan.
4. Scholars and other prominent citizens, who were able to leave the capital of the Byzantine empire, Constantinople [*Constantinopolis*], before it fell to the Ottoman Turks in 1453, carried with them religious objects and also Greek manuscripts, which were then studied, translated and safeguarded in Western Europe and primarily in Italy. The expansion of this early Byzantine "enlightenment" developed into the Italian Renaissance.
5. Late Hellenistic and Roman authors—Cicero, Strabo, Athenaios, etc.—and also most medieval Byzantine Greek historians (cf. Chapters V, VI) reversed the "y" and "i" and wrote the name of the largest city on Lesbos as *Mitylene*. Modern spelling has reverted to the ancient *Mytilene*. Both versions in Modern Greek sound exactly the same, all vowels being pronounced as a long "e," or like an Italian, Spanish, etc. "i": *Mitilini*.
6. **a.** King *Midas* of Phrygia remains famous for his magical—and destructive—"golden touch". *Gordios* was his father and their capital was named *Gordion* after him. Presumably the knot had been there for over 400 years before Alexander cut it.

    b. The planned publicity about Alexander, the Gordian knot and the pre-

dicted conquest of Asia, is an impressive example of a great leader's skill and need for popular image-making.
7. This crucial confrontation at the conclusion of the Roman Civil War took place in the region of *Thessaly*, in Central Greece, from where the Aeolian hero Lesbos had migrated to the island named after him (Chapter I-A).
8. The "lily" lines, in an English translation by Peter Jay, included in the "Greek Anthology" edited by P. Jay are attributed to a much later author, the "early Byzantine" Theophanes, of about 500–600 A.D. (Jay, P.: 1973, 1981, p. 366).
9. "Hellenistic" defines a period of history of at least 200–300 years (Grant, 1982), which was based on Alexander's successor states, but which, in terms of culture, aesthetics and life-styles did not end with the Roman conquest of these Greek kingdoms. In fact, the "hellenistic" mentality may still be as alive today, as are the classical, Renaissance or romantic spirits.
10. Achilles landed on Lesbos on his way to the Trojan war, probably to secure bases and supplies. The loot from his conquests on this island, including the "skilled and beautiful" women he took as slaves, became part of his dispute with the Greek leader, Agamemnon (Chapter I-A).
11. *Apollonios Rhodios* ("of Rhodes", the island where he spent his retirement years), third century B.C. Alexandrian (Egypt) author, poet and director [*Prostates*] of the Library. In his four-volume "*Argonautica*" he narrated in much detail the voyage of Jason and the Argonauts.
12. *Thetis*, a sea-nymph (Nereid, daughter of *Nereus*) was the mother of Achilles. *Aeacus* [*Aiakos*], reputedly a son of Zeus, was Achilles' grandfather. *Phthia* was the kingdom of Achilles in Central Greece. *Telamon*, a son of Aeacus like Peleus (the father of Achilles), was the uncle of Achilles and father of Ajax [the "great" *Aias*].
13. *Phanias* (see note II-20).
14. Outstanding examples of *Daphnis and Chloe* in twentieth-century art are the lithographs by Marc Chagall, drawings by Picasso, and the woodcuts of Aristide Maillol. The ballet, or "symphonie choreographique" by Maurice Ravel was first performed in Paris in 1912. Two orchestral suites by the same composer remain part of the popular symphonic repertory.
15. *Kronos* (Cronus, in Latin, Saturn), the son or Uranos and the father of Zeus, thus a "divine generation . . . before the Olympians" (Dict. Class. Myth.). The fact that he devoured his children and the near identity of the words, associated Kronos with Chronos, i.e. Time (Falliers, C.J.: Chronobiology in Relation to Allergy, in *Allergy Principles and Practice*, E. Middleton et al., editors, 1982).
16. A sudden and overwhelming fear is called *panic* because the god *Pan* could cause it with a blow of his whistle. *Syrinx* was an Arcadian tree-nymph who became a reed to avoid being seduced by Pan. This horned, goat-footed god then made a musical wind instrument from the reed, called syrinx (a reedpipe, or flute). Modern musical compositions by Claude Debussy, Elliott

Carter—"*Syringa*", 1978, based on a poem of John Ashbery—and others, refer to the story. Even the medical term *syringe* comes from the beloved nymph-reed of Pan.

17. *Apollonios of Tyre* [*Tyros*, a coastal city in eastern Mediterranean, now in Lebanon] should not be confused with *Apollonios of Rhodes* (note no. 11 above), or with the wandering teacher and miracle-worker, *Apollonios of Tyana* (Chapt. II-B), a contemporary and competitor of Jesus Christ, or with others, a mathematician, a grammarian, etc. of the same name.

18. The use of pre-existing stories in exact detail, was evidently not an uncommon practice by Shakespeare and his contemporaries.

19. After 465 years of Venetian rule, the Greek island of Crete was conquered by the Turks in 1669. Most Venetians and many Greeks left and only two fortified Venetian outposts remained on the island until 1715, when they too were surrendered to the Turkish Vizir (Norwich, 1982). The Greek folk epic of *Apollonios*, presumably written on Crete in the 16th century, was reprinted in Venice in the 1700's.

20. Currently both Kontianos and Temenos are considered simple copyists and not the original authors of the Cretan "Apollonios" (Wagner, C. *Medieval Greek Texts*, London, 1871 and *Carmina Graeca*, 1874, pp. 248-276, as stated by S. Kyriakides in the Greek "*Eleftheroudakis Encyclopedic Lexicon*).

21. The Greek language of this "*Apollonios*" is a linguistic jewel of folk art, regrettably not accessible to many. The fifteen-syllable verses are in the prevalent folk-song style and the spelling and grammar conform to contemporary rules, such as dropping an initial vowel [*Athenagoras* became *Thenagoras*] and switching declinations [*Arkhistrator* changed to *Arkhistratoras*]. The devout Christian spirit is shown by frequent references to the "Lord" and by placing the lost wife in a convent rather than the Temple of Diana [*Artemis*] on Ephesos.

22. The uproar of the crowd protesting against Saint Paul for fear of losing their business related to the worship of Artemis.

23. *Assos*, a city famous in ancient times especially in connection with Aristotle and Theophrastos (Chapter III-C) is now the Turkish village called Behramkale (*New York Times*, 11/9/86) about five miles from the north coast of Lesbos (cf. note VI-21).

24. The reference is to Amphion of Boeotia and to Arion of Lesbos (see Chapter II-A).

25. The *kykeon* (pronounced kee-kay-on) was an ancient Greek "cocktail," a thick mixed drink made of barley meal, grated cheese and special wine. The word *kykeon* later came to mean any confusing state of affairs, such as a "political kykeon."

26. *Eleusis* [meaning *arrival* in Greek], near Athens, was the place of worship of the annual return of Demeter's daughter, Persephone from the underworld. The Eleusinian mysteries involved a ritualistic initiation into a cult

with both Orphic and Dionysiac elements (Chapter I-B and note I-10).
27. *Mysia* was the region in northwest Asia Minor neighboring on the Troad and Phrygia (Ref. to king Midas, note no. IV-5a). The claim that Mysian girls became the first Muses has not been substantiated.

Chapter V

1. *Byzantium* [*Byzantion*], City of Byzas, founded about 660 B.C. by Megarian Greeks on the European side of the southern end of the Bosporos strait. Renamed Constantinople (City of Constantine) and, in the twentieth century officially (in Turkish) Istanbul, the city still gave its name, especially in the past 300 years, to the adjective "Byzantine" applied to the territory, manners and art of the Greek-speaking Christian East Roman Empire.
2. *Arian*: A follower of the unorthodox and "heretic" beliefs of the Alexandrian Christian presbyter Arius [*Arios*]—c. 260-336 A.D.—that Jesus, the Son, was subordinate to God the Father and also that Jesus Christ was subject to change with time.
3. *Greek Fire* [*Hygron Pyr*, Liquid Fire, in Greek]: A secret incendiary projectile weapon introduced about 673 A.D., probably containing petroleum, naphtha, pitch, resins and other flammable substances (Sewter, 1985, p. 517).
4. *Theme*: A major administrative and military subdivision of the East Roman Empire.
5. *Iconoclasm*: Opposition to the making and veneration of religious images of Jesus Christ, the Virgin Mary, saints, etc. pursued most intensely and violently by Byzantine rulers from 726 to 843 A.D. with the destruction [*iconoclasm* image-shattering] of holy icons and severe persecution of icon-worshipping [*iconolatry*].
6. *Indiction* (*indictio*, proclamation in Latin): A fifteen-year cycle beginning with an official proclamation about property values and tax obligations and used (at the time questionably—Ref. Ch. V-A) as a dating reference; medieval historians also dated events in reference to the "Creation of the World" (5500, or 5508 B.C.) and also the birth of Christ (Oxf. Class. Disc.; Magoulias, 1975, p. 264).
7. *Harun-al-Rashid* ("Aaron, the Well-directed" in Arabic): Fifth Abbasid Arab *caliph* ("successor" of the prophet Mohammed), famous for the brilliance of his court (786-809 A.D.) in Baghdad.
8. *Eunuch* [Greek: *eune*, couch, *-oukhos*, holder, keeper]: A castrated male trusted to guard and manage domestic affairs of royal families and thus often acquiring extraordinary privileges and executive power, but—being mutilated—not eligible to ascend the imperial throne. The chief eunuchs of empress Irene, Aetios and Stavrakios, may have changed the course of history by inhibiting a possible matrimonial link between the Byzantine and the Frankish "Roman" imperial rulers.
9. *Black shoes*: Ordinary footwear, not the purple buskins, which were the characteristic prerogative of the emperor (Sewter, 1984, p. 315).

10. *Logothete* [*logothetes*]: High administrator—literally accountant—and civil dignitary; *kouropalates*: palace head stewart, royal chamberlain; *sebastos*, fem. *sebaste*: honorable, highly respected (in awe), august, such as in the Roman imperial titles *Augustus*, *Augusta*.
11. *Triclinon* [Latin *triclinium*]: Greek and Roman dining room arrangement with couches holding three person each; wealthy homes often had two or more connecting *triclinia* (Oxf. Class. Dict.).
12. *Saint Sion* [Gk. *Ayia*—or *Ayhia*—*Sion*] presumably indicated the origin of the ancient icon, which was inscribed: MOTHER OF GOD SAINT SION (Kleombrotos, I.G., 1982, p. 10).
13. *Olympus* [Gk. *Olympos*]: Name—of unknown origin—of several prominent mountains in Greece, Asia Minor and the islands (Lesbos), the best known among them being the 3000-meter-high home of the Olympian Gods, on the border between Thessaly and Macedonia.
14. *Monomakhos* (meaning "Single Combatant" or "Dueller"): Family surname of a prominent line of Byzantine nobility; the mother of the Russian ruler Vladimir Monomakh (1113-25 A.D.) was a descendent of the Byzantine emperor Constantine IX. (Bobrick, B.: *Fearful Majesty: The Life and Reign of Ivan the Terrible*, G.P. Putnam, New York, 1987, p. 125).
15. *Orphanotrophos* (Guardian— "nourisher"— of the orphans): An official Byzantine title by which the Paphlagonian eunuch John was known.
16. *Kerularios* (in Latin, Cerularius): The surname of the ecumenical patriarch Michael, during whose tenure the Great Schism between the Eastern Orthodox and the Roman Catholic churches took place, in 1054 A.D.
17. *Skleros* (meaning "hard"): Surname of a noble Byzantine family, members of which aspired to the imperial throne; in feminine, *Skleraina* was the name of the devoted and ambitious young mistress of Constantine IX.
18. *Herodotos*: Classical Greek historian (484?-425? B.C.) quoted repeatedly in previous chapters of this book.
19. "You can't blame." Quote from Homer's *Iliad* (III, 153-157): As the leading Trojans saw Helen coming up the tower ... with lowered voices they said to each other: "You can't blame the Trojans and the strong-legged Achaeans for causing so much grief for so long on both sides for the sake of such a woman."
20. *Acarnanians*: Psellos referred to the Greek historian Thucydides, according to whom the rather primitive people of Acarnania, in west-central Greece, always continued to bear arms even in his time (Sewter, 1984, p. 270).

Chapter VI

1. *Alania*: The country of the mostly nomadic *Alans* (probably of Turkish origin) off the north-east coast of the Black Sea. More to the west were the *Scythians*, or *Scyths*, a name which the Greeks often applied to any "barbarians" —i.e. foreigners—from the north. The Greek-speaking citizens of the Byzantine empire continued to call themselves *Romans*, as heirs of the

Roman Empire and for them anyone from Italy and northwestern Europe was *Latin* or *Frank* (cf. Encycl. Brit. vol. VI, on the *Crusades*).
2. The Greek surnames *Komnenos* (masc.) and *Komnene* (fem.) have been transliterated (following a Latinizing tradition) as *Comnenus* and *Comnena*.
3. The fifteen-year *indiction* dating system and other chronological references are outlined in note no. 6, chapter V.
4. The *Patzinaks*, or *Pechenegs* (Encycl. Brit. *Vol. 17*) and the *Cumans*, or *Kumans* (Encyc. Brit. Vol. 13) were the dominant Turkish ethnic groups north of the Byzantine state in the 10th-12th centuries. The *Seljuk* or *Seljuq* (Ostrogorsky, p. 617) Turks penetrated the Greek territories from the east and south in Asia Minor. They were eventually displaced, absorbed or destroyed by the *Ottoman*—or *Osmanli*, descendants of Osman—Turks, who by the end of the fifteenth century had conquered all of Asia Minor and the Balkans.
5. Continuing a trend already noted in Strabo and Athenaios (chapt. II, notes 6 and 11) Greek authors reversed the "y" and "i" in the classical spelling of Mytilene and wrote *Mitylene*. In modern Greek (ch. VII) all the vowels sound like a long "ee" and in the Latin alphabet (tourist guides and maps) the name of the town is written *Mitilini*.
6. *Protonobilissimos*, meaning first and most noble, was one of the numerous titles applied—and often invented—by Byzantine rulers to honor or placate important and potentially dangerous persons, including foreigners.
7. Ancient *Epidamnos*—later called *Dyrrhakhion*, or, in Italian *Durazzo* and in Albanian *Durres*—was a major port of entry (now in Albania) from the west to the Balkans, both for trade and for foreign invasions.
8. In her History of Alexios, Anna quoted Homer in the original ancient Greek 38 times. The lines from the *Iliad* (VII, 279–282) describing how the herald Idaios (Idaeus) admonished the Greeks and the Trojans to stop the battle read (K.I.F. translation): "Fight no more . . . night has already fallen; and it is good to follow the night's rules." Sewter (p. 237) rendered this quote as: "Night is already upon us; it is good to heed the night."
9. Slavery did not exist officially in the profoundly Christian Byzantine State, but captured "barbarian" enemies were at times committed to bondage and forced to serve as slaves, mostly in military units.
10. The Latin Kingdom of Jerusalem was established after the forces of the first crusade captured the Holy City and Baldwin of Boulogne was crowned king in Bethlehem in 1100 A.D. (Runciman, 1951/92, Vol. I, p. 326).
11. Medieval Greek writers continued to use for their capital the ancient name Byzantion interchangeably with that of Constantinople [*Constantinoupolis*] and more commonly just *Polis*, the City (cf. note VII-2a).
12. *Gavras*, or *Gabras* was a member of "a turbulent family" (Sewter, 1969/85, p. 413) in Byzantine politics and military affairs.
13. *Sion* is the transliterated Greek spelling of Zion (in Hebrew pronounced *Tsiyon*), the hill in Jerusalem where the Temple was built. More broadly,

Sion or Zion indicated a holy place and it was the words Holy Sion—in Greek *Ayia Sion*—that led to the naming of the Lesbian village *Ayiasos*.

14. This site, or alternatively the promontory of Saint Phokas (chap. VII), have been considered as the possible locations of "The Triple Temple of Antiquity" (Paraskevaidis, M., in *Kathemerini*—"The Daily" newspaper of Athens, Sept. 6, 1970).
15. *Hesychast* was an eastern Christian monastic movement and belief in the ability to attain divine calm [*hesychia*, or *hesykhia*] through intense uninterrupted prayer involving even bodily functions such as vision and breath control. Although briefly adopted by higher church authorities, hesychasm was mostly ridiculed and its adherents were called belly-souls [*omphalopsychoi*].
16. The last name of the Genoese lords of Lesbos, mostly written *Gattilusio*, (cf. chap. VII, note 3) can also be found spelled *Gatilusio*, *Katalouso* and *Kataliuso*. Some first names have also been written differently by different authors. Nicolo has been called Nicorezo and Domenico Kyriakos [*Kyrios* = Dominus, Lord], or Ciriaco. Kritoboulos wrote *Dominiko* (p. 80) and incorrectly referred to Nicorezo as "the first . . . Gateliuso" (p. 86). The Genoese spelling of the plural *Gattilusj* has been preserved by Miller (1921).
17. Turkish names may be found spelled variously in both the Greek and the Latin alphabets, evidently in an effort to approximate the way they sounded. Orkhan may also be written Orchan, or Hyrkhan. Omu (Ostrogorsky) is the same as Umur (Magoulias) and Yunuz or Yunus (Magoulias) is also found as Yenis and (Kritoboulos) hellenized as *Ionouzis*.
18. *Doukas*, or variously *Ducas*, a family name meaning "Duke" belonged to a number of apparently unrelated Byzantines, including emperors, noblemen and the fifteenth century historian.
19. *Phokaia*, the prominent ancient "City of the Seals" was renamed *Foglia* by the Italian colonists. In the seventh century B.C. Greek colonists from Phokaia were among the first to colonize Italy!
20. *Mehmet* seems to be the most common transliteration of the name of many sultans and other Turks. The same name has been rendered from the Arabic or Turkish, as Mehmed, Mahmud, Mahomet, Mehemet, Mohammed and Muhammad. The name of the founder of Islam is generally written Mohammed and his followers are called Mohammedans and also Moslems, or Muslims ("those who submit").
21. *Assos*, the ancient city across the channel from Lesbos (associated with Aristotle and Saint Paul in antiquity) was by the time of the historian Doukas renamed *Makhran* and in modern Turkish it is known as *Behramkale* (*New York Times*: "Troy, Assos and Pergamum," 11/9/86).

Chapter VII

1. The tendency to call any western European and Latin Catholic "Frank"

[*Frangos*] has persisted among the Greeks since the Middle Ages (cf. chapt. VI, note 1).

2a. Greek writers, like the rest of the people, have continued to call Constantinople [*Konstantinoupolis*] simply "Polis", *The City* (cf. note VI-11).

2b. Galata [*Galatas*]: The district across the Golden Horn, northeast of Constantinople (probably from the word *gala*, milk).

3. In his folkish provincial style, this modern Greek writer decided on the spelling "Kateliuso" instead of the Italian *Gattilusio*. Kontoglou's historical information at times did not agree with established facts (cf. Table VI-1 and note VI-*16*).

4. Under Turkish rule, education in the Greek language and religion was only available—often in hiding— in obscure monasteries and churches.

5. The transliterated Greek spelling *Yais* may be only an approximation of the original.

6. For almost 1000 years Greek writers had to choose between an archaic classically "purist" style and the evolving, often unstructured "demotic" language of the people. The conflict had political as well as literary implications. In the 1980s the historically honored spelling (orthography) of the Greek language was altered by a political act and books like the 1989 "Compendium" displayed this amputated style deleting certain stress [*tones*] and aspiration marks.

7. After an eight-year revolutionary war against the Turkish conquerors, a small part of the original Greek territories became an independent state in 1829. Additional conflicts more than doubled modern Greece. After the post-World War I campaign into Asia Minor ended with a Greek Catastrophy in 1922, a "population exchange" took place, with the transfer and relocation of Greek and Turkish ethnic groups across the new borders to establish more homogeneous state populations.

8. The name Mytilene—often, especially by Medieval writers, spelled Mitylene and more recently Mitilini—has been used also to apply to the entire island of Lesbos.

9. Of the several Greek words for mother and baby, Eftaliotis' use of the colloquially familiar *mana* and *moro* warmly accentuate his metaphor.

10. Even in a small town and among long-time acquaintances, people of some education until very recently addressed each other as *mister* and *madame* [*kyrie, kyria*] and used the plural form (comparable to the French *vous*, etc.). Drivas speaks to the *daskala* in the polite plural all through the story.

11. Laurel—or bay—leaves not only form the wreaths for athletes and heroes, but also are the ingredients of sauces adding flavor to typical Greek dishes, such as the rabbit stew.

12. Vlach country—Vlakhia, or Wallachia— is the region in modern Romania north of the Danube and south of Moldavia.

13. *Anatolia*, the "Eastern Country", could refer to Asia Minor in general, but particularly to its eastern plateau (cf. chap. VI).

14. *Eleftherios Venizelos* (1864-1936), prominent liberal politician and prime minister of Greece 1910-15, 1917-20, 1928-33; *Ioakeim* (Joachim) was the ecumenical patriarch in Constantinople from 1878–84 and again in 1901–12, thus head of the Orthodox Church when Lesbos was liberated near the end of the Balkan wars.
15. Family names like Komnenos, Palaiologos and others identical with those of medieval imperial dynasties are still encountered in modern Greece.
16. *Stratis* (pronounced Strátis or Statís) is a common shortening of the name Efstratios (also sp. Eustratios).
17. The poet's line "... first cigarette free" (in freedom) has been mistranslated in recent publications as "my first free cigarette"! (Broumas, 1986, p. 33).
18. The large Greek island of Crete [*Krete*] remained under Venetian domination for more than 400 years until gradually (1645–1715 A.D.) it was conquered by the Turks. It regained autonomy under a Greek governor in 1897 and finally in 1912 it became part of Greece, which had become a newly independent state in 1829.
19. Family names ending in *-elis* are as prevalent on Lesbos (they may denote an Italian influence) as those in *-idis*, *-akis*, *-opoulos*, etc. in other parts of Greece.
20. Mikis Theodorakis (b. 1925): Prominent modern Greek composer of both light-popular songs and profoundly complex orchestral and choral music. He began composing the music for the *Axion Esti* in 1961 in Paris after he received the text from Elytis himself. They were both away from Greece due to the oppressive dictatorship of the military junta in Athens.
21. The lines of the short poem "Laconic" from *COMPUTERUS*, by Inos Phos, seem more succinct and *laconic* (!) compared to those of the "Laconic" by Elytis:

    Lac sans fond / Lac du néant / Lack of everything.
    Oh stranger, tell the Lacedemonians / that here I lie / Observant of their rules.
    (Copyright K.I. Fallieros, Denver, 1972)

22. Alexandros Papadiamantis (1851-1911), who has been called "a lay monk" (Pappageotes, 1972, pp. 163-72) for his austere lifestyle, came from the small island of Skiathos, across the Aegean west of Lesbos, and has been recognized as one of the most original and stylistically unique Greek novelists and storytellers of the past one hundred years.

REFERENCES

Abbot S, Love B: *Sappho was a Right-on Woman: A Liberated View of Lesbianism*, Stein & Day, New York, 1972.

Adrados F: *see* Rodriguez Adrados.

Aelian [*Ailianos*]: *The Properties of Animals*, cited by Edmonds, Vol. III, 1928.

Alcaeus [*Alkaios*]: in Bowra, 1961; Campbell, 1982; Edmonds 1928; Lobel & Page 1955-68.

Allen WF: *Tacitus: The Annals*, Books I-VI, in Latin, Ginn & Co. Boston 1890.

Anagnostopoulos A: *Maria Nephele: A poem in two voices by Odysseus Elytis*, trans. from the Greek: Boston, Houghton Mifflin, 1981.

Antonioz, M: *Verve: The Ultimate Review of Art and Literature*(1937–1960), H.N. Abrams, New York, 1988.

Apostolidis: *Anthology* (Modern Greek Poetry) 1708–1952, Estia, Athens, 1954.

Archilochus [*Arkhilokhos*]: in Edmonds, 1928; Rankin, 1977.

Arias, PE: Transl. & revised by B. Shefton: *Greek Vase Painting*, Abrams, New York, 1961.

Arion: in Edmonds, 1928.

Aristotle [*Aristoteles*]: *Poetics*, Greek text & Engl. transl. by WH Fyfe, Harvard Univ. Press, Cambridge 1927-82.

Aristotle [*Aristoteles*]: *Politics*, text & Engl. transl. by H. Rackham, Harvard, Cambridge, 1932-77.

Arrian [*Arrianos*]: *Alexander's Anabasis* (Ascent, Campaign), Greek text & Engl. transl. by E. Iliff Robson, Books 1-4, Vols. I-II, Harvard, Cambridge, 1976.

Athenaeus [*Athenaios*]: *Dining Scholars [Deipnosophists]*, Vols. I-IV, Greek text & Engl. transl. by CB Gulick, Harvard, Cambridge, 1969-71.

Axiotakis AS: *The New Monastery [Nea Moni] of Chios*, Holy Cathedral Publ., Chios [*Khios*], 1982.

Babbit FC: *Plutarch's Moralia*, Greek with Engl. transl. & notes, Harvard Univ. Press, Cambridge 1927-49.

Balasch M: *Safo—Obra Completa* (complete works), bilingual ed. Greek and Catalan, Escorpi/Edicions 62, Barcelona 1973- 85.

Balmer, Josephine: *Sappho—Poems and Fragments*, Carol Pub. Meadowland Books, Secaucus NJ 1988 (orig. Brilliance Books, London 1984).

Barnard, Mary: *Sappho—A New Translation*, University of California Press, Berkeley, 1958.

Barnstone, W.: *Sappho—Lyrics in the Original Greek with Translations*, New York Univ. Press, New York, 1965 (orig. pub. 1962).

Barnstone, W.: *Sappho and the Greek Lyric Poets*, Schocken Books, New York, 1988.

Barr S: *The Will of Zeus—A History of Greece from the Origins of Hellenic Culture to the Death of Alexander*, Lippincott, Philadelphia, 1961.

Baudelaire, Ch.: *Les Fleurs du Mal* (Flowers of Evil), in *An Anthology of French Poetry*, A. Flores ed., Doubleday, New York, 1958 (pp. 17–56 in English, pp. 294-323 in French); also Baudelaire Ch. *The Flowers of Evil*, in French, preceded by Engl. translations and notes, M & J Mathews, eds. New Directions, New York, 1955–89.

Beckly H (ed.): *Anthologia Graeca*, Books I-VI, E. Heineran, Munich, 1906.

Booth, Cathy: Rooting for "Michalis" (Michael Dukakis) *Time*, May 2, 1988, p. 30.

Bowder D: *Who Was Who in the Greek World, 776 B.C. – 30 B.C.*, Phaidon, Cornell Univ., Ithaca NY 1984.

Brehier L: *The Life and Death of Byzantium*, Engl. transl. by M Vaughan, N. Holland Publ. Co, Amsterdam & New York, 1977.

Broumas O: *What I Love: Selected Poems of Odysseas Elytis*, transl. from the Greek: Port Townsend, WA, Copper Canyon Press, 1986.

Broumas O: *Odysseas Elytis' The Little Mariner*, transl. from the Greek: Port Townsend, WA, Copper Canyon Press, 1988.

Brunt PA: *Arrian: History of Alexander and Indica*, Vols. I- II, Greek text & Engl. transl. Harvard Univ. Press, Cambridge 1929-76.

Bury JB: *A History of Greece*, Random House/Modern Library, New York, 1900-13, reprinted.

Caesar J: *The Civil Wars*, Latin text & Engl. transl. by A.G. Peskett, Harvard, Cambridge 1914-66, reprinted.

Campbell DA: *Greek Lyric* (Vol. I)—*Sappho, Alcaeus*, Harvard, Cambridge, 1982.

Campenhausen, von H: *The Fathers of the Greek Church*, Engl. transl. by S. Godman, Pantheon, New York, 1959.

Cantarella E: *Pandora's Daughters—The Role and Status of Women in Greek and Roman Antiquity*, Engl. transl. by MB Fant, Johns Hopkins Univ. Press, Baltimore 1987.

Casson L: *Ships and Seamanship in the Ancient World*, Princeton Univ. Press, Princeton NJ 1971.

Cedrenus, George [*Georgios Kedrenos*]: *Compendium [Synopsis] of History from the Beginning of the World to Isaac Comnenus*, DD Marcus ed., G. Xylandris Latin transl., Greek & Latin, Io. (John) Oporinus & Episcopios Bros. publ., Basel 1560; also in CSHB and MPG*.

Chalandon F: *Les Comnènes—Jean II et Manuel I*, orig. publ. by Picard, Paris, 1912, Burt Franklin Res. Series No. 2.
Choniates [*Khoniates*], Niketas (aka Acominatus): *History beginning from the Reign of King John Komnenos, son of Lord Alexios*, Greek with Latin transl. by H Wolfius, I. Oporinus pub. Basel 1557; also in CSHB.
Choniates [*Khoniates*], Niketas: *Annals—"O City of Byzantium"* Engl. transl. by HJ Magoulias, Wayne State Univ. Press, Detroit 1984.
Cicero MT: *Letters to Atticus*, Latin text & Engl. transl. by EO Winstedt, Vols. I–III, Harvard, Cambridge, 1912-67.
Cicero MT: *Pro Archia Poeta* (For Archias the Poet), Latin text & Engl. transl. by NH Watts, Harvard, Cambridge, 1923-65.
Cinnamus, John [*Ioannes Kinnamos*]: *Compendium [Epitome] of History from the Reign of John and Alexios Comnenos*, A Meineke ed., ED Weber publ., 1836.
Clement [*Clemes*] of Alexandria: *Exhortation to the Greeks [Protreptikos]*, Greek text & Engl. transl. by GW Butterworth, Harvard, Cambridge, 1960. pp. 1-263.
Cleomvrotos JG: *The Panayia (All-Holy Virgin Cathedral) of Ayiasos on Lesbos*, A. Altintzis Press, Thessaloniki/Mytilini, 1982 (in Greek).
Commentaries (Semeiographia), by many authors: *Stratis Myrivilis*: Athens, Euthyni, No. 27, 1987.
Comnena, Anna: *The Alexiad*, Engl. Transl. & Notes by ERA Sewter, Penguin, Middlesex & New York, 1969-85.
Comnene, Anna: *Alexiade*, Greek text & French transl. by B. Leib, Vol. I-II, Belles Lettres, Paris, 1943.
Critobulus: *Critobuli Imbriotae—Historiae*, DR Reinsch, ed. & German transl., CFHB, Vol. XXII, W. De Gruyter, Berlin, 1983.
Dalven R: *Anna Comnena*, Twayne Pub., New York, 1972.
Davenport G: *Archilochus, Sappho, Alkman: Three Lyric Poets of the Seventh Century B.C.*, Univ. Calif., Berkeley 1980, paperback 1984.
Dewing HB: *Procopius*, Vols. I-VII, Greek & Engl. transl., Harvard, Cambridge 1914-60.
Diehl Ch.: *Figures Byzantines*, Armand Colin, Paris 1909; Engl. transl. as *Byzantine Empresses* by H. Bell & Th. de Kerpely, AA Knopf, New York 1963.
Diodoros the Sicilian [*Diodoros Sikeliotes, or D. Siculus*]: *The Library of History*, Books I-XL, edited by CH Oldfather (I-VI), CL Sherman (VII), RM Greer (IX-X), FR Walton (XI) and FR Walton with RM Greer (XII), Greek & English text, Harvard, Cambridge,1935-70.
Diogenes Laertios: *Lives of Eminent Philosophers*. Greek text with Engl. transl. by RD Hicks, Vol. I-II, Harvard, Cambridge 1925-66.
Doukas M(?): *Decline and Fall of Byzantium to the Ottoman Turks*, annotated & transl. by HJ Magoulias, Waye State Univ. Press, Detroit, 1975.
Doukas: *Michaelis Ducae Nepotis—Historia Byzantina*, Im. Bekker ed., Greek with Latin transl., BG Niebuhr, Gen. Ed., CSHB, Bonn 1834.

DuBois P: Sappho and Helen, *Arethusa 11*:89-99, 1978.
Durant W: *The Life of Greece* in *The Story of Civilization*, Part II, Simon & Schuster, New York 1939, reprinted.
Durant W: *Caesar and Christ* in *The Story of Civilization*, Part III, Simon & Schuster, New York, 1944, reprinted.
Edmonds JM: *Daphnis and Chloe*, Greek text & Engl. transl. (orig. by G. Thornley), Harvard, Cambridge, 1916-78.
Edmonds JM: *Lyra Graeca*, Vols. I–III, Greek text & Engl. transl., Harvard, Cambridge, 1980 (first pub. 1922-28).
Edmonds JM: *The Characters of Theophrastus*, Greek text & Engl. transl., Harvard, Cambridge, 1946.
Eleftheriadis M: *Lesbos—History, Art, Folklore, Modern Life*, in Greek, English and other languages, Toubis pub., Athens 1986.
Elytis O: *The Little Mariner*, Engl. transl. by O. Broumas, Copper Canyon Press, Washington DC 1988.
Elytis O: *Selected Poems*, chosen and translated by E. Keeley, G. Savidis, Ph. Sherrard *et al.*, Viking, New York, 1981.
Elytis O: *The Sovereign Sun*, selected poems, Engl. transl. & notes by K. Friar, Temple Univ., Philadelphia, 1974.
Elytis O: *Theophilos, Now and Always* (in Greek), Introduction in *Theophilos— Paintings*, Theophilos Museum, City of Mytilene and Techne, Athens Eds., 1990.
Emery L: *Rose Macaulay: A Writer's Life*, J. Murray, London, 1991.
Falliers, CJ: Chronobiology in relation to allergy, chapt. in *Allergy Principles and Practice*, E. Middleton et al. eds., 2nd edition, Mosby, St. Louis 1983, pp. 457–483.
Ferrari F: *Saffo—Poesie*, Greek with Italian transl. & notes, Rizzoli, Milano, 1987.
Flores A; *An Anthology of French Poetry*, Doubleday Anchor, New York, 1958.
Friar K: *Modern Greek Poetry*: New York, Simon & Schuster, 1973.
Friar K: *Odysseus Elytis' The Sovereign Sun*, transl. from the Greek (selected poems): Philadelphia, Temple University, 1974.
Fyfe WH: *Aristotle: The Poetics; Longinus: On the Sublime; Demetrius: On Style*, Greek texts & Engl. transl., Harvard, Cambridge, 1927-80.
Gaselle S: *The Love Romances of Parthenius*, Greek text & Engl.transl., Harvard, Cambridge, 1916-78.
Gibbon E: *The Decline and Fall of the Roman Empire*, ed. & notes by JB Bury, Vols. I-VII, Methuen, London 1909-14, AMS Press, New York 1974.
Godley AD: *Herodotus*, Greek text, transl. & notes, Harvard Univ. Press, Cambridge 1920-66.
Godolphin FRB: *The Greek Historians: Herodotus, Thucydides, Xenophon, Arrian*, Vol. I-II, Random House, New York.
Goodrich NL: *Priestesses*, F. Watts, New York, 1989.
Goolden P: *The Old English Apollonius of Tyre* (Latin and Old English texts), Oxford Univ. Press, London 1958.

Grabar A, Manoussakas M: *L' Illustration du Manuscrit de Skylitzes de la Bibliothèque Nationale de Madrid*, Institut Hellenique de Venise, Venice, 1979.
Grant M: *From Alexander to Cleopatra: The Hellenistic World*, Scribner, 1982.
Grant M: *The Rise of the Greeks*, Scribner, New York 1987.
Grant M: *Julius Caesar*, M. Evans Co., New York, 1992.
Graves R: *The Greek Myths*, Vol. I-II, Brazillier, New York, 1955-57; Penguin 1962-86.
Graves R: *Homer's Daughter*, 1955, reprinted, Academy, Chicago, 1987.
Gregoras, Nikephoros: *Byzantine ["Romaic"] History*, Greek with Latin transl., BG Niebuhr ed., Vols. I-III, CSHB ED Weber publ. Bonn 1855.
Grimal P: *The Dictionary of Classical Mythology*, Engl. transl. AR Maxwell-Hyslop, Blackwell, New York, 1986.
Groden, Susie Q: *The Poems of Sappho*, Bobbs-Merrill, Indianapolis & New York, 1966.
Guidorizzi G (ed.): *Lirici Greci*, Greek text and Italian transl., O. Mondadori, Milano 1993.
Gulick CB: *Athenaeus: Deipnosophists*, Greek text & Engl. transl., Vols. I-VII, Harvard, Cambridge 1927-71.
Guthrie WKC: *Orpheus and Greek Religion*, 2nd ed., London, Methuen & Co., 1952.
Hammond NGL, Scullard HH (eds.): *The Oxford Classical Dictionary*, 2nd ed., Clarendon Press, Oxford 1978
Head C: *Imperial Byzantine Portraits*, Caratzas Bros., New Rochelle, NY 1982.
Henderson J: *The Maculate Muse—Obscene Language in Attic Comedy*, Yale Univ. Press, New Haven 1975.
Herodotus: *The History*, Engl. transl. by D Green, Univ. Chicago Press, Chicago 1987.
Herodotus [*Herodotos*]: *Histories [Historiai]*, Greek text, transl. & notes by AD Godley, Vols. I-IV, Harvard Univ. Press, Cambridge 1920-66.
Hicks RD: *Diogenes Laertius: Lives of Eminent Philosophers*, Greek text & Engl. transl., Harvard, Cambridge 1925-66.
Hogart RC: *The Hymns of Orpheus—Mutations*, Phanes Press, Grand Rapids, Michigan, 1993.
Homer [*Homeros*]: *The Iliad*, Vol. I-II,Greek text & Engl. transl. by AT Murray, Harvard, Cambridge, 1924-78.
Homer [*Homeros*]: *The Odyssey*, Vol. I-II, Greek text & Engl. transl. by AT Murray, Harvard, Cambridge 1919-84
Hughes JD: Theophrastus as ecologist, in *Theophrastean Studies on Natural Science, Physics and Metaphysics, Ethics, Religion, and Rhetoric*, WW Fortenbaugh, RW Shaples, eds., Transaction Books, New Brunswock (USA) & Oxford (UK) 1988.
Jaeger W: *Aristotle—Fundamentals of the History of his Development*, Engl. transl. by R Robinson, Oxford Univ. Press, New York 1967.

Jaspers K: *The Great Philosophers*, transl. by R Manheim, Harcourt, Brace & World 1962 (German orig. 1957)
Jay P (ed.): *The Greek Anthology and Other Ancient Epigrams*, Penguin, New York, 1981.
Jenkyns R: *Three Classical Poets: Sappho, Catullus and Juvenal*, Harvard, Cambridge 1982.
Jones HL: *The Geography of Strabo*, Vols. I-VIII, Harvard, Cambridge, 1928-61.
Julian [*Flavius Claudius Julianus*]: *The Works of the Emperor Julian*, Greek text & Engl. transl. by W. Cave Wright, Vol. I-III, Harvard, Cambridge 1913-69.
Karayiannis V, Molinos S: *Mytilene 1912*, Athens & Mytilene, Kastaniotis, 1984.
Kedrenos, Georgios: see Cedrenus, George.
Kinnamos, Ioannes: see Cinnamus, John.
Kirk CS, Raven JE: *The Presocratic Philosophers*, Cambridge Univ. Press, Cambridge UK, 1957-66.
Kontianos G, or Temenos K (eds.?): *Apollonios of Tyre—A Most Beautiful Tale*, N. Glykis, Venice 1745.
Kontoglou F: *He Ponemeni Romiosyne* (The Tormented "Romaic People"—i.e., Greeks), Astir, Athens, 1963, 7th ed., 1984.
Kordatos G: *Sappho and the Social Strife on Lesbos*, Epikairoteta Co., Athens 1982 (orig. pub. 1942), in modern Greek.
Kritoboulos: *see* Critobulus.
Lattimore R: *Greek Lyrics*, Univ. Chicago Press, Chicago 1960 (orig. pub. 1949).
Ledwidge B: *Sappho—La Première Voix de Femme* (in French with Greek text selections), Mercure de France, Paris 1987.
Lefkowitz Mary R: *The Lives of the Greek Poets*, Johns Hopkins, Baltimore 1981.
Leib B: *Anne Comnène: Alexiade*, edited Greek text and French transl., Vol. I-II, Belles Lettres, Paris 1943.
Leo the Deacon [*Diakonos*]: *Nikephoros Phokas and Joannes Tzimiskes*, in German, E Ivanka ed., F Loretto transl., Styria pub., Graz & Vienna 1961.
Leo Grammaticus: see Theophanes.
Levi P: *A History of Greek Literature*, Viking, New York 1985.
Lobel E, Page D: *Poetarum Lesbiorum Fragmenta*, Clarendon, Oxford, GB 1955-68.
Longinus [*Dionysios or Longinos*]: *On the Sublime (style)*, Greek text & Engl. transl. by WH Fyfe, Harvard, Cambridge 1927-82.
Longus: *Daphnis and Chloe—A Lesbiac Pastoral*, Greek text, Engl. transl. by G Thornley, revised & augmented by JM Edmonds 1916-78.
Louÿs P: *Les Chansons de Bilitis* (orig. 1895) J-P Goujon ed., Gallimard, Paris, 1990.
Maillol A: *Maillol Woodcuts: 303 Great Book Illustrations*, Eclogues, Daphnis and Chloe, and the Odes of Horace. Dover Publications, New York, 1979.
Mango CA: *Byzantium—The Empire of New Rome*, Chas. Scribner, New York, 1980.

Marcovich M: Sappho Fr. 31: Anxiety attack or love declaration? *Class. Quart.* N.S. *22*:19-32, 1972.
Marry JD: Sappho and the heroic ideal, *Arethusa 12*:71-92, 1979.
Mathews M & J (eds.): *Charles Baudelaire: The Flowers of Evil*, New Directions, New York 1955/89 (4th printing.).
Michaelidis KM: *Symboli sten Aioliki Bibliographia* (Contribution to the Aeolic Bibliography), Athens, 1940.
Miller W: *Essays on the Latin Orient*, Cambridge Univ. Press, Cambridge & London, GB, Macmillan, NY, 1921.
Mirmont, H de la Ville: Theophane de Mitylene, *Rev. Etudes Grecques, XVIII*: 165-206, 1905.
Moore G: *Daphnis and Chloe*, Engl. transl. with illustrations by Marc Chagall, Brazillier, New York 1977 (from *Les Editions Verve*, Paris 1961).
Mora, Edith: *Sappho*, in French, Flammarion, Paris, 1965.
Mountford JF, Winnington-Ingram RP: *Ancient Greek Music*, in *The New Oxford Companion to Music*, D Arnold gen. ed., Oxford Univ. Press, Oxford & New York, 1983-84, pp. 65-74.
Murray AT: *The Iliad*, vols I-II; *The Odyssey*, vols I-II, Greek with Engl. transl., Harvard, Cambridge 1919-84.
Myrivilis S: *He Daskala me ta Chrysa Matia* The Schoolteacher with the Golden Eyes, 21st ed., Kollaros & Co., Athens, 1986 (orig. 1933).
Myrivilis S: *He Panayia he Gorgona* (The Mermaid Madonna), 3rd ed., Kollaros & Co., Athens, 1960.
Nicol DM: *The Last Centuries of Byzantium, 1261-1453*, St. Martin Press, New York, 1972.
Nicol DM: *The End of the Byzantine Empire*, Holmes & Meier, New York, 1979.
Nilsson NA: *Die Apolonius-Erzahlung in den Slavischen Literaturen*, Almquist & Wiksells, Uppsala 1949.
Nims JF: *Sappho to Valery—Poems in Translation*, Princeton Univ. Press, Princeton, 1971.
Norwich JJ: *A History of Venice*, AA Knopf, New York, 1982.
Norwich JJ: *Byzantium—The Early Centuries*, AA Knopf, New York 1989.
Oldfather CH: *Diodoros of Sicily*, Greek text and Engl. transl. Vols I-XII, Harvard, Cambridge, 1933-68.
Ostrogorsky G: *History of the Byzantine State*, Engl. transl. by J Hussey, New Brunswick, New Jersey, Rutgers Univ. Press, 1969.
Page D: *Sappho and Alcaeus—An Introduction to the Study of Ancient Lesbian Poetry*, Clarendon Press, Oxford, 1959.
Papageotes GC: *The Story of Modern Greek Literature*, Athens Press, New York 1972.
Parthenius: *Love Romances [Erotika Pathemata]*, Greek text & Engl. transl. by S. Gaselee, Harvard, Cambridge, 1916-78.
Passas ID: *Ta Orfika* (The Orphic Works/Themes), Helios Publ., Athens, 1984.
Perrin B: *Plutarch's Lives,* Vols. I-XI, Greek with Engl. transl., Harvard,

Cambridge 1917-67.

Perry BE: *The Ancient Romances—A Literary-Historical Account of their Origins*, Univ. Calif. Press, Berkeley & Los Angeles, 1967.

Pesket AG: *Caesar: The Civil Wars*, Latin & Engl. transl., Harvard Univ. Press, Cambridge, 1914-66.

Plutarch [*Plutarkhos*]: *Parallel Lives*, Vols. I-XI, Greek with Engl. transl. & notes by Bernadette Perrin, Harvard Univ. Press, Cambridge 1917-68.

Plutarch: *Moralia [Ethika]*, Vols. I-XIV, Greek with Engl. transl. & notes by FC Babbitt, Harvard Univ. Press, Cambridge 1927-49.

Politis L: *A History of Modern Greek Literature*, Oxford Univ. Press, 1973.

Procopius of Caesaria: *Complete Works*, Vols. I-VII, Greek text, Engl. transl. by HB Dewing, Harvard, Cambridge 1914-60.

Procopius: *The Secret History*, Intro. & Engl. transl. by GA Williamson, Penguin, Middlesex & New York 1966-83.

Psellos M: *Chronographie [Khronographia]*, Greek with French transl. & notes by E. Renauld, Vols. I-II, Belles Lettres, Paris 1967.

Psellus [*Psellos*] M: *Fourteen Byzantine Rulers [Chronographia]*, Intro. & Engl. transl. by ERA Sewter, Penguin, New York 1966-84.

Quinn JD: Cape Phokas, Lesbos—Site of an archaic sanctuary for Zeus, Hera and Dionysus? *Amer J Archeol 65*:391-3, 1961.

Rackham H: *Aristotle: Politics*, Greek with Engl. transl. & notes, Harvard, Cambridge 1932-77.

Rankin HD: *Archilochus of Paros*, Park Ridge NJ 1977.

Rayor, Diane: *Sappho's Lyre—Archaic Lyric and Women Poets of Ancient Greece*, Intro. & Engl. transl., Univ. Calif. Press, Berkeley & Los Angeles, 1991.

Reinsch DR (ed): *Critobuli Imbriotae—Historiae*, CFHB, Vol. XXII, W. De Gruyter, Berlin 1983.

Rexroth K: *Poems from the Greek Anthology*, Univ. Mich. Press, Ann Arbor 1962.

Richter GMA: *The Portraits of the Greeks* (three-volume set) abridg. and revised by RRR Smith, Cornell Univ. Press, Ithaca NY 1984; orig. three-volume set, Phaidon, 1965.

Ridpath JC: *Cyclopaedia of Universal History*, Vol. I. The Ancient World, Jones/Riverside, Cincinnati & St. Louis, 1885.

Rilke RM: *Sonnets to Orpheus*, German with Engl. transl. by CF MacIntyre, Univ. Calif. Press, Berkeley 1960.

Rodriguez Adrados F: *Lirica Griega Arcaica*, Intro., Spanish transl. & notes, Gredos, Madrid 1980-86.

Rodriguez Tobal J: *Safo—Poemas y Fragmentos*, Greek with Spanish transl. & notes, Hiperion, Madrid 1990.

Runciman S: *Byzantine Civilization* (first pub. 1933), Meridian, Cleveland (11th printing) 1970.

Runciman S: *A History of the Crusades*, Vols. I-III, Cambridge Univ. Press, Cambridge 1951-92.

Russell B: *A History of Western Philosophy*, Simon & Schuster, New York 1945-72.
St. Clair W: *That Greece might still be Free—The Philhellenes in the War of Independence*, Oxford Univ. Press, London 1972.
Sappho: *Poems, Fragments & Commentaries*, in Barnstone 1965, Campbell 1982, Edmonds 1922-80, Lobel & Page 1955-68, Page 1959 and other international publications.
Sappho: *Fragmenta Nova* (from D Page: *Supplementum Lyricis Graecis*, Oxford 1974), with a "Note on the Text" by G Davenport, Arif Press, Berkeley 1981.
Sarton G: *A History of Science—Ancient Science through the Golden Age of Greece*, Harvard Univ. Press, Cambridge 1952-66.
Sathas KN: *Library of the Middle Ages [Mesaioniki Bibliotheke]*, Vols. I-VII, Venice/Paris 1872-79.
Savignac J-P: *Les Oracles de Delphes*, Orphée/La Difference, Giromagny, France 1989.
Sewter ERA: *The Alexiad of Anna Comnena*, Engl. transl. & notes, Penguin, Middlesex, UK & New York NY, 11969-85.
Sewter ERA: *Michael Psellus: Fourteen Byzantine Rulers*, Engl. transl. & notes, Penguin, Middlesex UK, New York NY, 1966-84.
Shakespeare W: *Pericles, Prince of Tyre*, in *The Complete Works*, Blakiston, Philadelphia, 1936 (and subsequent publications).
Skylitzes John [*Ioannes*]: *Synopsis of History*, Greek text, annotated, J Thurn ed., in Copr. Fontium Historiae Byzantinae (FSHB), H-G Beck, A Kambylis, R Keydell gen. eds., W. de Gruyter, Berlin 1973.
Smith CF: *Thucydides: History of the Peloponnesian War*, Vols. I-IV, Greek with Engl. transl. & notes, Harvard, Cambridge 1920-75.
Snyder, Jane McIntosh: *The Women and the Lyre—Women Writers in Classical Greece and Rome*, So. Illinois Univ. Press, Carbondale, Ill. 1991.
Sphrantzes G: *The Fall of the Byzantine Empire, A Chronicle, 1401-1477*, Engl. transl. by M. Philippides, Univ. Mass. Press, Amherst 1980.
Strabo [*Strabon*]: *Geography*, Greek text with Engl. transl. by HL Jones, Vols. I-VIII, Harvard, Cambridge 1928-61.
Tacitus C: *Annales*, Latin text, edited & introduced by WF Allen, Ginn & Co., Boston 1890.
Theophanes The Confessor: *Chronographia* (followed by Leo Grammaticus' *Chronographia*), Greek and Latin texts, RP Iacobus, Gour & RPF Combelis eds., Typo. Regia, Paris 1655; also in CSHB and MPG*.
Theophrastus: *The Characters*, ed. & transl. by JM Edmonds, Harvard, Cambridge 1929, revised 1946.
Thucydides: *Historiai (History of the Peloponnesian War)* Greek text edited & transl. by CF Smith, Harvard, Cambridge 1920-75.
Tobal J: *see* Rodriguez Tobal.
Toynbee AJ: *Greek Historical Thought*, Mentor, New York 1953, reprinted.
Toynbee AJ: *Greek Civilization and Character*, Mentor, New York 1953, reprinted.

Treu M: *Sappho Lieder (Songs)*, Greek with German transl. & notes, Munich & Zurich (7th edition), 1984.
Trypanis CA: *The Penguin Book of Greek Verse* (bilingual), Penguin, London, New York, 1971.
Trypanis CA: *Greek Poetry—From Homer to Seferis*, Faber, London & Boston, 1981.
Tsatsou J: *Empress Athenais-Eudocia*, Engl. transl. by J Demos, Holy Cross Orthodox Press, Brookline 1977.
Valetas G: *Aioliki Bibliographia* (Aeolic Bibliography) 1566–1939, Xenos Publ., Athens, 1939.
Vryonis S: *Byzantium and Europe*, Harcourt Brace & World, New York 1967.
Wallach L: *Diplomatic Studies of the Greek and Latin Documents from the Carolingian Age*, Cornell Univ. Press, Ithaca & London 1977.
Weigall A: *Sappho of Lesbos—Her Life and Times*, FA Stokes, New York 1932.
West ML: *The Orphic Poems*, Clarendon/Oxford, New York 1983-85.
White JT (ed.): *The Acts of the Apostles*, in White's Grammar School Texts, Greek text with a vocabulary, Longmans Green & Co. 1903.
Williamson GA (intro & transl.): *Procopius—The Secret History*, Penguin, Harmondsworth & New York, 1966/83.
Wilson NG: *Scholars of Byzantium*, Johns Hopkins, Baltimore, 1983.
Wilson NG: *An Anthology of Byzantine Prose*, W. de Gruyter, Berlin/New York, 1971.
Winstedt EO: *Cicero: Letters to Atticus*, Vols. I-III, Latin text with Engl. transl.& notes, 1912-67.
Wright WC: *The Works of Emperor Julian*, Intro., Greek text & Engl. translation, Harvard Univ. Press, Cambridge 1913-69.
Zalokostas ChP: *Gyro ap' ten Hellada* (Touring Greece), Pyrsos Publ. 1940.
Ziegler K, Sontheimer W: *Der kleine Pauly—Lexikon der Antike*, Vols. I-V, Deutscher Taschenbuch Verlag, Munich 1979 (entries, in German, on Lesbos, Lesbonax, Lesches, Orpheus, Sappho, etc.).
Zonaras J [*Ionannis*]: *Lives of the Christian Emperors from Constantine the Great to Alexios Comnenos*, Greek with Latin transl. by H Wolfius, I. Oporinus pub., Basel 1557; also in CSHB*.

---

*CSHB: *Corpus Scriptorum Historiae Byzantinae*
CFHB: *Corpus Fontium Historiae Byzantinae*
MPG: *Migne: Patrologia Graeca*
Other abbreviations in text
Ath.: Athenaios
MB: M. Barnard
WB: W. Barnstone
Bowra: C.M. Bowra
Cam.: D.A. Campbell
Dav.: G. Davenport
Diod.Sic.: Diodoros the Sicilian

Diog. Laer.: Diogenes Laertios
Edm.: J.M. Edmonds
Elef.: M. Eleftheriadis
SG: S. Groden
Lat: R. Lattimore
LP: Lobel-Page
Roc: P. Roche
  and
Class. Myth.: *Dictionary of Classical Mythology*, P. Grimal
Oxf. Class. Dict.: Oxford Classical Dictionary

Reference Tables

REFERENCE TABLE A

Chronology of Events Related to Lesbos

Neolithic human artifacts on Lesbos.	c. 3500 B.C.*
Greece settled by Greek-speaking peoples. Early bronze age in the Aegean islands.	c. 3000-2000
Pelasgian people on Lesbos. The flood of Deukalion destroys practically all life.	c. 1500
Mycenean-Achaean Greeks colonize Lesbos.	c. 1600-1100
Pelops stops on Lesbos on his way from Lydia to Greece.	c. 1300
Orpheus and the Argonauts.	c. 1225
Achaean Greeks with Achilles raid Lesbos on their way to the Trojan war.	c. 1200-1180
New Greek colonies on Lesbos: Aeolians and the sons of Penthilos.	1120-1000
Ionian Greeks colonize Asia Minor coast. Dorians conquer Greek mainland and send colonies to SW Asia Minor too. "Dark Ages" follow.	c. 1100-900
Epics of the Trojan war, the Iliad and the Odyssey of Homer.	c. 800
Date of the first Olympic Games in Olympia, Peloponnesos.	776**
Aristocracies and kings rule most Greek city-states.	c. 800-700
Midas king of Phrygia.	c. 700

Age of law-givers, sages and early philosophers; rise of "tyrannies" (dictatorships). Greek city of Naucratis founded in Egypt.	650-600
The last Penthilid ruler murdered, end of dynasty on Lesbos.	659
Lesbos prospering, becomes a major naval power. War with Athens over Sigeon by the Hellespont. Pittakos, Alkaios, Sappho at their peak [*acme*] in Mytilene.	c. 600
Croesus [*Kroisos*] king of Lydia, Amasis pharaoh of Egypt. Active trade and cultural exchange with Lesbos.	c. 560-546
Lydia and Greek cities on Asiatic coast conquered by Persia.	546-545
Coës of Mytilene helps the Persians against the Scythians and is made ruler of Mytilene. People revolt and kill him but Persians dominate.	513-491
Persians attempt to conquer Greece. Greek victory at Marathon.	490
Second Persian invasion of Greece. Persian fleet, including Asiatic Greek contingent, defeated in the straits of Salamis, near Athens.	480
Lesbos liberated from Persian rule, helps establish the Greek defensive "Delian" league.	479-478
Peloponnesian war between Athens and Sparta.	431-404
Revolt of Mytilene, surrender to Athens.	428-427
Battle of Mytilene: Spartans, Athenians, Lesbians.	407
Sea-battle of Arginousai.	406
Establishment of Schools of philosophy:	
The Academy	385 B.C.
The Lyceum	335
The Epicurean Garden	306
The Stoa	300
Aristotle on Lesbos	345-344
Alexander "the Great" of Macedon conquers Asia Minor.	334-333

Memnon, a Greek in charge of Persian troops attacks Lesbian cities.	334
Alexander dies in Babylon, Macedonian successors divide conquests.	323
Theophrastos of Eresos on Lesbos heads Lyceum in Athens.	322-288
Antiokhos I "Soter", Seleucid emperor.	280-262
First Macedonian war with Rome.	214-205
Pergamum [Pergamos] dominant under Eumenes II and Roman support.	197-160
Roman wars against Pontos—"Mithridatic" wars.	88-63
Roman Civil Wars—Caesar defeats Pompei at Pharsalus.	48
Octavian defeats Antony at Actium—Antony and Cleopatra die in Egypt.	30-31
Crucifixion of Jesus Christ—conversion of Paul the Apostle.	30 A.D.*
Third mission of Saint Paul, including visit of Lesbos.	55-57
Writing of the Four Gospels.	60-100
First Roman edict of Christian toleration.	260
Christian Council [*Synod*] of Nicaea [*Nikaia*]	325
Constantinople (Byzantium) made capital of the Roman empire.	330
End of the Olympic Games by edict of emperor Theodosius I.	394
Gothic, Vandal and Hun invasions.	c. 400-450...
Philosophical schools closed by emperor Justinian I.	529
Arabs conquer Palestine (including Jerusalem), Syria, Egypt and invade Asia Minor and the Aegean sea.	637-640
Four-year unsuccessful Arab siege of Constantinople.	674-678

Second Arab attempt to capture Constantinople.	717-718
Slavs begin to penetrate Balkans.	600-
Iconoclast rulers forbid veneration of holy icons, order their destruction and persecute icon-worshippers.	726-842
Charlemagne crowned Holy Roman Emperor.	800
Harun al-Rashid caliph of Baghdad; Arab power and culture at a peak.	786-809
Arabs conquer Crete, begin raids of Greek islands.	826-
Turkish mercenaries join Arab forces.	842-
Compilation of Greek "Suidas" —or "Suda"— encyclopedic lexicon.	c. 976
Greek Orthodox missions convert Russians to Christianity.	989
Emperor Basil II restores Byzantine power, domains and prestige.	976-1025
Ecclesiastical schism and growing separation of Greek Orthodox and Roman Catholic churches.	1054-
Turkish sultanate of Roum ("Roman") in Asia Minor.	1077-1327
Western Christian Crusades (I, II, III) cross Greek territories on their way trying to expel the Arabs from the Holy Land.	1096-1192
The Komnenos imperial dynasty reverses a downhill course of the Byzantine State, promotes culture and learning.	1081-1185
Riots against the Venetians in Greek lands; Venetians attack Greek islands.	1171
Latin forces of the Fourth Crusade capture Constantinople and establish Latin empire of the East.	1204-1261
Byzantine Civil Wars: Andronikos II vs. Andronikos III. John V Palaiologos vs. John VI Kantakouzenos.	1321-1328 1342-1347
Lesbos under Genoese rule. Italian republics control trade through Greek waters.	1354-1462

Mongols under Timur ("Tamerlane") invade and ravage Greek and Arab regions, reach the Aegean coast.	1368-1405
Ottoman Turks recover from Mongol onslaught, complete occupation of Asia Minor.	1390
Emperor Manuel II Palaiologos tours Europe for three years seeking in vain help against the Turks.	1399-1402
Greek scholars and artists fleeing the Turks settle in Italy, Spain and other parts of Europe.	14th-15th c.
Destruction of Christian (French, Hungarian, etc.) forces by the Turks in the Battle of Varna.	1444
Fall of Constantinople to the Ottoman Turks; end of the Greek-Byzantine empire, death of the last emperor, Constantine XI Palaiologos in the battle for the City.	1453
Turks capture Lesbos after heavy fighting, slaughter or enslave much of the population.	1462
Greeks find shelter in Russia; Maria Palaiologos, niece of the last Byzantine emperor, marries Russian czar Ivan III.	1472
Ottoman sultan Suleiman "The Magnificent" continues Turkish conquests, brings to his court counsellors, artists and scholars from other nations.	1520-66
Naval forces of Spain, the Italian Republics and the Papal States defeat the Turkish-Muslim fleet in the Battle of Lepanto [Gk. *Naupaktos*].	1571
Popular independence movements in America, France and elsewhere help ignite Greek aspirations to free themselves from the Turkish yoke.	1780-1820
Russo-Turkish war (1768-74) during which a Russian squadron enters the Aegean sea; naval battle near Lesbos and burning of Turkish navy ships in Mytilene harbor.	1771
Greek war of Independence against the Turks.	1821-29

Russo-Turkish war involves British navy in the Aegean and the Dardanelles [*Hellespont*]; Russians stopped from reaching Constantinople.	1877-78
Balkan wars force the Turks to abandon most of their European possessions. Lesbos liberated by Greek naval forces.	1912-13
World War I: Greece on the victorious side of the Allies, gains control of eastern Thrace and part of Asia Minor.	1914-18
Continuation of the Greek military campaign in Turkish Asia Minor ends with a catastrophy and over 1,500,000 refugees flee to Greece.	1922
Greek democracy abolished with the return of king George II to Greece and the establishment of a fascist-type dictatorship.	1936
World War II: Greece under German, Italian and Bulgarian occupation.	1941-44
Most of Greece under communist guerillas until nationalist forces regain control with British and American help.	1947-51
Greece and Turkey part of NATO (North Atlantic Treaty Organization).	1952
Military junta seizes Greek government; king Constantine fails to preserve democracy and flees Greece.	1967
Democracy restored in Greece; capitalist and socialist governments with notable developments and also failures.	1973-
Greece becomes a member of the European Community.	1981

---

*If preferable, the designations B.C. and A.D. can be taken to indicate Before Current date-system and Actual Date years.

**The ancient dating system was based on the Olympiads, which took place every four years, from 776 B.C. to (the 292nd) 393–4 A.D. over a period of 1162 years. The year 600 B.C. was around the 44th Olympiad, the 100th Olympiad was in 380–376 B.C. Later Byzantine historians used the indiction dating system (*cf.* Ch. V, note 6), or started their chronology from "the creation of the world" as well as from the birth of Christ.

REFERENCE TABLE B

OLYMPIAN GODS AND GODDESSES OF ANCIENT GREECE (1,2)

Name in English	Greek Spelling	Roman (Latin) Name	Main role and associations
Zeus also *Zas* (3) (gen. *Dios*)	ΖΕΥΣ (ΔΙΟΣ)	Jupiter	Lord of the Olympian Pantheon, of Heaven, Clouds and Thunder; the supreme God but often amorously involved with humans.
Hera (4)	ΗΡΑ	Juno	Wife of Zeus (succeeding others including Zeus' first wife, Metis, i.e. Wisdom); initially an independent goddess; queen of Heaven, protectress of females.
Aphrodite	ΑΦΡΟΔΙΤΗ	Venus	Goddess of Love, ideal or "pure" and also carnal; associated with erotic passion and with fertility, even in plants and animals.
Apollo	ΑΠΟΛΛΩΝ	Apollo	God of light, of divination and prophesy; also a musician god, protector of crops and new town building. As "Musagetes", leader of the Muses.

Ares	ΑΡΗΣ	Mars	God of War, of bravery (cf. Ref. Table "E") and destruction; lover of Aphrodite
Artemis	ΑΡΤΕΜΙΣ	Diana	Goddess of chase, forests and also, together with her brother Apollo, of light; a moon-goddess. Herself a virgin, she promoted fertility and presided over childbirth.
Athena	ΑΘΗΝΑ	Minerva	Goddess of Wisdom, intellect and the Arts of Peace; protectress of cities, esp. Athens.
Demeter	ΔΗΜΗΤΗΡ	Ceres	Goddess of the fertile Earth, of grain and agriculture; also a law-giver.
Hephaistos	ΗΦΑΙΣΤΟΣ	Vulcan	Divine personification of terrestrial - volcanic - fire; the divine blacksmith.
Hermes	ΕΡΜΗΣ	Mercury	Initially God of the Wind, later the Gods' messenger; protector of merchants and travellers.
Hestia	ΕΣΤΙΑ	Vesta	Goddess of the Hearth, of domestic fire, of the household and the family.
Poseidon	ΠΟΣΕΙΔΩΝ	Neptune	Brother of Zeus, master of the Seas and generally of water (helping vegetation); also connected with earthquakes.

Notes: (1) God [Theos] in ancient Greece was a superhuman, immortal but not necessarily a perfect or omnipotent being. The overseeing role of theos is reflected in the words theater, theory, etc.
(2) There were many other divinities, some of almost equal status to the twelve Olympians, among whom was Dionysos (Bacchus), God of wine and ecstasy.
(3) The sounds Z, D and Th were often interchangeable. The form Dios (of Zeus) can be traced to the Sanskrit and the Latin words for day and light, as well as for divinity.
(4) The Greek alphabet has no letter for the aspiration sound of H, as in Hera, Hermes, etc.

REFERENCE TABLE C

MUSICAL INSTRUMENTS OF ANCIENT GREECE

Aulos: Often translated as "flute", it was more like a clarinet or an oboe, with a vibrator inserted into a double- or single-reed pipe. The reed, or wood, bone, or ivory, open-ended pipe had three to six lateral holes, later increased to as many as sixteen. Pipes of different length were used for varying musical modes.

Barbitos: A variety of the lyre, with longer strings producing a deeper sound, used especially to accompany the convivial "party" songs of Alkaios and Sappho.

Cithara: see Kithara.

Harp: An early instrument with strings of unequal length, not usually employed for "serious" or sophisticated music.

Keras: A curved brass horn primarily for martial music.

Kithara: A more elaborate type of lyre, with a larger and sturdier vaulted wooden body. A simpler form was the Homeric kitharis or phorminx and a more advanced type was associated with Terpander of Lesbos (seventh century B.C.).

Lute: A type of lyre of later antiquity, introduced after the time of Alexander the Great.

Lyre: The dominant intrument of "lyric" poetry and song, with equal-length strings of gut or sinew varying in thickness and tension. Classically with seven strings strung vertically on a soundbox of wood or tortoise-shell, with oxhide stretched over the concave lower part. Fingering raised the pitch and produced harmonic sounds from the plucking of each string.

Magadis: A string instrument, possibly very similar to the pektis. Later it was renamed psalterion.

Pektis: String instrument, either like a lyre, or more probably a harp. Introduced by Sappho of Lesbos and often viewed as very similar to magadis.

Percussion: Cymbals, castanets, tambourine, triangles etc. used mostly for religious cult festivities and for light entertainment and rhythm.

Phorminx: Ancient instrument (ref. Homer, Orpheus) originally with 3–5 strings, but already by the 10th century and certainly by the 7th century B.C. with the standard seven strings, plucked with the right hand using a plectrum and with the left hand directly, perhaps to accompany the vocal melody. Later innovators, such as Phrynis of Mytilene (fifth century B.C.) added more (up to 12) strings.

Plagiaulos: Horizontally held aulos of late antiquity, possibly a genuine flute, or a reed-pipe with a lateral mouth opening.

Salpinx: A straight brass trumpet, with simple sounds suitable for military tunes.

Sambyke: Also called iambyke, a modified magadis with nine strings, used to accompany songs in the iambic meter, or rhythm.

Syrinx: High-pitched wind instrument resembling a recorder (flageolet), blown directly, with a single pipe or a raft of pipes of equal or graduated length (like a modern panpipe).

REFERENCE TABLE D

THE NINE MUSES AND THEIR FIELDS

Name*	Literal meaning	Associated activity
Calliope	Beautiful face	Epic poetry and eloquence
Clio	Celebrating glory	History
Erato	Lovely	Lyric poetry
Euterpe	Well-pleasing	Music
Melpomene	Singing powerfully	Tragedy (theater)
Polyhymnia	Much-chanting	Religious and heroic chant
Terpsichore	Delight in dance	Dance
Thalia	Blooming	Comedy (theater)
Urania	Heavenly	Astronomy**

---

*Muse, Greek *Mousa* [ΜΟΥΣΑ]: one of the sisters originally varying in number but later recognized as the nine daughters of *Zeus* and *Mnemosyne* (Memory]. From Mount Pieria in Thrace/Macedonia their cult spread to the slopes of Mount *Olympos* and further south to Mount *Helikon* in Boeotia. The "Muse" of a poet was the process of creative inspiration itself. Music became predominantly the art of the Muse. Museum has been a place where works of art and objects of permanent value are kept, displayed and studied.

**The inclusion of astronomy and the exclusion of visual arts are noteworthy.

REFERENCE TABLE E

CLASSICAL GREEK WORDS OF LASTING BRILLIANCE

(With a few exceptions such as *eros, logos, psyche*, only words that have not become part of the English vocabulary are listed).

Acme (n): the highest point, edge, peak of activity, prime of life.
Agape (n): affection, "pure" or "brotherly" love.
Agathos (adj): good, virtuous, noble, brave; later: kind.
Algos (n): pain, grief, sorrow - cf. analgesic; *algesidoros*, bringing pain.
Amousos (adj): ignorant of, or insensitive to the Muses, to art and beauty
Anexikakos (adj): enduring, or tolerating evil [*kakos, kakon*, evil, bad].
Ania (n): grief, trouble, annoyance, hence, now, boredom - cf. ennui.
Aphron (adj): mindless [*a-phron*], senseless - cf. schizo*phren*ia; not rel. to *aphros*, foam, as in Aphrodite.
Arete (n): virtue (Lat. vir, man), manly valor, skill, dignity; rel. to Ares, god of war - cf. aristos, aristocracy.
Askesis (n): exercise, practice, hence *asketes* (adj), ascetic, one who works hard at self-discipline and practices austere self-denial.
Ataraxia (n): unperturbability, freedom from emotional turmoil; *ataraktos* (adj), steady, untroubled.
Avros (adj): delicate, tender; *avrosyne* (n): delicate tenderness, luxuriousness.
Charis (n), pron. Harris, or Kharis*: charm, grace—cf. charisma.
Chrema (n): something useful, business matter, money.
Chresis (n): use, means, power.
Chresmos (n): oracle, oracular response, divination.
Chrestos (adj): useful, beneficial, favorable, kind, good.
Chrisma (n): a scented ointment, salve.

Christos (adj): annointed, as in Jesus Christ (Gk. transl. of the Hebrew *Messiah*, the annointed one).

Daimon (n): divine spirit, later an evil spirit—cf. Engl. demon; also the spirit or soul of the dead.

Dike (n): judgment, trial, lawsuit; *dikaios* (adj), righteous, just; *dikaioma* (n), just claim, right, justification.

Doxa (n): opinion, belief, from *dokein* (vb), to think, suppose; dogma, what one considers as true.

Enthusiasm (n): inspiration [*en-thusiasm*], excitement.

Eros (n): love, desire, mostly sexual; personified as Cupid.

Estros: see *oistros*.

Eudaemonia (n): happiness, prosperity, good spirit [*eu-daimonia*].

Eulogos (adj): of good reason, reasonable, sensible; *eulogia*; (n): praise, eulogy, blessing.

Eupsychia (n): good spirit, brave heart, courage; as a greeting, *eupsychei!*; (vb): be of good, brave mind; or on a tomb, farewell!

Hamartia (n): error, failure, sin; *hamartein*; (vb): to miss the mark, go wrong, fail, sin.

Hesychia, or *hesykhia* (n): stillness, quiet, rest; (adj): *hesychos.*

Himeros (n): longing, yearning, desire (esp. for something or someone far away); love (esp. not reciprocated).

Homonoia (n): concord, sameness of mind [*homo-, noia,* from *noos,* mind].

Logos (n): the "word", inner thought, reason, purpose.

Lysimeles (adj): loosener-of-limbs, i.e., Love; [*lysi-*, solving, dissolving; and *melos*, limb—not melos, song].

Makarios, also *macar* and *macarios* (adj): blessed, blissful, happy and for the dead, beyond pain; mod. Greek *makaritis.*

Malakos (adj): soft, gentle, hence effeminate.

Melete (n): attention, care, study, practice; *melema,* an object of care, loving attention, preoccupation, duty.

Meliphonos (adj): honey-voiced [*meli-, phone*].

Metanoia (n): change of mind, repentance [*meta-, noos*].

Methe (n): intoxication, drunkenness, also the drink itself—cf. amethyst.

Myron (n): sweet plant oil, balsam, perfume.

Mythoplokos (adj): weaver of myths, stories.

Nemesis (n): indignation, retribution, wrath.

Nomos (n): custom, convention, law; *nomisma* (numisma), coin (of recognized use).

Noos, also *nous* (n): mind, resolve, mood or temper; *noëmon,* of good mind.

Oistros, Lat. oestrus (n): gadfly, hence a sting, torment, passion, frenzy—cf. estrogen.

Pathos (n): suffering, calamity, passion.

Philos (adj): friend, dear, pleasing; *philia* (n), friendship, *philo-* (prefix), as in *philotheos*, loving God, *philopotes*, one who loves drinking, *philotimos*, one who values his honor.

Phren (n): the midriff muscle between the chest and the abdomen, hence the "heart" as the seat of life and also a mood, or the mind (wits); *phreneres* (adj), master of his mind - cf. schizophrenic; *phronema* (n): mind, resolve, pride; *phronesis* (n), thoughtfulness, good sense, prudence; *phronimos* (adj), sensible, steady, discreet.

Poikilos (adj): diversified, of varying colors and style; *poikilophron*, of changing mind.

Ponos (n): toil, hard labor and its result, work; also pain, stress and distress.

Pothos (n): desire, longing, yearning.

Prostates (adj): standing in front, protector, leader, patron.

Sophia (n): skill, cleverness, wisdom; *sophos* (adj), knowledgeable in one's art and also wise, prudent; *sophist* (adj), clever, crafty, one professing to teach wisdom.

Sophrosyne (n): practical wisdom, prudence.

Storghe (n): natural—e.g. parental—affection, love between family members.

Talaphron, short for *talasiphron* (adj): one with an enduring, patient mind, holding out, steadfast.

Thymos (n): breath-of-life, soul, "heart", mind-spirit; *thymiama* (n), smoking incense. Not rel. to *thymos,* the herb thyme.

Tlathymos (adj): same as *talaphron*.

Zelos (n): eager rivalry, zeal, also jealousy; *zelotes* (adj), a zealous antagonist, a zealot.

\# The masculine endings of adjectives, -os, -es, etc change in the feminine to -a, -e, etc.

* The Greek *chi* [χ], rendered as ch, sounds more like a soft kh, or h. The initial sound of h before a vowel—as in hero, hysteria, etc.—is written in Greek only with an aspiration mark, as there is no special letter for it.

REFERENCE TABLE F

THE SEVEN SAGES OF THE ANCIENT GREEK WORLD
About 650–550 B.C.

Name	Major work and declarations
Bias	Public leader in the Ionian city of Priene, which he saved from the Lydians. Revered for his justice, moderation and practical wisdom. He declared that "most people are bad" and advised "win by persuasion, not by force".
Chilon	Constitutional reformer in Sparta, raised the powers of the *ephors* (supervisors) above that of the kings. He repudiated tyranny, spoke only with few words and may have written elegiac verses.
Cleoboulos	Absolute ruler—"tyrant"—of Lindos, rebuilt its great temple of Athena and campaigned successfully in Lycia on the mainland. Noted for his wise sayings and also for the poetry and versified riddles of his famous daughter Cleobulina.
Periander [*Periandros*]	Tyrant of Corinth about 627-585 B.C. Built a boat passage through the straight of Corinth, expanded trade maintaining friendly relationships with other rulers and also encouraged the arts. Patron of the Lesbian poet and singer Arion. Quoted as saying "everything is [*melete*] study and practice".
Pittakos (Pittacus)	Elected absolute ruler of Mytilene he was able to overthrow the aristocratic tyranny—and consequently was hated by the poets of the nobility, including Alkaios and Sappho—and governed well

	for ten years, after which he insisted on retiring despite popular demand to stay on. Famous for his wise laws and for saying, among other quotations, "the office shows the man" and "forgiveness is better than vengeance". Wrote poetry and taught students from many distant lands, including the pioneer philosopher, Pherekydes.
Solon	Athenian civic leader, who, with arguments written as poems persuaded the citizens to continue a war to a successful end and also to adopt his political reforms. Elected *archon* [ruling officer] in 594 B.C. he introduced laws to relieve the poor, abolish debt-slavery and to grant more power to the people [*demos*] without yielding to some excessive demands. He resisted becoming a tyrant and in 584 B.C. left Athens to avoid conflicting pressures and to allow time for his laws to work. In old age he tried unsuccessfully to oppose the dictatorial drive of Peisistratos.
Thales	The first rational and empirical philosopher of Nature [*Physis*], of the Ionian city of Miletos. Studied in Egypt and brought home the knowledge of geometry and other sciences from there. Respected for his practical and political ingenuity, he prospered in commerce but his advice for an Ionian federation against the Persians was ignored with later disastrous results. Said to have predicted the solar eclipse of 585 B.C. and to have discovered electricity, connecting it with *electron* (amber). His sayings included the famous—later Delphic—"know thyself".

Sage [ΣΟΦΟΣ] in Greek antiquity was a wise, learned, judicious, prudent and generally prominent person. Later, the word *philosopher* reflected a certain humility regarding the possible attainment of absolute wisdom, so we had "lovers of wisdom" instead. The seven names listed were not unanimously accepted by all writers. Some included Pherekydes (student of Pittakos on Lesbos) and others.

References: Plato, "Protagoras" 343 A-B; Plutarch, "Banquet of the Seven Sages" in *Moralia* 146B-164D; Diogenes Laertios i 13, 28-33, 40-42. Also Bowder D.: *Who was Who in the Greek World*, 1982.

REFERENCE TABLE G

WOMEN WRITERS, POETS AND PHILOSOPHERS IN ANCIENT GREECE

Name	Background, life and works	References
Axiothea	One of the two women philosophers (the other was Lasthenia), who were students of Plato and continued with his successor, Speusippos, as members of the Platonic Academy in Athens, mid-fourth century B.C.	Diog.Laertios Book IV-1 Hicks 1966, p. 374.
Charixene	Flute-player, composer and poet (of undetermined date and place), proverbial for her "old-fashioned" style.	Edmonds 1927 quot. Etym. Mag. Vol.III, p. 42.
Cleobuline	Daughter of the philosopher Cleobulos of Lindos on the island of Rhodos, early sixth century B.C. Poems representing riddles, in hexameters.	Diog.Laertios Book I, 6. In Hicks, 1966, Vol. I, p.90.
Corinna	Lyric poetress of Tanagra (near Thebes) end of sixth century B.C., elder contemporary of Pindar, whom she rivalled successfully. Her texts rewritten in third century spelling.	Page, 1953; Oxf. Class. Dict. 1978, p. 290 Edmonds pp. 6-39.
Damophyle	Was part of Sappho's circle on Lesbos in the early sixth century B.C. then returned home to Pamphylia, on the	Philostatos, I, 30. Campbell 1982, p. 20, No. 21.

	south coast of Asia Minor, where she established a girls' school, like Sappho's. Composed hymns and love songs.	
Daphne	Daughter of the famous Theban seer Teiresias, taken captive to the temple at Delphi, c. 1200 B.C., she became a priestess and an oracle admired for the poetry of her lines. Homer was said to have expropriated her verses for use in his own epic poems. She was also called Sibylla.	Diod. Sic. IV. 66 p. 30. Graves, 1957, v. II, p. 24.
Erinna	Gifted young poetess, possibly student of Sappho c. 600 B.C. Died young at age 19, mourned in songs. Said to have surpassed Sappho in her hexameters. Possibly lived much later, in the fourth century B.C.	Cam. 1982, pp. 11, 35.
Hipparchina	Cynic philosopher from Thrace, follower of Crates, late fourth century B.C. May have been confused with Hipparina.	Diog. Laertios VI-7.
Hipparina	Cynic philosopher from Maroneia, near Thebes, around 300 B.C., follower (along with her brother) of Crates, who summed up his doctrines with "care for nothing". She declared: "not wasting time on the loom, I spent it in education".	Diog. Laertios Book VI-7.
Hypatia	Neoplatonist philosopher and astronomer, daughter of a Greek mathematician and astronomer in Alexandria, Egypt. First woman to teach philosophy in that city. Born 370 A.D., died 415 A.D. in the hands of rioting Christian fanatics.	Oxf. Class. Dict. 1978.
Lasthenia	Philosopher, mentioned in connection with Axiothea above.	

REFERENCE TABLES 437

Myrtis	Lyric poetess of Anthedon in Boeotia, sixth century B.C. Acknowledged for her "feminine tongue and sweet sound." Corinna and Pindar were her students.	Edmonds 1927, Vol. III, pp. 2-5.
Nossis	Like Erinna, mentioned as a contemporary of Sappho, but evidently she lived in Locri much later in the 2nd century B.C.	Cam. 1982, p. 11.
Pamphile (Lat. *Pamphila*)	A woman from Epidauros, south of Corinth, at the time of Nero (first century A.D.), scholar and historian whose main work "A collection of historical memoranda" included references to major philosophers and was also summarized in Latin.	Oxf. Class. Dict. 1978, p. 772. Diog. Laertios Book V - 2.
Praxilla	Mid-fifth century B.C. poetess of Sikyon in the Peloponnesos, wrote dithyrambs, hymns and drinking songs. Some of her lines widely considered as "silly".	Oxf. Class Dict. 1978, p. 874. Edmonds 1927, Vol. III, pp. 72-79.
Sappho	Most famous woman poet, musician and cultured personality in Greek antiquity. In Mytilene, on the island of Lesbos, she established a renowned school for girls. End of seventh, early sixth century B.C. Introduced new musical instruments and modes, wrote hymns, wedding songs and many love lyrics, often addressed to one of the young girls she loved.	Campbell 1982, pp. 1-205. Edmonds 1927, Vol. I, pp. 140-307. Bowra 1961 pp. 176-240. Barnstone 1965,pp. Oxf. Class. Dict. 1978, p. 950.
Sibylla	An archaic prophetic female, possibly historical, wandering and reciting her lines in verse form. By the sixth century B.C. she was considered mythical and the name was often used generically and in plural— the "Sibyls". *See also* Daphne.	Oxf. Class. Dict. 1978, p. 984.

REFERENCE TABLE H

MULTIPLE TRANSLATION SAMPLES OF POEMS BY SAPPHO
English and other languages, 1928-95

I. "Equal to the Gods": The ability to contemplate the beauty and charm of a young woman raises a person to a level "equal to the Gods" [*isos theoisin*]. In her much quoted poem (given in full, with comments, in Chapt. II-B), Sappho not only expressed her envy of the man who sat next to her beloved girl but also defined what it is to be like a God. Unlike the beautifully intense original Aeolian lyrics, some of the modern translations may seem pompous and silly but are cited for comparative study.

Original Aeolic Greek

φαίνεταί μοι κῆνος ἴσος θέοισιν ἔμμεν'
ὤνηρ ὄττις ἐνάντιός τοι ἰσδάνει καὶ πλά-
σιον ἆδυ φωνείσας ὑπακούει ⚘ καὶ γε-
λαίσας ἰμέροεν τό μ' ἦ μὰν καρδίαν ἐν
στήθεσιν ἐπτόαισεν·

Modern English translations

It is to be a God, methinks, to sit before you and listen close by to the sweet accents and winning laughter which have made the heart in my breast beat fast, I warrant you.
Edmonds 1928, Vol.I, p. 186

Peer of gods he seemeth to me, that man who sits before thee, and close beside thee listens to thy sweet voice and thy lovely laughter – this, this indeed, causes the heart in my breast to tremble.
Weigall 1932, p. 113

Peer of gods he seemeth to me, the blissful
Man who sits and gazes at thee before him,
Close beside thee sits, and in silence hears thee
    Silverly speaking.
Laughing love's low laughter. Oh this, this only
Stirs the troubled heart in my breast to tremble!
J. Addington Symmonds*

Peer of the gods, the happiest man I deem
Sitting before thee, rapt at thy sight, hearing
Thy soft laughter and thy voice most gentle,
    Speaking so sweetly.
Then in my bosom my heart wildly flutters.
Edwin M. Cox*

That one seems to me the equal of the gods, who sits in thy presence and hears near him thy sweet voice and lovely laughter; that indeed makes my heart beat fast in my bosom.
"Cox 2"*

Blest beyond earth's bliss, with heaven I deem him
    Blest, the man that in thy presence near thee
Face to face may sit, and while thou speakest,
    Listening may hear thee,
And thy sweet-voiced laughter: - In my bosom
    The rapt heart so troubleth, wildly stirred.
Walter Headlam*

O life divine! to sit before
Thee while thy liquid laughter flows
Melodious, and to listen close
To rippling notes from Love's full score.
O music of thy lovely speech!
My rapid heart beats fast and high.
David M. Robinson*
*In "Many Poets" 1942, pp. 15-18
(An anthology of earlier publications).

He is a god in my eyes –
the man who is allowed
to sit beside you – he
who listens intimately
to the sweet murmur
of your voice, the enticing

laughter that makes my own
heart beat fast.

Barnard 1958, p. 39

Fortunate as the gods he seems to me, that man who sits
    opposite you, and listens nearby to your sweet voice
And your lovely laughter; that, I vow, has set my heart
    within my breast a-flutter.

Page 1959, p. 19

Like the very gods in my sight is he who
sits where he can look in your eyes, who listens
close to you, to hear the soft voice, its sweetness
murmur in love and laughter, all for him. But it breaks my spirit;
underneath my breast all the heart is shaken.

Lattimore 1960, p. 39

That man seems to me to be the equal of the gods, who sits opposite you and, near to you, listens to you as you speak sweetly and laugh your lovely laughter; that in truth has set my heart fluttering in my breast.

Bowra 1961 (orig. 1936), p. 185

To me that man equals a god
as he sits before you and listens
closely to your sweet voice
and lovely laughter - which troubles
the heart in my ribs.

Barnstone 1965, p. 11

He is a god in my eyes, that man,
Given to sit in front of you
And close to himself sweetly to hear
The sound of your speaking.
Your magical laughter – this I swear –
Batters my heart.

Roche 1966, pp. 44-45

An equal to the gods, he seems to me,
the man who, with his face toward yours,
sits close and listens to the whispers of
your sweet voice and enticing laugh.
To watch has made my heart a pounding hammer in my breast.

Groden 1966, p. 10

Equal of the gods seems to me that man who sist opposite you and,
close to you, listens to your sweet words
And lovely laugh, which has passionately excited the heart in
my breast.
>							Trypanis 1971, p. 145-6

There's a man, I really believe, compares with
any god in heaven above! To sit there
knee to knee so close to you, hear your voice, your
cozy low laughter,
close to you – enough in the very thought to
put my heart at once in a palpitation.
>							Nims 1971, p. 291

He seems to be a god, that man
Facing you, who leans to be close,
Smiles, and, alert and glad, listens
To your mellow voice
And quickens in love at your laughter
That stings my breasts, jolts my heart.
>							Davenport 1980, p. 84

He seems as fortunate as the gods to me, the man who sits
opposite you and listens nearby to your sweet voice and lovely
laughter. Truly that sets my heart trembling in my breast.
>							Campbell 1982, p. 79

It seems to me that man is equal to the gods,
that is, whoever sits opposite you
and, drawing nearer, savours, as you speak,
the sweetness of your voice
and the thrill of your laugh, which have so stirred the heart
in my own breast
>							Balmer 1984/88, No. 20

He seems to me to be like the gods -
whatever man sits opposite you
and close by hears you talking sweetly
And laughing charmingly; which
makes the heart within my breast take flight.
>							Snyder 1991, p. 18

To me it seems
that man has the fortune of gods,

whoever sits beside you, and close,
who listens to you sweetly speaking
and laughing temptingly; my heart flutters in my breast
Rayor 1991, No. 8, p. 57

TO ME HE SEEMS EQUAL TO THE GODS
THAT MAN WHO SITS FACING YOU AND NEAR YOU
CAN LISTEN TO YOUR SWEET VOICE AND LOVELY LAUGHTER
THAT MAKES MY HEART INSIDE MY CHEST PALPITATE;
Fallieros, this volume, p. 52

French

Il me semble l'égal des dieux
L'homme qui est assis à côté de toi
Et entend de tout près ta douce voix.
Et ton rire qui m'emplit de désir.
Quand j'entends ce rire, mon coeur
Se retourne dans la poitrine;
Ledwidge 1987, p. 120

German

Scheinen will mir, dass er den Göttern gleich ist,
jener Mann, der neben dir sitzt, dir nahe
auf den süssen Klang deiner Stimme lauscht und,
wie du voll Liebreiz
ihm entgegenlachst: doch, fürwahr, in meiner
Brust hat dies die Ruhe geraubt dem Herzen.
Treu 1984, p. 25

Italian

A me pare uguale agli déi
chi a te vicino così dolce
suono ascolta mentre tu parli
e ridi amorosamente. Subito a me
il cuore si agita nel petto.
Quasimodo 1985 (orig. 1944), p. 9

A miei occhi e immagine di dei l'uomo,
lui che in te si specchia sedendo,
e s'avvicina a te si piega e coglie dolci voci
e riso di passione.
Il cuore dentro, fondo, mi precipita.
Savino 1983, p. 27

Mi sembra pari agli dei quell'uomo che siede di fronte
a te e vicino ascolta te che dolcemente parli
e ridi un riso che suscita desiderio. Questa visione veramente
mi ha turbato il cuore nel petto.
Ferrari 1987, p. 127

Mi pare simile a un dio l'uomo
che ti siede accanto e ti ascolta cosi,
mentre parli con lieve sussurro e ridi amabile:
questo mi stringe il cuore nel petto!
Guidorizzi 1993, p. 15

Spanish

Me parece igual a los dioses
aquel varon que esta sentado frente a ti
y a tu lado te escucha mientras le hablas dulcemente
y mientras ries con amor. Ello en verdad ha hecho desmayarse
a mi corazon dentro del pecho.
Adrados 1986, p. 361

Me parece igual a los dioses ese hombre
que ahora esta frente a ti sentado y tu dulce voz
a tu lado escucha mientras le ablas y tu amable risa;
lo cual, te juro, en mi pecho el alma saltar ha hecho.
Tobal 1990, p. 37

Catalan

Igual que els deus em sembla que aquest home
és, que et seu al davant, aquest que ara
escolta, a frec, la teva veu, car parles
molt delicada, i el teu riure agradós; de debò, dintre
del pit el cor em defalleix;
Balasch 1973/85, p. 31

Modern Greek

Θεὸς μοῦ φαίνεται στ' ἀλήθεια ἐμένα κεῖνος
ὁ ἄντρας ποὺ κάθεται ἀντικρύ σου κι ἀπὸ
κοντὰ τὴ γλύκα τῆς φωνῆς σου ἀπολαμβά-
νει ✵ καὶ τὸ γέλιο σου ἄχ ποὺ ξελογιάζει
καὶ ποὺ λιώνει στὸ στῆθος τὴν καρδιά μου
Elytis 1984, p. 79

II. **"Love has shaken ..."** Some of the simplest, yet most evocative verses of Sappho about Love [*Eros*], the "limb loosener", "bitter-sweet", "unmanageable serpent", compare the sudden erotic impulse to a stormy gust of wind. Some of the modern translations cited below miss both the linguistic and the languorous message of the Aeolic lines, preserved with admiration in antiquity by Maximus of Tyre (Campbell, 1982, p. 93).

Original Aeolic Greek

Ἔρος δ' ἐτίναξέ μοι φρέ-
νας ὡς ἄνεμος κὰτ ὄρος δρύσιν ἐμπέτων.

Modern English Translations

As for me, love has shaken my wits as a
down-rushing whirlwind that falls upon the oaks.
Edmonds 1928, Vol. I, No. v54, p. 222

Love shook my heart, like a wind falling on mountain-trees.
Page 1955, p. 136

As a whirlwind
swoops on an oak
Love shakes my heart
Barnard 1958, No. 44

Love shook my heart, like a wind falling on oaks on the mountain.
Bowra 1961 (orig. 1936), p. 184

Like a mountain whirlwind punishing the oak trees love has shattered my heart. left my heart	Love like a sudden breeze tumbling on the oak-tree leaves trembling.
Barnstone 1965 p. 9 and 1988 p. 67	Roche 1966, p. 42
Love shakes my heart like a wind sweeping down a mountain onto oaks.	Desire has shaken my mind As the wind in the mountain forests Roars through trees.
Groden 1966, p. 26	Davenport 1980, p. 83

Love shook my heart like a wind falling on oaks on a mountain.
Campbell 1982, p. 93

> Eros,
> sweet god ...
> shook my soul as the wind
> from the mountain fells trees ...
>
> <div align="right">Carter (lyrics for music) 1982 (LP record <i>Syringa</i>)</div>

> Love shook my heart
> like the wind on the mountain
> rushing over the oak trees.
>
> Balmer 1984/88, No. 1

> Eros shook my heart, like the wind
> assailing the oaks on a mountain
>
> Snyder 1991, p 27

> Love shook my senses,
> like wind crashing on mountain oaks.
>
> Rayor 1991, No 19, p 63

> LOVE [EROS] HAS SHAKEN MY MIND [PHREN]
> LIKE A MOUNTAIN WIND FALLING UPON THE OAK TREES.
>
> Fallieros 1995, this volume, p. 55

French

> L'amour a secoué mon coeur comme un orage
> deferlant sur les chênes en montagne.
>
> Ledwidge 1987, p. 159

German

> (es) hat geschüttelt die Sinne mir
> Eros, so wie ein Sturm in die Eichen des Bergwalds fällt.
>
> Treu 1984 (and earlier), p. 51

Italian

> Scuote l'anima mia Eros
> come vento sul monte
> che irrompe entro le querce;
>
> Quasimodo 1985 (orig.1944), p. 21

> Amore mi martella
> nelle vene. Come vento, in monte, batte querce.
>
> Savino 1983, p. 35

... Eros ha squassato il mio cuore, come raffica che irrompe sulle querce montane ...
Ferrari 1987, p 141

Eros ha scosso la mia mente
come vento che giu dal monte
batte sulle querce.
Guidorizzi 1993, p. 19

Spanish

... y Eros sacudió mis sentidos como el
viento que en los montes se abate sobre las encinas.
Adrados 1986, p. 365

... me ha agitado el Amor los sentidos
como en el monte se arroja a los pinos el viento.
Tobal 1990, p. 55

Catalan

... mes l'amor les entranyes
m'ha sacsejat com vent que en un munt bat els roures.
Balasch 1973/85, p. 41

Modern Greek

ὁ Ἔρωτας ποὺ παραμύθια πλάθει
μοῦ ἅρπαξε τὴν ψυχή μου καὶ τὴν τρά-
νταξε ἴδια καθὼς ἀγέρας ἀπὸ τὰ βουνὰ χυ-
μάει μέσα στοὺς δρῦς φυσομανώντας.

Elytis 1984, p. 35

Note: The practical impossibility of including several other translations in modern languages, even a few more in modern Greek, must be recognized.

Some earlier out-of-print French, Greek and Spanish translations could not be obtained. The very recent Italian publications appeared noteworthy.

REFERENCE TABLE I

PROMINENT HELLENISTIC RULERS
(Years of Reign, B.C.)

I. Alexander of Macedon, "The Great", 336-323 B.C.
II. Successors in three major parts of the divided empire.

MACEDON AND GREECE	EGYPT	SYRIA, BABYLONIA, PERSIA AND ADJACENT AREAS
Demetrios Poliorketes ("Besieger of Cities") 306–283	Ptolemy I Soter ("The Savior") 323–285	Seleukos I Nikator ("Victorious") 312–280
Antigonos II Gonatas 277–239	Ptolemy IV Philopator 221-205 with Arsinoe III, (sister & wife)	Antiokhos I Soter 280-261
Philippos V 220–179		Antiokhos II Theos 261–246
Perseus, last king of Macedon 179–168 Macedonia & Greece became Roman provinces.	Ptolemy XII Theos Auletes ("Flute Player") 80–51. Reigned with Roman support	Antiokhos III, The Great, 223-187
		Demetrios I Soter 162–150
	Ptolemy XIII Co-ruler with Cleopatra VII, 51–47	Antiokhos XIII 69–64, murdered after his kingdom was taken by the Romans of Pompey.
	Cleopatra VII (daughter of Ptolemy XII, sister & wife of Ptolemy XIII) 51-30: killed herself to avoid being captured by the Roman Octavian.	

447

REFERENCE TABLE J

MAJOR FOREIGN INVASIONS OF GREEK-BYZANTINE LANDS FROM THE FOURTH TO THE FIFTEENTH CENTURIES A.D.

Goths: After reaching Adrianople in 378 A.D. they came close but failed (398) to capture the capital of Constantinople. Ravaged the Greek mainland as far as Athens and Sparta. Induced by the Byzantines to mass-migrate to Italy (399). Sacked Rome in 410 A.D.

Vandals: From northern Europe they descended on Spain (409), then established their kingdom in North Africa. Raided repeatedly the Greek coast and islands from 440 on. Sacked Rome in 455 A.D. Vandal kingdom destroyed by a Byzantine "Roman" expedition 533-534 A.D.

Huns: Ravaged Greece, 440-446, North Italy and Gaul, 451-452. Their forces disintegrated after the death of their leader, Attila, in 453 A.D.

Persians: In constant war with the Greek-Byzantine "Romans" 340-363; escalated hostilities 526-532. They captured Antioch (540-544), Syria and Asia Minor reaching the coast across from Constantinople (603-9). The Byzantine emperor Heraclius in successive victorious campaigns recaptured Christian lands, including Jerusalem and caused the collapse of the Persian empire, 628 A.D.

Slavs: Following earlier invaders, by 582 Slavic tribes began to penetrate the Balkans, captured major cities and threatened Thessaloniki (584-6), the second city of the Byzantine empire. Serbs and Croats migrated south from 600 on and the Russians attempted to seize Constantinople (860). Slavic-speaking Bulgarians invaded imperial lands and also threatened the capital. A Serbian empire by 1330 covered large parts of Greece. The Turkish onslaught abolished the Bulgarian (1393), the Serbian and the Bosnian kingdoms (1459-63).

Arabs: Following the death of Mohammed in 632 they began expansionist wars; captured Jerusalem in 638, conquered Egypt, raided Greek coast and islands, 663-678. Two prolonged sieges of Constantinople by land and sea were unsuccessful but the Arabs made deep inroads into Greek territories. Arabs from

Spain captured Crete in 826 and for over 130 years launched from there attacks against other Greek islands, until Crete was retaken by Byzantine forces in 961. Fatimids from Egypt gained control of the Holy Land. Christian crusaders recaptured Jerusalem in 1099 but Moslems under Saladdin took it back. Gradually Turks replaced the Arabs as the ultimate threat to Byzantine survival.

Normans: After gaining control of Roman-Byzantine possessions in Italy and Sicily, they invaded Greece, 1081-82. In a second major invasion from the West, they crossed Macedonia and after capturing and ravaging Thessaloniki (Salonika) in 1185, they threatened Constantinople until Byzantine counterattacks and epidemic diseases forced them to withdraw.

Mongols: Advancing from Central Asia under their leader Timur, or Tamerlane (1398), they overran Persia, Mesopotamia and, after routing the Turks, reached the Aegean coast. Unexpectedly in 1403 they withdrew and Timur died on his expedition to China.

Turks: After subduing Persia, Mesopotamia (capturing the Arab capital, Baghdad) and Armenia (1065-67) the Seljuq Turks* defeated a large Byzantine army (1071) and established the Turkish Sultanate of Roum ("Rome") in Asia Minor, which lasted from 1077 to 1327. In 1101-4 the Turks recaptured Antioch and its surrounding area from the crusaders. By mid-thirteenth century the Ottoman Turks dominated over the Seljuqs, conquering more Byzantine territories. Finally in 1453 they captured Constantinople and then swept the remains of the Greek Orthodox Byzantine empire.

---

*Other Turkish ethnic groups invading Byzantium from the North included the Patzinaks (or Pechenegs), the Uzes and the Cumans.

REFERENCE TABLE K
BYZANTINE RULERS CONNECTED WITH LESBOS

Justinian I (527-565 A.D.). After his armies destroyed the Vandal kingdom in North Africa, he carried many prisoners back to Constantinople. A group of them escaped and their ships stopped on Lesbos before they reached Africa.

Irene the Athenian (regent 780-797, sole emperor 797-802). Following a palace coup she was dethroned and exiled on Lesbos, where she died less than a year later.

Nikephoros I (802-811). Renewing the iconoclastic policies of his predecessors he forced the hiding of holy icons, among them the venerable "Saint Sion" icon of the Virgin Mary, brought to Lesbos from Jerusalem.

Constantine VII (913-959). He exiled to Lesbos his brother-in-law Stephanos, who had attempted to seize the throne.

John I Tzimiskis (969-979). To safeguard his throne, he had the brother and the nephew of his predecessor (whom he had murdered) banished to Methymna, on Lesbos.

Michael IV (1034-41). Fearing the rumored imperial ambitions of Constantine Monomakhos, he had that nobleman—and future emperor—exiled on Lesbos.

Constantine IX Monomakhos (1042-55). Lived with his niece and beloved mistress Skleraina in exile on Lesbos, until the widowed empress Zoe chose him as her third husband and raised him to the throne. He, in turn, exiled the powerful brother and uncle of his two predecessors to Lesbos, where he had him first blinded and then executed.

Alexios I Komnenos (1081-1118). Saved Lesbos from capture and domination by the invading Turkish emir of Smyrna.

Manuel I Komnenos (1143-80). Held successive church councils to safeguard Christian Orthodoxy, which were regularly attended by bishops from Lesbos.

John III (1222-54). Took Lesbos and other islands back from the Latins.

Andronikos III (1328-41). Rescued Lesbos from an attempted seizure by Italian adventurers.

John V Palaiologos (1341-91). Gave Lesbos as dowry for his sister, whom he had marry the Genoese Francesco Gattilusio, to reward him for his help in regaining the throne. Later he sent the family of his other brother-in-law (and rival for the throne), Matthew Kantakouzenos, to live on Lesbos under the watchful eye of Gattilusio.

John VII (1390). Seized the throne for a year (with Turkish help) but mostly lived on Lesbos, near his father-in-law, the Genoese lord of Lesbos F. Gattilusio. Through French-Genoese connections, he sat on the throne again while his uncle, emperor Manuel II was in Europe for three years seeking help against the Turks.

Manuel II (1391-1425). Stayed on Lesbos after he had failed to defend the great city of Thessaloniki against the Turks. Later he traveled to major European cities, including Paris and London, desperately seeking help to save the emprire from total defeat.

Constantine XI (1449-53). Married the daughter of the Lord of Lesbos, Dorino Gattilusio. She was soon to die after a miscarriage on Lemnos, where her husband was fighting the Turks. As the last emperor of Byzantium, Constantine XI lost his life defending Constantinople against the final Turkish onslaught.

REFERENCE TABLE L

IDIOMATIC EXPRESSIONS IN MODERN GREEK
OFTEN QUOTED VERBATIM IN LITERARY TRANSLATIONS

daskála: a female school-teacher (masc. *dáskalos*); originally *didaskala, -os*, from the verb *didaskein*, to teach – cf. didactic.

gorgóna: from the ancient Greek *gorgon*, a monstrous medusa. Now it refers to any imaginary half-woman, half-fish creature, as does the word mermaid.

kafeneio: a simple coffee shop, or cafe, serving Greek- or Turkish-style coffee. The patrons, almost exclusively men, may sit for hours talking, playing cards or backgammon, or quietly rolling their worry-beads [*kombolóy*]. The *kafetzis*, or shop-keeper, often joins his customers' conversation and spirit.

kaiki: a small sailing boat, a caique [Turk. *kayik*], common in the eastern Mediterranean.

kéfi: a most untranslatable word referring to a characteristic state of good humor, high spirits, gay mood, enjoyment and fun.

kólyva: a dish of boiled whole wheat grains with raisins, nuts, candied almonds, pomegranate or other fruit and spices, topped with powdered sugar and served on a special – often silver – platter, with religious decorations. It is traditionally presented at memorial services, blessed and afterwards served to the congregation. The word may be traced to the ancient Greek kolyvos, a small coin and hence kolyva, small round cakes.

koumbáros*: probably from the Italian *compadre,* a person with a religious tie to someone, a best-man of a wedded couple, or the sponsor at a baby's christening. For the child this then would be his *nonós*, or in feminine *noná* (the parents' *kombára*).

lambáda*: a large ceremonial candle often decorated with ribbons, etc. for weddings, baptisms, funerals and other liturgical purposes.

makarios: blessed, blissful; *makaritis* (or *-es*), blessed among the dead, of blessed memory.

mezés (pl. *mezedes*): appetizers, hors d'oeuvres, often well-spiced.

nonós#, fem. *noná*: godfather, godmother, those who have christened a person, generally a baby. Also written *nounos, nouna*.

ouzeri: the French-sounding suffix *-eri* (Fr. *-erie*) after the word for the traditional Greek apperitif ouzo, describes a simple establishment serving a variety of *mezedes* to go with ouzo, or beer, or wine.

Panayia (also written *Panaghia*): the All Holy [*Pan*, Ayia, or Aghia] Mother of God, the Virgin Mary.

paximádi (pl. *paximadia*): dry durable toast, or a cross between a toast and a cookie, often flavored with spices and an herb such as anise, served traditionally after memorial services.

rakí (Arab. *arak*): strong distilled and slightly flavored alcoholic drink similar to ouzo, often drier and coarser.

skala: docking harbor (cf. French *escale,* port-of-call), often downhill from a village or town.

---

*The Greek spelling with mp is to be pronounced more like mb. In Modern Greek mp and nt are used for the foreign letters b and d, which have no equivalent in the Greek alphabet.

#When calling someone, the final s of the nominative is dropped, so one says "nonó!" (or "noné!"); Stratis is addressed as "Strati!", etc. Kyrios (mister, lord) becomes kyrie (*cf.* kyrie eleison, Lord have mercy).

REFERENCE TABLE M

English Word Choices in Translating Elytis's Poems

1. *trelée* (fem. - masc. *trelos*) can be rendered as crazy, or mad (Friar, 1973), insane and also foolish, or most excited.
2. *rhodiá*, the pomegranate tree (*rhodi*: pomegranate) is, like most trees in Greek, feminine (hence *she* in translation).
3. *áxion* (neut. – masc. *axios*) is a fundamental adjective (in the 88 pages of Elytis' poem it appears 15 times) referring to value (philos.: axiology, the study of values) and can be translated as worthy, valuable, or also capable, deserving. The liturgical connotations of *Axion Esti* (Worthy It Is) encourage a direct transliteration.
4. *akheiropóietos,* from *a* (not) *kheir* (or *cheir*, hand – cf. chirurgical, chiropractor) and *poietos* (made, created, cf. poetry) in Christian Orthodox tradition applied to sacred objects which could not have been the work of human hands but only divinely produced.
5. *cósmos,* the Greek word for the world, also refers to orderly arrangement, ornamentation, beauty (cf. cosmology vs cosmetology).
6. *zygós,* meaning yoke, or bondage in ancient Greek, has in modern Greek the broader sense of balance and more specifically scale (weighing).
7. *Yéra* (or *Gera*, as in geriatrics, with a soft gamma) is a small fishing village on Lesbos, near the end of a deep bay.
8. *oxidized:* binding oxygen and therefore rusty (the poet may have used the chemical term rather than the colloquial Greek for rust, to denote the positive aspects of oxidation).
9. prize is one way of translating *tímema*, which may variously mean value, worth, price, honor, distinction or even an estimate (for damages) and assessment (for taxes).
10. *daidalic* (not capitalized by Elytis) could mean ingenious, or challenging, from Daedalus [*Daidalos*], the mythical ancient builder of the labyrinth on Crete and of the wings of wax for him and his son Icarus [*Ikaros*] to escape from the control of king Minos.

11. *medén* in Greek is the word for zero, null, or etymologically "not-one" and hence nothingness, void.
12. *nephéle* (fem., from *néphos,* neut.) cloud. Also the name of a mythological woman who was created from a cloud by Zeus and then became the mother of the centaurs.

    Another Nephele in ancient Greek tradition was the mother of Phrixos and Helle (who drowned in the Hellespont, "Helle's Sea", known also as The Dardanelles).
13. *krimas,* or *crima,* is a modern Greek exclamation to declare that it's a pity, it's too bad; the word is the same as that for crime.
14. magic is the English noun closest to the Greek *mageia*, meaning enchantment, powerful charm, delight.
15. *énnoia,* lit. "in-the-mind" [*en-noia*] in modern Greek means concern, care, though basically it is the word for meaning, a concept or thought.

INDEX

Abdera, 298
Abydos, 231–2, 282
Academy, Platonic 105, 106ff., 110
Acheans, 3
Acre (city), 283
Actresses, 228
Adoption, 165, 178, 255
Adramyttion (-um), 284
Adrianople [*Adrianoupolis*], 284, 301, 302, 305–6, 311, 313
Adultery, 242
Aegean coast, islands, 230, 245, 283, 301, 363, 365, 391
Aeolians, 3ff., 85, 87
Aeolis, 14, 106, 390
Africa, 226, 229
Alexandria (Egypt), 30, 193
Alphabet
    Greek, 9, 27, 147
    Phoenician, 9
Amazons, 5–6, 143–4
America, 358, 367
Amputations, 232
Amputees, 350
Amusements, 261
Anatolia, 283
Anise, 56
Antibes, 343
Antioch [*Antiokhia*], 180, 222, 225
Antissa (city on Lesbos), 6, 14, 28, 138
Anxiety attack, 52

Apostasy, 221
Apostles, 192
Apotheosis, 221, 229
Appetizers, 370
Aqueducts, 377
Arabs, 230–2, 236, 237, 241, 248
Arianism (heresy), 227
Arcadian, 12
Arginousai (Arginusae), 97ff.
Argonauts, 17–18
Aristocracy, 40, 44, 50
Arkesilaos (Platonist), 105ff.
Armenia, Armenians, 123, 236, 323
Army volunteers, 345, 351
Arrogance, 120
Art styles, 377
Artemision (-um), 87
Asia, 226
Asia Minor, 133ff., 273ff.
Assassinations, 156, 158, 253
Assos, 105, 127, 193, 301, 307
Atheism, 194
Athens, 33–34, 86ff., 95ff., 105ff., 135, 193, 225, 327, 346, 351, 370
Atomic (theory), 124
Atrocities, 90
Attica, 88
Aulos (flute), 170

Babylonia, 84, 127
Bactria, 135

Balkan wars, 337
Barbarians, 135, 144, 224–5, 229, 278, 326
Basilika (Vasilika), village, 294, 374
Baths/bathing, 164–6, 178, 238, 336
Beauty, 37, 41, 56, 74, 193, 391
Beheadings, 232, 325, 326
Benediction, 330
Birthday
   celebrations, 125
Bishops, 224, 244, 254, 277–8, 291, 358
Black Sea, 303, 311–2, 357
Blasphemy, 48
Blindings, 237, 238, 243, 244, 247, 253–4, 257, 260
Blood-letting, 286
Bogomils (heretics), 287
Boorishness, 118
Booty, 312, 316
Boys for pleasure/sex, 176, 309
Breasts removed, 5, 143
Broadcasting, 346
Brothels, 180, 182–4, 228
Bronze age, 3
Bulgarians, 237, 246, 346
Burials, 97, 102–3, 156, 166, 258
Burning people, 326
Byzantines, 75, 322, 372
Byzantium, 224, 247, 282, 295, 297, 316, 317

Calendar
   islamic, 328
   new (Gregorian), 296
Calm, 28, 47
Caria, 134
Carthage, 229
Catalans, 302, 309
Catholics, 291–2, 296
Caucasus [*Kaukasos*], 142–4, 151
Chalkis [*Halkis*], 112, 138
Chaos, 126
Chariot
   race, 12;
   Venus's, 90
   winged, 12
Charm, indescribable, 265
Childbirth, 180, 303

Christ, love of, 329
Christening, 359
Christianity, 19, 111, 191, 221ff., 228, 248, 273, 274
Christians, 111, 129, 193, 294, 305, 321, 326, 328ff., 336
Circumcision, 310
Citizenship
   Athenian, 99
   Roman, 140, 144, 149
City, The, see Constantinople
Civil wars, 151ff., 157ff.
Clouds, 387
Coins, 149, 265, 292, 374
Colchis [*Kolkhis*], 142
Comedy, 44, 112
Comets, 257
Communications, 27ff.
Companions, female [*hetairai*], 46–47, 61
Concubines *see* Courtesans
Confiscation, 103, 232
Conspiracies, 228, 243, 251
Constantinople [*Konstantinoupolis*], 135, 221ff., 224, 225, 229, 245, 258, 283, 287–8, 294, 299, 302ff., 307, 311ff., 316
Constitutions, 79–81, 87, 336
Convents, 228, 234, 242, 274
Corfu [*Kerkyra*], 303
Corinth [*Korinthos*], 30–31, 40
Courtesans [*hetairai*], 46, 48, 63–65, 85, 109, 125, 228
Creation of the world, 83, 235, 298ff.
Creator, *The*, 195
Crete, 54, 185, 195, 247
Crimes vs. punishment, 91–93
Croton, 84
Crowds, 167
Cumans [*Komans*], 278
Cures, miraculous, 330, 374
Cyclades, 231–2, 391
Cyprus [*Kypros*], 281, 322
Cyrene (Kyrene) in Africa, 180

Dance, 167., 170, 179
Danube [*Istros*] river, 313
Death
   asthma, 266

children's, 243, 303–4
chosen, 99, 102, 139
for Christ, 329
in exile, 244
impending, 52
noble, 90
penalty, 92–93
predicted, 100
premature, 269
presumed, 180, 186
readiness for, 37
sentence, 253
sudden, 139
wish, 58, 153, 189–90
Delos, 20
Delphi, 39, 150
Democracy, 81, 89, 90;
    evils of, 246
Depression ["*distemperature*"], 183, 189
Desires, 172, 176
Destiny, 8
Dialectic, 108
Dictators, 35, 79, 83
Diplomacy, 146, 294
Diseases, 21, 257, 266, 267, 269
Disasters, 259
Dithyrambs (songs), 30–31
Divinity, 53
Dolphins, 13–14
Donkeys
    on parade, 251
    turning wild, 321
Dreams, 54, 100, 169, 178, 180
Drinking/drunkenness, 26, 28, 71–72,
    170, 176, 194, 282, 300, 360–1
Drowning, 364, 366, 368
Dynasties
    Komnenos, 273ff.
    Macedonian, 252
    Palaiologos, 290ff.

Earth, 50, 56, 83, 226
Earthquakes, 237, 294–5
Ecology, 110
Ecstasy, 20, 120
Education, 116, 221, 225, 248, 295
Effeminacy, 128
Eftalou (village), 373

Ego (self), 40–41
Egypt, 85, 133, 137, 157–8, 193, 248,
    295, 357
Elections, 336
Eleusinian
    "mysteries", 19, 194, 221
Embarrassment, 65, 263
Encyclopedia, 28, 44, 46, 248, 346
England, 341
Ephesos, 181–82, 192–3, 284, 288, 299
Epicureans, 105, 123ff.
Epidemics, 257
Epigrams, 47, 64, 141, 387
Equality, 81, 87
Eresos (or Eressos), 6, 44, 46, 64, 89,
    105–6, 111–12, 374
Eros 38, 41, 55, 58, 83
Erotic
    angle, 363
    fantasies, 59
    passion, 160ff.
    torment, 361
Ethics, 150
Ethnic
    diversity, 327
    identity, 321, 331–5
Eunuchs, 109, 233, 236, 239, 241, 254
Europe, 142, 226, 302
Evil
    elimination of, 105
    lack of, 106, 248
    prevalent, 225, 231, 257
Executions, 89, 95, 97, 103, 150, 223,
    257, 316
Exile, 44, 67, 80, 136, 322, 378
Extermination, 90, 93, 96, 278
Extortions, 144, 257
Extremes, 15
Eye
    gouging, *see* Blinding
    witnesses, 226, 285, 304

Fate, 100, 153–4, 190, 286
Festivals, 375
Figs, 121
Fire, liquid ("Greek"), 230, 232
Flanders, 276, 290
Flood, 3

Flute, 40
  (pipe), 166, 170, 179
Folklore, 332, 343
Ford Motor Co. ("Auto Works"), 358
France, 284–5, 290, 294, 302, 375ff., 378
Franks, 232, 240, 243, 290, 321ff.
Freedom, 90, 111, 381
Frenzy, 52
Freudian analysis, 52–53
Funerals, 103, 113

Gallipoli [*Kallipolis*] 306, 311ff., 314, 316
Gangrene, 347
Gastronomy, 108, 122, 159
Gaul, 151, 221
"Gay", 108
Genoa, 286, 291ff., 300
Genoese, 292, 302, 304, 309, 321ff., 374
Georgia, 303
Germans/Germany, 300, 340
Gifts, 262
Goats, 165ff., 344, 354
Godfather (nonos), 359ff.
Gold, 15, 80, 138, 234, 265
Gordian knot, 137
Gordion (Phrygia), 137
Gossip, 147
Goths, 224–5, 229
Gourmet, 115, 122
Gout, 257
Grammarians, 124
Guitar, 189

Halkis (Khalkis, Chalkis), 112, 138
Happiness, 123–24
Harems, 310
Harmony, 51
Hedone/hedonism, 123, 125
Hellespont (Dardanelles), 104, 306, 317
Heresies, 223, 287
Heretics, 275, 287
Hesychasm (Quietism), 296
Hios (Khios, Chios), 7, 10, 85, 102, 104, 108, 137, 283, 285–6, 290, 299, 302, 305, 307–8, 311, 323, 329
Historians, women, 159, 273
History, judgment of, 147
Hittites, 3

Holocaust
  Hellenic, 104
Holy
  Land, 284, 290
  Mountain (Mt. Athos), 300
  Roman Empire, 243
  Virgin [*Panayia*], 288, 327, 356ff., 368
Homage, 378
"Homocaust", 104
Homosexuality, 46, 48–49, 50, 52, 56, 61, 177
Hospitals, 345
Humor, 107, 116
Hungary, 332
Huns, 229
Hunting, 165
Hybris (hubris), 82
Hygeia, 21
Hypnotism, 353

Iambic singing, 42
Iconoclasm, 231
Icons
  destroyed, 305
  miraculous, 245
  venerated, 235ff., 288
Ideas, 391
Iliad, 8ff., 27, 51, 274
Illness, 381
Ignorance, 194
Imbros, 296, 310–11
Impiety, 112
Incest, 180, 186
Independence, 91, 93, 331–2, 337ff., 345
India, 123, 341
Individualism, 28, 51
Intellect, 106, 109, 265
Intercourse (sexual)
  frequent, 122
  "male type", 228
  promiscuous, 300
  unnatural, 228, 299
Ionia, 283
Issa, 4, 6
Italians, 304, 314, 316, 322
Italy, 30, 84, 145, 150, 151, 225, 274, 300, 316
Ithaca island, 10

INDEX **461**

Jerusalem, 193, 225, 230, 244, 284
Jewelry, 176, 186
Jews, 247, 327
Justice, 89–95, 261, 234

Kallipolis, *see* Gallipoli
Kalloni, town and bay, 374
Khazar princess, 235
Khios, *see* Hios
Kidnapping, 169
Kithara, 16, 28–28, 30, 232
Kissing, 168ff.
Klazomenai (-ae, town), 276
Kos, island, 323
Kylix (drinking cup), 26, 43
Kyme (Aeolian city), 5, 7, 96, 100, 102

Lacedaemon [*Lakedaimon*], 88, 98, 101
Laconia, 13
Lambs, 374
Lamentations, 241, 266, 269
Landscaping, luxurious, 267
Languages
   Arabic, 228
   "foreign", 48
   French, 48–49, 274
   Greek (archaic), 9, 17, 224;
     (spoken) 228; (official) 229, 274
   Latin, 38, 180–1, 228
   Old English, 180
   Slavonic, 228
Latins, 276, 285, 289, 290–1, 292ff., 305, 306, 321, 325
Lefkas (Leucas), island, 46
Lesbos
   ancient hero, 6
   island, 1–391, esp. 86, 88ff., 104ff., 111, 133–5, 136–8, 139ff., 149–50, 160ff., 164ff., 192, 224, 227, 231, 235, 244, 252, 253, 255, 256, 269–70, 308, 310, 312ff., 317, 322ff., 327, 331ff., 343–4, 345ff., 368ff., 375ff., 380–2, 391
Liberation, 337, 371
Liberty, statue of, 371
Libya, 227
Life, good, 123, 127
   just/unjust, 105

Lisvori (village), 294–5, 375
Liturgy, 346, 384
Loathsome, 119, 299
Logic, 107, 127
Logos, 287
Loom, 57
Looting, 290, 309, 312
Love
   after death, 368
   beauty and brilliance, 41
   duel, 51
   forbidden, 48
   passing, 47
   pure, 47
   shameful, 46, 47
   unnatural, 52
Lute, 22
Luxury, 58, 108, 115, 178, 263
Lyceum [*Lykeion*] of Athens, 105, 110, 112, 133
Lydia (kingdom of), 12, 40, 59, 80, 106, 283
Lyre, 22, 30, 41ff., 54, 107, 222

Macedonia, 15, 109, 133, 192, 243, 337, 345
Madrid, Spain, 246
Maenads [*Mainades*], 15–16, 20
Malevolence, 39
Mangana (monastery), 257
Manuscripts, ancient, 274, 309, 310
Marathon, 87
Marriages, 134, 186, 191, 236, 238, 240, 255, 256, 260, 262, 299, 303, 362, 366
Martyrdom, 326, 328ff.
Marxist, sociology, 50
Massacres, 9, 89ff., 289, 290, 291, 331
Mathematics, 83
Mating, animals, 172, 176
Medicine, 187
Mental therapy, 124
Merchants, 84, 286
Mercy, 278
Mermaids [*Gorgones*], 362
Mesa (town), 375
Methymna, 6, 14, 15, 30, 35, 88, 97, 133, 160, 169–70, 222, 253, 276, 287, 291, 308, 372–3

Migrations, 5
Miletos, 86–87, 193
Military service, 199
Mind lost, 103, 177
Mindlessness, 194
Miscarriage, 303
Mistra, 303
Mistresses, 262, 264–66
Mitilini, or Mitylene, *see* Mytilene
Modes, musical, 27
Molyvos (*see also* Methymna), 312, 322, 327, 372
Monarchy (rule of one), 80
Monasteries, 236, 245, 257, 258, 267, 297
Money, 27, 31, 240, 286
Mongols, 293, 301
Monks, 195, 229, 244–5, 250, 288, 289, 303, 326, 328ff.
Moon, 54, 55
Morality, 39, 43, 46, 48, 107, 127, 193, 361
Mosaics, 374
Moslems, 309, 321, 327, 328ff., 337
Mosques, 279, 309, 372, 375
Muses, 20–22, 42, 60, 194–5
Museums, 22, 114, 372, 373, 391
Music
  invention of, 16
  divine, 222
  strange, 222
Musical instruments, 41–42
Musician-poets [*melopoioi*], 27, 40, 50
Mutations, poetic, 20
Myrivili (mountain), 373
Mysteries, 221
Myths, 265
Mytilene, 4–6, 27, 29, 35–36, 40, 44, 67, 79ff., 85, 86–87, 88ff., 96, 99ff., 105, 122, 125–6, 144, 148–50, 165ff., 240, 244, 251, 252, 256, 257, 260, 276ff., 278ff., 288, 291, 297, 299, 303, 305ff., 310, 311ff., 314ff., 317–8, 322ff., 329, 334–5, 337ff., 346, 369–72

Nakedness, 166–7
National Academy, Athens, 327, 346
Naucratis (Greek city in Egypt), 84–85
Naval battles, 96ff., 286

Naxos, 322
Neolithic tools, 3
Newspapers, 345–6, 351
News, reporting, 39
Nicaea [*Nikaia*], 236, 241, 275, 282–3, 299
Normans, 273, 275, 278, 283
Noses, cut off (*rhinotomies*), 251
Nunneries, 242
Nymphs, 164–5, 167, 173–4

Occupations, 343–4
Odyssey, 9ff., 40, 342
Old age, 8, 110, 113, 126, 257
Olympic games (Olympiads), end of, 130
Olympus, Mountain
  Lesbos, 245, 374
  mainland Greece, 390
Oracles, 100
Orgies, 18, 116, 195, 249
Orthodoxy, 225, 227, 244–5, 248, 287, 291–2, 321–323, 328ff., 384
Ottomans (Turks), 290ff., 318, 321, 329ff., 334, 337ff.
Oysters, 123

Paean (battle song), 40, 98
Paganism, 193, 221
Palestine, 226, 230, 244, 283, 285
Pamphylia (in Asia Minor), 37, 49
Panayia (All-holy Virgin), 244–5, 327–8, 345ff., 368, 387
Panic, 170
Papacy, 248
Paphlagonia (in Asia Minor), 12, 240, 254
Parades, 240, 260, 264
Paradox, 15
Pardon, 80, 148
Paros (island), 28, 40, 223
Pashas, 325–6
Passions, 47, 93, 160
Patriarchs, 236, 238, 241, 247–9, 256, 257, 268, 331, 359
Patzinaks (*aka* Pechenegs), 276–8
Peace, 55, 158
Pearls, 123
Pectis (musical instrument), 27, 42
Pelasgians, 3, 6, 374
Pelopi (village), 373

INDEX   463

Peloponnesos (-us), 88ff., 97ff., 102, 236, 303–4
Penis "envy", 52
People, misled, 103–4
Perfection, 80, 83
Perfumes, 265
Pergamon (-um, *aka* Pergamos), 221, 307
Peripatetic, philosophy, 110
Persecution, 193
Persia, Persians, 85ff., 130, 133, 229–30, 301
Personalities, 259, 268
Petrified forest, 3
Phallic, awe, 52
Pharsala (*aka* Pharsalus), 152, 157
Philadelphia (in Asia Minor), 283
Philhellenes, 321
Philosophy
  Aristotelian, 109ff.
  Epicurean, 123ff.
  Platonic, 106ff.
  Pythagorean, 22, 83ff.
  Stoic, 126ff.
Phoenicia, 3, 9, 84, 133, 185
Phokaia (*aka* Foglia), 276, 301, 307–8, 322
Phorminx (musical instrument), 16, 18
Phrygia (in Asia Minor), 3, 9, 44, 283, 314, 347
Physicians, 109, 114, 181, 187
Piety, 231–2, 233
Pilgrims, 289
Pirates, 166, 181, 187, 245, 281, 288, 291, 302, 314
Pisa, 286, 371
Pitane (Aeolian city), 5, 106
Plagues, 226, 287, 306, 328, 331
Plants, medicinal, 369
Pleasures, excessive, 261
Plots, 156, 242
Poetry, 16, 27ff., 41, 48, 108
Poison, 145
Politics, 47, 65, 67, 80–82
Popes, 243, 295, 312, 323, 374
Populations, exchange, 334, 340
Poverty, 126, 127
Prayers, 119
Pregnancy, 143
Prejudice, 382

Priesthood, forced, 240
Prince's [*Prinkepos*] islands, 234, 235, 240
Prisoners, 278, 294
Prizes, Nobel, 382
Profits, 84
Property, confiscation, 103
Prophesy, 294
Prostitutes, 64, 84–85, 118, 194, 228
Protocol, imperial, 263
Prousa (in Asia Minor), 243
Providence, 243
Public
  service, 261
  works, 268
Punishment, 80–82
Purple, royal chamber, 273–4
Pyrrha (Lesbian city), 4, 67, 102, 112

Quietude [*hesykhia*], 47, 296

Raids, 286
Ransom, 308
Rationality, 120, 124, 127
Rebellions, 89, 102, 232, 242, 254, 255
Recycling the past, 390
Refugees, 340, 343, 339, 365
Religion, official, 19, 287
Renaissance, 273
Revenues, illegal, 257
Revolts/Revolutions, 81, 87, 89ff.
Rewards, 47, 263
Rhetoric, 90, 126, 139
Rhodos (island), 225, 285, 308, 312, 322, 323
Riddles, 270
Riots, 264, 288, 289
Riviera, French, 343, 378
Romans, 138ff., 160, 371–2
"Romans" (Byzantine Greeks), 226, 241ff., 274ff., 278, 300, 306, 316
Rome, 139ff., 150, 151ff., 156, 224, 248
Rules, flexible, 111
Russia, 331, 341
Russo-Turkish wars, 331

Sacrifices, 137, 176, 195
Sages, 14, 79–81
Saint Sophia (Holy Wisdom) cathedral,

233, 240
Salamis (island), 88
Samos (island), 84, 86, 96, 100, 124, 283, 290
Sanatorium, philosophical, 124
Saracens, 245
Sardis (city in Lydia), 80, 107, 145, 283
Satan, 287
Satyrs, 167
Savior
    Apollo, 21
    Jesus, 328ff.
    Zeus, 103, 177
Savoy, 295
Scythians, 275, 278
Seed (*sperma*), 84
Self (*ego*), 40
Self
    assessment, 390
    awareness, 40
    knowledge, 387
Selling one's body, 228
Semitic, 4, 231, 247
Serbs, 292
Sex
    education, 172–3
    play, 174
    unnatural, 109, 228
Sexual clumsiness, 168ff., 172
Sexuality, 48–49, 52–53
Shamelessness, 118
Sicily, 5, 30, 33, 36, 47, 95ff., 106, 237, 241
Sieges, 102, 279–81, 282, 312–3, 315–8, 324
Sins, 233, 234
Sirens, 17
Skepticism, 107
Slaughter, 278, 299, 308, 310, 316, 331, 349
Slavery, 89, 114, 158, 230, 278, 303, 309, 311, 325, 328, 336, 337
Slavs, 236, 248
Sleep, 54, 62, 171, 192
Smyrna [Turk. *Izmir*], 7, 273, 276ff., 279ff., 283, 301, 332
Sophia (city), 306
Sophistication, 265
Soul

eternal, 83
"right", 139
Spain, 146, 306
Spanish mission, 295
Sparta, 10, 28, 88ff., 96ff., 225
Speeches, 224, 260, 265, 349
Spirit, good [*eupsychia*], 139
Stadium [*stadion*], 35
Stars, 54, 55
Stoics, 105, 126ff., 135, 144, 150
Stress, 126, 128
Styles, 34, 51–52, 53–54, 265, 266
Suda (Suidas), encyclopedia, 28, 44, 46
Suicide, 46, 139, 365
Sultans, 302–3, 304, 305ff., 310ff., 318, 321, 324–5, 336
Superstition, 119
Surrender
    Mytilene, 309, 315–6
    Turkish, 339
Swimming pools, 267
Symposia, 116, 120
Synagogues, 327
Synod, 236, 239, 241, 253, 287
Syracuse [*Syrakousai*], 95ff.
Syros, island, 83

Tantalos, 11
Taxes, 85, 118, 140, 232, 311, 314, 316
Tenderness, 41
Tenedos, island, 10, 251, 292, 297, 300, 317
Testament
    Last Will and, 114
    New, 192, 341
Thasos, island, 306, 308
Theaters, 140, 341
Thera, island, 231
Therapy (care), 261
Thessaloniki (Salonica), 294, 296, 302
Thessaly, 3, 6, 152
Thrace, 15, 241, 243, 291–2, 294, 314
Thunderbolts, 8
Time [*Khronos*, Chronos], 83, 109, 113
Tongues, amputated, 237, 349
Topkapi, palace, 311
Torture, 138, 235, 326, 349
Tourists, 345, 368

Translations, 342, 346, 389, 390
Treasury, empty, 263
Treaties, 314
Trebizond [*Trapezous*], 303
Tribute, payment, 305–6, 314, 316, 324
Trojan war, 7–9, 14
Troy, 8, 27, 133, 192, 306, 314
Truth, 195, 391
Turks, 273, 275ff., 289, 290–4, 298ff., 302ff., 310ff., 321ff., 327ff., 355ff., 375
Tyrants (dictators), 30, 33, 66–68, 79–82, 86, 305ff.
Tyre (city), 179, 185ff., 285

University
  Athens, 381
  Constantinople, 258
Union of Soviet Socialist Republics (USSR), 381
United States of America (USA), 381
United States State Department, 381

Vandals, 224, 227
Variety, musical, 29
Varna (city), battle of, 303
Vatican library, 163
Venice, 185
Venetians, 215–6, 283, 285–6, 292, 304, 316ff., 322
Veterans, 349
Virgin, Holy
  chapel, 244
  pledge to, 368
Virginity, 61–62, 173, 178, 180, 182
Virtues of women, 39, 248
Visigoths, 225
Visions, 255, 266
Vlakhia, *see* Wallachia

Void of life, 113
Volcanoes, 231
Voluptuousness, 48, 172, 261

Wallachia [*Vlakhia*], 332, 357, 371
War
  Amazons, 5
  Balkan, 337
  Civil (Roman), 151ff., 157ff.
  Peloponnesian, 89ff.
  Russo-Turkish, 331
  Trojan, 7–9
  World (I or II), 331, 340
Weddings, 61–62, 179, 186, 300
Will and Testament, 114
Wines, 18, 30, 72–73, 113, 115–6, 167, 178
Wisdom, 84, 105, 127
  Holy (St. Sophia), 233, 240
Women
  deceived, 237
  desires of, 56–57
  helpless prey, 362
  free, 57, 85, 367
  Lesbian, 4–6, 42ff.
  lesbian, 42, 48–49, 52ff.
  loathsome, 299
  rulers, 239, 244, 250, 255, 259, 268
  sacrificed, 13–14
  slaves, 8
  traded, 8
  virtues of, 39, 248
  warriors, 5
Words
  common, 53
  final, 113
  immortal, 391
  right, 109
World, entire, 391
Worship, 245

INDEX OF PROPER NAMES

Abedin pasha ("Dino"), Turkish governor, 321
Achilles [*Akhilleus*], 3, 8, 10, 11, 160, 314
Aelian, writer, 33, 37
Aeolus [*Aiolos*], 3–6
Aëtios
    "heretic" bishop, 223–4
    palace eunuch, 233, 243
    medical authority, 223
Agamemnon, 8, 11, 12
Agathon, monk, 244–5, 288
Ajax [*Aias*], 11, 27, 314
Alaric, 224
Alcaeus [*Alkaios*], 12, 35, 79–81, 84, 223
Alcibiades, 96
Alexander of Macedon (The Great), 133ff.
Alexios I Komnenos (Comnenus), 273, 273ff.
Alexios II, 289
Amasis, Egyptian pharaoh, 85
Amphitrite, 13, 14
Anacreon, 38, 39, 41, 42, 223
Anactoria, 43, 56, 57, 391
Andromeda, 58, 59
Andronikos I Komnenos, 289–90
Andronikos II, 290–1, 296
Andronikos III, 290–1, 296
Anna Komnena, 273ff.
Anna (or Anne) of Savoy, 291, 299
Antiochus [*Antiokhos*], 180–1, 185
Aphrodite, 50, 57, 299, 365
Apollo, 16, 20, 371

Apollonios (-us) of Tyana, 36–37
Apollonios (-us) of Tyre, 179–80, 185ff.
Aquilius, 138–9
Arion, 30ff., 40, 221–2
Aristotle [*Aristoteles*], 29, 65, 70, 80–81, 105, 109–12, 133, 391
Arkhesilaos (-us), 105, 107–9
Arkhilokhos (Archilochus), 40, 223
Arrian [*Arrianos*], 135–7, 159
Asklepios (Aesculapius), 371
Athenaeus [*Athenaios*], 15, 30, 34, 41–42, 44, 59, 71ff., 115ff., 121ff., 138, 159
Athenais-Eudokia (wife of Theodosios II), empress, 129, 225–6, 246
Atthis, 46, 58–59, 391
Aydin, Turkish ruler, 299

Bacchus [*Bakkhos*], 16, 20, 73
Baldwin of Flanders, 290
Barsine (wife of Memnon, mistress of Alexander), 134
Basil I, 250
Basil II, 252, 254, 260
Beaudelaire, Charles, 48
Belisarius, general, 226–7
Benjamin of Tudella, 327
Boucicault, marshal, 294–5

Caesar, Julius, 139ff., 148ff., 157ff.
Callicratidas, 97–98
Carter, E., composer, 75
Cassander [*Kassandros*], 112

Catherine (wife of Constantine XI), 303
Catullus, 43
Chagall, Marc, 376, 379
Charlemagne, 232–3, 234, 236, 239, 240–1
Charles VI of France, 294
Chaucer, Geoffrey, 181
Choniates [*Khoniates*], Niketas, historian, 285, 287
Christopher [*Khristophoros*] of Mytilene, 269–70
Cicero, 38, 83, 140–1, 144, 147–8
Cinnamus [*Kinnamos*], John, historian, 284–6, 287
Clement [*Klemes*] of Alexandria, 30
Cleopatra VII of Egypt
Coës, 86–87
Conon, 97–98
Constantine I, The Great, 221, 232, 311
Constantine IV, 230
Constantine VI, 235ff., 246
Constantine VII Porphyrogennetos, 249–52
Constantine VIII, 252
Constantine IX Monomakhos, 255ff.
Constantine X Doukas, 273
Constantine XI Palaiologos (Palaeologus), 303, 311
Constantine Lekapenos, *see* Lekapenos
Constantius, 221
Cornelia (wife of Pompey), 150ff., 156

Dalassenos, Constantine, 276–77, 279
Damophyle of Pamphylia, 37
Darius of Persia, 86
Democritos (-us) of Abdera, 124
Deukalion, 3, 6
Diodoros of Sicily, 5–6, 70, 82, 87, 95ff., 104–5, 135, 159, 248
Diogenes Laertios (-us), 79–80, 83–84, 107ff., 112ff., 124ff., 124ff., 159
Dionysios of Halicarnassos, 51
Dionysos, 5, 12, 14, 20, 71, 73, 195
Dorikha (*aka* Rhodopis), 63–65, 87
Doukas (Ducas), John, 277, 279–80
Doukas (Ducas), Michael (historian), 298ff., 305ff., 309

Dukakis, Michael (U.S. presidential candidate), 373

Eftaliotis, Argyris, 341–3, 373
Eleanor of Aquitaine, 284
Electra, by Euripides, 128
Eleftheriadis, *see* Teriade
Elytis, Odysseas, 48, 370, 378, 380ff., 390–1
Enalos, 11, 13–15
Epicuros [*Epikouros*], 104–5, 123–5
Erygios, 43, 46, 134–5
Eudokia, empress, regent, 273
Eugene IX, pope, 295
Eugenia, *nee* Gattilusio, empress, 295
Euridice [*Euridike*], 18–19
Euripides, 100, 108
Eusebia, Byzantine empress, 221–2

Falier, Ordelafo, doge, 283

Galen [*Galenos*], 37
Gattilusio (also Kateluiso, Katalouzo, etc.)
    Domenico, 292, 310, 314, 324
    Dorino, 292, 303, 305, 311–2, 324
    Francesco I, 291–4, 297, 300
    Francesco II, 294–5, 321, 323
    Jacopo, 294
    Nicolo (Nicorezo), 307ff., 310, 314, 316, 325
Gavras, Michael, 286
George, Saint, 257
Gongyla, 43, 46, 55–56, 391
Gonzalez de Clavigo, R., 295
Grammatikos, Leo, 250
Gregoras, Nikephoros, historian, 296ff.
Gyrinno, 56, 391

Hadzidakis, Manos, composer, 89
Haraxos (Charaxus), 43, 46, 63, 84–85
Harun al-Rashid, 232, 241
Hector of Troy, 8
Helen
    of Troy, 9, 57, 381
    mother of Constantine I, 311, 323
    mother of Constantine XI, 311, 323
    wife of John V, 292, 297

Helena (wife of Constantine VII), 250, 252
Hellen (Greek hero), 4, 9
Hera, 73
Heracles (Hercules), 4–5
Heraclios (-us), 229–30
Hermarkhos, 105, 124, 126
Hermes, 370
Herodotos, 7, 31, 39, 46, 64, 67, 85, 87, 248, 261
Hesiod [*Hesiodos*], 32
Hipparkhos (-us), 17, 33
Homer [*Homeros*], 4, 6ff., 27, 57, 67, 265, 274, 277, 314
Hyrkan, *see* Orkhan

Iakovidis, George, painter, 371, 374
Ioakeim (Joachim), patriarch, 359
Irene the Athenian, empress, 232ff.
Isaac I Komnenos, 235
Ismael, Turkish leader, 312

Jason, Argonaut leader, 18
Jesus Christ [*Khristos*], 36
John I Tzimiskes, 252–3
John [*Ioannes*] V, 291–2, 296–8, 299, 323
John VI Kantakouzenos (Cantacuzene), 291, 296–8, 299–302, 323
John VII, 302
Julian [*Julianus*], the Apostate, 33, 54, 231ff.
Julius Caesar, *see* Caesar
Justinian I, 130, 226–7

Kantakouzenos, John, *see* John VI
Kantakouzenos, Matthew, 292, 297, 301
Katiluiso, *see* Gattilusio
Kedrenos (Cedrenus), George, 235ff., 238–40, 255–7, 264
Keroularios (Cerularius), Michael, patriarch, 257, 268
Kharis (Haris, Charis) of Mytilene, 138
Kleanthes, philosopher, 105, 127–9
Kontoglou, Photis, artist and writer, 322ff.
Kordatos, John, sociologist, 50
Kountouriotis, Paul, admiral, 337, 371
Krantor, philosopher, 107–8
Krates, philosopher, 107

Kritoboulos (Critobulus), Michael, historian, 310ff.
Kroisos (Croesus) of Lydia, 79–80

Lamb, Winifred, 372
Larihos (Larichus), 43, 44, 46, 134
Lekapenos
  Constantine, 250–2
  Stephanos, 250–2
Leo III the Isaurian, 230, 244
Leo IV the Khazar, 235
Leo V, 231
Leo VI, The Wise, 250
Leo the Deacon [*Diakonos*], 253
Lesbokles, 140
Lesbonax, 372
Lesbos, hero from Thessaly, 3, 6, 9
Leskhes (Lesches), 27
Linos (Linus), 17
Longinus, 52
Longos (Longus), 162–4, 354
Louis VII of France, 284, 290
Louis XIV, 285
Louÿs, Pierre, 49
Lucian [*Loukianos*], 16, 248
Luke, Saint, 192–3
Lysimakhos (Lysimachus), 181–4

Macar (also Macareus), 3–6, 9, 195
Macauley, Rose, 371
Mahmoud (Mahmud) Pasha, 314–5, 317–8
Manuel I Komnenos, 285–8
Manuel II Palaiologos (Palaeologus), 294–5, 301
Marcus Aurelius, 126
Maria of Alania, empress, 273
Maria Palaiologos-Gattilusio, 372
Marina, empress, 238, 242
Mary of Antioch, empress, 290
Matisse, Henri, 376, 378
Mehmed the Conqueror, sultan, 302–3, 305ff., 321, 326–7
Memnon, 133–4, 136–7
Menander [*Menandros*], 112, 371
Menelaos (-us), 10–12
Michael I, 246
Michael II, 246–7
Michael IV, 254–5

Michael V, 255–260
Michael VIII Palaiologos (Palaeologus), 290
Michael, metropolitan of Mytilene, 249
Midas, king of Phrygia, 3, 137
Mnasidika, 43, 49, 56–57, 391
Mohammed, religious leader, 330
Moskhos, John, 228–9
Museus, 17
Myrivilis, Stratis, 345ff., 371, 373
Myrsilos of Methymna, writer, 133

Nereus, 33
Nestor, 8, 10
Nikephoros II (Nicephorus), 233ff., 253
Noah, 3

Odysseus, 9, 10–11
Onomakritos, 17, 34
Orestes, 3, 11–13
Origen, church father, 18
Orpheus, 2, 3, 15ff., 29, 195
Orkhan (also Hyrkan), Turkish lord, 297–9
Ovid, 149

Palamedes, 9, 11
Pakhes, Athenian general, 89ff.
Pamphile, writer, 112
Pan (God), 20
Parthenios, 160–62
Paul, Saint, 191–3
Pausanias, historical geographer, 13–14, 38
Peisistratos (-us), Athenian ruler, 33
Pelops, 11–13, 373
Penthilos, 11, 12–13
Periander [*Periandros*], 30–31, 79
Pericles, Athenian commander, 101
Phainias (*aka* Phanias), 112, 120–1, 161–2, 374
Pherekydes, philosopher, 17, 83
Phillip [*Philippos*] of Macedon, 109, 133
Phineis, 13–15
Photios, ecumenical patriarch, 74–75, 160, 223, 247–9
Phrynis of Mytilene, 29
Picasso, Pablo, 378

Pittakos (Pittacus), 3, 14, 34, 35, 39, 79–83
Plato [*Platon*], philosopher, 37–38, 42, 105–7
Platon, Christian abbot, 242
Plutarch [*Plutarkhos*], 13, 24, 39, 82, 120, 134, 145, 150ff., 159
Polemon, philosopher, 107
Polykrates, tyrant of Samos, 86
Pompeios Markos, 149–50
Pompey [*Pompeius*] the Great, 139ff., 151ff., 372
Pope, Alexander, 48
Poseidon, 32
Potamon, 140, 372
Praxilla, writer, 159
Praxiteles, sculptor, 114
Priam [*Priamos*], king of Troy, 8
Prokopios (Procopius), historian, 276–8
Psellos, Michael, historian, 254, 258ff.
Ptolemy XI, king of Egypt, 155, 158
Ptolemy XIII, king of Egypt, 155
Ptolemy [*Ptolemaios*] "the black," epicurean philosopher, 105
Pyrrha, wife of Deukalion, 4
Pythagoras, philosopher, 17, 83–84, 86

Quasimodo, S., poet, 48

Rhodopis (*aka* Dorikha), Alexandrian courtesan, 63–65, 87
Romanos (-us) I Lekapenos, 250
Rutilius, Roman consul and district governor, 144–5

Sappho of Lesbos, 3, 27, 36–38, 40ff., 74, 79, 84–85, 111, 134, 354, 370–1, 374, 390–1
Seneca, 126
Shakespeare, William, 181ff.
Skleraina, mistress of Constantine IX, 257, 262–6
Skleros, Basil, 257, 260, 262
Skylitzes, John, historian, 246–7, 251ff., 255ff.
Sphrantzes (*aka* Frantzes), George, historian, 302–4
Socrates, 37, 97, 106

Solon of Athens, 37, 81, 83, 85, 88
Sophocles, 42, 155
Strabo [*Strabon*], historical geographer, 29, 34–36, 65, 111, 142
Swinburne, A.C., 57

Tamerlane, *see* Timur
Telemakhos (Telemachus), 10
Terpander [*Terpandros*], 28ff., 40, 221, 373
Teriade, Stratis, fine arts connoisseur, 375ff.
Thales of Miletos, 34
Theodora
  empress (wife of Justinian), 227–8
  empress (wife of Theophilos), 244, 273
  ruling empress (daughter of Constantine VIII), 254, 255, 259ff., 268
Theodore I Laskaris, 299
Theodore, Lesbian saint, 328ff.
Theodosius I, 130
Theodosius II, 225
Theophanes the Confessor, historian, 231ff.
Theophanes of Lesbos, political advisor, 140ff., 158
Theophilos, emperor, 244
Theophilos Hadjimichael, painter, 379–80
Theophrastos (Theophrastus), philosopher, 36, 105, 106, 109, 112ff., 370, 374
Thucydides [*Thukydides*], 89ff., 248
Timur, Mongolian ruler, 295, 301
Tzahas, Turkish rebel, 275ff., 279–81
Tzetzes, I., Byzantine historian, 75

Umur, Turkish lord, 299

Valerios, Konstantinos, governor of Lesbos, 288–9
Venezis, Elias, writer, 327–8
Venizelos, Eleftherios, political leader, 359
Verlaine, Paul, French poet, 48
Vernardakis, family, 333
Virgil (Vergil), 160

Zeno [*Zenon*], stoic philosopher, 105, 126–7
Zeus, 8, 12, 30, 71, 73, 83, 103, 144, 177
Zoe (wife of Leo VI) regent, 250–1
Zoe (daughter of Constantine VIII, wife of Constantine IX), empress, 254, 255ff., 259ff.
Zonaras, John, historian, 240ff.
Zoroaster [*Zarathustra*], 17

ISOS INTERNATIONAL, P.C.
360 South Garfield Street
Suite 670
Denver, Colorado 80209-3136
U.S.A.